Performance, Reliability, and Availability Evaluation of Computational Systems, Volume 1

This textbook intends to be a comprehensive and substantially self-contained two-volume book covering performance, reliability, and availability evaluation subjects. The volumes focus on computing systems, although the methods may also be applied to other systems. The first volume covers Chapter 1 to Chapter 14, whose subtitle is "Performance Modeling and Background". The second volume encompasses Chapter 15 to Chapter 25 and has the subtitle "Reliability and Availability Modeling, Measuring and Workload, and Lifetime Data Analysis".

This text is helpful for computer performance professionals for supporting planning, design, configuring, and tuning the performance, reliability, and availability of computing systems. Such professionals may use these volumes to get acquainted with specific subjects by looking at the particular chapters. Many examples in the textbook on computing systems will help them understand the concepts covered in each chapter. The text may also be helpful for the instructor who teaches performance, reliability, and availability evaluation subjects. Many possible threads could be configured according to the interest of the audience and the duration of the course. Chapter 1 presents a good number of possible courses programs that could be organized using this text.

Volume 1 is composed of the first two parts, besides Chapter 1. Part I gives the knowledge required for the subsequent parts of the text. This part includes six chapters. It covers an introduction to probability, descriptive statistics and exploratory data analysis, random variables, moments, covariance, some helpful discrete and continuous random variables, Taylor series, inference methods, distribution fitting, regression, interpolation, data scaling, distance measures, and some clustering methods. Part II presents methods for performance evaluation modeling, such as operational analysis, Discrete-Time Markov Chains (DTMC), and Continuous Time Markov Chains (CTMC), Markovian queues, Stochastic Petri nets (SPN), and discrete event simulation.

Performance, Reliability, and Availability Evaluation of Computational Systems, Volume 1

Performance and Background

Paulo Romero
Martins Maciel

CRC Press
Taylor & Francis Group
Boca Raton London New York

CRC Press is an imprint of the
Taylor & Francis Group, an **informa** business
A CHAPMAN & HALL BOOK

First edition published 2023
by CRC Press
6000 Broken Sound Parkway NW, Suite 300, Boca Raton, FL 33487-2742

and by CRC Press
4 Park Square, Milton Park, Abingdon, Oxon, OX14 4RN

CRC Press is an imprint of Taylor & Francis Group, LLC

© 2023 Taylor & Francis Group, LLC

ISBN: 978-1-032-29537-4 (hbk)
ISBN: 978-1-032-30639-1 (pbk)
ISBN: 978-1-003-30601-6 (ebk)

DOI: 10.1201/9781003306016

Typeset in Nimbus font
by KnowledgeWorks Global Ltd.

Publisher's note: This book has been prepared from camera-ready copy provided by the authors.

Dedication

———————————

To the One and Triune God, the Holy Mystery that is Wholly Love.

Contents

PART I   *Fundamental Concepts*

PART II Performance Modeling

Contents of Volume 2

Preface

This text intends to be a comprehensive and substantially self-contained two-volume book covering performance, reliability, and availability evaluation subjects. The volumes focus on computing systems, although the methods may also be applied to other systems. Like many other parallel or concurrent systems, computing systems often lead to conflicts because processes attempt to access resources simultaneously or with time overlapping. Such conflict may cause errors, processes congestion, and system deadlocks. Moreover, when planning a cost-effective system, the policies, mechanisms, systems' structures, and the respective phenomena are usually hard to represent by deterministic models. On the other hand, such systems commonly have statistical regularities that make them suitable for dealing with stochastic processes and statistics that quantify the collected data's central tendencies, variability, and shapes. Due to its size, the document was divided into two volumes. The first volume covers from Chapter 1 to Chapter 14, whose subtitle is "Performance Modeling and Background". The second volume encompasses from Chapter 16 to Chapter 26 and has the subtitle "Reliability and Availability Modeling, Measuring and Workload, and Lifetime Data Analysis".

This text is helpful for computer performance professionals for supporting planning, design, configuring, and tuning the performance, reliability, and availability of computing systems. Such professionals may use these volumes to get acquainted with specific subjects by looking at the particular chapters. Many examples in the textbook on computing systems will help them understand the concepts covered in each chapter. The text may also be helpful for the instructor who teaches performance, reliability, and availability evaluation subjects. Many possible threads could be configured according to the interest of the audience and the duration of the course. Chapter 1 presents a good number of possible courses programs that could be organized using this text. Students following a course organized by an instructor should observe the sequence proposed by the instructor. If the students need extra assistance on some particular background topic, they may go to the specific material shown in the text to fill the specific gaps. The performance analyst may also self-teach topics of interest. In such a case, the guidelines for students and instructors may serve them well. Each chapter has a good number of unsolved exercises to assist the students in consolidating the covered materials. In the case of self-teaching a particular topic of interest, a plausible direction is to adopt one of the threads suggested for students and instructors on Chapter 1.

The first chapter of Volume 1 introduces the text and provides a glimpse of performance evaluation planning, describes the intended public, suggests several threads for getting acquainted with the subjects covered in these volumes. This document comprises two volumes, each of which has two parts, totaling twenty-five chapters. Volume 1 is composed of the first two parts, besides Chapter 1. Part I gives the knowledge required for the subsequent parts of the text. This part includes six chapters. It covers an introduction to probability, descriptive statistics and exploratory data analysis, random variables, moments, covariance, some helpful discrete and continuous random variables, Taylor series, inference methods, distribution fitting, regression, interpolation, data scaling, distance measures, and some clustering methods. Part II presents methods for performance evaluation modeling, such as operational analysis, Discrete-Time Markov Chains (DTMC), and Continuous Time Markov Chains (CTMC), Markovian queues, Stochastic Petri nets (SPN), and discrete event simulation. Volume 2 is composed of the last two parts. Part III examines reliability and availability modeling by covering a set of fundamental notions, definitions, redundancy procedures, and modeling methods such as Reliability Block Diagrams (RBD) and Fault Trees (FT) with the respective evaluation methods, adopts Markov chains, Stochastic Petri nets and even hierarchical and heterogeneous modeling to represent more complex systems. Part IV discusses performance measurements and reliability data analysis. It first depicts some basic measuring mechanisms applied in computer systems, then discusses workload generation. After, we examine failure monitoring and fault injection, and finally, we discuss a set of techniques for reliability and maintainability data analysis. Several parts of the text have been used for performance, reliability, and availability evaluation courses for graduate and undergraduate students at Centro de Informática at Universidade Federal de Pernambuco, and as short courses and seminaries for students and companies.

The Mercury tool[1], which one that is adopted to model and evaluate many of the proposed examples and problems, can be obtained by contacting the author.

---

[1] https://www.modcs.org/

Acknowledgement

First and before all, I would like to thank the One and Triune God who gave strength and perseverance to his humblest slave to accomplish this task.

I thank my late father, Abelardo, who passed away in December, the 9th, 2016. His example as a self-made man, whose limitless capacity of work and discipline taught me persistence under all circumstances. I thank my mother, Aliete, for her love, care, immeasurable and unconditional support, and for what she went through with my father to bring me up to the man I am together with my brother Abelardo Jr., and my sisters Roberta and Fernanda.

I also thank my students, as I see them as a figure of other students who may benefit from this textbook. This document was carefully planned, conceived, and written thinking of you. My aim was to provide a comprehensive book and reasonably self-contained to support educating, teaching, training, and instructing students and professionals on performance, reliability, and availability evaluation.

When I was finishing writing the one before the last chapter, I got COVID-19. My case was critical. I was intubated, but the oxygen saturation level kept declining to the level that medical staff was setting up to use extracorporeal membrane oxygenation (ECMO). Dozen of prayer groups, hundreds of people prayed to the Lord. At that critical moment, my organism started to react, and in five more days, I was at home. I firmly believe that they were heard, and God gave me more time to be a better person and carry out tasks that I consigned to last priority.

Renata and my son Rodrigo, the greatest gifts in my life; thank you for your love and support. It is for you my struggle in this land. I try, fall, stand up, fall and stand again, and keep striving to follow the path to Life by the grace of God. I hope you follow the trail that leads to the Truth. To my wife, Teresa, I am in debt of having our most precious gifts, our son and daughter, by the grace of God. Teresa has supported me in the most painful and challenging moments of my life. Thank you for your love and care. Finally, I would like to thanks my in-laws Gilberto and Laélia for their love.

1 Introduction

This text aims to be self-contained to support one's instruction without requiring extra material, at least to some extent. Due to its size, the manuscript was divided into two volumes. The first volume covers Chapter 1 to Chapter 14, whose subtitle is "Performance Modeling and Background". The second volume encloses Chapter 16 to Chapter 26 and has the subtitle "Reliability and Availability Modeling, Measuring and Workload, and Lifetime Data Analysis". This chapter introduces the book by first providing an overview of how the text is divided and how the interested reader may use the document, and then a glimpse of Evaluation Planning. It also offers courses' configurations with the respective sequences of chapters, besides a list of possible short courses on specific subjects for instructors and students.

1.1 AN OVERVIEW

Performance evaluation refers to a set of methods for investigating the temporal behavior of systems. It has a long tradition in studying and designing communication and manufacturing systems, operational research, and computer systems. Reliability and availability evaluation refers to studying system behavior in the presence of failure and repair events of the system components. This book focuses on the performance, reliability, and availability evaluation of computational systems.

The computer systems may be broadly classified into two categories: real-time and resource-sharing systems. A real-time system is a system that provides its services subject to time constraints. Such systems may even be classified as soft real-time and hard real-time systems depending on if the constraints violation degrades the system performance or if the result is considered useless. On the other hand, many computational systems are resource-sharing systems due to cost-effectiveness and technological motivations. Some examples are online delivery services, streaming services, online reservation services, online content sharing, online ticket booking, communication networks, computer servers, manufacturing production systems, etc.

Sharing of system resources often leads to conflicts because processes attempt to access them simultaneously or with some time overlap what should be avoided to lead to reliable results. This, however, causes processes congestion and may even cause the system deadlock. Moreover, varying service times, error situations, arrival events, burst events, faults, and so forth make it extremely hard (if not impossible) to represent such phenomena by deterministic models. However, such systems and phenomena usually have statistical regularities that make them suitable to be defined by stochastic processes. Nevertheless, it is worth noting that depending on the abstraction level, a system may be viewed as a real-time system and in another as a resource-sharing system [177]. This book focuses on resource-sharing computational systems.

This text is divided into two volumes, and each volume is divided into two parts. The Volume 1 is composed of **Part I** and **Part II**. Volume 2 is divided into **Part III** and **Part IV**. Part I is composed of six chapters, Part II has seven chapters, Part III is divided into seven chapters, and Part IV has four chapters. Each chapter has many solved examples and questions for students to consolidate their knowledge on the topics covered in each chapter. This particular volume covers the first two parts.

Part I offers the background needed for the following parts of the document. This part contains six chapters. Chapter 2 presents an introduction to probability by encompassing algebra of sets, probability space, conditional probability, the law of total probability and independence, Bayes' Rule, and counting methods. Chapter 3 offers an extensive summary of descriptive statistics analysis by presenting statistics for measuring central tendency, variability, shape, and graphical description of data for exploratory data analysis. Chapter 4 gives the notion of random variables, discrete random variables and continuous random moments, joint random variables distribution, covariance, and other related measures. Chapter 5 presents some valuable discrete and continuous random variable distributions as well as describes the concepts of functions of random variables and Taylor series. Chapter 6 introduces a set of inference techniques for assessing system parameters with confidence, distribution fitting strategies, and methods for data fitting such as regression and interpolation. Finally, Chapter 7 presents the ideas of data scaling, distance measures, and some classical data clustering methods.

The system performance can be assessed via different methods and strategies depending on the context, criticality, and costs affected. In a general context, the performance evaluation may be conducted through Measuring, Analysis, and Simulation. Part II covers methods for performance evaluation modeling. Part II is organized into seven chapters. Chapter 8 presents the operational analysis. Chapter 9 and Chapter 10 introduce Discrete-Time Markov Chains (DTMC) and Continuous Time Markov Chains (CTMC). Chapter 11 depicts basic Markovian queue models. Chapter 12 and Chapter 13 detail Stochastic Petri Nets (SPN), and Chapter 14 introduces discrete event simulation. Measuring methods are discussed in Part IV.

The dependability of a system can be understood as the capability of carrying out a stipulated functionality that can be trustworthy. Due to the widespread provision of online services, dependability has become a requirement of primary concern. Providing fault-tolerant services is intrinsically attached to the adoption of redundancy. Replication of services is often supplied through distributed hosts across the world so that whenever the service, the underlying host, or the network fails, an alternative service is eager to take over. Among the dependability attributes, some critical ones are reliability and availability-related measures. A reliability or availability problem may be evaluated through combinatorial or state-space models, simulation, or lifetime data analysis.

Part III studies reliability and availability-related measures via combinatorial and state-space models. Simulation, which is introduced in Part II (Chapter 14), may also be adopted to evaluate the models presented in this part of the book. Lifetime data analysis is covered in Part IV. Part III is divided into seven chapters. Chapter 16 describes some early and pivotal works on reliability, availability, and dependability evaluation, a set of fundamental notions and definitions, the essential redundancy procedures, and the classification of modeling methods. Chapter 18 and Chapter 19 introduce the Reliability Block Diagrams (RBD) and Fault Trees (FT) and their applications. Their evaluation methods are discussed in Chapter 20. Chapter 21 studies more complex systems than those studied in the previous chapter. Markov chains are applied to model such systems, which are not well characterized by combinatorial models. Chapter 22 adopts SPN to model systems that are not precisely described by combinatorial methods and whose state spaces are large so that they turn out to be challenging to represent directly via Markov chains. In these two last chapters, multiple formalisms (RBD + CTMC, RBD + SPN, FT + CTMC + FT + SPN, for instance) are also employed to model even more convoluted systems through hierarchy and refinement.

Computer system performance measurements are founded on monitoring the system while being exposed to a workload. Such a workload could be observed during the system's typical operation or a workload test. Therefore, for obtaining meaningful measurements, the workload should be carefully characterized. The analyst may also ponder different workloads, how the system is monitored, and how the measured data are summarized and presented.

Contrasting performance, reliability, and availability-related measures are tougher to assess since system behavior depends on failure incidents. Nevertheless, as the mean time between failures (MTBF) in a dependable system is typically on the order of years, the fault occurrences have to be synthetically speeded up and injected into the system under test to analyze faults effects on the system behavior. Reliability data analysis concerns the analysis of observed product lifetimes. Such lifetime data can be of products in the market or associated with the system in operation. The data analysis and prediction are described as lifetime data analysis or reliability data analysis.

Part IV is divided into four chapters. Chapter 23 presents the basic performance measuring mechanism applied in computer systems. Chapter 24 discusses workload generation methods. Chapter 25 presents a set of methods for reliability and maintainability data analysis. Finally, Chapter 26 examines failure monitoring and fault injection procedures.

For Instructors

Here, we present some possible course configurations to support the instructor to define courses according to their aims, syllabus, and students' background. The suggestions are just alternatives that may serve as a road map to guide the interested instructor. Instructors may also choose alternative paths that better suit their courses' requirements.

Performance Measurement

This course plan aims at studying computer systems performance through measurements. This study supports comparing systems, upgrading, or tuning the system's performance or components by either replacing them with new devices with better capabilities or the whole system. More detailed descriptions of cases are briefly mentioned below.

A possible objective may be selecting systems from competing systems where some performance features are essential as decision criteria for the decision process.

Poor system performance could be either inadequate hardware devices or system management. Hence the performance study objective may be to identify and locate bottleneck devices or the cause of sluggish behavior. If an insufficient hardware device causes the problem, the system has to be upgraded, and if it is caused by poor management, the system has to be tuned up.

Assume the analyst team is confronted with several different computer system alternatives from which to choose. Furthermore, the analyst team may have several choices within each system that may affect economic value and performance, such as the dimension, main capacity, number of processor units, network interface, size and number of storage devices, etc. In such cases, the performance study goal might be to provide quantitative information about which configurations are best under specific conditions.

Consider that two or more computer system alternatives should be compared in terms of their performance. Therefore, the decision-maker is confronted with different systems from which one should be chosen. Furthermore, each system may have several other configuration options that impact both cost and performance, such as the size of the main memory, the number of processors, the type of network interface, the size and number of disk drives, the kind of system software, etc. The goal of the performance analysis, in this case, would be to provide quantitative information about which configurations are best under specific conditions.

Debugging a program for correct execution is a fundamental prerequisite for any application program. Once the program is functionally correct, the performance analysis may be required to find performance issues. For instance, consider that a program produces the right results, but such results are produced after a stipulated deadline. The goal of the performance analyst would be to apply the appropriate tools and analysis methods to find out why the program is not meeting performance requirements. All these cases are possible studies that could be tackled through the content covered in this course plan.

Content sequence

Chapter 1 → Chapter 23 (up to the first to two paragraphs of Section 23.6) → Chapter 3 → Chapter 2 → Chapter 4 → Chapter 5 → Chapter 6 → Chapter 8 → Chapter 23 (from Section 23.6 onwards) → Chapter 24.

Some sections of Chapter 4 may be omitted according to the depth of knowledge that is expected to be provided. In Chapter 5, the essential distributions are Bernoulli, Geometric, Binomial, Poisson, uniform, triangular, Student's t, and chi-square for this course. It is important to note that each specific content of Chapter 5 may be studied when needed.

Performance Evaluation: Measuring and Modeling

This course plan aims at studying computer systems' performance through modeling and measurements. Such a study supports modeling computational systems through stochastic models to tackle complexities related to conflicts, resource sharing, uncertainties, failures, discard, etc. Performance evaluation through models can be applied during the initial design stages of the system development activities to safeguard that the product meets the performance needs. Even when systems are already available and in operation, it may be too costly or unfeasible to stop the system to evaluate specific scenarios. The modeling portion covers Operational Analysis, Markov Chains, Markovian Queues, Stochastic Petri Nets, and Simulation. In such cases, the system performance may be assessed through measuring, but it represents the operational conditions of the system. It is impossible to create specific scenarios and test the system performance in such new scenarios. Having an accurate system model allows the analyst to evaluate such performance cases, better tuning system parameters, and planning system capacity. Besides, this course also covers the measuring process. This part covers the topics already seen in the previous plan.

Content sequence

Chapter 1 → Chapter 23 (up to the first to two paragraphs of Section 23.6) → Chapter 3 → Chapter 2 → Chapter 4 → Chapter 5 → Chapter 6 → Chapter 8 → Chapter 23 (from Section 23.6 onwards) → Chapter 24 → Chapter 5 → Chapter 9 → Chapter 10 → Chapter 11 → Chapter 12 → Chapter 13 → Chapter 14. Optional chapter: Chapter 7.

In the first passage of Chapter 5, the essential distributions to look at are Bernoulli, geometric, binomial, Poisson, uniform, triangular, Student's t, and chi-square. In the second passage of Chapter 5, the essential distributions to look at are the exponential, Erlang, hypoexponential, hyperexponential, and Cox distributions. Other distributions may be needed according to specific interests and studies. Chapter 23 and Chapter 24 may be summarized to cover only particular topics according to the course requirements and duration. However, it is worth mentioning that the specific contents of Chapter 5 may be covered when needed.

Performance Evaluation: Modeling

This course is the content of the course Performance Evaluation: Measuring and Modeling, removing the content of the course Performance Measurement. It focuses specifically on performance modeling by covering Operational Laws, Markov Chains, Markovian Queues, Stochastic Petri Nets, and Simulation.

Content sequence

Chapter 1 → Chapter 2 → Chapter 3 → Chapter 4 → Chapter 5 → Chapter 6 → Chapter 7 → Chapter 8 → Chapter 9 → Chapter 10 → Chapter 11 → Chapter 12 → Chapter 13 → Chapter 14.

It is worth mentioning that some parts of this chapter may be omitted according to the instructor's aim and the course duration. Each specific content of Chapter 5 may be studied when required.

Reliability and Availability Evaluation

Due to the widespread availability of services on the Internet, dependability has become a need of significant interest in system design and operation. Among the fundamental attributes of dependability, we have reliability and availability. The reliability of a system at a time instant t is the probability of that system performing its function accordingly without failure in the interval $t - t_0$, assuming t_0 is the instant the system begins to function. The most straightforward system availability in period T is the ratio between the period of which the system is operational, T_o, to the observation period T.

This course covers the topics of reliability and availability evaluation of systems. First, the necessary background is introduced (in case the students need an update on statistics and probability basis); otherwise, these chapters may be skipped. After that, the basic definitions of the subject are introduced. Then, a model classification is introduced, and later on, the combinatorial model is presented, that is, RBD and FT. This is followed by a description of several methods for evaluating non-state-based models. Markov chains are, then, adopted to represent reliability and availability problems that combinatorial models fail to describe accurately. Then, SPN is also assumed to model systems' reliability and availability features. Simulation may also be adopted as an alternative method of evaluation. Then, system reliability, availability, and maintainability are studied through parametric and nonparametric lifetime data analysis. Finally, an introduction to fault injection is presented.

Content sequence

Chapter 1 → Chapter 2 → Chapter 3 → Chapter 4 → Chapter 5 → Chapter 6 → Chapter 16 → Chapter 17 → Chapter 18 → Chapter 19 → Chapter 20 → Chapter 21 → Chapter 22 → Chapter 25 → Chapter 26.

If the students already know statistics and basic probability subjects, the respective chapters or parts of them may be skipped. If the class has no knowledge of Markov chain and stochastic Petri nets, an overview of Chapters 9, 10, 12, and 13 is required. Optional chapters: Chapters 7 and Chapters 14. The examples for Chapters 14 may be taken from Chapter 22.

Reliability and Availability Evaluation: Modeling

This course covers the background, fundamentals on dependability, reliability, availability and related metrics, and the modeling subjects of the previous course.

Content sequence

Chapter 1 → Chapter 2 → Chapter 3 → Chapter 4 → Chapter 5 → Chapter 6 → Chapter 16 → Chapter 17 → Chapter 18 → Chapter 19 → Chapter 20 → Chapter 21 → Chapter 22.

If the students are already versed in introductory statistics and probability subjects, the respective chapters or part of them may be skipped. If the class has no knowledge of Markov chain and stochastic Petri nets, an overview of Chapters 9, 10, 12, and 13 is required. Optional chapter: Chapters 14. The examples for Chapters 14 may be taken from Chapter 22.

Lifetime Data Analysis or Reliability and Availability Data Analysis

This course covers the background, fundamentals on dependability, reliability, availability and related metrics, and lifetime data analysis and fault injection subjects. In a general sense, there are two broad approaches for dealing with failure and repairing data: the parametric and nonparametric approaches. This course covers many methods of both general approaches.

Content sequence

Chapter 1 → Chapter 2 → Chapter 3 → Chapter 4 → Chapter 5 → Chapter 6 → Chapter 16 → Chapter 17 → Chapter 25 → Chapter 26.

Besides the long courses, a short course could be conceived from this document. This course is much more straightforward than the previous one. The background topics may be significantly reduced, or if the audience is already acquainted with the background, it could be skipped entirely, and the courses may start directly on the core subject. For instance, the list below summarizes a short course that the instructor may compose from the text.

- **Introduction to Statistics and Probability.**
  This course may be composed of Chapter 1, Chapter 2, Chapter 3, Chapter 4, Chapter 5, and Chapter 7 or specific part of them.

- **Operational Analysis: Bottleneck Analysis and Bounds.**
  Sequence of chapters: Chapter 1, Chapter 3, and Chapter 8.

- **Introduction to Markov Chain.**
  Sequence of chapters: Chapter 2, Chapter 5, Chapter 9, Chapter 10, and Chapter 11.

- **Performance Modeling with Markov Chain.**
  Sequence of chapters: Chapter 1, Chapter 2, Chapter 3, Section 4.1, Section 4.2, Chapter 6, Chapter 9, Chapter 10, and Chapter 11.

- **Performance Modeling with Stochastic Petri Nets.**
  Sequence of chapters: Chapter 1, Chapter 12, Chapter 13, and Chapter 14. Optional chapter: Chapter 22. Requirement: Course Performance Modeling with Markov Chain or Introduction to Markov Chain.

- **Performance Simulation.**
  Sequence of chapters: Chapter 1, Chapter 14 and examples from Chapter 13, and Chapter 22. Requirement: Course Performance Modeling with Stochastic Petri Nets.

- **Reliability, Availability, and Related Metrics Evaluation via RBD and FT.**
  This course may be formed of Chapter 1, Chapter 2, Chapter 5, Chapter 16, Chapter 17, Chapter 18, Chapter 19, and Chapter 20.

- **Reliability, Availability, and Related Metrics Evaluation with Markov Chain**
  This course may be composed of Chapter 1, Chapter 2, Chapter 5, Chapter 16, Chapter 17, Chapter 9, Chapter 10, and Chapter 21.

- **Reliability, Availability and Related Metrics Evaluation with Stochastic Petri Nets.**
  This course may composed of Chapter 12, Chapter 13, and Chapter 22. Requirement: Course Performance Modeling with Markov Chain or Introduction to Markov Chain.

- **Lifetime Data Analysis and Fault Injection.**
  This course may be defined of parts of Chapter 1, Chapter 2, Chapter 3, Chapter 4, Chapter 5 (Choose the distributions according your need), Chapter 25, and Chapter 26.

- **Introduction to to Workload Generation.**
  This course may be composed of parts of Chapter 1, Chapter 2, Chapter 3, Chapter 4, Chapter 5, Chapter 7, and Chapter 24.

For Students

Students following a course organized by an instructor should follow the sequence suggested by the instructor. For instance, if the instructor adopts the plan proposed for the course Reliability and Availability Evaluation: Modeling, the students should follow the steps depicted in the course plan. If the students need extra support on some specific background topic, they may go to the particular topic shown in the book (or on the references quoted) to fill the specific gaps. Each chapter has a good number of unsolved exercises to help the students to consolidate the covered subjects.

For self-studying, the interested person should first define the topic of interest. Such a topic of interest could be confined to a specific subject or broad as one other as one of the long courses proposed. In the latter case, we also suggest following the plans already defined. Next, the student should look at the core chapter of the topic of interest in specific subjects and check the necessary background. This book aims to be self-contained to support one's instruction without requiring extra material, at least to some extent.

For the Analyst

Analysts may use this book to get acquainted with specific subjects by looking at the particular chapters. A large number of examples will help them to understand the concepts covered in each chapter. The analyst may also self-teach topics of interest. In such a case, the guidelines for students and instructors may serve them well.

1.2 A GLANCE AT EVALUATION PLANNING

This section presents a general performance[1] (in the general sense) evaluation process of systems. Most performance system studies are unique since workload and the specificities of the environment can hardly be transferred for the next system to be studied. However, there are activities that performance studies are often required to execute. Hence, by cautiously carrying out such tasks, it will help the analyst avoid common mistakes. Furthermore, by following the steps of the proposed steps, it is expected to improve the success chances of achieving the aims of the performance studies [177, 188, 201].

Two general evaluation processes are depicted. These processes are introduced in a broad sense, without getting into details associated with any particular system. Instead, we focus on general features that are, in general, applied to many systems under study. The first process concerns the evaluation through **Measuring**, and the second covers the evaluation via **Modeling**. For the graphical representation of these processes, we adopted an activity-diagram-like notation[2]. In practical cases, these processes should be instantiated for each particular problem. In these specific problems, due to the simplicity of some particular macro-activity (or activity) or its complexity, such a macro-activity (or activity) may be merged with another or may be split into more than one macro-activity (or activity).

As a convention, we consider a rather informal definition of action, activity, and macro-activity in this chapter. However, it helps us to describe the proposed processes. An **action** is the lowest-level event executed by an actor (person, machine, tool) that modifies the state of a process. An **activity** is a set of actions. As a set could have only one action, an activity may be composed of only one action. Likewise, a **macro-activity** is a set of activities. Each macro-activity, activity, or action should be documented by specifying the following requirement. For the sake of brevity, whenever the explanation servers the three concepts and for avoiding mentioning "macro-activity, activity or action," we will call **task** (a generic name). When specific terms are needed, we adopt them.

---

[1] In such a broad context, it also denotes reliability and availability related attributes
[2] From UML (Unified Modeling Language) [444]

Table 1.1
Information for Each Task

Aims	Aim_1, Aim_2...
Stakeholder	Rodrigo
Preconditions	C_1, C_2 and C_3
Inputs	$Input_1$, $Input_2$...
Macro-Activity or Activity or Action	$Action_1$, $Action_2$, $Action_3$,...
Outputs	$Output_1$, $Output_2$...
Postconditions	C_7, C_9 or C_{10}

Each task must have clear **aims** (see Table 1.1). If they do not, they certainly are not needed. Therefore, for each task of the process, clearly and precisely define their aims. If an activity is composed of only one action, which is too simplistic, the analyst should consider joining such action to another activity. A **stakeholder** is responsible for a task; hence, they are accountable for the execution and issues related to the task. Carrying out a macro-activity, activity, or action demands a set requirement such as personnel, tools, documentation, etc. These are the **preconditions** for executing the task. Executing a task usually requires **inputs**, such as data, sensors, files, etc., which should also be readily available for carrying out the task. The task (**Macro-Activity or Activity or Action**) should be described to support the readability of the process and its replication and reproduction. If we describe a macro-activity (left column), you should probably have activities instead of actions on the right column. If we specify an activity on the left-hand side, we depict the actions that compose the respective activity. Executing the task generates **outputs** (products). Such expected products should also precisely be specified to support quality control. When a task is finished, a set of conditions should be reached to signal a correct state. If such a state is not achieved, the task was not rightfully executed, and some signal should be sent to inform that an issue occurred (**postconditions**). It is worth stressing that the activity-diagram notation represents the dependencies between tasks, such as precedences, choices, concurrent execution, and synchronization. However, other preconditions for carrying out a task, such as a specific set of tools required or a specific environmental condition, are not expressed in the activity diagram notation. The preconditions field for each task is the location for specifying such requirements. When a task is finished, it generates a product (an output), and such output may enable the next task in the activity diagram. However, the product generated may not conform to the specification; hence the task was indeed not finished. This is specified at the postcondition field of each task. Likewise, if a task is successfully finished, the postcondition field should state that. If the execution of the task demanded some specific tools, the postcondition field should also state that the tools are available for use.

It is worth mentioning that for both processes presented in the following, we strongly suggest that each macro activity, activity, and action should be documented using a template similar to the one shown in Figure 1.1 or at least a text document specifying the attributes depicted in the template.

Measuring Evaluation Process

Figure 1.1 depicts a general evaluation process based on **Measuring**. Such a process is broadly composed of six macro-activities, here called M_1, M_2, M_3, M_4, M_5, and M_6. In specific processes, some of these macro-activities may be simple enough to be merged with other macro-activities. On the other hand, some activities of a macro-activity might be complex enough to be considered macro-activities. The analyst should evaluate each case depending on the specific features of each project.

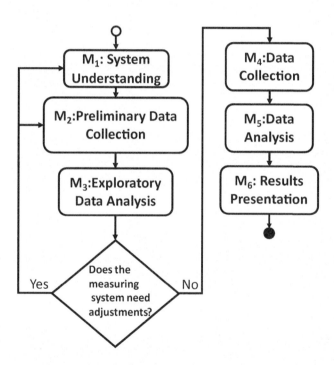

Figure 1.1 Evaluation through Measuring – Macro-Activities.

M_1: **System Understanding.** The first step of a system performance evaluation project is to define the performance aims of the study, define the boundaries of the system, and the system interfaces with other systems, the environment, and the customers. It is worth noting that each system provides a set of services; hence it is fundamental to list the set of services of the system that are of interest for the performance study. After that, for each of these services, the analyst should understand the system behaviors, considering the interaction between the system and the external actors (other systems, environment, and customers), and obtain a set of components that constitutes the system in the light of the performance aims of the study. For each service we intend to study, select a proper workload that represents conditions of interest for the evaluation (see Chapter 24). The system should be subdivided into parts only up to the level at which it is required to measure a component at its interface. If no information is needed to be measured at a finer grain, do not subdivide the system further. In other words, the level of details to which the system should be decomposed is equal to the subcomponent level that provides such information at its interface. The following list may represent the activities that compose M_1:

- $M_{1.1}$: Understanding the system and finding out the services of interest for the study.

- $M_{1.2}$: Defining **what** system service's parameters (factors that impact the system behavior) and their levels should be studied.

- $M_{1.3}$: Defining the performance boundaries.

- $M_{1.4}$: For each service to be evaluated, selecting a proper workload that represents conditions of interest (see Chapter 24).

- $M_{1.5}$: Figuring out the system's components **where** each measure of interest should be collected.

- $M_{1.6}$: Defining the collection frequency (**how often**) and the measuring period (**when**) each measure should be collected. If the data collection is not based on sampling (see Section 23.2), then all measures should be collected.

- $M_{1.7}$: Defining the strategy, method, and tools for collecting data from the system (**how**).

- $M_{1.8}$: Defining the one responsible for conducting the data collection (**who**).

M_2: **Preliminary Data Collection**. In the previous activity, we defined what we have to collect, where the data should be gathered, how the data should be collected, how often each measure should be collected, and the period of interest in which the data should be gathered. The stakeholder for carrying out the activity is also defined. Think of a system whose performance behavior is unknown. For gathering and analyzing data from such a system, it is essential first to figure out how the produced data are distributed, that is, if they are skewed or centralized, sharped at some point or flat, their variability, etc. Thus, preliminary data collection is an initial data gathering from the system to produce an initial sample (or initial samples) from the system's data to support exploratory data analysis. The activities that compose M_2 may be broadly summarized by:

- $M_{2.1}$: If the measuring method adopted is intrusive, insert a suitable probe device (sensor, piece of software, counter, etc.) to collect the data type at the specific locations where the data will be available (**how**). However, the required data may not be directly sensible by the probe device. In such a case, indirect measurement strategies are required (see Section 23.2). If the measurement method is not intrusive, the data should be gathered from the system interface with the environment or at the interface with other interacting systems. In such cases, the probe devices should be placed at those specific locations.

- $M_{2.2}$: Set up the measuring system to collect data for the period of interest (**when**) at the specified sampling frequency (**how often**). It is worth noting that the product of the sampling frequency by the period of interest leads to the sample size (see Chapter 23).

- $M_{2.3}$: Start the measuring process (**when**) (see Chapter 23).

- $M_{2.4}$: When the number of samples is equal to specified sample size (see Section 6), stop the measuring process (**when**). If the data collection is not based on sampling, stop the measuring process when all measures are obtained (**when**) (see Section 23.2).

- $M_{2.5}$: Make a backup of the collected data. It is one of the most commonly neglected activities in the process. Data storage and backup activity are some of the most neglected activities in the evaluation process, and it is a cause of great frustration since the whole set of collected data may be lost, and the collecting process may be required to be carried out again.

M_3: **Exploratory Data Analysis**. Exploratory Data Analysis (EDA) aims to analyze and investigate data sets and summarize their main characteristics, often employing data visualization methods. It helps determine how best to manipulate data sources to get the needed answers. EDA is primarily used to see what data can reveal; thus helping determine if the statistical techniques being considered for data analysis are appropriate. Exploratory data analysis is composed of non-graphical or graphical methods. Non-graphical methods generally involve calculating summary statistics, while graphical methods visually represent the collected data. Inference methods may also extend to EDA. It is worth noting that we also apply probability distribution Goodness of Fit methods at the stage whenever possible. EDA is a crucial activity when analyzing a data sample obtained from an experiment.

- $M_{3.1}$: Calculate the sample statistics and obtain the basic diagrams (see Chapter 3) according to the data type of the data set collected.

- $M_{3.2}$: If the data set is non-categorical, find out evidence to support inference statistic methods (see Chapter 6). Finding such pieces of evidence may be supported by probability distribution Goodness of Fit methods (see Section 6.6).

- $M_{3.3}$: Evaluate if the measuring system requires adjustments to carry out the data collection.

- $M_{3.4}$: Produce a short report describing how each service measures statistics and graphical summary, the respective information about the process of distribution fitting, and specify what, where, when, how, and how often to measure each service characteristic of interest.

Decision: Does the measuring system need adjustments?. If the measuring system does need adjustments, then go back to activity M_1 and M_2 to conduct the required adjustments, tuning, etc. Otherwise, we can execute the following activity of the process (M_4).

M_4: **Data Collection**. For each system service, we intend to study, select a proper workload that represents conditions of interest for the evaluation (see Chapter 24). We already know what, where, when, how, and how often to collect the data from the system at this stage. Therefore, use the short summary produced in $M_{4.4}$ to help to instrument, measure and, gather data from the system under study (see Chapter 23). The activities that compose M_4 are broadly summarized by:

- $M_{4.1}$: For each service to be evaluated, select a proper workload that represents conditions of interest (see Chapter 24).

- $M_{4.2}$: Include the set of suitable probes to gauge the metrics of interest (see Chapter 6).

- $M_{4.3}$: Set up the measuring system to collect data for the period of interest at the specified sampling frequency. Intrusive, non-intrusive, direct, indirect, sampling, or measuring all events methods may be required. The adopted method should already be specified at the short summary produced in $M_{3.4}$.

- $M_{4.4}$: Start the measuring process.

- $M_{4.5}$: When the number of measures is equal to the specified size, stop the measuring process.

- $M_{4.6}$: Make a backup of the collected data.

It is worth mentioning that data collection involves nothing more than following the measurement protocol when all goes well. Unfortunately, however, "going well" seems to be the exception rather than the rule. Therefore, those making measurements should maintain discipline to maintain careful logs of the data collection process.

M_5: **Data Analysis**. It is imperative to be conscious that the outcomes of measurements are random quantities; that is, the outcomes are different each time the experiment is repeated. Thus, the variability should be thoroughly handled to avoid inaccuracy and imprecision. The data analysis summarizes the collected data by descriptive statistics and inference methods for estimating system parameters.

- $M_{5.1}$: Use a good statistical tool to read the collected data sets obtained in M_4. It is often required to prepare a data file to be read by a statistical tool since the collected data set commonly has more than one metrics and other additional content. Hence, filtering those data sets´ content to select only the content of interest is a common procedure.

- $M_{5.2}$: Read the data set of interest.

- $M_{5.3}$: Carry out the statistical analysis according to the requirements of the study being conducted. Interpret the individual results and try to figure out possible cause-effect relations or at least some pieces of evidence that may lead us to investigate the system deeper (see Chapter 3, Chapter 6, and Chapter 7).

- $M_{5.4}$: Store the required statistics, graphics and make a backup of these gross results.

M_6: **Results Presentation**. The closing step of the evaluation process is to communicate the results to others. Depending on to whom the analyst needs to , the evaluation process results may require a distinct language style, graphics, and statistics to summarize the study for that specific audience. If the audience is a group of engineers, system administrators, or software developers, the adopted style might be technical enough to provide them the pieces of technical evidence that lead to the particular result. However, if the audience is members of the decision-making team, it is expected to present the results in a style and level of detail that people could easily understand. Usually, results depicted in graphic form and without statistical jargon are a better approach.

Often, at this point of the project, the knowledge gained by the study may require the analyst to go back and reconsider some of the decisions made in the previous steps or redefine the system boundaries, and include other factors and performance metrics not considered so far. Thus, the final project will typically be ready only after several iterations rather than in a single run.

Evaluation Process via Modeling

Figure 1.3 shows an evaluation process based on **Modeling**. This process is broadly composed of seven macro-activities, here called ME_1, ME_2, ME_3, ME_4, ME_5, ME_6, and ME_7. In particular processes, some of these macro-activities may be simple enough to be joined with other macro-activities. On the other hand, some activities might be too complex, so it is better to consider them as macro-activities. The analyst should judge each case depending on the particular characteristics of each project.

This evaluation process aims at studying systems' performance modeling. This evaluation process may be applied during the initial design stages of the system development activities to safeguard the product meets the performance needs. Figure 1.2

shows the interaction between the design team and the performance evaluation team. In this figure, ellipses denote design models. The ellipse at the bottom represents the final product, rectangles depict activities (performance evaluation and refinement), rectangles with rounded corners are performance models, and the rectangles with a folded corner are results from the performance evaluation activities. Performance evaluation through modeling allows the performance evaluation team to evaluate the system's performance, find design alternatives with distinct performance constraints, and provide feedback to the design team. The design team may disregard the poor design alternative considering the advice provided by the performance evaluation team and choose a more suitable option. Then, the design team may refine its specification and get a more detailed design model. Finally, the performance evaluation team may again produce another performance model and evaluate design alternatives from this new design model to help the design team rule out inadequate design alternatives. This process may go on and on until reaching the final product. It is worth mentioning that in this specific context, the aim of the performance evaluation, particularly at the earlier design stages, is not overly focused on the accuracy of the results since the performance data are still sparse, hypothetical, or at best we have some piece of data from previous projects, manufacturers, and service providers.

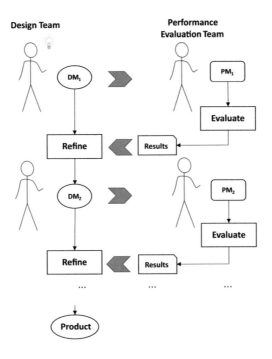

Figure 1.2   Interation Between the Design Team and the Performance Evaluation Team.

Performance evaluation via modeling, though, is not constrained to supporting the design process. In many practical cases, it is rather complex, if not economically impossible, to create scenarios for evaluating the performance of systems in operation. In some circumstances, it is simply impractical to stop the system from evaluating specific performance scenarios. For instance, consider an automobile production line. Stopping the production line for testing some specific performance condition such as injecting a fault to check if the fault tolerance mechanism will cope with the actual occurrence of failure when the system is in operation would cause substantial financial losses, and the companies would not afford such an experiment. Even in less expensive systems, in many cases, it is hard to create complex scenarios in the existing system; nevertheless, such a scenario may indeed occur, and their occurrence may be a cause of significant losses. In such cases, performance evaluation via modeling is a strategy of great help since it allows us to create a model of the system, validate such a model, and then set up the scenarios of interest and evaluate the models through a computer.

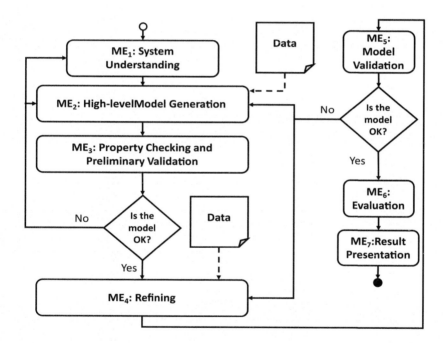

Figure 1.3   Evaluation through Modeling - Macro-Activities.

ME_1: **System Understanding**. The first step of a system performance evaluation project is to define the **performance aims** of the study, define the **boundaries of the system**, the system **interfaces** with other systems, the environment, and customers. Typically, each system provides a **set of services**; thus, specify the services of interest for the performance study. For each of these services, the analyst should understand the system's behavior and consider the system's interaction with other systems, the environment, and customers, as well as attempt to **define the components** that configure the system in light of the performance. The system should be split into components only up to the level at which it is required to evaluate metrics. If no information is required to be investigated at a finer grain, do not split the system further. In other words, the level to which the details the system should be decomposed is equal to the component level that provides such data at its interface.

The definition of **system boundaries**, as well as **workloads**, affects the system performance. Therefore, understanding the system boundaries and deciding the **proper workloads for each service** are a central activity of interest for a successful performance evaluation project. At this stage, **attempt to figure out the set of workload scenarios** that would be needed to explore the system performance features, and an **initial definition of the performance criteria** to be evaluated. The activities that compose ME_1 is broadly summarized by:

- $ME_{1.1}$: General understanding of the system, its services, its interfaces with other systems, and the environment.

- $ME_{1.2}$: Initial definition of performance criteria to be evaluated.

- $ME_{1.3}$: Identification of components of the system from the performance point of view.

- $ME_{1.4}$: Initial definition of the set of workload to be applied to the system.

ME_2: **High-level Model Generation**. Represent the system using high-level notations that help the analyst figure out the system structure, interfaces, and essential components considering the performance perspective. Therefore, first, represent the system structure using a structure diagram (see as an instance Figure 21.8.b) or stack models (see Figure 21.8.a, as an example). Besides, specify a high-level performance[3] notation (Abstract Model) like queue networks, high-level stochastic Petri nets, or a stochastic timed diagram. Then, generate a first version of the performance model of choice. The model chosen may depend on the kind of evaluation needed (reliability, availability, or performance - here in its particular sense), the type of problem particularly faced (see Figure 7.36 and Figure 15.1), and the analyst's acquaintance with each specific formalism. Assign some initial numbers to the Abstract Model's parameters. These numbers may be simple "guestimates" or rough numbers from previous projects, manufacturers, and services' providers. The list of activities that configure ME_2 may be summarized by:

---

[3]The term performance adopted here in a broad sense; that is, it may denote performance attributes such as throughput, response time, mean system size, etc.; or denote reliability and availability related measures.

- $ME_{2.1}$: Represent the system structure a using high-level notation. Aim at figuring out the system's interfaces and the essential components for the system performance study of interest.

- $ME_{2.2}$: Generate a first version of the performance behavior (Abstract Model) of the system by taking into account only those components that impact the system performance.

- $ME_{2.3}$: Assign some initial "guestimates" to the Abstract Model's parameters.

- $ME_{2.4}$: Refine the initial definition of performance criteria to be evaluated (see $ME_{1.2}$) and map these criteria to the abstract performance model.

ME_3: **Property Checking and Preliminary Validation. Check** the existence of some **desirable and undesirable properties** such the whether the state space is finite or infinite, the existence of deadlock states, reversibility to some initial state, etc. Besides, if the evaluation platform supports, **conduct** a debugging process, **a step-by-step**, or a token game **simulation** on the Abstract Model to check if the model functions as the system functions. A convincing result of such activity helps the performance team **gain confidence in the model** under construction.

Decision: **Does the model represent the system?** After checking the existence of some desirable and undesirable property, and conducting a step-by-step simulation on the Abstract Model to observe if the model works as the system, we ask if the model suitably represents the system at that level of abstraction. **If the model does not represent the system**, the performance team should **go back to** ME_1 and ME_2 and perform the due adjustment required. **Otherwise, proceed** to the Refining activity.

ME_4: **Refining** The measurement process was already introduced in Figure 1.1 and the respective explanatory text. The main aim of Refining is to **convert** the **Abstract Model** into a **Detailed Model** (Refined Model) by using as input the Abstract Model and the results obtained from the execution of the **Measurement Process** with manufacturers' data, services providers' data, previous projects' data, and "guestimates". It is worth noting that when we mean converting the Abstract Model to Refined Model, it implies representing the set of metrics of interest to be evaluated in the Refined Model.

This activity is one of the most complex tasks of the process. It may involve ingenuity to grasp the performance phenomena of interest at a specific detail level such that to allow the model to quantify the effects of the occurrences of that phenomena without generating a too detailed model that does not help deliver any additional performance measure of interest, however, producing a model computationally more complex to be evaluated.

Many strategies may be adopted to generate a refined model. The method summarized in Figure 7.36 and Figure 15.1 and the respective textual explanations propose two guidelines for obtaining a performance model and reliability/availability models besides stating the respective method of evaluation. As this activity is strongly dependent on the specific formalism the analyst may adopt, we prefer to stick to the guidelines that are undoubtedly useful when deciding on what class of models to adopt, their respective potential and strength, as well as the constraints, rather than providing a sequence of precise actions to be carried out.

ME_5: **Model Validation**. We name this macro-activity Model Validation; however, it is not accurate since the model will never be completely validated. This macro-activity aims to compare the performance model's results of a set of scenarios with the respective results of the existing system for the same set of scenarios. If the set of results is somewhat statistically equivalent, we say the model is "validated" for this set of scenarios and the respective boundary conditions. Nevertheless, we may bring a new scenario for which the model does not "replicate" the system output. Therefore, this activity is more precisely defined if we called it an *activity for gaining confidence in the model*. Nevertheless, such a name would be unappealing and perhaps confusing. Therefore, we adopted the name Model Validation, but the reader should be aware of the circumstances of the "validation" adopted in this setting.

Observing the remarks above, the Model Validation activity consists of comparing the performance behavior of the model, for a set of specified scenarios of interest, with the results produced by the system considering identical conditions (see comparing systems in Chapter 6).

It is also essential to highlight the type of measure and evaluation we are interested in, whether the measures are **transient** (dependent on the initial conditions) or **stationary** (independent of the initial conditions). Hence, when comparing the metrics measured and the values obtained from the model, they should be obtained accordingly.

Decision: **Does the model represent the system for the scenarios specified?** If a specific measure obtained from the system is statistically equivalent to the metrics' value obtained from the model for each scenario of interest, the model is "validated" for those metrics and the scenarios studied. If the same occurs for a set of metrics, the model is "validated" for the set of metrics and the scenarios evaluated. If the model is not "validated", the analyst should go back to ME_2 or ME_4 to fix the issues and repeat the process until getting the model "validated".

ME_6: **Evaluation**. Once the model is validated, we are ready to evaluate the set of metrics considering the performance scenarios of interest by examining different workload patterns and system configurations. The evaluation may be transient or stationary and assessed by analytic or numerical models and simulation.

ME_7: **Result Presentation**. The last step of the process is to deliver the results to the interested clients. Of course, the report and its language should conform to the specific audience. For example, if an audience is a group of system administrators, software developers, and engineers, the report may require technical details to help the audience understand and be convinced by the results found. Nonetheless, if the clients are from the decision-making team, the results may be better presented by focusing on the economic aspects of the finding, using graphical notations, and avoiding too much statistical jargon. Usually, at this point of the project, the experience obtained advises the analyst to go back and rethink some of the arrangements made in the previous round or redefine the system limits or incorporate additional factors and metrics. Consequently, the final project usually is ready after several rounds rather than in a single run.

Part I

Fundamental Concepts

This part of the book provides the background required for the subsequent chapters of the document. This part is divided into six chapters. Chapter 2 presents an introduction to probability by covering the basics of the algebra of sets, probability space, conditional probability, the law of total probability and independence, Bayes' Rule, and counting methods. Chapter 3 provides an extended summary of descriptive statistics analysis by depicting statistics for quantifying central tendency, variability, shape, and graphical representation of data valid for exploratory data analysis. Chapter 4 introduces the concept of random variables, moments, and joint random variables for discrete random variables and continuous random variables as well as covariance and other related measures. Chapter 5 introduces some important discrete and continuous random variable distributions as well as depicts the concepts of functions of random variables and Taylor series. Chapter 6 presents a set of inference methods for estimating system parameters with confidence, distribution fitting strategies, and methods for data fitting such as regression and interpolation. Finally, Chapter 7 introduces the concepts of data scaling, distance measures, and some classical data clustering methods.

2 Introduction to Probability

This chapter introduces probability, which is the base required for the book's subsequent chapters. This chapter covers the basics of the algebra of sets, probability space, conditional probability, the law of total probability and independence, Bayes' Rule, and counting methods.

2.1 SETS AND ALGEBRA OF SETS

Probability extensively uses sets and operations on sets, so let us start by introducing the notation for sets and some basics on the algebra of sets. A **set** is a collection of objects, usually called its members or elements, where the collection is regarded as a single object. The sentence $a \in A$ says that the element a is a **member of set** A, whereas $a \notin A$ states that a is not a member of A. For instance, consider the set A whose members are the prime numbers less than 10. The elements are, therefore, 1, 3, 5, and 7. The set is represented by listing the elements within curly brackets, that is

$$A = \{1, 3, 5, 7\}.$$

Hence, $3 \in A$ and $4 \notin A$. A set may have no element; in this case it is called an **empty set** and is denoted by $\emptyset$ or $\{\}$. Note that $\{\emptyset\} \neq \emptyset$, because $\emptyset \in \{\emptyset\}$ but $\emptyset \notin \emptyset$. This fact reflects that a car with an empty gas tank is better than a car without a gas tank since at least you have a gas tank [126].

If two sets have exactly the same members, then they are equal, that is $A = B$ if $x_i \in A$, then $x_i \in B$, and if $x_j \in B$, then $x_j \in A$. Therefore, if $B = \{1, 3, 5, 7\}$, then $A = B$, but $A \neq C$, if $C = \{1, 2, 3\}$.

Sets can be represented in many ways. For instance if a set S contains a finite number of elements, such as $x_1, x_2, ..., x_n$, we may represent the set by $S = \{x_1, x_2, ..., x_n\}$. If a set contains an infinite number of enumerable elements, let us say $x_1, x_2, ...$, the set may be represented by $S = \{x_1, x_2, ...\}$. Such a set in called countable infinite.

An alternative notation is $S = \{x_i \mid x_i \; satisfies \; P\}$, where "$\mid$" is read as "such as" and P is predicate or property. For instance the set A described above may be represented by $A = \{x_i \mid x_i \in \mathbb{N}, \; x_i \; is \; prime, \; x_i < 10, \; \forall x_i\}$.

Interval notation is a way of representing subsets of the real number line. A closed interval includes its endpoints. Consider, for example, the set $\{x \mid -10 \leq x \leq 5\}$. We denote this set in interval notation using closed brackets: $[-10, 5]$.

An open interval does not include its endpoints. For example, consider the set $\{x \mid -10 < x < 5\}$. For representing this set in interval notation, we use parenthesis: $(-10, 5)$. One can also have half-open and half-closed intervals, such as $(-10, 5]$.

If all element of set S are also elements of R, S is a **subset** of R, and is denoted by $S \subseteq R$ or $R \supseteq S$. A **proper subset** of a set S is a subset of S that is not equal to S. In other words, if R is a proper subset of S, then all elements of R are in S but S contains at least one element that is not in R. If S is a proper subset of R, it is denoted by $S \subset R$ or $R \supset S$. If $S \subset R$ and $R \subset S$, $S = R$, that is S and R are equal. If S is not equal to R, it is denoted by $S \neq B$.

The **universal set** is the set of conceivable elements of interest in a given context, and it is denoted by Ω. Therefore, having defined the context through the universal set, all set in that context, for instance, S (see Figure 2.1.a), is a subset of Ω.

The **complement set** of S in the universal set Ω are the elements in the universal set that do not belong to S. More formally, $S^c = \{x_i \in \Omega \mid x_i \notin S\}$ (see Figure 2.1.b). It is worth mentioning that $\Omega^c = \emptyset$.

The **union** of two sets, S and R, is the set of all elements that belong to S or R, that is $S \cup R = \{x_i \mid x_i \in S \vee x_i \in R\}$ (see Figure 2.1.c). The **intersection** of two sets, S and R, is the set of elements that belongs to S and R, that is $S \cap R = \{x_i \mid x_i \in S \wedge x_i \in R\}$ (see Figure 2.1.d).

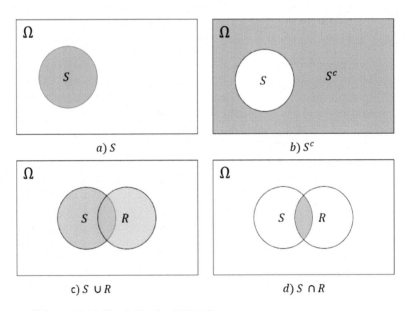

Figure 2.1   a) S, b) S^c, c) $S \cup R$, d) $S \cap R$.

Let $S = \{1,3,5,7\}$ and $R = \{2,3,4,5,9\}$, where $\Omega = \{0,1,2,3, 4,5,6,7,8,9\}$. Then, $S^c = \{0,2,4, 6,8,9\}$, $S \cup R = \{1,2,3,4,5,7,9\}$, and $S \cap R = \{3,5\}$.

When the number of sets considered in the union or intersection is large (n) or even infinite (∞), the following notation is useful:

$$\bigcup_{i=1}^{n} S_i = S_1 \cup S_2 \cup ... \cup S_n$$

and

$$\bigcup_{i=1}^{\infty} S_i = S_1 \cup S_2 \cup ... ,$$

and

$$\bigcap_{i=1}^{n} S_i = S_1 \cap S_2 \cap ... \cap S_n$$

and

$$\bigcap_{i=1}^{\infty} S_i = S_1 \cap S_2 \cap ... .$$

Two set S and R are said to be disjoint if $S \cap R = \emptyset$. A collection of sets of a set S is defined as a **partitions** of S if the subsets of S are disjoint and their union is S, that is $\bigcap_{i=1}^{n} S_i = \emptyset$, and $\bigcup_{i=1}^{n} S_i = S$, where S_i is a subset of S (see Figure 2.2).

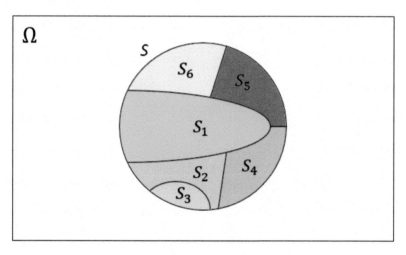

Figure 2.2 Partition of S.

Any set S has one or more subsets. If S has n elements, then S has 2^n subsets. The set of all subsets of S, is called the **power set** of S ($\mathscr{P}(S)$) of S. Let $S = \{a, b\}$, then $\mathscr{P}(S) = \{\emptyset, \{a\}, \{b\}, \{a,b\}\}$.

Algebra of Sets - Consider the sets S, R, and T in the universe Ω. The **set operations** have several properties. For example:

$$S \cup R = R \cup S.$$
$$S \cap (R \cup T) = (S \cap R) \cup (S \cap T).$$
$$(S^c)^c = S.$$
$$S \cup \Omega = \Omega.$$
$$S \cup (R \cup T) = (S \cup R) \cup T.$$
$$S \cup (R \cap T) = (S \cup R) \cap (S \cup T).$$
$$S \cap S^c = \emptyset.$$
$$S \cap \Omega = S.$$
$$S - R = S \cap R^c.$$
$$R - S = R \cap S^c.$$

The **De Morgan's law** states that

$$(S \cup R)^c = S^c \cap R^c,$$

which is generalized to

$$\left(\bigcup_i S_i \right)^c = \bigcap_i S_i^c.$$

It also states that

$$(S \cap R)^c = S^c \cup R^c,$$

which is also generalized to

$$\left(\bigcap_i S_i \right)^c = \bigcup_i S_i^c.$$

Another interesting law states that

$$S \cup R = S \cup (S^c \cap R).$$

The Venn diagram depicted in Figure 2.3 shows this property.

Example 2.1.1. Consider three sets $A = \{1,2,3\}$, $B = \{1,3,5\}$, and $C = \{4,5\}$ of a sample space $\Omega = \{1,2,3,4,5,6\}$.

$$A \cup B = \{1,2,3,5\}.$$
$$A \cap (B \cup C) = \{1,3\}.$$
$$A^c = \{4,5,6\}.$$

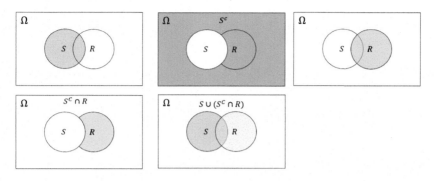

Figure 2.3 $S \cup R = S \cup (S^c \cap R)$.

$$A \cup (B \cup C) = \{1,2,3,4,5\}.$$
$$A \cup (B \cap C) = \{1,2,3,5\}.$$
$$A - B = \{2\}.$$
$$B - A = \{5\}.$$
$$A \cup (A^c \cap B) = \{1,2,3,5\}.$$

☐

2.2 PROBABILITY

A probability model is a mathematical description of the uncertainty of a system or situation. Probability is helpful in a wide variety of areas since it supports understanding and explaining variation, separating valid data from noise, and modeling complex phenomena [50, 441].

This mathematical representation is based on the concept of probability space. A probability space involves performing a random experiment. A **random experiment** is an experiment in which each realization can generate different results (**simple event**), even if the conditions are the same in each realization. The word "event" by itself reminds of something that occurred [413]. Each experiment has an outcome. A simple event is an **outcome** that cannot be broken down into simpler events. An **event** is any result set of an experiment, where the simplest events are called simple events.

A **probability space** consists of a tuple $(\Omega, \mathscr{P}(\Omega), P)$, where Ω is a sample space, which is the set of all possible outcomes of a random experiment, $\mathscr{P}(\Omega)$ is the **power-set of the sample space**, and P is the **probability function** that assigns an event $S \subseteq \Omega$ to a real number between zero and one, that is $P : S \rightarrow [0,1]$. It is worth mentioning that simple events of a sample space must be mutually exclusive. Summarizing, the function P must satisfy the following **axioms**:

$$P : S \rightarrow [0,1], \tag{2.2.1}$$

$$P(\emptyset) = 0, \quad P(\Omega) = 1, \tag{2.2.2}$$

and

$$P\left(\bigcup_{i=1}^{\infty} S_i\right) = \sum_{i=1}^{\infty} P(S_i), \quad \text{for } S_1, S_2, \ldots \text{ disjoint events.} \tag{2.2.3}$$

The concept of a random experiment is broad. For example, an experiment might be testing one server, two servers, three servers, measuring the time elapsed when a video file is downloaded or counting the number of discarded packages in a time interval. Therefore, the experiment should be defined according to the purpose of the study.

Example 2.2.1. Suppose an experiment consists of turning on an air conditioner for which the possible results of this experiment are: success (Up) or failure (Down). Success means that the air conditioner is appropriately working (Up – U); otherwise, it has a failure (Down – D). Therefore the possible results, represented in the sample space, are $\Omega = \{U, D\}$. The powerset of sample space is $\mathscr{P}(\Omega) = \{\emptyset, \{U\}, \{D\}, \{U, D\}\}$. Assume the probability of success is $P(U) = 0.95$; hence $P(D) = 0.05, P(\emptyset) = 0$, and $P(\Omega) = 1$. $\quad\square$

Example 2.2.2. Let us consider another example. Assume four servers (S_1, S_2, S_3, and S_4) were placed in an accelerated reliability test for a period. At the end of the test, each server may pass the test (Up - U) or may fail (F). Therefore, the result of the random experiment i may be represented by a 4-tuple $e_i = (s_i^{S_4}, s_i^{S_3}, s_i^{S_2}, s_i^{S_1})$, where $s_i^j = \{U, D\}, j \in \{S_1, S_2, S_3, S_4\}$. Therefore, the possible results are represented in the sample space

$$\begin{aligned}
\Omega = \{ & (D, D, D, D), (D, D, D, U), (D, D, U, D), (D, D, U, U), \\
& (D, U, D, D), (D, U, D, U), (D, U, U, D), (D, U, U, U), \\
& (U, D, D, D), (U, D, D, U), (U, D, U, D), (U, D, U, U), \\
& (U, U, D, D), (U, U, D, U), (U, U, U, D), (U, U, U, U)\},
\end{aligned}$$

where $|\Omega| = 16$. If $P(U) = 0.95$, then the probability of each simple event $e_i = (s_i^{S_4}, s_i^{S_3}, s_i^{S_2}, s_i^{S_1})$ is depicted in Table 2.1.

Hence, we have $P(D, D, D, D) = 0.05 \times 0.05 \times 0.05 \times 0.05 = 6.25 \times 10^{-6}$. Likewise, $P(U, D, D, U) = 0.95 \times 0.05 \times 0.05 \times 0.95 = 0.905$. The probability of having at least 2 servers functioning is $P(D, D, U, U) + P(D, U, D, U) + P(U, D, D, U) + P(D, U, U, D) + P(D, U, U, D) + P(U, U, D, D) + P(D, U, U, U) + P(U, U, U, D) + P(U, U, U, U) = 0.999519$. $\quad\square$

Table 2.1

Probability of Each Simple Event $e_i = (s_i^{S_4}, s_i^{S_3}, s_i^{S_2}, s_i^{S_1})$

e_i	$s_i^{S_4}$	$s_i^{S_3}$	$s_i^{S_2}$	$s_i^{S_1}$	$P(s_i^{S_4})$	$P(s_i^{S_3})$	$P(s_i^{S_2})$	$P(s_i^{S_1})$	$P(e_i)$
0	D	D	D	D	0.05	0.05	0.05	0.05	6.25×10^{-6}
1	D	D	D	U	0.05	0.05	0.05	0.95	1.19×10^{-4}
2	D	D	U	D	0.05	0.05	0.95	0.05	1.19×10^{-4}
3	D	D	U	U	0.05	0.05	0.95	0.95	2.26×10^{-3}
4	D	U	D	D	0.05	0.95	0.05	0.05	1.19×10^{-4}
5	D	U	D	U	0.05	0.95	0.05	0.95	2.26×10^{-3}
6	D	U	U	D	0.05	0.95	0.95	0.05	2.26×10^{-3}
7	D	U	U	U	0.05	0.95	0.95	0.95	4.29×10^{-2}
8	U	D	D	D	0.95	0.05	0.05	0.05	1.19×10^{-4}
9	U	D	D	U	0.95	0.05	0.05	0.95	2.26×10^{-3}
10	U	D	U	D	0.95	0.05	0.95	0.05	2.26×10^{3}
11	U	D	U	U	0.95	0.05	0.95	0.95	4.29×10^{-2}
12	U	U	D	D	0.95	0.95	0.05	0.05	2.26×10^{-3}
13	U	U	D	U	0.95	0.95	0.05	0.95	4.29×10^{-2}
14	U	U	U	D	0.95	0.95	0.95	0.05	4.29×10^{-2}
15	U	U	U	U	0.95	0.95	0.95	0.95	8.15×10^{-1}

Example 2.2.3. As a third example, consider a server placed in a reliability test and that we are interested in studying the time the server takes to present a failure. In this case, the sample space $\Omega = \mathbb{R}^+ = \{x \mid x > 0\}$. $\quad\square$

Some random experiment has an inherent sequential execution. For instance, assume the air conditioner mentioned in the first example is turned on and off three times. Each time the air conditioner is turned on, it may function (U) or not (D). Figure 2.4.a depicts the sample space in a 3-dimensional space, where the axes x, y, and z represent the first, the second, and the third activation, respectively. Each point of the cube represents a simple event of the sample space. Figure 2.4.b represents the sample space as a tree, which more naturally represents the sequential activations of the air conditioner and the respective results (Up - U or Down - D). In the tree notation, the simple events are represented in the leaves of the tree.

Probability has the following **properties**, for any events S and R:

1. $P(S^c) = 1 - P(S)$.

2. If $S \subseteq R$, then $P(S) \geq P(R)$.

3. $P(S \cup R) = P(S) + P(R) - P(S \cap R)$.

4. $P(S \cup R) = P(S) + P(S^c \cap R)$.

5. $P(S \cup R) \geq P(S) + P(R)$.

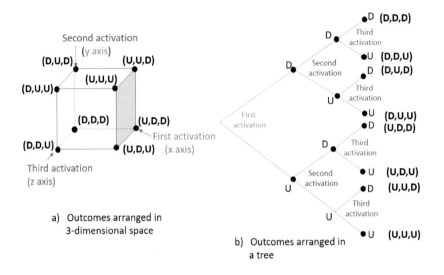

a) Outcomes arranged in 3-dimensional space

b) Outcomes arranged in a tree

Figure 2.4 Sample Space a) 3-dimensional space and b) as a tree structure.

The property number 3 is named **inclusion-exclusion** and can be generalized for

$$P\left(\bigcup_{i=1}^{n} S_i\right) = \sum_{i=1}^{n} P(S_i) - \sum_{i<j} P(S_i \cap S_j) + \qquad (2.2.4)$$

$$\sum_{i<j<k} P(S_i \cap S_j) \cap S_k) - \dots + (-1)^{n+1} P(S_1 \cap \dots \cap S_n).$$

For instance, consider three sets, A, B, and C; hence,

$$P(A \cup B \cup C) = P(A) + P(B) + P(C) - P(A \cap B) - P(A \cap C) - P(B \cap C) +$$

$$P(A \cap B \cap C).$$

The property number 4 is named **sum of disjoint products** and can be generalized for

$$P\left(\bigcup_{i=1}^{n} S_i\right) = P(S_1) + P(S_1^c \cap S_2) + P(S_1^c \cap S_2^c \cap S_3) + \qquad (2.2.5)$$

$$\dots + P(S_1^c \cap S_2^c \cap \dots \cap S_{n-1}^c \cap S_n).$$

Example 2.2.4. Consider the experiment depicted in Example 2.2.2 and its sample space Ω. Assume two events represented by sets A and B. The set A represents the event in which two or three servers are operational, whereas the set B denotes the event in which three or four servers are operational. Therefore, the set A is

$$A = \{(D, D, U, U)\, (D, U, D, U), (D, U, U, D), (D, U, U, U), (U, D, D, U),$$

$$(U, D, U, D), (U, D, U, U), (U, U, D, D), (U, U, D, U), (U, U, U, D)\}.$$

and the set B is

$$B = \{(D, U, U, U), (U, D, U, U), (U, U, D, U), (U, U, U, D)\}.$$

Thus

$$A \cap B = \{(U, D, U, U), (U, U, D, U), (U, U, U, D)\}.$$

Therefore, applying the inclusion-exclusion method, $P(A \cup B) = P(A) + P(B) - P(A \cap B)$, we have (from Table 2.1)

$$P(A) = 0.1850125,$$

$$P(B) = 0.98598125,$$

and

$$P(A \cap B) = 0.171475.$$

Hence, $P(A \cup B) = 0.1850125 + 0.98598125 - 0.171475 = 0.999519.$

Now, let us adopt the sum of disjoint products. From A, we obtain

$$A^c = \{(D, D, D, D), (D, D, D, U), (D, D, U, D), (U, D, D, D), (U, U, U, U)\}.$$

Hence,

$$A^c \cap B = \{(U, U, U, U)\}.$$

Thus, as $P(A \cup B) = P(A) + P(A^c \cap B)$, we obtain (from Table 2.1)

$$P(A) = 0.1850125,$$

$$P(A^c \cap B) = 0.81450625.$$

Therefore, $P(A \cup B) = P(A) + P(A^c \cap B) = 0.1850125 + 0.81450625 = 0.999519,$ which is the same result obtained when adopting the inclusion-exclusion method.

□

2.3 CONDITIONAL PROBABILITY

This section introduces the concept of conditional probability. Conditional probability aims at supporting reasoning on the outcome of an experiment based on incomplete information. Whenever we observe new evidence (more data), this information may affect our uncertainties. A new observation could be consistent with our beliefs or may question our prior knowledge. Conditional probability addresses how we should update our beliefs considering empirical evidence.

Before executing a random experiment, we cannot precisely know if an event A will occur. $P(A)$ is the **prior probability** of A. Now, if we are informed that an event B occurred, our knowledge of the probability of A occurring must be altered. The **conditional probability** of A given an event B occurred is denoted by $P(A \mid B)$.

Given an event B has taken place, the probability of the event A occurring must be renormalized by the probability of the given event (B) so that the sum of probabilities continues to sum 1. Therefore, the probability that the event A occurring given that the event B has occurred is the ratio between the occurring A and B ($A \cap B$) and the probability of B (since it already occurred). Hence

$$P(A \mid B) = \frac{P(A \cap B)}{P(B)}, \qquad (2.3.1)$$

where we assume $P(B) > 0$. If $P(B) = 0$, $P(A \mid B)$ is undefined.

For a defined event B, we have
1 -

$$P(\Omega \mid B) = \frac{P(\Omega \cap B)}{P(B)} = \frac{P(B)}{P(B)} = 1 \qquad (2.3.2)$$

2 - For any A and C disjoint, we have

$$P(A \cup C \mid B) = \frac{P((A \cup C) \cap B)}{P(B)} = \frac{P((A \cap B) \cup (C \cap B))}{P(B)}$$

$$P(A \cup C \mid B) = \frac{P(A \cap B)}{P(B)} + \frac{P(C \cap B)}{P(B)}$$

$$P(A \cup C \mid B) = P(A \mid B) + P(C \mid B). \qquad (2.3.3)$$

Generalizing, for A_i, $\forall i$, disjoints:

$$P(\bigcup_{i}^{n} A_i \mid B) = \sum_{i=1}^{n} P(A_i \mid B). \qquad (2.3.4)$$

3 -

$$P(A \cup C \mid B) \leq P(A \mid B) + P(C \mid B). \qquad (2.3.5)$$

Generalizing, we obtain

$$P(\bigcup_i^n A_i \,|\, B) \le \sum_{i=1}^n P(A_i \,|\, B). \tag{2.3.6}$$

Example 2.3.1. Assume the experiment depicted in Example 2.2.2. We already know the unconditional probability of the event A, that is $P(A) = 0.1850125$. Given at least two servers are functioning, $C = \{e_3, e_5, e_6, e_7, e_9, e_{10}, e_{11}, e_{12}, e_{13}, e_{14}, e_{15}\}$, what is the probability of having two or three servers operational, $P(A\,|\,C)$?

As

$$P(A\,|\,C) = \frac{P(A \cap C)}{P(C)}.$$

As $C = \{e_3, e_5, e_6, e_7, e_9, e_{10}, e_{11}, e_{12}, e_{13}, e_{14}, e_{15}\}$, $P(C) = 9.99519 \times 10^{-1}$. Now, we need to find $A \cap C$, and the calculating $P(A \cap C)$.

$$A \cap C = \{e_3, e_5, e_6, e_7, e_9, e_{10}, e_{11}, e_{12}, e_{13}, e_{14}\}$$
$$\cap \{e_3, e_5, e_6, e_7, e_9, e_{10}, e_{11}, e_{12}, e_{13}, e_{14}, e_{15}\} =$$
$$\{e_3, e_5, e_6, e_7, e_9, e_{10}, e_{11}, e_{12}, e_{13}, e_{14}\}.$$

Hence, $P(A \cap C) = 0.1850125$. Therefore,

$$P(A\,|\,C) = \frac{P(A \cap C)}{P(C)} = \frac{0.1850125}{9.99519 \times 10^{-1}} = 0.185102.$$

$\square$

Example 2.3.2. Assume again the experiment depicted in Example 2.2.2. Adopt, however, the probability of one server failing as $1 - p = 0.1$. If the number of failed servers is even (event B), calculate the probability of having only two failed servers (event A). Figure 2.5 shows the Venn diagram of such sets.

The unconditional probability of having only two servers in failure is

$$P(A) = P(e_3 \cup e_5 \cup e_6 \cup e_9 \cup e_{10} \cup e_{12}) =$$
$$P(A) = P(e_3) + P(e_5) + P(e_6) + P(e_9) + P(e_{10}) + P(e_{12}) = 0.0486.$$

The probability of having an even number of servers in failure is

$$P(B) = P(e_0 \cup e_3 \cup e_5 \cup e_6 \cup e_9 \cup e_{10} \cup e_{12}) =$$
$$P(B) = P(e_0) + P(e_3) + P(e_5) + P(e_6) + P(e_9) + P(e_{10}) + P(e_{12}) = 0.0487.$$

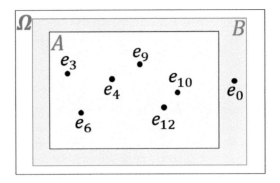

Figure 2.5 Venn Diagram - Example 2.3.2.

The probability of having an even number of failures (B) and exactly only two failures (A) is given by $P(A \cap B)$. Hence, we need

$$A \cap B = \{e_0 \cup e_3 \cup e_5 \cup e_6 \cup e_9 \cup e_{10} \cup e_{12}\} \cap$$

$$\{e_3 \cup e_5 \cup e_6 \cup e_9 \cup e_{10} \cup e_{12}\}.$$

Thus,

$$A \cap B = \{e_3 \cup e_5 \cup e_6 \cup e_9 \cup e_{10} \cup e_{12}\}.$$

Hence,

$$P(A \cap B) = 0.0486.$$

Therefore,

$$P(A \mid B) = \frac{P(A \cap B)}{P(B)} =$$

$$P(A \mid B) = \frac{0.0486}{0.0487} = 0.9979.$$

Summarizing, the unconditional probability of having precisely two failures is $P(A) = 0.0486$. However, if we know that the number of failures is even, the chances of having exactly only two failures significantly increases to $P(A \mid B) = 0.9979$.

$\square$

Example 2.3.3. Consider the sample space depicted in Figure 2.6, that is $\Omega = \{a, b, c, d, e, f, g, h, i, j, k, l, m, n, o, p, q, r, s, t\}$, $|\Omega| = 20$. Assume each simple event is equally likely, that is $P(e_i) = 0.05$, $e_i \in \Omega$. Consider the events $A = \{c, d, e, f, g, i, j, o, p, q\}$ and $B = \{g, p, q, r, s, t\}$. $|A| = 9$ and $|B| = 6$.

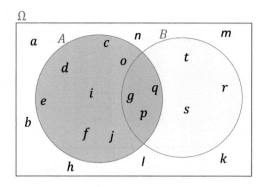

Figure 2.6   Venn Diagram - Example 2.3.3.

The unconditional probability of A and B are $P(A) = 0.45$ and $P(B) = 0.3$, respectively. The intersection set of A and B is $A \cap B = \{g, p, q\}$, $|A \cap B| = 3$. Thus, $P(A \cap B) = 0.15$. Assuming the event B occurred, the probability of A occurring is given by

$$P(A|B) = \frac{P(A \cap B)}{P(B)} = \frac{0.15}{0.3} = 0.5.$$

It is worth noting that given that we know the event B occurred, the probability of occurrence of the event A increases from $P(A) = 0.45$ to $P(A|B) = 0.5$.

$\square$

Example 2.3.4. A set of servers was monitored for a period aiming to detect failures (see Figure 2.7). Failures are represented by the event B. In addition, the monitoring system informs the occurrence of a failure by signaling an alarm (event A).
Assume a failure occurs (event B) with probability 0.15 ($P(B) = 0.15$). If the system is in failure, the monitoring system detects the failure and generates an alarm signal in 0.95 of the failures ($P(A|B)$); thus, in the case of failure (B), the monitoring system fails to report the failure 0.05 ($P(A^c|B)$). If the system is correctly functioning (event B^c), the monitoring system generates a false alarm (event A) with probability 0.1 ($P(A|B^c)$); hence when there is no failure the system does not send an alarm signal in 0.9 of the cases ($P(A^c|B^c)$) [441]. Figure 2.8 presents the sample space in tree format. The probability that the system is in failure, and the monitoring system does not detect the failure is

$$P(A^c \cap B) = P(A^c|B) \times P(B) = 0.05 \times 0.15 = 0.0075.$$

The probability that the system is in failure, and the monitoring system detects the failure is only

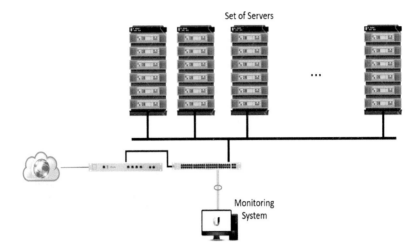

Figure 2.7   Servers with a Monitoring System - Example 2.3.4.

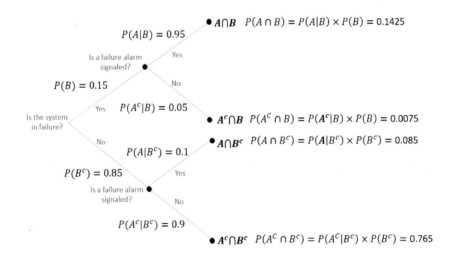

Figure 2.8   Sample Space - Example 2.3.4.

$$P(A \cap B) = P(A|B) \times P(B) = 0.05 \times 0.95 = 0.1425.$$

The probability that the system is appropriately functioning a false alarm is sent is

$$P(A \cap B^c) = P(A|B^c) \times P(B^c) = 0.85 \times 0.1 = 0.085.$$

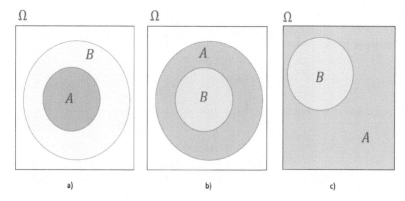

Figure 2.9   Venn Diagram - a) $A \subseteq B$, b) $B \subseteq A$ and c) $A \cap B = \emptyset$.

Finally, the probability that the system is properly functioning and no alarm is sent is

$$P(A^c \cap B^c) = P(A^c|B^c) \times P(B^c) = 0.85 \times 0.9 = 0.765.$$

$\square$

Three specific cases are worth stressing (Figure 2.9 shows the three first cases):

1. $P(A|B) = \frac{P(A)}{P(B)}$ if $A \subseteq B$.

2. $P(A|B) = 1$ if $B \subseteq A$.

3. $P(A|B) = 0$ if $A \cap B = \emptyset$.

The third case describes a case of two mutually exclusive events. Hence, if one occurs, the other does not occur.

The Axiom 2.2.3 states that if two events A and B are mutually exclusive, the sum of the probabilities of the events is

$$P(A \cup B) = P(A) + P(B).$$

2.4   INDEPENDENCE

Now, let us investigate the probability of the intersection of two events. First, consider the event B, where $P(B) > 0$. The event A is said to be independent of event B if

$$P(A|B) = P(A). \tag{2.4.1}$$

Hence, the knowledge of the occurrence of the event B does not change the probability of event A. Therefore, if event A is independent of event B, event B must also be independent of the event A. Thus, as

$$P(A \mid B) = \frac{P(A \cap B)}{P(B)},$$

and considering the Equation 2.4.1, we get

$$P(A \mid B) = \frac{P(A \cap B)}{P(B)} = P(A).$$

Hence

$$P(A \cap B) = P(A) P(B) \qquad (2.4.2)$$

if A and B are independent.

Generalizing for n independent events, A_i, $i = 1, 2, \ldots, n$, we have

$$P(\bigcap_{i=1}^{n} A_i) = \prod_{i=1}^{n} P(A_i). \qquad (2.4.3)$$

2.5 BAYES' RULE AND THE LAW OF TOTAL PROBABILITY

For any two events A and B, we know that

$$P(A \cup B) = P(A \mid B) P(B) = P(B \mid A) P(A). \qquad (2.5.1)$$

Therefore

$$P(A \mid B) = \frac{P(A \cup B)}{P(B)} = \frac{P(B \mid A) P(A)}{P(B)}. \qquad (2.5.2)$$

Equation 2.3.1 may be generalized for any events $A_1, \ldots, A_n$ with positive probabilities:

$$P(\bigcap_{i=1}^{n} A_i) = P(A_1) P(A_2 \mid A_1) P(A_3 \mid A_1 \cap A_2) \ldots P(A_n \mid A_1 \cap \ldots \cap A_{n-1}). \qquad (2.5.3)$$

Now, let $A_1, \ldots, A_n$ be a partition of sample space Ω and another event B (see Figure 2.10), then

$$P(B) = \sum_{i=1}^{n} P(B \mid A_i) P(A_i), \qquad (2.5.4)$$

which is called the Law of Total Probability, since $B = (B \cap A_1) \cup (B \cap A_2) \cup ... \cup (B \cap A_n)$, which leads to $P(B) = P(B \cap A_1) + P(B \cap A_2) + ... + P(B \cap A_n)$. It is worth mentioning that $(B \cap A_i) \cap (B \cap A_j) = \emptyset$ for any A_i and A_j of the partition.

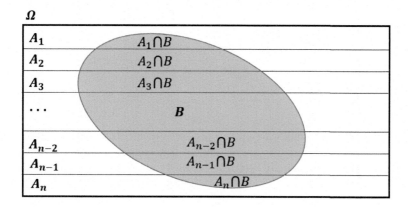

Figure 2.10 Partition $A_1, ... , A_n$ and an Event B.

Using Equation 2.5.2 and Equation 2.5.4, we obtain

$$P(A_i|B) = \frac{P(A_i \cap B)}{P(B)} = \frac{P(B|A_i)\,P(A_i)}{\sum_{i=1}^{n} P(B|A_i)\,P(A_i)}.$$

Hence

$$P(A_i|B) = \frac{P(B|A_i)\,P(A_i)}{\sum_{i=1}^{n} P(B|A_i)\,P(A_i)}, \tag{2.5.5}$$

which is named the Bayes' rule.

Example 2.5.1. Consider the system depicted in Example 2.3.4. In that example, a set of servers was monitored to detect failures (event B), and the monitoring system signals a failure by an alarm (event A). Figure 2.8 shows the sample space in a tree format. The probability the system is in failure, given an alarm signal is present, can be estimated by

$$P(B|A) = \frac{P(A|B) \times P(B)}{(P(A|B) \times P(B)) + (P(A|B^c) \times P(B^c))}.$$

Therefore,

$$P(B|A) = \frac{0.95 \times 0.15}{(0.95 \times 0.15) + (0.1 \times 0.85)} = 0.6264.$$

The probability the system is not in failure, given an alarm signal is present, is calculated using

$$P(B^c|A) = \frac{P(A|B^c) \times P(B^c)}{(P(A|B^c) \times P(B^c)) + (P(A|B) \times P(B))}.$$

Therefore,

$$P(B^c|A) = \frac{0.1 \times 0.85}{(0.1 \times 0.85) + (0.95 \times 0.15)} = 0.3736.$$

□

Example 2.5.2. A monitoring system periodically checks if a server is alive. The event D denotes the server is out of service. Two possible reasons may have taken the server down, the mutually exclusive events R_1 and R_2. Assume the probability of the server being out service as $P(D) = 0.1$; hence $P(D^c) = 0.9$. Consider the cause of R_1, given the failure occurred is $P(R_1|D) = 0.7$; thus $P(R_2|D) = 0.3$. Figure 2.11 shows the sequential description of the experiment.

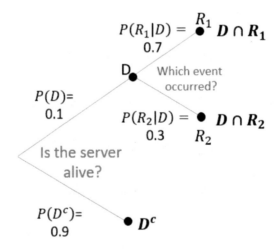

Figure 2.11 Sequential Description of the Experiment.

The probability the server is down given the event R_1 occurred is estimated by

$$P(D|R_1) = \frac{P(R_1|D)P(D)}{\sum_{i=1}^{2} P(R_i|D)P(D)}.$$

Hence,

$$P(D \mid R_1) = \frac{0.7 \times 0.1}{(0.7 \times 0.1) + (0.3 \times 0.1)} = 0.2059.$$

Likewise, The probability the server is down given the event R_2 occurred is estimated by

$$P(D \mid R_2) = \frac{P(R_2 \mid D) P(D)}{\sum_{i=1}^{2} P(R_i \mid D) P(D)}.$$

Thus,

$$P(D \mid R_2) = \frac{0.3 \times 0.1}{(0.3 \times 0.1) + (0.7 \times 0.1)} = 0.7941.$$

$\square$

Example 2.5.3. A system manager used an antivirus program to detect the "infection" of a computer of a data center concerning a new computer virus. Let us assume the new virus has infected 0.01 ($P(V)$) of computers of the data center; thus, the probability of a server not being infected is $P(V^c) = 0.99$. Consider V as the event that the computer has the virus. An antivirus program checks the computer software system and informs if the computer is infected. Let D denote the event that represents that the antivirus program detected the virus. Consider the antivirus program accurately detects the virus in 98% of the cases, that is $P(D \mid V) = 0.98$. Also assume the antivirus program informs the system is not infected by the virus (D^c) if the computer system actually does not have the virus (V^c) with probability 99%, that is $P(D^c \mid V^c) = 0.99$. Figure 2.12 shows the sample space of the experiment.

Hence, the probability of detecting the virus given the virus did not infect the computer is $P(D \mid V^c) = 0.01$. The probability the computer is infected by the virus given the antivirus program detected the infection is given by

$$P(V \mid D) = \frac{P(D \mid V) \times P(V)}{P(D)}.$$

$$P(V \mid D) = \frac{P(D \mid V) \times P(V)}{P(D \mid V) \times P(V) + P(D \mid V^c) \times P(V^c)}.$$

Therefore, the probability that the virus had infected the computer given the antivirus program detected the presence of the virus is only

$$P(V \mid D) = \frac{0.98 \times 0.01}{0.98 \times 0.01 + 0.02 \times 0.99} = 0.3311,$$

even though the antivirus program seems to be quite accurate. The probability the computer is not infected by the virus given the antivirus program detected the infection is given by

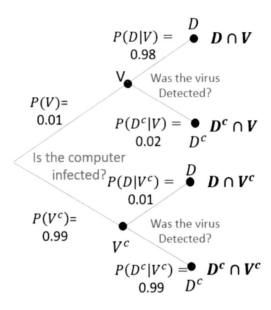

Figure 2.12 Sample Space of the Experiment - Virus Infection.

$$P(V^c|D) = \frac{P(D|V^c) \times P(V^c)}{P(D)}.$$

$$P(V^c|D) = \frac{P(D|V^c) \times P(V^c)}{P(D|V^c) \times P(V^c) + P(D|V) \times P(V)}.$$

Hence,

$$P(V^c|D) = \frac{0.02 \times 0.99}{(0.02 \times 0.99) + (0.98 \times 0.01)} = 0.6689.$$

The probability the computer is not infected by the virus given the antivirus program did not detect the infection is given by

$$P(V^c|D^c) = \frac{P(D^c|V^c) \times P(V^c)}{(P(D^c|V^c) \times P(V^c)) + (P(D|V^c) \times P(V^c))}.$$

Thus,

$$P(V^c|D^c) = \frac{0.99 \times 0.9}{(0.99 \times 0.9) + (0.01) \times 0.99} = 0.9802.$$

□

2.6 COUNTING

In many probability problems, it is required to determine the number of ways an event can occur. This section introduces methods for counting these possibilities. Such methods are usually described either by selection or allocation problems (see Figure 2.13). For example, the selection description may be well represented in how identifiable balls may be randomly chosen from a box. A random choice means each ball in the box is equally likely to be chosen in this context. These problems represented as allocation may be depicted, for instance, in terms of how indistinguishable balls may be inserted into identifiable boxes [413].

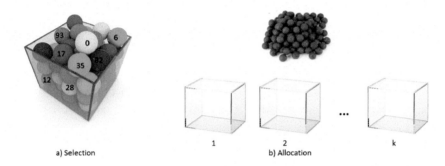

a) Selection   b) Allocation

Figure 2.13   a) Selection Problem and b) Allocation Problem.

In selection problems, once one ball is chosen, before selecting the next ball, a decision must be taken concerning the first ball chosen: 1) The ball is put back into the box (*with replacement*). In such a case, the same ball may be chosen many times. 2) The ball is set aside and never returned to the box (*without replacement*); hence a ball may occur only once.

Another concern is the order in which the balls are selected. In some cases, the order is essential, and in other cases, it is not. For example, one may know if a red ball was selected before a blue ball in some contexts. However, sometimes, it is not essential to know whether a red ball is selected before a blue one. The former case is called *permutation*, and the latter is known as *combination*.

2.6.1 N-PERMUTATION

An arrangement of n distinct balls without replacement is called an n-permutation, and the number of different arrangements is equal to

$$np(n) = n!. \qquad (2.6.1)$$

$np(n)$ is the number of distinct ways in which n identifiable balls can be organized.

Example 2.6.1. Consider three identified balls. The first ball has a label A, the second ball is labeled with B, and the third ball has a label C. Figure 2.14.a shows a box with the balls.

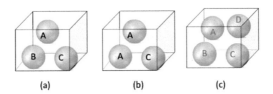

(a)   (b)   (c)

Figure 2.14   a) Three Balls. b) Three Balls with Repetition. c) Four Balls.

The number of arrangements of size 3 is

$$np(3) = 3! = 3 \times 2 \times 1 = 6.$$

The possible arrangements are ABC, ACB, BAC, BCA, CAB, and CBA.

□

Now assume the number of permutations without replacement, but in which the balls are not all distinct; that is, there are repetitions of the balls' identification. For instance, consider n balls, where we have n_1 balls of type 1, n_2 balls of type 2, n_3 balls of type 3, and so forth, such that $\sum_{i=1}^{k} n_i = n$. The number of different arrangements is equal to

$$np(n, n_1, n_2, ..., n_k) = \frac{n!}{\prod_{i=1}^{k} n_i!}. \tag{2.6.2}$$

Example 2.6.2. Consider three identified balls. The first ball has a label A, the second ball is labeled with A, and the third ball has a label C. Figure 2.14.b depicts a box with the respective balls. The number of arrangements of size 3 is

$$np(3, 2, 1) = \frac{3!}{2! \times 1!} = \frac{3 \times 2!}{2!} = 3.$$

The possible arrangement are AAC, ACA, and CAA.

□

Example 2.6.3. Assume six identified balls. The first ball is labeled A, the second ball is labeled with A, the third ball has a label B, the fourth ball has a label A, the fifth ball has a label B, and the sixth ball has a label C. The number of arrangements of size 6 is

$$np(6, 3, 2, 1) = \frac{6!}{3! \times 2!} = \frac{6 \times 5 \times 4 \times 3!}{3! \times 2!}$$

$$np(6,3,2,1) = \frac{6 \times 5 \times 4}{2} = 60.$$

□

2.6.2   K OUT OF N PERMUTATION WITH REPLACEMENT

In this case, the aim is to count the number of ways in which k balls may be selected from n distinct balls. Thus, the first ball is selected, their identity is recorded, and the ball is placed back in the box. Thus, the same ball may be chosen k times. Hence, the number of different arrangements is equal to

$$pr(n,k) = n^k. \tag{2.6.3}$$

Example 2.6.4. Consider ten balls, each one labeled with a single-digit number, such that each ball has the label 0, 1, 2, 3, 4, 5, 6, 7, 8, and 9. The number of different arrangements of size 3 is

$$pr(10,3) = 10^3 = 1000,$$

where the numbers recorded are from 000 to 999.

□

Now consider two boxes, where each Box_i, $i = \{1, 2\}$, has n_i distinguishable balls. Assume the first ball is selected from the first box, that is Box_1; hence, there are n_1 ways of choosing the first ball. Then, the second ball is chosen from the second box (Box_2). Thus, there are n_2 ways of choosing a second ball. Therefore, the number of distinct ordered pairs is equal to $n_1 \times n_2$. Generalizing for k boxes, where each Box_i, $i = \{1, 2, ..., k\}$, the number of distinct ordered k-tuples is

$$pr(n_1,n_2,...,n_k,k) = \prod_{i=1}^{k} n_i. \tag{2.6.4}$$

Example 2.6.5. Let us assume four boxes, Box_i, $i = \{1, 2, 3, 4\}$, where each Box_i has $n_1 = 4$, $n_2 = 7$, $n_3 = 3$, and $n_4 = 9$ identifiable balls, respectively. The number of different arrangements of size 4 is

$$pr(n_1,n_2,n_3,n_4,4) = \prod_{i=1}^{4} n_i = n_1 \times n_2 \times n_3 \times n_4 = 4 \times 7 \times 3 \times 9 = 756.$$

□

2.6.3   K OUT OF N PERMUTATION WITHOUT REPLACEMENT

Now move on to the problem of selecting k balls from n identifiable balls in a box, assuming that the chosen ball is not returned to the box. This problem is well represented by selecting k balls from a box with n distinguishable balls. The first of the k balls is chosen from a set of n balls, the second of the k balls is chosen from a set of $n - 1$ balls. Likewise, the third of the k balls is chosen from a set of $n - 2$ balls. This process continues until the selection of kth from those remaining $n - k + 1$. Therefore, for an arbitrary $k \leq n$, $k, n \in \mathbb{N}$, the number of arrangements is

$$p(n,k) = n \times (n-1) \times (n-2) \times ... \times, (n-k+1) = \frac{n!}{(n-k)!} \qquad (2.6.5)$$

Example 2.6.6. The number of arrangements of $k = 3$ balls from a box with $n = 4$ distinguishable balls, where each ball is labeled the by A, B, C, and D (see Figure 2.14.c) is

$$p(4,3) = \frac{4!}{(4-3)!} = \frac{4!}{1!} = 24.$$

The possible arrangements are $ABC, ABD, ACB, ACD, ADB, ADC, BAC, BAD, BCA, BCD, BDA, BDC, CAB, CAD, CBA, CBD, CDA, CDB, DAB, DAC, DBA, DBC, DCA,$ and DCB.

□

Example 2.6.7. Assume we need to calculate the number of arrangements that a five-digit code, in which all the digits are different, can be selected, where each digit is a hexadecimal number, that is from 0 to F. The number of ways these digits may be organized is

$$p(16,4) = \frac{16!}{(16-4)!} = \frac{16!}{12!}.$$

$$p(16,4) = \frac{16 \times 15 \times 14 \times 13 \times 12!}{12!}.$$

$$p(16,4) = 43,680.$$

□

2.6.4   K OUT OF N COMBINATION WITHOUT REPLACEMENT

Now assume the case in which balls are selected without replacement when the order in which they are selected is not important. In such a case, what matters is that a specific type of ball is chosen, but the order (first, second,...) is of no interest. As we have already seen, when selection order is not important, we have a combination problem instead of permutation.

Consider, for instance, a case where k balls are chosen from n balls in a box, and once a ball is chosen, it is not placed back into the box. Since the order is unimportant, we combine k out of n balls without replacement. Hence, for an arbitrary $k \leq n, k, n \in \mathbb{N}$, the number of combinations is given by

$$c(n,k) = \frac{n!}{k!\,(n-k)!} \tag{2.6.6}$$

which is equal to

$$c(n,k) = \frac{p(n,k)}{k!}. \tag{2.6.7}$$

The combination of k items out of n is also represented by the binomial coefficient $\binom{n}{k}$; hence

$$p(n,k) = \binom{n}{k} \times k!. \tag{2.6.8}$$

Example 2.6.8. Consider five (n) different colored balls, one red (R), one blue (B), one green (G), one black (B), and one white (W), from which two (k) are selected without replacement. The number of combinations is

$$c(5,2) = \frac{5!}{2!\,(5-2)!} = \frac{5!}{2!\,3!} = \frac{5 \times 4 \times 3!}{2!\,3!} = \frac{5 \times 4}{2} = 10.$$

$\square$

Example 2.6.9. Consider ten (n) servers identified by a label. The number of combinations without replacement of size five (k) is

$$c(10,5) = \frac{10!}{5!\,(10-5)!} = \frac{10 \times 9 \times 8 \times 7 \times 6 \times 5!}{5! \times 5!} = 252.$$

If the order is important (permutation), the number of arrangements is much higher:

$$p(10,5) = 252 \times 5! = 30,240.$$

$\square$

2.6.5 K OUT OF N COMBINATION WITH REPLACEMENT

The last case to be considered is a combination of taking into account replacements. Assume we need to select k out of n identifiable balls from a box, where after each selection, the chosen ball is placed back into the box. This problem is equivalent to selecting k out of $n+k-1$ distinguishable balls from a box. Therefore, the number of ways we may combine k out of n identifiable balls from a box with replacement is calculated by

$$cr(n,k) = \frac{(n+k-1)!}{(n-1)!\,k!} = \binom{n+k-1}{k}. \tag{2.6.9}$$

Example 2.6.10. Assume the box depicted in Figure 2.14.c. In that box, we find four balls ($n = 4$) identified by A, B, C, and D. The number of combinations of size three ($k = 3$) with replacement is

$$cr(4,3) = \frac{(4+3-1)!}{(4-1)!\,3!} = \frac{6!}{3!\,3!} = \frac{6 \times 5 \times 4!}{6} = 20.$$

The combinations are AAA, AAB, AAC, AAD, ABB, ABC, ABD, ACC, ACD, ADD, BBB, BBC, BBD, BCC, BCD, BDD, CCC, CCD, CDD, and DDD.

$\square$

Example 2.6.11. Assume the box depicted in Figure 2.14.c. Assume we select two (k) balls from those four balls in the box. A, B, C, and D are labels that identify the balls. The number of permutations, considering replacements and without replacements, and the group of combinations taking into account replacement or not, is shown. All possible sequences of strings for each type of problem are also depicted. The number of permutation of size 2 out of 4 balls with replacement is

$$pr(n,k) = n^k = 4^2 = 16$$

and respective arrangements are AA, AB, AC, AD, BA, BB, BC, BD, CA, CB, CC, CD, DB, DC, and DD. The number of permutation of size 2 out of 4 balls without replacement is

$$p(n,k) = \frac{n!}{(n-k)!} = \frac{4!}{(4-2)!} = 12,$$

and the arrangements are AB, AC, AD, BA, BC, BD, CA, CB, CD, DB, and DC.

The number of combinations of size 2 out of 4 balls with replacement is

$$cr(n,k) = \frac{(n+k-1)!}{(n-1)!\,k!} = \binom{n+k-1}{k} = \frac{5!}{3!\,2!} = 10,$$

and the combinations are AA, AB, AC, AD, BB, BC, BD, CC, CD, and DD. Finally, the number of combinations of size 2 out of 4 balls without replacement is

$$c(n,k) = \frac{n!}{k!\,(n-k)!} = \frac{4!}{2!\,(4-2)!} = 6.$$

and the combinations are AB, AC, AD, BC, BD, and CD. Besides, the number of permutations of size four (n) without replacement is

$$np(n) = n! = 4! = 24,$$

and the possible arrangements are ABCD, ABDC, ACBD, ACDB, ADBC, ADCB, BACD, BADC, BCAD, BCDA, BDAC, BDCA, CABD, CADB, CBAD, CBDA, CDAB, CDBA, DABC, DACB, DBAC, DBCA, DCAB, and DCBA.

$\square$

EXERCISES

Exercise 1. Let us consider three sets $A = \{1,3,4\}$, $B = \{1,2,5\}$ and $C = \{1,4,5,6\}$ of a sample space $\Omega = \{1,2,3,4,5,6,7,8\}$. Obtain (a) $A \cup B$, (b) $A \cap (B \cup C)$, (c) A^c, (d) $A \cup (B \cup C)$, (d) $A \cup (B \cap C)$, (e) $A - B$, (f) $B - A$, (g) $A \cup (A^c \cap B)$.

Exercise 2. Assume a product quality test, whose result is: success (s), partial success (ps), or failure (f). Success means that all functions of the product are appropriately functioning (s); if only one function of the system is not properly operating, the status is a partial success (ps). If more than one function is not properly working, the system is considered in failure (f). (a) Show the sample space of the experiment, (b) obtain the Powerset of sample space. If the probability of success is $P(s) = 0.85$ and the probability of partial success is $P(S) = 0.05$, (a) calculate the failure probability, (b) obtain the probability of the system being operational or partially operational, (c) calculate the probability of the system being in failure or partial success.

Exercise 3. Consider four servers $(S_1, S_2, S_3, S_4$ and $S_5)$ are tested for a period T. At the end of the test, each server may pass the test (P) or fail (F). (a) Construct a table that represents the sample space, (b) if $P(P) = 0.87$, calculate the probability of each simple event $e_i = \left(s_i^{S_1}, s_i^{S_2}, s_i^{S_3}, s_i^{S_4}, s_i^{S_5}\right)$ in the Table, (c) obtain the probability of at least three servers being operational.

Exercise 4. Consider the experiment depicted in Exercise 3 and its sample space Ω. Consider the set A represents the event in which two or three servers are operational, and the set B denotes the event in which three, four, or five servers are operational. (a) Applying the inclusion-exclusion method, $P(A \cup B)$, (b) adopt the sum of the disjoint product for calculating the probability of the same event.

Exercise 5. Assume the experiment depicted in Exercise 3. Given that at least three servers are functioning, what is the probability of having three or four servers operational?

Exercise 6. Consider again the experiment depicted in Example 3. Assume the probability of one server failing is $1 - p = 0.0.5$. If the number of failed servers is even, calculate the probability of having only two failed servers.

Exercise 7. Servers of a data center were monitored for detecting failures. Failures are denoted by the event F. The monitoring system signals a failure by sending an alarm (event A). Assume a failure occurs with a probability of 0.09. If the system fails, the monitoring system detects the failure and generates an alarm signal in 0.93 of the failures. In case of failure, the monitoring system fails to report 0.06 of failure $(P(A^c|F))$. If the system is correctly functioning (event F^c), the monitoring system generates a false alarm with probability 0.12 $(P(A|F^c))$. Hence when there is no failure, the system does not send an alarm signal with a probability of 0.9. (a) Obtain the probability that the system fails, and the monitoring system does not detect the failure. (b) Calculate the probability of the system being in failure, and the monitoring system detects the failure. (c) Calculate the probability that the system is appropriately functioning, a false alarm is sent, and finally (d) obtain the probability that the system is properly functioning and no alarm is sent.

Exercise 8. Assume the system described in Exercise 7. The servers were monitored, aiming at detecting failures (event F). The monitoring system signals a failure by setting the alarm (event A). (a) Calculate the probability the system is in failure, given that an alarm signal is present. (b) Obtain the probability that the system is not in failure, given that an alarm signal is present.

Exercise 9. A monitor periodically checks if a server is operational. The event F denotes the server is out of service. Two possible mutually exclusive causes may have taken the server down, C_1 and C_2. Assume the probability of the server being in failure is $P(F) = 0.15$; hence $P(F^c) = 0.85$. Consider the cause of C_1, given the failure occurred is $P(C_1|F) = 0.65$; thus $P(C_2|F) = 0.35$. (a) Calculate the probability the server is down, given the cause C_1. (b) Obtain the probability the server is down, given the cause C_2.

Exercise 10. A brand new antivirus program was installed in a data center to detect the "infection" of its servers concerning a new dangerous virus. Assume the virus has infected the data center computers infected 0.005 ($P(V)$). The antivirus program checks the computer software system and informs if the computer is infected. Let D denotes the event that represents that the antivirus program detected the virus. Consider the antivirus program accurately detects the virus 97% of the time. Also, assume the antivirus program informs that the virus does not infect the system (D^c) if the computer system does not have the virus (V^c) with a probability of 98%. Hence, the probability of detecting the virus given that the virus did not infect the computer is 0.02. (a) Obtain the probability that the computer is infected by the virus, given that the antivirus program detected the infection. (b) Calculate the probability that a server is not infected by the virus, given that the antivirus program detected the infection. (c) Obtain the probability that the computer is not infected by the virus, given that the antivirus program did not detect the infection.

Exercise 11. Consider a data center room with seven identified servers, $\{s_1, s_2, ..., s_7\}$. Calculate the number of arrangements of seven distinct servers without replacement.

Exercise 12. Now, consider a data center room with three classes of devices, $\{c_1, c_2, c_3\}$, and assume the number of devices of each class is ten, fifteen, and eight. First, calculate the arrangement of seven different servers without replacement. Next, calculate the number of arrangements of size thirty-three without replacement.

Exercise 13. Consider the data center room with seven identified servers, $\{s_1, s_2, ..., s_7\}$. Calculate the number of arrangements of seven distinct servers with replacement.

Exercise 14. Assume the data center room with three classes of devices, $\{c_1, c_2, c_3\}$. Assume the class c_1 has ten identifiable devices, the class c_2 has fifteen identifiable devices, and the class c_3 has eight identifiable devices. Calculate the number of different arrangements of size three.

Exercise 15. Consider twenty identified computers. Calculate the number of arrangements of four computers.

Exercise 16. Consider a code is composed of three letters (number of letters in the alphabet: twenty-six) and five digits (number of distinct digits: ten). What is the number of ways these letters and digits may be organized?

Exercise 17. Consider twenty (n) servers identified by a label. Obtain the number of combinations without replacement of size five (k).

Exercise 18. Assume we have twenty identified computers. Obtain the number of combinations of size four $(k = 4)$ with replacement.

3 Exploratory Data Analysis

Descriptive statistics summarize features of a data set (sample); hence descriptive statistics analysis aims to summarize a sample rather than use the statistics to learn about the population from which the data sample was obtained. The most common statistics quantify data central tendency, variability, and shape [77, 442]. Exploratory Data Analysis (EDA) builds upon descriptive data analysis by investigating discoveries, drifts, and relationships involving data to support the proposition of hypotheses. EDA is a crucial activity when analyzing a data sample obtained from an experiment. Such an analysis may support:

- detecting mistakes in the process,

- verifying the general characteristics of the system (population) from where the samples were obtained,

- delving into selection of possible suitable models, and

- gauging possible relations between variables.

The following sections summarize a set of statistics and of basic charts adopted to summarize samples collected from a system [287], [436],[178].

3.1 DIAGRAMS AND PLOTS

A statistical summary is a synthetic representation of a sample through numbers that summarize the general pattern (central tendency, dispersion, and shape) and the outliers of the measured data. Figure 3.1 presents a set of graphs used for data analysis, which helps to choose the graphical representations of the measured data. The following sections present their graphical notation and their applications.

Graphs for Categorical Variables:

Some charts for categorical variables relate the category to a count or percentage. The most important are:

- Bar Chart

- Pareto's Chart

- Pie Chart or Pizza Chart

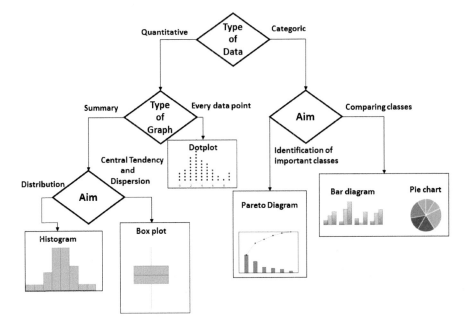

Figure 3.1 Types of Diagram, Plots and Data.

Example 3.1.1. Consider that a large communications system consists of several types of devices. A particular category has several models. Table 3.1 shows the number of defects observed in each category's devices during five (5) years. These devices were classified according to the models.

□

Bar Chart

The bar chart is used to compare measures of data categories. Each bar can represent the category's frequency, the function of a category (such as the mean, sum, or standard deviation), or summary values of a table. Creating a function requires numerical data and a categorical variable. The numerical data should represent the number (or percentage) of instances observed for each class. Considering the data in Table 3.1, the following bar chart (Figure 3.2a and Figure 3.2b) can be generated.

Pareto Chart

Pareto charts are a type of bar chart in which the horizontal axis represents the attributes of interest (classes). These classes are assigned counts or frequencies. In the Pareto graph, the bars are ordered from the highest count (or frequency) to the lowest count. A cumulative percentage line can also be included to assist in assessing the contribution of each category. Figure 3.3 shows the Pareto chart of the data presented in Table 3.1.

Table 3.1
Defects by Class

Type of Components	Failures	%
GS1	25	15.2
GS2	40	24.2
GS3	60	36.4
GS4	40	24.2

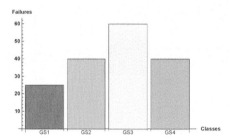

(a) Bar Chart (number of failures) - 1a

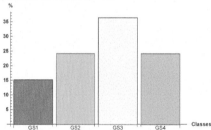

(b) Bar Chart (percentual) - 1b

Figure 3.2 Bar Charts.

Pie Chart

The pie chart is used to display proportions of data categories relative to the numeric data set. Categories can be organized into rows and their counts and percentages into columns. The resulting chart contains one sector for each category. Figure 3.4 shows a pie chart of the data shown in Figure 3.4. Within each sector, the percentage of the respective category was written.

Plots and Diagrams for Quantitative Variables

The distribution of a quantitative variable records its numerical values and the frequency of each value occurrence. The most important are:

- *Dot plot*

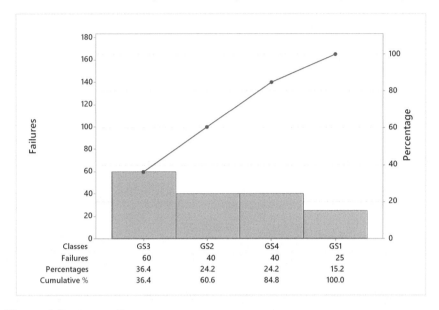

Classes	GS3	GS2	GS4	GS1
Failures	60	40	40	25
Percentages	36.4	24.2	24.2	15.2
Cumulative %	36.4	60.6	84.8	100.0

Figure 3.3   Pareto Chart.

- *Individual Value Plot*
- *Histogram*
- *Empirical Distribution Plot*
- *Box Plot*

These plots and the respective examples are presented in the following.

Individual Value Plot

The Individual Value Plot helps to compare the distributions of data samples. An individual value plot shows one point for each value of the sample. Thus, this plot supports the detection of outliers and data spread. The individual value plot is handy when one has relatively few observations or is important to assess each observation's effect.

Dot plot

Dot plots represent distributions of values along a number line. Dot plots are especially useful for comparing distributions. The abscissa of a dot plot is divided into intervals. Points represent the values that are in each range. A dot may represent an observation or a group of observations depending on the size of the sample. Consider the data set presented in Table 3.2. This dataset is a sample of a computational

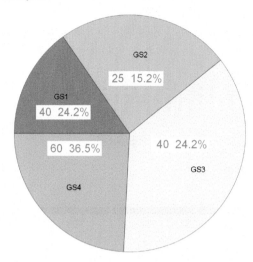

Figure 3.4   Pie Chart - Classes: GS1, GS2, GS3, and GS4.

system measurement's flow measurement (transactions per second-tps). Figure 3.5 shows the distribution of the data through the dot plot.

Table 3.2
Numerical Data – Throughput

	Data (tps)								
1	78.638	113.956	109.098	79.797	99.497	107.218	160.87	93.81	107.977
2	128.446	108.059	117.469	37.094	127.145	127.163	130.086	124.59	99.053
3	100.274	117.513	122.717	178.983	151.615	121.066	68.833	108.528	153.838
4	177.636	139.49	98.441	148.233	97.24	63.224	89.804	143.205	146.431
5	69.468	127.071	157.681	57.903	123.771	107.049	87.273	111.885	109.482
6	98.646	83.974	71.362	126.668	190.962	74.122	113.79	114.784	141.957
7	170.817	121.273	114.382	73.896	135.012	110.235	150.032	99.387	141.285
8	128.757	85.522	142.583	122.433	111.712	203.973	155.825	127.259	145.609
9	119.94	127.952	85.819	119.795	165.018	137.921	108.902	129.288	103.956
10	108.374	88.446	114.318	79.828	114.777	122.628	125.449	111.352	140.764

Individual Value Plot

The Individual Value Plot helps to compare the distributions of data samples. An individual value plot shows one point for each value of the sample. This plot supports the detection of outliers and data spread. The individual value plot is handy when one has relatively few observations or is important to assess each observation's effect. Figure 3.6 shows an individual value plot of the data sample presented in Table 3.2.

DotPlot

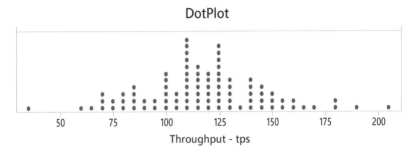

Throughput - tps

Figure 3.5 Dot plot

Figure 3.6 Individual Value Plot.

Histogram

Like a dot plot, a histogram is used to analyze the sample data's shape (central tendency, scatter, asymmetry, and flattening). If the sample size is small, it is recommended to use dot plots; otherwise, the histogram is more appropriate. In histograms, the sample values are divided into intervals (abscissa). The (ordinate) bars represent the number of observations included in each interval or their frequency.

Presenting a Histogram:

- Divide the interval of the data into classes of equal amplitude. There are several rules for determining the number of classes of a histogram. Two of these rules are: $NC = \lceil \sqrt{SS} \rceil$ and $NC = \lceil 1 + n \times \log_{10} SS \rceil$.[1] Statistical tools commonly use n = 3,4,5,6,7,8,9. Changing the number of classes changes the visual representation of the histogram. Count the number of observations in each interval (frequency table).

- The classes are arranged horizontally (abscissa) and the frequencies vertically (ordinate). There is no spacing between the intervals. Each interval is represented by a bar of height equal to the count or frequency.

The histogram of the data in Table 3.2 is shown in Figure 3.7. The number of classes of this histogram was calculated by:

$$NC = \lceil 1 + n \times \log_{10} SS \rceil = \lceil 1 + 8 \times \log_{10} 100 \rceil = 17. \qquad (3.1.1)$$

---

[1]NC- number of classes. SS - sample size.

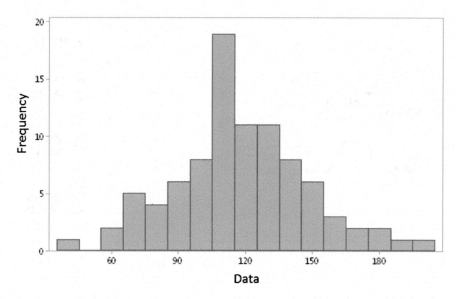

Figure 3.7 Histogram.

Empirical Cumulative Distribution

The empirical cumulative distribution graph shows the value of each observation, considering all values less than or equal to the value under evaluation, concerning the total percentage of sample values. Use cumulative empirical distribution function graphs to evaluate the distribution fit in the data or compare distributions of different samples. Many tools present the cumulative empirical distribution of sample data and an associated theoretical cumulative distribution function.

The staggered empirical cumulative distribution function graph resembles an accumulated histogram without bars. The cumulative empirical distribution of the data in Table 3.2 is shown in Figure 3.8. There are some alternatives to estimate the empirical cumulative distribution, such as

$$F_E(t_i) = \frac{i}{n}, \tag{3.1.2}$$

$$F_E(t_i) = \frac{i}{n+1} \tag{3.1.3}$$

and

$$F_E(t_i) = \frac{i-0.3}{n+0.4}, \tag{3.1.4}$$

where i is the quantile and n is the sample size.

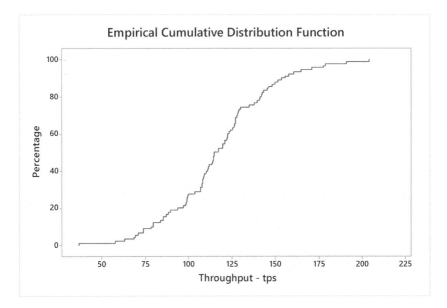

Figure 3.8   Empirical Cumulative Distribution.

3.2   STATISTICS OF CENTRAL TENDENCY

This section briefly summarizes some central tendency statistics: averages and the median.

Arithmetic Mean

The three classical Pythagorean means are the arithmetic, geometric, and harmonic mean [175]. The Pythagoreans studied the dependence of musical intervals on numerical ratios, and the theory of means was then developed concerning the theory of music, geometry, and arithmetic.

The arithmetic mean of a set of observations is obtained by summing up the individual measures and dividing the summation by the number of observations of the set.

$$\overline{X} = \frac{\sum_{x_i=1}^{n} x_i}{n} \tag{3.2.1}$$

An alternative notation is given by

$$E(X) = \frac{\sum_{x_i=1}^{n}}{n},$$ (3.2.2)

$n = |X|$, and E denotes the expected value of a sample X collected from a population (system).

The arithmetic mean of the data presented in Table 3.2 is $\overline{X} = 117.66tps$.

The mean is not immune to the influence of extreme observations, i.e., and it is said that the mean is not resistant to the presence of values that differ too much from the general pattern of the sample.

The arithmetic mean measures the central tendency to represent data whose quantities are summed to produce the total. For example, consider that an application has run 100 times and has logged the time of each run. The arithmetic mean of these measures is an appropriate central tendency since the total (total execution time) is obtained through the sum of the execution times.

Geometric Mean

When a "total" is obtained through a product, the average is best represented by the geometric mean. First, however, let us take a look at the term geometric mean. Consider a right triangle $\triangle ABC$. The measure of the altitude (BD) drawn from the vertex of the right angle to the hypotenuse (see Figure 3.9) is the square root of the product between the two segments of the hypotenuse (AD and DC), that is, by the geometric mean, $BD = \sqrt{AD \times DC}$.

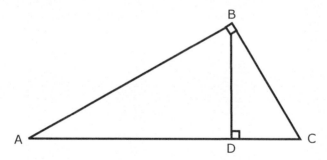

Figure 3.9 Right Triangle - Geometric Mean Interpretation.

The geometric mean $\overline{X}$, of a set of observations $X = \{x_i\}$ (sample) is obtained by the nth root of the product of the values of the observations ($n = |X|$ - cardinality of the set):

$$\overline{X} = \left(\prod_{x_i=1}^{n} x_i x_i \right)^{1/n}$$ (3.2.3)

Consider a database management system (DBMS) installed on an infrastructure composed of a server and an operating system (see Figure 3.10). The flow of this DBMS was monitored under stress conditions, and the maximum value obtained was 80 tps.

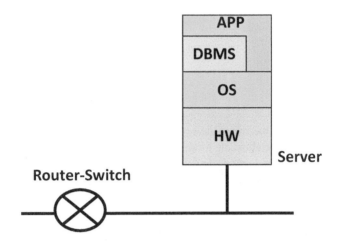

Figure 3.10 DBMS.

Some adjustments were applied to the system. More specifically, the hardware was updated; the operating system and *DBMS* were reconfigured. The hardware update increased the throughput by 22%. The adjustments in the operating system were responsible for an 8% increase in the *DBMS* throughput. Finally, the reconfiguration of the *DBMS* itself was responsible for increasing its throughput by 17 %.

$$\overline{X} = \sqrt[3]{1.22 \times 1.08 \times 1.17} = 1.1552 tps. \qquad (3.2.4)$$

The average increase in throughput is 1.1552 $(115.52\%) - 1.0000$ $(100\%) = 0.1552$ (15.52%).

Harmonic Mean

A frequency is the number of occurrences of a repeating event per time unit. A harmonic of a reference signal is an integer number multiple of the frequency of the reference signal. For instance, consider f as the fundamental frequency of a signal; the second harmonic signal has a frequency equal to $2 \times f$, the third harmonic signal has a frequency equal to $3 \times f$, and so forth. The harmonic mean is generally used to find the rates average. As frequencies are rates; hence the term harmonic mean.

As already stated, the harmonic mean is a central tendency statistic that must be adopted for averaging rates, that is, inversely proportional quantities, such as frequencies, flows, velocities. For example, consider that the data presented in Table 3.3 were transferred through a communication link at the respective transfer rate.

Table 3.3
Packages and Transfer Rate

Number of packages	Transfer rate (pps)
6400	280
6400	320
6400	480
6400	520

The average transfer rate is estimated by the harmonic mean, i.e.:

$$\overline{X} = \frac{n}{\sum_{x_i=1}^{n} \frac{1}{x_i}} \tag{3.2.5}$$

Note that if the link operated at the respective rates (280 pps, 320 pps, 480 pps, and 520 pps) for equal time intervals, the value of the harmonic average coincides with the value of the arithmetic mean. However, it should be noted that the number of packets transferred is no longer the same during each time interval.

Midrange

The midrange is the calculated average considering only the minimum and maximum values of a sample. Thus, the midrange can be particularly significant when working with tiny samples.

Consider a set of observations $X = \{x_i\}$ and $m = \min_{\forall x_i \in X}\{x_i\}$ e $M = \max_{\forall x_i \in X}\{x_i\}$, its minimum and its maximum, respectively. The center of the amplitude is obtained by:

$$MR = \frac{M+m}{2} \tag{3.2.6}$$

The midrange of the data presented in Table 3.2 is 120.53 tps.

Median

The median of a set of observations is the median point of distribution; that is, it is a number that divides observations by half. Half of the observations are below the median, and half are above the median. To estimate the median of a set of observations (X), do:

- Arrange all observations (x_i) in ascending order.

- If the number of observations (n) is odd, the median is in the $\frac{n+1}{2}$ observation from the smallest extent.

- If the number of observations is even, the median is the mean of the two central observations, and their position is also $\frac{n+1}{2}$.

The median of the data presented in Table 3.2 is 116.13 tps. Different from the means, the median is a statistic resistant to the presence of extreme values.

3.3 MEASURES OF DISPERSION

This section presents a set of statistics that express the dispersion of data. The statistics presented are the range, the standard deviation, the variance, the coefficient of variation, and the interquartile range.

Range

Range is the difference between the largest and smallest values of a dataset. The range can be instrumental when working with tiny samples. Consider a set of observations $X = \{x_i\}$ and $m = \min_{\forall x_i \in X} \{x_i\}$ e $M = \max_{\forall x_i \in X} \{x_i\}$, its minimum and its maximum, respectively. The range is obtained by

$$R = M - m. \tag{3.3.1}$$

The range of the data presented in Table 3.2 is 166.8 tps. The range is not immune to the influence of extreme observations.

Coefficient of Range

The coefficient of range (CoR) is a relative measure of dispersion based on the value of the range, which is also known as the range coefficient of dispersion. The CoR is defined by

$$CoR = \frac{M - m}{M + m}. \tag{3.3.2}$$

The coefficient of range of the data shown in Table 3.2 is $(203.973 - 37.094)/(203.973 + 37.094) = 0.692$.

Variance

The sample variance (Var) quantifies the dispersion of the sample data distribution around its mean. The variance of a sample X is defined by the ratio between the summation of the squared differences of each observation and the mean of the sample, and the number of observations minus one.

$$Var = \frac{\sum_{x_i=1}^{n} (x_i - \overline{X})^2}{n - 1}, \tag{3.3.3}$$

where $n = |X|$ is the sample size (cardinality of the set of observations). It is worth mentioning that variance is related to the second central moment of the sample or population (see Section 4.3). It is worth stressing that the variance of a population is defined by

$$Var = \frac{\sum_{x_i=1}^{n} \left(x_i - \overline{X}\right)^2}{n}. \tag{3.3.4}$$

The variance of the data sample presented in Table 3.2 is 896.09 tps^2 The variance is not immune to extreme observations.

Standard Deviation

One of the most used statistics to estimate the data sample X is the standard deviation (SD). The standard deviation measures the dispersion, considering how far the observations are from the mean (same unit of the mean). The sample standard deviation is calculated by the positive square root of the sample variance, i.e.:

$$SD = \sqrt{\frac{\sum_{x_i=1}^{n} \left(x_i - \overline{X}\right)^2}{n-1}} \tag{3.3.5}$$

$n = |X|$ is the sample size.

As for variance, the standard deviation of a population is defined by

$$SD = \sqrt{\frac{\sum_{x_i=1}^{n} \left(x_i - \overline{X}\right)^2}{n}} \tag{3.3.6}$$

The standard deviation is more intuitive than the variance since the result has the same data unit. The standard deviation of the data sample presented in Table 3.2 is 29.93 tps. The standard deviation is not immune to the influence of extreme observations.

Coefficient of Variation

The coefficient of variation is a statistic that estimates the dispersion of data sample X through relative variability and is calculated by the standard deviation to mean ratio.

$$CV = \frac{SD}{\overline{X}} \tag{3.3.7}$$

Because it is a dimensionless number, it is useful to compare the dispersion of populations with significantly different means. For example, the coefficient of variation of the data presented in Table 3.2 is 0.2544.

Interquartile Interval

Quartiles are values that divide a sample of data into four equal parts. With them, it is possible to assess the dispersion and trend of a data sample X.

First quartile Q_1: 25% of the data sample X is less than or equal to this value. Third quartile Q_3: 75% of the data sample X is less than or equal to this value. The second quartile of sample X is the median. The Interquartile Interval (range) (IIQ) is the difference between the third quartile and the first quartile; i.e., it covers the 50% intermediate of the data. Data from normally distributed $IIQ \cong \frac{4}{3} \times SD$.

$$IIQ = Q_3 - Q_1 \qquad (3.3.8)$$

The Interquartile Interval of the data sample presented in Table 2 is 36.44 tps. Notice that $\frac{4}{3} \times 29.93 = 39.91 \, tps$. This feature reinforces the possibility that the data in the table has been obtained from a system whose data are normally distributed. Please, check Figure 3.14.

3.4 STATISTICS OF SHAPE (ASYMMETRY AND KURTOSIS)

This section presents two shape statistics, skewness and kurtosis.

Skewness

The Fisher-Pearson skewness ($Skew_{FP}$) is statistics that quantify the asymmetry degree of a sample X. Assume a data sample X of size $n = |X|$. Such statistics are defined by

$$Skew_{FP} = \frac{(\sum_{i=1}^{n}(x_i - \overline{X})^3)/n}{SD^3} \qquad (3.4.1)$$

where $\overline{X}$ is the sample mean and SD is sample standard deviation. Nevertheless, most major software statistical packages adopt the adjusted Fisher-Pearson skewness. These statistics provide an adjustment to the original Fisher-Pearson skewness concerning the sample size. This statistics is defined by

$$Skew = \frac{\sqrt{n(n-1)}}{n-2} \times \frac{(\sum_{i=1}^{n}(x_i - \overline{X})^3)/n}{SD^3}. \qquad (3.4.2)$$

For large n $Skew_{FP}$ and $Skew$ provides similar results. It is worth stating that the skewness coefficients are related to the third central moment of sample or population (see Section 4.3).

Negative values (Skew <0) indicate that the tail is on the left. Positive values (Skew$>$ 0) indicate the right tail. SK = 0 indicates symmetry. Figure 3.11 shows density functions of two populations. Negative skewness shows a distribution with left asymmetry. Positive skewness is associated with the right asymmetry distribution. The skewness of the data is shown in Table 3.2 is 0.19. Therefore, the data distribution is slightly asymmetric to the right. It is also worth mentioning that such statistics are related to the third central moment of the sample or population (see Section 4.3).

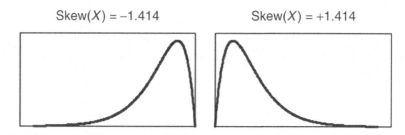

Figure 3.11   Skewness.

Kurtosis

Kurtosis is a statistic that estimates the "tailedness" of a sample. Assume a data sample X of size $n = |X|$ [195]. Such statistics are defined by

$$Kurt = \frac{\left(\sum_{i=1}^{n}(x_i - \overline{X})^4\right)/n}{SD^4} \qquad (3.4.3)$$

where $\overline{X}$ is the sample mean and SD is sample standard deviation. The normal distribution has a kurtosis of 3. Therefore, most statistical software packages adopted a variant that is defined by

$$Kurt = \frac{\left(\sum_{i=1}^{n}(x_i - \overline{X})^4\right)/n}{SD^4} - 3. \qquad (3.4.4)$$

It is worth mentioning that some authors call the later definition kurtosis excess (concerning normal distributions). Using the Statistics 3.4.4 (described above), negative values (Kurt <0) indicate longer tails than normal distributions. Positive values (Kurt> 0) indicate shorter tails than normal distributions. Kurt=0 indicates data distribution with similar tails to normal distribution (see Figure 3.12). The kurtosis of the data shown in Table 3.2 is 0.51, which indicates data distribution tails similar to a population normally distributed. The histogram of the data and the density function of the distribution are given in Figure 3.13.

It is worth stating the kurtosis coefficients are related to the fourth central moment of sample or population (see Section 4.3).

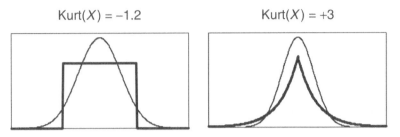

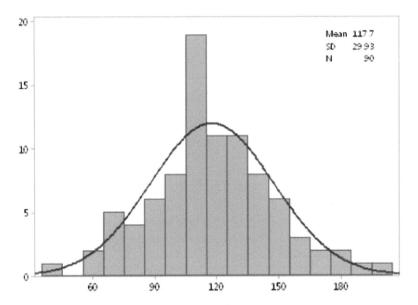

Figure 3.12   Kurtosis.

Figure 3.13   Histogram of Data and a Normal Distribution.

3.5   OUTLIERS

The statistics analyzed in the previous sections allow us to understand the general pattern of the sample obtained. It is essential, however, to highlight measures that profoundly diverge from this standard. These measures are called outliers. There is no absolute agreement among statisticians about defining outliers, but nearly everyone agrees that it is essential that they are identified and that appropriate analytic technique is used for data sets that contain outliers. An outlier may result from an error or improper interference or may be due to an intrinsic feature of the system.

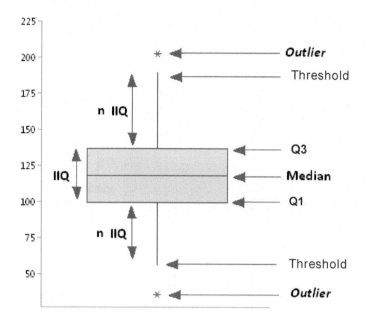

Figure 3.14   Box Plot.

Several criteria have been adopted to define an outlier candidate. One of the most ad-opted is based on IIQ (Interquartile Interval). Hence, data falling short of and beyond the following limits are considered candidate outliers:

$$LB = Q_1 - n \times IIQ \qquad\qquad (3.5.1)$$

$$UB = Q_3 - n \times IIQ \qquad\qquad (3.5.2)$$

Many authors consider n = 1.5 to define the limits of candidates for soft outliers and n = 3 to delimit the outliers' extremes.

The box plot is a summary diagram of the five numbers (median, first and third quartiles, smallest, and largest sample number). Some versions of the diagram, rather than depicting the maximum and minimum, record limits that demarcate what is con-sidered an outlier. In this case, the suspicious items are marked individually. Different criteria are adopted to define the outliers; however, it is common to adopt the rules of the $1.5 \times IIQ$ (interquartile range) and $3 \times IIQ$ to characterize soft and extreme outliers, respectively. Figure 3.14 shows a box plot for the data in Table 3.2.

The box plot is useful for graphing the outliers and for comparing sample distribu-tions. In the box plot, the boundaries are represented by points that are smaller than

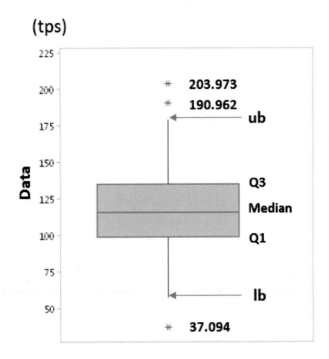

(tps)

Figure 3.15 Outliers.

$Q_1 - n \times IIQ^2$ or larger than $Q_3 + n \times IIQ^3$. These points are connected to the box through a line. Considering the data in Table 3.2 and $n = 1.5$, we detect three observations that stand out from the general pattern of the sample: $37.094\ tps$, 190.96, and $203.973\ tps$. These observations are presented in Figure 3.15. It is worth noting that statistical tools have adopted several variants of the box plot.

EXERCISES

Exercise 1. From a randomly selected sample of faculties from a university, a survey was conducted in which each faculty would choose his/her favorite personal computer brand from the six most relevant brands available in the market. The sample size was 150, and the result is shown in Table 3.4.

(a) Present this sample using pie charts.

(b) Depict the sample using a bar chart.

---

[2]LB -Lower Bound.
[3]UB -Upper Bound.

Table 3.4
Computer Brand Survey

Computer Brands	Quantity
CB_1	22
CB_2	35
CB_3	37
CB_4	28
CB_5	22
CB_6	6

(c) Write a short text describing the findings.

Exercise 2. Assume a scenario in a car manufactoring plant that analyzes the door panel defects of a specific automobile model. The study concentrates on door replacements due to painting defects of the car door panel. Over the last four months, the average doors substitution per month was forty-two. The monthly average defects per class of defects are shown in Table 3.5.

Table 3.5
Painting Defects

Types Defect	Quantity
Color variation	3
Line mark	57
Paint damage	8
Poor finishing	16
Rundown	8
Uncovareage	48

(a) Present this sample using a Pareto´s chart.

(b) Write a short text describing the findings.

Exercise 3. A program was executed 25 times and its execution times were recorded (*ms*). This sample is { 94.64, 92.13, 106.88, 95.39, 69.19, 104.21, 101.08, 100.82, 94.29, 111.41, 88.77, 112.13, 103.35, 101.24, 111.20, 78.21, 119.23, 95.08, 86.30, 94.00, 112.41, 126.58, 94.22, 107.37, 86.58 }. **(a)** Provide a statistic summary of this sample. **(b)** Present the dot plot and the box plot. **(c)** Using the summary and the graphs, interpret the collected sample.

Exercise 4. Four were executed, and their execution times were recorded as 50, 160, 100, and 400 ms. However, first, find their arithmetic mean and median.

Exercise 5. Consider the data presented in Table 3.6 were transferred through a communication link at the respective transfer rates. Next, calculate the mean transfer rate through the harmonic mean.

Table 3.6
Number of Packages Transferred - Transfer Rate

Number of Packages	Transfer Rate
12800	310
12800	290
12800	340
12800	270

Exercise 6. A set of adjustments was applied to a computer system. First, hardware updates increased throughput by 18%. Second, the new operating system setup increased the throughput by 9%. Finally, the DBMS reconfiguration was responsible for increasing the throughput by 12%. Calculate the average throughput increase (use the geometric mean).

Exercise 7. The times to transfer a data file between data centers were measured repeatedly. The times (s) were { 21.29, 23.75, 21.23, 24.20, 21.21, 16.10, 15.21, 24.68, 27.35, 12.95, 22.72, 22.68, 16.38, 13.34, 21.66, 24.65, 26.59, 26.19, 12.03, 16.44, 31.72, 41.49, 33.45, 25.20, 32.51 }. **(a)** Show a statistical summary of this sample. **(b)** Present the box plot. **(c)** Using the summary and the box plot, interpret the collected sample.

Exercise 8. A virtual machine startup times were recorded. The following times (in seconds) are shown in Table 3.7. **(a)** Calculate the sample mean, sample standard deviation, variance, and coefficient of variation, sample skewness, and kurtosis. **(b)** Calculate the sample median, the first and third quartile, and the interquartile interval. **(c)** Construct a box plot of the data. **(d)** Construct a histogram of the data.

Exercise 9. One script was executed on a computer for measuring the latency between a computer and a server hosting a website. A sample has one-hundred measures and was collected for four hours. The time between measures was $144\,s$. The sample is stored in Table 3.8. Analyze the sample, provide its statistic summary and suitable graphs, and comment on the findings.

Exercise 10. One script was executed to obtain a one-hundred-sample of processor utilization related to a process. This script collects two metrics: $\%usr$ and $\%system$. The total CPU-core utilization ($\%CPU$) is given by summing-up $\%usr$ and $\%system$.

Table 3.7
Virtual Machine Startup Time (s)

Startup Time (s)						
67.45	107.67	119.53	46.23	288.88	340.51	29.21
127.07	73.39	109.56	69.52	229.54	261.67	174.45
79.90	5398	108.28	70.96	155.37	155.74	256.50
59.66	65.94	51.48	74.52	236.84	160.52	3.99
96.40	72.54	96.98	46.97	158.52	257.21	5.52
117.92	105.96	63.13	86.43	83.32	154.74	33.61
132.83	86.14	135.23	116.40	282.67	213.38	209.17
85.73	84.93	79.50	94.37	212.06	360.13	31.14
101.47	92.90	128.06	97.66	321.05	25.25	377.00
88.94	104.94	76.53	81.62	312.62	108.04	263.58

Table 3.8
Latency (ms)

Ping Delay (ms)									
323	317	416	289	315	312	316	294	289	288
294	288	314	315	314	314	315	290	323	330
289	299	313	313	292	314	371	293	348	287
472	314	314	289	298	314	297	305	293	302
319	321	329	292	329	298	294	417	292	287
293	308	296	296	324	297	311	415	313	309
292	316	292	317	313	316	298	295	296	297
316	313	284	312	295	308	312	289	350	298
310	308	285	292	290	316	319	298	312	329
316	298	295	297	316	285	310	312	437	288

The sample was collected for eight hours, and the time between measures was $288\,s$. The sample is stored in Table 3.9. Analyze the metrics depicted in the sample (*%usr* and *%system*) and *%CPU*; provide the statistic summary, the graphs, and comment on the findings.

Exercise 11. A script was executed to measure a one-hundred-sample of memory usage related to the process. This script collects the virtual memory utilization of the entire process (*VSZ*), the non-swapped physical memory used by the process (*RSS*), and the process currently used shared physical memory (*%MEM*). The collected sample is depicted in Table 3.10. Analyze the sample's data, generate a statistical summary, plot suitable graphs to represent the sample, and write a short document interpreting the findings.

Table 3.9

Sample - *%usr* **and** *%system*

%usr	*%system*	*%usr*	*%system*	*%usr*	*%system*	*%usr*	*%system*	*%usr*	*%system*
0.40	0.07	0.41	0.06	0.19	0.22	0.46	0.30	0.58	0.16
0.37	0.30	0.34	0.40	0.32	0.29	0.28	0.31	0.27	0.16
0.41	0.28	0.39	0.05	0.46	0.16	0.27	0.29	0.45	0.09
0.32	0.09	0.37	0.13	0.36	0.16	0.36	0.20	0.38	0.17
0.45	0.23	0.18	0.15	0.50	0.20	0.32	0.18	0.29	0.05
0.47	0.08	0.32	0.21	0.42	0.21	0.41	0.09	0.47	0.15
0.30	0.28	0.35	0.24	0.32	0.40	0.45	0.02	0.46	0.22
0.43	0.25	0.37	0.16	0.40	0.22	0.26	0.08	0.12	0.33
0.20	0.19	0.28	0.24	0.42	0.05	0.36	0.27	0.28	0.26
0.31	0.28	0.51	0.19	0.36	0.08	0.39	0.17	0.41	0.21
0.31	0.33	0.37	0.19	0.42	0.28	0.29	0.30	0.45	0.18
0.35	0.11	0.58	0.25	0.33	0.09	0.39	0.20	0.25	0.24
0.35	0.18	0.29	0.23	0.34	0.29	0.17	0.10	0.33	0.02
0.46	0.41	0.50	0.20	0.42	0.01	0.43	0.16	0.31	0.04
0.63	0.02	0.25	0.17	0.45	0.08	0.33	0.20	0.44	0.02
0.36	0.17	0.13	0.02	0.28	0.26	0.45	0.20	0.32	0.16
0.44	0.09	0.44	0.28	0.49	0.22	0.39	0.13	0.52	0.24
0.25	0.18	0.50	0.37	0.36	0.02	0.52	0.36	0.48	0.06
0.36	0.17	0.38	0.21	0.43	0.20	0.37	0.05	0.38	0.24
0.42	0.33	0.41	0.10	0.28	0.25	0.38	0.34	0.41	0.28

Table 3.10
VSZ - RSS - %MEM
Virtual Memory Usage - Non-Swapped Physical Memory - Shared Physical Memory Used.

%MEM	VSZ (Kbytes)	RSS (Kbytes)	%MEM	VSZ (Kbytes)	RSS (Kbytes)	%MEM	VSZ (Kbytes)	RSS (Kbytes)
11.1	1221528	230352	8.5	1218640	175568	8.2	1221452	170960
11.1	1216752	229708	8.1	1218640	167400	8.3	1221452	171136
11.2	1217824	231988	7.9	1218648	164088	8.6	1222896	178936
11.2	1218640	232288	7.8	1218640	162140	8.8	1222784	181452
11.3	1218640	233936	7.8	1219796	161336	8.7	1221340	181368
11.1	1218640	229084	7.7	1221444	159052	8.7	1221572	181232
10.9	1218640	226120	7.5	1221444	156016	8.8	1221572	183356
10.3	1218640	213592	8.3	1218672	171224	8	1215428	166308
9.7	1218640	200460	8.2	1221444	170748	8.1	1216872	168164
9	1218640	185648	8.3	1221452	171492	8.2	1215428	169988
8.6	1213728	178924	8.7	1214752	180852	8.7	1214752	180828
8.6	1213728	179008	8.7	1214752	180852	8.7	1214752	180828
8.6	1213728	179008	8.7	1214752	180852	8.7	1214752	180828
8.6	1213728	179088	8.7	1214752	180772	8.7	1214752	180968
8.8	1214752	181644	8.7	1214752	180772	8.7	1214752	181232
8.8	1214752	181644	8.7	1214752	180772	8.8	1214752	181816
8.8	1214752	181644	8.7	1214752	180772	8.8	1214752	181816
8.7	1214752	180852	8.7	1214752	180772	8.8	1214752	181836
8.7	1214752	180852	8.7	1214752	180772	8.8	1214752	181920
8.7	1214752	180852	8.7	1214752	180828	8.8	1214752	182904
8.4	1215196	173364	8.3	1212528	171492	8.2	1212528	169900
8.4	1216640	173368	8.5	1212496	176588	8.8	1214752	182904
8.1	1216872	167844	8.5	1214000	177236	8.8	1214752	182904
8.1	1216872	167960	8.7	1213728	180108	8.8	1214752	182976
8.1	1216872	167496	8.6	1213728	178988	8.8	1214752	182772
8.1	1216992	167432	8.6	1213728	178988	8.8	1214752	182772
8.4	1220464	175032	8.6	1213728	179240	8.8	1214752	182772
8.2	1216280	171084	8.6	1213728	179240	8.8	1214752	182772
8.7	1232000	181112	8.6	1213728	178920	8.8	1214752	182772
8.8	1214752	182396	8.6	1213728	178920	8.8	1214752	182772
8.8	1214752	182396	8.8	1214752	182280	8.8	1214752	182280
8.8	1214752	182544	8.8	1214752	182368	8.8	1214752	182396
8.8	1214752	182544	8.8	1214752	182396	8.8	1214752	182396
						8.8	1214752	182396

4 Introduction to Random Variables

This chapter introduces the concept of random variables, moments, and joint random variables. Random variables are classified as discrete random variables or continuous random variables. This chapter covers discrete and continuous random variables and introduces moments, joint distributions, covariance, and other related measures.

4.1 DISCRETE RANDOM VARIABLES

This section introduces the basic concepts of discrete random variables and some of their characteristics. Many random experiments have numerical outcomes, such as times, lengths, speed, prices, etc. Other experiments provide non-numerical categoric results. For instance, consider a test of a program in which the outcome could be *pass* or *failed*. Other non-numerical results could be *true* or *false*, a color, or categories such as , *medium* or *large*, etc. In summary, random variables which take on values from a discrete set of numbers (countable set, but possibly infinite) are called discrete random variables.

A random variable (*RV*) is a function that assigns a real value to outcomes of a random experiment, that is

$$X : \Omega \to \mathbb{R}, \tag{4.1.1}$$

where Ω is the sample space of a random experiment. It is usual, but not required, to denote random variables by capital letters. Figure 4.1 (top of figure) shows a sample space of a random experiment, where each simple outcome (simple events) of the experiment is depicted by a dot. Two other more complex events are also highlighted in the figure: event A and event B, which are sets of simple events. Figure 4.1 also depicts the mapping of events E_k to their respective probabilities, $P(E_k) = p_{E_k}$, $0 \le p_{E_k} \le 1$. Figure 4.1 also shows the mapping of sample space events to real numbers, $X(E_k) = x$, $x \in \mathbb{R}$, that is a graphical representation of a random variable (bottom of the figure). Since the value of a random variable is determined by the outcome of the random experiment, we may assign probabilities of its possible values. Therefore, for each value the random variable X assumes, the respective probability mapping is also graphically depicted, $P(X = x_i) = p_i$, $0 \le p_i \le 1$. It is worth noting that the variable is random due to the random experiment. The mapping itself is a deterministic function, as shown in Figure 4.1. Besides, it is also important to mention that a function of a random variable is also a random variable.

Example 4.1.1. Consider the random experiment described in Example 2.2.2. In that example, four servers (S_1, S_2, S_3, and S_4) were evaluated in an accelerated reliability

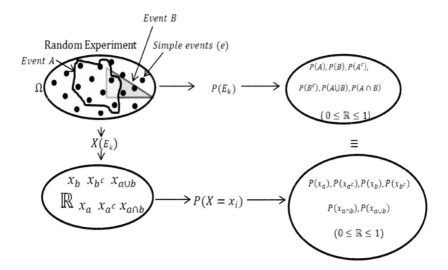

Figure 4.1   Mapping an Experiment to a Random Variable.

test. At the end of the test, each server may pass the test - Up (U) or fail (F). The result of the random experiment was represented by a 4-tuple $e = (s_1, s_2, s_3, s_4)$, where $s_i = \{U, D\}$ is the state of the server i after the test, $i \in \{1, 2, 3, 4\}$.

Let us define a random variable X that represents the number of servers that failed the test. Hence, $X : \Omega \to \mathbb{N}_{0-4}$, where $\mathbb{N}_{0-4} = \{0, 1, 2, 3, 4\}$. Figure 4.2 shows the mapping. It is worth observing that values X may assume are discrete.   □

Random variables that take on values from a discrete set of numbers are called discrete random variables. The set may be infinite but countable. Discrete random variables represent different indivisible items, like the number of faults, number of servers, number of users, number of devices that passed a test, etc.

Example 4.1.2. In Example 2.2.3, a random experiment consists of measuring the server time to failure by taking into account a reliability test. In this case, the sample space $\Omega = \mathbb{R}^+ = \{x \mid x > 0\}$. In this case, let us define a random variable T that represents the time to failure of the random experiment. In such a case, all possible results of the random experiment may already be considered the values of the counter-domain of the random variable T. Therefore, $T : \Omega \to \mathbb{R}^+$. Hence, in this case, T is a continuous random variable and an identity function.   □

Continuous random variables assume values from a continuous interval. For example, a random variable may represent the time between two successive arrivals to a queueing system, the time required to execute a program in a specific server, or the time required to repair a system. It is noteworthy that such random variables may

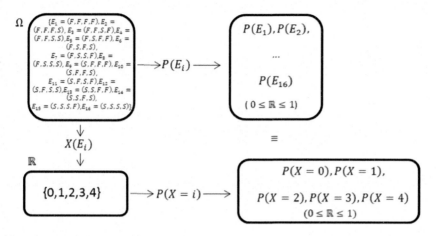

Figure 4.2 A Discrete Random Variable - $X : \Omega \rightarrow \mathbb{N}_{0-4}$, where $\mathbb{N}_{0-4} = \{0, 1, 2, 3, 4\}$.

be discretized, and suitable discrete random variables may be adopted to represent them. The subject of this section is discrete random variables. Continuous random variables are discussed in Section 4.2.

The *Probability Mass Function* (*pmf*) of a discrete random variable X is the function p_X defined by $p_X(x) = P(X = x)$ that assigns a probability, $p_X(x) \in [0, 1]$, to each to the possible values x of X. Note that $\sum_{\forall i} p_X(x_i) = 1$.

Example 4.1.3. A discrete random variable is completely specified by its probability mass function. In this example, the *pmf* is depicted in table form and as a graph. Figure 4.3 shows the graphic representation of random variable X, which is also depicted in Table 4.1.

Table 4.1
Random Variable and Its Probability Mass Function

x_i	0	1	2	3	4	5	6	7	8	9	10
$p_X(x_i)$	1/36	2/36	3/36	4/36	5/36	6/36	5/36	4/36	3/36	2/36	1/36

□

Example 4.1.4. Consider the random variable depicted in Example 4.1.1. The random variable X represents the number of servers that failed in a reliability test considering four servers. The random variable was defined as $X : \Omega \rightarrow \mathbb{N}_{0-4}$, where

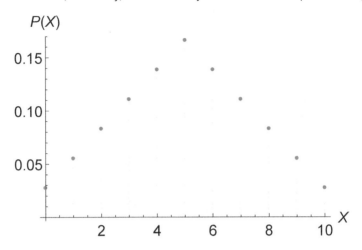

Figure 4.3 Probability Mass Function of X Depicted in Table 4.1.

$\mathbb{N}_{0-4} = \{0, 1, 2, 3, 4\}$. If the probability of one server presenting a failure is 0.2, and the occurrence of such a failure does not affect the probability of another server presenting a failure, the probabilities of having $X = 0$, $X = 1$, $X = 2$, $X = 3$, and $X = 4$ (see the sample space Ω on the top left corner of Figure 4.2 and Example 2.2.2):

$$P(X = 0) = (1 - p)^4,$$
$$P(X = 1) = 4p(1 - p)^3,$$
$$P(X = 2) = 6p^2(1 - p)^2,$$
$$P(X = 3) = 4p^3(1 - p),$$

and

$$P(X = 4) = p^4.$$

Therefore, $P(X = 0) = 0.4096$, $P(X = 1) = 0.4096$, $P(X = 2) = 0.1536$, $P(X = 3) = 0.0256$, and $P(X = 4) = 0.0016$. Figure 4.4 graphically depicts the probability mass function of X. It is worth highlighting that a function of a discrete random variable is another discrete random variable whose *pmf* may be obtained from the *pmf* of the original random variable. The probability of having at least three failed servers is $P(X \geq 3) = P(X = 3) + P(X = 4) = 0.0256 + 0.0016 = 0.0272$.

□

The *expected value* of random variable X provides the weighted average of its possible values. If X is a discrete random variable taking on the following values $\{x_1, x_2, \ldots\}$, then the expected value (also called *mean*) of X is defined by

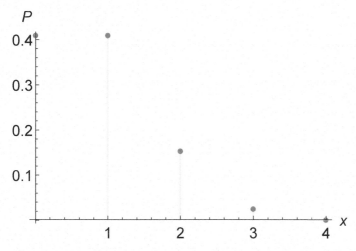

Figure 4.4   Probability Mass Function of X - Number of Failed Servers.

$$E(X) = \sum_i x_i P(X = x_i). \qquad (4.1.2)$$

If X is a discrete random variable, then the expected value of $g(X)$, a real-valued function, is defined by

$$E(g(X)) = \sum_i g(x_i) P(X = x_i). \qquad (4.1.3)$$

The *variance* of random variable X yields a measure of the dispersion of values around its mean, $E(X)$. If X is a random variable with mean $E(X)$, then the variance of X is defined by

$$Var(X) = E((X - E(X))^2), \qquad (4.1.4)$$

which leads to

$$Var(X) = E(X^2 - 2X E(X) + (E(X))^2).$$
$$Var(X) = E(X^2) - E(2X E(X)) + E((E(X))^2).$$
$$Var(X) = E(X^2) - 2E(X) E(E(X)) + (E(X))^2.$$
$$Var(X) = E(X^2) - 2E(X) E(X) + (E(X))^2.$$
$$Var(X) = E(X^2) - 2(E(X))^2 + (E(X))^2.$$
$$Var(X) = E(X^2) - (E(X))^2.$$

Therefore

$$Var(X) = E(X^2) - (E(X))^2. \qquad (4.1.5)$$

Hence, the variance of X is equal to the expected value of the square of X minus the square of the expected value of X. If X is a discrete random variable, the variance may be calculated by

$$Var(X) = \sum_i x_i^2 P(X = x_i) - (\sum_i x_i P(X = x_i))^2. \qquad (4.1.6)$$

The square root of its variance defines the *standard deviation* of X, $Var(x)$, that is

$$SD(X) = Var(X)^{\frac{1}{2}}. \qquad (4.1.7)$$

It is worth mentioning that standard deviation has the same unit of those values from the random variable, whereas the variance unit is the random variable unit squared. The *coefficient of variation* is a dimensionless measure of the variability of X. It is defined by

$$CoV(X) = \frac{SD(X)}{E(X)}. \qquad (4.1.8)$$

Example 4.1.5. Consider the discrete random variable X described in Example 4.1.3. In this example, the expected value, the variance of X, and the standard deviation are calculated according Equation 4.1.2, Equation 4.1.6, Equation 4.1.7 and Equation 4.1.8, respectively. Table 4.2 shows the respective terms adopted to calculate $E(X)$, $Var(X)$, $SD(X)$, and $CoV(X)$.

The expected value of X is $E(X) = 5$, the variance is $Var(X) = 5.8333$, $SD(X) = 2.4152$, and $CoV(X) = 0.4830$.

□

The *cumulative distribution function (cdf)*, or more simply the distribution function, $F_X(x)$ of a random variable X is defined as

$$F_X(x) = P(X \leq x). \qquad (4.1.9)$$

In words, $F_X(x)$ is the probability that a random variable X takes on a value that is less than or equal to x. If X is a discrete random variable,

$$F_X(x) = \sum_{\forall x_i, x_i \leq x} p_X(x_i). \qquad (4.1.10)$$

Every cumulative distribution function $F_X(x)$ is non-decreasing. Besides,

$$\lim_{x \to -\infty} F_X(x) = 0$$

Table 4.2

Expected Value and Variance of X - X is a Discrete Random Variable

x_i	x_i^2	$p_X(x_i)$	$x_i \times p_X(x_i)$	$x_i^2 \times p_X(x_i)$
0	0	0.03	0	0
1	1	0.06	0.0556	0.0556
2	4	0.08	0.1667	0.3333
3	9	0.11	0.3333	1
4	16	0.14	0.5556	2.2222
5	25	0.17	0.8333	4.1667
6	36	0.14	0.8333	5
7	49	0.11	0.7778	5.4444
8	64	0.08	0.6667	5.3333
9	81	0.06	0.5	4.5
10	100	0.03	0.2778	2.7778
			5	30.8333
			$E(X)$	$E(X)^2$

and

$$\lim_{x \to \infty} F_X(x) = 1.$$

If X is a discrete random variable whose domain is finite, then

$$F_X(x) = 0, x < \min\{x_i\}$$

and

$$F_X(x) = 1, x = \max\{x_i\}.$$

The notation $X \sim F$ is adopted to state that F is the distribution function of X. Probability questions related to X can be solved using its cdf, $F_X(x)$. For instance, consider the following cases:

1. $P(X \leq a) = F_X(a)$.

2. $P(X < a) = F_X(a) - P(X = a)$.

3. $P(X > a) = 1 - F_X(a)$.

4. $P(X \geq a) = 1 - P(X < a) = 1 - F_X(a) + P(X = a)$.

5. $P(a < X \leq b) = F_X(b) - F_X(a)$.

6. $P(a \leq X \leq b) = F_X(b) - F_X(a) + P(X = a)$.

The *complementary cumulative distribution function* (*ccdf*), or more simply the distribution function, $F_X^c(x)$ of a random variable X is defined as

$$F_X^c(x) = 1 - F_X(x) = P(X > x). \tag{4.1.11}$$

In words, $F_X^c(x)$ is the probability that a random variable X takes on a value that is higher than x. If X is a discrete random variable,

$$F_X^c(x) = 1 - \sum_{\forall x_i, x_i \leq x} p_X(x_i). \tag{4.1.12}$$

Example 4.1.6. Consider the discrete random variable X described in Example 4.1.3. Figure 4.4 and Table 4.1 depict the *pmf* of X. Table 4.3 and Figure 4.5 show the cumulative distribution function of the random variable X. Figure 4.6 depicts the complementary cumulative distribution function of X, $F_X^c(x)$.

Table 4.3
Cumulative Distribution Function of the Random Variable X

x_i	0	1	2	3	4	5
$F_X(x_i)$	0.02778	0.08333	0.16667	0.27778	0.41667	0.58333
x_i	6	7	8	9	10	
$F_X(x_i)$	0.72222	0.83333	0.91667	0.97222	1	

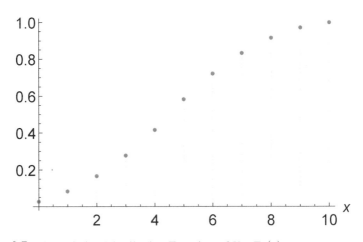

Figure 4.5   Cumulative Distribution Function of X - $F_X(x)$.

Table 4.4 presents some probabilities concerning X.

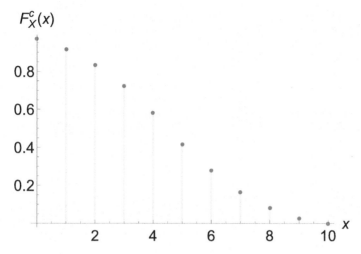

Figure 4.6 Complementary Cumulative Distribution Function of X - $F_X^c(x)$.

Table 4.4
Probabilities

a, b	Probability	Values
$a = 4$	$P(X \leq a)$	0.41667
$a = 4$	$P(X < a)$	0.27778
$a = 4$	$P(X > a)$	0.58334
$a = 4$	$P(X \geq a)$	0.72222
$a = 4, b = 8$	$P(a < X \leq b)$	0.5
$a = 4, b = 8$	$P(a \leq X \leq b)$	0.63889

Example 4.1.7. Example 4.1.4 presents a random variable X that denotes the number of servers failed during a reliability test. Four servers were used in the test. Figure 4.4 and Table 4.1 depict the *pmf* of X. Table 4.5 shows the *cdf* of X in table format, and Figure 4.7 shows it in the graphical format. The probability of at least three servers fail out of those four is $P(X \geq 3) = 1 - F_X(2) = 0.0272$, which is the same result obtained in Example 4.1.4 via *pmf*.

$\square$

Percentile Statistics - The percentiles and percentile ranks of a random variable X are calculated using its cumulative distribution function, $F_X(x)$. The percentile rank of value x is obtained from

$$p_x = 100 \times F_X(x) \tag{4.1.13}$$

and the percentile (the value x) of a specified rank p is obtained by

Table 4.5

$F_X(x)$ - X **is Number of Servers Failed.**

x	0	1	2	3	4
$F_X(x)$	0.4096	0.8192	0.9728	0.9984	1

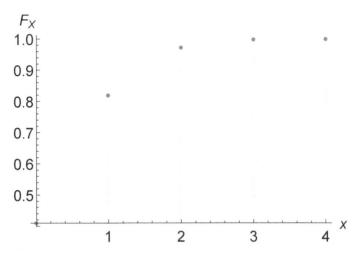

Figure 4.7 $F_X(x)$ - X is number of servers failed.

$$x_p = \arg F_X(x) = p. \tag{4.1.14}$$

For instance, the 50th percentile of a random variable X is the value that divides the distribution, $F_X(x)$, in half, and is known as the *median, Mdn*.

$$Mdn = x_{0.5} = \arg F_X(x) = 0.5. \tag{4.1.15}$$

If the number of values of the random variable X is even, then the median is the mean of the middle two numbers, that is

$$Mdn = \frac{x_{0.5^-} + x_{0.5^+}}{2}, \tag{4.1.16}$$

where $x_{0.5^-}$ is the percentile which for any $x > x_{0.5^-}$, $F_X(x) > 0.5$. Similarly, $x_{0.5^+}$ is the percentile which for any $x < x_{0.5^+}$, $F_X(x) < 0.5$.

The 25th percentile of a random variable X is the *first quartile* (Q_1).

$$Q_1 = x_{0.25} = \arg F_X(x) = 0.25 \tag{4.1.17}$$

If the number of values of the random variable X is even, then the first quartile is given by

$$Q_1 = \frac{x_{0.25^-} + x_{0.25^+}}{2} \qquad (4.1.18)$$

$x_{0.25^-}$ is the percentile which for any $x > x_{0.25^-}$, $F_X(x) > 0.25$. Similarly, $x_{0.25^+}$ is the percentile, which for any $x < x_{0.25^+}$, $F_X(x) < 0.25$.

The 75th percentile of a random variable X is the *third quartile* (Q_3).

$$Q_3 = x_{0.75} = \arg F_X(x) = 0.75. \qquad (4.1.19)$$

If the number of values of the random variable X is even, then the third quartile is given by

$$Q_3 = \frac{x_{0.75^-} + x_{0.57^+}}{2}, \qquad (4.1.20)$$

where $x_{0.75^-}$ is the percentile which for any $x > x_{0.75^-}$, $F_X(x) > 0.75$. Similarly, $x_{0.75^+}$ is the percentile, which for any $x < x_{0.75^+}$, $F_X(x) < 0.75$.

The second quartile is the median, $Q_2 = Mdn$. Another percentile-based statistic is the *interquartile range* (IQR), which is a measure of the spread of a distribution. The IQR is the difference between the 75th and 25th percentiles, that is

$$IQR = Q_3 - Q_1. \qquad (4.1.21)$$

Example 4.1.8. Consider the discrete random variable X described in Example 4.1.3, whose the cumulative distribution functions are depicted in Table 4.3 and Figure 4.5. Table 4.6 presents the statistics Min, Q_1, Mdn, Q_3, Max, and IQR for random variable X.

Table 4.6
Percentile Statistics

Measures	Min	Q_1	Mdn	Q_3	Max	IQR
Values	0	2	5	8	10	6

Example 4.1.9. Consider the discrete random variable Y whose cdf is depicted in Table 4.7 and in Figure 4.8. Table 4.8 presents the statistics Min, Q_1, Mdn, Q_3, Max, and IQR for random variable Y.

Section 5.1 shows a summary of some important discrete random variables.

Table 4.7
Cumulative Distribution Function $F_Y(y)$.

y	5	7	9	10	11	12	16	19	22	23
$F_Y(y)$	0.1	0.2	0.3	0.4	0.5	0.6	0.7	0.8	0.9	1

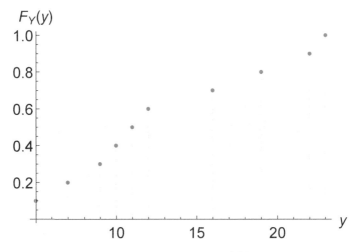

Figure 4.8 Cumulative Distribution Function $F_Y(y)$.

Table 4.8
Percentile Statistics of Y.

Measures	Min	Q_1	Mdn	Q_3	Max	IQR
Values	5	9	11.5	19	23	10

4.2 CONTINUOUS RANDOM VARIABLES

Now, let us turn our attention to continuous random variables. Continuous random variables take on any real value from a continuous interval. For example, the interval could be the entire real line, a half-line (also called a ray), or a line segment. Examples of such random variables are the time required to execute a task, the time to failure of a given class of system, the volume of liquid stored in the reservoir during a time interval, the temperature reached in an oven in a specified period, the waiting time in a queue, etc. Random variables that represent such measures may be discretized. However, our aim in this section is to study random variables defined on a continuous sample space.

Assume X is continuous random variable defined over the line of reals. The *cumulative distribution function* $F_X(x)$ is defined by

$$F_X(x) = P(X \leq x), \tag{4.2.1}$$

where $P(X \leq x)$ is the probability of X assuming a value smaller than x. The cumulative distribution functions has the following properties:

1. $0 \leq F_X(x) \leq 1$.

2. $F_X(x)$ is non-decreasing, that is, for any $a < b$, $F_X(a) < F_X(b)$.

3. $\lim_{x \to -\infty} F_X(x) = 0$, and $\lim_{x \to \infty} F_X(x) = 1$.

4. $P(a < X < b) = F_X(b) - F_X(a)$.

5. $F_X(x)$ is absolutely continuous. In other words, $dF_X(x)/dx$ is defined for every point in its domain, except at end points of a line interval or at the end point of a half-line.

As in the discrete case, the *complementary cumulative distribution function* $F_X^c(x)$ is defined by

$$F_X^c(x) = 1 - F_X(x) = 1 - P(X < x) = P(X > x), \tag{4.2.2}$$

where $P(X > x)$ is the probability of X assuming a value higher than x. The complementary cumulative distribution function has the following properties:

1. $0 \leq F_X^c(x) \leq 1$.

2. $F_X(x)$ is non-increasing, that is, for any $a < b$, $F_X^c(a) > F_X^c(b)$.

3. $\lim_{x \to -\infty} F_X^c(x) = 1$, and $\lim_{x \to \infty} F_X^c(x) = 0$.

4. $P(a < X < b) = F_X^c(a) - F_X^c(b)$.

5. $F_X^c(x)$ is absolutely continuous. In other words, $dF_X^c(x)/dx$ is defined for every point in its domain, except at end points of a line interval or at the end point of a half-line.

The hazard function is defined as (see Equation 16.2.12 in Section 16.2)

$$\lambda(x) = -\frac{dF_X^c(x)}{dx} \times \frac{1}{F_X^c(x)}. \tag{4.2.3}$$

From that, we have (see Equation 16.2.16 in Section 16.2)

$$F_X^c(x) = e^{-\int_0^x \lambda(x) \times dx} = e^{-H(x)}, \tag{4.2.4}$$

where

$$H(x) = \int_0^x \lambda(x) \times dx \qquad (4.2.5)$$

is the cumulative hazard function. Thus, we have

$$F_X(x) = 1 - e^{-\int_0^x \lambda(x) \times dx} = e^{-H(x)}. \qquad (4.2.6)$$

Example 4.2.1. Consider the random variable X that represents the time to execute a task. The domain of X is $(0, \infty)$. Table 4.9 depicts the cumulative distribution function, $F_X(x)$, of X. The time unity adopted to represent values of X is milliseconds (ms). Figure 4.10 shows the complementary cumulative distribution function of X, $F_X^c(x)$.

Table 4.9
Cumulative Distribution Function $F_X(x)$

X (ms)	$F_X(x)$	X (ms)	$F_X(x)$
0	0	550	0.911624
50	0.0143877	600	0.938031
100	0.0803014	650	0.956964
150	0.191153	700	0.970364
200	0.323324	750	0.979743
250	0.456187	800	0.986246
300	0.57681	850	0.990717
350	0.679153	900	0.993768
400	0.761897	950	0.995836
450	0.826422	1000	0.997231
500	0.875348		

Using Table 4.9, it is possible to calculate probabilities such as

$$P(X < 500\,ms) = F_X(500\,ms) = 0.875348,$$

$$P(X > 500\,ms) = 1 - F_X(500\,ms) = 1 - 0.875348 = 0.124652,$$

and

$$P(500\,ms < X < 800\,ms) = F_X(800\,ms) - F_X(500\,ms) =$$

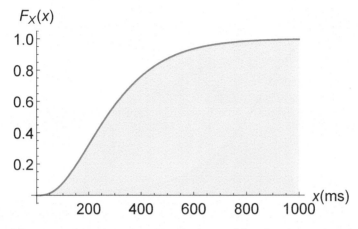

Figure 4.9 Cumulative Function Distribution $F_X(x)$ - Continuous Random Variable.

$$P(500\,ms < X < 800\,ms) = 0.986246 - 0.875348 = 0.110898,$$

which is also shown in Figure 4.11.

□

The derivative of the cumulative distribution function, $F_X(x)$, of continuous random variable X is called the probability density function (pdf) of X, which is denoted by $f_X(x)$. More formally

$$f_X(x) = \frac{dF_X(x)}{dx},\qquad(4.2.7)$$

where $f_X(x) \geq 0$ and $\int_{-\infty}^{\infty} f_X(x)\,dx = 1$, assuming X is defined in $(-\infty, \infty)$.

Probability questions related to X can also be solved using $f_X(x)$. Considering X is defined in $(-\infty, \infty)$, for instance, take into account the following cases:

1. $P(X < a) = \int_{-\infty}^{a} f_X(x)\,dx.$

2. $P(X > a) = 1 - \int_{-\infty}^{a} f_X(x)\,dx = \int_{a}^{\infty} f_X(x)\,dx.$

3. $P(a < X \leq b) = \int_{a}^{b} f_X(x)\,dx.$

It is worth mentioning that as X is continuous, $P(X = a) = \int_{a}^{a} f_X(x)\,dx = 0$; hence, $P(X < a) = P(X \leq a)$, for instance.

Example 4.2.2. Consider the random variable X represented in Example 4.2.1. Its probability density function, $f_X(x)$, is shown in Figure 4.12.

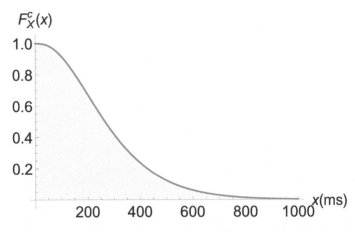

Figure 4.10   Complementary Cumulative Function Distribution $F_X^c(x)$.

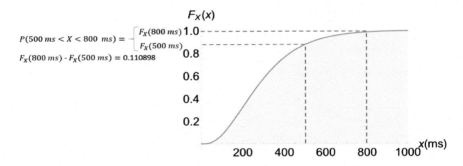

Figure 4.11 $P(500\,ms < X < 800\,ms)$ - Continuous Random Variable.

The probability of X assuming a value in the interval $(200\,ms, 400\,ms)$ is

$$P(200\,ms < X \leq 400\,ms) = \int_{200}^{400} f_X(x)\,dx = 0.438573,$$

which equates the red area depicted in Figure 4.13.

□

The *expected value* of continuous random variable X (also called *mean*) specified in an interval (a, b) is defined by

$$E(X) = \int_{a}^{b} x\,f_X(x)\,dx. \tag{4.2.8}$$

If X is a continuous random variable, then the expected value of $g(X)$, a real-valued function, specified in an interval (a, b), is defined by

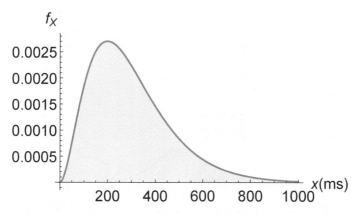

Figure 4.12   Probability Density Function $f_X(x)$ - Continuous Random Variable.

$$E(g(X)) = \int_a^b g(x) f_X(x) \, dx..$$ (4.2.9)

The *variance* of random variable X yields a measure of the dispersion of values around its mean, $E(X)$. If X is a random variable with mean $E(X)$, then the variance of X is defined by

$$Var(X) = E((X - E(X))^2),$$ (4.2.10)

which leads to

$$Var(X) = \int_a^b (x - E(X))^2 f_X(x) \, dx.$$ (4.2.11)

The square root of its variance defines the *standard deviation* of X, $Var(x)$, that is

$$SD(X) = Var(X)^{\frac{1}{2}} = \left(\int_a^b (x - E(X))^2 f_X(x) \, dx \right)^{1/2}.$$ (4.2.12)

As already mentioned, the standard deviation has the same unit of those values from the random variable, whereas the variance is the unit squared. The *coefficient of variation* is a dimensionless spread measure of X, which is defined by

$$CoV(X) = \frac{SD(X)}{E(X)}.$$ (4.2.13)

Example 4.2.3. Assume a continuous random variable X, whose domain is the interval $(0, 6)$, and *pdf* is defined as

$$f_X(x) = \frac{1}{144} \left(36 - x^2 \right).$$

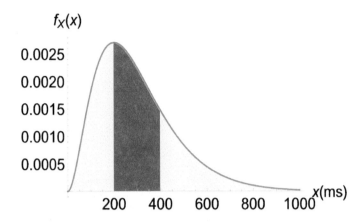

Figure 4.13 $P(200\,ms < X \leq 400\,ms) = \int_{200}^{400} f_X(x)\,dx.$

Figure 4.14 presents the density function. The expected value, the variance, the standard deviation, and the coefficient of variation of X are calculated according Equation 4.2.8, Equation 4.2.11, Equation 4.2.12 and Equation 4.2.13, respectively. The expected value of X is

$$E(X) = \int_0^6 x \frac{1}{144} \left(36 - x^2\right) dx = 2.25.$$

The variance is

$$Var(X) = \int_0^6 (x - E(X))^2 \frac{1}{144} \left(36 - x^2\right) dx = 2.1375.$$

The standard deviation is

$$SD(X) = (\int_a^b (x - E(X))^2 \frac{1}{144} \left(36 - x^2\right) dx)^{1/2} = 1.4620,$$

and, coefficient of variation

$$CoV(X) = \frac{SD(X)}{E(X)} = 0.6498.$$

□

Percentile Statistics - As in the discrete case, the percentiles and percentile ranks of a random variable X are calculated using its cumulative distribution function, $F_X(x)$. The percentile rank of value x is obtained from

$$p_x = 100 \times F_X(x) \tag{4.2.14}$$

and the percentile (the value x) of a specified rank p is obtained by

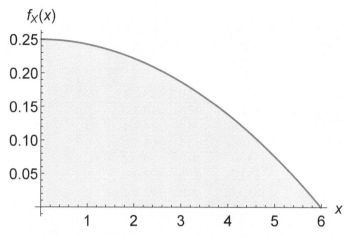

Figure 4.14 Probability Density Function of X - $f_X(x) = \frac{1}{144}\left(36 - x^2\right)$.

$$x_p = \min \arg F_X(x) \le p. \tag{4.2.15}$$

For instance, the 50th percentile of a random variable X is the value that divides the distribution, $F_X(x)$, in half, known as the *median, Mdn.*

$$Mdn = x_{0.5} = \min \arg F_X(x) = 0.5. \tag{4.2.16}$$

The 25th percentile of a random variable X is the *first quartile* (Q_1).

$$Q_1 = x_{0.25} = \min \arg F_X(x) = 0.25. \tag{4.2.17}$$

The 75th percentile of a random variable X is the *third quartile* (Q_3).

$$Q_3 = x_{0.75} = \min \arg F_X(x) = 0.75. \tag{4.2.18}$$

The second quartile is the median, $Q_2 = Mdn$. The *interquartile range* (*IQR*) is a measure of the spread of a distribution. The *IQR* is the difference between the 75th and 25th percentiles:

$$IQR = Q_3 - Q_1. \tag{4.2.19}$$

Example 4.2.4. Consider the random variable X represented in Example 4.2.1. Its probability density function, $f_X(x)$, is shown in Figure 4.12. Table 4.10 depicts the percentiles and the respective percentiles ranks of the random variable X.

Table 4.10
Percentiles and Percentile Ranks of X

x	$F_X(x)$	x	$F_X(x)$
0	0	288.26	0.55
81.7691	0.05	310.538	0.6
110.207	0.1	334.738	0.65
133.064	0.15	361.557	0.7
153.504	0.2	392.04	0.75
172.73	0.25	427.903	0.8
191.378	0.3	472.305	0.85
209.863	0.35	532.232	0.9
228.508	0.4	629.579	0.95
247.594	0.45	∞	1
267.406	0.5		

Table 4.11
Q_1, *Mdn*, Q_3, **and** *IQR* **for Random Variable** X

Measures	Q_1	*Mdn*	Q_3	*IQR*
Values	172.73	267.41	392.04	219.31

Table 4.11 presents the statistics Q_1, *Mdn*, Q_3, and *IQR* for random variable X, which were obtained from Table 4.10.

□

Section 5.2 summarizes some important continuous random variables.

4.3   MOMENTS

A random variable is characterized by its cumulative distribution function or its respective probability mass function (discrete variables) or density function (continuous variables). In many cases, however, this information may not be available or even necessary. In some instances, the availability of features such as some *moments* is sufficient. The term moment is taken from physics. Later on, some physical intuition is given to some particular moments. This section introduces the three classes of moments: *moments about the origin*, *central moments*, and *normalized central moments*; presents examples and also discusses *moment generation functions* and their use.

Let X be a random variable with mean $E(X)$ and variance $Var(X)$. The nth moment of X about the origin (*moment about zero*), $n \in \mathbb{N}$, is defined by

$$\mu'_n = E(X^n). \tag{4.3.1}$$

Thus, if X is a discrete random variable, we have

$$\mu'_n = E(X^n) = \sum_i x_i^n P(X = x_i). \tag{4.3.2}$$

If X is a continuous random variable with domain $(-\infty, \infty)$ (if the domain of X is (a, b), and the respective integral has a and b as limits), we get

$$\mu'_n = E(X^n) = \int_{-\infty}^{\infty} x^n f_X(x) \, dx. \tag{4.3.3}$$

The first moment about the origin of a random variable is; thus, either

$$\mu' = E(X) = \sum_i x_i P(X = x_i), \tag{4.3.4}$$

for discrete random variables, and

$$\mu' = E(X) = \int_{-\infty}^{\infty} x f_X(x) \, dx, \tag{4.3.5}$$

for continuous random variables. Hence, the first moment of a random variable, X, is its expectation or mean value, $E(X)$.

Example 4.3.1. Assume the discrete random variable specified in Example 4.1.3. The first and second moments about the origin are calculated using

$$\mu' = E(X) = \sum_i x_i P(X = x_i),$$

and

$$\mu'_2 = E(X^2) = \sum_i x_i^2 P(X = x_i).$$

Therefore, $\mu' = 5$ and $\mu'_2 = 30.83$. As the expected value of X is $E(X) = \mu'$, then $E(X) = 5$. The variance X is

$$Var(X) = \mu'_2 - (\mu')^2;$$

then $Var(X) = 5.8333$.

$\square$

We may understand the first moment (average) of a random variable as the center of mass of a set of objects with different weights distributed over a line segment (in practice, it can be seen as a plank). Figure 4.15 depicts this scenario.

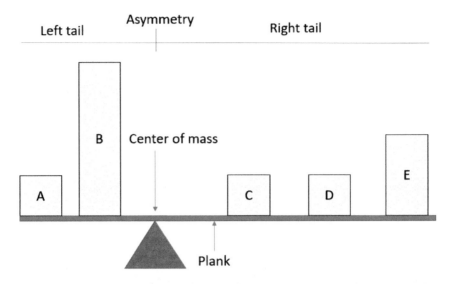

Figure 4.15   Center of Mass of Objects Distributed over a Plank.

Example 4.3.2. Assume a continuous random variable X defined in Example 4.2.3. The first and second moments about the origin are calculated using

$$\mu' = E(X) = \int_0^6 x f_X(x)\, dx,$$

and

$$\mu'_2 = E(X^2) = \int_0^6 x^2 f_X(x)\, dx.$$

Therefore, $\mu' = 2.25$ and $\mu'_2 = 7.2$. As the expected value of X is $E(X) = \mu'$, then $E(X) = 2.25$. The variance X is

$$Var(X) = \mu'_2 - (\mu')^2,$$

then $Var(X) = 2.1375$.

□

A random variable X with defined mean and variance has its nth *central moment*, $n \in \mathbb{N}$, defined as

$$\mu_n = E((X - E(X))^n).$$ (4.3.6)

If X is a discrete random variable, we have

$$\mu_n = E((X - E(X))^n) = \sum_i (x_i - E(X))^n P(X = x_i). \qquad (4.3.7)$$

When X is a continuous random variable with domain $(-\infty, \infty)$ (if the domain of X is (a, b), the respective integral has a and b as limits), the nth central moment is defined as

$$\mu_n = E((X - E(X))^n)) = \int_{-\infty}^{\infty} (x - E(X))^n f_X(x)\, dx. \qquad (4.3.8)$$

The second central moment (variance) corresponds to a random variable, in physical terms, which may be understood as the moment of inertia about the center of mass.

$$\mu_2 = E((X - E(X))^2) = \sum_i (x_i - E(X))^2 P(X = x_i) \qquad (4.3.9)$$

for discrete random variables, and

$$\mu_2 = E((X - E(X))^2)) = \int_{-\infty}^{\infty} (x - E(X))^2 f_X(x)\, dx \qquad (4.3.10)$$

for continuous random variables. Hence, the second central moment of a random variable, X, is its variance.

Example 4.3.3. Assume the discrete random variable specified in Example 4.1.3. Table 4.12 shows x_i, $P(X = x_i)$, and $(x_i - E(X))^2 \times p_X(x_i)$.

Table 4.12
Second Central Moment - Discrete Random Variable

x_i	$p_X(x_i)$	$(x_i - E(X))^2 \times p_X(x_i)$
0	0.0278	0.6944
1	0.0556	0.8889
2	0.0833	0.75
3	0.1111	0.4444
4	0.1389	0.1389
5	0.1667	0
6	0.1389	0.1389
7	0.1111	0.4444
8	0.0833	0.75
9	0.0556	0.8889
10	0.0278	0.6944

As the variance value of X is $Var(X) = \mu_2$, then $Var(X) = 5.8333$.

$\square$

The second center moment (variance) corresponds to the moment of inertia about the center mass (see Figure 4.15).

Example 4.3.4. Assume a continuous random variable X defined in Example 4.2.3. The second central moment is calculated using

$$\mu_2 = E((X - E(X))^2)) = \int_0^6 (x - E(X))^2 f_X(x)\,dx.$$

As $Var(X) = \mu_2$, then $Var(X) = 2.1375$ since $E(X) = 2.25$.

$\square$

The nth *normalized central moments* (or n^{th} *standardized central moment*) is the nth central moment divided by the square root of the second central moment to the nth power, $\mu_2^{n/2}$. In other words, the nth normalized central moment is defined as the nth central moment divided by the standard deviation to the nth power.

A random variable X with defined mean and variance has its nth *normalized central moments*, $n \in \mathbb{N}$, defined as

$$\tilde{\mu}_n = \left(\frac{E(X - E(X))^n}{\mu_2^{1/2}} \right)^n. \tag{4.3.11}$$

If X is a discrete random variable, we have

$$\tilde{\mu}_n = \left(\frac{E(X - E(X))^n}{\mu_2^{1/2}} \right)^n = \frac{\sum_i (x_i - E(X))^n P(X = x_i)}{\mu_2^{n/2}}. \tag{4.3.12}$$

When X is a continuous random variable with domain $(-\infty, \infty)$ (if the domain of X is (a, b), the respective integral has a and b as limits), the nth central moment is defined as

$$\tilde{\mu}_n = \left(\frac{E(X - E(X))^n}{\mu_2^{1/2}} \right)^n = \frac{\int_{-\infty}^{\infty} (x - E(X))^n f_X(x)\,dx}{\mu_2^{n/2}}. \tag{4.3.13}$$

Some distributions are known to have deviations on one side of the mean, others have deviations on the other side, and some are symmetrical. Any odd normalized central moment is a measure of the general concept of skewness. A random variable X has symmetric distribution about its mean, if $X - E(X)$ has the same distribution as $E(X) - X$. If X is not symmetric, it is said to be asymmetric. The skewness is a measure of the symmetry of a random variable. It is worth stressing that odd moments are positive when in presence of a tail to the right ($X - E(X) > 1$ - positive values), and they are negative when there is a tail to the left ($X - E(X) < 1$ - negative values). Thus, for any odd power $n \geq 3$, normalized central moments quantify a measure of a skewness type, with higher powers (n) giving greater weight to values that are far from the mean. As this phenomenon occurs for any odd $n \leq 3$ power, the natural choice to quantify the skewness of the X random variable is its third normalized central moment. However, it is worth mentioning that higher odd powers also measure skewness types, but with greater emphasis on values farther to the mean.

The third normalized central moment of a random variable is; thus, either

$$\tilde{\mu}_3 = \left(\frac{E(X - E(X))^n}{\mu_2^{1/2}} \right)^3 = \frac{\sum_i (x_i - E(X))^3 P(X = x_i)}{\mu_2^{3/2}}. \qquad (4.3.14)$$

for discrete random variables, or

$$\tilde{\mu}_3 = \left(\frac{E(X - E(X))^n}{\mu_2^{1/2}} \right)^3 = \frac{\int_{-\infty}^{\infty} (x - E(X))^3 f_X(x)\,dx}{\mu_2^{3/2}} \qquad (4.3.15)$$

for continuous random variables. The third normalized central moment of a random variable, X, is the *skewness* of X.

The larger the normalized central moment, the higher is the impact by values in the distribution tails. The fourth normalized central moment (defined as kurtosis) also measures the spread around the mean, as the second moment does (variance), but with a higher weighs on values of the distribution tails. Therefore, fourth normalized central moment provides information about the distribution "tailedness" [12] [462] [197]. Higher even normalized central moments ($n > 4$) give even more emphasis to values in distribution tails. However, as the fourth normalized central moment is the smallest normalized central moment that quantifies tailedness, it is a natural choice to quantify such a characteristic. It is worth mentioning that many authors and software packages usually describe kurtosis as a measure of the distribution peakedness. However, it indeed reflects the information on the distribution tail [12, 197, 462].

The fourth normalized central moment of a random variable is; thus, either

$$\tilde{\mu}_4 = \left(\frac{E(X - E(X))^4}{\mu_2^{1/2}} \right)^4 = \frac{\sum_i (x_i - E(X))^4 P(X = x_i)}{\mu_2^2}. \qquad (4.3.16)$$

for discrete random variables, or

$$\tilde{\mu}_4 = \left(\frac{E(X - E(X))^4}{\mu_2^{1/2}} \right)^4 = \frac{\int_{-\infty}^{\infty} (x - E(X))^4 f_X(x)\,dx}{\mu_2^2} \qquad (4.3.17)$$

for continuous random variables. The fourth normalized central moment of a random variable, X, is the *kurtosis* of X. The kurtosis is depicted in Equation 4.3.16 and Equation 4.3.17.

The fourth normalized central moment of a random variable normally distributed (see Section 5.2) is equal to $\tilde{\mu}_4 = 3$. The term excess kurtosis of random variable X is a statistic that represents how much larger is the random variable kurtosis than a random variable normally distributed. Therefore, the excess kurtosis *Kurt* is a comparative measure of tailedness between the random variable of interest and a random variable normally distributed (see Section 3.4).

$$Kurt = \tilde{\mu}_4 - 3. \tag{4.3.18}$$

Example 4.3.5. Assume the discrete random variable specified in Example 4.1.3. Table 4.13 shows x_i, $P(X = x_i)$, $(x_i - E(X))^3 \times p_X(x_i)$, and $(x_i - E(X))^4 \times p_X(x_i)$. From Example 4.3.3, we get $\mu_2^{1/2} = 2.42$. Hence, applying Equation 4.3.14 and Equation 4.3.16 we calculate the third and the fourth normalized central moments (also shown in Table 4.13), which are $\tilde{\mu}_3 = 0$ and $\tilde{\mu}_4 = 2.37$, respectively.

Table 4.13

Third and Fourth Normalized Central Moment - Random Variable - Example 4.1.3

x_i	$p_X(x_i)$	$(x_i - E(X))^3 \times p_X(x_i)$	$(x_i - E(X))^4 \times p_X(x_i)$
0	0.03	-3.47	17.36
1	0.06	-3.56	14.22
2	0.08	-2.25	6.75
3	0.11	-0.89	1.78
4	0.14	-0.14	0.14
5	0.17	0.00	0.00
6	0.14	0.14	0.14
7	0.11	0.89	1.78
8	0.08	2.25	6.75
9	0.06	3.56	14.22
10	0.03	3.47	17.36
		0	**2.37**
		$\tilde{\mu}_3$	$\tilde{\mu}_4$

□

Example 4.3.6. Consider the a continuous random variable X defined in Example 4.2.3. The third and fourth normalized central moments are calculated using Equation 4.3.15 and Equation 4.3.17, respectively. Therefore

$$\tilde{\mu}_3 = \frac{\int_0^6 \frac{1}{144} \left(36 - x^2\right) (x - \mu')^3 \, dx}{\sigma^3} = 0.3780,$$

and

$$\tilde{\mu}_4 = \frac{\int_0^6 \frac{1}{144} \left(36 - x^2\right) (x - \mu')^4 \, dx}{\sigma^4} = 2.1667,$$

where $\mu' = 2.25$ and $\sigma = 1.462$, which can be seen in the previous examples.

□

The *moment generating function* of a random variable X is defined as a function of $s, s \in \mathbb{R}$.

$$M_X(s) = E(e^{sX}) \qquad (4.3.19)$$

$M_X(s)$ exists if this expectation is finite for all $s \in (-c, c)$ where $-c \leq 0 \leq c$. Otherwise, $M_X(s)$ does not exist.

If X is a discrete random variable, then the moment generating function is

$$M_X(s) = \sum_{\forall x} e^{sx} P(X = x). \qquad (4.3.20)$$

If X is a continuous random variable, then $M_X(s)$ is specified by

$$M_X(s) = \int_{-\infty}^{\infty} e^{sx} f_X(x)\, dx, \qquad (4.3.21)$$

considering this integral exists.

$M_X(s)$ is called the moment generating function because all existing moments around the origin of X can be obtained by successively differentiating $M_X(s)$ by s, and then letting $s = 0$. For instance, the first moment around the origin of X is obtained by

$$\mu' = \frac{\partial M_X(s)}{\partial s}\Big|_{s=0}.$$

The second moment around the origin of X is obtained by

$$\mu'_2 = \frac{\partial^2 M_X(s)}{\partial^2 s}\Big|_{s=0}.$$

Likewise, the nth moment around the origin of X is obtained by

$$\mu'_n = \frac{\partial^n M_X(s)}{\partial^n s}\Big|_{s=0}.$$

Example 4.3.7. Assume the discrete random variable specified in Example 4.1.3. The moment generating function is calculated through Equation 4.3.20, which gives

$$M_X(s) = \frac{1}{36} + \frac{e^s}{18} + \frac{e^{2s}}{12} + \frac{e^{3s}}{9} + \frac{5e^{4s}}{36} + \frac{e^{5s}}{6} + \frac{5e^{6s}}{36} + \frac{e^{7s}}{9} + \frac{e^{8s}}{12} + \frac{e^{9s}}{18} + \frac{e^{10s}}{36}.$$

Differentiating $M_X(s)$ with respect to s, we obtain

$$\frac{\partial M_X(s)}{\partial s} = \frac{e^s}{18} + \frac{e^{2s}}{6} + \frac{e^{3s}}{3} + \frac{5e^{4s}}{9} + \frac{5e^{5s}}{6} + \frac{5e^{6s}}{6} + \frac{7e^{7s}}{9} + \frac{2e^{8s}}{3} + \frac{e^{9s}}{2} + \frac{5e^{10s}}{18}.$$

Now, let $s = 0$; then we get

$$\mu' = \frac{\partial M_X(s)}{\partial s}\Big|_{s=0} = 5.$$

It is worth noting that $E(X) = \mu'$; hence $E(X) = 5$. Now, let us obtain the second moment about the origin. As

$$\frac{\partial^2 M_X(s)}{\partial^2 s} = \frac{\partial \left(\frac{\partial M_X(s)}{\partial s} \right)}{\partial s},$$

then

$$\frac{\partial^2 M_X(s)}{\partial^2 s} = \frac{\partial \left(\frac{e^x}{18} + \frac{e^{2x}}{6} + \frac{e^{3x}}{3} + \frac{5e^{4x}}{9} + \frac{5e^{5x}}{6} + \frac{5e^{6x}}{6} + \frac{7e^{7x}}{9} + \frac{2e^{8x}}{3} + \frac{e^{9x}}{2} + \frac{5e^{10x}}{18} \right)}{\partial s},$$

which results in

$$\frac{\partial^2 M_X(s)}{\partial^2 s} = \frac{e^x}{18} + \frac{e^{2x}}{3} + e^{3x} + \frac{20e^{4x}}{9} + \frac{25e^{5x}}{6} + 5e^{6x} + \frac{49e^{7x}}{9} + \frac{16e^{8x}}{3} + \frac{9e^{9x}}{2} + \frac{25e^{10x}}{9}.$$

Now, let $s = 0$; then we get

$$\mu'_2 = \frac{\partial^2 M_X(s)}{\partial^2 s}\Big|_{s=0} = 30.8333.$$

As $Var(X) = \mu'_2 - (\mu')^2$, then $Var(X) = 30.8333 - 25 = 5.8333$ and $SD(X) = 2.4152$.

$\square$

Example 4.3.8. Assume a continuous random variable X introduced in Example 4.2.3. The central moment generating function is calculated through Equation 4.3.21, which gives

$$M_X(s) = -\frac{18s^2 - 6e^{6s}s + e^{6s} - 1}{72s^3}.$$

Differentiating $M_X(s)$ with respect to s, we obtain

$$\frac{\partial M_X(s)}{\partial s} = \frac{18s^2 - 6e^{6s}s + e^{6s} - 1}{24s^4} - \frac{36s - 36e^{6s}s}{72s^3}.$$

Applying $s = 0$ to the above expression results in an indeterminate form. Then, we opted to obtain an equivalent Taylor series (see Section 5.4) to the expression

$$-\frac{18s^2 - 6e^{6s}s + e^{6s} - 1}{72s^3},$$

which results in

$$1 + \frac{9s}{4} + \frac{18s^2}{5} + \frac{9s^3}{2} + \frac{162s^4}{35} + \frac{81s^5}{20} + O\left(s^6\right)$$

with five terms. Then, this new expression is differentiated concerning s,

$$\frac{\partial M_X(s)}{\partial s} = \frac{\partial(1 + \frac{9s}{4} + \frac{18s^2}{5} + \frac{9s^3}{2} + \frac{162s^4}{35} + \frac{81s^5}{20} + O\left(s^6\right))}{\partial s},$$

which results in

$$\frac{\partial M_X(s)}{\partial s} = \frac{9}{4} + \frac{36s}{5} + \frac{27s^2}{2} + \frac{648s^3}{35} + \frac{81s^4}{4} + O\left(s^5\right).$$

Now, let $s = 0$; then we get

$$\mu' = \frac{\partial M_X(s)}{\partial s}|_{s=0} = 2.25,$$

which is the expected value of X, $E(X) = \mu' = 2.25$. Now, let us obtain the second moment about the origin. As

$$\frac{\partial^2 M_X(s)}{\partial^2 s} = \frac{\partial(\frac{\partial M_X(s)}{\partial s})}{\partial s},$$

then

$$\frac{\partial^2 M_X(s)}{\partial^2 s} = \frac{\partial}{\partial s}\left(\frac{9}{4} + \frac{36s}{5} + \frac{27s^2}{2} + \frac{648s^3}{35} + \frac{81s^4}{4} + O\left(s^5\right)\right).$$

$$\frac{\partial^2 M_X(s)}{\partial^2 s} = \frac{36}{5} + 27s + \frac{1944s^2}{35} + 81s^3 + O\left(s^4\right).$$

Now, let $s = 0$; then we get

$$\mu'_2 = \frac{\partial^2 M_X(s)}{\partial^2 s}|_{s=0} = 7.2.$$

As $Var(X) = \mu'_2 - (\mu')^2$, then $Var(X) = 7.2 - 2.25^2 = 2.1375$ and $SD(X) = 1.4620$.

$\square$

The *central moment generating function* of a random variable X is defined as a function of s, $s \in \mathbb{R}$.

$$CM_X(s) = E(e^{s(X - \mu')}) \tag{4.3.22}$$

$CM_X(s)$ exists if this expectation is finite for all $s \in (-c, c)$ where $-c \leq 0 \leq c$. Otherwise, $CM_X(s)$ does not exist.

If X is a discrete random variable, then the moment generating function is

$$CM_X(s) = \sum_{\forall x} e^{s(x - \mu')} P(X = x). \tag{4.3.23}$$

If X is a continuous random variable, then $CM_X(s)$ is specified by

$$CM_X(s) = \int_{-\infty}^{\infty} e^{s(x - \mu')} f_X(x) \, dx, \tag{4.3.24}$$

considering this integral exists.

$CM_X(s)$ is called the central moment generating function because all existing central moments of X can be obtained by successively differentiating $CM_X(s)$ by s, and then letting $s = 0$. For instance, the second central moment of X is obtained by

$$\mu_2 = \frac{\partial^2 CM_X(s)}{\partial^2 s}\Big|_{s=0}.$$

Similarly, the nth central moment of X is obtained by

$$\mu_n = \frac{\partial^n CM_X(s)}{\partial^n s}\Big|_{s=0}.$$

Example 4.3.9. Assume the discrete random variable specified in Example 4.1.3. The central moment generating function is calculated through Equation 4.3.23, which gives

$$CM_X(s) = e^{-5x}\left(\frac{e^x}{18} + \frac{e^{2x}}{12} + \frac{e^{3x}}{9} + \frac{5e^{4x}}{36} + \frac{e^{5x}}{6} + \frac{5e^{6x}}{36} + \right.$$
$$\left. \frac{e^{7x}}{9} + \frac{e^{8x}}{12} + \frac{e^{9x}}{18} + \frac{e^{10x}}{36} + \frac{1}{36}\right).$$

Differentiating $CM_X(s)$ with respect to s, we obtain

$$\frac{\partial M_X(s)}{\partial s} = 25e^{-5s}\left(\frac{e^s}{18} + \frac{e^{2s}}{12} + \frac{e^{3s}}{9} + \right.$$
$$\left. \frac{5e^{4s}}{36} + \frac{e^{5s}}{6} + \frac{5e^{6s}}{36} + \frac{e^{7s}}{9} + \frac{e^{8s}}{12} + \frac{e^{9s}}{18} + \right.$$

$$\frac{e^{10s}}{36} + \frac{1}{36}) - 10e^{-5s}(\frac{e^s}{18} + \frac{e^{2s}}{6} + \frac{e^{3s}}{3} + \frac{5e^{4s}}{9} +$$

$$\frac{5e^{5s}}{6} + \frac{5e^{6s}}{6} + \frac{7e^{7s}}{9} + \frac{2e^{8s}}{3} + \frac{e^{9s}}{2} + \frac{5e^{10s}}{18})$$

$$+e^{-5s}(\frac{e^s}{18} + \frac{e^{2s}}{3} + e^{3s} + \frac{20e^{4s}}{9} + \frac{25e^{5s}}{6} + 5e^{6s} + \frac{49e^{7s}}{9}$$

$$+\frac{16e^{8s}}{3} + \frac{9e^{9s}}{2} + \frac{25e^{10s}}{9}).$$

Now, let $s = 0$, then we get

$$\mu_2 = \frac{\partial M_X(s)}{\partial s}\Big|_{s=0} = 5.8333.$$

□

Example 4.3.10. Assume the discrete random variable specified in Example 4.2.3. The central moment generating function is calculated through Equation 4.3.24, which gives

$$CM_X(s) = \int_0^6 e^{s(x-\mu')} \frac{1}{144} \left(36 - x^2\right) dx$$

$$CM_X(s) = \frac{e^{-9s/4} \left(-18s^2 + 6e^{6s}s - e^{6s} + 1\right)}{72s^3}.$$

Differentiating $CM_X(s)$ with respect to s,

$$\frac{\partial^2 M_X(s)}{\partial^2 s}\Big|_{s=0}$$

leads to an indeterminate form. Then, we opted to obtain an equivalent Taylor series (see Section 5.4) to the expression

$$\frac{e^{-9s/4} \left(-18s^2 + 6e^{6s}s - e^{6s} + 1\right)}{72s^3} = 1 + \frac{171s^2}{160} + \frac{63s^3}{320} + \frac{5913s^4}{14336} + \frac{8181s^5}{71680} + O\left(s^6\right).$$

Thus,

$$CM_X(s) = 1 + \frac{171s^2}{160} + \frac{63s^3}{320} + \frac{5913s^4}{14336} + \frac{8181s^5}{71680} + O\left(s^6\right).$$

Hence,

$$\frac{\partial^2 CM_X(s)}{\partial s^2} = \frac{171}{80} + \frac{189s}{160} + \frac{17739s^2}{3584} + \frac{8181s^3}{3584} + O\left(s^4\right).$$

Therefore

$$\mu_2 = \frac{\partial^2 CM_X(s)}{\partial^2 s}\Big|_{s=0} = 2.1375.$$

□

Methods for estimating distribution parameters are discussed in Section 25.3, and methods for generating random variates are presented in Section 14.3. The next sections introduce some useful discrete and continuous random variables.

4.4 JOINT DISTRIBUTIONS

Many modeling problems require representing a system through more than one random variable. For instance, one may be interested in relating the time between requests arrival to an input queue of a server and the time to process a request in the server. The joint probability distribution function defines the relationship between random variables, and through such a function, one can calculate the probability of statements concerning the random variables. It is worth mentioning that some of the random variable distributions introduced in the previous sections were already depicted as compositions of other random variables. This section, however, introduces more detailed examples and discusses some related characteristics not mentioned so far.

Let Ω be the sample space associated with an experiment E, and assume e is a result of experiment E. Consider X_1, X_2, ..., X_k to be random variables that are associated to each result e. $(X_1, X_2, ..., X_k)$ is called a k-dimensional random vector. Figure 4.16 depicts such a mapping.

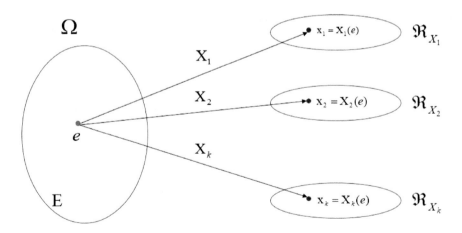

Figure 4.16   Multiple Random Variables.

Let us first start with two random variables, X and Y. Then, assume a two-dimensional random vector, (X, Y), representing X and Y for a given random experiment. If the possible values of (X, Y) form an enumerable finite or infinite set, (X, Y) is a discrete random vector. If the possible values of (X, Y) form a non-enumerable set of the Euclidean plane, (X, Y), is a continuous random vector.

The joint cumulative probability distribution function (*Joint CDF*) of the two-dimensional random vector, (X, Y), is defined by

$$F_{X,Y}(x,y) = P(X \leq x \wedge Y \leq y), \tag{4.4.1}$$

which is usually represented as

$$F_{X,Y}(x,y) = P(X \leq x, Y \leq y). \tag{4.4.2}$$

The joint cumulative probability distribution function of (X, Y) must have the following properties similar to those present in the cumulative probability distribution function of single random variables.

- $0 \leq F_{X,Y}(x,y) \leq 1,$ $\quad -\infty \leq x \leq \infty, \quad -\infty \leq y \leq \infty,$

- $F_{X,Y}(-\infty, -\infty) = 0,$

- $F_{X,Y}(\infty, \infty) = 1,$ and

- $F_{X,Y}(x_1, y_1) \leq F_{X,Y}(x_2, y_2)$ if $x_1 \leq x_2$ and $y_1 \leq y_2.$

4.4.1 JOINT DISCRETE RANDOM VARIABLES

As already mentioned, the knowledge of the joint cumulative probability distribution function, $F_{X,Y}(x,y)$, enables us to obtain the probability of statements related to the random variables that compose the random vector. Assume X and Y are discrete random variables related to a random experiment and form a two-dimensional random vector, (X, Y). The *joint probability mass function, Joint pdf*, is defined as

$$p_{X,Y}(x, y) = P(X = x, Y = y). \tag{4.4.3}$$

Generalizing to a k-dimensional random vector, $(X_1, X_2, ... X_k)$, the joint probability mass function is

$$p_{X_1,X_2,...X_k}(x_1, x_2, ... x_k) = P(X_1 = x_1, X_2 = x_2, ... X_k = x_k). \tag{4.4.4}$$

As the univariate probability mass functions, the sum of all possible probability values of X and Y is also one.

$$\sum_{\forall y} \sum_{\forall x} P(X = x, Y = y) = 1. \qquad (4.4.5)$$

For a k-dimensional random vector, $(X_1, X_2, ...X_i, ...X_k)$, we have

$$\sum_{\forall x_1} \sum_{\forall x_2} ... \sum_{\forall x_k} P(X_1 = x_1, X_2 = x_2, ...X_k = x_k) = 1. \qquad (4.4.6)$$

Example 4.4.1. Figure 4.17 shows the joint probability mass function, $p_{X,Y}(x, y)$, of a two-dimension discrete random vector composed of two variables $X \rightarrow \{0, 1, 2, 3, 4\}$ and $Y \rightarrow \{0, 1, 2, 3\}$ through a three-dimension plot. Table 4.14 shows the numerical values $p_{X,Y}(x, y)$ for each component of discrete random vector (X, Y). It is worth mentioning that $\sum_{y=0}^{3} \sum_{x=0}^{4} p_{X,Y}(x, y) = 1$.

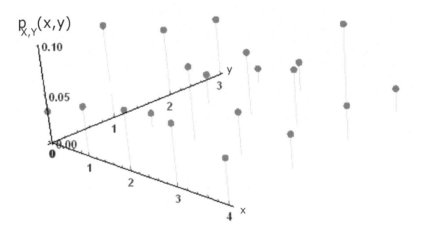

Figure 4.17 Joint Probability Mass Function, $p_{X,Y}(x, y)$.

The individual probability mass functions of X and Y, named *Marginal Probabilities - $P_X(x)$ and $P_Y(y)$* , may be obtained from the joint probability mass function, $p_{X,Y}(x, y)$, by

$$P_X(x) = \sum_{\forall y} P(X = x, Y = y), \qquad (4.4.7)$$

and

$$P_Y(y) = \sum_{\forall x} P(X = x, Y = y). \tag{4.4.8}$$

Table 4.14 shows the marginal probabilities $P_X(x)$ and $P_Y(y)$ on the rightmost column and in the last line, respectively. As an example, $P_X(2) = 0.2333$ and $P_Y(0) = 0.2417$. It important mentioning that $\sum_{x=0}^{4} P_X(x) = 1$ and $\sum_{y=0}^{3} P_Y(y) = 1$. The marginal probabilities functions, $P_X(x)$ and $P_Y(y)$, are also depicted in Figure 4.18.a and Figure 4.18.b, respectively.

Table 4.14
Joint Probability Mass Function and Marginal Probabilities.

$p_{X,Y}(x, y)$ and $P_X(x)$ and $P_Y(y)$.

X, Y	0	1	2	3	$P_X(x)$
0	0.0333	0.1000	0.0750	0.0667	0.2750
1	0.0500	0.0167	0.0333	0.0167	0.1167
2	0.0583	0.0750	0.0667	0.0333	0.2333
3	0.0583	0.0417	0.0583	0.0833	0.2417
4	0.0417	0.0333	0.0333	0.0250	0.1333
$P_Y(y)$	0.2417	0.2667	0.2667	0.2250	

Assuming a k-dimensional random vector, $(X_1, X_2, ..., X_k)$, the marginal probabilities are

$$P_{X_i}(x_i) = \sum_{\forall x_1} \sum_{\forall x_2} ... \sum_{\forall x_k} P(X_1 = x_1, X_2 = x_2, ...X_k = x_k), \qquad i \neq 1, 2, ..., k.$$
$$\tag{4.4.9}$$

The probability of X being higher or equal to three and Y smaller or equal to one is computed by summing up the probabilities in the gray cells of Table 4.14 since

$$P_{X,Y}(X \geq x_1, Y \leq y_1) = \sum_{x \geq x_1} \sum_{y \leq y_1} p_{X,Y}(x, y).$$

Hence,

$$P_{X,Y}(X \geq 3, Y \leq 1) = \sum_{x \geq 3} \sum_{y \leq 1} p_{X,Y}(x, y).$$

$$P_{X,Y}(X \geq 3, Y \leq 1) = p_{X,Y}(3, 0) + p_{X,Y}(3, 1) + p_{X,Y}(4, 0) + p_{X,Y}(4, 1).$$

$$P_{X,Y}(X \geq 3, Y \leq 1) = 0.0583 + 0.0417 + 0.0417 + 0.0333 = 0.1750.$$

□

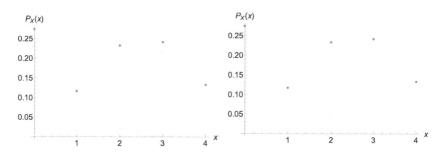

Figure 4.18   Marginal Probabilities Functions, $P_X(x)$ and $P_Y(y)$.

Now assume that given $X = x$, we would like to update the distribution of Y to contemplate this information. For this, the *conditional probability mass function*, the conditional *pdf*, should be adopted. The conditional probability mass function of Y given $X = x$ is defined as

$$P(Y = y \mid X = x) = \frac{p_{XY}(x,y)}{P_X(x)}, \tag{4.4.10}$$

where $P_X(x) = P(X = x) = \sum_{\forall y} P(X = x, Y = y)$.

Likewise, the conditional probability mass function of X given $Y = y$ is defined as

$$P(X = x \mid Y = y) = \frac{p_{XY}(x,y)}{P_Y(y)}, \tag{4.4.11}$$

where $P_Y(y) = P(Y = y) = \sum_{\forall x} P(X = x, Y = y)$.

Example 4.4.2. For instance, consider the joint distribution depicted in Table 4.14. $P(Y = 2 \mid X = 3)$ is given by

$$P(Y = 2 \mid X = 3) = \frac{p_{XY}(3,2)}{P(X = 3)} = \frac{0.0583}{0.2417} = 0.2414,$$

as $p_{XY}(3,2) = 0.0583$ (blue cell of Table 4.14) and

$$P(X = 3) = P_X(3) = \sum_{y=0}^{3} P(X = 3, Y = y) = 0.2417,$$

where $P_X(3)$ is provided in the pink cell of Table 4.14.

□

For a k-dimensional random vector, $(X_1, X_2, \ldots X_i, \ldots X_j, \ldots X_k)$, the conditional probability mass function of $(X_1, X_2, \ldots X_i, \ldots X_j, \ldots X_k)$, given $(X_i = x_i, X_j = x_j)$, is defined as

$$P(X_1, X_2, \ldots X_i, \ldots X_j, \ldots X_k \mid X_i = x_i, X_j = x_j) = \frac{p_{X_1, X_2, \ldots X_k}(x_1, x_2, \ldots x_k)}{P_{X_i, X_j}(x_i, x_j)}. \quad (4.4.12)$$

The random variables $X_1, X_2, \ldots X_k$ are independent, if

$$p_{X_1, X_2, \ldots X_k}(x_1, x_2, \ldots x_k) = P(X_1 = x_1)P(X_2 = x_2)\ldots P(X_k = x_k). \quad (4.4.13)$$

Considering a two-dimensional random vector, (X, Y), such that a random variable Z is specified as XY, if X and Y are independent, then

$$p_{X,Y}(x, y) = P(X = x)P(Y = y). \quad (4.4.14)$$

4.4.2 JOINT CONTINUOUS RANDOM VARIABLES

Now assume $X_1, X_2, \ldots, X_k$ are continuous random variables that are associated to a random experiment. $(X_1, X_2, \ldots, X_k)$ is the respective k-dimensional random vector. Consider a case in which only two continuous random variables are adopted, let us say X and Y; the random vector (X, Y) has a *Joint Probability Density Function* defined as

$$f_{X,Y}(x,y) = \frac{\partial^2 F_{X,Y}(x,y)}{\partial x \partial y}, \quad (4.4.15)$$

where $F_{X,Y}(x,y)$ is the joint cumulative probability distribution function of the random vector, (X, Y) - see Function 4.4.1. Therefore, we have

$$P((x,y) \in A) = \int\int_{(x,y)\in A} f_{X,Y}(x,y)dx\,dy, \quad (4.4.16)$$

where $A = \{(x, y) \mid x \in B, y \in C, \}$. If $B = (-\infty, x_1)$ and $C = (-\infty, y_1)$, then

$$P((x \in B, y \in C) = \int_{y \in C} \int_{x \in B} f_{X,Y}(x,y)dx\,dy, \quad (4.4.17)$$

As $P((x_1 \in B, y_1 \in C) = F(x_1, y_1)$, then

$$F(x_1, y_1) = \int_{-\infty}^{y_1} \int_{-\infty}^{x_1} f_{X,Y}(x, y) dx \, dy. \qquad (4.4.18)$$

Example 4.4.3. As an example, Figure 4.19 shows the plot of a joint probability density function specified by

$$f_{X,Y}(x, y) = \frac{\left(x^2 - 36\right)\left(y^2 - 81\right)}{69984}, \qquad x \in (0, 6), \quad y \in (0, 9).$$

The probability of X being larger or equal to four and of Y being smaller or equal to five is obtained by calculating

$$P(X \geq 4, Y \leq 5) = \int_0^5 \left(\int_4^6 \frac{\left(x^2 - 36\right)\left(y^2 - 81\right)}{69984} dx \right) dy = 0.11076.$$

Likewise, the probability of X being larger or equal to four and of Y being smaller or equal to five is obtained by calculating

$$P(X \leq 4, Y \leq 3) = \int_0^3 \left(\int_0^4 \frac{\left(x^2 - 36\right)\left(y^2 - 81\right)}{69984} dx \right) dy = 0.41015.$$

□

For a k-dimensional random vector $(X_1, X_2, ... X_k)$, the joint probability density function is defined as

$$f_{X_1, X_2, ... X_k}(x_1, x_2, ... x_k) = \frac{\partial^k F_{X_1, X_2, ... X_k}(x_1, x_2, ... x_k)}{\partial x_1 \partial x_2 ... \partial x_k}, \qquad (4.4.19)$$

where $F_{X_1, X_2, ... X_k}(x_1, x_2, ... x_k)$ is the joint cumulative probability distribution function of the random vector.

The individual probability density functions of X and Y, named *Marginal Density Functions* - $f_X(x)$ and $f_Y(y)$, may be obtained from the joint probability function, $f_{X,Y}(x, y)$, by integrating y or x over the respective domains, that is

$$f_X(x) = \int_{-\infty}^{\infty} f_{X,Y}(x, y) \, dy, \qquad (4.4.20)$$

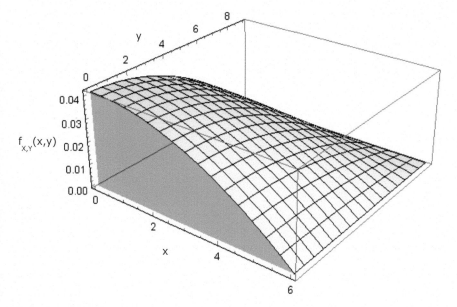

Figure 4.19 Joint Probability Density Function $f_{X,Y}(x,y)$.

and

$$f_Y(y) = \int_{-\infty}^{\infty} f_{X,Y}(x,y)\,dx. \qquad (4.4.21)$$

Example 4.4.4. Therefore, considering the joint density function

$$f_{X,Y}(x,y) = \frac{(x^2 - 36)(y^2 - 81)}{69984}, \qquad x \in (0,6), \quad y \in (0,9),$$

we have

$$f_X(x) = \int_0^9 \frac{(x^2 - 36)(y^2 - 81)}{69984}\,dy, \qquad x \in (0,6).$$

$$f_X(x) = -\frac{1}{144}(x-6)(x+6), \qquad x \in (0,6).$$

Similarly,

$$f_Y(y) = \int_0^6 \frac{(x^2 - 36)(y^2 - 81)}{69984}\,dx, \qquad y \in (0,9).$$

$$f_Y(y) = -\frac{1}{486}(y-9)(y+9), \qquad y \in (0,9).$$

It is worth noting that

$$\int_0^6 f_X(x)dx = 1$$

and

$$\int_0^9 f_Y(y)dy = 1.$$

Figure 4.20.a shows a graphical representation of $f_X(x)$, and Figure 4.20.b depicts $f_Y(y)$.

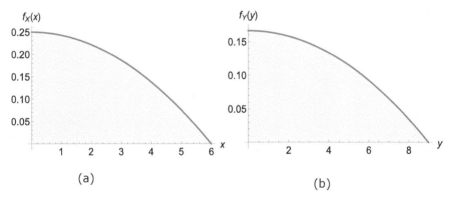

Figure 4.20   Marginal Density Functions $f_X(x)$ (a) and $f_Y(y)$ (b).

□

Now, generalizing for a k-dimensional random vector, $(X_1, X_2, ..., X_k)$ of continuous random variables, the marginal density function of X_i is defined as

$$f_{X_i}(x_i) = \int_{-\infty}^{\infty}\int_{-\infty}^{\infty} ... \int_{-\infty}^{\infty} f_{X_1,X_2,...X_k}(x_1, x_2, ...x_k)dx_1\,dx_2...dx_k, \qquad i \neq 1, 2, ..., k.$$

(4.4.22)

It is important to stress that

$$\int_{-\infty}^{\infty} f_{X_i}(x_i)dx_1 = 1.$$

Now assume we would like to find out the density function of Y given $X = x$. The conditional density function of Y given $X = x$ is defined as

$$f(Y = y \mid X = x) = \frac{f_{XY}(x,y)}{f_X(x)}. \qquad (4.4.23)$$

Likewise, the conditional density function of X given $Y = y$ is defined as

$$f(X = x \mid Y = y) = \frac{f_{XY}(x,y)}{f_Y(y)}. \qquad (4.4.24)$$

Generalizing for a k-dimensional random vector, $(X_1, X_2, \ldots X_i, \ldots X_j, \ldots X_k)$, the conditional density function of $(X_1, X_2, \ldots X_i, \ldots X_j, \ldots X_k)$, given $(X_i = x_i, X_j = x_j)$ is defined as

$$f(X_1, X_2, \ldots X_i, \ldots X_j, \ldots X_k \mid X_i = x_i, X_j = x_j) = \frac{f_{X_1, X_2, \ldots X_k}(x_1, x_2, \ldots x_k)}{f_{X_i, X_j}(x_i, x_j)}. \qquad (4.4.25)$$

A k-dimensional random vector, $(X_1, X_2, \ldots, X_k)$ is composed of continuous and independent random variables if

$$f_{X_1, X_2, \ldots X_k}(x_1, x_2, \ldots x_k) = f_{X_1}(x_1) f_{X_2}(x_2) \ldots f_{X_k}(x_k). \qquad (4.4.26)$$

Consider a two-dimensional random vector, (X, Y), the random variables X and Y are independent, if

$$f_{X,Y}(x, y) = f_X(x) f_Y(y). \qquad (4.4.27)$$

Example 4.4.5. Considering the joint density function and the respective marginal density function of X and Y given by

$$f_{X,Y}(x,y) = \frac{\left(x^2 - 36\right)\left(y^2 - 81\right)}{69984}, \qquad x \in (0,6), \quad y \in (0,9),$$

$$f_X(x) = -\frac{1}{144}(x - 6)(x + 6), \qquad x \in (0,6),$$

and

$$f_Y(y) = -\frac{1}{486}(y - 9)(y + 9), \qquad y \in (0,9),$$

respectively, as

$$f_{X,Y}(x,y) = f_X(x) \times f_Y(y), \qquad x \in (0,6), \quad y \in (0,9),$$

X and Y are independent.

□

The next two sections discuss the distribution of two specific types of random variable compositions, that is, (1) product and (2) sums of random variables.

4.4.3 CONVOLUTION

Consider the probability mass functions of two independent non-negative discrete random variables X and Y are given. The cumulative distribution probability function of their sum, $Z = X + Y$ is obtained through

$$P(Z = z) = P(X + Y = z) = \sum_{\forall u} p_Z(u, z - u).$$

$$P(Z = z) = P(X + Y = z) = \sum_{\forall u} p_{X+Y}(u, z - u).$$

As X and Y are independent, then $p_{X+Y}(u, z - u) = p_X(u)\, p_Y(z - u)$; hence

$$P(X + Y = z) = \sum_{\forall u} p_Y(z - u) \times p_X(u). \qquad (4.4.28)$$

The operation above is called discrete convolution, which is denoted by $(p_Y * p_X)(z)$; thus

$$(p_Y * p_X)(z) = \sum_{\forall u} p_Y(z - u) \times p_X(u). \qquad (4.4.29)$$

Example 4.4.6. Assume X is a discrete random variable defined over the domain $\{1, 2\}$ with probability mass function specified by

$$p_X(x) = \begin{cases} 0.5 & \text{if } x \in \{1,2\} \\ 0 & \text{otherwise.} \end{cases}$$

Also consider another discrete random variable, Y, defined over the domain $\{0, 1, 2\}$ with probability mass function specified by

$$p_Y(y) = \begin{cases} \frac{1}{3} & \text{if } y \in \{0, 1, 2\} \\ 0 & \text{otherwise.} \end{cases}$$

Now let us consider a random variable described by the sum of X and Y, that is $Z = X + Y$. Hence, Z is defined over $\{0, 1, 2, 3, 4\}$. The probability mass function of Z may be obtained through the discrete convolution $(p_X * p_Y)(z)$. Therefore,

$$P(Z = 0) = (p_Y * p_X)(0) = \sum_{u \in \{1,2\}} p_Y(0 - u) \times p_X(u),$$

$$P(Z = 0) = (p_Y * p_X)(0) = p_Y(0 - 1) \times p_X(1) + p_Y(0 - 2) \times p_X(2) =$$

$$P(Z = 0) = (p_Y * p_X)(0) = 0 \times 0.5 + 0 \times 0.5 = 0,$$

$$P(Z = 0) = 0,$$

$$P(Z = 1) = (p_Y * p_X)(1) = \sum_{u \in \{1,2\}} p_Y(1 - u) \times p_X(u),$$

$$P(Z = 1) = (p_Y * p_X)(1) = p_Y(1 - 1) \times p_X(1) + p_Y(1 - 2) \times p_X(2) =$$

$$P(Z = 1) = (p_Y * p_X)(0) = \frac{1}{3} \times 0.5 + 0 \times 0.5 = 0,$$

$$P(Z = 1) = \frac{1}{6},$$

$$P(Z = 2) = (p_Y * p_X)(2) = \sum_{u \in \{1,2\}} p_Y(2 - u) \times p_X(u),$$

$$P(Z = 2) = (p_Y * p_X)(2) = p_Y(2 - 1) \times p_X(1) + p_Y(2 - 2) \times p_X(2) =$$

$$P(Z = 2) = (p_Y * p_X)(2) = \frac{1}{3} \times 0.5 + \frac{1}{3} \times 0.5 = \frac{5}{3},$$

$$P(Z = 2) = \frac{1}{3},$$

$$P(Z = 3) = (p_Y * p_X)(3) = \sum_{u \in \{1,2\}} p_Y(3 - u) \times p_X(u),$$

$$P(Z = 3) = (p_Y * p_X)(3) = p_Y(3 - 1) \times p_X(1) + p_Y(3 - 2) \times p_X(2) =$$

$$P(Z = 3) = (p_Y * p_X)(2) = \frac{1}{3} \times 0.5 + \frac{1}{3} \times 0.5 = \frac{1}{3},$$

$$P(Z = 3) = \frac{1}{3},$$

and

$$P(Z = 4) = (p_Y * p_X)(4) = \sum_{u \in \{1,2\}} p_Y(4 - u) \times p_X(u),$$

$$P(Z = 4) = (p_Y * p_X)(4) = p_Y(4-1) \times p_X(1) + p_Y(4-2) \times p_X(2) =$$

$$P(Z = 4) = (p_Y * p_X)(2) = 0 \times 0.5 + \frac{1}{3} \times 0.5 = \frac{1}{6},$$

$$P(Z = 4) = \frac{1}{6}.$$

Hence, summarizing

$$p_Z(z) = \begin{cases} 1/6 & \text{if } z \in \{1,4\} \\ 1/3 & \text{if } z \in \{2,2\} \\ 0 & \text{otherwise.} \end{cases}$$

□

Section 5.1.3 presents the application of such an operation, for instance, when describing the binomial distribution.

Similar results are obtained for continuous random variables. Assume the probability density functions of two independent continuous random variables X and Y are given. The cumulative distribution probability function of their sum, $Z = X + Y$ is obtained through

$$F_Z(z) = F_{X+Y}(z) = P(X+Y \leq z) = \int_{-\infty}^{\infty} \int_{-\infty}^{z-x} f_{X+Y}(x, z-x) \, dy \, dx$$

$$F_{X+Y}(z) = P(X+Y \leq z) = \int_{-\infty}^{\infty} \left(\int_{-\infty}^{z-x} f_{X+Y}(x, z-x) \, dy \right) dx.$$

As $dF_Z(z)/dz = f_Z(z) = f_{X+Y}(z)$.

$$f_{X+Y}(z) = \frac{dF_Z}{dz} = \int_{-\infty}^{\infty} \frac{d}{dz} \left(\int_{-\infty}^{z-x} f_{X+Y}(x, z-x) \, dy \right) dx$$

$$f_{X+Y}(z) = \int_{-\infty}^{\infty} f_{X+Y}(x, z-x) \, dx.$$

As X and Y are independent, then $f_{X+Y}(x, z-x) = f_Y(z-x) f_X(x)$. Therefore

$$f_{X+Y}(z) = \int_{-\infty}^{\infty} f_Y(z-u) f_X(x) \, dx \qquad -\infty \leq z \leq \infty. \qquad (4.4.30)$$

The operation above is called continuous convolution and is denoted by $(f_Y * f_X)(z)$; hence

$$(f_Y * f_X)(z) = \int_{-\infty}^{\infty} f_Y(z-u) f_X(u) \, du \qquad -\infty \leq z \leq \infty. \qquad (4.4.31)$$

Example 4.4.7. Assume Y is a continuous random variable defined over the domain $(0, \infty)$ with probability density function specified by

$$f_Y(y) = \begin{cases} 2e^{-2y} & y \in (0, \infty) \\ 0 & \text{otherwise.} \end{cases}$$

Also consider another continuous random variable, X, defined over the domain $[0, 1]$ with probability density function specified by

$$f_X(x) = \begin{cases} 1 & \text{if } x \in [0, 1] \\ 0 & \text{otherwise.} \end{cases}$$

Now let us consider a random variable described by the sum of X and Y, that is $Z = X + Y$. Hence, Z is defined over $(0, \infty)$. The probability density function of Z may be obtained through the convolution $(f_X * f_Y)(z')$. Therefore,

$$f(Z = z') = (f_Y * f_X)(z') = \int_0^{z'} f_Y(z - u) f_X(u) \, du.$$

As $f_Y(z - u)$ is defined over $(0, \infty)$ and $f_X(u)$ is defined over $(0, 1)$ (see Figure 4.21), $f_Y(z - u) f_X(u) = 0$ for $u \notin (0, \min(1, z))$; so

$$f(Z = z') = (f_Y * f_X)(z') = \int_0^{\min(1, z')} 2e^{-2(z-u)} \, 1 \, du.$$

$$f(Z = z') = (f_Y * f_X)(z') = 2e^{-2z} \int_0^{\min(1, z')} e^{2u} \, du.$$

$$f(Z = z') = (f_Y * f_X)(z') = 2e^{-2z} \int_0^{\min(1, z')} e^{2u} \, du.$$

Thus,

$$f(Z = z') = (f_Y * f_X)(z') = 2e^{-2z} \left(\frac{1}{2} e^{2\min(1, z')} - \frac{1}{2} \right),$$

$$f(Z = z') = (f_Y * f_X)(z') = e^{-2z} (e^{2\min(1, z')} - 1);$$

thus

$$f_Z(z) = \begin{cases} e^{-2z} (e^{2\min(1, z)} - 1) & z \in (0, \infty) \\ 0 & \text{otherwise.} \end{cases}$$

□

Section 5.2.10 presents the application of continuous convolution, for instance, when describing the Erlang distribution.

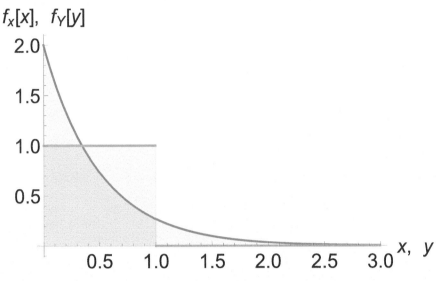

Figure 4.21 Probability Density Functions $f_X(x)$ (a) and $f_Y(y)$ (b).

4.4.4 EXPECTATION AND VARIANCE OF PRODUCTS OF RANDOM VARIABLES

This section discusses the product of random variables. Consider $Z = g(x,y) = XY$ is the product of two independent discrete random variables X and Y. Then the expected value of Z is obtained through $E(Z) = E(g(x,y)) = E(XY)$, that is

$$E(Z) = \sum_{\forall y}\sum_{\forall y} xy\,p_{X,Y}(x,y).$$

$$E(Z) = \sum_{\forall y}\sum_{\forall y} xy\,P(X=x)P(Y=y) = \sum_{\forall y}\sum_{\forall y} xP(X=x)yP(Y=y).$$

Hence,

$$E(Z) = E(XY) = E(X)E(Y). \tag{4.4.32}$$

Likewise, assume $Z = g(x,y) = XY$ is the product of two independent continuous random variables X and Y. Then the expected value of Z is obtained through $E(Z) = E(g(x,y)) = E(XY)$, that is

$$E(Z) = \int_{-\infty}^{\infty}\int_{-\infty}^{\infty} xy\,f_{X,Y}(x,y)\,dx\,dy.$$

If X and Y are independent, then

$$E(XY) = \int_{-\infty}^{\infty} \int_{-\infty}^{\infty} xy\, f_X(x) f_Y(y)\, dx\, dy.$$

$$E(XY) = \int_{-\infty}^{\infty} x\, f_X(x)\, dx \int_{-\infty}^{\infty} y\, f_Y(y)\, dy.$$

Thus,

$$E(Z) = E(XY) = E(X)E(Y). \tag{4.4.33}$$

Now, let us look at Definition 4.4.32 and Definition 4.4.33, but consider the covariance concept. Covariance is defined as the second joint moment about the mean values; that is, covariance is a measure of the joint variability of any two random variables X and Y, and it is defined by

$$Cov(X,Y) = E((X - E(X))(Y - E(Y))). \tag{4.4.34}$$

From the above equation, we have

$$Cov(XY) = E(XY - XE(Y) - YE(X) + E(X)E(Y)).$$

$$Cov(XY) = E(XY) - E(X)E(Y) - E(Y)E(X) + E(X)E(Y).$$

$$Cov(XY) = E(XY) - 2E(X)E(Y) + E(X)E(Y).$$

Hence,

$$Cov(XY) = E(XY) - E(X)E(Y). \tag{4.4.35}$$

From the expression above, we have

$$E(XY) = E(X)E(Y) + Cov(XY). \tag{4.4.36}$$

If X and Y are independent, $Cov(XY) = 0$, then

$$E(XY) = E(X)E(Y).$$

Now, let us obtain an expression for the variance of a product of two random variables, X and Y, that is $Var(XY)$. It is worth reminding that (see Equation 4.1.4 and Equation 4.1.5)

$$Var(X) = E(X - E(X))^2$$

and

$$Var(X) = E(X^2) - (E(X))^2.$$

If $Z = XY$, then

$$Var(Z) = Var(XY) = E(XY - E(XY))^2.$$
$$Var(XY) = E((XY)^2 - 2XY E(XY) + (E(XY))^2).$$
$$Var(XY) = E(XY)^2 - 2E(XY)E(XY) + (E(XY))^2.$$

As

$$Var(X) = E(X^2) - (E(X))^2$$

and

$$Var(Y) = E(Y^2) - (E(Y))^2,$$

then

$$E(X^2) = Var(X) + (E(X))^2$$

and

$$E(Y^2) = Var(Y) + (E(Y))^2.$$

Therefore,

$$Var(XY) = E(XY)^2 - 2E(XY)E(XY) + (E(XY))^2.$$
$$Var(X,Y) = E(XY)^2 - 2(E(XY))^2 + (E(XY))^2.$$
$$Var(X,Y) = E(XY)^2 - (E(XY))^2.$$
$$Var(X,Y) = E(X^2)E(Y^2) - (E(XY))^2.$$
$$Var(X,Y) = (Var(X) + (E(X))^2)(Var(Y) + (E(Y))^2) - (E(XY))^2.$$
$$Var(X,Y) = Var(X)Var(Y) + Var(X)(E(Y))^2 +$$
$$Var(Y)(E(X))^2 + (E(X))^2(E(Y))^2 - (E(XY))^2.$$

As

$$E(XY) = E(X)E(Y) + Cov(XY),$$

then

$$Var(XY) = Var(X)Var(Y) + Var(X)(E(Y))^2 +$$

$$Var(Y)(E(X))^2 + (E(X))^2(E(Y))^2 - (E(X)E(Y) + Cov(XY))^2.$$
$$Var(XY) = Var(X)Var(Y) + Var(X)(E(Y))^2 +$$
$$Var(Y)(E(X))^2 + (E(X))^2(E(Y))^2 - (E(X))^2(E(Y))^2 -$$
$$2E(X)E(Y)Cov(XY) - (Cov(XY))^2.$$
$$Var(XY) = Var(X)Var(Y) + Var(X)(EY))^2 +$$
$$Var(Y)(E(X))^2 - 2E(X)E(Y)Cov(XY) - (Cov(XY))^2.$$

As

$$Cov(XY) = E(XY) - E(X)E(Y),$$

then

$$Var(XY) = Var(X)Var(Y) + Var(X)(E(Y))^2 + Var(Y)(E(X))^2 -$$
$$2E(X)E(Y)Cov(XY) - (Cov(XY))^2.$$

$$Var(XY) = Var(X)Var(Y) + Var(X)(E(Y))^2 + Var(Y)(E(X))^2 -$$
$$2E(X)E(Y)(E(XY) - E(X)E(Y)) - (E(XY) - E(X)E(Y))^2.$$
$$Var(XY) = Var(X)Var(Y) + Var(X)(E(Y))^2 + Var(Y)(E(X))^2$$
$$2E(X)E(Y)(E(XY) - E(X)E(Y)) - (E(XY) - E(X)E(Y))^2.$$
$$Var(XY) = Var(X)Var(Y) + Var(X)(E(Y))^2 + Var(Y)(E(X))^2 -$$
$$2E(X)E(Y)E(XY) + 2(E(X))^2(E(Y))^2 - (E(XY) - E(X)E(Y))^2.$$
$$Var(XY) = Var(X)Var(Y) + Var(X)(E(Y))^2 + Var(Y)(E(X))^2 -$$
$$2E(X)E(Y)E(XY) + 2(E(X))^2(E(Y))^2 - (E(XY))^2 +$$
$$2E(XY)E(X)E(Y) - (E(X))^2(E(Y))^2.$$
$$Var(XY) = Var(X)Var(Y) + Var(X)(E(Y))^2 +$$
$$Var(Y)(E(X))^2 + (E(X))^2(E(Y))^2 - (E(XY))^2.$$

If X and Y are independent,

$$E(XY) = E(X)E(Y),$$

then

$$(E(XY))^2 = (E(X)E(Y))^2 = (E(X))^2(E(Y))^2.$$

Thus,

$$Var(XY) = Var(X)Var(Y) + Var(X)(E(Y))^2 +$$
$$Var(Y)(E(X))^2 + (E(X))^2(E(Y))^2 - (E(X))^2(E(Y))^2.$$

Therefore,

$$Var(XY) = Var(X)Var(Y) + Var(X)(E(Y))^2 + Var(Y)(E(X))^2. \qquad (4.4.37)$$

4.4.5 EXPECTATION AND VARIANCE OF SUMS OF RANDOM VARIABLES

If X and Y are two discrete random variables, then $E(Z) = E(X+Y)$ is obtained through

$$E(Z) = E(X+Y) = \sum_{\forall y}\sum_{\forall x}(x+y)p_{X,Y}(x,y).$$

$$E(Z) = E(X+Y) = \sum_{\forall y}\sum_{\forall x}(xp_{X,Y}(x,y) + yp_{X,Y}(x,y)).$$

$$E(Z) = E(X+Y) = \sum_{\forall x}xp_X(x) + \sum_{\forall y}yp_Y(y).$$

Hence,

$$E(Z) = E(Y) + E(X). \qquad (4.4.38)$$

Likewise, if X and Y are two continuous random variables, then $E(Z) = E(X+Y)$ is obtained through

$$E(Z) = E(X+Y) = \int_{-\infty}^{\infty}\int_{-\infty}^{\infty}(x+y)f_{X,Y}(x,y)\,dx\,dy.$$

$$E(Z) = E(X+Y) = \int_{-\infty}^{\infty}\int_{-\infty}^{\infty}(xf_{X,Y}(x,y) + yf_{X,Y}(x,y))\,dx\,dy.$$

$$E(Z) = E(X+Y) = \int_{-\infty}^{\infty}xf_X(x)\,dx + \int_{-\infty}^{\infty}yf_Y(y)\,dy.$$

Hence,

$$E(Z) = E(Y) + E(X).$$

Consider, for instance, the continuous random variables X and Y, and two constants $b, c \in \mathbb{R}$, where Y is defined as $Y = cX + b$. If $f_X(x)$ is the density function of X, the expected value of Y is defined as

$$E(Y) = \int_{-\infty}^{\infty} Y f_X(x) \, dx.$$

$$E(Y) = \int_{-\infty}^{\infty} (cX + b) f_X(x) \, dx.$$

$$E(Y) = c \int_{-\infty}^{\infty} X f_X(x) \, dx + \int_{-\infty}^{\infty} b f_X(x) \, dx.$$

$$E(Y) = c E(X) + b.$$

Similarly, if X and Y are discrete random variables and $p_X(x)$ is the probability mass function of X, the expected value of Y is defined as

$$E(Y) = \sum_{\forall x} Y p_X(x).$$

$$E(Y) = \sum_{\forall x} (cX + b) p_X(x).$$

$$E(Y) = c \sum_{\forall x} X p_X(x) + \sum_{\forall x} b p_X(x).$$

$$E(Y) = c E(X) + b. \tag{4.4.39}$$

Generalizing Equation 4.4.38 for k random variables, $(X_1, X_2, ..., X_k)$, k constants, $c_1, c_2, ..., c_k \in \mathbb{R}$, and k constants, $b_1, b2, ..., b_k \in \mathbb{R}$, if $Y = \sum_{i=1}^{k}(c_i X_i + b_i)$, the expected values of Y are

$$E(Y) = c_1 E(X_1) + c_2 E(X_2) + ... + c_k E(X_k) + b_1 + b2 + ... + b_k.$$

Thus,

$$E(Y) = \sum_{i=1}^{k} c_i E(X_i) + b_i. \tag{4.4.40}$$

Consider $Z = X + Y$ a random variable specified by the sum of two random variables, X and Y. The variance of Z may be calculated using

$$Var(Z) = Var(X + Y) = E((X + Y) - E(X + Y))^2$$

since

$$Var(X) = E(X - E(X))^2.$$

Hence,

$$Var(X + Y) = E(X + Y - E(X) - E(Y))^2.$$
$$Var(X + Y) = E((X - E(X)) + (Y - E(Y)))^2.$$
$$Var(X + Y) = E((X - E(X))^2 + 2(X - E(X))(Y - E(Y)) + (Y - E(Y))^2).$$
$$Var(X + Y) = E((X - E(X))^2) + E(2(X - E(X))(Y - E(Y))) + E((Y - E(Y))^2).$$
$$Var(X + Y) = E(X - E(X))^2 + 2E((X - E(X))(Y - E(Y))) + E(Y - E(Y))^2.$$

As

$$Cov(X, Y) = E((X - E(X))(Y - E(Y))).$$

Therefore,

$$Var(X + Y) = Var(X) + Var(Y) + 2Cov(X, Y). \quad (4.4.41)$$

If X and Y are independent, then $Cov(X, Y) = 0$; hence

$$Var(X + Y) = Var(X) + Var(Y). \quad (4.4.42)$$

It is worth noting that two independent random variables X and Y have $Cov(X, Y) = 0$. However, $Cov(X, Y) = 0$ does not imply X and Y are independent.

Generalizing for k independent random variables, $(X_1, X_2, ..., X_k)$, k constants, $c_1, c_2, ..., c_k \in \mathbb{R}$, and k constants, $b_1, b2, ..., b_k \in \mathbb{R}$, if $\sum_{i=1}^{k}(c_i X_i + b_i)$, the variance Y is

$$Var(\sum_{i=1}^{k}(c_i X_i + b_i)) = \sum_{i=1}^{k} c_i^2 Var(X_i). \quad (4.4.43)$$

4.5 SUMMARY OF PROPERTIES OF EXPECTATION AND VARI-ANCE

This section summarizes some of the most important properties of the expectation and variance of random variables. First, let us examine the properties related to the expected values of random variables.

1. If c and b are constants, then $E(cX + b) = cE(X) + b$.

2. $|E(X)| \leq E(|X|)$.

3. If $X \geq 0$, then $E(X) \geq 0$.

4. If $X \leq Y$, then $E(X) \leq E(Y)$.

5. If X and Y are two random variables, then $E(X + Y) = E(X) + E(Y)$.

6. If c_i and b_i are constants and X_i are random variables, then $E\left(\sum_{i=1}^{n}(c_i X_i + b_i)\right) = \sum_{i=1}^{n}(c_i E(X_i) + b_i)$.

7. If X and Y are two random variables, then $E(XY) = E(X)E(Y) + Cov(XY)$.

8. If X and Y are two independent random variables, then $E(XY) = E(X)E(Y)$.

Now, let us summarize some important properties related to variance.

1. If c is a constant, then $Var(c) = 0$.

2. $Var(X) = E(X - E(X))^2$

3. $Var(X) = E(X^2) - (E(X))^2$.

4. $Var(cX + b) = c^2 Var(X)$.

5. $Var(X + Y) = Var(X) + Var(Y) + 2Cov(X,Y)$.

6. If X and Y are independent random variables, then $Var(X + Y) = Var(X) + Var(Y)$.

7. If c_i and b_i are a constants and X_i are random variables, $Var(\sum_{i=1}^{k}(c_i X_i + b_i)) = \sum_{i=1}^{k} c_i^2 Var(X_i)$.

8. If X and Y are independent random variables, then $Var(X - Y) = Var(X + Y)$.

9. If X and Y are independent random variables, then $Var(XY) = Var(X)Var(Y) + Var(X)(E(Y))^2 + Var(Y)(E(X))^2$.

4.6 COVARIANCE, CORRELATION, AND INDEPENDENCE

As already defined, covariance is the second joint moment about the mean values. In other words, covariance is a linear measure of the joint variability of any two random variables, X and Y, and it is defined by

$$Cov(X,Y) = E((X - E(X))(Y - E(Y))). \qquad (4.6.1)$$

If X and Y are independent, then $Cov(X,Y) = 0$, but if $Cov(X,Y) = 0$, they can still be dependent since nonlinear relationship between random variables may not be detected through the covariance.

The correlation coefficient is a dimensionless measure that quantifies the linear relationship between two random variables. The correlation coefficient is often easier to interpret and is defined as

$$\rho_{XY} = \frac{Cov(X,Y)}{\sqrt{Var(X)Var(Y)}}. \qquad (4.6.2)$$

The correlation coefficient between X and Y is a values in the interval $(-1, 1)$. The correlation coefficient close to 1 indicates a strong linear positive relationship between X and Y, whereas values close to -1 indicate a strong linear negative relationship between X and Y. If the random variables are uncorrelated, the correlation coefficient is close to zero. It is worth mentioning that the correlation coefficient is close to zero and does not imply that X and Y are uncorrelated. If $\rho_{XY} = 0$ we say that X and Y are "uncorrelated". If X and Y are independent, their correlation will be 0, as with covariance. However, it does not go the other way. A correlation of 0 does not imply the independence of X and Y. The square of the correlation coefficient, ρ_{XY}^2, is called the coefficient of determination. Hence

$$\rho_{XY}^2 = \left(\frac{Cov(X,Y)}{\sqrt{Var(X)Var(Y)}} \right)^2, \qquad (4.6.3)$$

which ranges from 0 to 1. Values of ρ_{XY}^2 close to one indicate a strong linear relationship between X and Y. On the other hand, uncorrelated X and Y have ρ_{XY}^2 close to zero.

Figure 4.22.a shows a linear positive relation between X and Y. The $Cov(X,Y) = 28.4$, the correlation coefficient is $\rho_{XY} = 0.9798$, and correlation coefficient, $\rho_{XY}^2 = 0.9600$. Table 4.22 presents the set of data depicting the pairs assigned to X and Y. Figure 4.22.c depicts a perfect linear relation between X and Y ($\rho_{XY} = 1$, $Cov(X,Y) = 3.277$), whereas Figure 4.22.d presents a perfect negative linear relationship between X and Y ($\rho_{XY} = -1$, $Cov(X,Y) = -3.277$). The variables X and Y depicted in Figure 4.22.b are clearly correlated, but the covariance and correlation coefficient are zero, since the relationship X and Y is nonlinear.

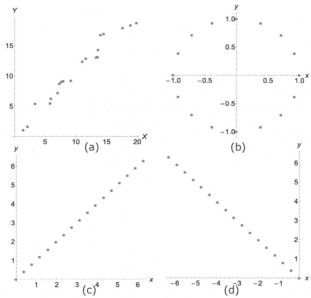

(a) $\rho_{XY} = 0.9798$ and $Cov(X,Y) = 28.4$.

(b) $\rho_{XY} = 0$, and $Cov(X,Y) = 0$.

(c) $\rho_{XY} = 1$ and $Cov(X,Y) = 3.277$.

d) $\rho_{XY} = -1$ and $Cov(X,Y) = -3.277$.

Figure 4.22 Covariance and Correlation Coefficient.

Table 4.15
Data Set Organized as Pairs (x, y)**.**

(x,	y)	(x,	y)
(1.51,	1.07)	(11.09,	12.36)
(2.22,	1.64)	(11.63,	12.86)
(3.44,	5.38)	(13.32,	13.02)
(5.83,	5.45)	(13.56,	13.10)
(5.99,	6.27)	(13.66,	14.30)
(7.05,	7.18)	(14.00,	16.72)
(7.32,	8.72)	(14.55,	16.94)
(7.63,	9.03)	(17.62,	17.94)
(7.96,	9.13)	(18.91,	18.37)
(9.20,	9.19)	(19.86,	18.74)

Example 4.6.1. An random experiment is mapped into two random variables, X and Y, whose values are depicted in Table 4.16. Figure 4.23 also shows the results of the random experiment. The covariance and the correlation coefficient of X and Y are

$$Cov(X, Y) = -1.136 \quad \text{and} \quad \rho_{XY} = -0.04.$$

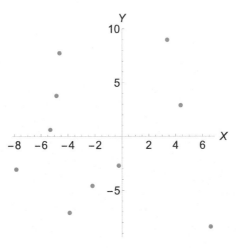

Figure 4.23 Covariance and Correlation Coefficient - $Cov(X, Y) = -1.136$ and $\rho_{XY} = -0.04$.

As the correlation coefficient is close to zero and as the graph, depicted in Figure 4.23, shows no correlation pattern, we may state that the X and Y are uncorrelated.

Table 4.16
Data Set Organized as Pairs (x, y)

(x,	y)
(− 7.86,	− 3.03)
(− 3.91,	− 7.1)
(− 4.85,	3.81)
(− 4.61,	7.75)
(− 2.19,	− 4.57)
(4.36,	2.94)
(− 5.33,	0.64)
(6.62,	− 8.37)
(3.34,	9.02)
(− 0.23,	− 2.69)

□

Below, a summary of some of the important properties related to the covariance of random variables is presented.

1. $Cov(X,X) = Var(X)$.

2. $Cov(X,Y) = Cov(Y,X)$.

3. $Cov(cX,Y) = c\,Cov(X,Y)$.

4. $Cov(X,Y + Z) = Cov(X,Y) + Cov(X,Z)$.

5. $Cov\left(\sum_{i=1}^{n} X_i, \sum_{j=1}^{m} Y_j\right) = \sum_{i=1}^{n} \sum_{j=1}^{m} Cov(X_i, Y_j)$.

6. $Var\left(\sum_{i=1}^{n} X_i\right) = \sum_{i=1}^{n} \sum_{j=1}^{m} Cov(X_i, Y_j)$.

A word of caution is still required about correlated variables. It is indispensable to realize the distinction between correlation and causation. A cause indicates that an observed change in the system or model output is directly related to a change in the input in the respective system or model's input. For instance, transferring a large data set takes longer than transmitting a small one because more packages are required to be sent. Hence, there is an expected high correlation between the transferring time and the data set size. However, the reverse is not always valid. In other words, the output can be highly correlated with the input without the input being the cause of the output. For example, it is possible to have a high correlation between the time required to transmit a file over the Internet at a time of day. Therefore, knowing the time of day allows us to forecast the time needed to send a file of a specific size. However, the time of day does not change the transmission time. What happens is that the number of people using the system changes throughout the day, according to the hours. These users' activities change the load on the network, which then causes the changes observed in the transmission periods of the files. Thus, although there is a strong correlation between the time required to send a file at a particular time of the day, the analyst must be cautious not to conclude that one causes the other. Therefore, the correlation does not imply causality [238].

EXERCISES

Exercise 1. The random variable X represents the number of servers that failed in a reliability test considering ten servers. The random variable was defined as $X : \Omega \rightarrow \mathbb{N}_{0-10}$, where $\mathbb{N}_{0-10}$ is the set of integer numbers between 0 and 10 and including them. If the probability of one server presenting a failure is 0.08, and the occurrence of such a failure does not affect the probability of other server presenting a failure, (a) what is the probability of having $X = 0$, $X = 1$, $X = 2$, $X = 3$, and $X = 4$? (b) What is the mean number of failed servers? (c) What is the respective standard deviation? (d) Plot the probability mass function of X.

Exercise 2. A random variable X is specified by the probability mass function depicted in Table 4.17.

Table 4.17

X **and PMF** $p_X(x)$ - $(x_i, p_X(x_i))$

x_i	0	1	2	3	4	5	6	7
$p_X(x_i)$	0.01	0.03	0.04	0.06	0.07	0.08	0.07	0.06
x_i	8	9	10	11	12	13	14	15
$p_X(x_i)$	0.04	0.12	0.04	0.03	0.17	0.11	0.06	0.01

(a) What is the expected value of X? (b) What is the variance of X and the respective standard deviation? (c) Calculate $CoV(X)$. (d) Plot the probability mass function of X. (e) Plot the cumulative probability function of X, and (e) plot the complementary cumulative distribution function of X.

Exercise 3. Calculate the following probabilities considering the random variable specified in Table 4.17: (a) $P(X \leq 8)$, (b) $P(X \geq 8)$, (c) $P(7 \leq X \leq 13)$, and (d) $P((X \leq 7) AND (X \geq 13))$.

Exercise 4. Consider the random variable X described in Table 4.17. Obtain the following statistics: Min, Q_1, Mdn, Q_3, Max, and IQR for random variable X.

Exercise 5. The random variable X that specifies the time to execute a function. The counter domain of X is $(0, \infty)$. Table 4.18 depicts the cumulative distribution function, $F_X(x)$, of X. The time unity adopted to represent values of X is milliseconds (ms).

Table 4.18

Cumulative Function Distribution $F_X(x)$

$x(ms)$	$F_X(x)$	$x(ms)$	$F_X(x)$	$x(ms)$	$F_X(x)$	$x(ms)$	$F_X(x)$
0	0	1400	0.52953	2800	0.87899	4200	0.96387
200	0.01444	1600	0.61655	3000	0.89902	4400	0.96929
400	0.03447	1800	0.6863	3200	0.9155	4600	0.97383
600	0.06672	2000	0.74245	3400	0.92908	4800	0.97765
800	0.13749	2200	0.78781	3600	0.94032	5000	0.98086
1000	0.28381	2400	0.82459	3800	0.94964	5200	0.98358
1200	0.42054	2600	0.85453	4000	0.9574	5400	0.98589

Using Table 4.9, (a) plot the cumulative distribution function, (b) plot the complementary cumulative distribution function, (c) calculate $P(X < 800 ms)$, (d) obtain $P(800\,ms < X < 2000\,ms)$, (e) $P(X > 2000\,ms)$, (f) calculate $P((X < 400\,ms)\,and\,(X > 5000\,ms))$, (g) estimate the median, the first and third quartile, and the interquartile range.

Exercise 6. Assume X is a continuous random variable defined over the interval $(0, 1000)$, whose cumulative distribution function is defined as

$$F_X(x) = 1.2 \times 10^{-3}x - 2. \times 10^{-10}x^3, \qquad x \in (0, 1000).$$

Obtain (a) the complementary cumulative distribution function $(F_X^c(x))$, (b) the respective density function $(f_X(x))$, (c) the hazard function $(\lambda_X(x))$, (d) the cumulative hazard function $(H_X(x))$(e) plot $F_X(x)$, $F_X^c(x)$, $f_X(x)$, $\lambda_X(x)$, and $H_X(x)$, (f) calculate the $E(X)$, (g) $Var(X)$, $SD(X)$, and $CoV(X)$, (h) Mdn, Q_1, Q_3, and IQR, and (i) $skewness(X)$ and $Kurt(X)$.

Exercise 7. Considering the random variable specified in Exercise 6, calculate (a) $P(X \leq 100)$, (b) $P(X \geq 800)$, (c) $P(200 \leq X \leq 800)$, and (d) $P((X \leq 50)\,AND\,(X \geq 950))$.

Exercise 8. Assume X is a continuous random variable defined over the interval $(0, \infty)$, whose cumulative hazard function is defined as

$$H_X(x) = -2.5 \times 10^{-7}x^2, \qquad x \in (0, \infty).$$

Obtain (a) the hazard function $(\lambda_X(x))$, (b) the complementary cumulative distribution function $(F_X^c(x))$, (c) the cumulative distribution function $(F_X(x))$, (d) the density function $(f_X(x))$, (e) plot $F_X(x)$, $F_X^c(x)$, $f_X(x)$, $\lambda_X(x)$, and $H_X(x)$, (f) calculate the $E(X)$, (g) $Var(X)$, $SD(X)$, and $CoV(X)$, (h) Mdn, Q_1, Q_3, and IQR, and (i) $skewness(X)$ and $Kurt(X)$.

Exercise 9. Considering random variable specified in Exercise 6, calculate (a) $P(X \leq 500)$, (b) $P(X \geq 2500)$, (c) $P(1200 \leq X \leq 2200)$, and (d) $P((X \leq 500)\,and\,(X \geq 2500))$.

Exercise 10. Considering the random variable specified in Table 4.17, (a) calculate the first and second moments about the origin, and (b) the variance and the standard deviation, (c) the second central moment, and (f) the third and the fourth normalized central moments.

Exercise 11. Assume a continuous random variable X whose cumulative distribution function is defined in Exercise 6. Calculate (a) the expected value, (b) the variance, the standard deviation, (c) the coefficient of variation, (d) the second central moment, and (e) the third and the fourth normalized central moments.

Exercise 12. For the random variable specified in Table 4.17 , obtain the moment generating function.

Exercise 13. Assuming the random variable whose cumulative distribution function is defined in Exercise 6, obtain its moment generating function.

Exercise 14. Table 4.19 shows the joint probability mass function, $p_{X,Y}(x,y)$, of a two-dimension discrete random vector composed of two variables $X \rightarrow \{0, 1, 2, 3, 4\}$ and $Y \rightarrow \{0, 1, 2, 3\}$.

Table 4.19
Joint Probability Mass Function, $p_{X,Y}(x,y)$.

X,Y	0	1	2	3
0	0.04	0.01	0.05	0.04
1	0.07	0.03	0.07	0.10
2	0.05	0.03	0.06	0.07
3	0.05	0.06	0.03	0.06
4	0.08	0.04	0.05	0.03

(a) Calculate $P((X \geq 3) \wedge (Y \leq 1))$. (b) Calculate the $P(Y = 3 | X = 2)$. (c) Obtain the marginal probability functions, $P_X(x)$ and $P_Y(y)$ and plot them. (d) Obtain $Cov(X,Y)$ and ρ_{XY}. (e) Are X and Y independent? (f) If X and Y are correlated, is it a linear correlation? (g) Calculate $P(X \geq 2)$. (h) Calculate $P(Y \leq 2)$. (i) Calculate $E(X+Y)$. (j) Obtain $Var(X+Y)$.

Exercise 15. Considering the joint density function of the random variables X and Y given by

$$f_{X,Y}(x,y) = 6.7799 \times 10^{-13} e^{-y \times 10^{-3}} (2 \times 10^6 + x^2),$$

$$x \in (0, 1000), \quad y \in (0, 1000).$$

(a) Calculate $P((X \leq 500) \wedge (Y \leq 400))$. (b) Obtain the marginal probabilities density functions, $f_X(x)$ and $f_Y(y)$ and plot them. (c) Obtain $Cov(X,Y)$, ρ_{XY} and ρ_{XY}^2. (d) Are X and Y independent? (e) If X and Y are correlated, is it a linear correlation? (f) Calculate $P(200 \leq X \leq 600)$. (g) $P(700 \leq X \leq 1000)$. (h) Are X and Y independent? (i) Calculate $E(XY)$. (j) Obtain $Var(XY)$.

Exercise 16. Assume the joint density function of the random variables X and Y specified by

$$f_{XY}(x,y) = \frac{6}{7}\left(x^2 + \frac{xy}{2}\right), \quad x \in (0,1) \quad y \in (0,2).$$

(a) Calculate the marginal probability density functions, $f_X(x)$ and $f_Y(y)$. (b) Are X and Y independent? (c) Obtain $Cov(X,Y)$, ρ_{XY} and ρ_{XY}^2. (d) If X and Y are correlated, is it a linear correlation? (e) Calculate $P(0 \leq X \leq 0.4)$. (f) $P(0.6 \leq y \leq 1.8)$. (g) Calculate $E(XY)$. (h) Obtain $Var(XY)$.

5 Some Important Random Variables

This chapter introduces some important discrete and continuous random variable distributions, presents the relations between some of these random variables, depicts the concepts of functions of random variables, and discusses the Taylor series, a powerful tool for approximating analytic functions.

5.1 SOME DISCRETE RANDOM VARIABLES

Certain types of random variables occur over and over again in applications. Some random variables are so ubiquitous in probability and statistics that they have names. This section introduces some of the most common discrete random variables adopted in the chapters of this book. Details related to some of these random variables may be left to be studied in more depth in the subsequent chapters, where they are applied. Other distributions may also be found in handbooks and textbooks such as [145, 221, 267, 365, 455].

5.1.1 BERNOULLI

Let us assume a random experiment that leads to possible results, such as success or failure, pass in a test our not pass, finished or not finished, available or unavailable, etc. Then, a *Bernoulli* random variable X is a discrete random variable that can assign zero (0) to one result and one (1) to the other result of the random experiment.

X is said to have the Bernoulli distribution with parameter p, $Bern(p)$, where $0 \leq p \leq 1$. Thus,

$$X = \begin{cases} 1 & \text{with} \quad P(X=1) = p \\ 0 & \text{with} \quad P(X=0) = 1-p. \end{cases} \tag{5.1.1}$$

$P(X = i)$, $i = i \in \{0, 1\}$ is the probability mass function. $X \sim Bern(p)$ denotes that X is distributed according to $Bern(p)$. The cumulative distribution function of a Bernoulli random variable is specified as

$$F_X(x) = \begin{cases} 0 & x < 0 \\ 1-p & 0 \leq x < 1 \\ 1-p & x \geq 1. \end{cases} \tag{5.1.2}$$

Figure 5.1.a depicts the probability mass function of a random variable distributed according to a Bernoulli distribution with parameter $p = 0.7$. Figure 5.1.b shows the respective cumulative distribution function.

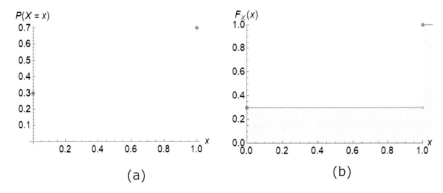

Figure 5.1   PDF (a) and CDF (b) of X - $X \sim Bern(p)$.

The expected value of X is given by

$$\mu' = 0 \times (1 - p) + 1 \times p = p. \tag{5.1.3}$$

The variance, the standard deviation, and the coefficient of variation are specified by

$$\mu_2 = p(1 - p), \tag{5.1.4}$$

$$(\mu_2)^{1/2} = \sqrt{p(1 - p)}, \tag{5.1.5}$$

and

$$CoV = \frac{\sqrt{(1 - p)p}}{p}, \tag{5.1.6}$$

respectively.

The skewness and the kurtosis (the fourth standardized central moment) are defined as

$$\tilde{\mu}_3 = \frac{1 - 2p}{\sqrt{(1 - p)p}} \tag{5.1.7}$$

and

$$\tilde{\mu}_4 = \frac{1 - 6(1 - p)p}{(1 - p)p}. \tag{5.1.8}$$

If the kurtosis is provided in comparison to a normal distribution (see Section 5.2), then we have

$$Kurt(X) = \frac{1 - 6(1 - p)p}{(1 - p)p} + 3. \tag{5.1.9}$$

The Bernoulli moment generating function is

$$M_X(s) = pe^s - p + 1,$$ (5.1.10)

and the central moment generating function is specified by

$$CM_X(s) = e^{-ps}(pe^s - p + 1).$$ (5.1.11)

More details and the application of the Bernoulli distribution are presented in Section 9.6, Section 25.3, and Section 16.2, for instance. Random variate generation based on the Bernoulli distribution is presented in Section 14.3. From the Bernoulli distribution, we may deduce several other probability distribution functions such as geometric, binomial, and negative binomial distributions.

5.1.2   GEOMETRIC

Assume a sequence of independent Bernoulli experiments (trials) with success probability equal to p. Let X represent the number of trials until the first success occurs. X has a geometric distribution with parameter p, $Geo(p)$, where $0 \leq p \leq 1$, which is usually denoted by $X \sim Geo(p)$. The probability mass function of X is specified by

$$P(X = k) = p(1 - p)^{k-1}, \quad k \in \mathbb{N}.$$ (5.1.12)

The respective cumulative distribution function is specified by

$$F_X(x) = \sum_{i=1}^{x}(1 - p)^{i-1}p, \quad i \in \mathbb{N},$$ (5.1.13)

which leads to

$$F_X(x) = 1 - (1 - p)^x, \quad x \in \mathbb{N}.$$ (5.1.14)

An alternate definition for X represents the number of failures before the first success. In such a case, the probability mass function of X is specified by

$$P(X = k) = p(1 - p)^k, \quad k \in \mathbb{N}.$$ (5.1.15)

Here, the second definition is adopted (Equation 5.1.15). The cumulative distribution function of a geometric random variable is specified as

$$F_X(x) = \sum_{i=0}^{x}(1 - p)^i p, \quad i \in \mathbb{N},$$ (5.1.16)

which leads to

$$F_X(x) = 1 - (1 - p)^{x+1}, \quad x \in \mathbb{N}.$$ (5.1.17)

Figure 5.2.a depicts the probability mass function of a random variable X distributed according to a geometric distribution with parameter $p = 0.25$. Figure 5.2.b shows the respective cumulative distribution function.

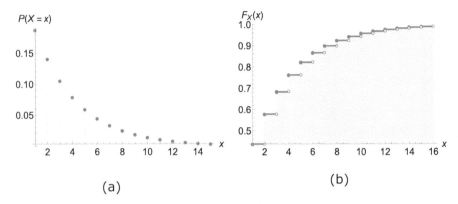

(a)   (b)

Figure 5.2   PDF (a) and CDF (b) of X - $X \sim Geo(p)$.

The expected value of X is given by

$$\mu' = \frac{1-p}{p}. \tag{5.1.18}$$

The variance, the standard deviation, and the coefficient of variation are specified by

$$\mu_2 = \frac{1-p}{p^2}, \tag{5.1.19}$$

$$(\mu_2)^{1/2} = \frac{\sqrt{1-p}}{p}, \tag{5.1.20}$$

and

$$CoV = \frac{1}{\sqrt{1-p}}, \tag{5.1.21}$$

respectively. The skewness and the kurtosis (the fourth standardized central moment) are defined as

$$\tilde{\mu}_3 = \frac{2-p}{\sqrt{1-p}} \tag{5.1.22}$$

and

$$\tilde{\mu}_4 = \frac{p^2 - 6p + 6}{1-p}. \tag{5.1.23}$$

If the kurtosis is provided in comparison to a normal distribution, then we have

$$Kurt(X) = \frac{p^2 - 6p + 6}{1 - p} + 3.$$ (5.1.24)

The geometric moment generating function is

$$M_X(s) = \frac{p}{1 - (1 - p)e^s},$$ (5.1.25)

and the central moment generating function is specified by

$$CM_X(s) = \frac{pe^{\left(1 - \frac{1}{p}\right)s}}{1 - (1 - p)e^s}.$$ (5.1.26)

Memoryless Property - Let X be a discrete random variable geometrically distributed that represents the time to failure (in days) of a software system. Its PDF is defined by Equation 5.1.15. The probability that the software system fails after s days ($s > t$, $s, t \in \mathbb{N}$), given the system survived t days is

$$P(X \geq t + s \,|\, X \geq t) = \frac{P((X \geq s) \cap (X \geq t))}{P(X \geq t)}$$

$$P(X \geq t + s \,|\, X \geq t) = \frac{P((X \geq s)}{P(X \geq t}$$

$$P(X \geq t + s \,|\, X \geq t) = \frac{(1 - p)^{s+t}}{(1 - p)^t}$$

$$P(X \geq t + s \,|\, X \geq t) = \frac{(1 - p)^t \times (1 - p)^s}{(1 - p)^t} = (1 - p)^s.$$

$$P(X \geq t + s \,|\, X \geq t) = (1 - p)^s = P(X \geq s).$$

Therefore, the fact of surviving t days (not failing in t days) does not affect the probability of surviving more s days since the unconditional probability of surviving s days is also $P(X > s) = (1 - p)^s$. It is worth mentioning that the geometric distribution is the only memoryless discrete distribution.

The geometric random variable median is defined as

$$Mdn = \frac{\log(0.5)}{\log(1 - p)} - 1.$$ (5.1.27)

The first and the third quartiles are defined as

$$Q_1 = \frac{\log(0.75)}{\log(1 - p)} - 1.$$ (5.1.28)

and

$$Q_3 = \frac{\log(0.25)}{\log(1 - p)} - 1.$$ (5.1.29)

Example 5.1.1. Finding a bug in a software system consists of executing the system with randomly selected data sets until the bug manifests itself. Using one data set does not affect the result provided from the next data set; that is, each Bernoulli experiment is independent. The probability that any specific data set isolates the bug is estimated as $p = 0.2$. Let X be the number of data sets considered in the test before the bug is revealed. This random variable is geometrically distributed with parameter p. The mean number of data sets used before the bug appears is estimated as

$$E(X) = \mu' = \frac{1-p}{p} = \frac{1-0.2}{0.2} = 4,$$

and its standard deviation is

$$SD(X) = (\mu_2)^{1/2} = \frac{\sqrt{1-p}}{p} = \frac{\sqrt{1-0.2}}{0.2} = 4.47214.$$

The probability of executing $k = 6$ data sets before the bug appears is $P(X \leq 6) = F_X(6) = 1 - (1 - 0.2)^7 = 0.790285$ since $P(X \leq k) = F_X(k) = 1 - (1 - p)^{k+1}$.
□

More details and an application of geometric distribution is presented in Chapter 9, for instance. Random variate generation based on geometric distribution is presented in Section 14.3.

5.1.3 BINOMIAL

We know that if X and Y are discrete random variables independently distributed, and $Z = Y + X$, the probability mass function of Z is the joint probability mass function of X and Y, which may be obtained by discrete convolution of the probability mass functions of X and Y.

$$P(X + Y = z) = \sum_{\forall u} P(Y = z' - u) \times P(X = u). \tag{5.1.30}$$

Now, consider that X and Y are distributed according to a Bernoulli distribution, $X \sim Bern(p)$ and $Y \sim Bern(p)$. The probability mass function of Z is the joint probability mass function of Y and X. Hence,

$$P(Z = z) = P(Y + X = z) = \sum_{u} P(Y = z - u, X = u).$$

As X and Y are independents, then

$$P(Z = z) = P(Y + X = z) = \sum_{u \in \{0,1,2\}} P(Y = z - u) P(X = u).$$

As we have two independent Bernoulli random variables (X and Y), then $Z = 0$, $Z = 1$ or $Z = 2$. Therefore, we have

$$P(Z = 0) = P(Y + X = 0) = P(Y = 0)P(X = 0) = (1 - p)(1 - p) = (1 - p)^2.$$

$$P(Z = 1) = P(Y + X = 1) = P(Y = 0)P(X = 1) + P(Y = 1)P(X = 0).$$

$$P(Z = 1) = (1 - p)p + p(1 - p) = 2p(1 - p).$$

Similarly,

$$P(Z = 2) = P(Y + X = 2) = P(Y = 1)P(X = 1) = p \times p = p^2.$$

Therefore,

$$\sum_{z=0}^{2} P(Z = z) = (1 - p)^2 + 2p(1 - p) + p^2,$$

which is equal to

$$\sum_{z=0}^{2} P(Z = z) = \sum_{z=0}^{2} \binom{2}{z} p^z (1 - p)^{2-z} = 1,$$

and

$$P(Z = k) = \sum_{z=0}^{k} \binom{2}{z} p^z (1 - p)^{2-z}, \qquad z, k \in \{0, 1, 2\}, \qquad (5.1.31)$$

which is a binomial distribution with parameter $n = 2$ and p, $Bin(2, p)$.

Now consider X to be a discrete random variable that specifies the number of failures in the n trials. X has binomial distribution with parameters n and p, which is denoted by $X \sim Bin(n, p)$.

$$P(X = k) = \binom{n}{k} p^k (1 - p)^{n-k}, \quad k \in \mathbb{N}, \qquad (5.1.32)$$

which a generalization of Equation 5.1.31. The cumulative distribution function of a binomial random variable is specified as

$$F_X(x) = \sum_{k=0}^{x} \binom{n}{k} p^k (1-p)^{n-k}, \quad k \in \mathbb{N}. \tag{5.1.33}$$

Figure 5.3.a depicts the probability mass function of a random variable X distributed according to a binomial distribution with parameters $n = 40$ and $p = 0.2$. Figure 5.3.b shows the respective cumulative distribution function.

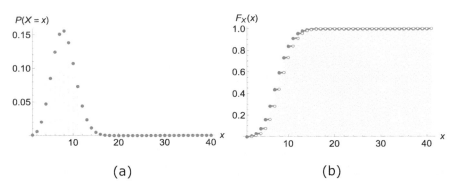

(a)   (b)

Figure 5.3   PDF (a) and CDF (b) of X - $X \sim Bin(n, p)$.

The expected value of X is given by

$$\mu' = np. \tag{5.1.34}$$

The variance, the standard deviation, and the coefficient of variation are specified by

$$\mu_2 = n(1-p)p, \tag{5.1.35}$$

$$(\mu_2)^{1/2} = \sqrt{n(1-p)p}, \tag{5.1.36}$$

and

$$CoV = \frac{\sqrt{n(1-p)p}}{np}, \tag{5.1.37}$$

respectively. The skewness and the kurtosis (the fourth standardized central moment) are defined as

$$\tilde{\mu}_3 = \frac{1-2p}{\sqrt{n(1-p)p}} \tag{5.1.38}$$

and

$$\tilde{\mu}_4 = \frac{1-6(1-p)p}{n(1-p)p}. \tag{5.1.39}$$

If the kurtosis is provided in comparison to a normal distribution, then we have

$$Kurt(X) = \frac{1 - 6(1 - p)p}{n(1 - p)p} + 3. \tag{5.1.40}$$

The binomial moment generating function is

$$M_X(s) = (p(e^s - 1) + 1)^n, \tag{5.1.41}$$

and the central moment generating function is specified by

$$CM_X(s) = e^{-nps}(p(e^s - 1) + 1)^n. \tag{5.1.42}$$

Example 5.1.2. Consider $n = 40$ similar computers are under an accelerated reliability test. The reliability test for each computer results in two possible outcomes: fail or pass. The execution of the reliability test in one computer does not affect the reliability result in another computer (independence). Assume the probability of failure for each computer is $p = 0.15$ (each Bernoulli trial). Let X be a random variable representing the number of failed computers when the reliability test ends. Hence, X is distributed according to a binomial distribution with parameters n and p.

The probability of having at most $i = 7$ computers in failure can be calculated using Equation 5.1.33. Hence,

$$P(X \leq i) = F_X(i) = \sum_{k=0}^{i} \binom{n}{k} p^k (1 - p)^{n-k}.$$

$$P(X \leq 7) = F_X(7) = \sum_{k=0}^{7} \binom{40}{k} 0.15^k (1 - 0.15)^{40-k} = 0.7559,$$

and the mean number of failed computers is estimated as $E(X) = \mu' = np = 40 \times 0.15 = 6$.

$\square$

5.1.4 NEGATIVE BINOMIAL

Consider the execution of the independent Bernoulli trial. Let X be a random variable that represents the number of failures until the rth success in the sequence of Bernoulli trials. This random variable is defined as having a negative binomial distribution with parameters p (failure probability) and r, ($X \sim NB(r, p)$), which is also called the Pascal distribution.

The negative binomial distribution can also be thought of a sequence of Bernoulli experiments implemented using a box filled with colored balls, in which X denotes the number of draws from the box until one gets r balls of a specific color, given p is the probability of having a ball of a different color. It is also assumed that Bernoulli's experiments are independent. The PDF of X is defined as

$$P(X = k) = \binom{k-1}{r-1} p^r (1-p)^{k-r}, \tag{5.1.43}$$

and cumulative distribution function of a geometric random variable is specified as

$$F(X) = \sum_{x=1}^{\infty} \binom{x-1}{r-1} p^r (1-p)^{x-r}. \tag{5.1.44}$$

Therefore, the probability of having at most k failures until the rth success is

$$P(X \leq k) = F(k) = \sum_{x=1}^{k} \binom{x-1}{r-1} p^r (1-p)^{x-r}. \tag{5.1.45}$$

Since for having r success, at most r trials are required, then

$$P(X \leq k) = \sum_{x=r}^{k} \binom{x-1}{r-1} p^r (1-p)^{x-r}. \tag{5.1.46}$$

Figure 5.4.a depicts the probability mass function of a random variable X distributed according to a negative binomial distribution with parameters $p = 0.4$ and $r = 10$. Figure 5.4.b shows the respective cumulative distribution function.

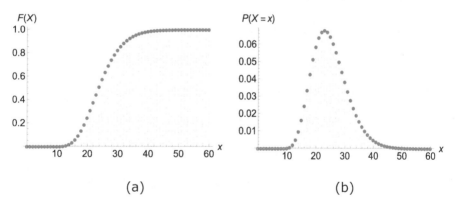

(a)   (b)

Figure 5.4   cdf (a) and pdf (b) of X - $X \sim NB(r, p)$.

The expected value of X is given by

$$\mu' = \frac{r}{p}. \tag{5.1.47}$$

The variance, the standard deviation, and the coefficient of variation are specified by

$$\mu_2 = \frac{(1-p)r}{p^2}, \tag{5.1.48}$$

$$(\mu_2)^{1/2} = \frac{\sqrt{(1-p)r}}{p}, \tag{5.1.49}$$

and

$$CoV = \frac{\sqrt{(1-p)r}}{r}, \tag{5.1.50}$$

respectively. The skewness and the kurtosis (the fourth standardized central moment) are defined as

$$\tilde{\mu}_3 = \frac{2-p}{\sqrt{(1-p)r}} \tag{5.1.51}$$

and

$$\tilde{\mu}_4 = \frac{p^2 - 6p + 6}{(1-p)r} + 3. \tag{5.1.52}$$

If the kurtosis is provided in comparison to a normal distribution, then we have

$$Kurt(X) = \frac{p^2 - 6p + 6}{(1-p)r}. \tag{5.1.53}$$

The negative binomial moment generating function is

$$M_X(s) = \left(\frac{pe^s}{1 - (1-p)e^s} \right)^r, \tag{5.1.54}$$

and the central moment generating function is specified by

$$CM_X(s) = e^{-\frac{rs}{p}} \left(\frac{pe^s}{1 - (1-p)e^s} \right)^r. \tag{5.1.55}$$

Example 5.1.3. Consider a large scale data center. Let us assume the probability of the server passing (success) an accelerated reliability test is $p = 0.15$. The probability of having at most $k = 50$ failures until $r = 10$ success is estimated by Equation 5.1.46, that is

$$P(X \leq k) = \sum_{x=r}^{k} \binom{x-1}{r-1} p^r (1-p)^{x-r}.$$

Hence,

$$P(X \leq 50) = \sum_{x=10}^{50} \binom{x-1}{10-1} 0.15^{10}(1-0.15)^{x-10} = 0.2089,$$

and the mean number of failures until obtaining 10 success is estimated using Equation 5.1.47, that is

$$E(X) = \mu' = \frac{r}{p} = \frac{10}{0.15} = 66.6667.$$

$\square$

Section 14.3.3 shows a method for generating a random variate based on the negative binomial distribution.

5.1.5 HYPERGEOMETRIC

The hypergeometric distribution arises in probabilistic experiments in which objects are divided into two distinct classes (class 1 and class 2). Such classes could be success or failure, passed or not passed, finished or not finished, male or female, etc. Now, assume a collection of N objects, in which r belongs to class 1 and $N - r$ are class 2. If we choose n objects from the collection of objects N without replacement, the random variable X that denotes the number of objects of class 1 from the selected n has a hypergeometric distribution. The PDF of X is defined as

$$P(X = k) = \frac{\binom{r}{k}\binom{N-r}{n-k}}{\binom{N}{n}}, \tag{5.1.56}$$

and otherwise is 0, where $k = max(0, n - N + r), \dots, min(n, r)$.

The cumulative distribution function of a hypergeometric random variable is specified as

$$F(X) = \sum_{i=0}^{r} \frac{\binom{r}{i}\binom{N-r}{n-i}}{\binom{N}{n}}. \tag{5.1.57}$$

Therefore, the probability of having at most k objects from class 1 from the selected n is

$$P(X \le k) = F(k) = \sum_{i=0}^{k} \frac{\binom{r}{i}\binom{N-r}{n-i}}{\binom{N}{n}}. \tag{5.1.58}$$

Figure 5.5.a depicts the probability mass function of a random variable X distributed according to a negative binomial distribution with parameters $N = 20$, $r = 5$ and $n = 8$. Figure 5.5.b shows the respective cumulative distribution function.

The expected value of X is given by

$$\mu' = \frac{nr}{N}. \tag{5.1.59}$$

The variance, the standard deviation, and the coefficient of variation are specified by

$$\mu_2 = \frac{nr(N-n)\left(1 - \frac{r}{N}\right)}{(N-1)N}, \tag{5.1.60}$$

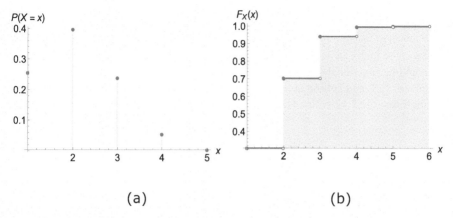

(a)　　　　　　　　　　　　　　　(b)

Figure 5.5 cdf (a) and pdf (b) of X - $X \sim HG(N,r,n)$.

$$(\mu_2)^{1/2} = \frac{\sqrt{\frac{nr(N-n)(N-r)}{N-1}}}{N}, \tag{5.1.61}$$

and

$$CoV = \frac{\sqrt{\frac{nr(N-n)(N-r)}{N-1}}}{nr}, \tag{5.1.62}$$

respectively. The skewness and the kurtosis (the fourth standardized central moment) are defined as

$$\tilde{\mu}_3 = \frac{\sqrt{N-1}(N-2n)(N-2r)}{(N-2)\sqrt{nr(N-n)(N-r)}} \tag{5.1.63}$$

and

$$\tilde{\mu}_4 = \frac{(N-1)N^2 \left(\frac{3r\left(n^2(-N)+(n-2)N^2+6n(N-n)\right)(N-r)}{N^2} - 6n(N-n) + N(N+1) \right)}{n(N-3)(N-2)r(N-n)(N-r)}. \tag{5.1.64}$$

If the kurtosis is provided in comparison to a normal distribution, then we have

$$Kurt(X) = \frac{(N-1)N^2 \left(\frac{3r\left(n^2(-N)+(n-2)N^2+6n(N-n)\right)(N-r)}{N^2} - 6n(N-n) + N(N+1) \right)}{n(N-3)(N-2)r(N-n)(N-r)} - 3. \tag{5.1.65}$$

Example 5.1.4. Consider a warehouse department of a company has forty items ($N = 40$) of specific type. Assume seven ($r = 7$) items are properly functioning and the rest are faulty ($N - r = 33$). The items are mixed, that is, when selecting an item, it could be functional or not functional. The probability of randomly selecting eight items ($n = 8$) and getting at least two non-functional items ($k = 2$) can be estimated using Equation 5.1.58, that is

$$P(X \geq k) = 1 - P(X < k) = 1 - F(k-1) = 1 - \sum_{i=0}^{k-1} \frac{\binom{r}{i}\binom{N-r}{n-i}}{\binom{N}{n}}.$$

$$P(X \geq 2) = 1 - P(X < 2) = 1 - F(1) = \sum_{i=0}^{1} \frac{\binom{7}{i}\binom{33}{8-i}}{\binom{40}{8}} = 0.4306.$$

□

5.1.6   POISSON

We have seen that if n independent Bernoulli experiments are executed, where each trial results in an event "occurrence" with probability p or event "non-occurrence" with probability $1 - p$, the discrete random variable X that specifies the number of event "occurrences" in n trials is binomially distributed with parameters n and p, $X \sim Bin(n, p)$. Hence, we have (see Equation 5.1.32):

$$P(X = k) = \binom{n}{k} p^k (1-p)^{n-k}, \quad k \in \mathbb{N}.$$

Now consider that the number of trials tends to infinity ($n \to \infty$), the probability p tends to zero ($p \to 0$), and that np tends to a constant value. Let us define $\lambda = np$ (a rate).

As $\lambda = np$, then $p = \lambda/n$; thus

$$P(X = k) = \binom{n}{k} \left(\frac{\lambda}{n}\right)^k \left(1 - \frac{\lambda}{n}\right)^{n-k}, \quad k \in \mathbb{N}.$$

Hence

$$P(X = k) = \frac{n!}{k!(n-k)!} \left(\frac{\lambda}{n}\right)^k \left(1 - \frac{\lambda}{n}\right)^{n-k}, \quad k \in \mathbb{N},$$

which is equal to

$$P(X = k) = \frac{\lambda^k}{k!} \frac{n!}{(n-k)!} \frac{1}{n^k} \left(1 - \frac{\lambda}{n}\right)^{n-k}, \quad k \in \mathbb{N}.$$

Now, let us take the second and third terms of the expression above and rewrite them as

$$\frac{n!}{(n-k)!}\frac{1}{n^k} = \frac{n(n-1)(n-2)\dots(n-k+1)(n-k)!}{(n-k)!\,n^k},$$

which is

$$\frac{n!}{(n-k)!}\frac{1}{n^k} = \frac{n(n-1)(n-2)\dots(n-k+1)!}{n^k}.$$

The numerator of the right-hand expression above has k terms, then

$$\frac{n!}{(n-k)!}\frac{1}{n^k} = \frac{n}{n}\frac{n-1}{n}\frac{n-2}{n}\dots\frac{n-k+1}{n},$$

which leads to

$$\frac{n!}{(n-k)!}\frac{1}{n^k} = 1\left(1-\frac{1}{n}\right)\left(1-\frac{2}{n}\right)\dots\left(1-\frac{k+1}{n}\right).$$

Therefore, we obtain

$$P(X=k) = \frac{\lambda^k}{k!}\left(1-\frac{1}{n}\right)\left(1-\frac{2}{n}\right)\dots\left(1-\frac{k+1}{n}\right)\left(1-\frac{\lambda}{n}\right)^{n-k}, \quad k \in \mathbb{N}.$$

$$P(X=k) = \frac{\lambda^k}{k!}\left(1-\frac{1}{n}\right)\left(1-\frac{2}{n}\right)\dots\left(1-\frac{k+1}{n}\right)\left(1-\frac{\lambda}{n}\right)^{n}\left(1-\frac{\lambda}{n}\right)^{-k},$$
$$k \in \mathbb{N}.$$

Now take the limit of n to the infinite; thus

$$\lim_{n\to\infty} P(X=k) = \lim_{n\to\infty}\frac{\lambda^k}{k!}\left(1-\frac{1}{n}\right)\left(1-\frac{2}{n}\right)\dots\left(1-\frac{k+1}{n}\right)\left(1-\frac{\lambda}{n}\right)^{n}\left(1-\frac{\lambda}{n}\right)^{-k}, \quad k \in \mathbb{N}.$$

$$P(X=k) = \frac{\lambda^k}{k!}\lim_{n\to\infty}\left(\left(1-\frac{1}{n}\right)\left(1-\frac{2}{n}\right)\dots\left(1-\frac{k+1}{n}\right)\right)\lim_{n\to\infty}\left(1-\frac{\lambda}{n}\right)^{n}\lim_{n\to\infty}\left(1-\frac{\lambda}{n}\right)^{-k}, \quad k \in \mathbb{N}.$$

Thus,

$$P(X=k) = \frac{\lambda^k}{k!}\times 1\times\lim_{n\to\infty}\left(1-\frac{\lambda}{n}\right)^{n}\times 1, \quad k \in \mathbb{N}.$$

As

$$e^{-\lambda} = \lim_{n\to\infty}\left(1-\frac{\lambda}{n}\right)^{n},$$

then

$$P(X = k) = \frac{\lambda^k e^{-\lambda}}{k!}, \quad k \in \mathbb{N}, \tag{5.1.66}$$

which is the Poisson probability mass function of X, denoted by $X \sim Pois(\lambda)$.

Therefore, when we have infinitely many independent Bernoulli trials, $\lim n \to \infty$, with probability p approaching zero ($p \to 0$), the discrete random variable X that specifies the number of event occurrences in n trials is distributed according to a Poisson probability distribution with parameters λ, that is $X \sim Pois(\lambda)$.

The cumulative distribution function of a Poisson random variable is specified as

$$F(X) = \sum_{i=0}^{\infty} \frac{\lambda^i e^{-\lambda}}{i!}, \quad i \in \mathbb{N}. \tag{5.1.67}$$

Therefore, the probability of having at most k event occurrence is

$$P(X \leq k) = F(k) = \sum_{i=0}^{k} \frac{\lambda^i e^{-\lambda}}{i!}, \quad i \in \mathbb{N}. \tag{5.1.68}$$

Therefore, the probability of having at least k event occurrence is

$$P(X \geq k) = 1 - \sum_{i=0}^{k-1} \frac{\lambda^i e^{-\lambda}}{i!}, \quad i \in \mathbb{N}. \tag{5.1.69}$$

Figure 5.6.a depicts the probability mass function of a random variable X distributed according to a Poisson distribution with parameters $\lambda = 20$. Figure 5.6.b shows the respective cumulative distribution function.

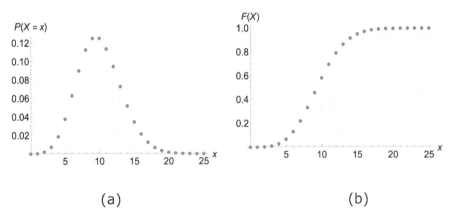

(a)   (b)

Figure 5.6   cdf (a) and pdf (b) of X - $X \sim Pois(\lambda)$.

The expected value of X is given by

$$\mu' = \lambda. \tag{5.1.70}$$

The variance, the standard deviation, and the coefficient of variation are specified by

$$\mu_2 = \lambda, \tag{5.1.71}$$

$$(\mu_2)^{1/2} = \sqrt{\lambda}, \tag{5.1.72}$$

and

$$CoV = \frac{1}{\sqrt{\lambda}}, \tag{5.1.73}$$

respectively. The skewness and the kurtosis (the fourth standardized central moment) are defined as

$$\tilde{\mu}_3 = \frac{1}{\sqrt{\lambda}} \tag{5.1.74}$$

and

$$\tilde{\mu}_4 = \frac{1}{\lambda} + 3. \tag{5.1.75}$$

If the kurtosis is provided in comparison to a normal distribution, then we have

$$Kurt(X) = \frac{3\lambda^2 + \lambda}{\lambda^2}. \tag{5.1.76}$$

The Poisson moment generating function is

$$M_X(s) = e^{\lambda(e^s - 1)}, \tag{5.1.77}$$

and the central moment generating function is specified by

$$CM_X(s) = e^{\lambda(e^s - 1) - \lambda s}. \tag{5.1.78}$$

Example 5.1.5. Consider a system that receives requests at the constant rate equal to $\lambda = 10s^{-1}$, and assume the probability of a request arriving in a second is very small (close to 0). If the number of requests observed in a period T is very large, the probability of at least fifteen requests ($X \geq 15$) arriving in a second may be estimated using Equation 5.1.69

$$P(X \geq k) = 1 - \sum_{i=0}^{k-1} \frac{\lambda^i e^{-\lambda}}{i!}, \quad i \in \mathbb{N}.$$

$$P(X \geq 15) = 1 - \sum_{i=0}^{14} \frac{10^i e^{-10}}{i!} = 0.0835.$$

$\square$

5.2 SOME CONTINUOUS RANDOM VARIABLES

So far, we have been working with discrete random variables. This chapter discusses continuous random variables, which can take on any real value in an interval. Such a interval could be the entire line, $(-\infty, \infty)$ or a semi-line as, for instance, $(0, \infty)$.

5.2.1 UNIFORM

A continuous random variable X that is equally likely to take any value in a range (a, b) is uniformly distributed with the probability density function given by

$$f_X(x) = \frac{1}{b-a}, \tag{5.2.1}$$

and zero for values outside the interval, that is $x \notin (a, b)$, $a, b \in \mathbb{R}$, $b > a$. A uniformly distributed random variable is usually denoted as $X \sim U(a, b)$. The cumulative distribution function of a uniform random variable is specified as

$$F_X(x) = \int_a^x f_X(x)\,dx = \int_a^x \frac{1}{b-a}\,dx = \frac{1}{b-a}\int_a^x dx,$$

which leads to

$$F_X(x) = \begin{cases} \frac{x-a}{b-a} & a \leq x \leq b \\ 1 & x > b. \end{cases} \tag{5.2.2}$$

Figure 5.7.a depicts the probability density function of a random variable X distributed according to a uniform distribution with parameter $a = -20$ and $b = 40$. Figure 5.7.b shows the respective cumulative distribution function.

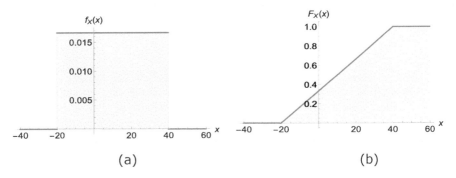

(a)   (b)

Figure 5.7   pdf (a) and cdf (b) of X - $X \sim U(-20, 40)$.

The expected value of X is given by

$$\mu' = \frac{a+b}{2}. \tag{5.2.3}$$

The variance, the standard deviation, and the coefficient of variation are specified by

$$\mu_2 = \frac{1}{12}(b-a)^2, \tag{5.2.4}$$

$$(\mu_2)^{1/2} = \frac{b-a}{2\sqrt{3}}, \tag{5.2.5}$$

and

$$CoV = \frac{b-a}{\sqrt{3}(a+b)}, \tag{5.2.6}$$

respectively. The skewness and the kurtosis (the fourth standardized central moment) are defined as

$$\tilde{\mu}_3 = 0. \tag{5.2.7}$$

and

$$\tilde{\mu}_4 = \frac{9}{5} = 1.8. \tag{5.2.8}$$

If the kurtosis is provided in comparison to a normal distribution, then we have

$$Kurt(X) = -\frac{6}{5} = -1.2. \tag{5.2.9}$$

The uniform moment generating function is

$$M_X(s) = \frac{e^{bs} - e^{as}}{s(b-a)}, \tag{5.2.10}$$

and the central moment generating function is specified by

$$CM_X(s) = \frac{e^{-\frac{1}{2}s(a+b)}\left(e^{bs} - e^{as}\right)}{s(b-a)}. \tag{5.2.11}$$

The uniform random variable median is defined as

$$Mdn = \frac{a+b}{2}. \tag{5.2.12}$$

The first and the third quartiles are defined as

$$Q_1 = \frac{1}{4}(3a+b), \tag{5.2.13}$$

and

$$Q_3 = \frac{1}{4}(a+3b). \tag{5.2.14}$$

Example 5.2.1. Let X be a random variable uniformly distributed in the interval $(0, 24)$. The probability of obtaining a value in interval $(4, 12)$ may be calculated using Equation 5.2.2; hence

$$F_X(x) = \begin{cases} \frac{x-a}{b-a} & a \le x \le b \\ 1 & x > b. \end{cases}$$

Therefore

$$P(4 < X < 9) = F_X(9) - F_X(4) = \frac{9-0}{24-0} - \frac{4-0}{24-0} = 0.2083.$$

□

5.2.2 TRIANGULAR

The triangular distribution is a continuous probability distribution that has a range defined by (a, b) and a mode c, where $a, b, c \in \mathbb{R}$ and $a \le c \le b$. The probability density function is given by

$$f_X(x) = \begin{cases} \frac{2(x-a)}{(b-a)(c-a)} & a \le x \le c \\ \frac{2(b-x)}{(b-a)(b-c)} & c < x \le b \end{cases} \tag{5.2.15}$$

and zero for values outside the interval (a, b), where $x \notin (a, b)$, $a, b \in \mathbb{R}$, $b > a$. A triangular distributed random variable is usually denoted as $X \sim Tr(a, b, c)$. The cumulative distribution function of a triangular random variable is specified as

$$F_X(x) = \begin{cases} \frac{(x-a)^2}{(b-a)(c-a)} & a \le x \le c \\ 1 - \frac{(b-x)^2}{(b-a)(b-c)} & c < x \le b \\ 1 & x > b \end{cases} \tag{5.2.16}$$

Figure 5.8.a depicts the probability density function of a random variable X distributed according to a triangular distribution with parameter $a = 10$, $b = 80$, and $c = 30$. Figure 5.8.b shows the respective cumulative distribution function.

The expected value of X is given by

$$\mu' = \frac{1}{3}(a+b+c). \tag{5.2.17}$$

The variance, the standard deviation, and the coefficient of variation are specified by

$$\mu_2 = \frac{1}{18}\left(a^2 - ab - ac + b^2 - bc + c^2\right), \tag{5.2.18}$$

$$(\mu_2)^{1/2} = \frac{\sqrt{a^2 - ab - ac + b^2 - bc + c^2}}{3\sqrt{2}}, \tag{5.2.19}$$

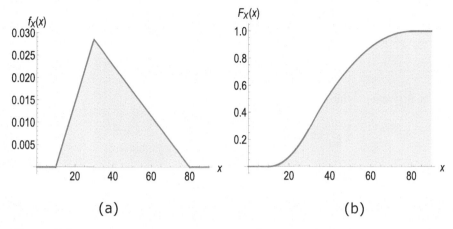

Figure 5.8   pdf (a) and cdf (b) of X - $X \sim Tr(10, 80, 30)$.

and

$$CoV = \frac{\sqrt{a^2 - ab - ac + b^2 - bc + c^2}}{\sqrt{2}(a+b+c)}, \qquad (5.2.20)$$

respectively. The skewness and the kurtosis (the fourth standardized central moment) are defined as

$$\tilde{\mu}_3 = \frac{\sqrt{2}(a+b-2c)(2a-b-c)(a-2b+c)}{5\left(a^2 - a(b+c) + b^2 - bc + c^2\right)^{3/2}}. \qquad (5.2.21)$$

and

$$\tilde{\mu}_4 = \frac{12}{5} = 2.4. \qquad (5.2.22)$$

If the kurtosis is provided in comparison to a normal distribution; then we have

$$Kurt(X) = -\frac{3}{5} = -0.6. \qquad (5.2.23)$$

The uniform moment generating function is

$$M_X(s) = \frac{2\left((a-b)e^{cs} + e^{as}(b-c) + (c-a)e^{bs}\right)}{s^2(a-b)(a-c)(b-c)}, \qquad (5.2.24)$$

and the central moment generating function is specified by

$$CM_X(s) = \frac{2e^{-\frac{1}{3}s(a+b+c)}\left((a-b)e^{cs} + e^{as}(b-c) + (c-a)e^{bs}\right)}{s^2(a-b)(a-c)(b-c)}. \qquad (5.2.25)$$

The triangular random variable median is defined as

$$
Mdn = \begin{cases} \dfrac{\sqrt{(b-a)(c-a)}}{\sqrt{2}} + a & \frac{1}{2} \le \frac{c-a}{b-a} \\ b - \dfrac{\sqrt{(b-a)(b-c)}}{\sqrt{2}} & \text{otherwise.} \end{cases} \tag{5.2.26}
$$

The first and the third quartiles are defined as

$$
Q_1 = \begin{cases} \frac{1}{2}\sqrt{(b-a)(c-a)} + a & \frac{1}{4} \le \frac{c-a}{b-a} \\ b - \frac{1}{2}\sqrt{3}\sqrt{(b-a)(b-c)} & \text{otherwise.} \end{cases} \tag{5.2.27}
$$

and

$$
Q_3 = \begin{cases} \frac{1}{2}\sqrt{3}\sqrt{(b-a)(c-a)} + a & \frac{3}{4} \le \frac{c-a}{b-a} \\ b - \frac{1}{2}\sqrt{(b-a)(b-c)} & \text{otherwise.} \end{cases} \tag{5.2.28}
$$

Example 5.2.2. A help desk department gives an account of an historical number of calls per day according to a triangular distribution with the following parameters $a = 100, b = 800, c = 300$, that is $X \sim Tr(100, 800, 300)$. The expected number of calls per day is calculated using Equation 5.2.17 and Equation 5.2.19, respectively. Thus,

$$
\mu' = \frac{1}{3}(a+b+c) = 400
$$

and

$$
(\mu_2)^{1/2} = \frac{\sqrt{a^2 - ab - ac + b^2 - bc + c^2}}{3\sqrt{2}} = 147.196.
$$

The probability of having more than 400 calls in a day may be estimated through Equation 5.2.16. Hence,

$$
P(X > 400) = 1 - F(400) = 0.4571.
$$

$\square$

5.2.3 NORMAL

The normal or Gaussian distribution function is ubiquitous throughout the world of statistics and probability. It is widely used in statistics because of the *central limit theorem*, which we discuss below without proof, that the sum of a large number of independent random variables is approximately normally distributed, regardless of the distribution of the individual random variables.

Consider a random variable X that represents the financial return from a sales campaign. Assume X is normally distributed with parameters μ (mean) and σ^2 (variance), shortly denoted by $X \sim N(\mu, \sigma^2)$, if its probability density function is

$$f_X(x) = \frac{1}{\sigma\sqrt{2\pi}} e^{-\frac{(x-\mu)^2}{2\sigma^2}}. \tag{5.2.29}$$

As is clear from Figure 5.9, the normal distribution is symmetric about its mean value μ, and it is short and flat when σ is large and tall and skinny when σ is small.

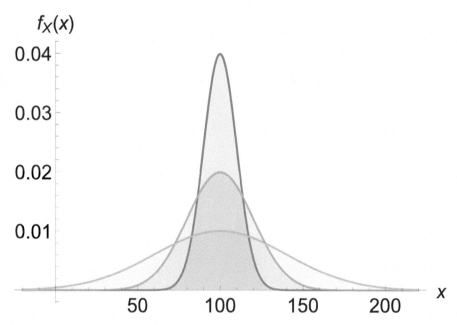

Figure 5.9 Probability Density Function $f_X(x)$ - $X \sim N(100, \sigma)$, $\sigma \in \{10, 20, 40\}$.

The cumulative distribution function for a random variable normally distributed has no closed-form; that is, we cannot write $F_X(x)$ in the form of an equation. The cumulative distribution function of a normal random variable may, however, be specified as

$$F_X(x) = \frac{1}{\sigma\sqrt{2\pi}} \int_{-\infty}^{\infty} e^{-\frac{(x-\mu)^2}{2\sigma^2}} dx. \tag{5.2.30}$$

This means that we must have recourse to numerical computation or precomputed tables; usually such tables provide data relating to the standard normal distribution, that is a normal random variable with mean $\mu = 0$ and standard deviation equal to $\sigma = 1$, $N(0, 1)$. Indeed, if a random variable X has the distribution $N(\mu, \sigma^2)$, then the random variable $Z = (x - \mu)/\sigma$ has a standard normal distribution. Therefore, the probability density function of a standard normal random variable, $N(0, 1)$, is reduced to

$$f_X(x) = \frac{1}{\sqrt{2\pi}} e^{-\frac{x^2}{2}}. \tag{5.2.31}$$

Figure 5.10 depicts the probability density function of a standard normal distribution, $N(0, 1)$.

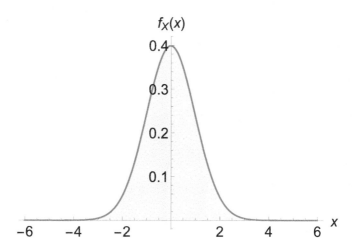

Figure 5.10 Probability Density Function of a Standard Normal Distribution $f_X(x) - X \sim N(0, 1)$.

Figure 5.11.a depicts the probability density function of a random variable X distributed according to a normal distribution with parameter $\mu = 200$ and $\sigma = 50$. Figure 5.11.b shows the respective cumulative distribution function.

The probability of an event occurring by x is

$$P(X \le x) = F_X(x) = \frac{1}{\sigma\sqrt{2\pi}} \int_{-\infty}^{x} e^{-\frac{(x-\mu)^2}{2\sigma^2}} dx. \tag{5.2.32}$$

The expected value of X is given by

$$\mu' = \mu. \tag{5.2.33}$$

The variance, the standard deviation, and the coefficient of variation are specified by

$$\mu_2 = \sigma^2. \tag{5.2.34}$$

The standard deviation and the coefficient of variation are specified by

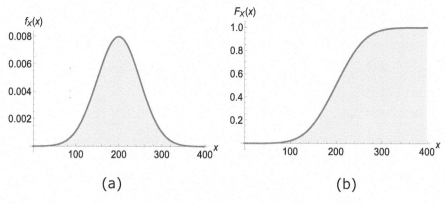

Figure 5.11 PDF (a) and CDF (b) of X - $X \sim N(200, 50)$.

$$(\mu_2)^{1/2} = \sigma, \tag{5.2.35}$$

and

$$CoV = \frac{\sigma}{\mu}, \tag{5.2.36}$$

respectively. The skewness and the kurtosis (the fourth standardized central moment) are defined as

$$\tilde{\mu}_3 = 0 \tag{5.2.37}$$

and

$$\tilde{\mu}_4 = 3. \tag{5.2.38}$$

If the kurtosis is provided in comparison to a normal distribution, then we have

$$Kurt(X) = 0. \tag{5.2.39}$$

The normal moment generating function is

$$M_X(s) = e^{\frac{s^2 \sigma^2}{2} + \mu s}, \tag{5.2.40}$$

and the central moment generating function is specified by

$$CM_X(s) = e^{\frac{s^2 \sigma^2}{2}}. \tag{5.2.41}$$

The normal random variable median is defined as

$$Mdn = \mu. \tag{5.2.42}$$

The first and the third quartiles are defined as

$$Q_1 = \mu - 0.67449\sigma, \tag{5.2.43}$$

and

$$Q_3 = \mu + 0.67449\sigma. \tag{5.2.44}$$

Example 5.2.3. Consider X is a normal random variable with mean $\mu = 100$ and variance $\sigma = 20$. The following probabilities are calculated using

$$P(X < 60) = F_X(60) = 0.02275,$$

$$P(X > 60) = 1 - F_X(60) = 0.97725,$$

and

$$P(60X < 90) = F_X(90) - F_X(60) = 0.28579.$$

$\square$

Central Limit Theorem

The central limit theorem, mentioned above, which we discuss here, but without presenting a proof, asserts that the sum of n independent random variables, $\{X_1, X_2, ..., X_n\}$, is approximated by a normal distribution with mean μ and variance σ^2 [178, 287, 413, 436]. More formally,

Theorem 5.2.1. *Let $X_1, X_2, ..., X_n$ be independent random variables whose expectation $E(X_i) = \mu_i$ and variances $Var(X_i) = \sigma_i^2$ are both finite. Let Y_n be the normalized random variable*

$$Y_n = \frac{\sum_{i=1}^n X_i - \sum_{i=1}^n \mu_i}{\sqrt{\sum_{i=1}^n \sigma_i^2}};$$

then $E(Y) = 0$ and $Var(Y) = 1$ when $n \to \infty$, that is $Y \sim N(0,1)$ when $n \to \infty$.

When the random variables are all identically distributed and independent, then Y_n simplifies to

$$Y_n = \frac{\sum_{i=1}^n X_i - n\mu}{\sigma\sqrt{n}},$$

where $\mu = (\sum_{i=1}^n \mu_i)/n$ and $\sigma^2 = (\sum_{i=1}^n \sigma_i^2)/n$.

More details about the normal distribution are in Chapter 6, where it is also extensively used. Section 14.3 and Section 25.3 also present other details related to random variate generation and parameter estimation. Besides, it is worth mentioning that the normal distribution is widely adopted in many other parts of this book.

5.2.4 CHI-SQUARE

The importance of chi-square (χ^2) random variables stems from the fact that the distribution of the sum of the squares, $X = \sum_{i=1}^{n} Y_i^2$, of a number of normal random variables, Y_i, is distributed according to a chi-square distribution. The chi-square distribution is one of the most important distribution in parametric statistics inference (see Chapter 6). We use de notation $X \sim \chi_{n-1}^2$ to state that X is distributed according to a chi-square distribution with $n-1$ degrees of freedom, where $n \in \mathbb{N}, n > 1$.

The concept of degrees of freedom can be understood with this simple example. Consider n a natural number, let us say $y_1, y_2, ..., y_n$. If the mean of such numbers is the number $\bar{y}$, we can choose $n-1$ values for y_i, $i = \{1,2,...,n\}$, but once you freely choose $n-1$ values, the last value is already specified. Hence, the degrees of freedom (for you freely choosing values) is $n-1$.

The probability density function of a random variable that follows a chi-square distribution with $n-1$ degrees of freedom is

$$f_X(x) = \frac{2^{\frac{1}{2}-\frac{n}{2}}e^{-x/2}x^{\frac{n-3}{2}}}{\Gamma\left(\frac{n-1}{2}\right)} \qquad x > 0, \qquad (5.2.45)$$

where $\Gamma(n)$ is a gamma function, which is defined by

$$\Gamma(n) = \begin{cases} (n-1)! & \text{if } n \in \mathbb{N}^+ \\ \int_0^\infty x^{n-1}e^{-x}dx & \text{if } n \notin \mathbb{N}^+, \mathbb{R}(n) > 0. \end{cases} \qquad (5.2.46)$$

The gamma function has some interesting properties, among them:

- $\Gamma(1) = 1$,
- $\Gamma\left(\frac{1}{2}\right) = \sqrt{\pi}$, and
- $\Gamma(n) = (n-1)\Gamma(n-1) \qquad n > 0.$

The cumulative distribution function values can be obtained in tables available in the literature or may be calculated through

$$F_X(x) = \int_0^x \frac{2^{\frac{1}{2}-\frac{n}{2}}e^{-\frac{x}{2}}x^{\frac{1}{2}(n-3)}}{\Gamma\left(\frac{1}{2}(n-1)\right)}dx \qquad x > 0. \qquad (5.2.47)$$

Figure 5.12.a depicts the probability density function of a random variable X distributed according to a chi-square distribution with parameter $n-1 = 99$. Figure 5.12.b shows the respective cumulative distribution function.

Figure 5.13 presents probability density functions for random variables distributed according to χ_2^2, χ_8^2, and χ_{32}^2, respectively.

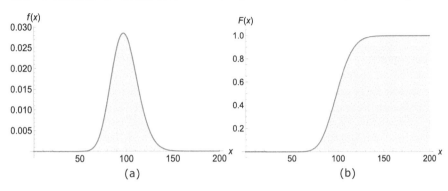

Figure 5.12   pdf (a) and cdf (b) of X - $X \sim \chi^2_{99}$.

The probability of an event occurring by x is

$$P(X \leq x) = F_X(x) = \int_0^x \frac{2^{\frac{1}{2}-\frac{n}{2}} e^{-\frac{x}{2}} x^{\frac{1}{2}(n-3)}}{\Gamma\left(\frac{1}{2}(n-1)\right)} \, dx \qquad x > 0, \qquad (5.2.48)$$

and the percentile (the value x) of a specified rank p is obtained by

$$x_p = \arg_x F_X(x) = \arg_x p, \qquad (5.2.49)$$

and the probability of an event occurring in the interval (x_1, x_2) is

$$P(x_1 \leq X \leq x_2) = \int_{x1}^{x2} \frac{2^{\frac{1}{2}-\frac{n}{2}} e^{-\frac{x}{2}} x^{\frac{1}{2}(n-3)}}{\Gamma\left(\frac{1}{2}(n-1)\right)} \, dx. \qquad (5.2.50)$$

The expected value of X is given by

$$\mu' = n - 1. \qquad (5.2.51)$$

The variance, the standard deviation, and the coefficient of variation are specified by

$$\mu_2 = 2(n-1), \qquad (5.2.52)$$

$$\mu_2^{1/2} = \sqrt{2}\sqrt{n-1}, \qquad (5.2.53)$$

and

$$CoV = \frac{\sqrt{2}}{\sqrt{n-1}}, \qquad (5.2.54)$$

respectively. The skewness and the kurtosis (the fourth standardized central moment) are defined as

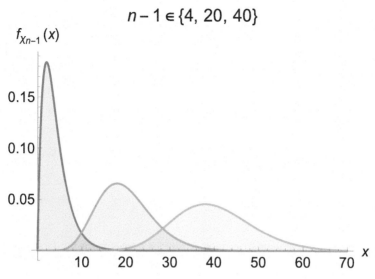

Figure 5.13 pdf X - $X \sim \chi^2_{n-1}$, $n \in \{5, 21, 41\}$.

$$\tilde{\mu}_3 = 2\sqrt{2}\sqrt{\frac{1}{n-1}} \qquad (5.2.55)$$

and

$$\tilde{\mu}_4 = \frac{12}{n-1} + 3. \qquad (5.2.56)$$

If the kurtosis is provided in comparison to a normal distribution, then we have

$$Kurt(X) = \frac{12}{n-1}. \qquad (5.2.57)$$

The chi-square moment generating function is

$$M_X(s) = (1-2s)^{\frac{1-n}{2}}, \qquad (5.2.58)$$

and the central moment generating function is specified by

$$CM_X(s) = e^{(1-n)s}(1-2s)^{\frac{1-n}{2}}. \qquad (5.2.59)$$

Example 5.2.4. Consider X is a chi-square random variable with sample size equal to $n = 100$. The value of X for $F_X(x) = 0.975 = (1 - \alpha/2)$ is estimated by Equation 5.2.49, that is

$$x_p = \arg_x F_X(x) = \arg_x p = \arg_x(1 - \frac{\alpha}{2}) = \arg_x(0.975).$$

$$x_{0.975} = 128.422,$$

and the probability is calculated using the Formula 5.2.48, that is

$$P(X \leq 73.361) = F(73.361) = \int_0^{x2} \frac{2^{\frac{1}{2}-\frac{n}{2}} e^{-\frac{x}{2}} x^{\frac{1}{2}(n-3)}}{\Gamma\left(\frac{1}{2}(n-1)\right)} dx = 0.025.$$

□

Other information about the chi-square distribution is depicted in Section 6.2, Section 6.6.2, Section 14.3 and Section 16.3, for instance.

5.2.5 STUDENT'S T

The importance of Student's t random variables comes from the fact that they resemble the normal distribution and are extensively applied in statistic inference. Consider two independent random variables Z and S such that $Z \sim N(0,1)$ and $nS^2 \sim \chi^2_{n-1}$, where $n \in \mathbb{N}$, $n > 1$ is the sample size. Assume a third random variable X_n defined as a function of Z and nS^2, such that

$$X_n = \frac{Z}{S\sqrt{n}}$$

is distributed according to a Student's t distribution with degree of freedom $n-1$ (usually denoted by $X \sim t(n-1)$), whose probability density function is defined by

$$f_X(t) = \frac{\left(\frac{n-1}{x^2}\right)^{n/2} \left(\frac{n+x^2-1}{x^2}\right)^{-n/2} \Gamma\left(\frac{n}{2}\right)}{\sqrt{\pi}\sqrt{n-1}\Gamma\left(\frac{n}{2}-\frac{1}{2}\right)}. \tag{5.2.60}$$

As the density function of a standard random variable (Z), the density function of X (Student's t random variable) is symmetric about zero. Besides, as n becomes large, the $f_X(t)$ approaches the standard normal density function. It is worth mentioning that if X is the sum of n independent squared standard normal variables, $X \sim \chi^2_{n-1}$ (see χ^2_{n-1} random variable); hence

$$X = \sum_{i=1}^{n} Z_i^2.$$

Dividing both sides by n, we obtain

$$\frac{X}{n} = \frac{\sum_{i=1}^{n} Z_i^2}{n} = \frac{Z_1^2 + Z_2^2 + \dots + Z_n^2}{n}.$$

As n gets large, $\frac{X}{n} \to 1$, and

$$\frac{Z_1^2 + Z_2^2 + \ldots + Z_n^2}{n} = 1.$$

Therefore, for n large, $X_n = \frac{Z}{S\sqrt{n}}$ approaches a standard normal distribution.

The cumulative distribution function values can be obtained in tables available in the literature or may be calculated through

$$F_X(x) = \frac{\Gamma\left(\frac{n}{2}\right)}{\sqrt{n-1}\sqrt{\pi}\Gamma\left(\frac{n-1}{2}\right)} \int_{-\infty}^{x} \left(\frac{n-1}{x^2}\right)^{n/2} \left(\frac{x^2+n-1}{x^2}\right)^{-\frac{n}{2}} dx. \qquad (5.2.61)$$

The probability of an event occurring by x is

$$P(X \le x) = F_X(x) = \frac{\Gamma\left(\frac{n}{2}\right)}{\sqrt{n-1}\sqrt{\pi}\Gamma\left(\frac{n-1}{2}\right)} \int_{-\infty}^{x} \left(\frac{n-1}{x^2}\right)^{n/2} \left(\frac{x^2+n-1}{x^2}\right)^{-\frac{n}{2}} dx.$$
$$(5.2.62)$$

Figure 5.14.a depicts the probability density function of a random variable X distributed according to a Student's t distribution with parameter $n - 1 = 29$. Figure 5.14.b shows the respective cumulative distribution function.

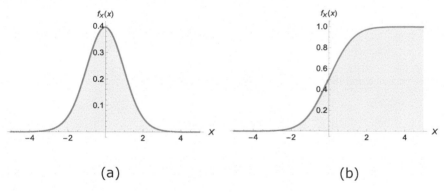

(a)							(b)

Figure 5.14   PDF (a) and CDF (b) of X - $X \sim t(29)$.

Figure 5.15 presents probability density functions for random variables distributed according to $t(2)$, $t(8)$, and $t(32)$, respectively.

The percentile (the value x) of a specified rank p is obtained by

$$x_p = \arg_x F_X(x) = \arg_x p. \qquad (5.2.63)$$

The expected value and the median of X are given by

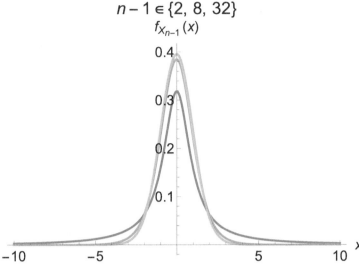

Figure 5.15   pdf X - $X \sim t(n-1)$, $n \in \{3, 9, 33\}$.

$$\mu' = 0, \tag{5.2.64}$$

and

$$Mdn = 0. \tag{5.2.65}$$

The variance and the standard deviation are specified by

$$\mu_2 = \frac{n-1}{n-3}, \quad n \geq 3, \tag{5.2.66}$$

$$\mu_2^{1/2} = \sqrt{\frac{n-1}{n-3}}, \quad n \geq 3. \tag{5.2.67}$$

respectively. The skewness and the kurtosis (the fourth standardized central moment) are defined as

$$\tilde{\mu}_3 = 0 \tag{5.2.68}$$

and

$$\tilde{\mu}_4 = \frac{6}{n-5} + 3 \quad n \geq 5. \tag{5.2.69}$$

If the kurtosis is provided in comparison to a normal distribution, then we have

$$Kurt(X) = \frac{6}{n-5} \quad n \geq 5. \tag{5.2.70}$$

Example 5.2.5. Consider X is a Student's t random variable with sample size equal to $n = 30$. The value of X for $F_X(x) = 0.95\,(1 - \alpha)$ is estimated by Equation 5.2.63, that is

$$x_p = \arg_x F_X(x) = \arg_x p = \arg_x(1 - \alpha) = \arg_x(0.95).$$

$$x_{0.95} = 1.69913,$$

and the probability is calculated using the Formula 5.2.62, that is

$$P(X \leq 1) = F(1) = 0.837209.$$

$\square$

Other information about the Student's t distribution is also presented in Chapter 6 and Section 14.4.

5.2.6 F DISTRIBUTIONS

Assume W and Y are independent random variables distributed according chi-square distribution with n and m degrees of freedoms, respectively, that is

$$W \sim \chi_n^2 \qquad \text{and} \qquad Y \sim \chi_m^2;$$

then the random variable

$$X_{n,m} = \frac{\frac{W}{n}}{\frac{Y}{m}}$$

is distributed according to F probability distribution with n and m degrees of freedom, $n > 0, m > 0, n, m \in \mathbb{N}$, that is $X \sim F(n,m)$. The F probability distribution is also known as Snedecor's F distribution or the Fisher–Snedecor probability distribution. The probability density function of an $X_{n,m}$ distribution is given by

$$f_X(x) = \frac{m^{m/2} n^{n/2} x^{\frac{n}{2}-1}(m+nx)^{\frac{1}{2}(-m-n)}\Gamma\left(\frac{m+n}{2}\right)}{\Gamma\left(\frac{m}{2}\right)\Gamma\left(\frac{n}{2}\right)}, \qquad n > 0, m > 0, x > 0.$$

(5.2.71)

Figure 5.16 presents the probability density functions for random variables Xs distributed according to $F(n,m)$, for $n \in \{2,5,10\}$ and $m \in \{2,5,10\}$, respectively.

The cumulative distribution function values can be obtained in tables available in the literature or may be calculated through

$$F_X(x_1) = \frac{m^{m/2} n^{n/2} \Gamma\left(\frac{m+n}{2}\right)}{\Gamma\left(\frac{m}{2}\right)\Gamma\left(\frac{n}{2}\right)} \int_0^{x_1} x^{\frac{n-2}{2}}(m+nx)^{-\frac{1}{2}(m+n)}\,dx.$$

(5.2.72)

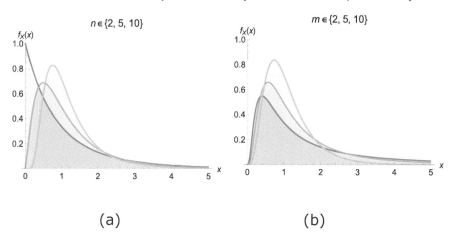

$n \in \{2, 5, 10\}$ $m \in \{2, 5, 10\}$

(a)   (b)

Figure 5.16   pdf $n \in \{2,5,10\}$ (a) and pdf $m \in \{2,5,10\}$ (b) of X - $X \sim F(n,m)$.

Figure 5.17 presents the cumulative distribution function for random variables Xs distributed according to $F(n,m)$, for $n \in \{2,5,10\}$ and $m \in \{2,5,10\}$, respectively. The probability of an event occurring by x_1 is

$$P(X \leq x_1) = F_X(x_1) = \frac{m^{m/2} n^{n/2} \Gamma\left(\frac{m+n}{2}\right)}{\Gamma\left(\frac{m}{2}\right) \Gamma\left(\frac{n}{2}\right)} \int_0^{x_1} x^{\frac{n-2}{2}} (m + nx)^{-\frac{1}{2}(m+n)} \, dx. \quad (5.2.73)$$

The percentile (the value x) of a specified rank p is obtained by

$$x_p = \arg_x F_X(x) = \arg_x p. \quad (5.2.74)$$

The expected value of X is given by

$$\mu' = \frac{m}{m-2}, \qquad m > 2. \quad (5.2.75)$$

The variance and the standard deviation are specified by

$$\mu_2 = \frac{2m^2(m+n-2)}{(m-4)(m-2)^2 n} \qquad m > 4, \quad (5.2.76)$$

$$\mu_2^{1/2} = \frac{\sqrt{2}m\sqrt{m+n-2}}{\sqrt{m-4}(m-2)\sqrt{n}}, \qquad m > 4, \quad (5.2.77)$$

respectively. The skewness and the kurtosis (the fourth standardized central moment) are defined as

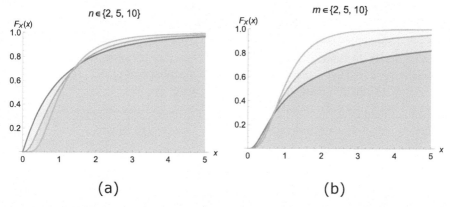

Figure 5.17   cdf $n \in \{2,5,10\}$ (a) and cdf $m \in \{2,5,10\}$ (b) of X - $X \sim F(n,m)$.

$$\tilde{\mu}_3 = \frac{2\sqrt{2}\sqrt{m-4}(m+2n-2)}{(m-6)\sqrt{n}\sqrt{m+n-2}}, \qquad m > 6 \qquad (5.2.78)$$

and

$$\tilde{\mu}_4 = \frac{12\left((5m-22)n(m+n-2)+(m-4)(m-2)^2\right)}{(m-8)(m-6)n(m+n-2)} + 3, \qquad m > 8. \quad (5.2.79)$$

If the kurtosis is provided in comparison to a normal distribution, then we have

$$Kurt(X) = \frac{12\left((5m-22)n(m+n-2)+(m-4)(m-2)^2\right)}{(m-8)(m-6)n(m+n-2)}, \qquad m > 8. \quad (5.2.80)$$

Example 5.2.6. Consider X is a random variable distributed according to an F probability distribution with parameters $n = 10$ and $m = 20$. The value of X for $F_X(x) = 0.1$ is estimated by Equation 5.2.74, that is

$$x_p = \arg_x\{F_X(x) = p\},$$
$$x_{0.1} = \arg_x\{F_X(x) = 0.1\},$$
$$x_{0.1} = 0.445729, \qquad \qquad .$$

and $P(X \leq 0.44573) = 0.1$ is calculated using the Formula 5.2.73.   □

More information about this distribution and its applications are presented, for instance, in Section 25.3.4.

5.2.7 EXPONENTIAL

The exponential random variable is continuous is the analog discrete random variable geometrically distributed. This distribution is central in performance and reliability modeling and in other distributions composed of exponential phases. Hence, the exponential distribution is adopted in many chapters of this text.

Assume a random variable Y has a geometric distribution with parameter p, $Geo(p)$, where $0 \leq p \leq 1$, which is usually denoted by $Y \sim Geo(p)$. Hence,

$$P(Y > k) = (1 - p)^k, \quad k \in \mathbb{N}.$$

Now assume, as we did for the Poisson random variable, the event per time unit (a rate) is constant and defined as $\lambda = np$ (see Section 5.1.6). Consider one time unit (original interval - $[0, 1]$) is divided into a large number of sub-intervals, n, such that each sub-interval is very small and denoted by $\tau = 1/n$. Thus, the probability of an event occurrence in a sub-interval τ approaches zero, $p \to 0$, such that $p = \lambda/n = \lambda \tau$. Therefore, the probability of more than k events occurring in the original time unit is

$$P(Y > nk) = \left(1 - \frac{\lambda}{n}\right)^{nk}.$$

Now, let $Y = X/n$

$$P\left(\frac{X}{n} > k\right) = \left(1 - \frac{\lambda}{n}\right)^{nk}.$$

considering $n \to \infty$; we obtain

$$P\left(\frac{X}{n} > k\right) = \lim_{n \to \infty} \left(1 - \frac{\lambda}{n}\right)^{nk} = e^{-\lambda k},$$

which is a continuous random variable exponentially distributed with parameter λ. A random variable X exponentially distributed with parameters λ is usually denoted by $X \sim Exp(\lambda)$. The cumulative distribution function of X is

$$F_X(x) = P(X \leq x) = 1 - e^{-\lambda x}, \qquad x \geq 0, x \in \mathbb{R}, \qquad (5.2.81)$$

Deriving $F_X(x)$ in terms of x $(dF_X(x)/dx = f_X(x))$ results in the probability density function

$$f_X(x) = \lambda e^{-\lambda x}, \qquad x \geq 0, x \in \mathbb{R}. \qquad (5.2.82)$$

It is worth mentioning that if Z is a Poisson random variable with parameter λ, which denotes the constant rate (frequency of events), X is a random variable that represents the time between the occurrence of events.

Let us also consider a different approach. We know from Equation 4.2.6 that

$$F_X(x) = 1 - e^{-\int_0^x \lambda(x) \times dx} = e^{-H(x)}.$$

If the hazard function $\lambda(x)$ is constant, that is $\lambda(x) = \lambda$ for all $x \geq 0$, then we get

$$F_X(x) = 1 - e^{-\lambda t}.$$

Thus, the only continuous random variable with a constant hazard function is the exponential random variable.

Now, let us consider the reverse process. Assume a a continuous random variable $Y \sim Exp(\lambda)$. A discrete random variable X may be obtained by discretizing Y, such that $X = \lceil Y \rceil$. Therefore,

$$P(X = x_i) = F_X)(x_i) - F_X)(x_i - 1) = (1 - e^{-\lambda x_i}) - (1 - e^{-\lambda(x_i - 1)}).$$

$$P(X = x_i) = 1 - e^{-\lambda x_i} - 1 + e^{-\lambda(x_i - 1)}.$$

$$P(X = x_i) = -e^{-\lambda x_i} + e^{-\lambda(x_i - 1)}.$$

$$P(X = x_i) = e^{-\lambda(x_i - 1)}(1 - e^{-\lambda}).$$

As $p = (1 - e^{-\lambda})$ and $(1 - p)^{x_i - 1} = e^{-\lambda(x_i - 1)}$, then

$$P(X = x_i) = (1 - p)^{x_i - 1} p,$$

which is the PDF of a geometrically distributed random variable.

Memoryless Property - Let X be a continuous random variable exponentially distributed that represents the time to failure of a system. Consider two time instants, t and s. The time interval that represents that the system did not fail until t is (t, ∞), and the time interval that represents that the system survived the instant s is (s, ∞). As $t < s$, then $(t, \infty) \subset (s, \infty)$; Hence, $(t, \infty) \cap (s, \infty) = (s, \infty)$.

From the cumulative distribution function presented in Equation 5.2.81, the probability that the system fails after the instant s given the system survived t is

$$P(X \geq t + s \mid X \geq t) = \frac{P((X \geq s) \cap (X \geq t))}{P(X \geq t)}$$

$$P(X \geq t + s \mid X \geq t) = \frac{P(X \geq s)}{P(X \geq t)}$$

$$P(X \geq t + s \mid X \geq t) = \frac{e^{-\lambda(t+s)}}{e^{-\lambda t}}$$

$$P(X \geq t + s \mid X \geq t) = \frac{e^{-\lambda t} e^{-\lambda s}}{e^{-\lambda t}}.$$

$$P(X \geq t + s \mid X \geq t) = e^{-\lambda s},$$

which shows that the probability of an event occurring after $t + s$, since it did not occur until t depends only on s, and the time passed (t) does not influence the probability of an event occurring. Section 16.3 also shows that the only memoryless continuous random variable is the exponential random variable (see Equation 16.3.4).

Figure 5.18.a shows the probability density function of $X \sim Exp(\lambda)$, $\lambda \in \{4, 6, 10\}$. Likewise, Figure 5.18.b depicts the cumulative probability function of X.

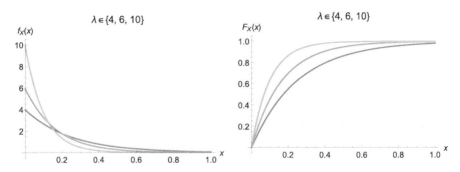

Figure 5.18   pdf (a) cdf (b) of X. $X \sim Exp(\lambda)$, $\lambda \in \{4, 6, 10\}$.

The expected value of X is given by

$$\mu' = \frac{1}{\lambda}. \tag{5.2.83}$$

The variance is specified by

$$\mu_2 = \frac{1}{\lambda^2}. \tag{5.2.84}$$

The standard deviation and the coefficient of variation are specified by

$$(\mu_2)^{1/2} = \frac{1}{\lambda}, \tag{5.2.85}$$

and

$$CoV = 1, \tag{5.2.86}$$

respectively. The skewness and the kurtosis (the fourth standardized central moment) are defined as

$$\tilde{\mu}_3 = 2 \tag{5.2.87}$$

and

$$\tilde{\mu}_4 = 9. \tag{5.2.88}$$

If the kurtosis is provided in comparison to a normal distribution, then we have

$$Kurt(X) = 6. \tag{5.2.89}$$

The exponential moment generating function is

$$M_X(s) = \frac{\lambda}{\lambda - s}, \tag{5.2.90}$$

and the central moment generating function is specified by

$$CM_X(s) = \frac{\lambda e^{-\frac{s}{\lambda}}}{\lambda - s}. \tag{5.2.91}$$

The exponential random variable median is defined as

$$Mdn = \frac{\ln(2)}{\lambda}. \tag{5.2.92}$$

The first and the third quartiles are defined as

$$Q_1 = \frac{\ln\left(\frac{4}{3}\right)}{\lambda}. \tag{5.2.93}$$

and

$$Q_3 = \frac{\ln(4)}{\lambda}. \tag{5.2.94}$$

Example 5.2.7. Consider X is an exponential random variable representing the time to failure (in hours) of a system. Assume the distribution parameter (failure rate) is $\lambda = 10^{-4} h^{-1}$. The probability the system only fails after $4000h$ may be estimated using Equation 5.2.81; hence

$$P(X > x) = 1 - F_X(x) = 1 - (1 - e^{-\lambda x}).$$

$$P(X > 4000h) = 1 - F_X(4000h) = 1 - 1 + e^{-10^{-4} \times 4000} = 0.67032.$$

The mean time to failure of the system may be estimated using Equation 5.2.83, which is

$$\mu' = \frac{1}{\lambda} = 10000h.$$

$\square$

The reader is also invited to read Section 16.3, where more information about this distribution is introduced. The exponential distribution is the fundamental distribution underlying the study of continuous time Markov chains (see Chapter 10), Markovian queues (see Chapter 11) and stochastic Petri nets (see Chapter 13). The random variate generation method based on exponential distribution is depicted in Section 14.3.

5.2.8 GAMMA

The gamma distribution is a family of continuous probability distributions. For instance, the exponential, Erlang, and χ^2 distributions are some particular cases of gamma distributions. The gamma distribution has this name because the gamma function is in the denominator of the gamma density function. The most common representation of the gamma density function of a random variable X has two parameters; γ is the shape parameter, and β is the scale parameter. Some variants also have a location parameter. The probability density function of random variable X distributed according to a two-parameter gamma distribution is

$$f_X(x) = \frac{e^{-\frac{x}{\beta}} x^{\gamma-1} \beta^{-\gamma}}{\Gamma(\gamma)}, \qquad x, \gamma, \beta \geq 0, \qquad (5.2.95)$$

and the respective cumulative distribution function is

$$F_X(x_1) = \int_0^{x_1} \left(\frac{e^{-\frac{x}{\beta}} x^{\gamma-1} \beta^{-\gamma}}{\Gamma(\gamma)} \right) dx, \qquad x, \gamma, \beta \geq 0. \qquad (5.2.96)$$

Figure 5.19.a shows the probability density function of $X \sim Gamma(\gamma, \beta)$, $\gamma \in \{1, 2.5, 4, 6.8\}$ and $\beta = 2$. Likewise, Figure 5.19.b shows the probability density function of $X \sim Gamma(\gamma, \beta)$, $\beta \in \{1, 2.5, 4, 6.8\}$, and $\gamma = 2$.

Figure 5.20.a shows the cumulative probability function of $X \sim Gamma(\gamma, \beta)$, $\gamma \in \{1, 2.5, 4, 6.8\}$ and $\beta = 2$; and Figure 5.20.b the cumulative probability function of $X \sim Gamma(\gamma, \beta)$, $\beta \in \{1, 2.5, 4, 6.8\}$, and $\gamma = 2$.

The expected value of X is given by

$$\mu' = \beta\gamma. \qquad (5.2.97)$$

The variance, the standard deviation, and the coefficient of variation are specified by

$$\mu_2 = \beta^2\gamma, \qquad (5.2.98)$$

$$(\mu_2)^{1/2} = \beta\sqrt{\gamma}, \qquad (5.2.99)$$

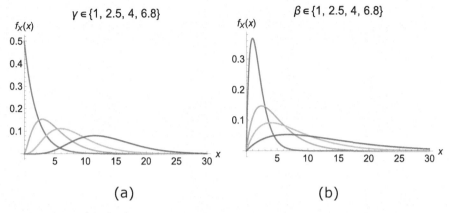

Figure 5.19 pdf (a) pdf (b) of X. $X \sim Gamma(\gamma, \beta)$.

and

$$CoV = \frac{1}{\sqrt{\gamma}}, \tag{5.2.100}$$

respectively. The skewness and the kurtosis (the fourth standardized central moment) are defined as

$$\tilde{\mu}_3 = \frac{2}{\sqrt{\gamma}} \tag{5.2.101}$$

and

$$\tilde{\mu}_4 = \frac{6}{\gamma} + 3. \tag{5.2.102}$$

If the kurtosis is provided in comparison to a normal distribution, then we have

$$Kurt(X) = \frac{6}{\gamma}. \tag{5.2.103}$$

The gamma moment-generating function is

$$M_X(s) = (1 - \beta s)^{-\gamma}, \tag{5.2.104}$$

and the central moment generating function is specified by

$$CM_X(s) = e^{\beta \gamma(-s)}(1 - \beta s)^{-\gamma}. \tag{5.2.105}$$

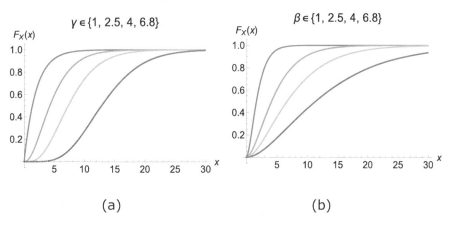

Figure 5.20 cdf (a) cdf (b) of X. $X \sim Gamma(\gamma, \beta)$.

Example 5.2.8. Consider X is a gamma random variable that represents the time of execution of a complex system function (in seconds). Assume the distribution parameters are $\gamma = 4.8$ and $\beta = 100\,s$. The probability the system function is executed in less than $300\,s$ ($P(x_1 < 300\,s)$) may be estimated using Equation 5.2.96, that is

$$P(X < x_1) = F_X(x_1) = \int_0^{x_1} \left(\frac{e^{-\frac{x}{\beta}} x^{\gamma-1} \beta^{-\gamma}}{\Gamma(\gamma)} \right) dx, \qquad x, \gamma, \beta \geq 0.$$

Hence

$$P(X < 300\,s) = \int_0^{300} \left(\frac{e^{-\frac{x}{100}} x^{4.8-1} 100^{-4.8}}{\Gamma(4.8)} \right) dx = 0.21275.$$

The mean time to execute the system function may be estimated using Equation 5.2.97; thus

$$\mu' = \beta\gamma = 100 \times 4.8 = 480\,s.$$

$\square$

For certain parameter values, a gamma distributed random variable $X \sim Gamma(\gamma, \beta)$ is equal to

- an exponential random variable, $X \sim Exp\left(\frac{1}{\beta}\right)$,   when $\gamma = 1$,

- an Erlang random variable, $X \sim Erl(\gamma, \beta)$,   when $\gamma > 1$, $\gamma \in \mathbb{N}$, (See next.)

- a chi-square random variable, $X \sim \chi^2_{2 \times \gamma}$,   if $\beta = 2$.

5.2.9 PHASE-TYPE

Exponential random variables are widely adopted in performance and reliability modeling. The main reason for adopting this distribution is twofold. First, the exponential distribution indeed well represents some phenomena in that field. Second is its mathematical tractability due to its memoryless property. Nevertheless, in many cases, the exponential distribution is simply not suitable to represent the system. An alternative to consider in such cases is adopting more general distributions that phases of exponential distributions can represent. Such a class of distribution is usually called phase-type [413] distributions (phases of exponential distributions) or expolinomial [179]. Additionally, as we shall see in Section 13.3.8, for instance, phase-type distributions are very useful when it is required to represent a probability distribution, and the only data available are the mean value and the standard deviation. In this family of distributions, we have

- Exponential,

- Erlang,

- Hypoexponential,

- Hyperexponential,

- Generalized Erlang, and

- Cox distributions.

Some of these distributions are presented in this chapter and applied and discussed in more depth in specific chapters.

5.2.10 ERLANG

As mentioned when describing the gamma distribution, the Erlang random variable is a particular case of the gamma distribution, when the shape parameter of the gamma distribution is $\gamma > 1$, $\gamma \in \mathbb{N}$. When $\gamma = 1$, the gamma distribution, and consequently the Erlang distribution, is an exponential distribution with parameter $1/\beta$. The notation adopted when presenting the gamma distribution considered the shape parameter, γ - number of phases, and the scale parameter, in this case, the mean value of each phase. In this section, we adopt λ as the shape parameter, where $\lambda = 1/\beta$; thus λ is the rate of each exponential phase.

Before presenting the main characteristics of the Erlang distribution, let us stress two aspects: (1) its coefficient of variation is smaller than one, and (2) the inverse of its square coefficient of variation is a natural number larger than one.

The probability density function of random variable X distributed according to an Erlang distribution is

$$f_X(x) = \frac{e^{-x\lambda}x^{\gamma-1}\lambda^{\gamma}}{(\gamma-1)!}. \tag{5.2.106}$$

and the respective cumulative distribution function is

$$F_X(x_1) = \frac{\lambda^{\gamma}}{(\gamma-1)!}\int_0^{x_1} e^{-x\lambda}x^{-1+\gamma}dx. \tag{5.2.107}$$

The Erlang random distribution can also be thought of as a succession of exponential phases. For instance, consider the random variable $X \sim Erl(\gamma, \lambda)$; it can be graphically shown as in Figure 5.21, in which we see a sequence of size γ of exponential phases. Each exponential phase has λ, $Exp(\lambda)$, as its parameters, and $1/\lambda$ is the mean time between two successive arrivals.

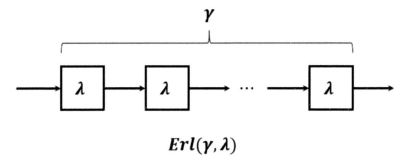

$$Erl(\gamma, \lambda)$$

Figure 5.21 $Erl(\gamma, \lambda)$ Represented as γ Exponential Phases, $Exp(\lambda)$,in Tandem.

For instance, consider two continuous, independent, non-negative and identically distributed random variables X and Y, and a third random variable that is defined by the sum of X and Y, that is $Z = Y + X$. Assume $X, Y \sim Exp(\lambda)$ $x, y \geq 0$; then the density function of Z if obtained by the convolution $f_Z(z) = (f_Y * f_X)(z)$, $z \geq 0$. For continuous non-negative random variables, we have

$$(f_Y * f_X)(z) = \int_0^z f_Y(z-u)f_X(u)du. \tag{5.2.108}$$

As

$$f_X(x) = \lambda e^{-\lambda x} \quad \text{and} \quad f_Y(y) = \lambda e^{-\lambda y},$$

and $Y = Z - X$, then

$$f_Z(z) = (f_Y * f_X)(z) = \int_0^z \left(\lambda e^{-\lambda(z-u)}\right)\left(\lambda e^{-\lambda u}\right)du.$$

$$f_Z(z) = (f_Y * f_X)(z) = \int_0^z \lambda e^{-\lambda z} e^{\lambda u} \lambda e^{-\lambda u} \, du.$$

$$f_Z(z) = (f_Y * f_X)(z) = \int_0^z \lambda^2 e^{-\lambda z} \, du.$$

$$f_Z(z) = (f_Y * f_X)(z) = \left(\lambda^2 e^{-\lambda z}\right) \int_0^z du.$$

$$f_Z(z) = (f_Y * f_X)(z) = \lambda^2 z e^{-\lambda z},$$

which is the same if we take Equation 5.2.106 for $\gamma = 2$ and λ

$$f_Z(z) = \frac{e^{-z\lambda} z^{\gamma-1} \lambda^{\gamma}}{(\gamma-1)!}.$$

$$f_Z(z) = \frac{e^{-z\lambda} z^{2-1} \lambda^2}{(2-1)!}.$$

$$f_Z(z) = \lambda^2 z e^{-z\lambda} \qquad z \geq 0.$$

Figure 5.22.a shows the probability density function of $X \sim Erl(\gamma, \lambda)$, $\gamma \in \{1, 3, 4, 7\}$ and $\lambda = 0.5$. Similarly, Figure 5.22.b shows the probability density function of $X \sim Erl(\gamma, \lambda)$, $\lambda \in \{1, 1/3, 1/4, 1/7\}$ and $\gamma = 2$.

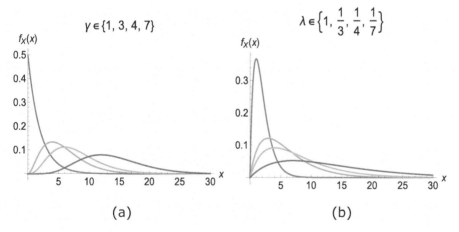

Figure 5.22 pdf (a) pdf (b) of X. $X \sim Erl(\gamma, \lambda)$.

Figure 5.23.a shows the cumulative probability function of $X \sim Erl(\gamma, \lambda)$, $\gamma \in \{1, 3, 4, 7\}$ and $\lambda = 0.5$; and Figure 5.23.b shows the cumulative probability function of $X \sim Erl(\gamma, \lambda)$, $\lambda \in \{1, 1/3, 1/4, 1/7\}$ and $\gamma = 2$.

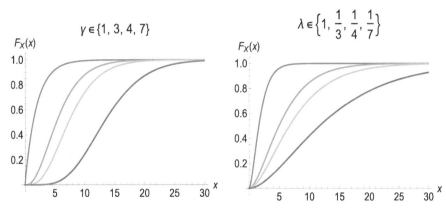

Figure 5.23   cdf (a) cdf (b) of X. $X \sim Erl(\gamma, \lambda)$.

The expected value of X is given by

$$\mu' = \frac{\gamma}{\lambda}.$$
(5.2.109)

The variance, the standard deviation, and the coefficient of variation are specified by

$$\mu_2 = \frac{\gamma}{\lambda^2},$$
(5.2.110)

$$(\mu_2)^{1/2} = \frac{\sqrt{\gamma}}{\lambda},$$
(5.2.111)

and

$$CoV = \frac{1}{\sqrt{\gamma}}, \qquad CoV < 1, \qquad \frac{1}{Cov^2} \in \mathbb{N}^+, \qquad \frac{1}{Cov^2} > 1,$$
(5.2.112)

respectively. The skewness and the kurtosis (the fourth standardized central moment) are defined as

$$\tilde{\mu}_3 = \frac{2}{\sqrt{\gamma}}$$
(5.2.113)

and

$$\tilde{\mu}_4 = \frac{6}{\gamma} + 3.$$
(5.2.114)

If the kurtosis is provided in comparison to a normal distribution, then we have

$$Kurt(X) = \frac{6}{\gamma}.$$
(5.2.115)

The Erlang moment-generating function is

$$M_X(s) = \left(1 - \frac{s}{\lambda}\right)^{-\gamma}, \tag{5.2.116}$$

and the central moment generating function is specified by

$$CM_X(s) = e^{-\frac{\gamma s}{\lambda}}\left(1 - \frac{s}{\lambda}\right)^{-\gamma}. \tag{5.2.117}$$

Example 5.2.9. Assume a system in which the time between transaction requests (X) is distributed according to $Erl(\gamma, \lambda)$, where $\gamma = 6$ and $\lambda = 0.01\,s^{-1}$, $X \sim Erl(\gamma, \lambda)$. The probability of having a request arrival by $450\,s$ is $P(X \leq 450\,s)$ may be calculated via Equation 5.2.107; hence

$$P(X \leq t) = F_X(x_1) = \frac{\lambda^{\gamma}}{(\gamma - 1)!}\int_0^{x_1} e^{-x\lambda}x^{\gamma-1}\,dx.$$

$$P(X \leq 450\,s) = F_X(450\,s) = \frac{0.01^6}{(6-1)!}\int_0^{450} e^{-0.01x}x^{6-1}\,dx.$$

$$P(X \leq 450\,s) = 0.29707,$$

and the mean time between request arrivals may be calculated using Equation 5.2.109, that is

$$\mu' = \frac{\gamma}{\lambda}.$$

$$\mu' = \frac{6}{0.01\,s^{-1}} = 600\,s.$$

$\square$

The Erlang distribution is adopted in many modeling problems throughout this book. More information on the Erlang distribution is presented in Section 16.3. A moment matching method using the Erlang distribution and empirical data is presented in Section 13.3.8. A method for random variate generation based on Erlang distribution is presented in Section 14.3.

5.2.11 HYPOEXPONENTIAL

As we have for Erlang random variables, we can use a sequence of exponential phases to model random variables that have less variability than an exponentially distributed random, that it $CoV < 1$. Therefore, hypoexponential can be seen as a generalization of the Erlang distribution in which the rates of each exponential phase are not constrained to be equal. However, the inverse of its square coefficient of variation even being larger than one, it is not natural number, $1/CoV^2 > 1$, $1/CoV^2 \notin \mathbb{N}$.

Consider two continuous, independent, non-negative distributed random variables X and Y, and a third random variable that is defined by the sum of X and Y, that is $Z = Y + X$. Assume $X, \sim Exp(\lambda_1)$ and $Y \sim Exp(\lambda_2)$, $x, y \geq 0$; then the density function of Z is the joint density functions of X and Y. Such a function is obtained by the convolution $f_Z(z) = (f_Y * f_X)(z)$, $z \geq 0$. For continuous non-negative random variables, we have (see Equation 5.2.108)

$$(f_Y * f_X)(z) = \int_0^z f_Y(z - u) f_X(u) \, du.$$

As

$$f_X(x) = \lambda_1 e^{-\lambda_1 x} \quad \text{and} \quad f_Y(y) = \lambda_2 e^{-\lambda_2 y},$$

and $Y = Z - X$, then

$$f_Z(z) = (f_Y * f_X)(z) = \int_0^z \left(\lambda_2 e^{-\lambda_2(z-u)} \right) \left(\lambda_1 e^{-\lambda_1 u} \right) du.$$

$$f_Z(z) = (f_Y * f_X)(z) = \int_0^z \lambda_2 e^{-\lambda_2 z} e^{\lambda_2 u} \lambda_1 e^{-\lambda_1 u} du.$$

$$f_Z(z) = (f_Y * f_X)(z) = \lambda_1 \lambda_2 e^{-\lambda_2 z} \int_0^z e^{\lambda_2 u - \lambda_1 u} du.$$

$$f_Z(z) = (f_Y * f_X)(z) = \lambda_1 \lambda_2 e^{-\lambda_2 z} \int_0^z e^{(\lambda_2 - \lambda_1)u} du.$$

$$f_Z(z) = (f_Y * f_X)(z) = \frac{\lambda_1 \lambda_2 e^{-\lambda_2 z} \left(1 - e^{z(-\lambda_1 + \lambda_2)} \right)}{\lambda_1 - \lambda_2}.$$

$$f_Z(z) = (f_Y * f_X)(z) = \frac{\lambda_1 \lambda_2 \left(e^{-z\lambda_2} - e^{-z\lambda_1} \right)}{\lambda_1 - \lambda_2}.$$

Hence,

$$f_Z(z) = (f_Y * f_X)(z) = \frac{\lambda_1 \lambda_2 e^{-z\lambda_2}}{\lambda_1 - \lambda_2} - \frac{\lambda_1 \lambda_2 e^{-z\lambda_1}}{\lambda_1 - \lambda_2}, \qquad z \geq 0. \qquad (5.2.118)$$

The cumulative distribution function is then obtained by

$$F_Z(x) = \int_0^x \left(\frac{e^{-z\lambda_2} \lambda_1 \lambda_2}{\lambda_1 - \lambda_2} + \frac{e^{-z\lambda_1} \lambda_1 \lambda_2}{-\lambda_1 + \lambda_2} \right) dz, \qquad z \geq 0,$$

which leads to

$$F_Z(x) = \frac{\lambda_1 - e^{-x\lambda_2}\lambda_1 + \left(-1 + e^{-x\lambda_1}\right)\lambda_2}{\lambda_1 - \lambda_2}.$$

$$F_Z(x) = \frac{\lambda_1 - \lambda_1 e^{-x\lambda_2}}{\lambda_1 - \lambda_2} + \frac{\lambda_2 e^{-x\lambda_1} - \lambda_2}{\lambda_1 - \lambda_2}.$$

$$F_Z(x) = \frac{\lambda_1}{\lambda_1 - \lambda_2} - \frac{\lambda_1 e^{-x\lambda_2}}{\lambda_1 - \lambda_2} + \frac{\lambda_2 e^{-x\lambda_1}}{\lambda_1 - \lambda_2} - \frac{\lambda_2}{\lambda_1 - \lambda_2}.$$

$$F_Z(x) = \frac{\lambda_1 - \lambda_2}{\lambda_1 - \lambda_2} - \frac{\lambda_1 e^{-x\lambda_2}}{\lambda_1 - \lambda_2} + \frac{\lambda_2 e^{-x\lambda_1}}{\lambda_1 - \lambda_2}.$$

Thus,

$$F_Z(x) = 1 - \frac{\lambda_1 e^{-x\lambda_2}}{\lambda_1 - \lambda_2} + \frac{\lambda_2 e^{-x\lambda_1}}{\lambda_1 - \lambda_2}. \tag{5.2.119}$$

Now, if we consider random variable $Z \sim Hypo(\lambda_1, \lambda_2)$ (see the PDF 5.2.118) and $V \sim Exp(\lambda_3)$, where Z and V are non-negative, $z \geq 0$ and $v \geq 0$, and independent, then the distribution of $W = Z + V$ is

$$f_W(w) = (f_Z * f_V)(w) = \frac{\lambda_1 \lambda_2 \lambda_3 e^{-\lambda_3 w}}{(\lambda_1 - \lambda_3)(\lambda_2 - \lambda_3)} + \frac{\lambda_1 \lambda_2 \lambda_3 e^{-\lambda_1 w}}{(\lambda_2 - \lambda_1)(\lambda_3 - \lambda_1)} + \tag{5.2.120}$$

$$\frac{\lambda_1 \lambda_2 \lambda_3 e^{-\lambda_2 w}}{(\lambda_1 - \lambda_2)(\lambda_3 - \lambda_2)}. \qquad w \geq 0.$$

Generalizing for a hypoexponential random variable X with γ exponential independent phases, $X \sim Hypo(\lambda_1, \lambda_2, \dots \lambda_\gamma)$, the probability density function of random variable X is

$$f_X(x) = \sum_{i=1}^{\gamma} \prod_{j=1, j \neq i}^{\gamma} \frac{\lambda_i \lambda_j e^{-\lambda_i x}}{\lambda_j - \lambda_i}, \qquad x \geq 0, \quad i \leq j \leq \gamma. \tag{5.2.121}$$

Now, we present some measures for a random variable distributed according to a hypoexponential function with two phases, $X \sim Hypo(\lambda_1, \lambda_2)$. The expected value of X is given by

$$\mu' = \frac{1}{\lambda_2} + \frac{1}{\lambda_1}. \tag{5.2.122}$$

The variance, the standard deviation, and the coefficient of variation are specified by

$$\mu_2 = \frac{1}{\lambda_2^2} + \frac{1}{\lambda_1^2}, \tag{5.2.123}$$

$$(\mu_2)^{1/2} = \sqrt{\frac{1}{\lambda_2^2} + \frac{1}{\lambda_1^2}}, \tag{5.2.124}$$

and

$$CoV = \frac{\lambda_1 \lambda_2 \sqrt{\frac{1}{\lambda_2^2} + \frac{1}{\lambda_1^2}}}{\lambda_1 + \lambda_2}, \tag{5.2.125}$$

respectively. The skewness and the kurtosis (the fourth standardized central moment) are defined as

$$\tilde{\mu}_3 = \frac{2\left(\frac{1}{\lambda_2^3} + \frac{1}{\lambda_1^3}\right)}{\left(\frac{1}{\lambda_2^2} + \frac{1}{\lambda_1^2}\right)^{3/2}} \tag{5.2.126}$$

and

$$\tilde{\mu}_4 = \frac{6\left(\lambda_1^4 + \lambda_2^4\right)}{\left(\lambda_1^2 + \lambda_2^2\right)^2} + 3. \tag{5.2.127}$$

If the kurtosis is provided in comparison to a normal distribution, then we have

$$Kurt(X) = \frac{6\left(\lambda_1^4 + \lambda_2^4\right)}{\left(\lambda_1^2 + \lambda_2^2\right)^2}. \tag{5.2.128}$$

The $Hypo(\lambda_1, \lambda_2)$ moment-generating function is

$$M_X(s) = \frac{\lambda_1 \lambda_2}{(s - \lambda_1)(s - \lambda_2)}, \tag{5.2.129}$$

and the central moment generating function is specified by

$$CM_X(s) = \frac{\lambda_1 \lambda_2 e^{\left(\frac{1}{\lambda_2} + \frac{1}{\lambda_1}\right)(-s)}}{(s - \lambda_1)(s - \lambda_2)}. \tag{5.2.130}$$

Example 5.2.10. Assume the time to repair a system is represented by random variable X distributed according to $Hypo(\lambda_1, \lambda_2)$, where $\lambda_1 = 0.06 h^{-1}$ and $\lambda_2 = 0.15 h^{-1}$. The probability of having a repairing of the system by $10 h$ may be calculated using Function 5.2.119; hence

$$P(X \le x) = F_X(x) = 1 - \frac{\lambda_1 e^{-x\lambda_2}}{\lambda_1 - \lambda_2} + \frac{\lambda_2 e^{-x\lambda_1}}{\lambda_1 - \lambda_2}.$$

$$P(X \le 10h) = F_X(10h) = 1 - \frac{0.06 \times e^{-10 \times 0.15}}{0.06 - 0.15} + \frac{0.15 \times e^{-10 \times 0.06}}{0.06 - 0.15} = 0.234067.$$

The mean time to repair, the standard deviation of the time to repair, and the respective coefficient of variation are calculated using Equation 5.2.122, and Equation 5.2.125, respectively.

$$\mu' = \frac{1}{\lambda_2} + \frac{1}{\lambda_1} = 23.33\,h,$$

$$(\mu_2)^{1/2} = \sqrt{\frac{1}{\lambda_2^2} + \frac{1}{\lambda_1^2}} = 17.95\,h,$$

and

$$CoV = \frac{\lambda_1 \lambda_2 \sqrt{\frac{1}{\lambda_2^2} + \frac{1}{\lambda_1^2}}}{\lambda_1 + \lambda_2} = 0.77.$$

The probability density function of X is depicted in Figure 5.24.

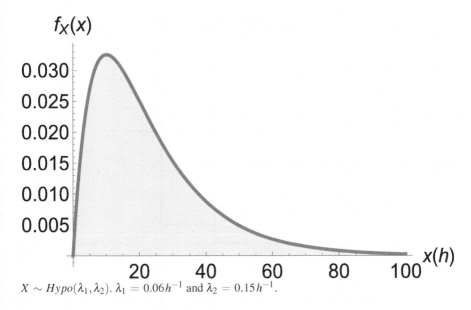

$X \sim Hypo(\lambda_1, \lambda_2)$. $\lambda_1 = 0.06h^{-1}$ and $\lambda_2 = 0.15h^{-1}$.

Figure 5.24   Probability Density Function of X.

A moment matching method using the hypoexponential distribution and empirical data is presented in Section 13.3.8.

5.2.12 HYPEREXPONENTIAL

The hyperexponential distribution describes n exponential processes in parallel. This distribution can be used to approximate empirical distributions with a coefficient of variation larger than one ($CoV > 1$). Assume X is a continuous random variable whose probability density function is composed of n parallel phases of exponential probability density functions. The probability density function of X is defined by

$$f_X(x) = \sum_{i=1}^{n} \alpha_i \lambda_i e^{-\lambda_i x} \qquad x \geq 0, \qquad (5.2.131)$$

where α_i is the probability of choosing phase i and $\sum_{i=1}^{n} \alpha_1 = 1$. The probability distribution of X is a hyperexponential distribution with n phases, whose parameters are α_i and λ_i, $1, \leq i \leq n$, $i \in \mathbb{N}$. A short notation to express that X is distributed according to a hyperexponential distribution with n phases is $X \sim Hyperexp(\alpha_1, ..., \alpha_n, \lambda_1, ..., \lambda_n)$. Figure 5.25 shows a graphical representation of this distribution.

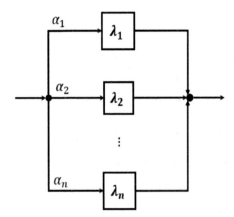

Figure 5.25 $X \sim Hyperexp(\alpha_1, ..., \alpha_n, \lambda_1, ..., \lambda_n)$

The cumulative distribution function is

$$F_X(x) = \sum_{i=1}^{n} \alpha_i (1 - e^{-\lambda_i x}) \qquad x \geq 0. \qquad (5.2.132)$$

Now assume X is a continuous random variable distributed according to a hyperexponential distribution with two phase, and the respective parameters: α, $(1 - \alpha)$, λ_1 and λ_2. The probability density function of X is defined by

$$f_X(x) = \alpha\lambda_1 e^{\lambda_1(-x)} + (1-\alpha)\lambda_2 e^{\lambda_2(-x)} \qquad x \geq 0, \qquad (5.2.133)$$

and the cumulative distribution function is

$$F_X(x) = 1 - (1-\alpha)e^{-x\lambda_2} - \alpha e^{-x\lambda_1}, \qquad x \geq 0. \qquad (5.2.134)$$

Figure 5.26.a shows the probability density function of $X \sim Hyperexp(\alpha, 1 - \alpha, \lambda_1, \lambda_2)$, where $\lambda_1 = 10$, $\lambda_1 = 20$, and $\alpha \in \{0.1, 0.5, 0.9\}$. Similarly, Figure 5.26.b shows the cumulative probability function of X.

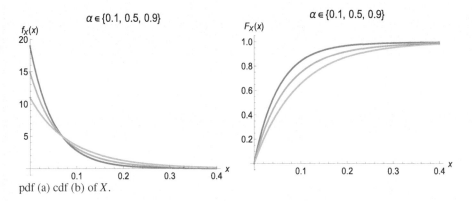

pdf (a) cdf (b) of X.

Figure 5.26 $X \sim Hyperexp(\alpha, 1 - \alpha, \lambda_1, \lambda_2)$, $\lambda_1 = 10$, $\lambda_1 = 20$, $\alpha \in \{0.1, 0.5, 0.9\}$.

The expected value of X is given by

$$\mu' = \frac{\alpha}{\lambda_1} + \frac{1-\alpha}{\lambda_2}. \qquad (5.2.135)$$

The variance, the standard deviation, and the coefficient of variation are specified by

$$\mu_2 = \frac{(\alpha-2)\alpha}{\lambda_1^2} + \frac{1-\alpha^2}{\lambda_2^2} + \frac{2(\alpha-1)\alpha}{\lambda_1\lambda_2}, \qquad (5.2.136)$$

$$(\mu_2)^{1/2} = \sqrt{\frac{1-\alpha^2}{\lambda_2^2} + \frac{2(\alpha-1)\alpha}{\lambda_1\lambda_2} - \frac{(\alpha-2)\alpha}{\lambda_1^2}}, \qquad (5.2.137)$$

and

$$CoV = -\frac{\lambda_1\lambda_2\sqrt{\frac{1-\alpha^2}{\lambda_2^2} + \frac{2(\alpha-1)\alpha}{\lambda_1\lambda_2} - \frac{(\alpha-2)\alpha}{\lambda_1^2}}}{(\alpha-1)\lambda_1 - \alpha\lambda_2}, \qquad (5.2.138)$$

respectively.

The $Hyperexp(\alpha, 1 - \alpha, \lambda_1, \lambda_2)$ moment-generating function is

$$M_X(s) = \frac{\alpha \lambda_1}{\lambda_1 - s} + \frac{(1 - \alpha)\lambda_2}{\lambda_2 - s}, \tag{5.2.139}$$

and the central moment generating function is specified by

$$CM_X(s) = e^{-s\left(\frac{\alpha}{\lambda_1} + \frac{1-\alpha}{\lambda_2}\right)} \left(\frac{\alpha \lambda_1}{\lambda_1 - s} + \frac{(1 - \alpha)\lambda_2}{\lambda_2 - s} \right). \tag{5.2.140}$$

Example 5.2.11. Assume the time between request arrivals (X) in a system is distributed according to $X \sim Hyperexp(\alpha, 1 - \alpha, \lambda_1, \lambda_2)$, $\alpha = 0.35$, $\lambda_1 = 10 s^{-1}$, and $\lambda_1 = 20 s^{-1}$. The probability of having a request arrival by $x_1 = 0.15 s$ $(150 ms)$ is $P(X \leq 0.15 s)$ which may be calculated via Equation 5.2.134; hence

$$P(X \leq x_1) = F_X(x_1) = 1 - (1 - \alpha)e^{-x\lambda_2} - \alpha e^{-x\lambda_1}.$$

$$P(X \leq 0.15 s) = F_X(0.15 s) = 1 - (1 - 0.35)e^{-0.15 s \times 20 s^{-1}} - 0.35 e^{-0.15 s \times 10 s^{-1}}.$$

$$P(X \leq 0.15 s) = 0.8895.$$

The mean time between request arrivals, the standard deviation, and the coefficient of variation may be calculated using Equation 5.2.135, Equation 5.2.137, and Equation 5.2.138, respectively.

$$\mu' = \frac{\alpha}{\lambda_1} + \frac{1 - \alpha}{\lambda_2} = 67.5 ms,$$

$$(\mu_2)^{1/2} = \sqrt{\frac{1 - \alpha^2}{\lambda_2^2} + \frac{2(\alpha - 1)\alpha}{\lambda_1 \lambda_2} - \frac{(\alpha - 2)\alpha}{\lambda_1^2}} = 75 ms,$$

and

$$CoV = -\frac{\lambda_1 \lambda_2 \sqrt{\frac{1 - \alpha^2}{\lambda_2^2} + \frac{2(\alpha - 1)\alpha}{\lambda_1 \lambda_2} - \frac{(\alpha - 2)\alpha}{\lambda_1^2}}}{(\alpha - 1)\lambda_1 - \alpha\lambda_2} = 1.1179.$$

□

The hyperexponential random variable is adopted in many modeling problems throughout this book when $CoV > 1$. More details about the hyperexponential distribution are discussed in Section 16.3. A moment matching method using the hyperexponential distribution and empirical data is depicted in Section 13.3.8. Finally, a method for random variate generation based on hyperexponential distribution is presented in Section 14.3.

5.2.13 COX

A Cox random variable has a phase-type distribution that is a mixture of hypoexponential and hyperexponential distributions [83]. It can be adopted to represent an empirical distribution whose coefficient of variation is smaller, equal to or greater than one. The model consists of n sequential exponential phases, each phase with parameter λ_i, $1 \leq i \leq n$, $i \in \mathbb{N}$, and probabilities (α_i) that allows finishing the sequence at phase i or continuing the sequence by continuing to the next phase $(i+1)$, α_i, $1 \leq i \leq n-1$, $i \in \mathbb{N}$. At the last phase, the sequence is concluded anyway. Figure 5.27.a presents a graphical notation of how such a phase-type distribution is arranged.

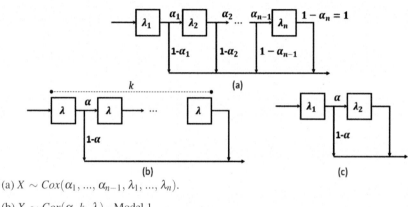

(a) $X \sim Cox(\alpha_1, ..., \alpha_{n-1}, \lambda_1, ..., \lambda_n)$.

(b) $X \sim Cox(\alpha, k, \lambda)$ - Model 1.

(c) $X \sim Cox(\alpha, \lambda_1, \lambda_2)$ - Model 2

Figure 5.27 Cox Distribution.

As $\lambda_i \in \mathbb{R}^+$ and $\alpha_i \in [0, 1]$, the number of configurations (particular Cox distribution instances) is infinity. We concentrate our study on two more specific Cox distribution configurations, which are depicted in Figure 5.27.b (Model 1) and Figure 5.27.c (Model 2) [52, 414]. The model depicted in Figure 5.27.b has k sequential exponential phases, each with a rate parameter equal to λ, and only two exit possibilities of sequence, that is, after executing phase 1, the model may proceed in the sequence by executing the subsequent phases with probability α or exit the sequence after executing the first phase only. The probability of leaving after the first phase is $1 - \alpha$. The second exit possibility is after executing the complete sequence of exponential phases.

The second specific Cox model has only two exponential phases, each with parameter λ_1 and λ_2, respectively. As in the previous model, we have two possibilities for exiting the sequence. First, after the execution of the first phases with $1 - \alpha$, the other exiting point is after the execution of the second exponential phase. Figure 5.27.c depicts this model.

The model depicted in Figure 5.27.b, *Cox Model 1*, may have the parameter values carefully chosen to represent empirical data with coefficient of variation smaller or equal to one ($CoV \leq 1$), although it may also represent data with $CoV \leq 1.20416$. The respective CoV maximal value is obtained for $\alpha = 0.107143$.

On the other hand, the model depicted in Figure 5.27.c, *Cox Model 2*, may have the parameter values chosen to represent empirical data with coefficient of variation higher than one ($CoV > 1$). Indeed, the *Cox Model 2* allows representing empirical data with $CoV \geq \frac{1}{\sqrt{2}}$.

Cox Model 1 - A random variable that obeys the Cox distribution depicted in Figure 5.27.b is denoted by $X \sim Cox(\alpha, k, \lambda)$. The probability density function of random variable X distributed according to a *Cox Model 1* distribution is

$$f_X(x) = e^{-x\lambda}\lambda - e^{-x\lambda}\alpha\lambda + \frac{e^{-x\lambda}x^{k-1}\alpha\lambda^k}{(k-1)!}, \qquad x \geq 0, \qquad (5.2.141)$$

and the respective cumulative distribution function is

$$F_X(z) = \frac{x^k\alpha\lambda^k(x\lambda)^{-k}\left((k-1)! - \int_{z\lambda}^{\infty}x^{k-1}e^{-x}dx\right)}{(k-1)!} - e^{-z\lambda}\left(e^{z\lambda} - 1\right)(\alpha - 1),$$
$$z \geq 0. \qquad (5.2.142)$$

The expected value of X is given by

$$\mu' = \frac{1 + (k-1)\alpha}{\lambda}. \qquad (5.2.143)$$

The variance, the standard deviation, and the coefficient of variation are specified by

$$\mu_2 = \frac{1 + (k-1)(k - (k-1)\alpha)\alpha}{\lambda^2}, \qquad (5.2.144)$$

$$(\mu_2)^{1/2} = \frac{\sqrt{1 + (k-1)(k - (k-1)\alpha)\alpha}}{\lambda}, \qquad (5.2.145)$$

and

$$CoV = \frac{\sqrt{1 + (k-1)(k - (k-1)\alpha)\alpha}}{1 + (k-1)\alpha}. \qquad (5.2.146)$$

The *Cox Model 1* moment-generating function is

$$M_X(s) = \frac{2(\alpha - 1)}{\lambda^2} + \frac{-(1+k)k\alpha}{\lambda^2} + \frac{(\alpha - k\alpha - 1)^2}{\lambda^2} + \qquad (5.2.147)$$

$$\frac{2(\alpha - k\alpha - 1)\left(-\frac{\alpha-1}{\lambda} + \frac{k\alpha}{\lambda}\right)}{\lambda}, \qquad s \geq 0.$$

Example 5.2.12. The time to repair a system is represented by *Cox Model 1*, that is $X \sim Cox(\alpha, k, \lambda)$, where $\alpha = 0.9$, $k = 5$, and $\lambda = 0.2\,h^{-1}$. The probability that time to repair is higher than $30\,h$ may be computed using Equation 5.2.142, such that

$$P(X > 30h) = 1 - F(30h) = 0.2568.$$

The mean time to repair and the respective coefficient of variation may be calculated using Equation 5.2.143 and Equation 5.2.146, respectively.

$$\mu' = 23\,h,$$

and

$$CoV = 0.5343.$$

$\square$

A moment matching method using *Cox Model 1* and empirical data is depicted in Section 13.3.8.

Cox Model 2 - A random variable that obeys the Cox distribution depicted in Figure 5.27.c is denoted by $X \sim Cox(\alpha, \lambda_1, \lambda_2)$. The probability density function of random variable X distributed according to an *Cox Model 2* distribution is

$$f_X(x) = \frac{e^{-\lambda_2 x}\alpha\lambda_1\lambda_2}{\lambda_1 - \lambda_2} + e^{-\lambda_1 x}\lambda_1\left(1 - \alpha + \frac{\alpha\lambda_2}{\lambda_2 - \lambda_1}\right), \qquad x \geq 0, \quad (5.2.148)$$

and the respective cumulative distribution function is

$$F_X(x) = \frac{e^{-\lambda_2 x}\alpha\lambda_1\lambda_2}{\lambda_1 - \lambda_2} + e^{-\lambda_1 x}\lambda_1\left(1 - \alpha + \frac{\alpha\lambda_2}{\lambda_2 - \lambda_1}\right), \qquad x \geq 0. \quad (5.2.149)$$

The expected value of X is given by

$$\mu' = \frac{1}{\lambda_1} + \frac{\alpha}{\lambda_2}. \qquad (5.2.150)$$

The variance, the standard deviation, and the coefficient of variation are specified by

$$\mu_2 = \frac{1}{\lambda_1^2} - \frac{\alpha(\alpha - 2)}{\lambda_2^2}, \tag{5.2.151}$$

$$(\mu_2)^{1/2} = \sqrt{\frac{1}{\lambda_1^2} - \frac{\alpha(\alpha - 2)}{\lambda_2^2}}, \tag{5.2.152}$$

and

$$CoV = \frac{\lambda_1 \lambda_2 \sqrt{\frac{1}{\lambda_1^2} - \frac{1}{\alpha(\alpha-2)} \lambda_2^2}}{\alpha \lambda_1 + \lambda_2}. \tag{5.2.153}$$

The *Cox Model 2* moment-generating function is

$$M_X(s) = \frac{\lambda_1 \left(s(\alpha - 1) + \lambda_2 \right)}{(s - \lambda_1)(s - \lambda_2)}, \tag{5.2.154}$$

and the respective central moment-generating function is

$$CM_X(s) = \frac{e^{-s\left(\frac{1}{\lambda_1} + \frac{\alpha}{\lambda_2}\right)} \lambda_1 \left(s(\alpha - 1) + \lambda_2 \right)}{(s - \lambda_1)(s - \lambda_2)}. \tag{5.2.155}$$

Example 5.2.13. The time to repair a system is represented by *Cox Model 2*, that is $X \sim Cox(\alpha, \lambda_1, \lambda_2)$, where $\alpha = 0.7$, $\lambda_1 = 3.2\,h^{-1}$ and $\lambda_2 = 30.854 \times 10^{-3}\,h^{-1}$. The probability that time to repair is higher than $30\,h$ may be computed using Equation 5.2.149, such that

$$P(X > 30h) = 1 - F(30h) = 0.2801.$$

The mean time to repair and the respective coefficient of variation may be calculated using Equation 5.2.150 and Equation 5.2.153, respectively.

$$\mu' = 23\,h,$$

and

$$CoV = 1.3443.$$

$\square$

A moment matching method using *Cox Model 2* and empirical data is presented in Section 13.3.8.

5.2.14   WEIBULL

The Weibull distribution has the noteworthy characteristics that it can represent decreasing, constant, and increasing hazard functions (see Section 16.2), a property that makes it very appealing for reliability modeling.

We know that a general cumulative distribution function, for non-negative random variables, may be represented by (see Equation 4.2.6)

$$F_X(x) = 1 - e^{-\int_0^x \lambda(x) \times dx},$$

where $\lambda(x)$ the hazard function. The hazard function is defined as (see Function 4.2.3)

$$\lambda(x) = -\frac{dF_X^c(x)}{dx} \times \frac{1}{F_X^c(x)}, \qquad x \geq 0.$$

Hence, the parameters of the cumulative distribution function may be chosen so that $\lambda(x)$ (the hazard function) may be decreasing, constant, or increasing. We already have seen that when $\lambda(x)$ is constant, we have an exponential distribution, since $\lambda(x) = \lambda$

$$\int_0^x \lambda \times dx = \lambda x,$$

which results in $F_X(x) = 1 - e^{-\lambda x}$.

Let Y be a continuous random variable exponentially distributed, $Y \sim Exp(\lambda)$, where $\lambda = 1$. Hence, the probability density function of Y is

$$f_Y(y) = \lambda e^{-\lambda y} = e^{-y}, \qquad y \geq 0$$

and the cumulative distribution function is

$$F_Y(y) = 1 - e^{-\lambda y} = 1 - e^{-y}.$$

Now, let us define another continuous random variable, X, so that

$$X = \beta Y^{\frac{1}{\alpha}} + \mu, \qquad \alpha > 0, \quad \beta > 0, \quad x > \mu.$$

Hence

$$Y^{1/\alpha} = \frac{X - \mu}{\beta}.$$

Now take the natural logarithm of both sides, that is

$$\ln Y^{1/\alpha} = \ln\left(\frac{X - \mu}{\beta}\right).$$

$$\frac{\ln Y}{\alpha} = \ln\left(\frac{X - \mu}{\beta}\right).$$

$$\ln Y = \alpha \ln\left(\frac{X - \mu}{\beta}\right).$$

$$\ln Y = \ln\left(\frac{(X - \mu)^\alpha}{\beta}\right).$$

Hence,

$$Y = \left(\frac{X - \mu}{\beta}\right)^\alpha.$$

As $F_Y(y) = 1 - e^{-y}$, then

$$F_X(x) = 1 - e^{-\left(\frac{x-\mu}{\beta}\right)^\alpha}, \qquad x \geq \mu, \qquad (5.2.156)$$

which is the cumulative distribution function of X. Such a distribution is named the three-parameter Weibull distribution after Swedish physicist Waloddi Weibull, where β is the scale parameter, α is the shape parameter, and μ is the location parameter, $Weibull(\alpha, \beta, \mu)$.

Deriving the cumulative distribution function, $F_X(x)$, in relation to x, $dF_X(x)/dx$, we obtain the probability density function

$$f_X(x) = \frac{\alpha}{\beta}\left(\frac{x - \mu}{\beta}\right)^{\alpha-1} e^{-\left(\frac{x-\mu}{\beta}\right)^\alpha}, \qquad x \geq \mu. \qquad (5.2.157)$$

If $\mu = 0$, then the Function 5.2.156 is simply

$$F_X(x) = 1 - e^{-\left(\frac{x}{\beta}\right)^\alpha}, \qquad x \geq 0 \qquad (5.2.158)$$

which is the two-parameter Weibull cumulative distribution function, where β is the scale parameter and α is the shape parameter, $Weibull(\alpha, \beta)$.

Deriving the Function 5.2.158, in relation to x, $dF_X(x)/dx$, we obtain the two-parameter Weibull probability density function

$$f_X(x) = \frac{\alpha}{\beta}\left(\frac{x}{\beta}\right)^{\alpha-1} e^{-\left(\frac{x}{\beta}\right)^\alpha}, \qquad x \geq 0. \qquad (5.2.159)$$

If the shape parameter, α, is equal to one, then we get

$$F_X(x) = 1 - e^{-\frac{x}{\beta}}, \qquad\qquad x \geq 0$$

and

$$f_X(x) = \frac{1}{\beta} e^{-\frac{x}{\beta}}, \qquad\qquad x \geq 0,$$

which are the cumulative distribution function and the density function of a random variable exponentially distributed, respectively, and $\lambda = 1/\beta$.

Now, consider the hazard function definition

$$\lambda(x) = -\frac{dF_X^c(x)}{dx} \times \frac{1}{F_X^c(x)}, \qquad\qquad x \geq 0.$$

From the cumulative distribution function, we obtain

$$\lambda(x) = \frac{\alpha}{\beta} \left(\frac{x}{\beta}\right)^{\alpha-1}. \qquad\qquad (5.2.160)$$

Consider X is random variable that represents the time to execute a task. Also assume that X is distributed according to a two-parameter Weibull distribution, $X \sim Weibull(\alpha, \beta)$. Figure 5.28 shows, as an example, the hazard function in the interval $(0, 1.5t.u.)$ - $t.u.$ is time unity - considering the shape parameter $\alpha \in \{0.4, 0.8, 1, 2, 4, 8\}$ and $\beta = 0.25t.u..$

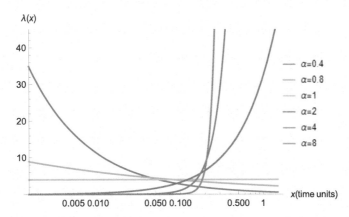

Figure 5.28   Hazard Function, $\lambda(x)$, $\alpha \in \{0.4, 0.8, 1, 2, 4, 8\}$, $\beta = 0.25t.u..$

The expected value of X is given by

$$\mu' = \beta\,\Gamma\left(1 + \frac{1}{\alpha}\right) = \beta \int_0^\infty y^{1/\alpha}\,dy. \tag{5.2.161}$$

The variance, the standard deviation, and the coefficient of variation are specified by

$$\mu_2 = \beta^2\left(-\Gamma\left(1 + \frac{1}{\alpha}\right)^2 + \Gamma\left(1 + \frac{2}{\alpha}\right)\right) = \left(\int_0^\infty y^{1+\frac{1}{\alpha}-1}e^{-y}\,dy\right)^2, \tag{5.2.162}$$

$$(\mu_2)^{1/2} = \beta\sqrt{-\Gamma\left(1 + \frac{1}{\alpha}\right)^2 + \Gamma\left(1 + \frac{2}{\alpha}\right)} = \tag{5.2.163}$$

$$\beta\sqrt{-\left(\int_0^\infty y^{1+\frac{1}{\alpha}-1}e^{-y}\,dy\right)^2 + \int_0^\infty y^{1+\frac{2}{\alpha}-1}e^{-y}\,dy},$$

and

$$CoV = \frac{\sqrt{-\Gamma\left(1+\frac{1}{\alpha}\right)^2 + \Gamma\left(\frac{2+\alpha}{\alpha}\right)}}{\Gamma\left(1+\frac{1}{\alpha}\right)} = \frac{\sqrt{-\left(\int_0^\infty y^{1+\frac{1}{\alpha}-1}e^{-y}\,dy\right)^2 + \int_0^\infty y^{1+\frac{2}{\alpha}-1}e^{-y}\,dy}}{\int_0^\infty y^{1/\alpha}e^{-y}\,dy}. \tag{5.2.164}$$

The two-parameter Weibull random variable median is defined as

$$Mdn = \beta\,\sqrt[\alpha]{\ln 2}. \tag{5.2.165}$$

The first and the third quartiles are defined as

$$Q_1 = \beta\,\sqrt[\alpha]{\ln\left(\frac{4}{3}\right)}, \tag{5.2.166}$$

and

$$Q_3 = \beta\,\sqrt[\alpha]{\ln 4}. \tag{5.2.167}$$

Example 5.2.14. The time to failure of a system is represented by $X \sim$ $Weibull(\alpha, \beta)$, where $\alpha = 0.4$, $\beta = 6000h$. The probability the system fails before the $1000h$ may be computed using Equation 5.2.158, such that

$$P(X < 1000h) = F(1000h) = 0.4369.$$

The mean time to failure and the respective standard deviation may be calculated using Equation 5.2.161 and Equation 5.2.163, respectively.

$$\mu' = 13293.4\,h$$

and

$$(\mu_2)^{1/2} = 41752.7\,h.$$

$\square$

Example 5.2.15. Similarly to the previous example, assume the time to failure of a system is represented by $X \sim Weibull(\alpha, \beta)$, where $\alpha = 1$, $\beta = 6000\,h$. The probability the system fails before the $1000\,h$ may be computed using Equation 5.2.158, such that

$$P(X < 1000h) = F(1000h) = 0.2212.$$

The mean time to failure and the respective standard deviation may be calculated using Equation 5.2.161 and Equation 5.2.163, respectively.

$$\mu' = 4000\,h.$$

and

$$(\mu_2)^{1/2} = 4000\,h.$$

$\square$

Example 5.2.16. As in the two previous examples, the time to failure of a system is represented by $X \sim Weibull(\alpha, \beta)$, where $\alpha = 4$, $\beta = 6000\,h$. The probability the system fails before the $1000\,h$ may be computed using Equation 5.2.158, such that

$$P(X < 1000h) = F(1000h) = 0.0039.$$

The mean time to failure and the respective standard deviation may be calculated using Equation 5.2.161 and Equation 5.2.163, respectively.

$$\mu' = 3625.61\,h.$$

and

$$(\mu_2)^{1/2} = 1017.14\,h.$$

$\square$

Other distributions such as log-normal, loglogistic, Dagun, Gumbel, Laplace, logistic, Pareto, Cauchy, Rayleigh, Pert, and beta distribution are introduced throughout this text, in particular in Section 16.3 and Section 14.3. It is worth mentioning again that the methods for estimating distribution parameters are presented in Section 25.3, and strategies for generating random variates are introduced in Section 14.3. More details and many other probability distributions can be found in probability distribution compendiums, and handbooks such as these references [145, 221, 267, 455].

5.3 FUNCTIONS OF A RANDOM VARIABLE

A random variable is sometimes defined as a function of one or more random variables. Consider a random variables X defined over $\{1, 2, 3, 4\}$, and another random variable $Y = g(X)$ defined in terms of X. For instance, assume $Y = 3X^2 + 4$. The random variable Y is a derived random variable from X. If X is a discrete random variable whose probability mass function is defined as

$$p_X(x) = \begin{cases} 1/10, & x = 1, \\ 2/10, & x = 2, \\ 3/10, & x = 3, \\ 4/10, & x = 4, \\ 0, & otherwise, \end{cases}$$

then

$$p_y(y) = \begin{cases} 1/10, & y = 2, \\ 2/10,, & y = 17, \\ 3/10, & y = 42, \\ 4/10, & y = 77, \\ 0, & otherwise. \end{cases}$$

Figure 5.29.a and Figure 5.29.b depict the probability mass function of X defined over $\{1, 2, 3, 4\}$ and $Y = 3X^2 + 4$.

Now assume X is defined over $\{-2, -1, 1, 2\}$, and another random variable $Y = g(X)$ X^2 is defined in terms of X. If X is a discrete random variable with probability mass function defined as

$$p_X(x) = \begin{cases} 2/10, & x = -2, \\ 3/10, & x = -1, \\ 3/10, & x = 1, \\ 2/10, & x = 2, \\ 0, & otherwise, \end{cases}$$

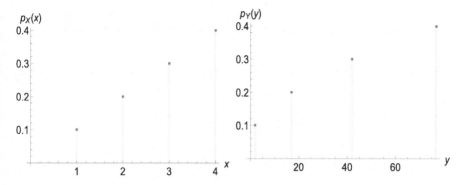

Figure 5.29 (a) $p_X(X)$ and (a) $p_Y(y)$ - $Y = 3X^2 + 4$.

then

$$p_y(y) = \begin{cases} 4/10, & y = 1, \\ 6/10, & y = 4, \\ 0, & otherwise. \end{cases}$$

Figure 5.29.a and Figure 5.29.b depict the probability mass function of X defined over $\{-2, -1, 1, 2\}$ and the probability mass function of Y. Therefore, we observe that the probability mass function of Y is obtained from this general relation

$$p_y(y) = \sum_{x:g(x)=y} p_X(x). \tag{5.3.1}$$

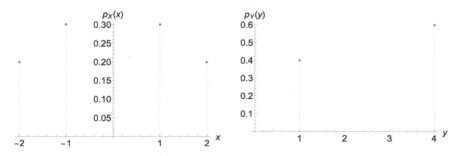

Figure 5.30 (a) $p_X(X)$ and (a) $p_Y(y)$ - $Y = X^2$.

For the continuous random variable, a general approach for obtaining the probability density function ($f_Y(y)$) of a random variable, $Y = g(x)$, derived from another random variable, X, consists of first obtaining the cumulative probability function of Y, ($F_Y(y)$), from the cumulative probability function of X, ($F_X(x)$), and then finding out the probability density function of Y.

Consider as an example the random variable X exponentially distributed with parameter λ. Its cumulative distribution function is specified by

$$F_X(x) = \begin{cases} 1 - e^{-\lambda x}, & x \geq 0, \\ 0, & otherwise. \end{cases}$$

Assume a random variable Y is defined as $Y = X^2$. Now, we derive the probability density function of Y by first finding the cumulative distribution function of Y, and then obtaining the probability density function $f_Y(y)$. As $Y = X^2$, then $X = \pm\sqrt{Y}$. However, as $x \geq 0$, $X = \sqrt{Y}$. Hence,

$$F_Y(y) = \begin{cases} 1 - e^{-\lambda \sqrt{y}}, & y \geq 0, \\ 0, & otherwise. \end{cases}$$

As $f_Y(y) = dF_Y(y)/dy$, then

$$f_Y(y) = \begin{cases} \frac{\lambda e^{-\lambda \sqrt{y}}}{2\sqrt{y}}, & y \geq 0, \\ 0, & otherwise. \end{cases}$$

Figure 5.31.a and Figure 5.31.b show the cumulative probability function of X and the respective probability density function.

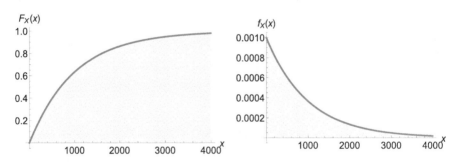

Figure 5.31   (a) $F_X(x)$ and (a) $f_X(x)$ - $X \sim Exp(\lambda)$.

Figure 5.32.a and Figure 5.32.b (linear-log plot) show the cumulative probability function of Y and the respective probability density function.

For the random variable uniformly distributed or for random variables $Y = g(x)$ that are increasing or decreasing, a simpler approach may be adopted for calculating $f_Y(y)$. Such an approach allows us to obtain $f_Y(y)$, given $f_X(x)$ is provided, without having to obtain $F_Y(y)$ first.

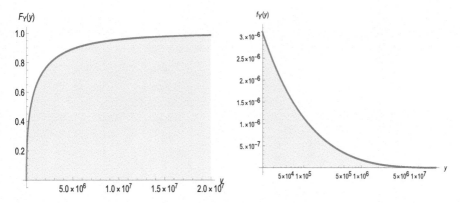

Figure 5.32   (a) $F_Y(y)$ and (a) $f_Y(y)$ - $Y = X^2$.

Consider X is a random variable uniformly distributed over the range (x_l, x_u), $f_X(x) = 1/(x_u - x_l)$. Hence, if Y is obtained from X using a scaling factor a $(a > 0,$ $a \in \mathbb{R})$ and shifting by b $(b \in \mathbb{R})$, that is $Y = aX + b$, the distribution of Y is also uniformly distributed over the range (y_l, y_u), where $y_l = ax_l + b$ and $y_u = ax_u + b$. Thus, $f_Y(y) = 1/(y_u - y_l) = 1/a(x_u - x_l)$.

As an example, let us adopt this simpler approach first. Consider a continuous random variable X defined over $(-2, 2)$, and another random variable $Y = g(X) = 4X + 3$ defined in terms of X. Assume the probability density function of X is

$$f_X(x) = \begin{cases} 0.25, & -2 \leq x \leq 2, \\ 0, & otherwise. \end{cases}$$

The domain of Y is $(-5, 11)$, and as Y is also uniformly distributed, then

$$f_Y(y) = \begin{cases} 0.0625, & -5 \leq x \leq 11, \\ 0, & otherwise. \end{cases}$$

For any continuous random variable X multiplied by a positive constant a and shifted by b, that is $Y = aX + b$, the following relation always holds

$$f_Y(y) = \frac{1}{a} f_X \left(\frac{y - b}{a} \right) \tag{5.3.2}$$

and

$$F_Y(y) = F_X \left(\frac{y - b}{a} \right). \tag{5.3.3}$$

Figure 5.33.a and Figure 5.33.b show the probability density function of X and the probability density function of Y, respectively.

Figure 5.33 (a) $f_X(X)$ and (a) $f_Y(y)$ - $Y = 4X + 3$.

Now assume X is a random variable that represents the time required to drive a car for $1000\,m$. If $X \sim Exp(\lambda)$, where $E(T) = 1/\lambda = 40\,s$; hence $\lambda = 2.5 \times 10^{-2}\,s^{-1}$. Let $Y = d/X$ be a random variable that represents the speed of the car in route over distance $d = 1000\,m$.

As $X \sim Exp(\lambda)$, then

$$F_X(x) = \begin{cases} 1 - e^{-\lambda x}, & x \geq 0, \\ 0, & otherwise. \end{cases}$$

As $Y = d/X$, then $X = 10^3\,Y^{-1}$ and $x \geq 0$, then $y \geq 0$; hence

$$F_Y(y) = \begin{cases} 1 - e^{-\frac{\lambda 10^3}{y}}, & y \geq 0, \\ 0, & otherwise. \end{cases}$$

As $f_Y(y) = dF_Y(y)/dy$, then

$$f_Y(y) = \begin{cases} \frac{10^3 \lambda e^{-\frac{10^3 \lambda}{y}}}{y^2}, & y \geq 0, \\ 0, & otherwise. \end{cases}$$

The probability of a car speed being in the interval (70 m/s, 110 m/s) may be calculated through

$$P(70m/s \leq Y \leq 110m/s) = \int_{70}^{110} \frac{10^3 \lambda e^{-\frac{10^3 \lambda}{y}}}{y^2}\,dy = 0.1304,$$

and the probability of a car speed being higher than $80ms$ is

$$P(Y \geq 80m/s) = \int_{80}^{\infty} \frac{10^3 \lambda e^{-\frac{10^3 \lambda}{y}}}{y^2}\,dy.$$

$$P(Y \geq 80\,m/s) = 1 - \int_0^{80} \frac{10^3 \lambda e^{-\frac{10^3 \lambda}{y}}}{y^2}\, dy = 0.3935.$$

Let us consider another example. Assume X is a random variable with a probability density function specified by

$$f_X(x) = \frac{1}{144}\left(36 - x^2\right), \qquad x \in (0, 6).$$

If Y is another random variable derived from X that is equal to $Y = 3X^2$, then

$$F_X(x) = \int_0^6 \frac{1}{144}\left(36 - x^2\right) dx = x/4 - x^3/432, \qquad x \in (0, 6).$$

As $Y = 3X^2$, $x = \pm\sqrt{y/3}$. But, as $x \geq 0$, then $x = \sqrt{y/3}$. Therefore,

$$F_Y(y) = \frac{\sqrt{y}}{4\sqrt{3}} - \frac{y^{3/2}}{1296\sqrt{3}}, \qquad y \in (0, 108),$$

$$F_Y(y) = \frac{(324 - y)\sqrt{y}}{1296\sqrt{3}}, \qquad y \in (0, 108),$$

since $x = 0$ implies $y = 0$ and $x = 0$ results in $y = 108$. As $f_Y(y) = dF_Y(y)/dy$, then

$$f_Y(y) = \frac{324 - y}{2592\sqrt{3}\sqrt{y}} - \frac{\sqrt{y}}{1296\sqrt{3}}, \qquad y \in (0, 108).$$

The probability of $Y \leq 50$ is

$$P(Y \leq 50) = \int_0^{50} \left(\frac{324 - y}{2592\sqrt{3}\sqrt{y}} - \frac{\sqrt{y}}{1296\sqrt{3}} \right) dy = 0.8631.$$

5.4 TAYLOR SERIES

Many functions can be approximated by power series. Such functions are called analytic functions. The Taylor-Maclaurin series are potent tools for approximating analytic functions that can be difficult to calculate. Such series were named after Brook Taylor, and Colin Maclaurin [106, 171, 193]. The Taylor-Maclaurin series provides a means of predicting a function value at one point in terms of the function value and its derivatives at another point.

A useful way to understand the Taylor series is to build it term by term. For instance, consider

$$f(x_{i+1}) \approx f(x_i), \quad x_{i+1} = x_i + \triangle x, \quad \triangle x \to 0.$$

This relationship is intuitive since it indicates that the value of f at x_{i+1} is very close to its value at x_i if $\triangle x \to 0$. If f is constant, indeed $f(x_{i+1}) = f(x_i)$. However, if a function changes over the interval, the terms $f(x_{i+1})$ and $f(x_i)$ are not exactly the same. Hence, the Taylor series provides additional terms to obtain a better estimate. For instance, assume a function f is defined over a interval (a, b), that f'' exists on the interval (a, b), and $x_i \in (a, b)$; thus consider a first-order approximation given by

$$f(x_{i+1}) \approx f(x_i) + f'(x_i)(x_{i+1} - x_i), \tag{5.4.1}$$

where the additional term consists of a slope, $f'(x_i)$, multiplied by the distance between x_i and x_{i+1}. Hence, the new expression is a straight line, which allows predicting linear changes of the function between the points x_i and x_{i+1}. Such a prediction is exact if the function f is a straight line, but if the function has some curvature, additional terms allow more accurate estimates. For instance, a second-order term may be added to the series to capture quadratic trends (see Figure 5.34). Such an estimate is obtained through

$$f(x_{i+1}) \approx f(x_i) + f'(x_i)(x_{i+1} - x_i) + \frac{f''(x_i)}{2!}(x_{i+1} - x_i)^2.$$

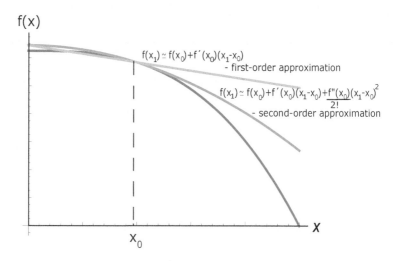

Figure 5.34 Taylor Series – First and Second-Order Approximations.

Likewise, additional terms can be included to obtain the complete Taylor series:

$$f(x_{i+1}) = f(x_i) + f'(x_i)(x_{i+1} - x_i) + \frac{f''(x_i)}{2!}(x_{i+1} - x_i)^2 +$$

$$+ \frac{f'''(x_i)}{3!}(x_{i+1} - x_i)^3 + ... + \frac{f^n(x_i)}{n!}(x_{i+1} - x_i)^n + ...$$

Thus

$$f(x_{i+1}) = \sum_{n=0}^{\infty} \frac{f^n(x_i)}{n!}(x_{i+1} - x_i)^n. \qquad (5.4.2)$$

The series presented above may be presented as

$$f(x_{i+1}) = P_n(x_{i+1}) + R_n(x_{i+1}), \qquad (5.4.3)$$

where

$$P_n(x_i) = \sum_{k=0}^{n} \frac{f^k(x_i)}{k!}(x_{i+1} - x_i)^k, \qquad (5.4.4)$$

and

$$R_n(x_i) = \frac{f^{n+1}(\xi(x))}{(n+1)!}(x_{i+1} - x_i)^{n+1}, \qquad (5.4.5)$$

where $P_n(x)$ is called the nth Taylor polynomial for f about x_i, and $R_n(x_i)$ is the remainder term that specifies the error. $\xi(x)$ is a function of x, which we do not expect to be able to specify. The Taylor series is often called the Maclaurin series when $x_i = 0$. Likewise, in such a case, the Taylor polynomial is also called the Maclaurin polynomial. It is worth mentioning that, in general, the nth-order Taylor series expansion will be exact for an nth-order polynomial. However, in most cases, the inclusion of only a few terms results in good approximation for practical purposes.

Example 5.4.1. The Taylor series about $x_0 = 2$ for

$$f(x) = \frac{x^2}{1 - 2x},$$

considering 10 terms, is given by first computing $f^i(x) i \in \{1, 2, ..., 10\}$. Hence,

$$f'(x_0) = \frac{2x_0}{1 - 2x_0} + \frac{2x_0^2}{(1 - 2x_0)^2},$$

$$f''(x_0) = \frac{2}{1 - 2x_0} + \frac{8x_0}{(1 - 2x_0)^2} + \frac{8x_0^2}{(1 - 2x_0)^3},$$

$$f'''(x_0) = \frac{12}{(1 - 2x_0)^2} + \frac{48x_0}{(1 - 2x_0)^3} + \frac{48x_0^2}{(1 - 2x_0)^4},$$

$$f^4(x_0) = \frac{96}{(1 - 2x_0)^3} + \frac{384x_0}{(1 - 2x_0)^4} + \frac{384x_0^2}{(1 - 2x_0)^5},$$

$$f^5(x_0) = \frac{960}{(1 - 2x_0)^4} + \frac{3840x_0}{(1 - 2x_0)^5} + \frac{3840x_0^2}{(1 - 2x_0)^6},$$

$$f^6(x_0) = \frac{11520}{(1 - 2x_0)^5} + \frac{46080x_0}{(1 - 2x_0)^6} + \frac{46080x_0^2}{(1 - 2x_0)^7},$$

$$f^7(x_0) = \frac{161280}{(1 - 2x_0)^6} + \frac{645120x_0}{(1 - 2x_0)^7} + \frac{645120x_0^2}{(1 - 2x_0)^8},$$

$$f^8(x_0) = \frac{2580480}{(1 - 2x_0)^7} + \frac{10321920x_0}{(1 - 2x_0)^8} + \frac{10321920x_0^2}{(1 - 2x_0)^9},$$

$$f^9(x_0) = \frac{46448640}{(1 - 2x_0)^8} + \frac{185794560x_0}{(1 - 2x_0)^9} + \frac{185794560x_0^2}{(1 - 2x_0)^{10}},$$

and

$$f^{10}(x_0) = \frac{928972800}{(1 - 2x_0)^9} + \frac{3715891200x_0}{(1 - 2x_0)^{10}} + \frac{3715891200x_0^2}{(1 - 2x_0)^{11}}.$$

Substituting $x_0 = 2$ in $f^i(x_0)$, in $(x - x_0)^i$ and considering $1/i!$ in the Polynomial 5.4.4, that is

$$P_{10}(x) = \sum_{i=0}^{10} \frac{f^i(2)}{i!} (x - 2)^i,$$

we obtain the values depicted in Table 5.1.

Hence, using the values of the columns $f^i(x_0)$ and $1/i!$, we obtain

$$P(x) = -1.3333 - 0.4444(x - 2) - \frac{0.07407(x - 2)^2}{2!} + \frac{0.1481(x - 2)^3}{3!} -$$

$$\frac{0.3951(x - 2)^4}{4!} + \frac{1.3168(x - 2)^5}{5!} - \frac{5.2674(x - 2)^6}{6!} + \frac{24.5816(x - 2)^7}{7!} -$$

$$\frac{131.102(x - 2)^8}{8!} + \frac{786.612(x - 2)^9}{9!} - \frac{5244.08(x - 2)^{10}}{10!}.$$

Thus, $P(x)$ for $x = 2.1$ is $P(2.1) = -1.378122$, and as we know the true value of $f(x)$ for $x = 2.1$, $f(2.1) = -1.378125$, then we have $R(10) = f(2.1) - P(2.1) = -3.38 \times 10^{-6}$.

$\square$

Table 5.1
Ten terms - $f^i(x_0)$, $(x-2)^i$, $i!$, **and** $(i!) \times f^i(x_0) \times (x-x_0)^i$ **for** $x_0 = 2$.

i	$f^i(2)$	$(x-x_0)^i$	$i!$	$(1/i!) \times f^i(2) \times (x-2)^i$ for $x = 2.1$
0	-1.33333	1	1	-1.3333333
1	-0.44444	0.1	1	-0.0444444
2	-0.07407	0.01	2	-0.000370371
3	0.14815	0.001	6	2.46913×10^{-5}
4	-0.39506	0.0001	24	-1.64609×10^6
5	1.31687	0.00001	120	1.09739×10^{-7}
6	-5.26749	10^{-6}	720	-7.31596×10^{-9}
7	24.58160	10^{-7}	5040	4.8773×10^{-10}
8	-131.10200	10^{-8}	40320	-3.25154×10^{-11}
9	786.61200	10^{-9}	362880	2.16769×10^{-12}
10	-5244.08000	10^{-10}	3628800	-1.44513×10^{-13}

Example 5.4.2. Assume a function $f(x) = e^{x^2}$, and consider we are required to calculate

$$\int_0^1 f(x)\,dx = \int_0^1 e^{x^2}\,dx.$$

As we do not know an analytic solution to this integral, we represent $f(x)$ by a Taylor series and then integrate the Taylor polynomial to obtain an approximated result, that is

$$f(x) = P_n(x) + R_n(x).$$

Hence

$$f(x) \simeq P_n(x),$$

and

$$\int_0^1 P_n(x)\,dx \simeq \int_0^1 f(x)\,dx.$$

Therefore, let us first obtain a Taylor polynomial with, for instance, ten terms, that is $P_{10}(x)$. Thus, considering $f(x) = e^{x^2}$ for $x_0 = 0$, we get

$$f(0) = 1.$$

Now, let us take the first derivative of $f(x)$:

$$f'(x) = 2e^{x^2}x$$

Assigning $x_0 = 0$, $f'(0) = 0$, the second derivative of $f(x)$ is

$$f''(x) = 2e^{x^2} + 4e^{x^2}x^2.$$

For $x_0 = 0$, $f''(0) = 2$. Likewise, we obtain the derivatives $f'''(x)$, $f^4(x)$, $f^5(x)$, $f^6(x)$, $f^7(x)$, $f^8(x)$, $f^9(x)$, and $f^{10}(x)$. Therefore

$$f'''(x) = 12e^{x^2}x + 8e^{x^2}x^3.$$
$$f'''(0) = 0.$$
$$f^4(x) = 12e^{x^2} + 48e^{x^2}x^2 + 16e^{x^2}x^4.$$
$$f^4(0) = 12.$$
$$f^5(x) = 120e^{x^2}x + 160e^{x^2}x^3 + 32e^{x^2}x^5.$$
$$f^5(0) = 0.$$
$$f^6(x) = 120e^{x^2} + 720e^{x^2}x^2 + 480e^{x^2}x^4 + 64e^{x^2}x^6.$$
$$f^6(0) = 120.$$
$$f^7(x) = 1680e^{x^2}x + 3360e^{x^2}x^3 + 1344e^{x^2}x^5 + 128e^{x^2}x^7.$$
$$f^7(0) = 0.$$
$$f^8(x) = 1680e^{x^2} + 13440e^{x^2}x^2 + 13440e^{x^2}x^4 + 3584e^{x^2}x^6 + 256e^{x^2}x^8.$$
$$f^8(0) = 1680.$$
$$f^9(x) = 30240e^{x^2}x + 80640e^{x^2}x^3 + 48384e^{x^2}x^5 + 9216e^{x^2}x^7 + 512e^{x^2}x^9.$$
$$f^9(0) = 0.$$
$$f^{10}(x) = 30240e^{x^2} + 302400e^{x^2}x^2 + 403200e^{x^2}x^4 +$$
$$161280e^{x^2}x^6 + 23040e^{x^2}x^8 + 1024e^{x^2}x^{10}.$$
$$f^{10}(0) = 30240.$$

Now, using Function 5.4.4, and considering $x_0 = 0$, we get

$$P_{10}(x) = 1 + x^2 + \frac{x^4}{2} + \frac{x^6}{6} + \frac{x^8}{24} + \frac{x^{10}}{120}.$$

Now, calculate

$$\int_0^1 \left(1 + x^2 + \frac{x^4}{2} + \frac{x^6}{6} + \frac{x^8}{24} + \frac{x^{10}}{120}\right) dx = 1.46253.$$

□

Table 5.2

Fourteen Terms of Taylor Polynomial of $f_X(x) = \frac{1}{10}e^{-\left(\frac{x}{10}\right)^3}3\left(\frac{x}{10}\right)^2$.

k	$f^k(0)$	$k!$	$f^k(0)/k!$
0	0	1	0
1	0	1	0
2	6.00×10^{-3}	2	3.00×10^{-3}
3	0	6	0
4	0	24	0
5	-3.60×10^{-4}	120	-3.00×10^{-6}
6	0	720	0
7	0	5040	0
8	$/6.048 \times 10^{-5}$	40320	1.50×10^{-9}
9	0	362880	0
10	0	3628800	0
11	-1.99584×10^{-5}	39916800	-5.00×10^{-13}
12	0	479001600	0
13	0	6227020800	0
14	1.08973×10^{-5}	87178291200	1.25×10^{-16}

Example 5.4.3. Assume a random variable X is distributed according to a Weibull distribution with parameters $\alpha = 3$ and $\beta = 10$. The probability density function of X is

$$f_X(x) = \frac{1}{10}e^{-\left(\frac{x}{10}\right)^3}3\left(\frac{x}{10}\right)^2.$$

The Taylor series, considering fourteen terms ($n = 14$) and $x_i = x_0 = 0$ is obtained using the Polynomial 5.4.4; hence

$$P_{14}(x) = \sum_{k=0}^{14}\frac{f^k(x_0)}{k!}(x_k - x_0)^k.$$

Table 5.2 shows $f^k(x_0)$ and $f^k(x_0)/k!$, for $x_0 = 0$, and $k = \{1, 2, ..., 14\}$.

Using the terms presented in Table 5.2 (Column $f^k(x_0)/k!$), we obtain the Taylor polynomial:

$$P_{14}(x) = \frac{3x^2}{10^3} - \frac{3x^5}{10^6} + \frac{1.5x^8}{10^9} - \frac{5x^{11}}{10^{13}} + \frac{1.25x^{14}}{10^{16}}.$$

The probability of having $0 < X < 7$ may be calculated using

$$P(0 < X < 7) = \int_0^7 P_{14}(x)\,dx.$$

$$P(0 < X < 7) = \int_0^7 \left(\frac{3x^2}{10^3} - \frac{3x^5}{10^6} + \frac{1.5x^8}{10^9} - \frac{5x^{11}}{10^{13}} + \frac{1.25x^{14}}{10^{16}} \right) dx.$$

$$P(0 < X < 7) = 0.290364.$$

□

EXERCISES

Exercise 1. Calculate the probability of observing the first success at the 10th trial when the success probability is 0.8.

Exercise 2. A random experiment, represented by a random variable X, is composed of Bernoulli experiments. The random experiment finishes when the first result of a Bernoulli experiment is a failure. Find the number of Bernoulli experiments executed before the first failure, k, when the success probability is $p = 0.6$ such that $P(X \leq k) = 0.8$.

Exercise 3. Why is the geometric distribution the only memoryless discrete distribution?

Exercise 4. Finding a bug in a new software system version consists of executing the system with randomly selected data sets until a bug appears. The data sets are independent, so using one data set does not affect the result obtained from another data set. The probability that any specific data set isolates a bug is $p = 0.15$. Let X be the number of data sets considered before a bug occurs. (a) Calculate the mean number of data sets used before a bug occurrs. (b) Calculate the coefficient of variation of the number of data sets used before a bug occurs. (c) Obtain the probability of executing $k = 10$ data sets before a bug occurs.

Exercise 5. Assume $n = 50$ indistinguishable servers placed in an accelerate reliability test. When the test finishes, each server is either functional or in failure. Consider that the test execution in one server does not affect the test in any other server. Suppose the probability of failure for each computer is $p = 0.12$. (a) Calculate the probability of having at most $i = 7$ servers in failure. (b) Calculate the probability of having more than 15 servers in failure. (c) Find out the probability of having between 6 and 16 servers in failure. (d) Obtain the mean number of failed servers.

Exercise 6. In a large data center, consider the probability of a server passing an accelerate reliability test is $p = 0.85$. Calculate the probability of having at most $k = 10$ failures until $r = 50$ success.

Exercise 7. A mobile operator receives batches of many mobile phones and submits them to inspection. The company inspection policy consists of checking samples (of each batch) of not more than twenty-five mobile phones. Once the third defective phone is detected, the inspection of the batch is finished. Such a batch is then rejected. Otherwise, the inspection of the batch continues until twenty-five mobile phones have been checked, when the batch is accepted. What is the probability of rejecting a batch if it indeed has 10% defective phones?

Exercise 8. A warehouse has forty items of a specific type. Consider that fifteen of these items are indeed faulty, and the rest are functional. What is the probability of randomly selecting twelve items and getting at least two non-functional items?

Exercise 9. Why may a binomial distribution approximate the Poisson distribution?

Exercise 10. Assume a system receives a number of requests in a period and considers the request rate is constant. Besides, let the probability of a request arriving in a second to be close to zero. If the constant request rate is $\lambda = 15 s^{-1}$, calculate the probability of at least ten requests arriving in a second.

Exercise 11. What is the relation between the Poisson and the exponential distributions?

Exercise 12. Let the transaction request rate be, on average, 30 requests per minute. Then, assuming the Poisson process well approximates this arrival traffic, what is the probability of receiving at least 90 transactions in four minutes?

Exercise 13. Let a random variable $X \sim U(0, 1000)$. Calculate (a) the expected value of X, (b) its coefficient of variation, and (c) $P(250 \leq X \leq 520)$.

Exercise 14. What is the importance of the continuous uniform distribution in simulation processes?

Exercise 15. The number of calls to a help desk department is specified by a random variable $X \sim Tr(50, 300, 120)$. (a) Calculate the expected number of calls per day and (b) the probability of having more than 350 calls in a day.

Exercise 16. What is the relation between the triangular and the uniform distributions?

Exercise 17. Why is normal distribution so widely used in statistics? Explain and give examples.

Exercise 18. A disk storage manufacturer reports that the average lifetime of a specific type of disk is $40000 h$ with a standard deviation of $4200 h$. If the disk lifetime is normally distributed, obtain: (a) the percentage of disks that last at least $15000 h$, (b) the probability of disks with a lifetime between $10000 h$ and $25000 h$, and (c) the 85th percentile of the life hours.

Exercise 19. What is the relation between the chi-square and the normal distributions?

Exercise 20. What is the relation between the chi-square and the Erlang distributions?

Exercise 21. What is the relation between the chi-square and the Student's t distributions?

Exercise 22. Why is the chi-square distribution important in statistical inference? Explain and give examples.

Exercise 23. Let X be a chi-square random variable with a degree of freedom equal to 500. (a) What is the value of X for $F_X(x) = 0.90$? (b) What is the value of X for $F_X(x) = 0.05$? (c) Calculate $P(450 \leq X \leq 550)$.

Exercise 24. Why is the Student's t distribution important for statistical inference? Explain and give examples.

Exercise 25. What is the relation between the normal and the Student's t distributions?

Exercise 26. Let X be a Student's t random variable with a degree of freedom equal to 80. (a) What is the value of X for $F_X(x) = 0.975$? (b) What is the value of X for $F_X(x) = 0.025$? (c) Calculate $P(X \geq 2.7)$.

Exercise 27. What is the relation between the F and the Erlang distributions?

Exercise 28. Let X be a random variable distributed according to a F distribution with parameters $n = 15$ and $m = 20$. (a) Obtain the value of X for $F_X(x) = 0.05$ and for $F_X(x) = 0.95$. (b) Obtain the probability of $P(X \leq 0.4)$

Exercise 29. Why is the exponential distribution widely adopted in performance and reliability modeling?

Exercise 30. Why is the exponential distribution the only memoryless continuous distribution?

Exercise 31. What is the relation between the exponential and the geometric distributions?

Exercise 32. What is the relation between the exponential and the Erlang distributions?

Exercise 33. What is the relation between the exponential and the hyperexponential distributions?

Exercise 34. Assume X is an exponential random variable that represents the time to failure of a router. Assume the distribution parameter (failure rate) is $\lambda = 2 \times 10^{-4} h^{-1}$. (a) Calculate the probability the server survives $3000 h$. (b) Calculate the server's mean time to failure.

Exercise 35. Show the relationship among the gamma distribution and following distributions: (a) Erlang, (b) hypoexponential, (c) chi-square, (d) exponential.

Exercise 36. Let X be a gamma random variable that represents the time to repair of a system (in hours) with parameters $\gamma = 2$ and $\beta = 15 h$. (a) What is the probability of a failed system being repaired by $X \leq 24 h$? (b) Calculate the mean time to repair.

Exercise 37. Is it possible to use gamma random variables to represent decreasing, constant, and increasing hazard functions? Explain.

Exercise 38. What is the importance of exponential phase-type distributions in performance and reliability modeling? Explain.

Exercise 39. Explain why the following distributions are called phase-type distributions: (a) Erlang, (b) hypoexpoential, (c) hyperponential, and (d) Cox distributions.

Exercise 40. Why the probability of the Erlang density function can be obtained through the convolution of exponential density functions?

Exercise 41. Let $X \sim Erl(\gamma, \lambda)$ be a random variable that represents the time to process a transaction. Consider $\gamma = 4$ and $\lambda = 0.01\,s^{-1}$. (a) Obtain the mean time to process a transaction and its coefficient of variation. (b) Calculate the probability of a transaction being processed by $200\,ms$?

Exercise 42. What is the relation between the hypoexponential and the Erlang distribution?

Exercise 43. Let $X \sim Hypo(\lambda_1, \lambda_2)$ be a random variable that represents the time to repair a storage system. Assume $\lambda_1 = 0.05\,h^{-1}$ and $\lambda_2 = 0.1\,h^{-1}$. (a) Calculate the mean time to repair the storage system, and its coefficient of variation. (b) What is the probability of the storage system being repaired after $40\,h$?

Exercise 44. A mobile device manufacturer specifies that the device´s time to failure is distributed according to $X \sim Hyperexp(\alpha, 1 - \alpha, \lambda_1, \lambda_2)$, $\alpha = 0.28$, $\lambda_1 = 2 \times 10^{-5}\,h^{-1}$, and $\lambda_1 = 2.5 \times 10^{-4}\,h^{-1}$. (a) Obtain the mean time to failure, its variance, and coefficient of variation. (b) Calculate the probability of a mobile device not failing by $12000\,h$.

Exercise 45. The time to process an electronic purchase transaction is distributed according to a random variable $X \sim Cox_1(\alpha, k, \lambda)$ (*Cox Model 1*). Let $\alpha = 0.8$, $k = 5$, and $\lambda = 80\,s^{-1}$. (a) Obtain the average time to process a purchase transaction and the respective coefficient of variation. (b) Calculate the probability of the time to process a transaction being shorter than $20\,ms$.

Exercise 46. Let $X \sim Cox_2(\alpha, \lambda_1, \lambda_2)$ (*Cox Model 2*) represent the time to failure of a switch. Assume that $\alpha = 0.7$, $\lambda_1 = 0.4\,h^{-1}$, and $\lambda_2 = 2 \times 10^{-5}\,h^{-1}$. (a) Calculate the probability that the system fails only after $20000\,h$. (b) Obtain the mean value and the coefficient of variation of X.

Exercise 47. Why is the Weibull distribution so attractive for reliability modeling?

Exercise 48. What is the relation between the Weibull and the exponential distribution?

Exercise 49. Consider a line of electronic product whose infant mortality is represented by $X \sim Weibull(\alpha, \beta)$, where $\alpha = 0.3$, $\beta = 5000\,h$. (a) What is the probability of an item of this product line surviving $500\,h$ in a reliability test? (b) Obtain the respective hazard function.

Exercise 50. Let $Y = \frac{X^3}{8} + 3$, where Y is a derived random variable from X. If X is a discrete random variable whose probability mass function is defined as

$$p_X(x) = \begin{cases} 1/10, & x = 1, \\ 2/10, & x = 2, \\ 5/10, & x = 3, \\ 2/10, & x = 4, \\ 0, & otherwise \end{cases}$$

(a) Obtain $F_X(x)$. (b) Calculate $F_Y(y)$. (c) Obtain $p_Y(y)$. (d) Plot all these functions.

Exercise 51. Let X be a continuous random variable defined by the cumulative probability distribution

$$F_X(x) = 1 - e^{-\frac{4.0656x^{0.4}}{10^2}}, \qquad x \geq 0.$$

and let $Y = X^2 + 3$. (a) Find cumulative probability distribution of Y and the respective domain. (b) Obtain the probability density function of Y. (c) Calculate $F_Y(3.5)$. (d) Calculate $\int_3^{3.5} f_y(y)\, dy$. (e) Obtain the mean value of Y.

Exercise 52. Considering the previous exercise, (a) find the Taylor polynomial with three terms ($P_3(y)$) for $F_Y(y)$. (b) Calculate $P_3(3.1)$ and compare with $F_Y(3.1)$ (obtained in the previous exercise). (c) Find the Taylor polynomial with six terms ($P_6(y)$) for $f_y(y)$. (d) Calculate $\int_3^{3.5} P_6(y)\, dy$ and compare with the result obtained in letter (d) of the previous exercise.

Exercise 53. Let X be a random variable defined by the probability density function

$$f(x) = 0.938192e^{-3.2x} + 0.0218081e^{-0.030854x}, \qquad x \geq 0.$$

(a) Find the Taylor polynomial with ten terms ($P_{10}(x)$). (b) Calculate $\int_0^1 P_{10}(x)\, dx$ and compare with the result of $\int_0^1 f(x)\, dx$.

Exercise 54. From the probability density function of the previous exercise, obtain the respective cumulative probability function ($F(x)$). (a) Find the Taylor polynomial with ten terms ($P_{10}(x)$) of $F(x)$. (b) Calculate $P_{10}(1)$ and compare with the result of $F(1)$.

6 Statistical Inference and Data Fitting

This chapter presents inference methods for estimating system parameters with confidence, distribution fitting strategies, and methods for data fitting such as regression and interpolation. Figure 6.1 presents a diagram summarizing the measurement process, descriptive analysis of the data (see Chapter 3), and the estimation of population parameters. Each method is described and illustrated in this chapter through small examples to help the reader gain the intuition behind the formalism. Some methods for distribution parameters´ estimation are also presented in Section 25.3.

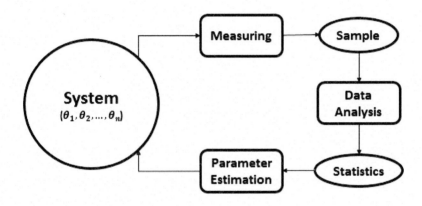

Figure 6.1 Measurement and Estimation of Parameters.

6.1 PARAMETRIC CONFIDENCE INTERVAL FOR MEAN

Figure 6.2 describes a guideline to support the process of choosing suitable statistical methods for estimating the population's mean as a function of the data sample. It is assumed the system has been measured, the suitable sample was collected, and the exploratory data analysis was already conducted. Distributions fitting tests may also have been performed (two methods are presented in Section 6.6).

At this stage, the analyst has data to answer the first of the questions of the diagram depicted in Figure 6.2. The question is: "Do we have evidence to assert that the data measured can come from a population normally distributed?" If the answer is yes, a

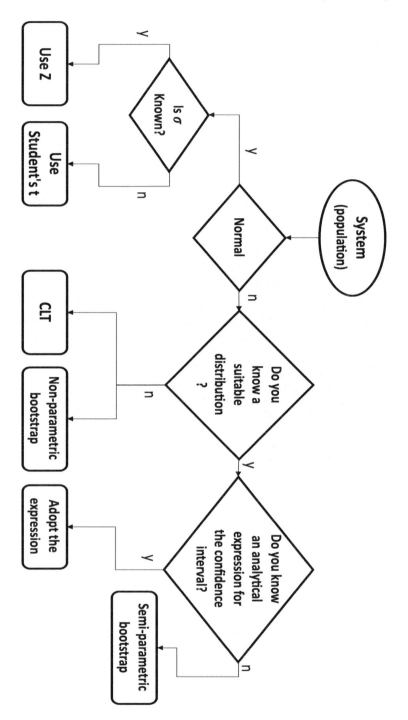

Figure 6.2 Orientation for Statistical Inference of Means.

question follows: "Do we know the population standard deviation (σ)?" If we know it, use Z^1 (Section 6.1.1) [178, 287, 436].

If we do not know the population standard deviation, apply Student's t method (Section 6.1.1) [178, 287, 436]. If we reject the normality of the data, we might ask one of these questions:

- Is it possible to transform the data set into another data set that is normally distributed? One may try to transform the original data set into another data set that is normally distributed by applying the transformation methods introduced in Section 7.1. Some handy methods are the Box-Cox and the Yeo-Johnson transformations. Hence, the transformed data set is normally distributed; as explained above, one may apply the Z or the Student's t distribution. Nevertheless, if you do not know any transformation method that can transform the original data set into a normally distributed data set, we may still ask:

- Do we know a distribution that suitably represents the population from which the sample comes?

If the answer is yes, ask, "Do you know a specific parametric inference method for this distribution?" If the answer is yes, use such a method [269]. If the answer to the last question is no, but you indeed know a distribution suitable to represent the data set, we may resort to the semi-parametric bootstrap (Section 6.5.3) [118, 120, 121].

If you are neither able to transform the data set into another data set that is normally distributed nor are aware of theoretical distribution that suitably represents the data, I would suggest two options:[2]

1. use the central limit theorem [178, 287, 436] or

2. use nonparametric bootstrap (Section 6.5.1) [118, 120, 121].

This section presents the classical parametric methods for estimating the confidence interval for means. The first method should be applied when the population variance is known; the second is suitable when the variance is unknown.

6.1.1 CONFIDENCE INTERVAL WHEN VARIANCE IS KNOWN

This section presents the parametric method to estimate the confidence interval of the mean. In order to apply this method, there should be no evidence to refute the normal distribution as an appropriate probability distribution to represent the population. Furthermore, the variance of the population, σ^2, should be known. Assuming these requirements, consider a system was measured, and one sample of size n was

---

[1] Standard normal distribution. $Z \equiv N(0.1)$.

[2] Pragmatically speaking, adopt the second option.

obtained. Let $\overline{X}$ be the mean of the sample, and $\sigma_{\overline{X}} = \sigma/\sqrt{n}$ that be the standard deviation of the sample means (standard error) according to the central limit theorem. The statistic

$$Z = \frac{\overline{X} - \mu}{\sigma_{\overline{X}}} \tag{6.1.1}$$

is distributed according to a standard normal distribution ($N(0,1)$), where μ is the system (population) mean. Therefore,

$$P\left(-z_{\frac{\alpha}{2}} \leq Z \leq z_{\frac{\alpha}{2}}\right) = 1 - \alpha,$$

where α is the significance level. Hence

$$-z_{\frac{\alpha}{2}} \leq Z \leq z_{\frac{\alpha}{2}}.$$

$$-z_{\frac{\alpha}{2}} \leq \frac{\overline{X} - \mu}{\sigma_{\overline{X}}} \leq z_{\frac{\alpha}{2}}.$$

After some algebra, we obtain

$$\overline{X} - z_{\frac{\alpha}{2}} \times \frac{\sigma}{\sqrt{n}} \leq \mu \leq \overline{X} + z_{\frac{\alpha}{2}} \times \frac{\sigma}{\sqrt{n}}.$$

Therefore, the confidence interval is calculated by:

$$\mu \in \left(\overline{X} - z_{\frac{\alpha}{2}} \times \frac{\sigma}{\sqrt{n}}, \overline{X} + z_{\frac{\alpha}{2}} \times \frac{\sigma}{\sqrt{n}}\right), \tag{6.1.2}$$

where $\overline{X}$ is the sample mean, n is the sample size, σ is the population standard deviation, and $z_{\alpha/2}$ is the value of Z for probability $\alpha/2$, where $1 - \alpha$ is the requested confidence level. The confidence interval shown above is called two-tailed.

When a mean interval has $1 - \alpha$ of confidence, it means that if 100 samples (each with n measures) are obtained, and if the confidence interval for each of these samples is calculated, $1 - \alpha$ of these intervals would contain the correct mean value. In the two-tailed confidence interval, α is divided by two for finding the upper and lower bounds of the interval that contains the population mean.

The confidence interval can also be one-tailed[3]. In this case, the interval can be either obtained by:

$$\mu \in \left(-\infty, \overline{X} + z_{\alpha} \times \frac{\sigma}{\sqrt{n}}\right) \tag{6.1.3}$$

---

[3]The one-tailed confidence interval indicates that one has $(1 - \alpha)\%$ confidence that the mean population value is above or below a threshold.

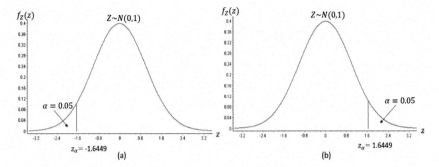

Figure 6.3   Values of z_α for Single-Valued Intervals with $\alpha = 0.05$.

or

$$\mu \in (\overline{X} - z_\alpha \times \frac{\sigma}{\sqrt{n}} \, , \, \infty).$$
(6.1.4)

In the first case, the mean is said to be above

$$\overline{X} - z_\alpha \times \frac{\sigma}{\sqrt{n}}$$

with $(1 - \alpha)\%$ of confidence. In the second case, the mean value is said to be below

$$\bar{X} + z_\alpha \times \frac{\sigma}{\sqrt{n}}$$

with $(1 - \alpha)\%$ of confidence.

Figure 6.3 shows z_α for one-tailed intervals, considering $\alpha = 0.05$.

Example 6.1.1. Consider that there is no evidence to refute the claim that the data in Table 3.2 follows a normal distribution. Also, consider that we know the population standard deviation and that its value is $\sigma = 30$ tps.

The sample mean is $\overline{X} = 119.28 tps$ and $n = 100$. For computing the confidence interval, we only need to specify the value of Z respective to the degree of significance α, that is z_α. Many statistical tables as well as tools provide z_α. The respective $P(Z < z\alpha/2) = \alpha/2$ is depicted in Figure 6.4.

The value of $z_{\alpha/2}$ is tabulated and is available in several texts. It can also be obtained by means of several statistical tools, where $Z_{critical}\% = z_{\alpha/2}$ through $P(Z < z_{critical}) = \alpha/2$. In other words, we want to find out the value of Z that satisfies $P(Z < z_{critical}) = \alpha/2$. In this specific case, $Z = z_{\alpha/2}$ that is $P(Z < z_{\alpha/2}) = 0.025$. Hence, $z_{\alpha/2} = z_{0.025} = -1.96, |z_{0.025}| = 1.96$.

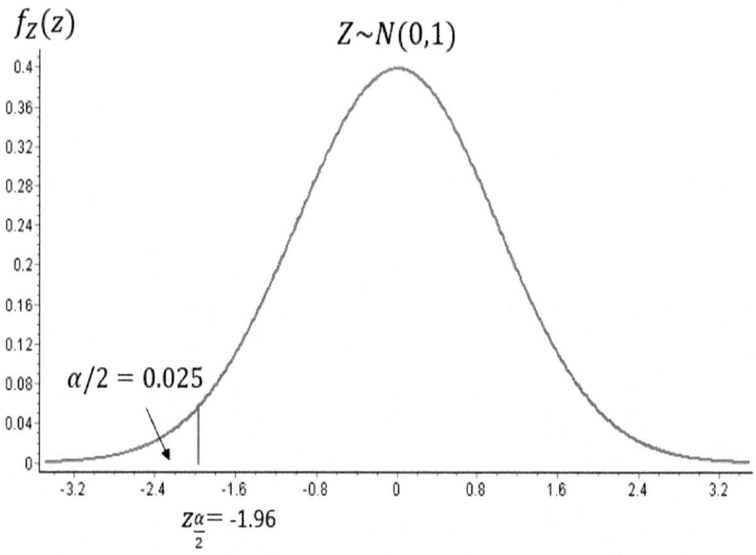

Figure 6.4 $z_{critical} - z_{\alpha/2}$.

Now, we can estimate a confidence interval for the mean by

$$\mu \in \left(119.28 - 1.96 \times \frac{30}{\sqrt{100}} \ , \ 119.28 + 1.96 \times \frac{30}{\sqrt{100}} \right)$$

$$\mu \in \left(113.40 \ , \ 125.1 \right).$$

The sample size may be estimated by:

$$n \geq \left(\frac{z_{critical} \times \sigma}{\varepsilon} \right)^2, \tag{6.1.5}$$

where ε is the accepted error.

Example 6.1.2. Consider that we want to estimate the required sample size to estimate the confidence interval for the 95% confidence interval. Assume that we know the population standard deviation ($\sigma = 30 tps.$). If the margin of error considered is $\varepsilon = 8 tps$, we have:

$$n \geq \left(\frac{z_{\frac{\alpha}{2}} \times \sigma}{\varepsilon} \right)^2 = \left(\frac{1.96 \times 30}{8} \right)^2 = 54.0225. \tag{6.1.6}$$

6.1.2 CONFIDENCE INTERVAL WHEN VARIANCE IS UNKNOWN

This section presents a parametric method to estimate the confidence interval of the mean when system (population) variance is unknown. The requirement to apply this method is that there is no evidence to refute the normal distribution as suitable to represent the population. This method does not require the population variance to be known; instead, the population variance is estimated through the sample variance. This method uses the Student's t distribution. Assuming these requirements, consider a system was measured, and one sample of size n was obtained. Let $\overline{X}$ be the mean of the sample, and SD be the sample standard deviation. The statistic

$$T = \frac{\overline{X} - \mu}{SD/\sqrt{n}} \tag{6.1.7}$$

is distributed according to a standard Student's t distribution with $n - 1$ degrees of freedom (t_{n-1}), where μ is the system (population) mean. Therefore,

$$P(-t_{\frac{\alpha}{2},n-1} \leq T \leq t_{\frac{\alpha}{2},n-1}) = 1 - \alpha,$$

where α is the significance level. Hence

$$-t_{\frac{\alpha}{2},n-1} \leq T \leq t_{\frac{\alpha}{2},n-1}.$$

$$-t_{\frac{\alpha}{2},n-1} \leq \frac{\overline{X} - \mu}{SD/\sqrt{n}} \leq t_{\frac{\alpha}{2},n-1}.$$

After some algebra, we obtain

$$\overline{X} - t_{\frac{\alpha}{2},n-1} \times \frac{SD}{\sqrt{n}} \leq \mu \leq \overline{X} + t_{\frac{\alpha}{2},n-1} \times \frac{SD}{\sqrt{n}}.$$

The two-tailed confidence interval is calculated by:

$$\mu \in \left(\overline{X} - t_{\frac{\alpha}{2},n-1} \times \frac{SD}{\sqrt{n}}, \overline{X} + t_{\frac{\alpha}{2},n-1} \times \frac{SD}{\sqrt{n}} \right), \tag{6.1.8}$$

where $\overline{X}$ is the average mean, n is the sample size, SD is the sample standard deviation. $t_{\alpha/2,n-1}$ is the t value obtained when Student's t distribution with $n - 1$ degree of freedom is $\alpha/2$.

As in the case of the previous section, the one-tailed confidence interval can be calculated by:

$$\mu \in \left(\overline{X} - t_{\frac{\alpha}{2},n-1} \times \frac{SD}{\sqrt{n}}, \overline{X} + t_{\frac{\alpha}{2},n-1} \times \frac{SD}{\sqrt{n}} \right), \tag{6.1.9}$$

where $\overline{X}$ is the sample average, n is the sample size, SD is the sample standard deviation. $t_{\alpha/2,n-1}$ is the t value obtained when Student's t distribution with $n-1$ degree of freedom, and α is the degree of significance.

Example 6.1.3. Assume there is no evidence to refute the claim that the data in Table 3.2 comes from a normal distribution. Besides, take into account the population standard deviation is unknown. The sample mean is $\overline{X} = 119.28\,tps$, the sample standard deviation is $29.23\,tps$, and $n = 100$. Therefore, in order to calculate the confidence interval for the mean, we only need to know $t_{\alpha/2,n-1}$. For a two-tailed confidence interval equal $1 - \alpha = 95\%$ ($\alpha = 5\%$ of significance), we have $\alpha/2 = 2.5\%$. $t_{\alpha/2,n-1}$ is tabulated and is available in several tables. It can also be obtained by means of many statistical tools (see Figure 6.5) through $P(t < t^*) = \alpha/2$. In this specific case, we need to find out the value of t^*, such that $P(t < t^*) = 0.025$, considering a degree of freedom equal to $99\,(n-1 = 100 - 1 = 99)$. For this example, $t_{\alpha/2,n-1} = t_{0.025,99} = -1.9842$. $|t_{0.025,99}| = 1.9842$.

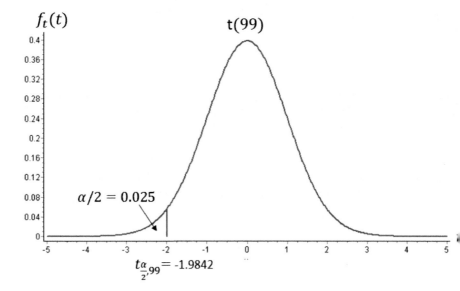

Figure 6.5 $t_{critical} - t_{\frac{\alpha}{2}}, n - 1$.

The two-tailed confidence interval for the mean is

$$\mu \in \left(119.28 - 1.9842 \times \frac{29,23}{\sqrt{100}} \ , \ 119.28 + 1.9842 \times \frac{29.23}{\sqrt{100}} \right) \qquad (6.1.10)$$

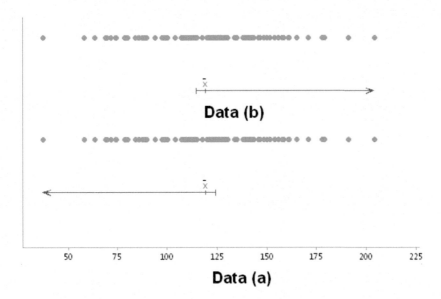

Figure 6.6   Dot Plot and One-Tailed Confidence Interval.

$$\mu \in (113.48 \text{ s} , \quad 125.08 \text{ s}). \tag{6.1.11}$$

Considering the same degree of confidence, that is, 95%, we have no evidence to refute that

$$\mu \in (-\infty , \quad 124.13 \text{ s}). \tag{6.1.12}$$

Likewise, we have no evidence to refute

$$\mu \in (114.42 \text{ s} , \quad \infty). \tag{6.1.13}$$

Figure 6.6 shows the dot plot and the respective one-tailed confidence intervals.

The size of the sample can be estimated by

$$n' \geq \left(\frac{t_{\frac{\alpha}{2}, n-1} \times SD}{\varepsilon} \right)^2, \tag{6.1.14}$$

where ε is the margin of error considered and n is the size of the preliminary sample used to estimate σ through SD.

Example 6.1.4. Consider that a sample size should be estimated taking into account a given degree of confidence of 95%. If the population standard deviation is unknown, a preliminary sample of size $n = 10$ may be adopted to estimate the population standard deviation (σ) from the sample standard deviation (SD). If the preliminary sample standard deviation is $42.5 tps$ and the specified error is $\varepsilon = 8 tps$, the sample size may be estimated by:

$$n' \geq \left(\frac{t_{\frac{\alpha}{2},n-1} \times SD}{\varepsilon} \right)^2 = \left(\frac{t_{0.025,9} \times SD}{\varepsilon} \right)^2 = \left(\frac{2.2281 \times 42.5}{8} \right)^2 = 140.11.$$

$$(6.1.15)$$

Hence, in this particular example:

$$n' \geq 141. \tag{6.1.16}$$

Since $n = 10$ are already available (from the preliminary sample), at least 131 more measurements should be obtained, since $n' = n + n_{addition}$. Hence, $n_{addition} = 131$.

6.2 PARAMETRIC CONFIDENCE INTERVAL FOR VARIANCE AND STANDARD DEVIATION

This section presents the classical parametric method for estimating the confidence interval for variance and standard deviation. Figure 6.7 presents a diagram that guides the choice of the statistical methods. Therefore, using this guideline, the question is: Do we have enough evidence to support non-rejecting the normal distribution as a suitable distribution to represent the population? If sufficient evidence is available, the normal distribution must be rejected, and the chi-square distribution should not be adopted to estimate the population confidence interval of the variance and the standard deviation. On the other hand, if the evidence is not sufficient to support the rejection, the chi-square distribution (see Figure 6.8) may be adopted for estimating the confidence intervals.

Assuming the requirements described above, consider that a system was measured, and one sample of size n was collected. Let SD^2 denote the sample variance and σ^2 be the system (population) variance. The statistic

$$\chi^2 = \frac{(n-1)SD^2}{\sigma^2}$$

is distributed according to a χ^2 distribution with $n-1$ degrees of freedom. Hence

$$P(\chi^2_{\left(\frac{\alpha}{2},n-1\right)} \leq \chi^2 \leq \chi^2_{\left(1-\frac{\alpha}{2},n-1\right)}) = 1 - \alpha.$$

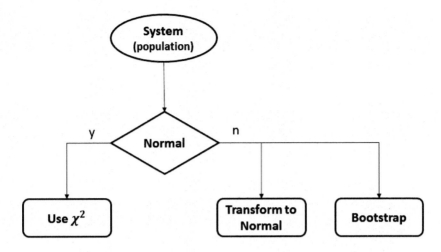

Figure 6.7   Choosing the Method to Estimate the Variance Confidence Interval

Thus

$$\chi^2_{\left(\frac{\alpha}{2},n-1\right)} \leq \chi^2 \leq \chi^2_{\left(1-\frac{\alpha}{2},n-1\right)}.$$

$$\chi^2_{\left(\frac{\alpha}{2},n-1\right)} \leq \frac{(n-1)SD^2}{\sigma^2} \leq \chi^2_{\left(1-\frac{\alpha}{2},n-1\right)}.$$

After some algebra, we obtain

$$\frac{(n-1)SD^2}{\chi^2_{\left(1-\frac{\alpha}{2},n-1\right)}} \leq \sigma^2 \leq \frac{(n-1)SD^2}{\chi^2_{\left(\frac{\alpha}{2},n-1\right)}}.$$

The method presented here may be implemented by the following steps:

1. Verify whether the data (collected sample) suggests the population may be properly represented by a normal distribution.

2. Using $n-1$ degrees of freedom (sample size minus one) and the required degree of confidence $(1-\alpha)$, find $\chi^2_{\left(\frac{\alpha}{2},n-1\right)}.$ and $\chi^2_{\left(1-\frac{\alpha}{2},n-1\right)}$

3. Calculate the upper and lower bounds of the interval by:

$$\sigma^2 \in \left(\frac{(n-1) \times SD^2}{\chi^2_{1-\frac{\alpha}{2},\,n-1}}, \frac{(n-1) \times SD^2}{\chi^2_{\frac{\alpha}{2},\,n-1}} \right) \tag{6.2.1}$$

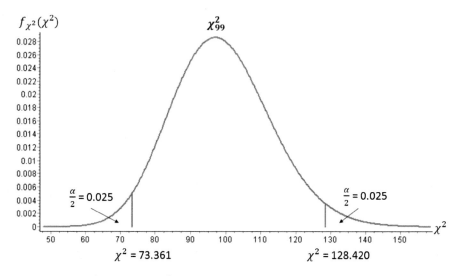

Figure 6.8 $\chi^2_{1-\frac{\alpha}{2},n-1}$ and $\chi^2_{1-\frac{\alpha}{2},n-1}$.

The confidence interval of σ is obtained by:

$$\sigma \in \left(\sqrt{\frac{(n-1) \times SD^2}{\chi^2_{1-\frac{\alpha}{2},\,n-1}}}, \sqrt{\frac{(n-1) \times SD^2}{\chi^2_{\frac{\alpha}{2},\,n-1}}} \right) \tag{6.2.2}$$

$\chi^2_{\alpha/2}$, and $\chi^2_{1-\alpha/2}$ are the values of χ^2, obtained through the distribution χ^2 with degree of freedom $n-1$ and the probabilities $\alpha/2$ and $1-\alpha/2$, respectively. The values $\chi^2_{\alpha/2}$, and $\chi^2_{1-\alpha/2}$ are tabulated and are available in several texts. They can also be obtained through statistical tools (see Figure 6.8) through $P(\chi^2_{n-1} < \chi^2_{\alpha/2,n-1}) = \alpha/2$ and $P(\chi^2_{n-1} < \chi^2_{1-\alpha/2,n-1}) = 1 - \alpha/2$.

The one-tailed confidence intervals are

$$\sigma^2 \in \left(-\infty, \frac{(n-1) \times SD^2}{\chi^2_{\alpha,n-1}} \right), \tag{6.2.3}$$

$$\sigma^2 \in \left(\frac{(n-1) \times SD^2}{\chi^2_{1-\alpha,n-1}}, \infty \right), \tag{6.2.4}$$

$$\sigma \in \left(-\infty, \sqrt{\frac{(n-1) \times SD^2}{\chi^2_{\alpha,n-1}}} \right), \tag{6.2.5}$$

and

$$\sigma \in \left(\sqrt{\frac{(n-1) \times SD^2}{\chi^2_{1-\alpha,n-1}}}, \infty \right).$$ (6.2.6)

Example 6.2.1. Consider that there is no evidence to refute the claim that the data in Table 3.2 ($n = 100$) come from a normal distribution. The confidence interval for variance and for the population standard deviation with 95% may be calculated. $SD = 29,23\,tps$, $Var = 854,36\,tps^2$. Since $1 - \alpha = 95\%$, hence $\frac{\alpha}{2} = 2.5\%$. As $\chi^2_{\frac{\alpha}{2},\,n-1} = 73.361$ and $\chi^2_{1-\frac{\alpha}{2},\,n-1} = 128.42$ (See Figure 6.8); thus :

$$\sigma^2 \in \left(\frac{(n-1) \times SD^2}{\chi^2_{\frac{\alpha}{2},n-1}}, \frac{(n-1) \times SD^2}{\chi^2_{1-\frac{\alpha}{2}\,n-1}} \right) = \left(\frac{99 \times 854.36}{128.42}, \frac{99 \times 854.36}{73.361} \right).$$ (6.2.7)

$$\sigma^2 \in (658.63\,tps^2, 1152,95\,tps^2),$$ (6.2.8)

and

$$\sigma \in (25.66\,tps, 33.96\,tps).$$ (6.2.9)

□

6.3 PARAMETRIC CONFIDENCE INTERVAL FOR PROPORTION

This chapter presents three methods for estimating confidence intervals of proportions. This section introduces two parametric methods since they are likely to provide narrower intervals than those computed by bootstrap (see Section 6.5). The first parametric method is based on the binomial distribution, and the second adopts the normal distribution as a suitable approximation of the binomial probability distribution. The latter demands less computational effort but requires additional criteria. The criteria required for adequately representing the binomial probability are described later.

6.3.1 PARAMETRIC CONFIDENCE INTERVAL FOR PROPORTION USING THE BINOMIAL DISTRIBUTION

This section presents the parametric method to estimate the confidence interval of proportions (p) based on the binomial distribution, $b(n,k)$. Consider a sample of size n with k successes (events of interest). The point estimate of the proportion is obtained through

$$p' = \frac{k}{n}.$$ (6.3.1)

Now, take into account that:

$$S_{\leq \frac{\alpha}{2}} = \left\{ k_l \,|\, k_l = \max_{k'}\{k'\}, P(X \leq k') \leq \frac{\alpha}{2}, k' \in \mathbb{N} \right\}, \qquad (6.3.2)$$

where $S_{\leq \frac{\alpha}{2}}$ is a unity set that has the maximal k', that is k_l, satisfying $P(X \leq k') \leq \frac{\alpha}{2}$. It is known that

$$P(X \leq k_l) \leq \frac{\alpha}{2} \qquad (6.3.3)$$

$$\Longleftrightarrow$$

$$P(X \leq k_l) = \sum_{k'=1}^{k_l} \binom{n}{k'} \times p'^{k'} \times (1 - p')^{n-k'} \leq \frac{\alpha}{2}. \qquad (6.3.4)$$

Therefore, the lower limit of the confidence interval (two-tailed) with $(1 - \alpha)\%$ is

$$p_l = \frac{k_l}{n}. \qquad (6.3.5)$$

Now consider

$$S_{\leq 1 - \frac{\alpha}{2}} = \left\{ k_u \,|\, k_u = \max_{k'}\{k'\}, P(X \geq k') \leq 1 - \frac{\alpha}{2}, k' \in \mathbb{N} \right\}, \qquad (6.3.6)$$

that is, $S_{\leq 1 - \frac{\alpha}{2}}$ is a unity set that has the maximal k', that is k_u, which satisfies $P(X \leq k') \leq 1 - \frac{\alpha}{2}$.

Hence,

$$P(X \leq k_u) \leq 1 - \frac{\alpha}{2} \qquad (6.3.7)$$

$$\Longleftrightarrow$$

$$P(X \leq k_u) = \sum_{k'=1}^{k_u} \binom{n}{k'} \times p'^{k'} \times (1 - p')^{n-k'} \leq 1 - \frac{\alpha}{2}. \qquad (6.3.8)$$

Therefore, the upper limit of the confidence interval (two-tailed) with the degree of significance equal to $(\alpha)\%$ is

$$p_u = \frac{k_u}{n}. \tag{6.3.9}$$

The confidence interval of the ratio $((1 - \alpha)\%$ confidence) is:

$$p \in (p_l, p_u) = \left(\frac{k_l}{n}, \frac{k_u}{n} \right). \tag{6.3.10}$$

Example 6.3.1. Consider that $m = 25843$ location sensors of mobile phones were tested last month. A total of 342 faulty devices has been found. The confidence interval for the proportion of defects with $1 - \alpha = 95\%$ confidence needs to be calculated; hence :

$$p' = \frac{m}{n} = \frac{342}{25843} = 0.013234.$$

If all devices are of the same model and they were tested in similar conditions throughout an evaluation period, we get:

$$S_{\leq 0.025} = \{k \mid P(X \leq k) \leq 0.025\} = \{305\},$$

since $k = 305$ is the greater integer that fulfills $P(X \leq k) < 0.025$, because $P(X \leq 305) = F_{b(25843)}(305) = 0.02197[4]$ and $P(X \leq 306) = F_{b(25843)}(306) = 0.0251$. Therefore, a k greater than 305 violates $P(X \leq k) < 0.025$. Observe the probability mass function $f_{b(n)}(k)$ depicted in Figure 6.9, where $n = 25843$.

Thus

$$pl = \frac{k}{n} = \frac{305}{25843} = 0.011802.$$

Now consider

$$S_{\leq 0.975} = \{k \mid P(X \geq k) \leq 0.975\} = \{378\},$$

since $k = 378$ is the largest integer that does not violate $P(X \leq k) \leq 0.975$, because

$$P(X \leq 378) = F_{b(25843)}(378) = 0.97511$$

and

$$P(X \leq 377) = F_{b(25843)}(377) = 0.97188.$$

---

[4]$F_{b(n)}(k)$ is the binomial cumulative distribution function.

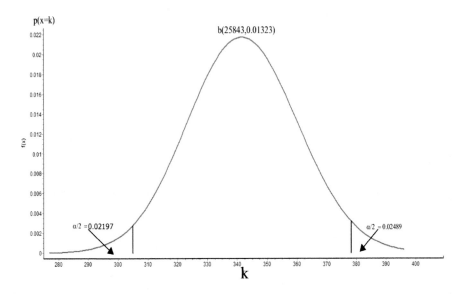

Figure 6.9 $S_{\leq 0.025} = \{305\}$ and $S_{\leq 0.975} = \{378\}$.

So:

$$pu = \frac{k}{n} = \frac{378}{25843} = 0.01463.$$

As

$$p \in (p_l \ , \ p_u) = \left(\frac{k_l}{n}, \frac{k_u}{n}\right), \tag{6.3.11}$$

then

$$p \in \left(\frac{305}{25843}, \frac{378}{25843}\right) = (0.011802, 0.01463),$$

taking into account 95% confidence.

It is important to stress, however, that the actual degree of confidence is $F_{b(n)}(378) - F_{b(n)}(304) = 0.9552$, since $F_{b(n)}(378) = 0.97511$ and $F_{b(n)}(304) = 0.01668$, for $n = 25843$.

6.3.2 PARAMETRIC CONFIDENCE INTERVAL FOR PROPORTION BASED ON NORMAL APPROXIMATION

This method is suitable when a normal distribution can approximate a binomial distribution. Remember, though, that the binomial distribution is discrete, whereas the normal distribution is continuous. The shape of binomial distributions varies significantly depending on their parameters (n and p). If p is close to 0.5 and n is large, the binomial distribution can be approximated by a normal distribution. For the even larger value of n, it is still possible to approximate the binomial distribution by the normal distribution, albeit p departs from 0.5. Below, a procedure for calculating the confidence interval of proportion is presented,$(p)^5$:

1. Check if there is no evidence to refute the normal distribution as a suitable approximation of the binomial distribution (see conditions below).

2. Find the critical value, $Z^* \left(Z_{\frac{\alpha}{2}} \right)$.

3. Calculate the error interval, $\varepsilon \leq Z_{\frac{\alpha}{2}} \times \sqrt{\frac{p'q'}{n}}$.

4. Find $p \in (p' - \varepsilon, \ p' + \varepsilon)$.

Conditions for a normal distribution to approximate a binomial distribution:

- The procedure must have a fixed number of repetitions (n).

- Repetitions should be independent.

- Each repetition should have all results classified into two categories.

- The probabilities (p and q) must remain constant for each repetition.

- $n \times p' \geq 5$ or $n \times q' \geq 5$, where ($p' = 1 - q'$).

If these conditions are satisfied, the mean value (μ) and the standard deviation (σ) of the normal distribution can be estimated by:

$$\mu = n \times p' \qquad (6.3.12)$$

$$\sigma = \sqrt{n \times p' \times q'} \qquad (6.3.13)$$

The formal proof of this equivalence is known as DeMoivre-Laplace approximation [343] [167].

$^5 p'$ − (sample ratio) and $p' + q' = 1$.

The confidence interval for proportion may also be one-tailed[6]. In such a case, the interval is estimated by:

$$p \in (-\infty \ , \quad p' + \varepsilon) \tag{6.3.14}$$

or

$$p \in (p' - \varepsilon \ , \quad \infty), \tag{6.3.15}$$

where $\varepsilon \leq Z_\alpha \times \sqrt{\frac{p'q'}{n}}$.

Example 6.3.2. Suppose 829 computers were evaluated to check if their respective operating systems were defective in the last ten days. In this sample, it was observed that 426 shown some defect in their operating systems. However, the other equipment did not present defects. Therefore, we wish to calculate the confidence interval for the proportion of defects with 95% confidence using the normal distribution.

From the above description, we know that $n = 829$ and we observed 426 defects (m). Therefore:

$$p' = \frac{m}{n} = \frac{426}{829} = 0.513872.$$

Let's consider that all computers are similar (have the same characteristics) and that they were in similar conditions throughout the evaluation period. Observe that $n \times p' \geq 5$, because $829 \times 0.513872 = 426 \gg 5$. These are basic features needed to support the normal distribution as an approximation binomial distribution. The mean value, as well as the standard deviation of the normal distribution, is estimated by:

$$\mu = 829 \times 0.513872 = 426.$$

$$\sigma = \sqrt{829 \times 0.513872 \times 0.486128} = 14.39.$$

Since $|Z_{0.025}| = 1.96$,

the confidence interval is:

$$(p' - E, \ p' + E) = \left(p' - Z_{\frac{\alpha}{2}} \times \sqrt{\frac{p'q'}{n}}, \ p' + Z_{\frac{\alpha}{2}} \times \sqrt{\frac{p'q'}{n}} \right) =$$

---

[6]The one-tailed confidence interval specifies that one has $(1 - \alpha)\%$ confidence that the population means is above or below the respective threshold.

$$(0.513872 - 1.96 \times \sqrt{\frac{0.513872 \times 0.486128}{829}} ,$$

$$0.513872 + 1.96 \times \sqrt{\frac{0.513872 \times 0.486128}{829}}) =$$

$$p \in (0.4798 , 0.5479).$$

6.4 PARAMETRIC CONFIDENCE INTERVAL FOR DIFFERENCE

This section presents two parametric methods for calculating the confidence interval of differences. These methods help compare the performance of two systems. The methods presented are the paired comparison and the comparison of the non-corresponding measurements method.

6.4.1 CONFIDENCE INTERVAL FOR PAIRED COMPARISON

This section introduces the parametric method for calculating the confidence interval for paired measurements. In order to apply this method, the paired observations should be normally distributed, but it is resistant to moderate deviation from normality [287]. Furthermore, this method compares the mean of the difference of two sets of paired observations. Therefore, it is appropriate to compare the performance between the two systems. This method is usually called the paired t-test or t-test using a matched pairs.

This method is useful for analyzing cases like this:

1. Differences between two systems (S_1 and S_2) that have been studied, considering different workloads (wl_1, wl_2, wl_3, wl_4, ..., wl_n).

2. Differences in performance of a system before (b) and after (a) a "treatment" (improvement, upgrade, etc.). As in the previous case, different workloads should be considered.

Method

1. Set up a table (see Table 6.1) with four (4) columns and the number of rows equal to the number of workloads (treatments) to be considered in the study.

   a. In the first column, identify the workloads.

   b. In the second and third columns, identify the performance metric of interest (m) obtained from system S_1 (or S_b), here called m_i^1, and system S_2 (or S_a), called m_i^2, respectively.

   c. The fourth column should store the difference of the values contained in the cells of the second and third columns, that is, $d_1 = m_1^1 - m_1^2$.

Caution: Keep the same reference for all subtractions stored in the cells of the fourth column; i.e., if for the first cell calculate $d_1 = m_1^1 - m_1^2$, consider m_i^1 as minuend from the other differences in the table.

2. For each workload (wl_i), obtain the value of the metric of interest (m) in the system S_1 (or S_b) and the system S_2 (or S_a), that is m_i^1 and m_1^2, respectively.

   Caution: The execution order of the experiments must be random to avoid favoring one of the systems.

3. Fill in the table.

4. Calculate the differences: $d_i = m_i^1 - m_i^2$.

5. Calculate the mean of differences, $\bar{d} = \frac{\sum_i^n d_i}{n}$, and the standard deviation of the differences, $SD_{d_i} = \frac{\sum_i^n (d_i - \bar{d})}{n-1}$.

6. Find the critical value of $t_{\alpha/2, n-1}$, where α is the significance level and n is the number of differences (matches the number of workloads or treatments).

7. Calculate the confidence interval of the differences by:

$$\left(\bar{d} - t_{\frac{\alpha}{2}, n-1} \times \frac{SD_{\bar{d}}}{\sqrt{n}} , \ \bar{d} + t_{\frac{\alpha}{2}, n-1} \times \frac{SD_{\bar{d}}}{\sqrt{n}} \right).$$

8. If

$$0 \in \left(\bar{d} - t_{\frac{\alpha}{2}, n-1} \times \frac{SD_{\bar{d}}}{\sqrt{n}} , \ \bar{d} + t_{\frac{\alpha}{2}, n-1} \times \frac{SD_{\bar{d}}}{\sqrt{n}} \right),$$

there is no evidence to refute the equivalence between the performances of the systems S_1 and S_2.

9. If

$$0 \notin \left(\bar{d} - t_{\frac{\alpha}{2}, n-1} \times \frac{SD_{\bar{d}}}{\sqrt{n}} , \ \bar{d} + t_{\frac{\alpha}{2}, n-1} \times \frac{SD_{\bar{d}}}{\sqrt{n}} \right),$$

there is evidence to refute the equivalence between the systems.

Example 6.4.1. Consider the performance evaluation of two servers $(S_1$ and $S_2)$ in relation to the execution time of a benchmark composed of ten (10) programs $(\{p_i | 1 \leq i \leq 10, \ i \in N\})$. It is required to find out if the servers have equivalent performance. Adopt 95% degree of confidence.

Each program p_i was properly executed on each server, that is S_1 and S_2, and their execution times (et) were stored in columns 2 and 3 of Table 6.1.

The mean and the standard deviation of differences are

$$\bar{d} = \frac{\sum_i^n d_i}{n} = \frac{0.09}{10} = 0.01 \ s,$$

Table 6.1

Comparison between S_1 and S_2

Workload i	System S_1 Measure (m_i^1)	System S_2 Measure (m_i^2)	Differences $d_i = m_i^1 - m_i^2$
wl_1	m_1^1	m_1^2	$d_1 = m_1^1 - m_1^2$
wl_2	m_2^1	m_2^2	$d_1 = m_2^1 - m_2^2$
wl_3	m_3^1	m_3^2	$d_1 = m_3^1 - m_3^2$
...	...	...	...
wl_n	m_n^1	m_n^2	$d_n = m_n^1 - m_n^2$

Table 6.2

Comparison between S_1 and S_2

Program p_i	$et_{S_1}(p_i)$ (s)	$et_{S_2}(p_i)$ (s)	$di = et_{S_1}(p_i) - et_{S_2}(p_i)$ (s)
p1	98.328	99.974	-1.64554
p2	108.359	107.311	1.04864
p3	90.017	86.999	3.01828
p4	122.155	115.502	6.65252
p5	140.675	140.189	0.48578
p6	91.444	90.756	0.68831
p7	89.56	93.506	-3.945
p8	158.992	163.837	-4.84573
p9	100	99	1
p10	131.062	133.431	-2.36

$$SD_{\bar{d}} = \frac{\sum_i^n (d_i - \bar{d})}{n-1} = 3.39 \ s,$$

$$n = 10.$$

Since $1 - \alpha = 0.95$; thus $\alpha/2 = 0.025$.

Find out $\left| t_{\frac{\alpha}{2}, n-1} \right|$ using a table or use a statistics tool. Notice that $\left| t_{\frac{\alpha}{2}, n-1} \right| = \left| t_{0.025;9} \right| = 2.2622$. Hence:

$$\left(\bar{d} - t_{\frac{\alpha}{2}, n-1} \times \frac{SD_{\bar{d}}}{\sqrt{n}}, \ \bar{d} + t_{\frac{\alpha}{2}, n-1} \times \frac{SD_{\bar{d}}}{\sqrt{n}} \right) =$$

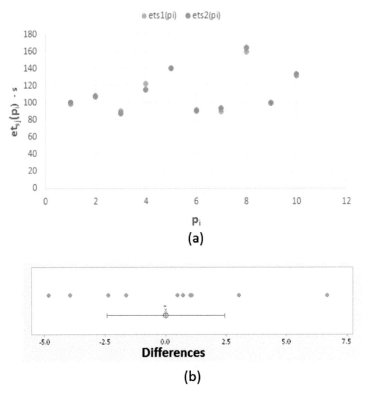

Figure 6.10 Paired Comparison.

$$\left(0.01 - 2.2622 \times \frac{3.39}{\sqrt{10}}, \ 0.01 + 2.2622 \times \frac{3.39}{\sqrt{10}}\right) =$$

$$(-2.42 \ s, \ 2.44 \ s).$$

As $0 \in (-2.42 \ s, \ 2.44 \ s)$, there is no evidence that shows a difference between the performances of the servers in relation to the execution times of these ten (10) programs. Figure 6.10 (a) shows the execution times $(et_{S_j}(p_i))$ of each program (p_i) on the servers S_1 and S_2. Figure 6.10 (b) shows the respective execution time differences (d_i), and the confidence interval of the difference.

$P (t \geq \bar{d})$ is calculated using Student's t distribution with nine $(n-1 = 9)$ degrees of freedom. The result is $P (t \geq \bar{d}) = P (t \geq 0.01) = 0.49612$, which can be observed in Figure 6.11. As $P (t \geq 0.01)$ is greater than the chosen degree of significance $\alpha/2 = 0.025$, we have no evidence to state a difference between the systems.

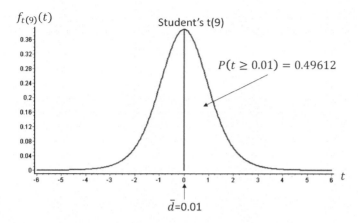

Figure 6.11 $P(t \geq 0.01) = 0.49612$.

6.4.2   CONFIDENCE INTERVAL FOR COMPARISON OF NON-CORRESPONDING MEASUREMENTS

This section introduces the method for calculating the confidence interval of differences of unpaired samples. This method is more general than the one described in the previous section since pairing is not required. Nevertheless, the intervals tend to be wider. Here we are interested in finding out if the two sample means are significantly different from one another. This method is also usually named the unpaired t-test.

This method compares the difference of the means of two sets of observations. Therefore, it is appropriate to compare the performance between two systems (S_1 and S_2). Data from both sets are required to be normally distributed, but moderate departures from normality do not adversely affect the procedure [287]. The method also adopts the Student's t distribution. The procedure is described below.

Method:

1. Set up the table (see Table 6.3) with two (2) columns. Each column will be used to store the observations of each system (S_1 and S_2), respectively. The number of rows in each column should equal the number of observations (measurements) to be made in each system. The number of observations in each system may be different.

2. Get the metric of interest (m) in the system S_1 and system S_2, that is m_i^1 and m_i^2, respectively and fill in the table [7].

---

[7]Caution: As already mentioned, the measurement process must be meticulous to avoid bias that invalidates the experiment. It is essential to pay particular attention to the order of execution of the experiments. This order must be random so as not to privilege one of the evaluated systems.

3. Calculate the averages of each set of measurements:

$$\bar{X}_{S_1} = \frac{\sum_i^k m_i^1}{k}$$

and

$$\bar{X}_{S_2} = \frac{\sum_i^l m_i^2}{l}$$

4. Calculate the variances of each set of observations:

$$Var_{S_1} = \frac{\sum_i^k \left(m_i^1 - \bar{X}_{S_1}\right)^2}{k-1}$$

and

$$Var_{S_2} = \frac{\sum_i^l \left(m_i^2 - \bar{X}_{S_2}\right)^2}{l-1}$$

5. Calculate the differences of means:

$$d = \overline{X}_{S_1} - \overline{X}_{S_2}$$

6. Calculate the combined standard deviation of the difference:

$$SD_d = \sqrt{\frac{Var_{S_1}}{k} + \frac{Var_{S_2}}{l}}$$

7. Calculate the degree of freedom:

$$df = \left[\frac{\left(\frac{Var_{S_1}}{k} + \frac{Var_{S_2}}{l}\right)^2}{\frac{\left(\frac{Var_{S_1}}{k}\right)^2}{k-1} + \frac{\left(\frac{Var_{S_2}}{l}\right)^2}{l-1}} \right]$$

8. Find the critical value[8] of $t_{\alpha/2,df}$, where α is the degree of significance and df is the degree of freedom.

9. Calculate the confidence interval of the difference by:

$$\left(d - t_{\frac{\alpha}{2},df} \times SD_d \quad , \quad d + t_{\frac{\alpha}{2},df} \times SD_d\right).$$

10. If $0 \in (d - t_{\alpha/2,df} \times SD_d \quad , \quad d + t_{\alpha/2,df} \times SD_d)$, there is no evidence to refute the equivalence between the performances of the S_1 and S_2 systems.

Table 6.3

Measurements and Means

Measures System S_1 (m_i^1)	Measures System S_2 (m_i^2)
m_1^1	m_1^2
m_2^1	m_2^2
m_3^1	m_3^2
...	...
m_k^1	m_k^2
	...
	m_l^2

11. If $0 \notin (d - t_{\alpha/2,df} \times SD_d \ , \ d + t_{\alpha/2,df} \times SD_d)$, there is evidence to refute the equivalence between the performances of the S_1 and S_2 systems.

Example 6.4.2. Consider the performance evaluation of two servers (S_1 and S_2). The metric of interest is the execution time of a program p. We are interested in identifying if the servers have equivalent performance or if it is possible to detect a difference between their performances, adopting 95% degree of confidence. The program p was executed eighty (80) times on server S_1 and sixty (60) times on server S_2. The time of each execution (in seconds) is presented in Table 6.4 and Table 6.5, respectively.

The mean execution times were: $\bar{X}_{S_1} = 129.29\ s$ and $\bar{X}_{S_2} = 96.48\ s$. The variances of the execution times in each server were: $Var_{S_1} = 335.62\ s^2$ and $Var_{S_2} = 229.96\ s^2$. The difference between the means is: $d = \bar{X}_{S_1} - \bar{X}_{S_2} = 129.29 - 96.48 = 32.81\ s$. $k = 80$ and $l = 60$. Hence:

$$SD_d = \sqrt{\frac{Var_{S_1}}{k} + \frac{Var_{S_2}}{l}} = \sqrt{\frac{335.62}{80} + \frac{229.96}{60}} = 2.8334\ s.$$

The degree of freedom is:

$$df = \left\lceil \frac{\left(\frac{Var_{S_1}}{k} + \frac{Var_{S_2}}{l}\right)^2}{\frac{\left(\frac{Var_{S_1}}{k}\right)^2}{k-1} + \frac{\left(\frac{Var_{S_2}}{l}\right)^2}{l-1}} \right\rceil = \left\lceil \frac{\left(\frac{335.62}{80} + \frac{229.96}{60}\right)^2}{\frac{\left(\frac{335.62}{80}\right)^2}{79} + \frac{\left(\frac{229.96}{60}\right)^2}{69}} \right\rceil = \lceil 136.61 \rceil = 137$$

[8]See Figure 6.5

Table 6.4

Execution Times of p in S_1 (s)

128.8889	131.9825	146.6564	152.4132	108.8858	120.9392
135.3684	100.3032	130.3808	143.8752	135.3981	131.9884
124.8359	100.2743	126.0511	126.0745	139.8403	166.4441
169.4574	71.59124	124.2379	100.0792	141.5367	136.9231
132.4383	121.9959	129.7074	129.4364	120.5112	124.0616
127.1439	116.4275	98.49064	147.132	147.6174	126.0622
133.3001	154.0759	129.5195	129.6519	157.1947	109.3149
122.161	119.1393	133.177	139.383	124.2305	109.8805
138.4465	132.2861	146.1545	136.2227	123.1625	134.906
131.7068	108.4131	147.4526	121.4935	117.4007	138.3835
101.4498	170.9016	101.8073	87.1168	156.0243	124.4304
122.519	147.404	127.9268	125.4507	118.192	128.8633
120.2534	160.9791	105.14	152.7198	128.9949	128.1379
162.0163	120.346				

The critical value is $|t_{0.025,\ 137}| = 1.9774$. Observe the critical value in the density function of t_{137} shown in Figure 6.12.

The two-tailed confidence interval is:

$$\left(d - t_{\frac{\alpha}{2},df} \times SD_d \quad , \quad d + t_{\frac{\alpha}{2},df} \times SD_d \right) =$$

$$(32.81 - 1.9774 \times 2.8334 \quad , \quad 32.81 + 1.9774 \times 2.8334) =$$

Table 6.5
Execution Times of p in S_2 (s)

97.0976	96.7093	75.9953	111.2402	96.3580	75.0536
86.7689	71.0738	90.4117	115.2223	85.0790	96.8029
75.1732	111.0476	85.3946	105.0384	85.1352	118.5020
102.0201	112.8616	113.5483	99.8367	100.2675	124.9278
71.9474	97.626	80.0626	103.6038	121.8776	105.6923
110.7070	69.1854	110.1512	105.0958	87.8749	96.3081
98.0096	103.9656	106.0298	100.7254	98.1204	113.2560
98.0467	97.0015	118.2828	108.0790	96.696	64.6555
102.7555	73.2157	126.6669	98.9518	68.4163	98.9400
96.7998	84.4191	93.6163	91.3953	68.3368	90.5625

$$(27.21 \ s \quad , \quad 38.41 \ s).$$

As $0 \notin (27.21 \ s, \quad 38.41 \ s)$, we have evidences that shows a significant difference between the performances of the servers in relation to the execution time of the program p.

We can also calculate $P(t \geq d)$ through the tabulated values of the density function of t_{137}[9]. It is observed that:

$$P(t \geq d) = P(t \geq 32.81) \simeq 0.0.$$

As $P(t \geq 32.81)$ is smaller than the chosen degree of significance -$\alpha/2$ (0.025), there is enough evidence to reject the hypothesis of equivalence between the systems with respect to the execution time of program p. With the same degree of significance, that is, 95%, we also have enough evidence to state that the execution time of the program p on server S_1 is higher than the execution time on server S_2, since $d \in (28.12 \quad , \quad \infty)$. We can also calculate $P(t \geq 28.12)$ through the density function of t_{137}. We have:

$$P(t \geq d) = P(t \geq 28.12) \simeq 0.0.$$

---

[9]Use table or statistical tool to get value. The process is already presented previously through several figures of this text.

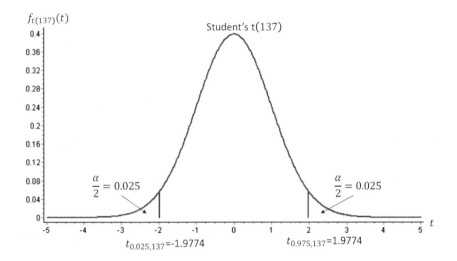

Figure 6.12 Critical Values - $t_{0.025,\,137} = -1.9774$ and $t_{0.975,\,137} = 1.9774$.

6.5 BOOTSTRAP

The publication in 1979 of Bradley Efron's paper on bootstrap methods [119] was an important event in statistics since it synthesized earlier ideas on resampling and defined a new framework for parameter estimation [96, 120]. Bootstrap can be thought of as a strategy that can be applied to estimate parameters of distributions. It may be applied, for instance, when parametric inference methods are not suitable. The following sections present three variants of this strategy.

6.5.1 BASIC BOOTSTRAP

This section presents the basic method proposed by Efron [118, 120, 121]. This method generates resamples with repetition of a sample. Figure 6.13 shows the main activities performed in the bootstrap.

Consider that a sample of size m has been obtained (measured) from a system under study. From this sample, n resamples of size m are generated. These resamples are obtained through random selections with replacement from the original sample. For each resample, the statistic of interest is calculated. Therefore, we have n values of the statistics of interest, each of which coming from one resample. These values are, then, sorted in ascending order, that is $\{\hat{\theta}^1, \hat{\theta}^2, ..., \hat{\theta}^i, ..., \hat{\theta}^{n-1}, \hat{\theta}^n\}$, where $\hat{\theta}^1$ is the smallest value and $\hat{\theta}^n$ is the largest value. After that, the values corresponding to the percentiles $\alpha/2 \times 100\%$ ($\hat{\theta}^{\alpha/2 \times 100\%}$) and $(1 - \alpha/2) \times 100\%$ ($\hat{\theta}^{1 - \alpha/2 \times 100\%}$) are obtained. These two values correspond to the lower and upper bounds of the two-

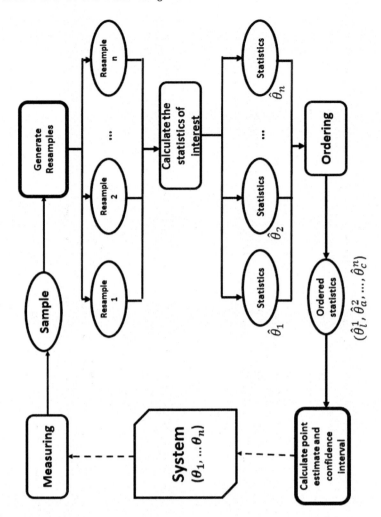

Figure 6.13   Basic Bootstrap.

tailed confidence interval, respectively. The steps related to this process are described here:

If the confidence interval of interest is one-tailed, perform one of the following options instead of steps 6 and 7 described above. The alternatives are:

- If the confidence interval is one-tailed, such as (LB, ∞), determine the lowest value higher than $\alpha \times 100\%$ lower values of ordered statistics, that is $LB = \hat{\theta}^{\alpha \times 100\%}$

- If the confidence interval is one-tailed, such as $(-\infty, UB)$, determine the low-

---

Algorithm 1 Bootstrap

1: Select a random sample of size m.
2: Select a sample from the sample (a resample) of size m with replacement.
3: Calculate the statistics of interest (the mean, variance, etc.) of the resample.
4: Repeat steps 2 through 3 n times. (Consider a large n, that is $n = 1000$ or $10,000$).
5: Sort the n values of the statistics obtained in ascending order.
6: Depending on the desired degree of confidence $(1 - \alpha)$, determine the values that are $\frac{\alpha}{2} \times 100\%$ ($\hat{\theta}^{\frac{\alpha}{2} \times 100\%}$) above the lowest value and $(1 - \frac{\alpha}{2}) \times 100\%$ ($\hat{\theta}^{(1 - \frac{\alpha}{2}) \times 100\%}$) below the highest value.
7: These values are the lower ($LB = \hat{\theta}^{\frac{\alpha}{2} \times 100\%}$) and higher ($UB = \hat{\theta}^{(1 - \frac{\alpha}{2}) \times 100\%}$) limits of the two-tailed confidence interval of the parameter estimated by the statistics.

---

est value higher than $(1 - \alpha) \times 100\%$ lower values of ordered statistics, that is $UB = \hat{\theta}^{(1-\alpha) \times 100\%}$.

Code 2 reads data from an Excel spreadsheet, then generates 10,000 resamples, and computes the two-tailed 95% confidence interval for the population mean.

Algorithm 2 Bootstrap - Mathematica Code

1: *Degree of Significance *
2: $\alpha = 0.05$;
3: *Reading Excel Spreadsheet *
4: data = Sort[Flatten[Import["data.xlsx"]]];
5: *Resample Generation*
6: meandata = Table[Mean[RandomChoice[data, Length[data]]], 10000];
7: *Confidence Interval*
8: Quantile[meandata, $\alpha/2$, 1 -$\alpha/2$]

Example 6.5.1. In an experiment, the round trip time (RTT) two hosts take to communicate with one another (in milliseconds) was recorded in Table 6.6. Bootstrap was applied to calculate the 95% two-tailed confidence interval of the mean round trip time ($MRTT$).

In this process, 1000 resamples were generated, each with 100 observations (the same size as the measured sample). For each resample, the mean was calculated. Afterward, the means were sorted in ascending order. Table 6.7 presents the thirtieth (30) lowest and thirtieth (30) highest means of the thousand (1000) means calculated. This table is organized into one hundred (100) columns by ten (10) rows. The eleventh lowest value (percentile 1.1%) is in the first row of the second column. The 2.5% and 97.5% percentiles were highlighted in the table. These numbers correspond to the lower and upper confidence interval bounds of the population mean:

Table 6.6
Round Trip Time (RTT) - ms

104.7196	203.7221	300.6923	414.4022	92.62806	223.9594	240.0018	359.2983	90.12639	271.8118
150.1113	178.5311	315.1238	408.7179	109.5103	164.6566	297.2719	362.3586	109.5103	297.2719
100.3835	200.897	310.9478	340.4307	110.5069	233.6339	233.9412	383.5152	54.60123	295.4758
100.3835	200.897	310.9478	340.4307	131.1631	215.1761	335.1037	389.7702	119.0568	288.5545
113.178	187.1229	248.7397	387.3934	119.0568	200.7713	288.5545	395.6357	90.12639	271.8118
150.1113	178.5311	315.1238	408.7179	122.0549	224.5178	353.3375	424.2734	231.4049	360.6798
113.178	187.1229	248.7397	387.3934	45.64294	236.1018	260.9277	425.6914	164.6566	362.3586
122.0549	224.5178	353.3375	424.2734	102.3655	208.8814	300.3518	392.5326	205.8156	371.1171
71.14753	179.5134	298.2135	373.203	102.3655	208.8814	300.3518	392.5326	200.7713	395.6357
101.2945	194.6917	349.3317	408.462	113.178	187.1229	248.7397	387.3934	231.4049	360.6798

Table 6.7
1000 Means of RTT Resamples - ms.

Percentile 1.1%

Order	Re-sample Means (RTTs) - ms							Order
1	219.4824	223.4537	226.3741	...	267.0436	269.0550	271.5726	991
2	220.1019	223.5243	226.8582	...	267.1355	269.1284	271.8501	992
3	221.1571	223.8250	226.9718	...	267.1458	269.3089	271.9283	993
4	221.1669	224.5263	227.0758	...	267.3872	269.4367	272.5213	994
5	221.3548	224.8856	227.2045	...	268.1536	269.5028	274.0738	995
6	221.4677	225.1398	227.3389	...	268.2307	269.6058	274.7871	996
7	222.1898	225.3195	227.5026	...	268.3850	269.6312	275.0265	997
8	222.2909	225.5932	227.6497	...	268.4529	270.7355	275.7150	998
9	222.8687	225.8579	227.7573	...	268.5014	271.1182	276.1098	999
10	223.4337	226.0685	227.8660	...	269.0524	271.5453	279.6191	1000

Percentile 2.5% — Percentile 97.5%

$$MRTT \in (227.2045ms, 268.1536\,ms).$$

[10]

6.5.2 BOOTSTRAP-T

This section introduces the bootstrap-t method for computing confidence interval [104] of a parameter θ. This method generates n resamples (y_i) from a sample x obtained from the population. The original sample, x, provides a first point estimate of the parameter θ, that is $\hat{\theta}$. These resamples are generated through random selections with replacement. The statistic of interest is calculated for each resample ($\hat{\theta}(y_i)$) as well as their respective standard error of each resample, $\hat{\sigma}_{\hat{\theta}(y_i)}$.

---
[10]Mean round trip time.

Table 6.8
Ordered T^j.

	Ordered T^j								
1	-4.61708	-3.15017		-1.95411		1.94907		2.963562	3.165526	9991
2	-4.24591	-3.11513		-1.95342		1.950774		2.967662	3.220371	9992
3	-3.67061	-3.07185		-1.95327		1.951398		2.968347	3.24969	9993
4	-3.63842	-3.07076		-1.95231		1.953135		2.968403	3.269064	9994
5	-3.24268	-3.06897	...	-1.94825	...	1.953964	...	2.990184	3.271247	9995
6	-3.21399	-3.05748		-1.94261		1.954028		2.993854	3.3308	9996
7	-3.19045	-3.04147		-1.94233		1.954138		3.037479	3.370192	9997
8	-3.18792	-3.03455		-1.94213		1.954202		3.048682	3.390946	9998
9	-3.18111	-3.01453		-1.94185		1.956683		3.07554	3.477022	9999
10	-3.15019	-3.00988		-1.93935		1.958164		3.109424	4.457258	10000

Percentile 2.5% (under -1.95411 column)   Percentile 97.5% (under 1.94907 column)

It is worth noting that $\hat{\sigma}_{\hat{\theta}(y_i)}$ may not have a closed form solution. If the parameter θ is the mean, then $\hat{\sigma}_{\hat{\theta}(y_i)}$ is the standard deviation. However, if θ is another statistics, the standard error needs to be somewhat estimated.

Then, the statistics obtained from resamples $((\hat{\theta}(y_i)))$ are standardized (T^i - the standardized statistics) by considering the standard error of each resample ($\hat{\sigma}_{\hat{\theta}(y_i)}$) and the estimate obtained from the population's sample, θ. This set of standardized statistics ($\{T^i\}$) is then sorted in ascending order. After, the percentiles of interest of standardized statistics are obtained, and the interval bounds are computed. The procedure presented in this section is particularly tailored for estimating the confidence interval of means. Figure 6.14 and the pseudo-code 3 depict the steps of this process.

The steps of this process are described below:

Example 6.5.2. In this example, a confidence interval of the mean round trip time ($MRTT$) is calculated using bootstrap-t, considering a degree of confidence of 95%. The system was measured, and the sample presented in Table 6.6 was obtained. The sample mean is $\hat{\theta} = 247.034ms$ and its standard deviation is $\hat{\sigma} = 10.7306ms$. $10,000$ resamples were generated, and the respective means were calculated ($1,000$ means). The standardized means of each resample y_i is then obtained by

$$T^i = \frac{\hat{\theta}(y_i) - \hat{\theta}}{\hat{\sigma}_{\hat{\theta}(y_i)}},$$

and are summarized in Table 6.8. $\hat{\sigma}_{\hat{\theta}(y_i)}$ is the standard deviation of the resample y_i.

Hence, for instance, considering the resample y_{5351}, that has mean equal to $\hat{\theta}(y_{5351}) = 247.94ms$ and standard deviation $\hat{\sigma}(y_{5351}) = 10.83$, the respective stand-

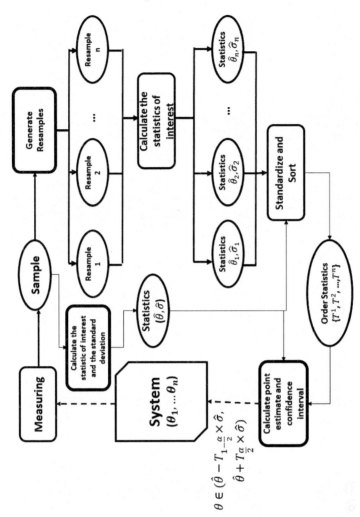

Figure 6.14 Bootstrap-t.

ardized mean is $T^{5351} = (247.94 - 247.034)/10.83 = 8.366 \times 10^{-2}$.

After standardizing each resample mean, the standardized means are sorted in ascending order. Then, using the ordered set, the percentiles 2.5% and 97.5% are obtained, that is $T_{2.5\%} = -1.93935$ and $T_{97.5\%} = 1.95816$, and the confidence interval bounds are calculated:

$$(247.034 - (1.95816) \times 10.7306 \ , \ 247.034 - (-1.93935) \times 10.7306).$$

Thus,

Algorithm 3 Bootstrap-t.

1: Select a random sample (x) of size m.
2: Using x, compute the point estimate of θ, $\hat{\theta}$, and $\hat{\sigma}$ (standard deviation of the sample).
3: Select a sample from the sample x (a resample - y_i) of size m (the same size of x) with replacement.
4: For the resample (y_i), estimated θ by computing $\hat{\theta}(y_i)$ and $\hat{\sigma}_{\hat{\theta}(y_i)}$ (standard deviation of the resample y_i).
5: Repeat steps 3 through 4 n times. (Consider a large n, that is $n = 1000$ or $10,000$).
6: For every resample (y_i), compute $T^i = \frac{\hat{\theta}(y_i) - \hat{\theta}}{\hat{\sigma}_{\hat{\theta}(y_i)}}$.
7: Considering the degree of significance α and all computed T^i, find

$$T_{1-\frac{\alpha}{2}} \text{ and } T_{\frac{\alpha}{2}}$$

(For two-sided confidence interval)

    or

$$T_{1-\alpha}$$

(For one-sided confidence interval)

8: Calculate the confidence interval by:

$$\theta \in (\hat{\theta} - T_{1-\frac{\alpha}{2}} \times \hat{\sigma} \ , \ \hat{\theta} - T_{\frac{\alpha}{2}} \times \hat{\sigma}).$$

(Two-sided confidence interval)

    or by

$$\theta \in (\hat{\theta} - T_{1-\alpha} \times \hat{\sigma} \ , \ \infty)$$

(One-sided confidence interval)

$$RTT \in (226.022ms \ , \ 267.844ms).$$

6.5.3 SEMI-PARAMETRIC BOOTSTRAP

This section introduces the semi-parametric bootstrap method. This method uses a sample of size n, obtained from the system, to estimate the population distribution parameters (see Figure 6.15.). Samples of the same sample size are then generated by a random number generation method (represented in the figure by $t = F^{-1}(U)$), which represents data from the population distribution. After obtaining m resamples, the same steps adopted in the basic bootstrap are applied; for each resample, the statistics of interest are calculated, and then these statistics are ordered. Afterward, the upper and lower bounds of the confidence interval are obtained. The steps for estimating a two-tailed semi-parametric bootstrap are described in the pseudo-code 4. The one-tailed confidence interval may be implemented by adapting this procedure to the respective method described in Section 6.5.1.

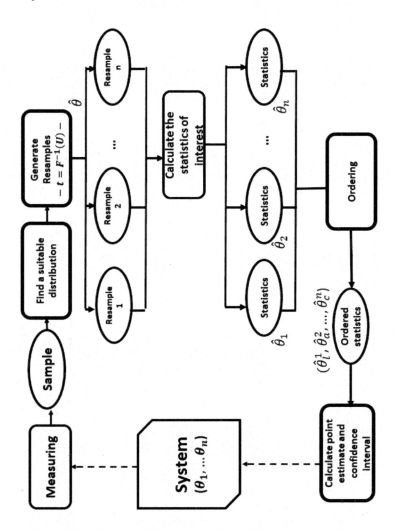

Figure 6.15   Semi-Parametric Bootstrap.

Algorithm 4 Semi-Parametric Bootstrap

1: Select a random sample of size n.
2: Use the sample to find a suitable probability distribution to represent the population.
3: Apply a method for generating a random variate and use probability distribution to generate a resample of size n ($\{t_i|t_i = F^{-1}(U), |\{t_i\}| = n\}$).

4: Calculate the statistic of interest for the resample.
5: Repeat steps 3 and 4 m times. Adopt a "big" number, (say $m = 1000$ or $10,000$).
6: Sort the m statistics in ascending order.
7: Considering the desired degree of confidence, $(1 - \alpha)$, determine the percentiles $\frac{\alpha}{2} \times 100\%$ and $\left(1 - \frac{\alpha}{2}\right) \times 100\%$. These values are the lower and upper limits of

the two-parameter confidence interval of the population parameter.

Example 6.5.3. Let us consider again the example presented in Section 6.5.1. After collecting the sample (presented in Table 6.6), this sample was evaluated, and a distribution that can represent the population was chosen (Exploratory Data Analysis and Goodness of Fit).

Figure 6.16 shows the histogram of the sample. A set of probability distributions was analyzed, and the best candidate distribution (among those evaluated) was the uniform distribution $U(45.6049, 425.754)$. The Kolmogorov-Smirnov (KS) Goodness of Fit test did not reject this distribution.

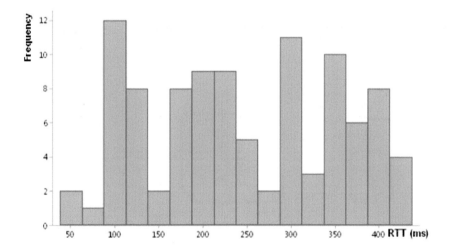

Figure 6.16 Histogram of the Sample Presented in Table 6.6.

From the original sample, 10,000 resamples were generated. For each of these resamples, the mean (the statistic of interest) was calculated, the set of averages was ordered, and the percentiles 2.5% and 97.5% were found. These two values were adopted as the upper and lower bounds, respectively, of the two-tailed confidence interval of the population's mean. Hence, the interval is:

$$MRTT \in (214.1924 \, ms \quad , \quad 234.9661 \, ms).$$

Code 5 imports data from an Excel spreadsheet into Mathematica, chooses a probability distribution function, and performs the Goodness of Fit test, then generates 10,000 resamples, and computes the two-tailed 95% confidence the interval for the population mean.

Algorithm 5 Semi-Parametric Bootstrap - Mathematica Code.

1: *Reading Excel Spreadsheet *
2: data = Flatten[Import["data.xlsx"]];
3: D=EmpiricalDistribution[data];
4: *Choosing a Probability Distribution and the Goodness of Fit *
5: estimatedD=FindDistribution[data];
6: Print["Estimated Distribution: ",estimatedD]
7: alpha=0.05;
8: KolmogorovSmirnovTest[data,estimatedD,"ShortTestConclusion",   Significance Level → alpha]
9: *Resample Generation and Confidence Interval*
10: numberofresamples=10000;
11: meandata1=Table[Mean[RandomVariate[estimatedD,Length[data]]], numberof resamples];
12: Print["SPBCI - Mean= ",Quantile[meandata1,alpha/2,(1-alpha)/2]]

6.6 GOODNESS OF FIT

This section presents two methods for checking if probability distributions are suitable for representing a set of measured data. The methods introduced are $P - P$ plot method, χ^2 [80, 327] and the Kolmogorov-Smirnov [105, 222] Goodness of Fit (GoF) methods.

6.6.1 PROBABILITY–PROBABILITY PLOT METHOD

This method assesses how close two distributions, two data sets; one data set and one distribution are from each other [149]. When testing the goodness of fit of a theoretical distribution for a data set, the theoretical cumulative distribution and the empirical cumulative distribution are plotted against each other. The parameter values for the theoretical distributions may be estimated from the data set. As the probability distributions ranges are $[0, 1]$, the range of the graph is the unit square $[0, 1] \times [0, 1]$. If the theoretical distribution is suitable for the data set, the plot should be close to a straight line. Statistics such as coefficient of determination, r^2, may be used to quantify how close the two distributions are to one another.

The following steps may summarize the method for testing goodness of fit of a theoretical distribution for a data set:

1. Collect the sample $s = \{t\}$, $|s| = n$.

2. Sort the sample in ascending order. Therefore, we have $s = \{t_1, t_2, ..., t_i, ..., t_n\}$, where t^1 is the smallest measure, t_2 is the second smallest measure, and so forth; and t_n is the largest measure of the sample.

3. Compute the empirical distribution - $F_E(t_i) = i/(n+1)$ or i/n or $(i-0.3)/(n+0.4))$.

4. Choose the theoretical distribution, F_T.

5. Estimate the parameters of F_T from the sample s.

6. Plot F_T against F_E.

7. Check how close the dots are to a $45°$ straight line ($y = ax + b$) starting from a point close to point $(0, 0)$. In case they deviate, the distributions differ. Therefore, check the angular coefficient (a) of the linear regression ($a \rightarrow 1$), and the intercept ($b \rightarrow 0$). The coefficient of determination, r^2, shows how close the dots are to a straight line.

Example 6.6.1. Assume a system composed of a computer server and a program. A sample of size $n = 100$ of the execution time of the program was collected. The ordered sample is shown in Table 6.9. The cumulative empirical distribution is depicted in Column $F_E(t_i) = i/(n+1)$. First, we tested the goodness of fit of the Normal distribution ($F_N(t_i, \mu, \sigma)$) with mean and the standard deviation estimated from the sample mean and sample standard deviation, respectively, $\hat{\mu} = 1050\,ms$ and $\hat{\sigma} = 220\,ms$.

Table 6.9

Ordered Sample - Execution Time in *ms*

i	t_i	$F_E(t_i)$	$F_N(t_i, \mu, \sigma)$	$F_{Exp}(t_i, \lambda)$
1	636	0.02	0.0301	0.4540
2	656	0.039	0.0365	0.4638
3	686	0.059	0.0490	0.4791
4	725	0.078	0.0696	0.4979

Continued on next page

Table 6.9 – *Continued from previous page*

i	t_i	$F_E(t_i)$	$F_N(t_i,\mu,\sigma)$	$F_{Exp}(t_i,\lambda)$
5	766	0.098	0.0987	0.5174
6	778	0.118	0.1080	0.5226
7	778	0.137	0.1081	0.5227
8	798	0.157	0.1256	0.5315
9	809	0.176	0.1368	0.5366
10	847	0.196	0.1783	0.5531
11	859	0.216	0.1932	0.5583
12	867	0.235	0.2033	0.5616
13	913	0.255	0.2669	0.5802
14	932	0.275	0.2961	0.5878
15	940	0.294	0.3083	0.5908
16	947	0.314	0.3196	0.5935
17	969	0.333	0.3564	0.6019
18	991	0.353	0.3941	0.6102
19	1005	0.373	0.4190	0.6154
20	1009	0.392	0.4269	0.6170
21	1020	0.412	0.4454	0.6207
22	1050	0.431	0.4993	0.6313
23	1066	0.451	0.5288	0.6370
24	1070	0.471	0.5367	0.6385
25	1071	0.49	0.5372	0.6386
26	1093	0.51	0.5769	0.6461
27	1110	0.529	0.6074	0.6519
28	1113	0.549	0.6128	0.6529
29	1121	0.569	0.6270	0.6556
30	1140	0.588	0.6589	0.6617
31	1140	0.608	0.6591	0.6617
32	1152	0.627	0.6789	0.6656
33	1158	0.647	0.6884	0.6674
34	1160	0.667	0.6913	0.6680
35	1177	0.686	0.7181	0.6734
36	1181	0.706	0.7240	0.6746
37	1186	0.725	0.7310	0.6760
38	1189	0.745	0.7363	0.6771
39	1197	0.765	0.7479	0.6795
40	1201	0.784	0.7544	0.6809
41	1205	0.804	0.7594	0.6819
42	1218	0.824	0.7770	0.6857
43	1225	0.843	0.7863	0.6878
44	1241	0.863	0.8069	0.6925

Continued on next page

Table 6.9 – *Continued from previous page*

i	t_i	$F_E(t_i)$	$F_N(t_i, \mu, \sigma)$	$F_{Exp}(t_i, \lambda)$
45	1248	0.882	0.8157	0.6946
46	1324	0.902	0.8939	0.7161
47	1335	0.922	0.9023	0.7189
48	1336	0.941	0.9032	0.7192
49	1456	0.961	0.9674	0.7493
50	1504	0.98	0.9804	0.7605

After computing $F_E(t_i)$ and $F_N(t_i, \mu, \sigma)$, $\forall t_i \in s$, plot the graph $F_E(t_i) \times F_N(t_i, \mu, \sigma)$, $\forall t_i \in s$. This plot is shown in Figure 6.17.

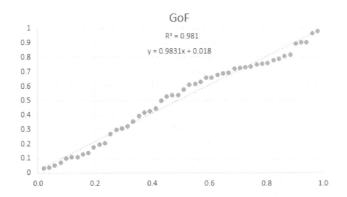

Figure 6.17 Probability–Probability Plot - $F_E(t_i) \times F_N(t_i, 1050\,ms, 220\,ms)$.

The angular coefficient calculated is $a = 0.9831$, and the linear coefficient is $b = 0.018$. It is worth noting that the dots are close to a $45°$ degree ($a = 0.9831$) straight line with the intercept at $b = 0.018$. Besides, the coefficient of determination, r^2, is 0.981.

Now, let us test the goodness of fit of the exponential distribution ($F_{Exp}(t_i, \lambda)$) with rate (λ) estimated from the sample, where $\hat{\lambda} = 1/\hat{\mu} = 9.51 \times 10^{-4}\,ms^{-1}$. The plot $F_E(t_i) \times F_{Exp}(t_i, \lambda)$ is shown in Figure 6.18. The angular coefficient calculated is $a = 0.2511$, and the linear coefficient is $b = 0.4996$. Hence, the dots are far from a $45°$ degree straight line, even having a coefficient of determination, r^2, for a linear model as 0.9362.

6.6.2 χ^2 METHOD

The χ^2 method should be adopted for checking if a sample comes from a population with a specific probability distribution function [80, 105, 327, 342]. However, the method considers that data is binned; hence, the test statistics depend on grouped data.

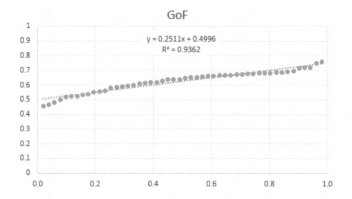

Figure 6.18 Probability–Probability Plot - $F_E(t_i) \times F_{Exp}(t_i, 9.51 \times 10^{-4} ms^{-1})$.

The χ^2 test is based on Q^2 statistics. This statistic measures the distance between the observed values and those we would expect to obtain if the sample came from a particular probability distribution. In other words, the fit test compares the frequency of the sample and respective data that comes from a theoretical probability distribution. This method is well suited for categorical data but may also be applied to numerical data. This test presents better results for discrete distributions since the sample should be first grouped into bins for applying the method for continuous data, and the test is susceptible to the choice of bins. Moreover, the test is dependent on:

- number of bins,

- sample size, and

- bin size.

There is no optimal method for defining the bin width, and the number of bins since the optimal bin width depends on the distribution, even though most reasonable alternatives should produce a similar outcome. This method should not be applied if samples are small or some bin counts are too small (less than five). In such a case, one may combine some bins in the tails.

The χ^2 test aim is:

- compare observed frequencies with expected frequencies, and

- decide whether the observed frequencies seem to agree or disagree with the expected frequencies assigned to a probability distribution of interest.

For a random sample of size n, consider a hypothesis (null hypothesis – H_0) that this sample comes from a population with a probability distribution function $F_T(\Theta, t)$, where Θ is the set of parameters of the distribution and t is the index variable. The alternative hypothesis (H_1) states that the sample does not come from a population with a distribution $F_T(\Theta, t)$. Now, consider that we wish to check if the sample probability distribution ($F(\Theta, t)$) may be represented by $F_T(\Theta, t)$, that is, H_0: $F(\Theta, t) = F_T(\Theta, t)$, where the parameters θ_i were estimated from the sample. The steps of this process are described below:

1: Select the random sample of size n, $S = \{x_1, x_2, \ldots, x_n\}$. This sample is obtained from a population with distribution function $F(\Theta, t)$ of unknown parameters. $\theta_i \in \Theta$.

2: Divide S into a set of disjoint intervals or categories, that is, $IS = \{I_i | \ I_i = (lb_i, ub_i), \ lb_i, ub_i \in \mathbb{R}, \ lb_i < ub_i, \ I_i \cap I_j = \varnothing, \ \forall I_i, I_j \in IS, \ I_i \neq I_j\}$. And, let o_z be the number of values that belongs to the interval I_z ($z = 1, 2, \ldots, k$).

3: Find $P(I_z) = F(\Theta, ub_z) - F(\Theta, lb_z)$ and let $e_z = n \times P(I_z)$[11] be the expected frequency of the interval I_z.

4: Calculate the test statistic $Q^2 = \sum_{z=1}^{k} \frac{(o_z - e_z)^2}{e_z}$.

5: The statistic Q^2 is distributed approximately according to χ^2_{k-1}, where k is the number of classes ($k - 1$ degree of freedom.).

6: Considering a degree of confidence equal to $1 - \alpha$, reject the null hypothesis (H_0) if $Q^2 \geq \chi^2_{1-\alpha, k-1}$.

Example 6.6.2. Consider that every day a software company tested one hundred ($n = 100$) appliances. Considering a period of one hundred (100) days, the total number of appliances tested was $100 \times 100 = 10000$. The daily mean number of defects (MND) observed in 100 days was $MND = \sum_{i=1}^{100} d_i / 100 = 19.86$, where d_i is the number of observed defects in day i. Since we tested 100 products every day, the point estimate of the defect probability is $\hat{p} = 19.86/100 = 0.1986$.

Table 6.10 presents the number of days in which we observed the respective number of defects that belongs to a bin [12]. We adopted a bin size equal to (see footnote). Therefore there were $(0 - 14), (15 - 17), (18 - 20), (21 - 23), (24 - 26)$, and $(27 - 100)$ defects per day. Hence, we have six (6) bins (classes), that is $i = \{1, 2, 3, 4, 6\}$. It is worth mentioning that the first and the last bins (classes) are wider since the number of defects is much rarer. The number of defects observed in each bin is depicted by o_i.

Our aim is to check if we have evidences to refute the binomial distribution probability with parameters $Bin(n, p)$, where $n = 100$ and $p = 0.1986$, as a suitable distribution for representing the observed data. The expected number of defects for each bin i is therefore $e_i = n \times P_B(bin_i, \hat{p}, n)$, where n is the daily sample size, bin_i is a bin or class, $\hat{p}$ is the point estimate of the defect probability, and $P_B(bin_i, \hat{p}, n)$ is the probability of the number of defects of a bin_i.

---

[11] Consider $e_j \geq 5$, $\forall I_z$ ($z = 1, 2, \ldots, k$).

[12] $m \log_{100} n - 1 = 3$. The daily sample size (n) is $= 100$ and we considered $m = 2$.

Table 6.10
Observed and Expected Data

bin	o_i	e_i	$\frac{(o_i-e_i)^2}{e_i}$
$(0-14)$	7	8.56	0.28
$(15-17)$	20	19.72	0.00
$(18-20)$	30	29.06	0.03
$(21-23)$	26	24.71	0.07
$(24-26)$	11	12.77	0.24
$(27-100)$	6	5.18	0.13

The test statistic Q^2 is calculated by summing up the values of column $(o_i-e_i)^2/o_i$, that is, $Q^2 = \sum_{i=1}^{k}(o_i-e_i)^2/e_i$, where $k=6$. In this example, $Q^2=0.76$. If we consider a degree of confidence of $1-\alpha=95\%$, then $\chi^2_{1-\alpha,k-1} = \chi^2_{95\%,5} = 1.1455$, where $k=6$ is the number of bins. As $Q^2 < \chi^2_{\alpha,k-1}$, we have no evidence to reject the binomial distribution as suitable for representing the observed data taking into account a 95% of degree of confidence. It is worth mentioning, however, that the bin range was carefully chosen. If we change the ranges, we may obtain a result in which we have enough evidence to reject the $Bin(n,p)$, $n-100$ and $p=0.1986$, as suitable distribution to represent the data.

□

Example 6.6.3. A set of servers was observed for one hundred (100) weeks. The observation period was divided into five ($k=5$) classes. The first class range is fourteen (14) weeks, the three (3) subsequent classes have a range of three (3) weeks. The last class has a range of seventy-seven (77) weeks. The number of failures observed in each class is shown in Column o_i of Table 6.11, $i \in \{1,2,3,4,5\}$. The aim is to check if if there is enough evidence to refute the binomial distribution $B(p,n)$, where $p=0.2$ and $n=100$ as a suitable distribution to represent the observed server failures. Column $B((xl_i \leq X \leq xh_i,n,p)$ depicts the probability of each class i, that is, $B((X \leq xh_i,n,p) - B((X \leq xl_i,n,p)$, where xl_i and xh_i are respectively the lower and upper bound of each class i. Column e_i is the expected value for the class i, considering $B(p,n)$, that is $B((xl_i \leq X \leq xh_i,n,p) \times n$. Column $(o_i-e_i)^2/e_i$ presents the normalized squared difference between the observed data and the expected value of the class i.

Column $Q^2 = \sum_{i=1}^{k}\frac{(o-ie_i)^2}{e_i}$ is the calculated statistic from the data and $\chi^2_{1-\alpha,k-1}$ is obtained from the χ^2_{k-1} distribution, considering $1-\alpha=95\%$ degree of confidence and $k=5$ as the number of classes. As $Q^2 = 13.74 > \chi^2_{1-\alpha,k-1} = 9.49$, there is evidence to reject $B(p,n)$, $p=0.2$ and $n=100$, as a suitable distributions to represent the data set. We even have enough evidence to reject $B(p,n)$, $p=0.2$ and $n=100$, as fitting to the data since $\chi^2_{1-\alpha,k-1} = 13.28$ for $1-\alpha=99\%$. Nevertheless, if we

Table 6.11

Goodness of Fit - Binomial distribution - $B(n = 100, p = 0.2)$

Class: (i,xl_i,xh_i)			o_i	$B((xl_i \leq X \leq xh_i, n, p)$	e_i	$(o_i - e_i)^2/e_i$	Q^2	$\chi_{1-\alpha,k-1}$
1	0	14	7	0.1137	11.37	1.680	13.74	11.07
2	15	17	15	0.2273	22.73	2.628		
3	18	20	18	0.2970	29.70	4.607		
4	21	23	14	0.2238	22.38	3.137		
5	24	100	9	0.1382	13.82	1.683		

want to only reject $B(p,n)$, $p = 0.2$ and $n = 100$, only if we are $1 - \alpha = 99.9\%$ sure of its inadequacy; thus we not have enough evidence to achieve such a high degree of confidence since $\chi_{1-\alpha,k-1}^2 = 18.47$, and in such a case $Q^2 < \chi_{1-\alpha,k-1}^2$ (13.74 < 18.47).

□

Example 6.6.4. A set of one hundred (100) servers was observed during an accelerate reliability test. The observation period was divided into nine ($k = 9$) classes. The first class range is one hundred and fifty-one 151 days, whereas the subsequent seven (7) classes have a range of twelve (12) days. The last class has a range of 36 days. The number of failures observed in each class is shown in Column o_i of Table 6.12, $i \in \{1,2,3,4,5,6,7,8,9\}$. The aim is to check if there is enough evidence to refute the normal distribution $N(\mu,\sigma)$, where $\mu = 196$ days and $\sigma = 30$ days, as a suitable distribution to represent the observed lifetime data. Column $N((xl_i \leq X \leq xh_i, \mu, \sigma)$ depicts the probability of each class i, that is, $N((X \leq xh_i, \mu, \sigma) - N((X \leq xl_i, \mu, \sigma)$, where xl_i and xh_i are respectively the lower and upper bound of each class i. Column e_i is the expected value for the class i, considering $N(\mu,\sigma)$, that is $N((X \leq xh_i, \mu, \sigma) - N((X \leq xl_i, \mu, \sigma) \times n$. Column $(o_i - e_i)^2/e_i$ depicts the normalized squared difference between the observed data and the expected value of the class i.

Column $Q^2 = \sum_{i=1}^{nc} \frac{(o-ie_i)^2}{e_i}$ is the calculated statistic from the data and $\chi_{1-\alpha,k-1}^2$ is obtained from χ_{k-1}^2 distribution, considering $1 - \alpha = 95\%$ degree of confidence and $k = 9$ as the number of classes. As $Q^2 = 5.2075$ and $\chi_{1-\alpha,k-1}^2 = 15.5073$ ($Q^2 < \chi_{1-\alpha,k-1}^2$), there is no evidence to reject $N(\mu,\sigma)$, $\mu = 36$ days and $\sigma = 30$ days, as suitable distributions to represent the servers' time to failure under the accelerate reliability test with such a degree of confidence.

□

6.6.3 KOLMOGOROV-SMIRNOV METHOD

The Kolmogorov-Smirnov test (KS test) seeks to determine whether two sets of data differ significantly [105, 222]. The KS test has the advantage of making no assump-

Table 6.12
GoF - Server Time to Failure in Accelerate Reliability Test - $N(196\,days, 30\,days)$

Class: i, xl_i, xh_i			o_i	$N((xl_i \leq X \leq xh_i, \mu, \sigma)$	e_i	$(o_i - e_i)^2/e_i$	Q^2	$\chi_{1-\alpha, nc-1}$
1	0	151	9		0.0668	6.67	0.8138	6.6770	16.9190
2	151	163	8		0.0689	6.88	0.1832		
3	163	175	8		0.1063	10.62	0.6462		
4	175	187	12		0.1401	14.00	0.2867		
5	187	199	12		0.1577	15.77	0.9013		
6	199	211	13		0.1516	15.17	0.3094		
7	211	223	8		0.1245	12.46	1.5939		
8	223	235	7		0.0873	8.74	0.3450		
9	235	271	8		0.0906	9.08	0.1279		

tions about data distribution. This test can compare two empirical distributions of data, an empirical distribution, and a theoretical distribution, or even two theoretical distributions. This test uses cumulative probability distributions. When applying the Kolmogorov-Smirnov GoF test to check if a theoretical distribution ($F_X(p_1, ..., p_n)$) represents a data set requires knowing in advance the parameters $(p_1, ..., p_n)$ of the theoretical distribution. However, the parameter estimation can be accomplished by using the methods introduced in Section 25.3.

The set of steps below depicts a process for comparing an empirical distribution and a theoretical distribution, but it can be easily adapted to evaluate the other mentioned cases.

Procedure for the KS test:

1. Define two hypotheses:

    - $H0$: the sample distribution and the theoretical distribution approach one another.
    - $H1$: the distributions do not approach one another.

2. From one sample $Y = (y_1, y_2, ..., y_i, ..., y_n)$ and a theoretical distribution, obtain:

    - the empirical cumulative distribution functions of Y ($ecdf$),
    - and the theoretical cumulative distribution of interest, named $F(t_i)$).

3. Calculate $D_{calc} = \max_{1 \leq i \leq n}(F_t(t) - \frac{i-1}{n}, \frac{i}{n} - F_t(t))$. (See Figure 6.19).

4. Get $D_{critical, \alpha}$.

5. Compare D_{calc} with $D_{critical, \alpha}$:

    - If D_{calc} is smaller than or equal to $D_{critical, \alpha}$, the null hypothesis ($H0$) is not rejected, considering the degree of confidence $(1 - \alpha)\%$.

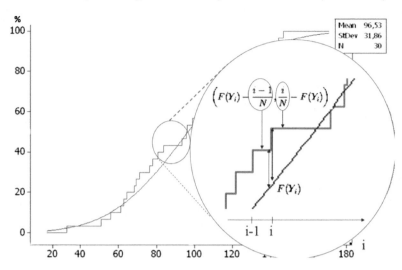

Figure 6.19 Comparison Between Distributions.

Table 6.13
Values of $c(\alpha)$ **for** $n > 35$

$n > 35$	$(1 - \alpha) = 0.9$	$(1 - \alpha) = 0.95$	$(1 - \alpha) = 0.99$
$c(\alpha)$	1.224	1.358	1.6280

- If D_{calc} is greater than to $D_{critical.\alpha}$, the null hypothesis ($H0$) is rejected, since we have enough evidence supporting discrepancies between the evaluated distributions.

The $D_{critical,\alpha}$ can be obtained through Table 6.14, statistical tools, or through the formulas [396] such as:

$$D_{critical,\alpha} = \frac{c(\alpha)}{\sqrt{n}}. \qquad (6.6.1)$$

For samples larger than 35 (n), $c(\alpha)$ can be obtained through Table 6.13.

Example 6.6.5. Consider a system composed of an application server and a program. An experiment was executed. This experiment consists of one hundred (100) executions of the program. Each time execution was recorded in Table 6.15, which shows a fragment of the complete sample. Column i shows the execution order, so 1 (one) means the shortest time, 2 (two) denotes the second shortest time, etc.

Table 6.14
Values of $D_{critical,\alpha}$

$1-\alpha$ n	0.9	0.95	0.99
1	0.950	0.975	0.995
2	0.776	0.842	0.929
3	0.636	0.708	0.829
4	0.565	0.624	0.734
5	0.510	0.563	0.669
6	0.468	0.520	0.617
7	0.436	0.483	0.576
8	0.410	0.454	0.542
9	0.387	0.430	0.513
10	0.369	0.409	0.489
11	0.352	0.391	0.468
12	0.338	0.375	0.450
13	0.325	0.361	0.432
14	0.314	0.349	0.418
15	0.304	0.338	0.404
16	0.295	0.327	0.392
17	0.286	0.318	0.381
18	0.279	0.309	0.371
19	0.271	0.301	0.361
20	0.265	0.294	0.352

$1-\alpha$ n	0.9	0.95	0.99
21	0.259	0.287	0.344
22	0.253	0.281	0.337
23	0.247	0.275	0.330
24	0.242	0.269	0.323
25	0.238	0.264	0.317
26	0.233	0.259	0.311
27	0.229	0.254	0.305
28	0.225	0.250	0.300
29	0.221	0.246	0.295
30	0.218	0.242	0.290
31	0.214	0.238	0.285
32	0.211	0.234	0.281
33	0.208	0.231	0.277
34	0.205	0.227	0.273
35	0.202	0.224	0.269
> 35	$\dfrac{1.224}{\sqrt{n}}$	$\dfrac{1.358}{\sqrt{n}}$	$\dfrac{1.628}{\sqrt{n}}$
	$D_{critical,\,\alpha}$		

Table 6.15
KS Goodness of Fit test

i	t_i	$F_E^-(t_i)$	$F_E^+(t_i)$	$Ft(t_i)$	$L_i = F_i - F_E^-$	$H_i = F_E^+ - F_i$	$D_i = max\{|L_i|, |H_i|\}$
1	142.8	0.000	0.010	0.002	0.002	0.008	0.008
2	146.2	0.010	0.020	0.011	0.001	0.009	0.009
3	147.7	0.020	0.030	0.020	0.000	0.010	0.010
4	147.7	0.030	0.040	0.021	-0.009	0.019	0.019
5	149	0.040	0.050	0.034	-0.006	0.016	0.016
6	149.1	0.050	0.060	0.035	-0.015	0.025	0.025
7	150.5	0.060	0.070	0.056	-0.004	0.014	0.014
8	151.3	0.070	0.080	0.073	0.003	0.007	0.007
9	151.5	0.080	0.090	0.077	-0.003	0.013	0.013
10	151.8	0.090	0.100	0.085	-0.005	0.015	0.015
11	151.9	0.100	0.110	0.089	-0.011	0.021	0.021
12	154.5	0.110	0.120	0.180	0.070	-0.060	0.070
13	154.6	0.120	0.130	0.185	0.065	-0.055	0.065
14	154.8	0.130	0.140	0.193	0.063	-0.053	0.063
15	155	0.140	0.150	0.203	0.063	-0.053	0.063
16	155.3	0.150	0.160	0.218	0.068	-0.058	0.068
17	155.4	0.160	0.170	0.222	0.062	-0.052	0.062
18	155.5	0.170	0.180	0.227	0.057	-0.047	0.057

Table 6.15 continued from previous page

i	t_i	$F_E^-(t_i)$	$F_E^+(t_i)$	$Ft(t_i)$	$L_i = F_i - F_E^-$	$H_i = F_E^+ - F_i$	$D_i = max\{|L_i|, |H_i|\}$
19	155.5	0.180	0.190	0.229	0.049	-0.039	0.049
20	155.6	0.190	0.200	0.230	0.040	-0.030	0.040
21	155.6	0.200	0.210	0.231	0.031	-0.021	0.031
22	155.6	0.210	0.220	0.231	0.021	-0.011	0.021
23	155.7	0.220	0.230	0.237	0.017	-0.007	0.017
24	156.1	0.230	0.240	0.259	0.029	-0.019	0.029
25	156.3	0.240	0.250	0.271	0.031	-0.021	0.031
26	156.9	0.250	0.260	0.300	0.050	-0.040	0.050
27	156.9	0.260	0.270	0.301	0.041	-0.031	0.041
28	157	0.270	0.280	0.311	0.041	-0.031	0.041
29	157.4	0.280	0.290	0.333	0.053	-0.043	0.053
30	157.4	0.290	0.300	0.334	0.044	-0.034	0.044
31	157.6	0.300	0.310	0.343	0.043	-0.033	0.043
32	157.6	0.310	0.320	0.344	0.034	-0.024	0.034
33	157.7	0.320	0.330	0.350	0.030	-0.020	0.030
34	157.7	0.330	0.340	0.352	0.022	-0.012	0.022
35	157.9	0.340	0.350	0.361	0.021	-0.011	0.021
36	158	0.350	0.360	0.372	0.022	-0.012	0.022
37	158.2	0.360	0.370	0.379	0.019	-0.009	0.019
38	158.4	0.370	0.380	0.394	0.024	-0.014	0.024
39	158.5	0.380	0.390	0.400	0.020	-0.010	0.020
40	159.1	0.390	0.400	0.438	0.048	-0.038	0.048
41	159.2	0.400	0.410	0.448	0.048	-0.038	0.048
42	159.2	0.410	0.420	0.449	0.039	-0.029	0.039
43	159.4	0.420	0.430	0.458	0.038	-0.028	0.038
44	159.5	0.430	0.440	0.467	0.037	-0.027	0.037
45	159.6	0.440	0.450	0.472	0.032	-0.022	0.032
46	159.6	0.450	0.460	0.473	0.023	-0.013	0.023
47	159.8	0.460	0.470	0.485	0.025	-0.015	0.025
48	159.8	0.470	0.480	0.488	0.018	-0.008	0.018
49	160	0.480	0.490	0.499	0.019	-0.009	0.019
50	160	0.490	0.500	0.502	0.012	-0.002	0.012
51	160.3	0.500	0.510	0.519	0.019	-0.009	0.019
52	160.3	0.510	0.520	0.519	0.009	0.001	0.009
53	160.3	0.520	0.530	0.522	0.002	0.008	0.008
54	160.4	0.530	0.540	0.529	-0.001	0.011	0.011
55	160.5	0.540	0.550	0.533	-0.007	0.017	0.017
56	160.5	0.550	0.560	0.534	-0.016	0.026	0.026
57	160.7	0.560	0.570	0.548	-0.012	0.022	0.022
58	160.7	0.570	0.580	0.549	-0.021	0.031	0.031
59	160.9	0.580	0.590	0.562	-0.018	0.028	0.028
60	161.3	0.590	0.600	0.588	-0.002	0.012	0.012
61	161.4	0.600	0.610	0.595	-0.005	0.015	0.015
62	161.7	0.610	0.620	0.610	0.000	0.010	0.010
63	161.8	0.620	0.630	0.616	-0.004	0.014	0.014
64	161.9	0.630	0.640	0.622	-0.008	0.018	0.018
65	162.1	0.640	0.650	0.635	-0.005	0.015	0.015
66	162.3	0.650	0.660	0.649	-0.001	0.011	0.011
67	162.3	0.660	0.670	0.649	-0.011	0.021	0.021
68	162.7	0.670	0.680	0.674	0.004	0.006	0.006
69	162.8	0.680	0.690	0.677	-0.003	0.013	0.013
70	162.9	0.690	0.700	0.683	-0.007	0.017	0.017

Table 6.15 continued from previous page

i	t_i	$F_E^-(t_i)$	$F_E^+(t_i)$	$Ft(t_i)$	$L_i = F_t - F_E^-$	$H_i = F_E^+ - F_t$	$D_i = max\{|L_i|, |H_i|\}$
71	162.9	0.700	0.710	0.684	-0.016	0.026	0.026
72	162.9	0.710	0.720	0.685	-0.025	0.035	0.035
73	162.9	0.720	0.730	0.687	-0.033	0.043	0.043
74	162.9	0.730	0.740	0.688	-0.042	0.052	0.052
75	163.1	0.740	0.750	0.699	-0.041	0.051	0.051
76	164.1	0.750	0.760	0.752	0.002	0.008	0.008
77	164.1	0.760	0.770	0.755	-0.005	0.015	0.015
78	164.5	0.770	0.780	0.772	0.002	0.008	0.008
79	164.5	0.780	0.790	0.775	-0.005	0.015	0.015
80	164.6	0.790	0.800	0.777	-0.013	0.023	0.023
81	164.9	0.800	0.810	0.791	-0.009	0.019	0.019
82	165	0.810	0.820	0.796	-0.014	0.024	0.024
83	165	0.820	0.830	0.798	-0.022	0.032	0.032
84	165.3	0.830	0.840	0.811	-0.019	0.029	0.029
85	165.4	0.840	0.850	0.816	-0.024	0.034	0.034
86	165.4	0.850	0.860	0.816	-0.034	0.044	0.044
87	165.5	0.860	0.870	0.822	-0.038	0.048	0.048
88	166	0.870	0.880	0.841	-0.029	0.039	0.039
89	166.3	0.880	0.890	0.854	-0.026	0.036	0.036
90	166.3	0.890	0.900	0.854	-0.036	0.046	0.046
91	166.4	0.900	0.910	0.856	-0.044	0.054	0.054
92	166.7	0.910	0.920	0.867	-0.043	0.053	0.053
93	167.2	0.920	0.930	0.885	-0.035	0.045	0.045
94	167.7	0.930	0.940	0.900	-0.030	0.040	0.040
95	168.2	0.940	0.950	0.914	-0.026	0.036	0.036
96	170.2	0.950	0.960	0.955	0.005	0.005	0.005
97	170.6	0.960	0.970	0.962	0.002	0.008	0.008
98	171.4	0.970	0.980	0.972	0.002	0.008	0.008
99	173.4	0.980	0.990	0.987	0.007	0.003	0.007
100	179.9	0.990	1.000	1.000	0.010	0.000	0.010

The column t_i presents the execution time of the ith shortest time. $F_E(t)$ denotes that empirical distribution of execution time. This information is represented in milliseconds. In column $F_E^-(t_i)$, the data obtained through the expression $\frac{i-1}{n}$ are presented. Column $F_E^+(t_i)$, presents the data obtained by $\frac{i}{n}$. The column $F_t(t_i)$ shows the values of the distribution that is tested as a possible distribution for the respective values of t. In this example, the distribution considered was $normal(\mu, \sigma)$, where $\mu = 159.92\ ms$ and $\sigma = 5.9368\ ms$. The values of t were classified in ascending order. The columns $L_i = F_t - F_E^-$ and $H_i = F_E^+ - F_t$ present the respective differences $F_t(t_i) - F_E^-(t_i)$ and $F_E^+(t_i) - F_t(t_i)$. The column $D_i = max\{|L_i|, |H_i|\}$ shows the larger difference between these two differences. The maximal difference among these differences is called $D_{calc} = max_i\{D_i\}$. In this case, $D_{calc} = 0.07$.

Considering 95% of degree of confidence, $D_{critical,5\%} = c(\alpha)/\sqrt{n} = 1.358/100 = 0.1358$. Since D_{calc} (0.07) is smaller than $D_{critical,5\%}$ (0.1358), the null hypothesis is not rejected. Figure 6.20 shows the graphs of cumulative empirical and normal distributions, $D_{critical,5\%}$, D_{calc}, and the test result.

$F_E(t), F_t(t)$

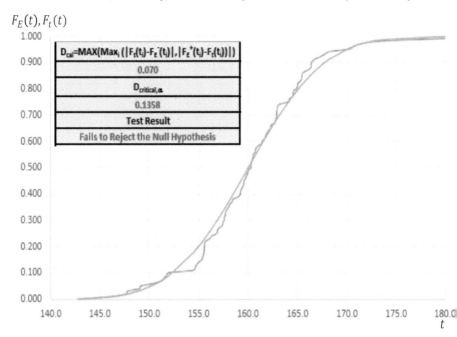

Figure 6.20 Empirical (Blue) and Normal (Gray) Distributions.

6.7 DATA FITTING

Curve fitting is the process of finding suitable models for data and analyzing the models' accuracy. Hence, the aims are to find out trends that allow having predictive analytic functions through the available data set. It is, however, worth stressing that an essential aspect of data fitting is data collection. Any analysis method is only as good as the data on which it is based. This section introduces linear, polynomial, and exponential regressions models, and Lagrange´s interpolation [165, 288, 316, 356, 477].

6.7.1 LINEAR REGRESSION

This section presents the simple linear regression model. In other words, it introduces a linear model that relates a response variable y (dependent variable) with a single regressor x (independent variable or predictor).

Before entering into details, it is worth mentioning that the observations on the response variable x are assumed to be random observations from the population, and the regressor variables $(y - f(x))$ are assumed to be constants for a given population of interest. Assume a straight line function represented by

$$f(x) = Ax + B, \qquad (6.7.1)$$

where A and B are the unknown angular coefficient and the intercept. Now, consider a data set of size n represented by pairs of points, such as $(x_1, y_1), (x_1, y_1), ..., (x_k, y_k),$ ..., (x_n, y_n) that has a linear trend (see Figure 6.21), where $X = \{x_1, x_2, ...x_n\}$ and $Y = \{y_1, y_2, ...y_n\}$ are the set of ordered values of x_k and y_k, respectively. The general aim here is to figure out what are the best values of A and B that minimize the error, E, between the real points and respective points obtained through the linear function $f(x)$.

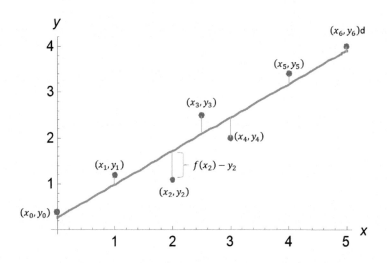

Figure 6.21 Linear Regression

Many different metrics may quantify errors. In regression models, one of the most adopted is the Root Mean Square Error (RMSE). The RMSE (Below, we adopt just E to denote RMSE.) is defined by the square root of the mean of squares of distances between actual data points and the respective points provided by the prediction function. More formally,

$$E = \sqrt{\frac{1}{n} \sum_{k=1}^{n} (f(x_k) - y_k)^2}. \tag{6.7.2}$$

Figure 6.21 presents a data set with seven points and highlights the difference $f(x_2) - y_2$. Our aim is to find estimates for A and B that minimize the error E. Hence,

$$\min E \Rightarrow \min \varepsilon = \min \sum_{k=1}^{n} (f(x_k) - y_k)^2,$$

where

$$\varepsilon = \sum_{k=1}^{n} ((Ax_k + B) - y_k)^2, \qquad (6.7.3)$$

where ε is usually named the *residual* or *sum of square errors*. It is worth stressing that there is no maximal error, but specific values exist for A and B that provide a minimal error. Therefore, deriving ε for A and B and equally each expression to zero allows us to obtain the minimal values of A and B that minimize the error. Thus, deriving ε for A and B, we get

$$\frac{\partial \varepsilon}{\partial A} = 0 \qquad (6.7.4)$$

and

$$\frac{\partial \varepsilon}{\partial B} = 0 \qquad (6.7.5)$$

equalling them to zero, and then solving both equations for the two unknowns (A and B), we have

$$\frac{\partial}{\partial A} \left(\sum_{k=1}^{n} ((Ax_k + B) - y_k)^2 \right),$$

which leads to

$$\sum_{k=1}^{n} \left(Ax_k^2 + Bx_k - y_k x_k \right) = 0.$$

Hence

$$A \sum_{k=1}^{n} x_k^2 + B \sum_{k=1}^{n} x_k = \sum_{k=1}^{n} y_k x_k.$$

Likewise, from Equation 6.7.5, we have

$$\frac{\partial}{\partial B} \left(\sum_{k=1}^{n} ((Ax_k + B) - y_k)^2 \right)$$

which take us to

$$\sum_{k=1}^{n} 2\left(Ax_k + B - y_k\right) = 0. \tag{6.7.6}$$

Thus,

$$A \sum_{k=1}^{n} x_k + nB = \sum_{k=1}^{n} y_k, \tag{6.7.7}$$

which is equivalent to this linear matrix system

$$\begin{pmatrix} \sum_{k=1}^{n} x_k^2 & \sum_{k=1}^{n} x_k \\ \sum_{k=1}^{n} x_k & n \end{pmatrix} \begin{pmatrix} A \\ B \end{pmatrix} = \begin{pmatrix} \sum_{k=1}^{n} y_k x_k \\ \sum_{k=1}^{n} y_k \end{pmatrix}. \tag{6.7.8}$$

Then, we estimate A and B by

$$\hat{A} = \frac{n \sum_{k=1}^{n} y_k x_k - \sum_{k=1}^{n} y_k \sum_{k=1}^{n} x_k}{n \sum_{k=1}^{n} x_k^2 - \left(\sum_{k=1}^{n} x_k\right)^2} \tag{6.7.9}$$

and

$$\hat{B} = \frac{\sum_{k=1}^{n} y_k \sum_{k=1}^{n} x_k^2 - \sum_{k=1}^{n} x_k \sum_{k=1}^{n} y_k x_k}{n \sum_{k=1}^{n} x_k^2 - \left(\sum_{k=1}^{n} x_k\right)^2} \tag{6.7.10}$$

since we have all x_k and y_k. The correlation coefficient between the data sets x_k and y_k, $k \in \{1, 2, ..., n\}$, is a values in the interval $(-1, 1)$ (see Equation 4.6.2) that indicates a linear relationship between the data sets.

$$\rho_{XY} = \frac{Cov(X, Y)}{\sqrt{Var(X) Var(Y)}}.$$

Likewise, the coefficient of determination also provides information about the linear relationship between the data sets, where values of ρ_{XY}^2 close to one indicate a strong linear relation between X and Y, and uncorrelated X and Y have ρ_{XY}^2 close to zero (see Equation 4.6.3).

$$\rho_{XY}^2 = \left(\frac{Cov(X, Y)}{\sqrt{Var(X) Var(Y)}}\right)^2.$$

Table 6.16

Data Set (x_k, y_k)

k	x_k	y_k	x_k^2	$x_k y_k$	$f(x_k)$	$(f(x_k) - y_k)^2$
1	0.00	0.40	0.00	0.00	0.2643	0.0184
2	1.00	1.20	1.00	1.20	0.9929	0.0429
3	2.00	1.10	4.00	2.20	1.7214	0.3862
4	2.50	2.50	6.25	6.25	2.0857	0.1716
5	3.00	2.00	9.00	6.00	2.4500	0.2025
6	4.00	3.40	16.00	13.60	3.1786	0.0490
7	5.00	4.00	25.00	20.00	3.9071	0.0086

Table 6.17

Data Summary

$\sum_{k=1}^{n} x_k$	$\sum_{k=1}^{n} y_k$	$\sum_{k=1}^{n} x_k^2$	$\sum_{k=1}^{n} x_k y_k$	$\sum_{k=1}^{n} x_k \sum_{k=1}^{n} y_k$	n	A	B
17.50	14.60	61.25	49.25	255.50	7	0.7286	0.2643

Example 6.7.1. Assume a data set composed of seven pairs depicted in Columns x_k and y_k of Table 6.16. The respective points are also shown in Figure 6.21. Table 6.17 shows the data summary calculated from data in Table 6.16.

Using the information available in Table 6.16 and Table 6.17, and applying in Equation 6.7.9 and Equation 6.7.10, we estimate $A = 0.7286$ and $B = 0.2643$ as also shown in Table 6.17. Therefore, the linear model is estimated by

$$\hat{y} = \hat{A}x + \hat{B}, \tag{6.7.11}$$

hence,

$$\hat{y} = 0.7286x + 0.2643,$$

where $E = 0.3544$ and $\varepsilon = 0.8793$. The correlation coefficient is $\rho = 0.9558$ and the coefficient of determination is $\rho^2 = 0.9135$; hence, both denote a strong linear relationship between the data sets x_k and y_k, $k \in \{1, 2, ..., n\}$. $\square$

Example 6.7.2. Let us consider a data set composed of twenty pairs, (x_k, y_k), depicted in Columns x_k and y_k of Table 6.18. The respective points are also shown in Figure 6.22.

Table 6.18
Data Set Composed of Twenty Pairs

k	x_k	y_k	k	x_k	y_k
1	0.3855	78.2658	11	9.4302	35.7762
2	0.4484	73.6320	12	10.3725	35.6596
3	1.3584	71.9883	13	10.3732	34.5777
4	1.4620	70.7748	14	11.7744	30.7041
5	5.2846	63.8734	15	16.7460	30.6425
6	5.3833	58.0750	16	16.9578	26.7791
7	6.1245	57.3510	17	17.7499	22.2907
8	6.8050	50.2785	18	18.1667	22.0439
9	8.7149	44.4071	19	19.1345	10.4765
10	9.4110	39.1079	20	19.1875	4.4540

Table 6.19
Data Summary - Data Set Composed of Twenty Pairs

$\sum x_k$	S yk	$\sum x_k^2$	$\sum x_k y_k$	$\sum x_k \sum y_k$	n	A	B
195.2701	861.1584	2699.701195	5839.8223	168158.5116	20	-3.2377	74.6695

E	ε	ρ	ρ^2
5.3549	573.4950	-0.9672	0.9355

Considering the data available in Table 6.18 and Table 6.19, and using Equation 6.7.9 and Equation 6.7.10, $A = -3.2377$ and $B = 74.6695$ are estimated. Hence, the linear model estimated by Equation 6.7.11 is

$$\hat{y} = -3.2377x + 74.6695,$$

where $E = 5.3549$ and $\varepsilon = 573.4950$. The linear model is also plot in Figure 6.22. The correlation coefficient is $\rho = -0.9672$ and the coefficient of determination is $\rho^2 = 0.9355$; thus, both denote a strong linear relationship between the data sets x_k and $y_k, k \in \{1, 2, ..., n\}$. However, as ρ is negative, we have, indeed, a negative linear relationship between the data sets.

□

Generalizing for Multiple Linear Regression

The strategy applied above may also be adopted for the case when a linear model relates the response variable y with more than one regressor, $\mathbf{x} = (x_1, x_2, ..., x_m)$. As before, consider a data set composed of n tuples $(y_k, x_1^k, x_2^k, ..., x_m^k)$. For such cases, the linear model has this format:

$$f(\mathbf{x}) = f(\mathbf{x}, C_0, C_1, ..., C_m) = C_1 x_1 + C_2 x_2 + C_3 x_3 + ... C_m x_m + C_0. \quad (6.7.12)$$

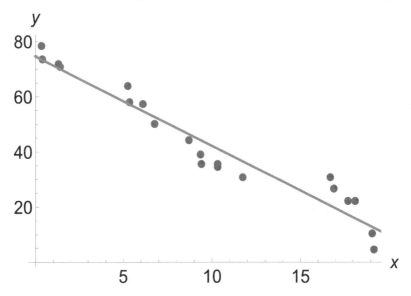

Figure 6.22 Linear Regression.

The general setting for solving this problem is the same adopted for single linear regression, but, now, considering each coefficient C_i, $i \in \{0, 1, ..., m\}$. Hence, the aim is finding each C_i that minimizes the error, ε, which is a function of C_i, $i \in \{0, 1, ..., m\}$. Hence

$$min\, \varepsilon(C_0, C_1, ..., C_m) = min \sum_{k=1}^{n} (f(\mathbf{x}, C_0, C_1, ..., C_m) - y_k)^2. \qquad (6.7.13)$$

Therefore, deriving $\varepsilon(C_0, C_1, ..., C_m)$ for each C_i and equally each expression to zero, we have a $(m+1) \times (m+1)$ system of linear equations that allows us to obtain the minimal values of each C_i (unknown) that minimizes the error, $\varepsilon(C_0, C_1, ..., C_m)$. Thus, we have

$$\frac{\partial \varepsilon(C_0, C_1, ..., C_m)}{\partial C_0} = 0,$$

$$\frac{\partial \varepsilon(C_0, C_1, ..., C_m)}{\partial C_1} = 0,$$

$$\frac{\partial \varepsilon(C_0, C_1, ..., C_m)}{\partial C_2} = 0,$$

$$\vdots$$

$$\frac{\partial \varepsilon(C_0, C_1, ..., C_m)}{\partial C_m} = 0,$$

which is the system of $m+1$ linear equations with $m+1$ unknowns $(C_0, C_1, ..., C_m)$. Hence, solving this system of equations, we find C_0, C_1, ..., C_m that minimize $\varepsilon(C_0, C_1, ..., C_m)$.

Example 6.7.3. Assume a data set composed of fifteen tuples depicted in Columns x_k, y_k, and z_k of Table 6.20. The respective points are also shown in Figure 6.23. The format of the linear model is

$$f(x,y) = Ax + By + C.$$

Table 6.20
Data Set $\{(x_k, y_k, z_k)\}$ $k \in \mathbb{N}$, $k \in [0, 15]$ **- Multiple Linear Regression**

k	x_k	y_k	z_k	k	x_k	y_k	z_k
1	1.00	4.00	8.00	9	9.00	9.80	23.00
2	2.00	1.80	9.00	10	10.00	9.20	19.00
3	3.00	2.70	10.00	11	11.00	11.80	25.00
4	4.00	4.30	8.00	12	12.00	12.90	22.00
5	5.00	5.20	13.00	13	13.00	13.30	26.00
6	6.00	5.70	16.00	14	14.00	14.80	24.00
7	7.00	7.60	14.00	15	15.00	13.00	27.00
8	8.00	7.80	18.00				

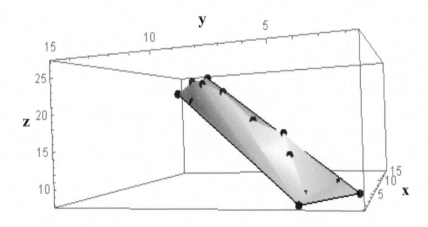

Figure 6.23 Data Set - $\{(x_k, y_k, z_k)\}$ $k \in \mathbb{N}$, $k \in [0, 15]$

We aim to find estimates of A, B, and C that minimize ε. Thus,

$$min \, \varepsilon(A,B,C) = min \sum_{k=1}^{15} (f(x_k,y_k) - z_k)^2.$$

Hence, deriving $\varepsilon(A,B,C)$ for A, B, and C and equally each expression to zero, we have a system of linear equations that allows us to obtain the minimal values of A, B, and C that minimize the error. Thus, deriving

$$\frac{\partial \varepsilon(A,B,C))}{\partial A} = 0,$$

$$\frac{\partial \varepsilon(A,B,C))}{\partial B} = 0,$$

$$\frac{\partial \varepsilon(A,B,C))}{\partial C} = 0,$$

and solving the system of equations for A, B and C, we obtain $\hat{A} = -1.0110$, $\hat{B} = 2.3714$, and $\hat{C} = 17.4395$, for where $E = 2.9132$ and $\varepsilon = 127.301$. Therefore, the estimated model is

$$f(x,y) = -1.0110x + 2.3714y + 17.4395.$$

$\square$

6.7.2 POLYNOMIAL REGRESSION

The strategy adopted for linear regression may also be broadly adopted as a general setting to estimate parameters of more complex curve fitting. The whole idea behind curve fitting is taking your data, (x_k, y_k), $k \in \{1, 2, ..., n\}$, and assuming you have a function, $f(x)$, that is parameterized by a set of parameters (coefficients), C_i, $i \in \{0, 1, ..., m\}$, such that $f(x) = f(x, C_0, C_1, ..., C_m)$. The curve may be a straight line, a parabola, an exponential function, sines, cosines etc. Hence, we have to choose values for these parameters that embody the respective curve fit.

In linear regression, the aim was to find the angular coefficient and the intercept of the curve to minimize ε. Now, $\varepsilon = \varepsilon(C_0, C_1, ..., C_m)$ is a function of the parameters (like multiple linear regression), which is defined as

$$\varepsilon(C_0, C_1, ..., C_m) = \sum_{k=1}^{n} (f(x_k, C_0, C_1, ..., C_m) - y_k)^2, \quad (6.7.14)$$

and our aim is to minimize $\varepsilon(C_0, C_1, ..., C_m)$. The general process we have adopted so far is also considered here. Thus, for finding the value of parameters C_i, $i \in \{0, 1, ..., m\}$ that minimize $\varepsilon(C_0, C_1, ..., C_m)$, we first derive the function

$\varepsilon(C_0, C_1, ..., C_m)$ for each parameter C_i, equalize each algebraic expression to zero, and find the value of each parameter that minimizes $\varepsilon(C_0, C_1, ..., C_m)$. Hence,

$$\frac{\partial \varepsilon(C_0, C_1, ..., C_m)}{\partial C_j} = 0, \qquad j = 0, 1, ..., m, \qquad (6.7.15)$$

so that we get $m+1$ equations. The problem with these equations is that they could be linear or non-linear equations. Hence, if $f(x_k, C_0, C_1, ..., C_m)$ is a polynomial, then we have an $m+1$ set of linear equations with $m+1$ parameters that can be easily solved. However, if $f(x_k, C_0, C_1, ..., C_m)$ is a more complex function, we may obtain an $m+1$ set of non-linear equations that may be too complex to find a global minimum. We may use some iterative method that starts with guesses that hopefully converge to a global minimum for such cases. In this particular section, however, we consider only polynomial functions.

Example 6.7.4. Consider the data set composed of fifteen pairs depicted in Columns x_k and y_k of Table 6.21. The respective points are also shown in Figure 6.24. Let us assume the following function is a good model for representing such a data set

$$f(x) = Ax^2 + Bx + C.$$

Table 6.21
Data Set (x_k, y_k), $k = \{1, 2, ..., 15\}$

k	x_k	f(x)	y_k	k	x_k	f(x)	y_k
0	0	8	12	8	8	176	163
1	1	15	10	9	9	215	190
2	2	26	23	10	10	258	305
3	3	41	35	11	11	305	250
4	4	60	80	12	12	356	350
5	5	83	60	13	13	411	420
6	6	110	102	14	14	470	540
7	7	141	95	15	15	533	550

Our aim is finding estimates of A, B, and C that minimize $\varepsilon(A, B, C)$. Thus,

$$min\,\varepsilon(A, B, C) = min \sum_{k=1}^{15} (f(x_k, y_k) - z_k)^2.$$

Hence, deriving $\varepsilon(A, B, C)$ for A, B, and C, and equalling them to zero, that is

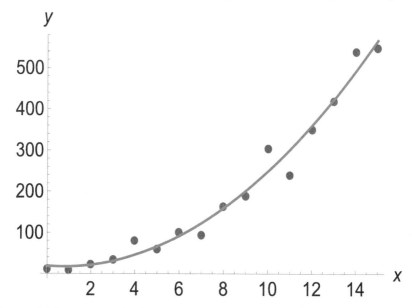

Figure 6.24 Data Set (x, y) - Polynomial Regression.

$$\frac{\partial \varepsilon(A,B,C))}{\partial A} = 0,$$

$$\frac{\partial \varepsilon(A,B,C))}{\partial B} = 0,$$

$$\frac{\partial \varepsilon(A,B,C))}{\partial C} = 0,$$

we get

$$\frac{\partial \varepsilon(A,B,C))}{\partial A} = 16(-55982 + 22289A + 1800B + 155C) = 0,$$

$$\frac{\partial \varepsilon(A,B,C))}{\partial B} = 16(-4529 + 1800A + 155B + 15C) = 0,$$

and

$$\frac{\partial \varepsilon(A,B,C))}{\partial C} = -6350 + 2480A + 240B + 32C = 0,$$

which is equivalent to

$$\begin{pmatrix} 22289 & 1800 & 155 \\ 1800 & 155 & 15 \\ 2480 & 240 & 32 \end{pmatrix} \begin{pmatrix} A \\ B \\ C \end{pmatrix} = \begin{pmatrix} 55982 \\ 4529 \\ 6350 \end{pmatrix}$$

Solving this system of linear equations for A, B, and C, we obtain $\hat{A} = 2.71376$, $\hat{B} = -4.17847$, and $\hat{C} = 19.4596$. Therefore, the model is

$$f(x) = 2.71376x^2 - 4.17847x + 19.4596,$$

and $E = 27.3372$ and $\varepsilon = 11957.2$. The curve is also plotted in Figure 6.24.

$\square$

A turning point in a curve is a point of the respective graph where the curve changes its concavity, either from increasing to decreasing or decreasing to increasing. A polynomial of degree n is at most $n-1$ turning points of the curve. Therefore, if a curve has three turning points, check at most the polynomial of the 4th order.

6.7.3 EXPONENTIAL REGRESSION

Now, let us apply the general data fitting approach to find parameters of a model that fit a data set that may be represented by an exponential behavior. Exponential regression may be adopted to represent data sets with slow initial growth that then accelerates rapidly without bound. Another possible situation is when we have a fast-decaying start. After that, it slows down to reach values closer and closer to zero. Such a curve may be represented by a function such as

$$f(x) = y = Ce^{Ax}. \qquad (6.7.16)$$

The function that specifies ε is defined as

$$\varepsilon(A,C) = \sum_{k=1}^{n} \left(Ce^{Ax_k} - y_k \right)^2, \qquad (6.7.17)$$

for a data set (x_k, y_k), $k \in \{1,2,...,n\}$. The problem with the model above is that when $\varepsilon(A,C)$ is derived for A and C, we no longer obtain a system of linear equations as in previous cases. For instance, let us take the derivative of $\varepsilon(A,C)$ for A; thus

$$\frac{\partial \varepsilon(A,C)}{\partial A} = \sum_{k=0}^{n} 2Ce^{Ax_k} x_k \left(Ce^{Ax_k} - y_k \right),$$

and then equaling the derivative to zero, we get

$$\sum_{k=0}^{n} 2Ce^{Ax_k} x_k \left(Ce^{Ax_k} - y_k \right) = 0.$$

Likewise, if we derive $\varepsilon(A,C)$ for C and then equal the expression to zero, we obtain

$$\sum_{k=0}^{n} 2e^{Ax_k}\left(Ce^{Ax_k} - y_k\right) = 0.$$

These two equations are a non-linear system of equations, which may be too complex to find a global minimum. Therefore, we may adopt iterative algorithms that start with guesses that may converge to a global minimum in these cases. However, the exponential models may be transformed into a linear model by applying a logarithm for this particular case.

Thus, let us define a function $Y = g(y) = \ln(y)$. As

$$y = Ce^{Ax},$$

then

$$\ln(y) = \ln(Ce^{Ax}).$$
$$\ln(y) = \ln(C) + \ln(e^{Ax}).$$
$$\ln(y) = \ln(C) + Ax\ln(e).$$
$$\ln(y) = \ln(C) + Ax.$$

Now, let us define $B = \ln(C)$; hence

$$\ln(y) = Ax + B, \tag{6.7.18}$$

which is

$$Y = Ax + B. \tag{6.7.19}$$

Therefore, the original data set is transformed into

$$(x_k, \ln(y_k)), \qquad k \in \{1, 2, ..., n\}.$$

Now, we may use the linear regression (depicted in Section 6.7.1) to estimate A and B, and from them, estimate C since $B = \ln C$; thus

$$C = e^B. \tag{6.7.20}$$

Example 6.7.5. Let us consider a data set composed of fifteen pairs, (x_k, y_k), depicted in Columns x_k and y_k of Table 6.22. The respective points are also shown in Figure 6.25. For this data set, we adopted an exponential regression. Hence, we need to estimate the parameters C and A of the model (see Function 6.7.16)

$$y = Ce^{Ax}.$$

Table 6.22
Data Set Composed of Fifteen Pairs - Exponential Regression

k	x_k	y_k	$\ln(y_k)$	x_k^2	$x_k y_k$
1	1	3	1.0986	1	1.0986
2	2	3.8	1.3350	4	2.6700
3	3	3.7	1.3083	9	3.9250
4	4	4.5	1.5041	16	6.0163
5	5	4.9	1.5892	25	7.9462
6	6	5	1.6094	36	9.6566
7	7	5.2	1.6487	49	11.5406
8	8	5.8	1.7579	64	14.0629
9	9	6.5	1.8718	81	16.8462
10	10	8	2.0794	100	20.7942
11	11	8.6	2.1518	121	23.6694
12	12	9.4	2.2407	144	26.8885
13	13	11	2.3979	169	31.1726
14	14	13	2.5649	196	35.9093
15	15	14	2.6391	225	39.5859

The original data set is, then, first transformed into the data set depicted in Columns x_k and $\ln(y_k)$ of Table 6.22. The transformed data set is also depicted in Figure 6.26.

$$\ln(y) = Ax + B,$$

Using the linear regression approach presented in Section 6.7.1, A and B are estimated, $\hat{A} = 0.1050$ and $\hat{B} = 1.0129$. Table 6.23 shows the information summary for estimating A, B, and C.

Table 6.23
Data Summary and $\hat{A}$, $\hat{B}$, and $\hat{C}$.

$\sum x_k$	$\sum y_k$	$\sum x_k^2$	$\sum x_k y_k$	$\sum x_k \sum y_k$	n	A	B	C
120.00	27.80	1240.00	251.78	3335.62	15	0.1050	1.0129	2.7536

The straight line equation is

$$Y = \ln(y) = 0.1050x + 1.0129,$$

which is also shown in Figure 6.26. The correlation coefficient is $\rho = 0.9905$ and the coefficient of determination is $\rho^2 = 0.9810$. Using $\hat{B}$, we estimate C using (see Equation 6.7.20)

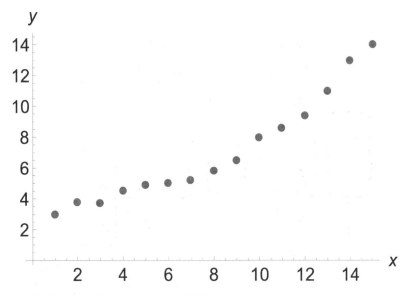

Figure 6.25 Data Set Composed of Fifteen Pairs.

$$\hat{C} = e^{\hat{\beta}}.$$

Hence, $\hat{C} = e^{1.0129} = 2.7536$. Therefore, we get

$$y = 2.7536\,e^{0.1050x},$$

where $E = 0.0631$ and $\varepsilon = 0.0598$. This curve is presented in Figure 6.27.

□

Regression techniques are one of the most popular statistical techniques used for prediction. Indeed, many regression methods could be applied to various types of data set trends. Let us, however, point out the logarithmic and the logistic regression models. The logarithmic regression may be to model situations where growth or decay accelerates rapidly at first and then slows over time. The logistic model represents a data set whose growth starts increasing over time. However, the growth steadily slows at a certain point, and the function approaches a limiting value. For a broad view on regression methods, the reader may refer to [477]

6.7.4 LAGRANGE'S POLYNOMIAL

The last sections introduced some curve fitting methods that provide the smallest error. It is worth mentioning, however, that these methods do not necessarily go

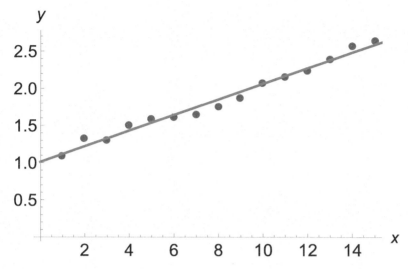

Figure 6.26   Transformed Data Set Composed of Fifteen Pairs.

through any point of the data set (see Figure 6.28.a). On the other hand, this section sets forth a method that adopts a function that goes through all data set points. The approach discussed here is a polynomial fitting approach that is not the best fit in the sense that it reduces the error; instead, the polynomial goes through all data points of the data set (see Figure 6.28.b). Hence, the error obtained when using such an approach is zero.

This is a very different approach to what we have seen in the previous section. Although the error here is zero since the polynomial goes through all data points, the polynomial's degree (n) is equal to the $n - 1$ turning points. For instance, the polynomial depicted in Figure 6.28.b has a degree equal to six since it has five turning points. Therefore, if we have a data set with one hundred points, the polynomial may have ninety-nine turns to fit the data. The phenomenon is usually called *polynomial wiggle*. Hence, such an approach is very sensitive to the presence of outliers and data fluctuation. Besides, this approach may provide reasonable estimates for data interpolation, that is, for estimating missing points within the collected data set, but we may see massive fluctuation in the data set edges; hence it does not work well for data extrapolation (estimating missing points beyond the data set boundaries).

Consider a data set $\{(x_0, y_0), (x_1, y_1), \dots (x_n, y_n)\}$ and assume a polynomial $P_n(x) = a_0 + a_1 x + a_2 x^2 + \dots, a_n x^n$. Then, we have a polynomial system with $n + 1$ unknowns $(a_0, a_1, \dots, a_n)$ and $n + 1$ constraints $(\{(x_0, y_0), (x_1, y_1), \dots (x_n, y_n)\})$. Thus, considering all data points (x_i, y_i), $i \in \{0, 1, \dots, n\}$, we get

$$P_n(x_0) = y_0 = a_0 + a_1 x_0 + a_2 x_0^2 + \dots, + a_n x_0^n,$$
$$P_n(x_1) = y_1 = a_0 + a_1 x_1 + a_2 x_1^2 + \dots, + a_n x_1^n,$$

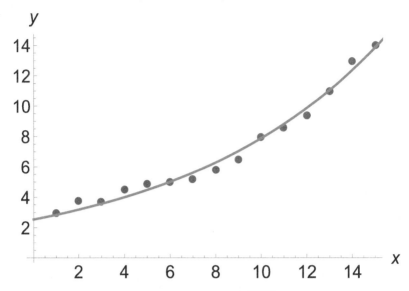

Figure 6.27 Exponential Curve $-y = 2.7536e^{0.1050x}$.

$$\vdots$$

$$P_n(x_n) = y_1 = a_0 + a_1 x_n + a_2 x_n^2 + ..., + a_n x_n^n,$$

which is a system of $n + 1$ linear equations with $n + 1$ unknowns. This system, represented in matrix form, is

$$\begin{pmatrix} 1 & x_0 & x_0^2 & \cdots & x_0^n \\ 1 & x_1 & x_1^2 & \cdots & x_1^n \\ \vdots & \vdots & \vdots & \cdots & \vdots \\ 1 & x_n & x_n^2 & \cdots & x_n^n \end{pmatrix} \begin{pmatrix} a_0 \\ a_1 \\ \vdots \\ a_n \end{pmatrix} = \begin{pmatrix} y_0 \\ y_1 \\ \vdots \\ y_n \end{pmatrix},$$

which is equal to

$$XA = Y.$$

As we have the data set $\{(x_0, y_0), (x_1, y_1), ... (x_n, y_n)\}$, we obtain $a_0, a_1, ..., a_n$ by solving the system of linear equations.

One drawback of such an approach is that if we add one more data point, we have to reconstruct the whole system of linear equations. An alternative to the process presented above adopts the *Lagrange's Polynomial*. Lagrange's polynomial is defined as

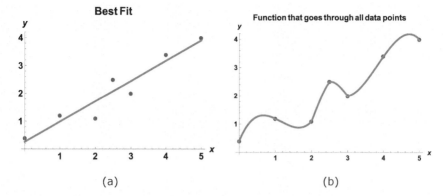

Figure 6.28   (a) Error Reduction. (b) Function That Goes Through All Data Points.

$$P_n(x) = \frac{(x - x_1)(x - x_2)\dots(x - x_{n-1})}{(x_0 - x_1)(x_0 - x_2)\dots(x_0 - x_{n-1})} y_0 + \qquad (6.7.21)$$

$$\frac{(x - x_0)(x - x_2)\dots(x - x_{n-1})}{(x_1 - x_0)(x_1 - x_2)\dots(x_1 - x_{n-1})} y_1 +$$

$$\vdots$$

$$+ \frac{(x - x_0)(x - x_2)\dots(x - x_{n-2})}{(x_{n-1} - x_0)(x_{n-1} - x_2)\dots(x_{n-1} - x_{n-2})} \cdot y_{n-1},$$

which may be encapsulated by

$$P(x) = \sum_{j=0}^{n-1} \left(y_j \prod_{k=0,k\neq j}^{n-1} \frac{x - x_k}{x_j - x_k} \right). \qquad (6.7.22)$$

Example 6.7.6. Assume a data set composed of seven pairs depicted in Columns x_k and y_k of Table 6.16. The respective points are also shown in Figure 6.28. Using this data set on Function 6.7.22, we obtain the polynomial

$$P(x) = 0.0013(x-5)(x-4)(x-3)(x-2.5)(x-2)(x-1) +$$

$$0.1833(x-5)(x-4)(x-3)(x-2.5)x(x-1) -$$

$$0.7111(x-5)(x-4)(x-3)(x-2)x(x-1) +$$

$$0.3333(x-5)(x-4)(x-2.5)(x-2)x(x-1) -$$

$$0.0944(x-5)(x-3)(x-2.5)(x-2)x(x-1) -$$

Table 6.24

Data Set - (x_k, y_k), $k = \{1, 2, ..., 15\}$

k	x_k	y_k	k	x_k	y_k
1	1.0	7.50	9	800.0	16.35
2	100.0	12.50	10	900.0	16.41
3	200.0	14.50	11	1000.0	16.31
4	300.0	15.00	12	1100.0	16.21
5	400.0	15.50	13	1200.0	16.32
6	500.0	15.70	14	1300.0	16.48
7	600.0	16.20	15	1400.0	16.46
8	700.0	16.32	16		

$$0.0333(x-5)(x-4)(x-3)(x-2.5)(x-2)x,$$

which may be simplified to

$$P(x) = 0.4 + 39.71x - 87.4369x^2 + 70.5833x^3 -$$
$$26.3756x^4 + 4.62667x^5 - 0.307556x^6.$$

The interpolation at $x = 2.3$ is $P(2.3) = 2.1448$.

□

Example 6.7.7. Let us consider a data set composed of fifteen pairs depicted in Columns x_k and y_k of Table 6.24. The respective points are also shown in Figure 6.29.

Using this data set on Function 6.7.22, we obtain the polynomial

$$P(x) = 8.2884 - 0.8142x + 0.0260x^2 - 3.3 \times 10^{-4}x^3$$
$$+2.3 \times 10^{-6}x^4 - 1.0 \times 10^{-8}x^5 + 3.2\,10^{-11}x^6$$
$$-6.8 \times 10^{-14}x^7 + 1,1 \times 10^{-16}x^8 - 1.2 \times 10^{-19}x^9$$
$$+9.3 \times 10^{-23}x^{10} - 5.2 \times 10^{-26}x^{11} + 1.9 \times 10^{-29}x^{12}$$
$$-4.2 \times 10^{-33}x^{13} + 4.2 \times 10^{-37}x^{14}.$$

Assume $x = 650$, $P(650) = 16.3098$. Figure 6.30 depicts the polynomial in the range $(0, 1400)$. It is worth noting the fluctuation in the data set edges. In such regions, neither interpolation nor extrapolation may be accurate. Figure 6.31 depicts the polynomial in the range $(0, 1288)$.

□

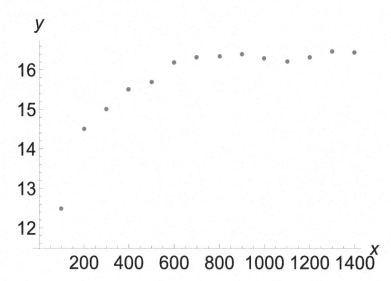

Figure 6.29   Data Plot - (x_k, y_k), $k = \{1, 2, ..., 15\}$.

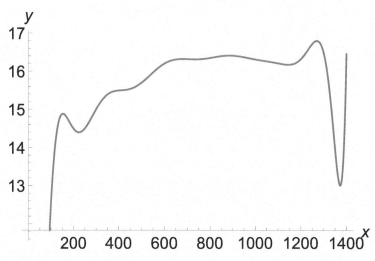

Figure 6.30   Interpolation Graph - $x \in (0, 1400)$.

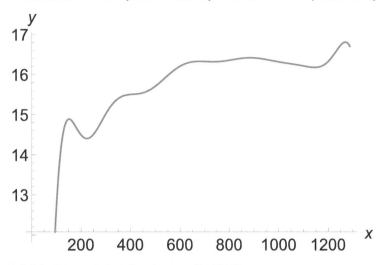

Figure 6.31 Interpolation Graph - $x \in (0, 1288)$.

EXERCISES

Exercise 1. A benchmark was executed in a server 100 times. The execution times (*ms*) were recorded and are presented in Table 6.25. Considering the population standard deviation as $\sigma = 21\,ms$, calculate the point estimation and the confidence interval of the mean execution time, taking into account a degree of significance of 5%. Use the Diagram 6.2 to guide you when choosing the estimation method.

Table 6.25
Execution Times

Execution Times (ms)									
214.8777	169.0455	186.7581	198.5695	176.7429	151.6902	155.2821	177.6468	189.3394	140.4914
230.5956	172.1261	161.7645	177.967	175.5629	169.3852	184.2131	203.4329	153.589	216.4846
200.2888	153.9862	145.0239	180.9114	177.0588	166.5817	186.5075	212.8107	181.4893	213.1504
169.4907	185.9838	178.3342	171.4	180.9375	139.1942	185.1725	170.5479	156.7214	172.3999
192.8169	200.2045	193.1399	201.591	161.7344	172.8991	177.9039	182.3208	193.9169	173.3422
169.2228	165.4883	193.4375	167.9258	196.5666	181.7794	155.6137	171.8709	166.8734	193.5451
205.1235	148.93	197.3692	165.3406	168.9155	186.844	136.0245	165.6926	161.2294	213.6312
156.0236	197.9636	185.005	195.4825	184.5736	193.0583	153.7238	177.1794	162.4607	147.3295
164.3414	199.0529	154.0574	160.9904	165.5579	211.2347	173.3051	165.2122	173.3131	197.7244
170.618	181.4616	179.0411	148.729	240.763	192.5364	186.5608	200.0143	176.0633	197.6362

Exercise 2. A user calls a service deployed in an application server. The user called the service 60 times, and each round trip time was recorded in Table 6.26. Next,

compute the point estimation and the confidence interval of the mean round trip time, taking into account a degree of significance of 1%. Use Diagram 6.2 to help you when defining the estimation method to be adopted.

Table 6.26
Round Trip Time

Round Trip Time (ms)					
186.4978	232.57	216.5795	226.0516	162.6561	251.6661
306.4696	262.5679	178.5637	214.7398	196.4679	204.5006
246.8279	229.2001	215.9115	228.1066	203.9529	239.5076
242.3109	256.1409	220.0037	261.5842	257.2282	223.1867
227.8811	221.9513	275.9563	292.2176	231.6957	214.8416
278.1708	268.2424	221.868	226.7751	214.5121	193.993
249.6557	257.8084	246.065	200.2462	239.846	255.3547
253.292	201.4026	180.2109	243.5119	216.7897	216.7973
208.1038	266.9491	189.6811	241.9945	274.2512	216.0063
238.7719	230.4372	229.2552	195.8083	211.2262	249.4203

Exercise 3. Considering the sample presented in Table 6.26, estimate how many more measures are required to estimate the confidence interval of the mean if we require a degree of confidence of 99% and an absolute error of $5\,ms$.

Exercise 4. Using the sample depicted in Table 6.25, estimate the confidence interval of the population standard deviation, taking into account a degree of confidence of 95%. Explain why you adopted this specific method.

Exercise 5. The time to transfer a small file between two sites was recorded 100 times. This sample is shown in Table 6.27. Estimate the confidence interval of time to transfer this file between these two locations, considering a degree of confidence of 95%. Justify the adoption of the method considered for estimation.

Exercise 6. Considering the sample shown in Table 6.27, calculate the confidence interval of the population skewness, taking into account a significant degree of 10%.

Exercise 7. Compare the performance of two servers (s_1 and s_2) concerning the execution time of a program. The program was executed 30 times on s_1 and 50 times on s_2. The execution times are shown in Table 6.28. It is required to find out if the servers have equivalent performance. Adopt a 95% of degree of confidence.

Table 6.27
Time to Transfer

Time to Transfer (ms)									
74.63	22.50	2.58	500.90	20.61	106.10	410.35	137.35	108.42	19.97
247.74	90.64	216.23	212.64	110.50	188.69	343.77	221.97	87.04	229.77
84.87	647.30	233.43	229.14	444.72	265.68	94.05	432.13	340.21	140.00
355.44	106.81	154.56	97.32	25.66	162.06	80.99	127.67	105.69	48.44
171.98	185.63	95.92	62.58	181.47	204.91	333.11	9.32	17.21	33.57
128.17	192.91	12.53	57.10	11.09	239.69	68.10	424.93	41.85	30.26
427.93	29.96	8.95	384.85	148.57	198.51	27.17	132.13	684.23	66.20
60.72	504.88	495.43	5.56	7.94	392.28	79.00	200.16	101.02	144.98
14.55	234.08	397.87	26.62	490.42	243.13	1.96	65.77	67.57	50.08
185.90	31.15	192.49	23.74	14.21	114.24	82.29	62.01	79.58	33.10

Exercise 8. A mobile phone manufacturer is qualifying a new model. This model is qualified if the percentage of mobile phones that fail when applying a stress test does not exceed 2%. A random sample of 250 mobile phones contains six defective phones. Estimate the confidence interval for proportion, considering 95% of degree of confidence, and inform if the new model is qualified or not.

Exercise 9. Elaborate a methodology to evaluate and compare the performance of two personal computers (computers at your disposal), considering as workload four programs. Each of the programs should explore one aspect of the computational system:

1. Program 1: integer operations

2. Program 2: floating-point operations

3. Program 3: operations with matrices

4. Program 4: graphical operations

The choice of each program is your responsibility. Define the methodology steps through an activity diagram and a document that describes the respective activities. Besides, specify the tools required to execute each activity, the inputs, the products, and the conditions that signal the completion of each of the activities of the process. Adopt the execution time of the programs as the primary metric for comparing the computer's performance.

Exercise 10. Adopt the methodology defined in the previous exercise (define a test-bed, computers, operating system, workload ...) and apply it for comparing the performance of two computers at your disposal. Evaluate the systems appropriately, present the results and your diagnosis.

Exercise 11. In your opinion, what are the main difficulties for applying the bootstrap-t method for estimating confidence intervals statistics in general?

Table 6.28
Program Execution Times in s_1 and s_2

Server s_1 (ms)			Server s_2 (ms)				
125.302	125.364	129.491	121.232	127.403	147.043	150.086	152.947
119.026	130.156	127.737	153.124	140.478	149.328	154.216	145.887
104.935	155.090	119.950	128.966	144.881	139.455	148.273	130.305
135.941	110.225	133.981	137.399	133.041	152.535	138.691	140.942
108.729	138.692	101.700	145.377	136.206	126.793	154.545	138.180
128.676	127.857	121.650	152.801	128.337	136.467	157.890	141.825
112.271	98.488	130.685	151.294	113.529	148.484	139.141	150.223
131.733	120.388	107.406	138.821	134.362	143.290	130.566	121.223
105.687	110.473	115.235	151.899	151.412	134.370	134.963	145.848
129.847	92.796	155.956	147.644	123.404	137.720	148.617	144.529

Exercise 12. A software tester claims that at least 10% of all software functions from a software infrastructure have severe defects. A sample of 200 functions revealed that 16 contained such defects. Does this finding support the tester's claim? Adopt a degree of significance of 1%.

Exercise 13. A software company is examining the effectiveness of two different programming languages in improving programming performance. Fifteen of its expert programmers, familiar with both languages, were required to code a specified function in both languages. The times required to implement the function in each programming language were recorded (in minutes). Table 6.29 shows the respective time each programmer spent implementing the function. Is there evidence to support better performance programming in any of the languages?

Exercise 14. Consider a data set composed of fifteen pairs depicted in Columns x_k and y_k of Table 6.30. (a) Obtain a linear regression model for this data set, and plot the data set and the estimated line. (b) Calculate E and ε. (c) Obtain ρ and ρ^2, and comment. (d) Find $y = \hat{f}(50)$ and $y = \hat{f}(93)$.

Exercise 15. Assume a data set composed of fifteen tuples depicted in Columns x_1^k, x_2^k and y_k of Table 6.31. (a) Obtain a multi-linear regression model for this data set. (b) Calculate E and ε. (c) Find $y = \hat{f}(10, 40)$ and $y = \hat{f}(40, 80)$.

Exercise 16. Consider a data set composed of fifteen pairs depicted in Columns x_k and y_k of Table 6.32. (a) Obtain a polynomial regression model of degree $n = 3$ for this data set, and plot the data set and the estimated curve. (b) Calculate E and ε. (c) Find $y = \hat{f}(17)$ and $y = \hat{f}(32)$.

Table 6.29
Time to Program

Programmer	Time (min) PL$_1$	PL$_2$
1	17	18
2	16	14
3	21	19
4	14	11
5	18	23
6	24	21
7	16	10
8	14	13
9	21	19
10	23	24
11	13	15
12	18	20
13	13	15
14	18	21
15	15	16

Table 6.30
Data Set - Exercise 14

x_k	y_k	x_k	y_k
4.5	18.3	46.6	9.1
11.4	17.7	61.6	8.4
11.5	14.5	77.1	6.5
16.6	12.3	81.7	5.8
37.1	12.3	83.3	2.3
39.0	12.2	85.6	1.9
40.2	12.0	89.3	0.0
40.8	9.1		

Exercise 17. Assume a data set depicted in Columns x_k and y_k of Table 6.33. (a) Obtain an exponential regression model for this data set, and plot the data set and the estimated curve. (b) Calculate E and ε. (c) Find $y = \hat{f}(15)$ and $y = \hat{f}(25)$.

Exercise 18. Consider a data set composed of fifteen pairs depicted in Columns x_k and y_k of Table 6.34. (a) Obtain polynomial regression models of degree1 1, 2, 3, and 4 for this data set, and plot the data set and the estimated curve. (b) Calculate E and ε. (c) Which model provides smaller error? (d) Using the best model, find $y = \hat{f}(9.2)$ and $y = \hat{f}(22)$.

Table 6.31
Data Set - Exercise 15

x_1^k	x_2^k	y_k	x_1^k	x_2^k	y_k
0.7	3.7	-2.3	21.9	2.1	41.8
1.1	3.4	-1.2	22.5	2.0	43.0
3.3	3.2	3.3	25.7	1.2	50.2
4.5	3.2	5.9	26.2	0.6	51.7
12.1	2.6	21.7	26.5	0.6	52.5
12.9	2.4	23.3	32.3	0.6	64.0
19.9	2.2	37.5	36.4	0.2	72.6
19.9	2.2	37.6			

Table 6.32
Data Set - Exercise 16

k	x_k	y_k	k	x_k	y_k
0	0.3	0.0	8	15.4	-227.2
1	1.3	-3.9	9	19.5	-208.7
2	4.2	-35.5	10	23.4	-88.7
3	7.4	-96.6	11	26.0	66.9
4	9.1	-130.4	12	26.1	71.6
5	9.1	-130.9	13	26.1	78.2
6	9.5	-138.5	14	26.4	96.3
7	14.7	-222.1			

Exercise 19. A data set is composed of fifteen pairs depicted in Columns x_k and y_k of Table 6.34. (a) Obtain the Lagrange's polynomial for this data set. (b) Plot the data set and the polynomial. (c) Using the polynomial, find $y = \hat{f}(5.0)$ and $y = \hat{f}(9.2)$.

Table 6.33
Data Set - Exercise 17

k	x_k	y_k	k	x_k	y_k
1	4.9	1.87×10^2	9	23.1	5.58×10^{14}
2	6.4	4.64×10^4	10	25.0	8.00×10^{15}
3	8.7	1.21×10^6	11	25.9	2.64×10^{16}
4	11.2	3.80×10^7	12	28.8	1.48×10^{18}
5	17.5	2.52×10^{11}	13	31.5	6.42×10^{19}
6	18.2	6.73×10^{11}	14	32.6	2.84×10^{20}
7	21.0	3.11×10^{13}	15	36.0	3.54×10^{22}
8	21.2	4.26×10^{13}			

Table 6.34
Data Set - Exercise 18

k	xk	yk	k	xk	yk
1	1.1	7.00	9	8.9	18.40
2	2.3	14.00	10	10.3	18.70
3	2.8	13.00	11	11.4	17.80
4	4.3	15.40	12	11.9	18.60
5	5.4	16.90	13	13.2	19.00
6	4.9	16.70	14	14.3	21.00
7	7.1	18.00	15	14.9	20.00
8	8.2	17.80			

7 Data Scaling, Distances, and Clustering

This chapter introduces the concepts of data scaling and its application. Afterward, the concepts of the distance between data points and some essential distance measures are presented. After that, the chapter depicts some classical clustering methods, k-means (and k-median), k-medoids, and agglomerative hierarchical clustering. Finally, a set of examples are shown to support the explanation of each concept.

7.1 DATA SCALING

Many statistical methods are deeply dependent on the ranges of distinct parameters of interest. For instance, suppose we are interested in applying a specific statistical method to decide which computer system component should prioritize when tuning the system. Furthermore, assume that we consider the memory utilization (measured in multiples of bytes) and the response time (measured in (sub)multiples of seconds) related to the system workload among the parameter of interest. The collected sample measures have different units and ranges. Applying a statistical method that combines these two distinct sets of parameter values may decisively affect the outcome. In such a case, it is critical to first scale the parameters' values before applying the statistical technique [351].

Some standard useful scaling method are

1. Min-Max Scaling,

2. Mean and Standard Deviation Scaling,

3. Absolute Maximal Scaling,

4. Median-Interquartile Scaling,

5. Quantile Scaling,

6. Power Transform Scaling, and

7. Vector Scaling.

Transformations For Better Normal Distribution

Min-Max Scaling transforms a data set, $\{x_i\}$, $|\{x_i\}| \in \mathbb{N}$, by scaling each individual measure to a range between zero and one by

$$x_i' = m \times \frac{x_i - Min}{Max - Min} + s, \qquad (7.1.1)$$

where $Min = \min\{x_i\}$ and $Max = \max\{x_i\}$ are the minimal and the maximal values of the set $\{x_i\}$, respectively; and $m = 1$ and $s = 0$ $(m, s \in \mathbb{R})$. If $m \neq 1$ and $s \neq 0$, the scaling is generalized to distinct ranges.

Example 7.1.1. Assume a data sample depicted in Table 7.1. The scaled data set considering the *Min-Max* method (through the scaling Expression 7.1.1), for $m = 1$ and $s = 0$ is shown in Table 7.2, where $Min = -4.67$, $Max = 94.01$, and $Max - Min = 98.47$. The histogram of this data set depicted is shown in Figure 7.1.

Table 7.1
Original Data Set

Data									
93.21	78.57	31.89	80.81	63.37	7.21	40.21	68.39	86.59	37.63
21.62	60.79	1.66	43.09	-0.79	54.54	77.68	11.43	67.73	5.25
39.69	25.14	52.10	9.89	52.49	55.32	37.16	18.27	54.65	40.17
52.52	20.91	35.19	75.83	48.10	44.94	92.58	90.57	51.60	90.82
32.20	51.69	91.79	47.08	31.38	89.39	26.08	43.04	91.32	16.50
30.76	1.51	27.00	71.75	11.78	-1.52	72.33	84.13	19.44	24.87
-4.16	86.25	88.53	-4.46	8.07	46.81	5.17	-4.47	26.19	38.59
47.54	-2.67	5.92	41.68	71.92	16.35	6.30	16.63	83.73	45.71
13.92	14.43	87.38	68.03	76.72	90.09	10.76	59.45	74.43	35.15
13.56	23.40	73.36	92.73	59.97	94.01	3.42	46.59	72.47	17.53

Table 7.2
Scaled Data - Min-Max Scaling

Scaled Data									
0.99	0.84	0.37	0.87	0.69	0.12	0.45	0.74	0.92	0.43
0.26	0.66	0.06	0.48	0.04	0.60	0.83	0.16	0.73	0.10
0.45	0.30	0.57	0.15	0.58	0.61	0.42	0.23	0.60	0.45
0.58	0.26	0.40	0.82	0.53	0.50	0.99	0.97	0.57	0.97
0.37	0.57	0.98	0.52	0.36	0.95	0.31	0.48	0.97	0.21
0.36	0.06	0.32	0.77	0.17	0.03	0.78	0.90	0.24	0.30
0.00	0.92	0.94	0.00	0.13	0.52	0.10	0.00	0.31	0.44
0.53	0.02	0.11	0.47	0.78	0.21	0.11	0.21	0.90	0.51
0.19	0.19	0.93	0.74	0.82	0.96	0.15	0.65	0.80	0.40
0.18	0.28	0.79	0.99	0.65	1.00	0.08	0.52	0.78	0.22

The histogram of the scaled data set, $\{x_i'\}$, $|\{x_i'\}| \in \mathbb{N}$, depicted is shown in Figure 7.2.

□

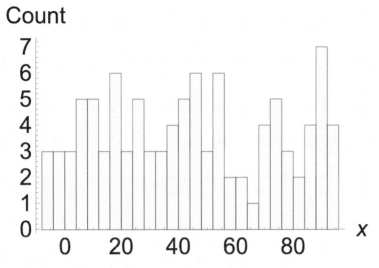

Figure 7.1   Histogram of Data Set $\{x_i\}$, $|\{x_i\}| \in \mathbb{N}$.

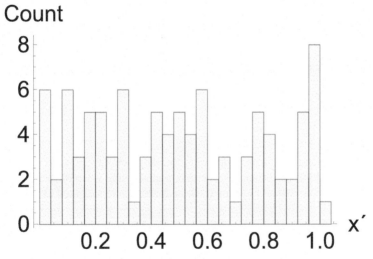

Figure 7.2   Histogram of Min-Max Scaled Data Set $\{x_i'\}$, $|\{x_i'\}| \in \mathbb{N}$.

Mean and Standard Deviation Scaling transforms data set, $\{x_i\}$, $|\{x_i\}| \in \mathbb{N}$, by scaling each individual measure by

$$x_i' = m \times \frac{x_i - \overline{X}}{SD} + s, \tag{7.1.2}$$

where $m, s \in \mathbb{R}$, $\overline{X}$ is the mean value, and SD is the standard deviation values of the set $\{x_i\}$, respectively. If $m = 1$ and $s = 0$, the original data is scaled to zero mean and standard deviation equal to one. However, if $m \neq 1$ and $s \neq 0$, the scaling is generalized to distinct ranges.

Example 7.1.2. Assume a data sample depicted in Table 7.1. The scaled data set considering the *Mean and Standard Deviation Scaling* method, for $m = 1$ and $s = 0$ (adopting Expression 7.1.2) is shown in Table 7.3, where *Mean* = 44.28 and *SD* = 30.17. The histogram of the scaled data set, $\{x_i'\}$, $|\{x_i'\}| \in \mathbb{N}$, depicted is shown in Figure 7.3.

Table 7.3
Scaled Data by the Mean and Standard Deviation

Scaled Data by the Mean and SD									
1.62	1.14	-0.41	1.21	0.63	-1.23	-0.14	0.80	1.40	-0.22
-0.75	0.55	-1.41	-0.04	-1.49	0.34	1.11	-1.09	0.78	-1.29
-0.15	-0.63	0.26	-1.14	0.27	0.37	-0.24	-0.86	0.34	-0.14
0.27	-0.77	-0.30	1.05	0.13	0.02	1.60	1.53	0.24	1.54
-0.40	0.25	1.57	0.09	-0.43	1.49	-0.60	-0.04	1.56	-0.92
-0.45	-1.42	-0.57	0.91	-1.08	-1.52	0.93	1.32	-0.82	-0.64
-1.61	1.39	1.47	-1.62	-1.20	0.08	-1.30	-1.62	-0.60	-0.19
0.11	-1.56	-1.27	-0.09	0.92	-0.93	-1.26	-0.92	1.31	0.05
-1.01	-0.99	1.43	0.79	1.08	1.52	-1.11	0.50	1.00	-0.30
-1.02	-0.69	0.96	1.61	0.52	1.65	-1.35	0.08	0.93	-0.89

□

Absolute Maximal Scaling transforms the data set, $\{x_i\}$, $|\{x_i\}| \in \mathbb{N}$, by scaling each individual measure such that the maximal absolute value of the data set is one. This can be accomplished by using the transformation represented by the Expression 7.1.3.

$$x_i' = m \times \frac{x_i}{Max} + s, \tag{7.1.3}$$

where $Max = \max\{x_i\}$ are the maximal values of the set $\{x_i\}$, $m = 1$ and $s = 0$ ($m, s \in \mathbb{R}$). If $m \neq 1$ and $s \neq 0$, the scaling is generalized to different ranges.

Example 7.1.3. Consider the data set shown in Table 7.1. The scaled data set considering the *Absolute Maximal Scaling* method (through the scaling Expression 7.1.3), for $m = 1$ and $s = 0$ is shown in Table 7.4, where $Max = 94.01$. The histogram of the scaled data set, $\{x_i'\}$, $|\{x_i'\}| \in \mathbb{N}$, depicted is shown in Figure 7.4.

□

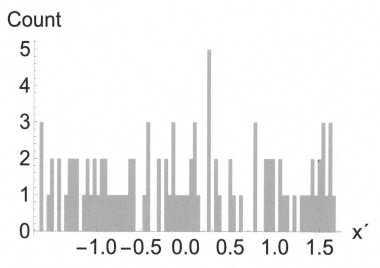

Figure 7.3 Histogram of Scaled Data by the Mean and Standard Deviation $\{x_i'\}$, $|\{x_i'\}| \in \mathbb{N}$

Table 7.4
Scaled Data - Absolute Maximal Scaling

Scaled Data by the Absolute Maximal									
0.99	0.84	0.34	0.86	0.67	0.08	0.43	0.73	0.92	0.40
0.23	0.65	0.02	0.46	-0.01	0.58	0.83	0.12	0.72	0.06
0.42	0.27	0.55	0.11	0.56	0.59	0.40	0.19	0.58	0.43
0.56	0.22	0.37	0.81	0.51	0.48	0.98	0.96	0.55	0.97
0.34	0.55	0.98	0.50	0.33	0.95	0.28	0.46	0.97	0.18
0.33	0.02	0.29	0.76	0.13	-0.02	0.77	0.89	0.21	0.26
-0.04	0.92	0.94	-0.05	0.09	0.50	0.05	-0.05	0.28	0.41
0.51	-0.03	0.06	0.44	0.77	0.17	0.07	0.18	0.89	0.49
0.15	0.15	0.93	0.72	0.82	0.96	0.11	0.63	0.79	0.37
0.14	0.25	0.78	0.99	0.64	1.00	0.04	0.50	0.77	0.19

Median-Interquartile Scaling transforms the data set, $\{x_i\}$, $|\{x_i\}| \in \mathbb{N}$, by scaling each individual measure by

$$x_i' = m \times \frac{x_i - Med}{IQR} + s, \qquad (7.1.4)$$

where $m, s \in \mathbb{R}$, Med is the median value, and IQR is the interquartile range values of the set $\{x_i\}$, respectively. If $m = 1$ and $s = 0$, the original data is scaled to zero mean and standard deviation equal to one. When $m \neq 1$ and $s \neq 0$, the scaling is generalized to distinct ranges.

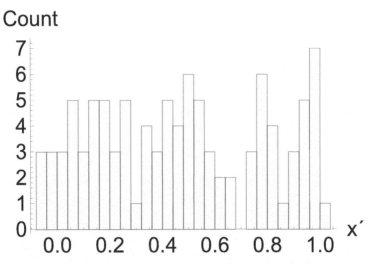

Figure 7.4 Histogram of Scaled Data by Absolute Maximal $\{x_i'\}$, $|\{x_i'\}| \in \mathbb{N}$.

Example 7.1.4. Assume a data sample depicted in Table 7.1. The scaled data set considering the *Median-Interquartile Scaling* method, for $m = 1$ and $s = 0$ (adopting Expression 7.1.4) is shown in Table 7.5, where *Median* $= 43.06$ and *IQR* $= 54.71$. The histogram of the scaled data set, $\{x_i'\}$, $|\{x_i'\}| \in \mathbb{N}$, depicted is shown in Figure 7.5.

Table 7.5
Median-Interquartile Scaling

Scaled Data by the Interqualtile								
0.92	0.65	-0.20	0.69	0.37	-0.66	-0.05	0.46	0.80	-0.10
-0.39	0.32	-0.76	0.00	-0.80	0.21	0.63	-0.58	0.45	-0.69
-0.06	-0.33	0.17	-0.61	0.17	0.22	-0.11	-0.45	0.21	-0.05
0.17	-0.40	-0.14	0.60	0.09	0.03	0.91	0.87	0.16	0.87
-0.20	0.16	0.89	0.07	-0.21	0.85	-0.31	0.00	0.88	-0.49
-0.22	-0.76	-0.29	0.52	-0.57	-0.81	0.53	0.75	-0.43	-0.33
-0.86	0.79	0.83	-0.87	-0.64	0.07	-0.69	-0.87	-0.31	-0.08
0.08	-0.84	-0.68	-0.03	0.53	-0.49	-0.67	-0.48	0.74	0.05
-0.53	-0.52	0.81	0.46	0.62	0.86	-0.59	0.30	0.57	-0.14
-0.54	-0.36	0.55	0.91	0.31	0.93	-0.72	0.06	0.54	-0.47

□

Quantile Scaling transforms the data set, $\{x_i\}$, $|\{x_i\}| \in \mathbb{N}$, with its empirical cumulative distribution function, $F_E(x_i)$ (see Section 3.1), into another data set $\{z_i\}$,

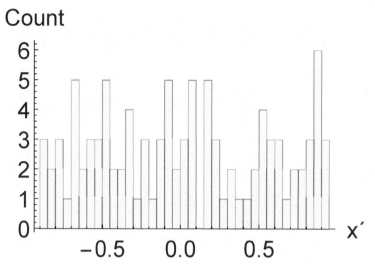

Figure 7.5   Histogram of Scaled Data by Median-Interquartile $\{x_i'\}$, $|\{x_i'\}| \in \mathbb{N}$.

$|\{z_i\}| \in \mathbb{N}$ that is represented by another cumulative distribution function, $F_T(x_i)$. Therefore, assume a data set, $\{x_i\}$, $|\{x_i\}| \in \mathbb{N}$, its empirical cumulative distribution

$$F_E(x_i) = \frac{i}{n+1}$$

(see also Function 3.1.3) and a theoretical distribution $F_T(z_i, \Theta)$, where Θ is the set of parameters of $F_T(z_i)$. Equaling $F_E(x_i)$ to $F_T(z_i)$, and then, using the inverse of $F_T(z_i)$, we get z_i (see Section 14.3.2). Hence

$$z_i = F_T^{-1}(F_E(x_i), \Theta). \tag{7.1.5}$$

Example 7.1.5. Assume the data set, $\{x_i\}$, $|\{x_i\}| = 100$, and its empirical cumulative distribution $F_E(x_i)$ the respective columns of Table 7.6. Figure 7.6 shows the histogram of the data set $\{x_i\}$.

Scaling this data set to the $U(0,1)$ is accomplished by

$$u_i = F_{U(0,1)}^{-1}(F_E(x_i)).$$

Applying the content of columns $F_E(x_i))$ as the function $F_{U(0,1)}^{-1}$ independent values, we get scaled data set according to the uniform distribution $U(0,1)$. The scaled data set is shown in columns u_i.

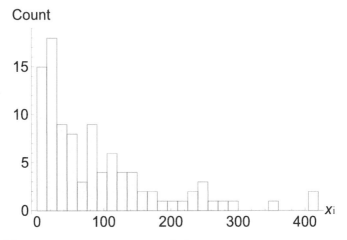

Figure 7.6   Histogram of the Data Set $\{x_i\}$.

Table 7.6

Quantile Scaling - Uniform, $U(0,1)$, and Normal, $N(0,1)$, Distributions

i	x_i	$F_E(x_i)$	u_i	z_i	i	x_i	$F_E(x_i)$	u_i	z_i
1	1.122	0.010	0.010	-2.330	51	63.322	0.505	0.505	0.012
2	1.180	0.020	0.020	-2.058	52	67.403	0.515	0.515	0.037
3	3.223	0.030	0.030	-1.885	53	71.317	0.525	0.525	0.062
4	5.175	0.040	0.040	-1.755	54	77.688	0.535	0.535	0.087
5	5.451	0.050	0.050	-1.650	55	79.130	0.545	0.545	0.112
6	5.529	0.059	0.059	-1.560	56	82.313	0.554	0.554	0.137
7	7.877	0.069	0.069	-1.481	57	82.704	0.564	0.564	0.162
8	8.185	0.079	0.079	-1.410	58	83.445	0.574	0.574	0.187
9	8.803	0.089	0.089	-1.346	59	84.523	0.584	0.584	0.213
10	10.876	0.099	0.099	-1.287	60	84.790	0.594	0.594	0.238
11	10.910	0.109	0.109	-1.232	61	85.161	0.604	0.604	0.264
12	12.220	0.119	0.119	-1.181	62	85.858	0.614	0.614	0.289
13	12.240	0.129	0.129	-1.132	63	92.561	0.624	0.624	0.315
14	13.210	0.139	0.139	-1.087	64	95.306	0.634	0.634	0.342
15	13.833	0.149	0.149	-1.043	65	101.410	0.644	0.644	0.368
16	15.313	0.158	0.158	-1.001	66	104.113	0.653	0.653	0.395
17	16.119	0.168	0.168	-0.961	67	108.413	0.663	0.663	0.422
18	16.839	0.178	0.178	-0.922	68	111.060	0.673	0.673	0.449
19	17.229	0.188	0.188	-0.885	69	111.126	0.683	0.683	0.477
20	17.323	0.198	0.198	-0.849	70	117.350	0.693	0.693	0.505
21	18.048	0.208	0.208	-0.814	71	117.509	0.703	0.703	0.533
22	18.057	0.218	0.218	-0.780	72	118.801	0.713	0.713	0.562
23	18.692	0.228	0.228	-0.746	73	122.060	0.723	0.723	0.591
24	21.413	0.238	0.238	-0.714	74	125.619	0.733	0.733	0.621
25	21.820	0.248	0.248	-0.682	75	129.924	0.743	0.743	0.651
26	25.051	0.257	0.257	-0.651	76	130.074	0.752	0.752	0.682
27	25.054	0.267	0.267	-0.621	77	142.891	0.762	0.762	0.714
28	25.375	0.277	0.277	-0.591	78	143.206	0.772	0.772	0.746

Table 7.6
Quantile Scaling - Uniform, $U(0,1)$, and Normal, $N(0,1)$, Distributions

i	x_i	$F_E(x_i)$	u_i	z_i	i	x_i	$F_E(x_i)$	u_i	z_i
29	25.849	0.287	0.287	-0.562	79	144.620	0.782	0.782	0.780
30	26.861	0.297	0.297	-0.533	80	144.807	0.792	0.792	0.814
31	27.138	0.307	0.307	-0.505	81	150.222	0.802	0.802	0.849
32	28.104	0.317	0.317	-0.477	82	164.385	0.812	0.812	0.885
33	28.256	0.327	0.327	-0.449	83	175.629	0.822	0.822	0.922
34	31.826	0.337	0.337	-0.422	84	175.919	0.832	0.832	0.961
35	33.855	0.347	0.347	-0.395	85	193.530	0.842	0.842	1.001
36	38.659	0.356	0.356	-0.368	86	206.702	0.851	0.851	1.043
37	40.075	0.366	0.366	-0.342	87	216.828	0.861	0.861	1.087
38	40.402	0.376	0.376	-0.315	88	235.608	0.871	0.871	1.132
39	41.989	0.386	0.386	-0.289	89	239.522	0.881	0.881	1.181
40	42.928	0.396	0.396	-0.264	90	241.631	0.891	0.891	1.232
41	43.269	0.406	0.406	-0.238	91	254.163	0.901	0.901	1.287
42	44.907	0.416	0.416	-0.213	92	254.273	0.911	0.911	1.346
43	45.375	0.426	0.426	-0.187	93	261.204	0.921	0.921	1.410
44	46.744	0.436	0.436	-0.162	94	280.507	0.931	0.931	1.481
45	49.844	0.446	0.446	-0.137	95	290.604	0.941	0.941	1.560
46	53.910	0.455	0.455	-0.112	96	345.692	0.950	0.950	1.650
47	54.915	0.465	0.465	-0.087	97	413.847	0.960	0.960	1.755
48	57.030	0.475	0.475	-0.062	98	415.113	0.970	0.970	1.885
49	58.462	0.485	0.485	-0.037	99	534.261	0.980	0.980	2.058
50	59.830	0.495	0.495	-0.012	100	673.648	0.990	0.990	2.330

Figure 7.7 shows the histogram of the scaled data set $\{u_i\}$.

Likewise, we scale the data set, $\{x_i\}$, $|\{x_i\}| = 100$, and its empirical cumulative distribution $F_E(x_i)$ using distribution $N(0,1)$ by adopting

$$z_i = F_{N(0,1)}^{-1}(F_E(x_i)).$$

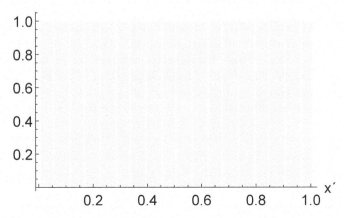

Figure 7.7 $U(0,1)$ Quantile Scaling - Histogram of the Scaled Data Set $\{u_i\}$.

The scaled data set is depicted in columns z_i of Table 7.6. Figure 7.8 depicts the histogram of the scaled data set $\{z_i\}$.

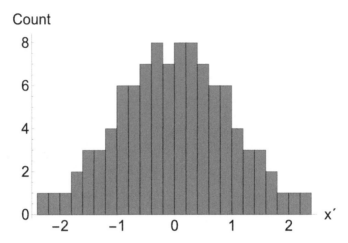

Figure 7.8 $N(0,1)$ Quantile Scaling - Histogram of the Scaled Data Set $\{z_i\}$.

□

Power Transformation Scaling - The power transformation scaling methods help model skewed data sets, data sets with high variability, or circumstances where normality is desired. Power transform scaling aims at stabilizing variance and minimizing skewness. Log, Box-Cox, and Yeo-Johnson transformation scaling are some of the most adopted power scaling methods of such a class [57, 474].

■ *Log Transformation Scaling* may be adopted to reshape a highly skewed data set into a less asymmetrical set of data. Some of the most adopted bases are 10, 2, and ε.

One of such functions is the *Log Transformation*. In cases where the data samples are highly skewed or non-normal due to outliers, log transformations may be a suitable approach. In log transformation each sample value $\{x_i\}$, $|\{x_i\}| \in \mathbb{N}$, is transformed by $log(x_i)$ with a different base. The most common bases are 10, base 2, or ε. Figure 7.9.a shows the individual plot of the data set depicted in Table 7.6, whose histogram is shown in Figure 7.6. Figure 7.9.b, Figure 7.9.c, and Figure 7.9.d shows the individual plots when the original data set is transformed using $\log_{10} x_i$, $\log_2 x_i$, and $\ln x_i$.

Figure 7.10.a, Figure 7.10.b, and Figure 7.10.d shows the histograms for the scaled data sets obtained by the respective functions $\log_{10} x_i$, $\log_2 x_i$, and $\ln x_i$.

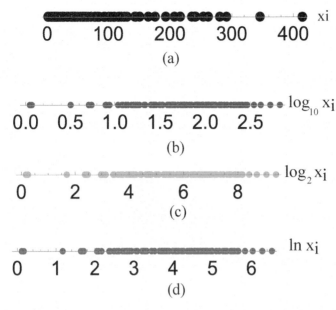

Figure 7.9 Original Data Set ($\{x_i\}$) and Scaled Data Sets - $\{\log_{10} x_i\}$, $\{\log_2 x_i\}$ and $\{\ln x_i\}$.

■ Another useful method is the *Box-Cox transformation*. This transformation aims to set the data into normalized scaled data by stabilizing variance and reducing skewness. Box-Cox needs input data to be strictly positive. The first definition of this transformation is

$$y_i(\lambda, x_i) = \begin{cases} \frac{x_i^{\lambda}-1}{\lambda}, & \text{if } \lambda \neq 0 \\ \log x_i, & \text{if } \lambda = 0 \end{cases} \tag{7.1.6}$$

since

$$\lim_{\lambda \to 0} \frac{x_i^{\lambda}-1}{\lambda} = \log x_i.$$

Box and Cox also introduced an alternative transformation in which $gm^{-(\lambda-1)}$ was included, where gm is the geometric mean of the original data set, $\{x_i\}, |\{x_i\}| \in \mathbb{N}$. Hence, the alternate definition is

$$y_i(\lambda, x_i) = \begin{cases} \frac{x_i^{\lambda}-1}{\lambda \, gm^{(\lambda-1)}}, & \text{if } \lambda \neq 0 \\ gm \log x_i, & \text{if } \lambda = 0 \end{cases} \tag{7.1.7}$$

as

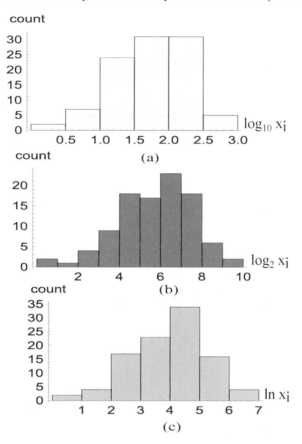

Figure 7.10 Histograms of the Scaled Data Sets - $\{\log_{10} x_i\}$, $\{\log_2 x_i\}$ and $\{\ln x_i\}$

$$\lim_{\lambda, \to 0} \frac{y_i^{\lambda} - 1}{\lambda \, gm^{(\lambda - 1)}} = gm \log y_i.$$

The inclusion of the $gm^{-(\lambda - 1)}$ simplifies the interpretation of $y_i(\lambda)$ since the units of measurement do not change as λ changes. Practically, we analyze λ in the interval $(-5, 5)$ to find a value of λ that provides the least skewed transformed data set.

Example 7.1.6. Assume the data set, $\{x_i\}$, $|\{x_i\}| = 100$, shown on Table 7.6. Figure 7.6 shows the histogram of the data set $\{x_i\}$. The geometric mean of the data set is $gm = 53.3422$. Applying the data set to the Transformation 7.1.7 for $\lambda \in \{-1, -0.5, -0.2, 0.2, 0.5, 1\}$, we get the respective data sets depicted by the histograms shown in Figure 7.11. When assigning $\lambda = 0.1$, the scaled data set is shown through its histogram depicted in Figure 7.12.a. Figure 7.12.b shows the histogram of the scaled data set for $\lambda = 0.17$.

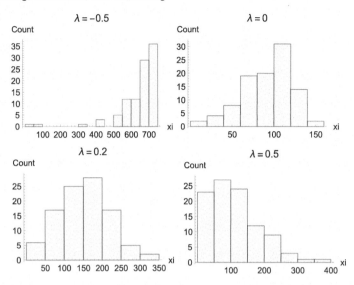

Figure 7.11 Scaled Data Sets - $\lambda = -0.5$, $\lambda = 0$, $\lambda = 0.2$, and $\lambda = 0.5$.

The original data set has a *skew* = 2.3158. As expected, considering the KS goodness of fit, there is enough evidence to reject the normal distribution as suitable for representing the original data set even with an 80% degree of confidence. The scaled data set obtained from the Box-Cox transformation considering $\lambda = 0.17$ has a *skew* = −0.0120. Besides, the KS goodness of fit does not reject the normal distribution for 80% degree of confidence. Likewise, the normal distribution was rejected for representing the original data set for 95% degree of confidence. On the other hand, the scaled data set was also not rejected.

□

The Box-Cox transformation method was a significant step towards scaling the data set to fit a normal distribution. As already stated, the Box-Cox transformation is only valid for positive x_i. A shifting parameter (δ) can indeed be introduced to handle data sets which are negative values, such that all values x_i become positive. Hence, we may have

$$y_i(\lambda, x_i) = \frac{(x_i + \delta)_i^\lambda - 1}{\lambda}. \tag{7.1.8}$$

It is worth stressing, however, that when adopting the Box-Cox model for regression, the introduction of δ makes the process of estimating λ harder to solve [474].

■ Another neat method is the *Yeo-Johnson Power Transformations*, which handles negative values x_i, neither requiring first transforming the data set values to positive

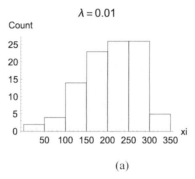

(a)

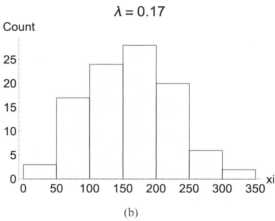

(b)

Figure 7.12 Histograms of Box-Cox Scaled Data Sets - $\lambda = 0.1$ and $\lambda = 0.17$.

values nor facing issues related to parameter estimation when adopting the regression model as in the Box-Cox method. This transformation is defined by

$$
y_i(\lambda, x_i) = \begin{cases} \frac{(x_i+1)^{\lambda}-1}{\lambda} & \text{if } \lambda \neq 0 \wedge x_i \geq 0 \\ \log_{10}(x_i+1) & \text{if } \lambda = 0 \wedge x_i \geq 0 \\ -\frac{(1-x_i)^{2-\lambda}-1}{2-\lambda} & \text{if } \lambda \neq 2 \wedge x_i < 0 \\ -\log_{10}(1-x_i) & \text{if } \lambda = 2 \wedge x_i < 0 \end{cases} \tag{7.1.9}
$$

If $\forall x_i \in \{x_i\}$, x_i is strictly positive, then the Yeo-Johnson transformation is simplified to the Box-Cox method.

Example 7.1.7. Let us adopt the data set, $\{x_i\}$, $|\{x_i\}| = 100$, shown on Table 7.7. Figure 7.13.a shows the histogram of the data set $\{x_i\}$. Applying *Yeo-Johnson Power Transformations* for $\lambda = 0.956$ we get the respective data sets shown in Columns $\{y_i\}$ presented in Table 7.7. Figure 7.13.b shows the histogram of the scaled data.

Table 7.7
Yeo-Johnson Power Transformations - $\lambda = 0.956$

x_i	y_i	x_i	y_i	x_i	y_i	x_i	y_i
-964.564	-1250.48	-39.4064	-44.5864	334.0422	270.3086	632.0149	497.4869
-804.388	-1034.59	-39.4064	-44.5864	346.8717	280.2339	649.1826	510.4048
-800.934	-1029.95	-15.8744	-17.3453	347.3919	280.636	652.6055	512.9786
-760.583	-975.857	-15.8744	-17.3453	416.6007	333.9116	654.1782	514.161
-565.813	-716.655	12.53263	11.57642	424.5007	339.9669	654.5122	514.412
-565.813	-716.655	22.85605	20.6573	438.5694	350.7382	654.5122	514.412
-490.652	-617.614	24.66486	22.22793	446.2472	356.6101	654.5764	514.4603
-417.126	-521.371	30.54302	27.30009	498.9009	396.7635	666.5522	523.4594
-417.126	-521.371	30.54302	27.30009	510.1128	405.2889	836.9704	650.8056
-358.677	-445.389	51.41343	45.01454	531.0343	421.1755	853.9648	663.4381
-354.545	-440.037	51.41343	45.01454	531.0343	421.1755	1082.461	832.2968
-354.545	-440.037	80.03232	68.8125	531.1868	421.2912	1082.461	832.2968
-318.345	-393.27	80.03232	68.8125	538.6058	426.9181	1307.77	997.2594
-315.788	-389.975	98.23217	83.74343	546.4357	432.8529	1317.255	1004.175
-315.788	-389.975	106.2538	90.28468	550.4273	435.8769	1328.17	1012.131
-304.511	-375.457	123.7201	104.4551	557.3475	441.1175	1475.737	1119.413
-277.577	-340.882	146.1633	122.5369	577.0472	456.0201	1482.927	1124.627
-277.577	-340.882	150.6669	126.1501	586.1799	462.9213	1607.905	1215.098
-232.773	-283.698	165.6064	138.1027	590.0953	465.8785	1610.396	1216.898
-185.316	-223.659	175.3744	145.8921	602.8126	475.4777	1702.207	1283.157
-185.316	-223.659	284.4596	231.7861	607.6993	479.164	1714.981	1292.363
-170.326	-204.826	284.4596	231.7861	608.8591	480.0386	1729.008	1302.47
-147.9	-176.789	284.4596	231.7861	620.1753	488.5691	1896.598	1422.939
-121.727	-144.304	334.0422	270.3086	622.5731	490.3758	2053.66	1535.415
-44.541	-50.6448	334.0422	270.3086	623.3651	490.9725	2053.66	1535.415

The skewness of the original data set is $Skew = 0.60396$, whereas the skewness of the scaled data set is $Skew = 0.0041$. The visual representation of both data sets also shows that the scaled data set is much more symmetric than the original data set.

□

Unit Vector Scaling modifies a vector $\vec{v}$ by holding the primary orientation but adjusting its length by a scale factor, so that the original vector space may shrink or expand. A vector $\vec{v}$ may be obtained through a tuple, t_e and t_o (a coordinate vector) in a given dimension n. For instance, assuming a two-dimension space, a vector $\vec{v}$ may be represented by the coordinate vector (tuple) $(v_{e_x} - v_{o_x}, v_{e_y} - v_{o_y})$. Considering the coordinate vector t_o as the origin of the vector space, $(0,0)$, $\vec{v} = \vec{v_x} + \vec{v_y}$, where $\vec{v_x}$ is represented by a coordinate vector (tuple) $(v_{e_x} - v_{o_x}) = (v_{e_x} - 0) = v_{e_x}$, which may be simplified to v_x. Likewise, $v_{e_y} - v_{o_y}$ is denoted by v_y. Hence, in a two-dimension space, the vector $\vec{v}$ can be represented by the tuple (v_x, v_y). For instance, the vector $\vec{v} = 2\vec{i} + 3\vec{j}$ is represented in two-dimension cartesian space by the pair $(2,3)$ as shown in Figure 7.14, where $\vec{i}$ and $\vec{j}$ are the unity vectors of each dimension. Considering a normed space vector, a unit vector of length one, a normalized vector $\vec{i}$ of a non-zero vector $\vec{x}$ is the unit vector in the direction of $\vec{x}$ and is obtained by

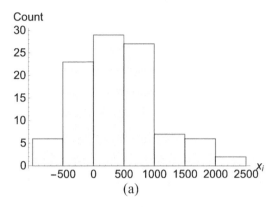
(a)

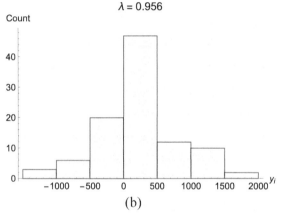
(b)

Figure 7.13   (a) Original Data Set $\{x_i\}$ and (b) Scaled Data Set $\{y_i\}$.

$$\vec{i} = \frac{\vec{x}}{\|\vec{x}\|}, \tag{7.1.10}$$

where $\|\vec{x}\|$ is the norm (length) of $\vec{x}$.

A normed vector space is a vector space on which a norm is defined. A norm of a vector space is a function $\|.\| : \mathbb{R} \mapsto \mathbb{R}$ called the *norm of a vector* if it has the following properties:

- $\|\vec{v}\| \geq 0$ for any $\vec{v} \in \mathbb{R}^n$, and $\|\vec{v}\| = 0$ if and only if $\vec{v} = \vec{0}$.

- $\|\alpha\vec{v}\| = |\alpha| \|\vec{v}\|$ for any $\vec{v} \in \mathbb{R}^n$, and any scalar $\alpha \in \mathbb{R}$.

- $\|\vec{v} + \vec{w}\| \leq \|\vec{v}\| + \|\vec{w}\|$ for any $\vec{v}, \vec{w} \in \mathbb{R}$.

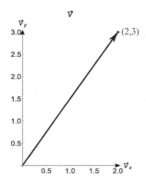

Figure 7.14   Vector $\vec{v}$ Represented by the Coordinate Vector $(2,3)$.

The most usual vector norms belong to the p-norm class (also called the *Minkowski norm*), which are defined by

$$\|\vec{v}\|_p = \left(\sum_{i=1}^{n} |v_i|^p \right)^{\frac{1}{p}}.$$ (7.1.11)

Some specific cases of the p-norm class are the 1-norm, *Manhattan norm*, which is defined as

$$\|\vec{v}\|_1 = |v_1| + |v_2| + \ldots + |v_n|,$$ (7.1.12)

the 2-norm, *Euclidean norm*, which is defined as

$$\|\vec{v}\|_2 = \sqrt{x_1^2 + v_2^2 + \ldots + v_n^2},$$ (7.1.13)

and the ∞-norm (*Chebyshev-norm*), which is defined as

$$\|\vec{v}\|_\infty = \max_{1 \le i \le n} |v_i|.$$ (7.1.14)

By adopting each specific norm, a set of vectors may be scaled in many distinct ways. For instance, the original set of vectors, $\{\vec{v}_k\}$, may be scaled according to the vector whose length is the largest, the shortest, the average length, the median length, and so forth. Therefore, if we adopt the vector of maximal length assuming a specific norm, each scaled vector is obtained by

$$\vec{u}_k = \frac{\vec{v}_k}{m_p},$$ (7.1.15)

where m_p the length of the largest vector in the set $\{\vec{v}_k\}$ for the specific p-norm.

Example 7.1.8. Consider a data set of vectors represented by thirty two-dimension vectors depicted in Column 1 and Column 2 of Table 7.8 - $\{(x_i, y_i)\}$. In this example, we adopted the 1-norm, 2-norm, and ∞-norm spaces and obtained the respective normalized space vector by scaling the vectors by the vector of maximal length in each respective norm. It is worth stressing that other normalized vector spaces could be obtained when other criteria (the shortest, the average length, or adopting the median length, for instance) are adopted for scaling.

The coordinate vectors are shown in the other columns of Table 7.8. For the *Manhattan norm*, the maximal vector length is 437.30. Likewise, when adopting the *Euclidean norm*, the maximal vector length is 394.49. Similarly, for the *Chebyshev-norm*, the maximal vector length is 391.90. The respective normalized vectors are shown on the third and fourth ($\{(u_i, v_i)\}$ - 1-norm), fifth and sixth ($\{(u_i, v_i)\}$ - 2-norm), and seventh and eighth columns ($\{(u_i, v_i)\}$ - ∞-norm) of that table, respectively.

Table 7.8

Original Data Set, $1 - norm$, $2 - norm$ **and** $\infty - norm$.

x_i	y_i	u_i - 1-norm	v_i - 1-norm	u_i - 2-norm	v_i - 2-norm	u_i - ∞-norm	v_i - ∞-norm
62.08	356.34	0.13	0.74	0.15	0.88	0.16	0.90
38.19	391.90	0.08	0.81	0.09	0.96	0.10	0.99
53.86	183.02	0.11	0.38	0.13	0.45	0.14	0.46
84.78	180.28	0.18	0.37	0.21	0.44	0.21	0.45
73.39	159.66	0.15	0.33	0.18	0.39	0.18	0.40
43.08	283.97	0.09	0.59	0.11	0.70	0.11	0.71
13.70	321.07	0.03	0.67	0.03	0.79	0.03	0.81
99.23	162.79	0.21	0.34	0.24	0.40	0.25	0.41
86.15	204.13	0.18	0.42	0.21	0.50	0.22	0.51
82.82	128.71	0.17	0.27	0.20	0.32	0.21	0.32
91.59	289.60	0.19	0.60	0.23	0.71	0.23	0.73
50.64	286.65	0.11	0.60	0.12	0.71	0.13	0.72
47.37	280.86	0.10	0.58	0.12	0.69	0.12	0.71
90.57	93.76	0.19	0.19	0.22	0.23	0.23	0.24
40.59	88.39	0.08	0.18	0.10	0.22	0.10	0.22
87.33	269.64	0.18	0.56	0.21	0.66	0.22	0.68
74.71	160.00	0.16	0.33	0.18	0.39	0.19	0.40
50.72	73.02	0.11	0.15	0.12	0.18	0.13	0.18
20.42	147.32	0.04	0.31	0.05	0.36	0.05	0.37
66.49	62.41	0.14	0.13	0.16	0.15	0.17	0.16
82.64	294.00	0.17	0.61	0.20	0.72	0.21	0.74
96.68	71.11	0.20	0.15	0.24	0.17	0.24	0.18
45.44	391.86	0.09	0.81	0.11	0.96	0.11	0.99
96.41	245.54	0.20	0.51	0.24	0.60	0.24	0.62
57.09	145.13	0.12	0.30	0.14	0.36	0.14	0.36

Figure 7.15 graphically depicts the original vector space, and Figure 7.16 shows the Euclidean scaled vector space.

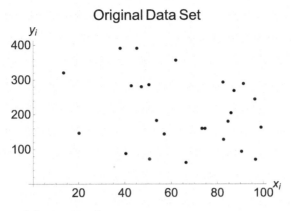

Figure 7.15   Original Vector Space.

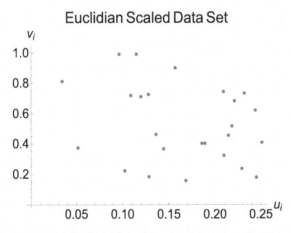

Figure 7.16   Euclidean Scaled Vector Space Adopting the Vector of Maximal Length.

7.2   DISTANCE AND SIMILARITY MEASURES

In many problems we are required to estimate the proximities between entities or objects [133]. Such proximities are usually quantified by similarity measures or distance measures. The entities or objects may be well represented by tuples (coordinate vectors) in a given vector space. Consider a set of coordinate vectors represented by $\{x, y\}$, where $x = (x_1, x_2, ..., x_n)$ and $y = (y_1, y_2, ..., y_n)$, where x and y represent samples and x_i and y_i, $1 \leq i \leq n$, are values of x and y for the dimension i.

Hence, the p-distance (*Minkowski distance*) between x and y is defined as

$$d_p = \sqrt[p]{|x_1 - y_1|^p + |x_2 - y_2|^p + ... + |x_n - y_n|^p}$$

which is equal to

$$d_p = \sqrt[p]{\sum_{i=1}^{n} |x_i - y_i|^p}. \tag{7.2.1}$$

It is worth stressing that each term i may also be weighted ($\omega_i \in [0,1]$) so that

$$d_p = \sqrt[p]{\sum_{i=1}^{n} \omega_i |x_i - y_i|^p}, \tag{7.2.2}$$

where $\sum_{i=1}^{n} \omega_i = 1$. Hence, the 1-distance (*Manhattan distance*) between two tuples of dimension n, named x and y, is defined as

$$d_1 = \sum_{i=1}^{n} |x_i - y_i| \tag{7.2.3}$$

or the weighted version

$$d_1 = \sum_{i=1}^{n} \omega_i |x_i - y_i|. \tag{7.2.4}$$

Weighting an object (value, observation, element) gives greater or lesser importance than other variables when determining the proximity between two objects.

The Manhattan distance is useful when calculating the distance between two data points in a grid-like path since it considers the sum of absolute distances between two points. Let us graphically illustrate the Manhattan distance concept using a chessboard depicted in Figure 7.17.a. In a chess game, the distance between squares may be measured as the number of moves required from a specific piece to reach a given position if it is in another position. For instance, assume a rook is in a position of $d5$. However, the rook's shortest number of moves required to reach position $c6$ is two since the rook cannot move in diagonal directions. The rook may either first reach positions $d6$ or $c4$, and then reach position $e6$. Likewise, bishops use the Manhattan distance on the chessboard rotated $45°$ degrees, with its diagonals as coordinate axes.

The *Euclidean distance* (2-distance) between the tuples of dimension n, named x and y, is defined as

$$d_2 = \sqrt{\sum_{i=1}^{n} (x_i - y_i)^2}, \tag{7.2.5}$$

which is the straight line distance between two data points in space. Figure 7.18 and the example below show the Euclidean distance between points $\{(2,3), (1,5)\}$ in a plan.

The weighted *Euclidean distance* is defined as

$$d_2 = \sqrt{\sum_{i=1}^{n} \omega_i (x_i - y_i)^2}, \qquad (7.2.6)$$

The ∞-distance (*Chebyshev distance*) between the tuples of dimension n is defined as

$$d_\infty = \max_{1 \le i \le n} \{|x_i - y_i|\}. \qquad (7.2.7)$$

Likewise, the weighted *Chebyshev distance* is defined by

$$d_\infty = \max_{1 \le i \le n} \{\omega_i |x_i - y_i|\}, \qquad (7.2.8)$$

which is a distance measure between two points calculated as the maximum difference over any of their dimensions. Let us again use the chessboard to illustrate the concept of Chebyshev distance graphically. Kings and queens use Chebyshev distance. For example, assume Figure 7.17.b. The king is in position $d5$ (the same position adopted when we considered the rook). The king's shortest number of moves required to reach position $c6$ is one since it can move diagonally.

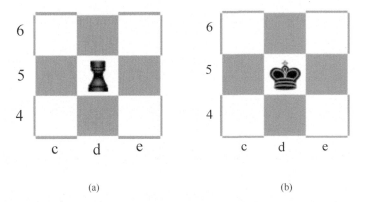

(a)   (b)

Figure 7.17 Manhattan and Chebyshev Distances.

Assume the set of two pairs $\{(2, 3), (1, 5)\}$ ((coordinate vectors)) representing the two physical vectors ($\vec{y}$ and $\vec{x}$) shown in Figure 7.18.

The *p*-distance class (*Minkowski distance*) between the coordinate vectors $(1, 5)$ and $(2, 3)$ is

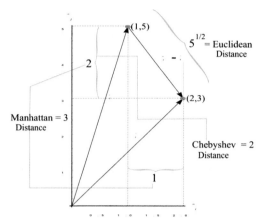

Figure 7.18   Physical Vectors $\vec{y}$, $\vec{x}$ and $\vec{y} - \vec{x}$.

$$d_p = \sqrt[p]{|1 - 2|^p + |5 - 3|^p} = \sqrt[p]{1^p + 2^p},$$

which is the length of the difference of the physical vector $\vec{y} - \vec{x}$ taking into account the p-norm. If $p = 3$, then

$$d_3 = \sqrt[3]{|1 - 2|^3 + |5 - 3|^3} = \sqrt[3]{1^3 + 2^3} = 3^{\frac{2}{3}}.$$

If $p = 2$, we calculate the *Euclidean distance*, that is

$$d_2 = \sqrt{(1 - 2)^2 + (5 - 3)^2} = \sqrt{1^2 + 2^2} = \sqrt{5},$$

which is the Euclidean length of the physical vector $\vec{y} - \vec{x}$.

For $p = 1$, we estimate the *Manhattan distance* is

$$d_1 = |1 - 2| + |5 - 3| = 1 + 2 = 3,$$

and for $p \to \infty$, the *Chebyshev distance* is calculated. Thus,

$$d_\infty = \max\{|1 - 2|, |5 - 3|\} = \max\{1, 2\} = 2.$$

Besides the distances introduced above, we also discuss the *Hamming* and the *Jaccard* distances. The *Hamming distance* quantifies a distance measure between two sequences of symbols of equal span is the number of locations where the corresponding symbols are different. For instance, assuming two data strings, the Hamming distance provides the total number of different symbols in each string's position.

The Hamming distance between two binary strings ($s_a := s_{a,1}s_{a,1} \dots s_{a,i} \dots s_{a,n}$ and $s_b := s_{b,1}s_{b,1} \dots s_{b,i} \dots s_{b,n}$) of equal length ($n$) is formally defined as

$$d_h = \sum_{i=1}^{n}(s_{a,i} \veebar s_{b,i}), \tag{7.2.9}$$

which is the summation of distinct characters between both strings[1]. Assume two strings represented by $s_a := 10011$ and $s_b := 00101$. Hence

$$10011 \veebar 00101 = 10110 = s_c.$$

Hence

$$d_h = \sum_{i=1}^{5}s_{c,i} = 3.$$

Similar approaches are applied to calculate the Hamming distance between two strings of symbols such as strings of text.

The *Jaccard distance* is used to find how different two sets are. The Jaccard index compares members for two sets to measure similarity between the two sets of data. The index ranges from 0 to 1, where the higher the number, the more similar the two sets are. This measure is sensitive to small set sizes; it works better for large sets than for small sets.

Consider two sets A and B; the Jaccard index is defined as

$$i_j = \frac{|A \cap B|}{|A \cup B|}. \tag{7.2.10}$$

The Jaccard distance between two sets is defined as

$$d_j = 1 - i_j = 1 - \frac{|A \cap B|}{|A \cup B|}. \tag{7.2.11}$$

As an example, consider two sets $A = \{a,b,c,d,e\}$ and $B = \{d,e,f,g,h\}$. The Jaccard index between these two sets is

$$i_j = \frac{|\{a,b,c,d,e\} \cap \{d,e,f,g,h\}|}{|\{a,b,c,d,e\} \cup \{d,e,f,g,h\}|}.$$

---

[1] $\veebar$ is the exclusive-or symbol.

$$i_j = \frac{|\{d,e\}|}{|\{a,b,c,d,e,f,g,h\}|}$$

$$i_j = \frac{2}{8} = 0.25.$$

Therefore, the Jaccard distance between the sets is

$$d_j = 1 - i_j = 1 - 0.25 = 0.75.$$

Many other distances are also available, such as the *sine, cosine, chi-squared,* and *Mahalanobis* distances, among others. For instance, the cosine angle between the two vectors ranges from 0 to 1, where 1 means the two vectors are perfectly similar [351].

7.3 CLUSTER DISTANCES

Previously, we studied proximity measures between two items (individuals, elements, points). Clustering is dividing a set of data into groups whose elements within these groups are more similar than the elements in other groups. Clustering methods often require quantifying the distance between groups of items.

Here, we introduce four widely adopted distance measures (similarities) between clusters (also known as linkage measures). Many other measures may be derived or extended from the basic measures. Consider two clusters (a cluster is a set of data points whose elements share some similarities), named C_a and C_b. Also assume two elements belonging to each cluster, that is, $m_a^i \in C_a$ and $m_b^j \in C_b$, and the distance between these two points is defined as $d^m(m_a^i, m_b^j)$. It is worth stressing that $d^m(m_a^i, m_b^j)$ could be any distance measures — similarities — between points (d^m) is described in Section 7.2. In other words, the distance could be Manhattan, Euclidian, Chebyshev, Hamming, Jaccard (with or without weights), and other distances (distance name — d^m) depending on the problem and context [150, 206, 214]. For the sake of simplicity, we will adopt d instead of d^m whenever the context is clear. Therefore, the minimal distance between clusters C_a and C_b assuming the distance measures d between points (see Section 7.2) is defined by

$$CD_{min}(C_a, C_b) = \min_{\forall i,j}\{d(m_a^i, m_b^j)\}. \tag{7.3.1}$$

The maximal distance between clusters C_a and C_b considering the distance measures d between points is defined as

$$CD_{max}(C_a, C_b) = \max_{\forall i,j}\{d(m_a^i, m_b^j)\}. \tag{7.3.2}$$

The mean distance between clusters C_a and C_b considering the distance measures d between points is defined as

$$CD_{mean}(C_a, C_b) = d(\overline{m_a}, \overline{m_b}), \qquad (7.3.3)$$

where $\overline{m_a}$ and $\overline{m_b}$ are the means of cluster C_a and C_b, respectively. It is worth stressing that m_a^i and m_b^i may be multidimensional.

Finally, let us define the average distance between clusters C_a and C_b considering the distance measures d between points is defined as

$$CD_{avg}(C_a, C_b) = \frac{1}{|C_a| \times |C_b|} \sum_{\forall i \in \{1,2,\dots,n\}, \forall j \in \{1,2,\dots,q\}} d(m_a^i, m_b^j), \qquad (7.3.4)$$

where $|C_a| = n$ and $|C_b| = q$; $n, q \in \mathbb{N}$.

Example 7.3.1. Assume a measure is composed of two other simpler measures. Two samples of this pair of measurements were collected, $G_1 = \{(m_{1,x}^i, m_{1,y}^i)\}$ and $G_2 = \{(m_{2,x}^j, m_{2,y}^j)\}$, where $|G_1| = n$, $|G_2| = q$, $n, q \in \mathbb{N}$, $i \in \{1, 2, \dots, n\}$, and $j \in \{a, b, \dots, q\}$. These two sets of measures are depicted in Table 7.9. These pairs of measurements area also depicted by points in Figure 7.19. The red points belong to G_1, and the blue points are measures represented by G_2.

Table 7.9

$G_1 = \{(m_{1,x}^i, m_{1,y}^i)\}$ **and** $G_2 = \{(m_{2,x}^j, m_{2,y}^j)\}$

i, j	$\overrightarrow{m_1^i}$		$\overrightarrow{m_2^j}$	
	$m_{1,x}^i$	$m_{1,y}^i$	$m_{2,x}^j$	$m_{2,y}^j$
1,a	20.51	81.12	97.08	51.92
2,b	28.32	61.55	68.76	161.32
3,c	6.70	82.84	73.49	98.21
4,d	13.49	7.72	72.97	132.03
5,e	25.08	47.63	94.67	93.22
6,f	21.07	81.26	85.67	112.61

The Euclidian length of each vector, represented by the points $(m_{1,x}^i, m_{1,y}^i)$ and $(m_{2,x}^j, m_{2,y}^j)$ are shown in Figure 7.20.

From these two sets of composite measures, we calculated two sets of measures that summarize each of these pairs. These two new set of measures are obtained by using

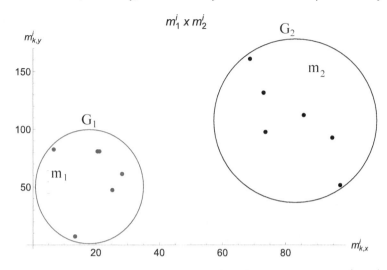

Figure 7.19 Points Belonging to $G_1 = \{(m_{1,x}^i, m_{1,y}^i)\}$ and $G_2 = \{(m_{2,x}^j, m_{2,y}^j)\}$.

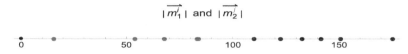

Figure 7.20 Euclidian Length of Vectors $\{(m_{1,x}^i, m_{1,y}^i)\}$ and $\{(m_{2,x}^j, m_{2,y}^j)\}$.

the Euclidean norm ($p = 2$) for each pair so as to get the length of each m_1^i and m_2^j. Therefore, for each pair $(m_{k,x}^i, m_{k,y}^i)$, $k \in \{1, 2\}$, we calculate $|\vec{m_k^i}|$ by

$$|\vec{m_k^i}| = \sqrt{(m_{k,x}^i)^2 + (m_{k,y}^i)^2}.$$

Table 7.10 presents $|\vec{m_1^i}|$ and $|\vec{m_2^j}|$. In the table we adopted a simplified notation; hence instead of $|\vec{m_k^i}|$, we adopted m_k^i.

Table 7.10
Summary of m_1^i **and** m_2^i, $i \in \{1, 2, 3, 4, 5, 6\}$, **and** $j \in \{1, 2, 3, 4, 5, 6\}$.

m_1^i	83.67	67.75	83.11	15.54	53.83	83.95
m_2^j	110.09	175.36	122.66	150.85	132.86	141.50
i, j	1	2	3	4	5	6

The means of m_1^i and m_1^i are

$$\overline{m_1} = Mean(m_1^i) = \frac{\sum_{i=1}^{6} m_1^i}{6} = 64.64$$

and

$$\overline{m_2} = Mean(m_2^j) = \frac{\sum_{j=1}^{6} m_2^j}{6} = 138.89.$$

Thus, using the Manhattan distance ($p = 1$), and Expression 7.3.3, we get

$$CD_{mean}^1(G_1, G_2) = d_1(\overline{m_1}, \overline{m_2}) = |\overline{m_1} - \overline{m_2}| = 74.25.$$

From the measures shown in Table 7.10, we can compute the distances (similarities) between measures as defined in Formula 7.3.1, 7.3.3, and 7.3.4. The distance between m_k^i and $m_{k'}^j$ is denoted by $d_{k,k'}^{i,j}$ and is defined according to the formulas mentioned above. Table 7.11 presents the distances between each pair of measures (m_1^i, m_2^j), $i \in \{1,2,3,4,5,6\}$, $j \in \{1,2,3,4,5,6\}$.

Table 7.11
Distances Between Pair of Measures (m_1^i, m_2^j): $d_{1,2}^{i,j} = d(m_1^i, m_2^j)$

D	i	1	2	3	4	5	6
j	$d_{1,2}^{i,j}$	$d_{1,2}^{1,j}$	$d_{1,2}^{2,j}$	$d_{1,2}^{3,j}$	$d_{1,2}^{4,j}$	$d_{1,2}^{5,j}$	$d_{1,2}^{6,j}$
1	$d_{1,2}^{i,1}$	26.42	91.69	38.99	67.18	49.19	57.82
2	$d_{1,2}^{i,2}$	42.34	107.61	54.91	83.10	65.11	73.74
3	$d_{1,2}^{i,3}$	26.99	92.25	39.55	67.74	49.76	58.39
4	$d_{1,2}^{i,4}$	94.55	159.82	107.12	135.31	117.32	125.96
5	$d_{1,2}^{i,5}$	56.27	121.54	68.83	97.03	79.04	87.67
6	$d_{1,2}^{i,6}$	26.15	91.42	38.71	66.91	48.92	57.55

Using Equation 7.3.1 on Table 7.11, we obtain

$$CD_{min}^1(G_1, G_2) = \min_{\forall i,j}\{d_{1,2}^{i,j}\} = 26.15.$$

Likewise, adopting Equation 7.3.2 on Table 7.11, we obtain

$$CD_{max}^1(G_1, G_2) = \max_{\forall i,j}\{d_{1,2}^{i,j}\} = 159.82.$$

Considering Expression 7.3.4 on Table 7.11, we get

$$CD_{avg}^1(G_1, G_2) = \frac{\sum_{i=1}^{2}\sum_{j=1}^{6} d_{1,2}^{i,j}}{6 \times 6} = 74.25,$$

since $|G_1|$ $|G_2| = 6$. Table 7.12 presents the Euclidean distances between the pair of points of G_1 and G_2 in the plane depicted in Figure 7.19. Figure 7.21 shows the difference vector between vectors $\vec{m}_2^j - \vec{m}_1^3$, that is $\vec{d}_{1,2}^{1,3} = \vec{m}_2^1 - \vec{m}_1^3$.

Table 7.12
Euclidian Distances Between Pairs of Vectors (Points).

$d_{1,2}^{i,j}$	$d_{1,2}^{1,j}$	$d_{1,2}^{2,j}$	$d_{1,2}^{3,j}$	$d_{1,2}^{4,j}$	$d_{1,2}^{5,j}$	$d_{1,2}^{6,j}$
$d_{1,2}^{i,1}$	81.9536	69.4348	95.5205	94.5585	72.1304	81.4771
$d_{1,2}^{i,2}$	93.5947	107.6521	100.0525	163.2430	121.7956	93.1884
$d_{1,2}^{i,3}$	55.6679	58.1717	68.5311	108.5735	102.6261	55.0904
$d_{1,2}^{i,4}$	73.1021	83.4310	82.5301	137.8083	97.0431	72.6037
$d_{1,2}^{i,5}$	75.1427	73.5217	88.5770	117.9026	75.1427	74.5653
$d_{1,2}^{i,6}$	72.3784	76.7920	84.3997	127.3326	72.3784	71.8124

Applying Equation 7.3.1 on Table 7.12, we get

$$CD_{min}^2(G_1, G_2) = \min_{\forall i,j}\{d_{1,2}^{i,j}\} = 55.09.$$

Likewise, adopting Equation 7.3.2 on Table 7.12, we obtain

$$CD_{max}^2(G_1, G_2) = \max_{\forall i,j}\{d_{1,2}^{i,j}\} = 88.10.$$

Using Expression 7.3.4 on Table 7.12, we obtain

$$CD_{avg}^2(G_1, G_2) = \frac{\sum_{i=1}^{2}\sum_{j=1}^{6} d_{1,2}^{i,j}}{6 \times 6} = 74.25,$$

$\square$

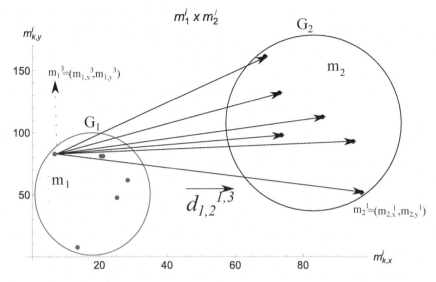

Figure 7.21   Difference Vectors Between Vector of G_1 and G_2.

7.4   CLUSTERING: AN INTRODUCTION

Many authors have tried to formalize the definition of a cluster. However, it is a daunting task since their efforts led to numerous and diverse criteria [133, 215]. Nevertheless, we will informally consider a cluster as a set of related objects grouped. The criteria for grouping such objects could be diverse and are dependent on problem-solving aims. Cluster analysis is a generic name given for many statistical methods that detect groups (cluster) in a sample of objects [465, 475]. Hence, detecting such groups reduces the dissimilarities between objects by classifying them into more homogeneous groups.

There are a vast and diverse number of clustering methods. These techniques have been evolving according to several trends, emerging optimization methods, and application areas. Such diversity makes it challenging to classify clustering methods because such categories may overlap so that a method may have characteristics from various classes. Two of the most important clustering strategy classes are *Partitioning* and *Hierarchical Clustering*.

The methods based on partitioning organizes objects into clusters, where each cluster is formed to optimize a partitioning criterion based on similarity among objects within a cluster and distinction between objects of different clusters. Hierarchical clustering may be subdivided into agglomerative and divisive methods. Agglomerative methods execute a series of successive fusions of the individuals into groups, whereas divisive methods successfully separate individuals into more refined groups.

Before introducing some classical clustering methods, let us look at the graphical representation of data that may also be an attractive tool to provide insights related to a sample's data item. Such an exploratory analysis may be useful for suggesting that the data set may contain subsets of data items (objects) somewhat related. The graphical tools support the human visual capacity of detecting patterns. On the other hand, we should be careful with such an analysis since one may suppose some relation between objects with no statistical evidence of such relation.

Histogram, the dot plot, the individual plot, and scatter plots are simple graphical mechanisms that may support one´s detecting data patterns. For instance, consider the data set depicted in Table 7.13. This data set has eighty measures. The data set's statistic summary is shown on the second and sixth rows of Table 7.14. It is worth checking the coefficient of variation of the data set ($CoV = 0.541$) and the inter-quartile range ($IQR = 184.5$).

Table 7.13
Data Set

Data Set							
94.91	120.50	280.35	108.72	128.18	98.22	76.74	125.69
90.63	288.22	284.67	101.71	58.40	58.87	316.73	80.13
288.21	136.17	119.49	310.89	109.88	89.64	104.06	284.43
308.43	278.03	282.33	64.60	132.88	109.69	135.07	113.48
104.70	153.31	317.13	55.71	310.13	107.19	139.37	277.83
298.98	324.28	89.41	313.19	112.82	274.90	107.78	85.12
102.97	102.54	118.76	99.57	92.29	134.59	279.29	97.53
103.58	288.98	298.19	117.52	113.98	92.47	120.10	306.20
88.44	319.16	136.65	69.07	303.12	270.05	293.31	275.90
286.26	272.77	113.05	83.53	95.90	317.68	126.97	315.84

The histogram of the data set shown in Table 7.13 is shown in Figure 7.22.a, which clearly shows two groups (clusters) of data apart from each other. Besides, the dot plot (Figure 7.22.b) and the individual plot (Figure 7.22.c) also depict the two groups of data.

The original data set was divided into two data set subgroups (Group 1 and Group 2), whose statistic summaries are shown on the third, fourth, seventh, and eighth rows of Table 7.14. The Group 1 size is fifty, and the size of the data set Group 2 is thirty. Hence, the Group 1 data set size is 0.625 of the original data set, and the Group 2 size is 0.375. The respective histograms of each subgroup are shown in Figure 7.23.a and Figure 7.23.b. One should now compare both groups' coefficient of variation and the inter-quartile ranges with the original data set's respective statistics. It is worth highlighting the histogram form of the groups and the histogram of the original data set.

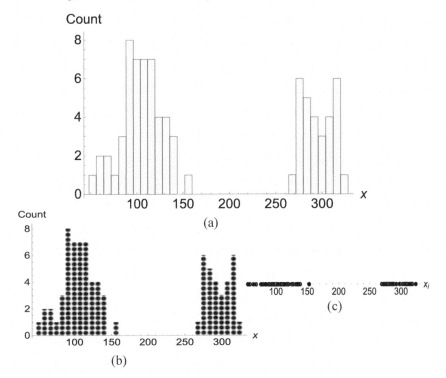

Figure 7.22   (a) Histogram, (b) Data Plot and (c) Individual Plot of Data Depicted in Table 7.13.

Table 7.14
Statistic Summaries - (a) Original Data Set (b) Group 1 and (c) Group 2

Sets	N	Mean	SD	Var	CoV	Min	Q1
Original Data Set	80	176.1	95.3	9075.2	0.541	55.7	100.1
Group 1	50	104.45	22.31	497.86	0.2136	55.71	90.38
Group 2	30	295.52	16.68	278.27	0.0564	270.05	280.09
Sets	Med	Q3	Max	Range	IQR	SK	Kurt
Original Data Set	123.1	284.6	324.3	268.6	184.5	0.45	-1.63
Group 1	104.38	119.64	153.31	97.6	29.26	-0.25	-0.14
Group 2	291.14	11.47	324.28	54.23	31.38	0.18	-1.43

The *scatter plot* combines numerical data with one variable on each axis to find a relationship. Occasionally the data points in a scatter plot form distinct groups or clusters. For instance, consider two identical samples of fifty gadgets of several brands; each sample has one gadget of each specific brand (model). The first sample was analyzed in a stress reliability test until they failed (in days). M_2 denotes the

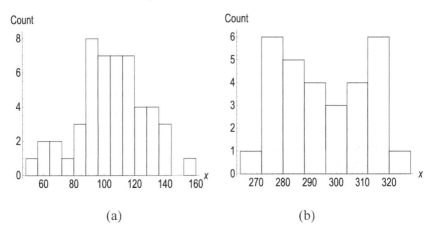

(a)   (b)

Figure 7.23   Histogram of Group 1 (a) and Group 2 (b).

time to failure (TTF) of each device evaluated in the stress test. Likewise, the second (identical) sample of fifty gadgets was observed until all components failed. These times to failure are represented by M_1 (in days). Table 7.15 shows for each specific gadget pair (each specific model was evaluated in the stress test and normal operation), their respective times to failure. Table 7.16 presents the statistic summaries of M_1 and M_2.

The scatter plot shown in Figure 7.24 shows three clusters (groups) of devices. The cluster $G1$ shows models that had a short time to failure in the stress test and during regular operation. The cluster $G2$ shows gadgets that had a long time to failure in the stress test, but the time to failure in usual conditionals was not high. The cluster $C3$ groups gadgets that reached a long times to failure in regular operation and during the stress test.

Table 7.17 shows the statistical summary of M_1 and M_2 for each cluster, that is $G1$, $G2$, and $G3$. It is worth noting the coefficient of variation and the skewness of of each measure for each cluster. Figure 7.25 shows the respective histograms for each variable (M_1 and M_2) of each cluster ($G1$, $G2$, and $G3$)

When we have a multivariate data set with three or more dimensions, the scatter plots of each pair of variables may still be helpful as a basis for an initial data exploration for evidence of some cluster structure. For instance, consider the three-dimension sample depicted in Figure 7.26, where we may even see three groups of data.

Figure 7.27 shows the three two-dimension scatter plots from the front, above, and left points of view. Such views help in identifying possible data clusters. However, it is worth noting that the left view only detects two clusters instead of three. The reader

Table 7.15

M_1 — TTF **in Regular Operation.** M_2 — TTF **in the Stress Test.**

M_1 (days)	M_2 (days)	M_1 (days)	M_2 (days)	M_1 (days)	M_2 (days)
92.14	53.39	106.60	44.08	1009.66	187.24
93.60	54.66	107.54	45.79	1014.77	195.81
95.72	53.38	108.64	61.20	1016.74	191.98
97.34	44.80	947.45	190.75	1021.89	201.01
97.54	53.31	955.87	197.31	1025.24	191.63
97.82	54.55	970.91	205.93	1031.02	201.91
99.27	47.19	978.72	196.94	2231.66	201.34
99.35	53.17	980.57	204.23	2601.07	198.82
99.71	50.71	984.01	196.33	2700.80	199.73
100.51	53.99	984.44	192.86	2717.32	202.11
101.65	39.87	990.43	196.14	2723.22	207.32
102.00	49.34	994.14	203.66	2770.94	194.21
102.70	54.22	994.62	196.31	2849.54	202.91
103.36	58.05	995.84	195.76	2854.44	199.05
103.51	46.74	1002.64	201.04	2898.39	196.01
104.91	54.12	1003.06	203.44	2900.61	199.86
105.26	56.42	1007.27	201.15		

Table 7.16

Statistic Summary of M_1 **and** M_2.

Measures	Mean	SD	Var	CoV	Min	Q1	
M_1	1002	973	946986	0.9715	94	103	
M_2	141.4	72.6	5267.1	0.5133	39.9	54.1	
Measures	**Med**	**Q3**	**Max**	**Range**	**IQR**	**SK**	**Kurt**
M_1	984	1024	2901	2807	921	0.92	-0.4
M_2	194.2	200.4	207.3	167.4	146.4	-0.47	-1.83

is also invited to check the scatter plot matrices, which are matrices with scatter plots [133].

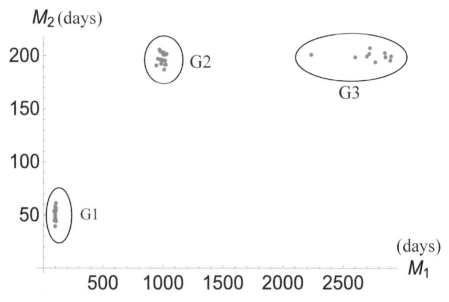

Figure 7.24 Scatter Plot — Clusters $G1$, $G2$, and $G3$.

Table 7.17
Statistic Summary of M_1 and M_2 for Cluster $G1$, $G2$ and $G3$.

Measures	Mean	SD	Var	CoV	Min	Q1		
M1_G1	100.96	4.51	20.33	4.47	92.14	97.61		
M2_G1	51.45	5.27	27.81	10.25	39.87	46.85		
M1_G2	995.46	22.22	493.87	2.23	947.45	981.43		
M2_G2	197.57	5.11	26.07	2.58	187.24	193.59		
M1_G3	2724.8	198.5	39407.6	7.29	2231.7	2675.9		
M2_G3	200.14	3.65	13.33	1.82	194.21	198.12		
Measures	**Med**	**Q3**	**Max**	**Range**	**IQR**	**SK**	**Kurt**
M1_G1	101.08	104.56	108.64	16.5	6.95	-0.17	-0.53
M2_G1	53.34	54.47	61.2	21.33	7.61	-0.45	-0.11
M1_G2	995.23	1013.49	1031.02	83.57	32.06	-0.46	-0.11
M2_G2	196.63	201.72	205.93	18.69	8.13	-0.18	-0.72
M1_G3	2747.1	2865.4	2900.6	669	189.6	-1.9	4.34
M2_G3	199.8	202.31	207.32	13.11	4.19	0.34	0.9

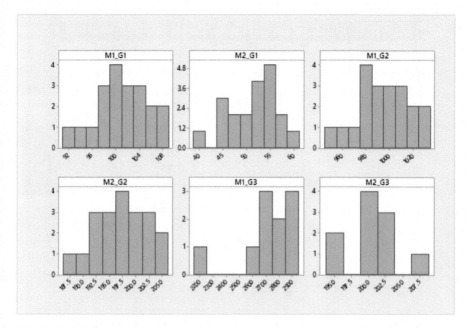

Figure 7.25   Histograms of M_1 and M_2 for $G1$, $G2$, and $G3$.

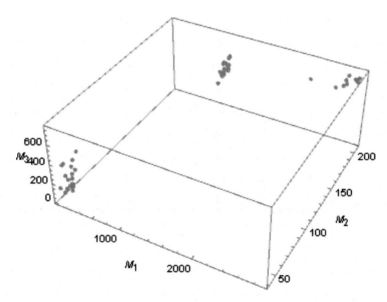

Figure 7.26   Three Dimension Sample.

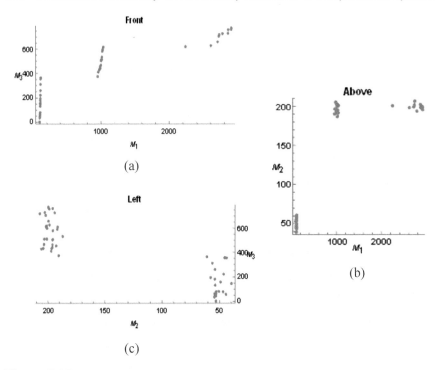

Figure 7.27 Scatter Plots: (a) Front, (b) Above, and (c) Left.

7.5 K-MEANS

The *k-means* is likely the most widely applied non-hierarchical clustering method [249, 316]. K-means clustering partitions a data set into a set of k pre-specified groups (clusters). The objects within the same group are similar, whereas objects from different clusters are dissimilar. In other words, the k-means method attempts to minimize the variability within each cluster and consequently maximize the variability between clusters. It is worth stressing, however, that there are many variants of the k-means method. Perhaps, the simplest k-means method variant has the following steps:

1. Suppose a data set, D, containing n elements (objects), that is $D = \{o_1, o_2, \ldots o_n\}$, $|D| = n$.

2. Specify the number of clusters, K.

3. Select an initial partition of the objects contained in D in the K clusters. Hence, $C_1, C_2, \ldots, C_K$, such that $\bigcup_{i=1}^{K} C_i = D$ and $\bigcap_{i=1}^{K} C_i = \emptyset$.

4. Calculate each cluster's centroid (c_i) — explained below — and the distances between each observation ($o_j \in D$) and centroid, $d(c_i, o_j)$, $\forall c_i$. If an

observation $o_j \in C_K$ is nearer the centroid of a cluster (C_W) other than the one it currently belongs to ($d(c_W, o_j) < d(c_K, o_j)$), re-assign o_j to the nearer cluster, so that ($C_K = C_K - \{o_j\}$ and $C_W = C_W \cup \{o_j\}$).

5. Repeat Step 4 until all observations are nearest the centroid of the cluster to which they belong; that is when no reassignment is required.

6. If the number of clusters cannot be specified with confidence in advance, repeat Steps 2 to 5 with a different number of clusters and evaluate the results.

In many clustering applications, the variables describing the individual (objects, elements) are not measured in the same units. For instance, one variable may represent the execution time; another may represent memory usage; others may represent a finance cost or density. In such cases, the set of observations should be scaled (see Section 7.1), and the distances (with or without weights) calculated for carrying out the clustering process.

In some applications, the problem to be addressed already clearly defines the number of clusters. For instance, we intend to assign a given number of processes to the processors available in the system. In such a case, the number of clusters would be the number of processors. Nevertheless, in most applications, the analyst needs to estimate the number of clusters required. Some such methods may be found in [133].

Once the number of clusters has been determined, the next step is to define the initial partition. The first simple method consists of taking the K observations (points, elements) and assigning them a center point (centroid) of each cluster C_i, $i = \{1, 2, ..., K\}$., and then assigning the remaining elements to the cluster that they are closest to using a distance measure. A second straightforward method assigns partitions to the units so that the first n_1 elements are initially assigned to cluster C_1, the next n_2 elements are initially assigned to cluster C_2, and so forth. The last n_k elements are assigned to cluster C_K, such that $\bigcup_{i=1}^{K} C_i = D$. A third method randomly chooses the K data points from the data set (D). Then, the K points are adopted as centroids of the K clusters. The remaining points are then assigned in the cluster C_i so that each point is closest to using a distance measure. There are many other possible approaches. The reader is invited to check [214].

The term *centroid* (moment about the origin) is adopted as a replacement for the expressions "center of gravity," "center of mass," and "barycenter" when the geometrical aspects of that point are essential to be stressed [417]. The mean of a set of numbers is the centroid of this set of observations. The centroid of a set of n points in a plane ((x_c, y_c)) may be calculated by merely calculating the means of their coordinates. Hence,

$$x_c = \frac{\sum_{i=1}^{n} x_i}{n}, y_c = \frac{\sum_{i=1}^{n} y_i}{n}. \tag{7.5.1}$$

An interesting approach to finding the centroid of irregular figures and volumes is the decomposition strategy. Details about "center of gravity" and "center of mass" may be found in calculus books [236, 415, 417].

Example 7.5.1. This is a small example that aims at presenting the steps of the method described above. Here, we adopt a small sample of two-dimension measures represented by the set of pairs $v_i = (x_i, y_i)$ such that $D = \{(x_i, y_i)\}$, $|D| = 6$. This data set is shown in the second column of Table 7.18. The Euclidean length of each vector $|\vec{v}_i|$ is shown in the fourth column.

The centroid of the original data $(v_{\vec{D},c} - (x\,D,c, \; y\,D,c))$ set is

$$x_{D,c} = \frac{4.5 + 9 + 15 + 3 + 18 + 2}{6} = 8.5833,$$

$$y_{D,c} = \frac{9 + 3 + 7 + 11 + 4 + 7}{6} = 6.8333.$$

Thus, $(x_{D,c}, y_{D,c}) = (8.5833, 6.8333)$. Hence the centroid length is $|v_{\vec{D},c}|$ $\sqrt{8.5833^2 + 6.8333^2} = 10.9712$. The sum of the squared error (*SSE*) of the original data set is

$$SSE = \sum_{i=1}^{6} (|\vec{v}_i| - |v_{\vec{D},c}|)^2 = 103.7636.$$

As a first step, we normalized each original vector according to Min-Max scaling (see Equation 7.1.1). The normalized vectors are depicted in the third column of Table 7.18. It is worth mentioning that this step may be avoided. However, for some specific cases, it may be advisable to normalize the data set. Then, the Euclidean length of each normalized vector $|v_{n,i}^{\rightarrow}|$ was calculated. These lengths are shown in the fifth column of Table 7.18.

Table 7.18

$\{(x_i, y_i)\}$, $\{(x_{n,i}, y_{n,i})\}$, $\sqrt{x_i^2 + y_i^2}$ **and** $\sqrt{x_{n,i}^2 + y_{n,i}^2}$

i	x_i	y_i	$x_{n,i}$	$y_{n,i}$	$\sqrt{x_i^2 + y_i^2}$	$\sqrt{x_{n,i}^2 + y_{n,i}^2}$
1	4.5	9	0.1563	0.75	10.0623	0.7661
2	9	3	0.4375	0	9.4868	0.4375
3	15	7	0.8125	0.5	16.5529	0.9540
4	3	11	0.0625	1	11.4018	1.0020
5	18	4	1	0.125	18.4391	1.0078
6	2	7	0	0.5	7.2801	0.5

As the second step, let us define the number of clusters as $K = 2$. Then, we randomly define the initial partition as $C_1 = \{\vec{v}_1, \vec{v}_2, \vec{v}_4\}$, and $C_2 = \{\vec{v}_3, \vec{v}_5, \vec{v}_6\}$, where $v_1 = (4.5, 9)$, $v_2 = (9, 3)$, $v_4 = (3, 11)$, $v_3 = (15, 7)$, $v_5 = (18, 4)$, and $v_6 = (2, 7)$. The respective normalized coordinate vectors are $v_{n,1} = (0.15625, 0.75)$, $v_{n,2} = (0.4375, 0)$, $v_{n,4} = (0.0625, 1)$, $v_{n,3} = (0.8125, 0.5)$, $v_{n,5} = (1, 0.125)$, and $v_{n,6} = (0, 0.5)$. Such an approach is the second basic method described earlier. Nevertheless, it is also worth stressing that some other specific and wiser method may be adopted.

Then, adopting the normalized coordinates, we calculate the centroid of each cluster. Thus,

$$x_{c1} = \frac{0.15625 + 0.4375 + 0.0625}{3} = 0.21875, \ y_{c1} = \frac{0.75 + 0 + 1}{3} = 0.5833$$

and

$$x_{c2} = \frac{0.8125 + 1 + 0}{3} = 0.6042, \ y_{c2} = \frac{0.5 + 0.125 + 0.5}{3} = 0.375.$$

Hence, $(x_{c1}, y_{c1}) = (0.21875, 0.5833)$, and $(x_{c2}, y_{c2}) = (0.6042, 0.375)$. After that, we calculate the Euclidean distance (it could be another depending on the study), of each coordinate vector $(x_{n,i}, y_{n,i})$ to the centroid of each cluster, in this specific case, $K = 2$. The centroids of each cluster are (x_{c1}, y_{c1}) and (x_{c2}, y_{c2}), respectively. Therefore, considering $i = 1$, we have

$$d_2((x_{n,1}, y_{n,1}), (x_{c1}, y_{c1})) = \sqrt{(x_{n,1} - x_{c1})^2 + (y_{n,1} - y_{c1})^2},$$

$$d_2((x_{n,1}, y_{n,1}), (x_{c1}, y_{c1})) = \sqrt{(0.15625 - 0.21875)^2 + (0.75 - 0.5833)^2} = 0.1780,$$

and

$$d_2((x_{n,1}, y_{n,1}), (x_{c2}, y_{c2})) = \sqrt{(x_{n,1} - x_{c1})^2 + (y_{n,1} - y_{c1})^2},$$

$$d_2((x_{n,1}, y_{n,1}), (x_{c2}, y_{c2})) = \sqrt{(0.15625 - 0.6042)^2 + (0.75 - 0.375)^2} = 0.5842.$$

As $d_2((x_{n,1}, y_{n,1}), (x_{c1}, y_{c1})) < d_2((x_{n,1}, y_{n,1}), (x_{c2}, y_{c2}))$, the pair (x_{c1}, y_{c1}) stays in cluster C_1. Now, assume $i = 2$; then we have to calculate the distance between $(x_{n,2}, y_{n,2})$ and each centroid, that is (x_{c1}, y_{c1}) and (x_{c2}, y_{c2}). Hence, we have

$$d_2((x_{n,2}, y_{n,2}), (x_{c1}, y_{c1})) = \sqrt{(x_{n,2} - x_{c1})^2 + (y_{n,2} - y_{c1})^2},$$

$$d_2((x_{n,2},y_{n,2}),(x_{c1},y_{c1})) = \sqrt{(0.4375 - 0.21875)^2 + (0 - 0.5833)^2} = 0.6230$$

and

$$d_2((x_{n,2},y_{n,2}),(x_{c2},y_{c2})) = \sqrt{(x_{n,2} - x_{c1})^2 + (y_{n,2} - y_{c1})^2},$$

$$d_2((x_{n,2},y_{n,2}),(x_{c2},y_{c2})) = \sqrt{(0.4375 - 0.6042)^2 + (0 - 0.375)^2} = 0.4104.$$

As $d_2((x_{n,2},y_{n,2}),(x_{c2},y_{c2})) < d_2((x_{n,2},y_{n,2}),(x_{c1},y_{c1}))$, the pair $(x_{n,2},y_{n,2}))$ moves to cluster C_2. Hence, the clusters are updated to $C_1 = \{\vec{v}_1, \vec{v}_4\}$, and $C_2 = \{\vec{v}_2, \vec{v}_3, \vec{v}_5, \vec{v}_6\}$.

Now, we calculate the new centroid of C_1 and C_2. The centroids of each cluster are $(x_{c1}, y_{c1}) = (0.1094, 0.875)$, and $(x_{c2}, y_{c2}) = (0.5625, 0.2812)$. Now, we have to calculate the distances between the coordinate vectors and each centroid. We always followed the sequence $i := 1,2,3,4,5,6$. However, other strategies may be adopted to speed up the clustering process. Adopting the sequence, the next pair $(x_{n,i},y_{n,i}))$ to move to another cluster is $(x_{n,6},y_{n,6}))$ since $d_2((x_{n,6},y_{n,6}),(x_{c1},y_{c1})) < d_2((x_{n,6},y_{n,6}),(x_{c2},y_{c2}))$ as $d_2((x_{n,6},y_{n,6}),(x_{c1},y_{c1})) = 0.3906$ and $d_2((x_{n,6},y_{n,6}),(x_{c2},y_{c2})) = 0.6035$.

Considering this result, the clusters are updated to $C_1 = \{\vec{v}_1, \vec{v}_4, \vec{v}_6\}$, and $C_2 = \{\vec{v}_2, \vec{v}_3, \vec{v}_5\}$.

As the clusters changed, we have to calculate each respective centroid. The new centroids are $(x_{c1}, y_{c1}) = (0.0729, 0.75)$, and $(x_{c2}, y_{c2}) = (0.75, 0.2083)$. Then, we calculate the distances between the coordinate vectors, $(x_{n,i},y_{n,i}))$ for $i := 1,2,3,4,5,6$, and each centroid. The distances of any coordinate vectors belonging to a specific cluster were larger than the distance to the other centroid. This implies no move from one cluster to the other cluster is required. Hence, the process finishes, and the resulting clusters (see Figure 7.28) are

$$C_1 = \{\vec{v}_1, \vec{v}_4, \vec{v}_6\},$$

and

$$C_2 = \{\vec{v}_2, \vec{v}_3, \vec{v}_5\}.$$

This process was also executed using Mathematica through the Code 6. The set of pairs D is defined on the first line of the code. The second line, through function *FindCluster[]* takes the set *data* (we adopted *data* instead of D because D is a reserved word in Mathematica.), specify the number of clusters to be found ($K = 2$ - second parameter), defines the distance type to be considered (*EuclideanDistance* -

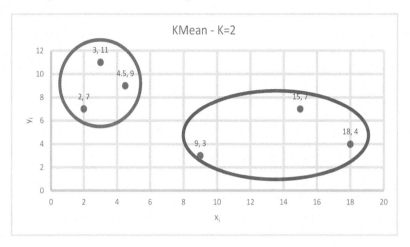

Figure 7.28   Cluster C_1 and C_2.

Algorithm 6 K-Means

1: ClearAll;
2: data = $\{\{4.5,9\},\{9,3\},\{15,7\},\{3,11\},\{18,4\},\{2,7\}\}$;
3: FindClusters[data, 2, DistanceFunction $\rightarrow$ EuclideanDistance, Method $\rightarrow$ "KMeans"]

---

third parameters), and defines the clustering method to be adopted ("KMean" - fourth parameter).

Executing this piece of code, we got the same clusters obtained through the process depicted in detail above. The centroids of each cluster considering the original data set are $(x_{c1}, y_{c1}) = (3.1666, 9)$ and $(x_{c2}, y_{c2}) = (14, 4.6666)$. The sums of the squared error (SSE_j, $j \in \{1,2\}$) of each element of a cluster to its centroids are

$$SSE_1 = \sum_{i\in\{1,4,6\}} \left(|\vec{v}_i| - |v\vec{C}_{1,c}| \right)^2 = 8.8458,$$

$$SSE_2 = \sum_{i\in\{2,3,5\}} \left(|\vec{v}_i| - |v\vec{C}_{2,c}| \right)^2 = 44.5577,$$

and $SSE_1 + SSE_2 = 53.4036$.

The k-means method does not assure convergence to the global optimum. Usually, the process finishes at a local optimum. Besides, the results may depend on the initial partition of the objects [133, 215]. As already specified in step 6 of the method described earlier, executing the k-means methods multiple times with different initial partitions in practice is common.

□

Example 7.5.2. The piece of code depicted in 6 did not explicitly specify the initial partition. In such a case, Mathematica functions automatically specified the initial partition. Many other options are available to allow the analyst to have more control over the clustering process [468]. One of such options supports specifying the initial centroids of each cluster. The code lines depicted in 7 adopt such an option, and two pairs are assigned as the initial centroids of each cluster considered.

Algorithm 7 K-Means

1: ClearAll;
2: data = $\{\{4.5,9\},\{9,3\},\{15,7\},\{3,11\},\{18,4\},\{2,7\}\}$;
3: FindClusters[data, 2, DistanceFunction $\rightarrow$ EuclideanDistance, Method $\rightarrow$
4: {"KMeans", "InitialCentroids" $\rightarrow$ $\{\{4.5,9\},\{9,3\}\}\}$]

Executing the piece of Code 7, we get the following clusters:

$$C_1 = \{\{4.5,9\},\{3,11\},\{2,7\}\}$$

and

$$C_2 = \{\{9,3\},\{15,7\},\{18,4\}\}.$$

If, instead, we define initial centroids as $\{\{2,7\},\{18,4\}\}\}$, and execute the piece of Code 7, we obtain the following clusters:

$$C_1 = \{\{4.5,9\},\{9,3\},\{3,11\},\{2,7\}\}$$

and

$$C_2 = \{\{15,7\},\{18,4\}\}.$$

□

The k-means method is affected by outliers' presence since such measures are far from the mean of the data set. Hence, when outliers are assigned to clusters, they can considerably misrepresent their central values and increase the squared error sum.

7.6   K-MEDOID AND K-MEDIAN

The k-means method may be slightly modified to reduce the sensitivity to outliers by substituting the clusters by either the respective medoids or the medians. This leads us to two alternative methods called *k-medoid* and *k-median* methods.

A *medoid* of a data set (or cluster) is the element whose average dissimilarity to all the elements in the data set is minimal. Hence, assuming a data set D, whose cardinality is $|D| = n$, $n \in \mathbb{N}$, its medoid is defined by

$$x_{medoid} = \arg\min_{\forall x_j \in D} \sum_{i=1}^{n} d_p(x_i, x_j), \qquad (7.6.1)$$

where $d_p(x_i, x_j)$ is a p distance (see Section 7.2) between the element x_i and x_j.

Example 7.6.1. Assume a data set $D = \{10.0623, 9.4868, 16.5529, 11.4018, 18.4391, 7.2801\}$ of measures. Table 7.19 shows the distances between any point (measure) $x_j \in D$ to any other point ($x_i \in D$), that is $d(x_j, x_i) = x_j - x_i$, and the average of such distances for each $x_j \in D$ (9th column).

Table 7.19
Average Distance Between x_j **and** x_i, $x_j, x_i \in D$, $\forall x_j \in D$.

$d(x_j,x_i)$	i	1	2	3	4	5	6	$\frac{\sum_{i=1}^{6}(x_i-x_j)}{6}$
j	$x_j \ x_i$	10.0623	9.4868	16.5529	11.4018	18.4391	7.2801	
1	10.0623	0.0000	-0.5755	6.4906	1.3394	8.3768	-2.7822	2.1415
2	9.4868	0.5755	0.0000	7.0661	1.9149	8.9523	-2.2067	2.7170
3	16.5529	-6.4906	-7.0661	0.0000	-5.1512	1.8861	-9.2728	-4.3491
4	11.4018	-1.3394	-1.9149	5.1512	0.0000	7.0373	-4.1216	0.8021
5	18.4391	-8.3768	-8.9523	-1.8861	-7.0373	0.0000	-11.1590	-6.2352
6	7.2801	2.7822	2.2067	9.2728	4.1216	11.1590	0.0000	4.9237

The shortest distance average is

$$\frac{\sum_{i=1}^{6}(x_i - x_4)}{6} = 0.8021,$$

whose point $x_j = x_4$ is 11.4018, which is the medoid of D. The median of D is $Med = 10.7320$.

$\square$

The k-means method presented in the previous section may have the fourth step adapted to calculate either the clusters´ medoid or the respective medians. Both alternatives are not sensitive to the presence of outliers in the data set.

Table 7.20
Sample of Execution Times of a Set of Applications

Execution Times (s)					
67.92	468.58	692.70	785.43	863.78	1112.14
74.43	541.04	704.07	788.33	901.90	1115.28
75.07	552.61	709.60	804.06	953.50	1119.98
75.87	568.34	727.43	805.21	995.40	1164.64
101.54	580.48	729.34	807.47	1005.82	1231.06
107.13	591.04	733.13	822.52	1027.45	1278.22
115.91	606.25	735.71	829.59	1056.51	1282.15
116.25	629.15	749.39	833.93	1070.23	1304.15
123.78	649.84	774.22	841.43	1087.15	1346.03
128.60	672.44	776.15	858.22	1102.90	1598.00

Example 7.6.2. Assume a data set of multiple measures representing the time to execute (in seconds) a given set of applications. This means that each application was measured several times. The number of measures for each application is unknown. The sample size is sixty (60) and is shown in Table 7.20. Figure 7.29 and Figure 7.30 show the individual value plot and the histogram of the sample.

Original Data Set

$$0 \qquad 500 \qquad 1000 \qquad 1500 \qquad x_i(s)$$

Figure 7.29 Individual Value Plot of the Sample.

The statistical summary of the sample is shown in Table 7.21.

Analyzing the histogram of the sample and particularly the individual value plot, we may intuitively guess the sample is composed of two or three clusters. It is worth stressing that it is just a visual observation of the sample. Nevertheless, we adopt $k = 3$ and applied the k-*medoid* method for obtaining the clusters. This process was implemented using the Mathematica code depicted in Code 8. The sample is stored file "datamedoid.xlsx". The execution of Line 6 reads the sample and stores it in

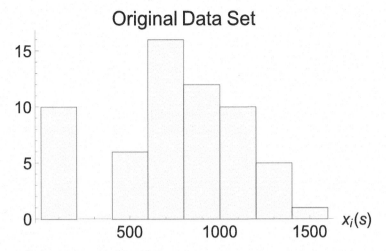

Figure 7.30 Histogram of the Sample.

Table 7.21
Statistic Summary of the Sample

Sample	
Mean (s)	749.51
Standard Deviation (s)	369.86
Sample Variance (s^2)	136799.79
CoV	0.49
Minimum (s)	67.92
Maximum (s)	1598.00
Range (s)	1530.07
Median (s)	780.79
Q1 (s)	588.40
Q3 (s)	1011.23
IQI (s)	422.83
Kurtosis	-0.23
Skewness	-0.34
Count	60.00

data. The number of clusters is defined in Line 5 (= 3). Executing the statement defined in Line 7 generates three clusters using the medoid process and adopting the Euclidean distance for generating three ($k = 3$) clusters, which are stored in *cl*. The three clusters are shown in Table 7.22 (C_1, C_2, and C_3).

Table 7.23 shows the statistical summary of each cluster (C_1, C_2, and C_3). Figure 7.31 show the individual value plot of each cluster.

Algorithm 8 K-Medoid

1: Clear[data];
2: Clear[cl];
3: Clear[k];
4: ClearAll;
5: k = 3;
6: data = Flatten[Import["C:datamedoid.xlsx"]];
7: cl = FindClusters[data, k, DistanceFunction → EuclideanDistance, Method → "KMedoids"];

Table 7.22

Clusters C_1, C_2, **and** C_3

C_1 (s)	C_2 (s)				C_3 (s)	
67.92	468.58	692.70	785.43	863.78	953.50	1119.98
74.43	541.04	704.07	788.33	901.90	995.40	1164.64
75.07	552.61	709.60	804.06		1005.82	1231.06
75.87	568.34	727.43	805.21		1027.45	1278.22
101.54	580.48	729.34	807.47		1056.51	1282.15
107.13	591.04	733.13	822.52		1070.23	1304.15
115.91	606.25	735.71	829.59		1087.15	1346.03
116.25	629.15	749.39	833.93		1102.90	1598.00
123.78	649.84	774.22	841.43		1112.14	
128.60	672.44	776.15	858.22		1115.28	

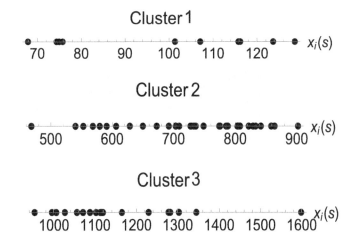

Figure 7.31 Individual Value Plot of Each Cluster.

Table 7.23
Statistic Summary of Each Cluster

Statistics	C_1	C_2	C_3
Mean (s)	98.65	722.92	1158.37
Standard Deviation (s)	23.15	109.71	158.20
Sample Variance (s^2)	535.74	12036.32	25026.63
CoV	0.23	0.15	0.14
Minimum (s)	67.92	468.58	953.50
Maximum (s)	128.60	901.90	1598.00
Range (s)	60.67	433.32	644.50
Median (s)	104.33	734.42	1113.71
Q1 (s)	75.27	692.70	1059.94
Q3 (s)	116.16	805.78	1266.43
IIQ (s)	40.89	113.08	206.49
Kurtosis	-1.90	-0.55	2.15
Skewness	-0.16	-0.53	1.29
Count	10	32	18

It is worth comparing the coefficient of variations (CoV) of the clusters and the original data set (sample) CoV. The clusters' CoVs are much smaller than the original sample CoV.

□

7.7 HIERARCHICAL CLUSTERING

Hierarchical clustering could be classified into two classes: *agglomerative* and *divisive* approaches. The agglomerative strategies consist of steps (the hierarchy) that start with many clusters equal to the number of observations (n) and apply a series of successive fusions of such observations into groups until reaching only one group. The divisive strategy starts from a single group containing all (n) observations, divides this group into groups, and keeps dividing them (the hierarchy) until reaching n groups. If the analysts are not interested in building the entire hierarchical structure, they must decide when the clustering process should stop. Both strategies (*agglomerative* and *divisive*) adopt a proximity (similarity) matrix.

Differently from the methods introduced in previous sections, fusions or divisions are irrevocable. Hence, once two observations are joined, they cannot subsequently be separated. Likewise, once two observations are split, they cannot be rejoined.

The agglomerative approaches are likely the most adopted hierarchical methods. Such approaches produce a series of data partitions by fusion. In the first phase, the n observations are represented by n clusters. The last phase generates a single group containing all n observations. The basic operations of all agglomerative methods are similar. Differences between these methods arise because of the different ways of defining the distance (or similarity) between an individual and a group of observations, or between two groups of observations (see Section 7.2 and Section 7.3).

As already mentioned, the variables describing the objects (elements) may not be quantified in the same units for many clustering problems. For example, one variable may represent the time to failure; another may represent memory usage; others may represent prices or throughput. In such cases, the set of observations (the tuples) should be scaled (as introduced in Section 7.1), the distances (with or without weights) should be calculated, and then the clustering process should start.

In hierarchical clustering, it is usual to represent the distances (or similarities) between objects through a distance matrix. Assume a set of objects $OS = \{o_i\}$, $|OS| = n, n, i \in \mathbb{N}$, represented by the set of values $MS = \{m_i\}$, $|MS| = n; n, i \in \mathbb{N}$ and $m_i \in \mathbb{R}$. The distance matrix of such measures is defined as a symmetric matrix such that

$$D_{i,j} \subseteq n \times n, \ \ d_{i,j} = d_{j,i}, \text{ and } d_{i,i} = 0, \tag{7.7.1}$$

where $d_{i,j} \Leftrightarrow d_p(i,j)$ is a distance function (see Section 7.2) between objects i and j. It is also important to mention some of the many different techniques available to support the object's selection. Some standard methods adopted in hierarchical clustering are the nearest neighbor (*single linkage*) method [143], the furthest neighbor (*complete linkage*) method [403], the *group average* method [196], and *Ward's method*. Hence, assuming two clusters represented by two disjoint sets X and Y, the *single-linkage* clustering is implemented by finding the elements in each cluster $x \in X$ and $y \in Y$ that has the shortest inter-cluster distance (*icd*).

$$icd = \min_{\forall x \in X, \forall d \in Y} \{d_p(x,y)\}. \tag{7.7.2}$$

The *complete-linkage* clustering is implemented by finding the elements in each cluster $x \in X$ and $y \in Y$ that have the farthest distance.

$$icd = \max_{\forall x \in X, \forall d \in Y} \{d_p(x,y)\}. \tag{7.7.3}$$

The *group average* clustering is implemented by finding the distance between any two clusters X and Y by taking the average of all distances $d_p(x,y)$ between pairs of elements of $x \in X$ and $y \in Y$ and calculating the mean distance. Hence

$$icd = \frac{1}{|X||Y|} \sum_{\forall x \in X} \sum_{\forall y \in Y} d(x,y). \tag{7.7.4}$$

Other well-known linkage methods are the centroid, the median-based linkages (may be adopted when elements are represented by tuples), and the linkage based on Ward's criterion. Ward-linkage aims at minimizing the total within-cluster variance [133, 214]. Lance and Williams proposed a flexible formula that provides the inter-cluster distances between a cluster k and a cluster (i, j) formed by joining the cluster i and j as

$$icd_{(k,(i,j))} = \alpha_i d_{(k,i)} + \alpha_j d_{(k,j)} + \beta d_{(i,j)} + \gamma |d_{(k,i)} - d_k|, \qquad (7.7.5)$$

where $d_{(i,j)}$, $d_{(k,i)}$, and $d_{(k,j)}$ are the pairwise distances between clusters C_i, C_j, and C_k, respectively. Besides, α_j, α_i, β , and γ are parameters [226]. Table 7.24 shows the Lance–Williams' parameter values for defining each linkage method.

Table 7.24
Lance–Williams Parameters for Each Linkage Method.

Method	Lance–Williams Parameters			
	α_i	α_j	β	γ
Single linkage	0.5	0.5	0	−0.5
Complete linkage	0.5	0.5	0	0.5
Average linkage	$(n_i)/(n_i + n_j)$	$(n_j)/(n_i + n_j)$	0	0
Centroid linkage	$(n_i)(n_i + n_j)$	$(n_j)/(n_i + n_j)$	$-(n_i n_j)/(n_i + n_j)^2$	0
Median linkage	0.5	0.5	−0.25	0
Ward's method	$(n_i + n_k)/(n_i + n_j + n_k)$	$(n_j + n_k)/(n_i + n_j + n_k)$	$-(n_k)/(n_i + n_j + n_k)$	0

The *agglomerative hierarchical clustering* process has the following steps:

Algorithm 9 Agglomerative Hierarchical Clustering

1: $\Sigma_0 = \{\{o_i\}\}$, $|\Sigma_0| = n, i \in \mathbb{N}$;
2: $X = \{x_j\}$, $|X| = n, j \in \mathbb{N}$;
3: $D_0 = CalculateInitialDistanceMatrix(\Sigma_0, X)$
4: For $i = 1, i \leq n, i + +$
5:     If (StopCriteria=TRUE); the process may stop when a given number of clusters were defined.
6:     $CS = FindCluster(\Sigma_{i-1}, \Sigma_0)$
7:     Break;
8:     $(p_l, p_r) = FindNextPair(\Sigma_{i-1}, D_{i-1}, LinkageMethod)$
9:     $\Sigma_i = (\Sigma_{i-1} \cup (p_l, p_r)) \setminus \{\{p_l\}, \{p_r\}\}$
10:     $D_i = CalculateDistanceMatrix(\Sigma_i, D_{i-1}\}$
11: If $(|\Sigma_i| = 1)$
12:     $CS = FindCluster(\Sigma_i, CuttingDistance)$; if the process stops with one single set, then find the cluster set based on $CuttingDistance$
13: Print(CS) ; set of clusters

Step 1 defines each object, o_i, as a specific cluster. The set of initial clusters is then Σ_0; hence $|\Sigma_0| = n$, $n \in \mathbb{N}$. Step 2 assigns to each object o_i a measure $x_i \in X$ (X is the set of measures assigned to each object o_i). The third steps calculated the initial distance matrix, D_0, using Σ_0 and X. The fourth step is a "for" control loop. If this loop is completely executed, that is, we have n iterations, we finish the loop body with $|\Sigma_n| = 1$, that is, one cluster. Step 5 checks if a stop criterion was reached. An example of stop criterion might be $|\Sigma_i| = k$, that is, having grouped k objects. Many other criteria might be conceived depending on the problem being solved. Step 7 finds the next pair of objects (clusters) to be combined (joined) based on the agglomerative step reached so far, Σ_{i-1}, the distance matrix, D_{i-1}, and on the *LinkageMethod* adopted. Step 8 generates Σ_i based on the new pair found in step 7. If the for loop is totally executed (n iterations), $|\Sigma_i| = 1$; thus the process finishes with one cluster. Such a cluster may be divided based on a *CuttingDistance*, such that *CS* has the set of clusters. If the for loop was finished because a stop criterion was reached, the set of clusters is defined based on *stop criterion*, Σ_i and Σ_0.

Example 7.7.1. This example aims at explaining the agglomerative hierarchical process by study a specific case. In this example, the only criterion for finding the cluster is the *CuttingDistance* = 5.5. Therefore, the for loop is completely executed. Assume six application programs $AP = \{a_1, a_2, a_3, a_4, a_5, a_6\}$ were executed in a specific computer system. The execution times (in seconds) that each application program took to be executed in the computer are shown in $X = \{3.0s, 6.0s, 17.0s, 11.0s, 28.0s, 21.0s\}$. As an example, let us illustrate the agglomerative hierarchical clustering by grouping application programs that are similar in terms of execution times.

From the set of execution times, X, and the set of application programs, AP, we calculate the initial distance matrix (D_0) by adopting the Euclidean distance, that is $d(x_j, x_i) = \sqrt{(x_i - x_j)^2}$. The distance matrix is shown in Table 7.25.

Table 7.25
Initial Distance Matrix (D_0) - $d(x_j, x_i) = \sqrt{(x_i - x_j)^2}$

$d(x_j, x_i)$ (s)	a_i	a_1	a_2	a_3	a_4	a_5	a_6
a_j	x_j (s) / x_i (s)	3.0	6.0	17.0	11.0	28.0	21.0
a_1	3.0	0.0	3.0	14.0	8.0	25.0	18.0
a_2	6.0	3.0	0.0	11.0	5.0	22.0	15.0
a_3	17.0	14.0	11.0	0.0	6.0	11.0	4.0
a_4	11.0	8.0	5.0	6.0	0.0	17.0	10.0
a_5	28.0	25.0	22.0	11.0	17.0	0.0	7.0
a_6	21.0	18.0	15.0	4.0	10.0	7.0	0.0

As the study aims at grouping similar programs in terms of execution times, we adopted the *single-linkage* method since it finds the elements with the shortest inter-cluster distance (*icd*). As we adopted the agglomerative approach, the first set of clusters (Σ_0) is defined as

$$\Sigma_0 = \{\{a_1\}, \{a_2\}, \{a_3\}, \{a_4\}, \{a_5\}, \{a_6\}\}.$$

Then, examining the distance matrix shown in Figure 7.25, we find the elements that have the shortest distance. These application programs are a_1 and a_2 because $d(x_1, x_2) = 3\,s$. Thus, we join the clusters $\{a_1\}$ and $\{a_2\}$ and obtain a new cluster defined as

$$(a_1, a_2) = \{a_1\} \cup \{a_2\} = \{a_1, a_2\}.$$

Therefore, the new set of clusters is

$$\Sigma_1 = (\Sigma_0 \cup \{(a_1, a_2)\}) \setminus \{\{a_1\}, \{a_2\}\},$$

which leads to

$$\Sigma_1 = \{\{(a_1, a_2)\}, \{a_3\}, \{a_4\}, \{a_5\}, \{a_6\}\}.$$

Now, using Equation 7.7.2 ((*single linkage*)), we compute the distance matrix (D_1) by considering the new cluster and the removed cluster. This matrix is shown in Table 7.26.

Table 7.26
The Distance Matrix D_1

$d(x_j, x_i)$ (s)	(a_1, a_2)	a_3	a_4	a_5	a_6
(a_1, a_2)	0	11	5	22	15
a_3	11	0	6	11	4
a_4	5	6	0	17	10
a_5	22	11	17	0	7
a_6	15	4	10	7	0

Now, we examine the distance matrix shown in Figure 7.26 and find the elements that have the shortest distance. These programs are a_3 and a_6 since $d(x_3, x_6) = 4\,s$. Thus, we join the clusters $\{a_3\}$ and $\{a_6\}$ and obtain another new cluster defined as

$$(a_3, a_6) = \{a_3\} \cup \{a_6\} = \{a_3, a_6\}.$$

Hence, the new set of clusters is

$$\Sigma_2 = (\Sigma_1 \cup \{(a_3, a_6)\}) \setminus \{\{a_3\}, \{a_6\}\}.$$

$$\Sigma_2 = \{\{(a_1, a_2)\}, \{(a_3, a_6)\}, \{a_4\}, \{a_5\}\}.$$

Assuming this new set of clusters, Σ_3 and using Equation 7.7.2 (*single linkage*), we compute the distance matrix (D_2), which is depicted in Table 7.27.

Table 7.27
The Distance Matrix D_2

$d(x_j, x_i)$ (s)	(a_1, a_2)	(a_3, a_6)	a_4	a_5
(a_1, a_2)	0	11	5	22
(a_3, a_6)	11	0	6	7
a_4	5	6	0	17
a_5	22	7	17	0

The distance matrix depicted in Figure 7.27 shows that the elements (clusters) that have the shortest distance are (a_1, a_2) and a_4 since $d((a_1, a_2), a_4) = 45\,s$. Hence, we join the clusters $\{(a_1, a_2)\}$ and $\{a_4\}$ and obtain a new cluster defined as

$$((a_1, a_2), a_4)) = (a_1, a_2) \cup \{a_4\} = \{a_1, a_2, a_4\}.$$

Then, another set of clusters is obtained and defined as

$$\Sigma_3 = (\Sigma_2 \cup ((a_1, a_2), a_4)) \setminus \{\{(a_1, a_2)\}, \{a_4\}\}.$$

$$\Sigma_3 = \{\{((a_1, a_2), a_4)\} \{(a_3, a_6)\}, \{a_5\}\}.$$

Considering Σ_3 and using Equation 7.7.2, we compute the distance matrix (D_3) (Table 7.28).

Table 7.28
The Distance Matrix D_3

$d(x_j, x_i)$ (s)	$((a_1, a_2), a_4)$	(a_3, a_6)	a_5
$((a_1, a_2), a_4)$	0	6	17
(a_3, a_6)	6	0	7
a_5	17	7	0

The shortest distance in the matrix depicted in Figure 7.28 is $d(((a_1,a_2),a_4),(a_3,a_6)) = 6s$. Thus, we join the clusters $\{((a_1,a_2),a_4\}$ and $\{(a_3,a_6)\}$ and obtain

$$\Sigma_4 = (\Sigma_3 \cup (((a_1,a_2),a_4),(a_3,a_6)) \setminus \{\{((a_1,a_2),a_4)\}, \{(a_3,a_6)\}\}.$$

$$\Sigma_4 = \{\{(((a_1,a_2),a_4),(a_3,a_6))\}, \{a_5\}\}.$$

Finally, from Σ_4 and using Equation 7.7.2, the last distance matrix (D_4) (Table 7.29) is obtained.

Table 7.29
The Distance Matrix D_4

$d(x_j,x_i)$ (s)	$(((a_1,a_2),a_4),(a_3,a_6))$	a_5
$(((a_1,a_2),a_4),(a_3,a_6))$	0	7
a_5	7	0

This distance matrix leads us finally to one cluster composed of

$$\Sigma_5 = \{\{((((a_1,a_2),a_4),(a_3,a_6)),a_5)\}\}.$$

Looking at Σ_5, we see the clustering order.

□

The agglomerative hierarchical clustering is commonly displayed as a tree-like diagram called a dendrogram. The dendrogram shows the joining ordering of compound elements (clusters) in hierarchical clustering. Each cluster fusion is denoted by joining two compound elements through two branches and forming a parent node (a new compound element). A compound element is formed by joining individual elements or existing compound clusters. The individual element of the dendrogram are the leaf nodes. At each dendrogram node, we have a right and left sub-branch of clustered compounds. The vertical axis represents the distance measure between clusters. The height of a node (compound element - cluster) represents the distance value between the right and left clusters.

Figure 7.32 shows the dendrogram related to the clustering example depicted above. Hierarchical clustering does not explicitly define the number of clusters. Instead, we may consider, for instance, a distance value that will yield an appropriate number of clusters. In this specific case, let us assume the cutting distance is 5.5, represented by the dashed red line. This criterion generates three (3) clusters: $\{(((a_1,a_2),a_4)\}$, $\{(a_3,a_6)\}$, and $\{a_5\}$.

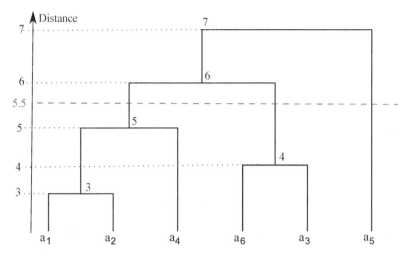

Figure 7.32 Dendrogram - $\Sigma_5 = \{\{((((a_1,a_2),a_4),(a_3,a_6)),a_5)\}\}$.

Another possibility is defining a cutting-cost function that calculates values assuming the dendrogram was cut at a specific level, leading to a set of clusters composed of the respective elements. The value provided by such a cost function would be dependent on the number of clusters and the composition of each cluster. For instance, such a function could consider processors´ utilization, memory usage, throughput, execution times, etc.

Example 7.7.2. Assume a set of programs, $sop = \{p_i\}$, $|sop| = 10$, $i \in \{i \in \mathbb{N} \mid 1 \le i \le 10\}$, is required to run uninterruptedly to sustain data center management and security services. Each of these programs was monitored for a period T in a server with m cores. The overall processors´ utilization of a server for each program in the interval T is shown in Table 7.30.

Table 7.30
The Overall Server´s Utilization of Each Program p_i during T.

i	1	2	3	4	5	6	7	8	9	10
u_{p_i}	0.1528	0.9287	0.6071	0.6359	0.6129	0.2253	0.0556	0.1668	0.7121	0.8851

Using Table 7.30, generate the initial distance matrix D_0 using the Euclidean distance. This distance matrix shows the differences between utilization of each program (at the initial phase, every program p_i is a cluster - a set). The subsequent distance matrices, D_k, are obtained considering the (*complete linkage*) method, that is, considering the furthest neighbor elements. Thus, the grouping process aims to join programs with high utilization and low utilization to find a balanced configuration. In this specific study, we adopted only two servers to execute the set of services ($j \in \{1,2\}$).

At each step, k (iteration), we take the largest compound element (the set (s_k) with the largest number of elements joined up to the step k), assign to server $j = 1$ and compute

$$w_1(s_k) = \sum_{\forall p_i \in s_k} u_{p_i},$$

which is the total utilization assigned to server 1 at the step k.

Likewise, take the complement set of s_k, that is s_k^c, and assign the programs in this set to server $j = 2$. Then, calculate

$$w_2(s_k^c) = \sum_{\forall p_i \in s_k^c} u_{p_i}.$$

It is worth stressing that $w_2(s_k^c)$ is the total utilization assigned to server 2 at the step k. After that, compute the average workload difference between servers at step k, that is

$$wld_k = \frac{|w_1(s_k) - w_2(s_k^c)|}{2}.$$

The clustering process is carried out until every element is joined. At each step k, d_k is computed for $w_1(s_k)$ and $w_2(s_k)$. The program allocation to the server is the one that provides the smallest d_k. In other words, at step k, we found a program allocation, programs in s_k assigned to server 1 and programs in s_k^c assigned to server 2, (among those analyzed) that is the least unbalanced. More formally,

$$k = \arg\min_{\forall k}\{wld_k\},$$

such that the programs represented in s_k are assigned to server 1, and the programs represented in s_k^c are assigned to server 2. Now, let us show each step of this process. In the first step, $\Sigma_0 = \{ \{p_1\}, \{p_2\}, \{p_3\}, \{p_4\}, \{p_5\}, \{p_6\}, \{p_7\}, \{p_8\}, \{p_9\}, \{p_{10}\}\}$. Then, using the utilization of each program depicted in Table 7.30, we generate the initial distance matrix D_0, where $d_{p_i,p_j}^0 = \sqrt{(u_j - u_i)^2}$. This matrix is shown in Table 7.31.

The first ($k = 1$) of the clustering process starts finding out the largest distance in D_0. Hence, $d_{max} = \max_{\forall p_i,p_j}\{d_{p_i,p_j}^0\} = 0.8730$. The programs that have this distance are p_2 and p_7. Thus, we obtain

Table 7.31

The Initial Distance Matrix D_0

D_0	p_i	p_1	p_2	p_3	p_4	p_5	p_6	p_7	p_8	p_9	p_{10}
p_j	u_j / u_i	0.1528	0.9287	0.6071	0.6359	0.6129	0.2253	0.0556	0.1668	0.7121	0.8851
p_1	0.1528	0	0.7758	0.4542	0.4830	0.4601	0.0725	0.0972	0.0140	0.5592	0.7322
p_2	0.9287	0.7758	0	0.3216	0.2928	0.3158	0.7034	0.8730	0.7619	0.2166	0.0436
p_3	0.6071	0.4542	0.3216	0	0.0288	0.0058	0.3818	0.5514	0.4403	0.1050	0.2780
p_4	0.6359	0.4830	0.2928	0.0288	0	0.0229	0.4105	0.5802	0.4690	0.0762	0.2492
p_5	0.6129	0.4601	0.3158	0.0058	0.0229	0	0.3876	0.5573	0.4461	0.0992	0.2722
p_6	0.2253	0.0725	0.7034	0.3818	0.4105	0.3876	0	0.1697	0.0585	0.4867	0.6597
p_7	0.0556	0.0972	0.8730	0.5514	0.5802	0.5573	0.1697	0	0.1112	0.6564	0.8294
p_8	0.1668	0.0140	0.7619	0.4403	0.4690	0.4461	0.0585	0.1112	0	0.5452	0.7183
p_9	0.7121	0.5592	0.2166	0.1050	0.0762	0.0992	0.4867	0.6564	0.5452	0	0.1730
p_{10}	0.8851	0.7322	0.0436	0.2780	0.2492	0.2722	0.6597	0.8294	0.7183	0.1730	0

$$\Sigma_1 = \Sigma_0 \cup \{(p_2, p_7)\} \setminus \{\{p_2\}, \{p_7\}\}.$$

Hence, we get $s_1 = \{p_2, p_7\}$, and from s_1, we obtain s_1^c. Thus,

$$w_1(s_1) = u_{p_2} + u_{p_7} = 0.9843, \text{ and } w_2(s_1^c) = 3.9979$$

and as

$$wld_1 = \frac{|w_1(s_1) - w_2(s_1^c)|}{2} = \frac{|0.9843 - 3.9979|}{2} = 1.5068.$$

Using Σ_1, we generate D_1 by considering the *complete linkage* approach. Matrix D_1 is shown in Table 7.32. The farthest pair of elements is (p_2, p_7) and p_{10}, because $d^1_{(p_2, p_7), p_{10}} = 0.8294$.

Table 7.32

Step $k = 1$. Matrix D_1

D_1	(p_2, p_7)	p_1	p_3	p_4	p_5	p_6	p_8	p_9	p_{10}
(p_2, p_7)	0	0.7758	0.5514	0.5802	0.5573	0.7034	0.7619	0.6564	0.8294
p_1	0.7758	0	0.4542	0.4830	0.4601	0.0725	0.0140	0.5592	0.7322
p_3	0.5514	0.4542	0	0.0288	0.0058	0.3818	0.4403	0.1050	0.2780
p_4	0.5802	0.4830	0.0288	0	0.0229	0.4105	0.4690	0.0762	0.2492
p_5	0.5573	0.4601	0.0058	0.0229	0	0.3876	0.4461	0.0992	0.2722
p_6	0.7034	0.0725	0.3818	0.4105	0.3876	0	0.0585	0.4867	0.6597
p_8	0.7619	0.0140	0.4403	0.4690	0.4461	0.0585	0	0.5452	0.7183
p_9	0.6564	0.5592	0.1050	0.0762	0.0992	0.4867	0.5452	0	0.1730
p_{10}	0.8294	0.7322	0.2780	0.2492	0.2722	0.6597	0.7183	0.1668	0

Then, we get

$$\Sigma_2 = \Sigma_1 \cup \{((p_2,p_7),p_{10})\} \setminus \{\{(p_2,p_7)\}, \{p_{10}\}\}.$$

Thus, we get $s_2 = \{p_2, p_7, p_{10}\}$. From s_2, we obtain s_2^c. Hence,

$$w_1(s_2) = 1.8694, \quad \text{and} \quad w_2(s_2^c) = 3.1129$$

and as

$$wld_2 = \frac{|w_1(s_2) - w_2(s_2^c)|}{2} = \frac{|1.8694 - 3.1129|}{2} = 0.6217.$$

From Σ_2, we obtain D_2. Matrix D_2 is shown in Table 7.33.

Table 7.33

Step $k = 2$. Matrix D_2

D_2	$((p_2,p_7),p_{10})$	p_1	p_3	p_4	p_5	p_6	p_8	p_9
$((p_2,p_7),p_{10})$	0	0.7758	0.5514	0.5802	0.5573	0.7034	0.7619	0.6564
p_1	0.7758	0	0.4542	0.4830	0.4601	0.0725	0.0140	0.5592
p_3	0.5514	0.4542	0	0.0288	0.0058	0.3818	0.4403	0.1050
p_4	0.5802	0.4830	0.0288	0	0.0229	0.4105	0.4690	0.0762
p_5	0.5573	0.4601	0.0058	0.0229	0	0.3876	0.4461	0.0992
p_6	0.7034	0.0725	0.3818	0.4105	0.3876	0	0.0585	0.4867
p_8	0.7619	0.0140	0.4403	0.4690	0.4461	0.0585	0	0.5452
p_9	0.6564	0.5592	0.1050	0.0762	0.0992	0.4867	0.5452	0

Then, we find out the largest distance in D_2, which is $d^2_{((p_2,p_7),p_{10}),p_1} = 0.7619$. Hence, we join $((p_2,p_7),p_{10})$ and p_1. Therefore

$$\Sigma_3 = \Sigma_2 \cup \{(((p_2,p_7),p_{10}),p_1)\} \setminus \{\{((p_2,p_7),p_{10})\}, \{p_1\}\}.$$

Thus, we get $s_3 = \{p_2, p_7, p_{10}, , p_1\}$. From s_3, we obtain s_3^c. Hence,

$$w_1(s_3) = 2.0222 \quad \text{and} \quad w_2(s_3^c) = 2.9600,$$

and as

$$wld_3 = \frac{|w_1(s_3) - w_2(s_3^c)|}{2} = \frac{|2.0222 - 2.9600|}{2} = 0.4689.$$

Considering Σ_3, generate D_3. Matrix D_3 is shown in Table 7.34.

The farthest pair of elements considering D_3 are $(((p_2,p_7),p_{10}),p_1)$ and p_8 since $d^3_{((((p_2,p_7),p_{10}),p_1),p_8)} = 0.7619$. Hence, joining the elements $(((p_2,p_7),p_{10}),p_1)$ and p_8, we get

Table 7.34

Step $k = 3$. Matrix D_3

D_3	$(((p_2,p_7),p_{10}),p_1)$	p_3	p_4	p_5	p_6	p_8	p_9
$(((p_2,p_7),p_{10}),p_1)$	0	0.5514	0.5802	0.5573	0.7034	0.7619	0.6564
p_3	0.5514	0	0.0288	0.0058	0.3818	0.4403	0.1050
p_4	0.5802	0.0288	0	0.0229	0.4105	0.4690	0.0762
p_5	0.5573	0.0058	0.0229	0	0.3876	0.4461	0.0992
p_6	0.7034	0.3818	0.4105	0.3876	0	0.0585	0.4867
p_8	0.7619	0.4403	0.4690	0.4461	0.4461	0	
p_9	0.6564	0.1050	0.0762	0.0992	0.0992	0.4867	0

$$\Sigma_4 = \Sigma_3 \cup \{((((p_2,p_7),p_{10}),p_1),p_8)\} \setminus \{\{(((p_2,p_7),p_{10}),p_1)\}, \{p_8\}\}.$$

This process was carried out until getting Σ_9. Table 7.36, Table 7.37, Table 7.38, and Table 7.39 are the respective distance tables obtained at steps $k \in \{5, 6, 7, 8\}$.

Table 7.35

Step $k = 4$. Matrix D_4

D_4	$((((p_2,p_7),p_{10}),p_1),p_8)$	p_3	p_4	p_5	p_6	p_9
$((((p_2,p_7),p_{10}),p_1),p_8)$	0	0.5514	0.5802	0.5573	0.7034	0.6564
p_3	0.5514	0	0.0288	0.0058	0.3818	0.1050
p_4	0.5802	0.0288	0	0.0229	0.4105	0.0762
p_5	0.5573	0.0058	0.0229	0	0.3876	0.0992
p_6	0.7034	0.3818	0.4105	0.3876	0	0.4867
p_9	0.6564	0.1050	0.0762	0.0992	0.4867	0

$\Sigma_9 = \{(((((((((p_2,p_7),p_{10}),p_1),p_8),p_6),p_9),p_4),p_5),p_3)\}$. The values of the function wld_k, for $k \in \{1, 2, ... 9\}$ is shown in Table 7.40 and Figure 7.33. It is worth noting that the $wld(k)$ reaches its smallest value for $k = 5$. In this configuration, we

Table 7.36

Step $k = 5$. Matrix D_5

D_5	$(((((p_2,p_7),p_{10}),p_1),p_8),p_6)$	p_3	p_4	p_5	p_9
$(((((p_2,p_7),p_{10}),p_1),p_8),p_6)$	0	0.5514	0.5802	0.5573	0.6564
p_3	0.5514	0	0.0288	0.0058	0.1050
p_4	0.5802	0.0288	0	0.0229	0.0762
p_5	0.5573	0.0058	0.0229	0	0.0992
p_9	0.6564	0.1050	0.0762	0.0992	0

Table 7.37
Step $k = 6$. Matrix D_6

D_6	$((((((p_2, p_7), p_{10}), p_1), p_8), p_6), p_9)$	p_3	p_4	p_5
$((((((p_2, p_7), p_{10}), p_1), p_8), p_6), p_9)$	0	0.5514	0.5802	0.5573
p_3	0.5514	0	0.0288	0.0058
p_4	0.5802	0.0288	0	0.0229
p_5	0.5573	0.0058	0.0229	0

Table 7.38
Step $k = 7$. Matrix D_7

D_7	$(((((((p_2, p_7), p_{10}), p_1), p_8), p_6), p_9), p_4)$	p_3	p_5
$(((((((p_2, p_7), p_{10}), p_1), p_8), p_6), p_9), p_4)$	0	0.5514	0.5573
p_3	0.5514	0	0.0058
p_5	0.5573	0.0058	0

Table 7.39
Step $k = 8$. Matrix D_8

D_8	$((((((((p_2, p_7), p_{10}), p_1), p_8), p_6), p_9), p_4), p_5)$	p_3
$((((((((p_2, p_7), p_{10}), p_1), p_8), p_6), p_9), p_4), p_5)$	0	0.5514
p_3	0.5514	0

obtain the least unbalanced program allocation among those evaluated. This configuration assigns programs p_1, p_2, p_6, p_7, p_8, and p_{10} to Server 1 (Cluster 1), and allocates programs p_3, p_4, p_5, and p_9 to Server 2 (Cluster 2).

Table 7.40
Average Workload Difference ($wld(k)$) Between Servers at Step k

k	1	2	3	4	5	6	7	8	9
$wld(k)$	1.5068	0.6217	0.4689	0.3021	0.0768	0.6353	1.2711	2.1876	2.1876

Figure 7.34 shows the dendrogram generated, the cutting line based on function wld, the two clusters with their respective programs. The total workload assigned to Server 1 and Server 2 are

$$w_l(s_5) = \sum_{i \in \{1,2,6,7,8,10\}} u_{p_i} = 2.4143$$

and

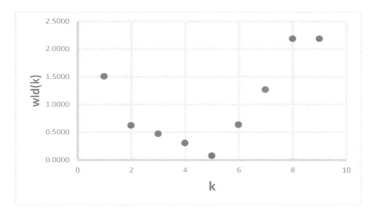

Figure 7.33 Average Workload Difference ($wld(k)$) Between Servers at Step k.

$$w_2\left(s_5^c\right) = \sum_{i \in \{3,4,5,9\}} u_{p_i} = 2.5679,$$

respectively.

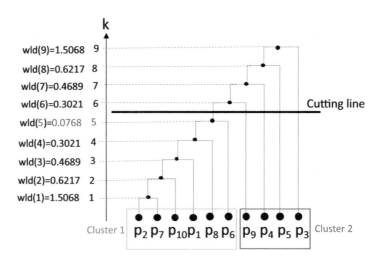

Figure 7.34 Dendrogram and Clusters.

Hierarchical clustering can provide ambiguous results distance ties, that is, clusters that are equidistant from clusters. A simple and usually adopted method for breaking the ties is the random selection of a cluster. The main shortcoming of hierarchical clustering methods is that once two objects are joined, they can never be divided. Nevertheless, hierarchical clustering methods are quite popular since they are relatively simple to understand and implement.

EXERCISES

Exercise 1. Why do we need scaling data sets? Explain.

Exercise 2. What are the aims, advantages, and constraints of the following scaling methods: (a) Min-Max Scaling, (b) Mean and Standard Deviation Scaling, (c) Absolute Maximal Scaling, (d) Median-Interquartile Scaling, (e) Quantile Scaling, (f) Box-Cox transformation, and (g) Yeo-Johnson transformation.

Exercise 3. Assume a data sample depicted in Table 7.41. Scale the data set considering the Min-Max method and shows the individual plot of the scaled data set.

Table 7.41
Data Set 1

Data Set 1		
266.3221	266.0667	56.33376
345.581	361.5453	275.4429
369.2548	427.3882	271.7463
323.7195	286.2254	390.1033
404.4847	323.9181	386.7435
285.6356	458.7889	334.0986
334.4928	315.0503	406.2339
323.2607	311.8316	122.3915
277.3464	371.3818	283.0629
262.5769	290.6228	255.516

Exercise 4. Consider the data sample depicted in Table 7.41. Scale the data set adopting the *Mean and Standard Deviation Scaling* method and show the scaled data set histogram.

Exercise 5. Adopt a data sample depicted in Table 7.42. Scale the data set considering the *Absolute Maximal Scaling* method and draws the individual plot of the scaled data set.

Exercise 6. Use a data sample depicted in Table 7.43. Scale the data set considering the *Median-Interquartile Scaling* method and show the scaled data set's histogram.

Table 7.42
Data Set 2

Data Set 2		
418.0399	1102.352	352.0158
522.1638	433.4566	669.2888
455.2294	655.9011	662.3701
210.4155	211.7876	103.7925
354.5415	839.8115	173.41
1202.122	16.64458	133.0276
114.2533	300.8692	6.769031
469.1167	69.35457	106.5759
21.27715	409.6026	110.5438
144.103	52.1883	378.8726

Table 7.43
Data Set 3

Data Set 3		
131.3897	276.5173	676.8088
1291.176	1467.828	2.02509
171.4232	1425.03	771.1034
11.31401	138.1161	17.1154
12.01165	745.4979	111.1283
152.7772	359.3603	314.9674
388.1342	169.2149	129.3603
859.0171	9.272153	124.2079
1435.373	324.6425	227.5352
129.7257	4.594087	1020.581

Exercise 7. Assume a data sample depicted in Table 7.44. Scale the data set considering the *Quantile Scaling* method and presents the individual plot of the scaled data set.

Exercise 8. Consider a data sample depicted in Table 7.42 and transform this sample using the log function adopting the base 2, 10, and ε. Show individual plots of the transformed data sets.

Exercise 9. Assume the data set shown in Table 7.44 and apply the Box-Cox transformation and generates a transformed data set for $\lambda = -1$, $\lambda = 0$, and $\lambda = 0.4$. Show the histogram of the scaled data sets.

Exercise 10. Consider the data set shown in Table 7.45 and apply the Yeo-Johnson transformation and generates a transformed data set for $\lambda = 0.5$. Show individual

Table 7.44
Data Set 4

Data Set 4		
3.665915	108.9517	375.3578
29.98981	247.8977	444.1713
352.46	49.59171	425.819
99.85297	108.452	438.0852
55.55388	384.1982	351.5588
463.3974	377.8049	378.7381
43.23063	397.7636	416.6455
37.69437	469.9167	372.2283
23.55327	351.7379	407.1985
5.661005	470.0508	290.1143

plots of the transformed data sets.

Table 7.45
Data Set 5

Data Set 5		
105.9066	36.5269	102.0831
23.7381	106.6991	55.0761
77.6693	0.1769	-19.8573
136.6926	-63.3947	198.0456
91.8604	128.8150	24.3920
-3.0583	233.5761	200.7793
93.1615	67.5000	112.4049
-0.2628	129.4585	-50.3669
-52.0904	137.8371	8.8641

Exercise 11. What do you understand to be the norm of a vector?

Exercise 12. Explain with examples what the Minkowski, Euclidean, Manhattan, and Chebyshev norms are.

Exercise 13. Adopting the data set depicted in Table 7.46 obtain the normalized data sets according to Manhattan, Euclidean, and Chebyshev norms.

Exercise 14. Explain the concepts and the purposes of the following distance measures: (a) Manhattan, (b) Euclidean, (c) Jaccard, and (d) Hamming.

Exercise 15. Describe the concept of cluster distance. Show examples.

Table 7.46

Data Set: $\{((x_i, y_j))\}, |\{(x_i, y_j)\}| = 20$

i	x_i	y_i	i	x_i	y_i
1	308.79	585.03	11	801.11	74.95
2	200.70	837.13	12	377.83	101.82
3	33.93	11.55	13	462.98	80.20
4	168.76	187.07	14	330.38	38.74
5	511.87	128.58	15	425.59	20.56
6	271.74	15.77	16	506.90	317.00
7	544.71	76.95	17	449.40	226.57
8	291.90	249.60	18	415.34	240.99
9	468.77	520.63	19	486.32	78.99
10	609.34	612.07	20	479.01	444.92

Exercise 16. Using the vectors presented in Table 7.46, calculate (a) the Manhattan distances, (b) the Euclidean distances, and (d) the Chebyshev distances between the following vectors: (1) (x_1, y_1) and (x_9, y_9), and (2) (x_6, y_6) and (x_{18}, y_{18}).

Exercise 17. Let us consider a sample of pairs of measures shown in Table 7.47. Use graphical tools such as scatter plot, histogram, dot plot, or individual plot to detect clusters' possible existence. If there are clusters, provide, for each of them, their statistical summary and interpret them.

Table 7.47

Data Sample - Clusters

i	x_i	y_i	i	x_i	y_i	i	x_i	y_i
1	9.93	7.50	11	46.22	19.89	21	93.77	103.15
2	6.28	7.41	12	26.88	34.57	22	78.02	88.12
3	8.44	6.70	13	36.41	26.53	23	124.54	95.53
4	9.90	13.16	14	2.70	26.15	24	88.89	81.58
5	15.72	15.24	15	23.95	35.88	25	109.10	131.08
6	7.15	13.03	16	22.14	29.43	26	112.10	72.89
7	12.35	10.84	17	21.81	39.80	27	74.84	73.87
8	9.65	10.70	18	28.31	26.89	28	82.48	71.88
9	15.93	11.47	19	34.05	32.70	29	94.73	104.85
10	11.42	17.65	20	39.08	11.92	30	93.14	119.69

Exercise 18. Assuming the previous exercise, calculate (a) the minimal Euclidean distances (CD_{min}), (b) the maximal Euclidean distances (CD_{max}), (c) the mean Euclidean distances (CD_{mean}), and (d) the average Euclidean distances (CD_{avg}) between

each pair of clusters found.

Exercise 19. Consider the twenty computers configurations represented by the respective availability and cost ($). The availability and the cost of each configuration are shown in Table 7.48. Using the k-means clustering method, find a set of configurations that provides the highest availabilities and the lowest costs. As an initial cluster partition, divide the twenty configurations into two clusters, each with ten configurations.

Table 7.48

Availability $(0-100)$ **and Its Implementation Cost ($)**

i	A_i	C_i ($)	i	A_i	C_i ($)
1	86.34	4459.79	11	98.07	6832.42
2	85.54	9529.28	12	83.67	6278.70
3	91.08	5384.87	13	95.15	7606.37
4	92.78	4233.47	14	93.86	7947.45
5	92.04	9623.04	15	98.81	3980.53
6	83.59	4097.23	16	92.57	6629.29
7	86.29	7398.85	17	97.43	4684.90
8	91.75	9363.51	18	97.92	5773.80
9	93.34	7734.06	19	83.40	4952.97
10	96.24	4215.40	20	98.26	7434.25

Exercise 20. Find out the solution required in the previous exercise, now applying the k-medoid approach.

Exercise 21. Adopt the agglomerative hierarchical clustering and find a cluster with the four best configurations according to the criteria described in Exercise 19.

Exercise 22. Use the agglomerative hierarchical clustering and find three clusters with the closest measures of the data set presented in Table 7.44. Show the respective dendrogram, the mean, and the standard deviation of each cluster.

System performance can be evaluated through different methods and strategies depending on the context (criticality, costs involved) in which it is inserted and if the system is still under conception or already operational. Therefore, in a broad context, the performance evaluation of a system may be carried out through:

1. Measuring,

2. Analysis, and

3. Simulation.

Measuring is an alternative when the system is already in operation. Even then, however, it may not be feasible to conduct a performance experiment since the system may not be interrupted to evaluate specific scenarios since the costs involved or the criticality of agents involved prevents suspending its operations for studying performance issues. *Analysis* and *Simulation*, on the other hand, consider a model instead of an actual system. The system performance is evaluated through a model that represents the system. Hence, we must have confidence that the system is well represented by the model that is evaluated. The activity that aims at finding pieces of evidence for rejecting a model as a representation of the system is usually called *Validation*. If we do not find evidence to reject a model, in practice, we accept the model as a representation of the system until new pieces of evidence support the rejection.

Analysis can be sub-divided into two broad classes: *Analytic/Algebraic Methods* and *Numerical Methods*. Analytic/algebraic models are specified by relations (equations, inequations, functions, formulas) between system parameters and performance criteria, which are analyticly solved. It is important to stress, however, that *closed form* analytic solutions are only possible for a few classes of systems, usually small or specified by regular (well-formed) structures (see Chapter 11). For more complex system, though, models solved by numerical methods may be the alternative (see Chapter 9, Chapter 10, and Chapter 13). If the state space is too big or infinite, the system lacks regularity, or even if non-phase-type distributions should be represented, the evaluation option may fall into *Simulation*. With simulation, there are no fundamental restrictions towards the models that can be evaluated. Nevertheless, the simulation does have pragmatic constraints since the amount of computer time and memory running a simulation can be prohibitively large. Therefore, the general advice is to pursue an analytic model wherever possible, even if simplifications and/or decompositions are required (these simplifications must not undermine the model´s objective). Nevertheless, if the model is not tractable, numerical methods may be applied to find a solution. However, if the model is yet too costly and big, the option of predicting system performance is the simulation. Figure 7.35 depicts a general relation between the time to obtain a solution and the evaluation approach.

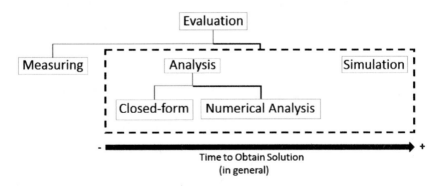

Figure 7.35   Evaluation Methods *vs.* Time to Obtain Solution.

Figure 7.36 provides a guideline that may help the analyst decide the evaluation approach to follow, considering the class of probability distributions required, the state-space size, and the availability of the known analytic solution. This guideline aims at supporting the representation capacity and the time to obtain a solution inherent to the models as depicted in Figure 7.35. Once a performance problem is evaluated through a model, the first question is if a phase-type distribution is suitable to represent the events and tasks represented in the model. If they are not suitable, simulation is the alternative. If phase-type distribution represents well the events and tasks, one should ask if an analytic model represents the system. If the analyst is aware of such a model, he/she should resort to such a model. If an analytic model is not known, the analyst should ask if the state space size is finite and, if it is, if the evaluation platform (computers) has enough memory to represent the state space. If these two last questions are affirmatively answered, numerical solutions are likely to be the best choice; otherwise, the analyst should employ simulation.

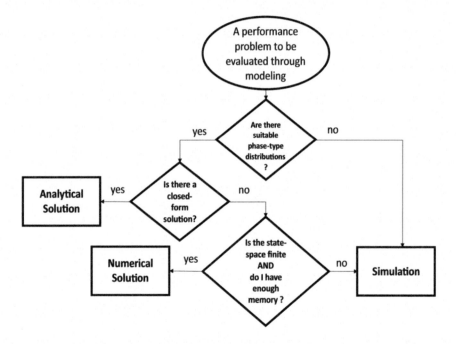

Figure 7.36   Guideline for Choosing the Performance Model Solution.

This part is composed of seven chapters. Chapter 8 introduces the operational analysis. Chapter 9 and Chapter 10 present Markov chains. Chapter 11 describes basic Markovian queue models. Chapters 12 and Chapter 13 detail stochastic Petri nets. Finally, Chapter 14 closes the part by introducing discrete event simulation.

Part II

Performance Modeling

8 Operational Analysis

Many day-to-day problems in performance analysis of computer systems can be solved by using some simple relationships that do not require any assumption about the distribution of service times or interconnection times. Several of these relations, called operational laws, were initially identified by Buzen and later extended by Denning and Buzen [98, 188]. This chapter presents an introduction to Operational Analysis.

It is worth mentioning the meaning of the term Operational Analysis. The word operational refers to data measured directly from a running system, that is, a functioning system. Therefore, operational requirements can be verified by measurements. The operational quantities are the data that can be measured during a finite **period of observation**, T. For example, consider a system represented by a "black box" shown in Figure 8.1. If such a system has K components, it may well be described with its components as in Figure 8.2.

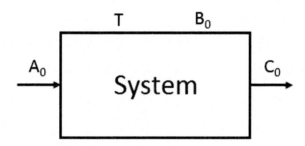

Figure 8.1 Simple System - "Black Box".

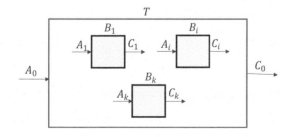

Figure 8.2 System with K Components.

If we monitored the device i for a period of T, we could measure the **number of arrivals** at i that is A_i (transactions, operations, packets), the **number of finalizations** C_i (transactions, operations, packets, etc.), and its **busy time** B_i during the period T. The number of arrivals and conclusions (jobs finished) performed by the system in the period is denoted by A_0 and C_0, respectively. These *quantities* are assigned to variables named **operational variables**. Operational variables are either basic quantities, which are directly measured during the observation period, or derived quantities, which are computed from the basic quantities. The basic quantities are: A_0, C_0, A_i, C_i, B_i and T.

The operational variables of the system should be measurable, and its validity depends on the assumption that can be tested by observing the system for a finite observational period, T, large enough to minimize fluctuations. The system must be flow-balanced; that is, the number of arrivals at a given device must be close to its number of departures, $A_i \approx C_i$; thus :

$$\frac{C_i - A_i}{C_i} \to 0. \tag{8.0.1}$$

From measurable data (basic quantities), we can directly calculate the following derived quantities:

- The **arrival rate** of component i,

$$\lambda_i = \frac{A_i}{T}, \tag{8.0.2}$$

- The **throughput** of component i,

$$X_i = \frac{C_i}{T}, \tag{8.0.3}$$

- The **utilization** of component i,

$$U_i = \frac{B_i}{T}, \tag{8.0.4}$$

- The **mean service time** of the component i,

$$S_i = \frac{B_i}{C_i}, \tag{8.0.5}$$

- The **system arrival rate**,

$$\lambda_0 = \frac{A_0}{T}, \text{and} \tag{8.0.6}$$

- The **system throughput**,

$$X_0 = \frac{C_0}{T}. \tag{8.0.7}$$

Example 8.0.1. A processor was monitored for 1 min. It was observed that it was busy for $36\,s$. The total number of transactions that reached the processor was 1800, and it also executed 1800 transactions over the same period.

a) What is the processor arrival rate, $\lambda_{CPU} = \frac{A_{CPU}}{T}$?

b) What is the processor throughput, $X_{CPU} = \frac{C_{CPU}}{T}$?

c) What is the processor utilization, $U_{CPU} = \frac{B_{CPU}}{T}$?

d) What is the mean service time of transactions served by the processor, $S_{CPU} = \frac{B_{CPU}}{C_{CPU}}$?

It is important to note that the only system resource is the CPU, so the metrics associated with the CPU will be the same as those associated with the system. Therefore:

$$\lambda_{CPU} = \frac{A_{CPU}}{T} = \frac{1800\,trans}{60\,s} = 30\,tps,$$

$$X_{CPU} = \frac{C_{CPU}}{T} = \frac{1800\,trans}{60\,tps} = 30\,tps,$$

$$U_{CPU} = \frac{B_{CPU}}{T} = \frac{36\,s}{60\,s} = 60\%,$$

$$S_{CPU} = \frac{B_{CPU}}{C_{CPU}} = \frac{36\,s}{1800\,trans} = 0.02\,s.$$

$\square$

As we have seen, the basic quantities are collected during an observation period, and the derived quantities are computed from the basic quantities. All these quantities are assigned to operational variables, which may change from one observation to another.

8.1   UTILIZATION LAW

Now, consider the components i of the system presented in Figure 8.2. If during observation period T, the number of completed operations in i was C_i, and the component's i busy time was B_i, the following operational variable is available (as we have already seen):

$$U_i = \frac{B_i}{T}.$$

Then, multiplying and dividing by the operational variable C_i, we obtain

$$U_i = \frac{B_i}{T} = \frac{B_i}{T} \times \frac{C_i}{C_i} = \frac{B_i}{C_i} \times \frac{C_i}{T},$$

which is

$$U_i = S_i \times X_i. \tag{8.1.1}$$

An equation such as this, which depicts an identity among operational quantities, is called an operational law and must hold in every observation period. This specific relation is named the utilization law. We will introduce other operational laws later in this chapter.

Example 8.1.1. Consider a network gateway; measurements show that packets arrive at an average rate of $125\,pps$ (packets per second), and the gateway takes about $2\,ms$ to route them. What is the utilization of the link?

As the system is balanced, $X_i = \lambda_i$; hence : $U_i = 2 \times 10^{-3}\,s \times 125\,pps = 0.25 = 25\%$.

When experimenting with a system that measures the utilization of all its resources, considering the representative workload, the "bottleneck" of the system is that component that presents higher utilization. In other words, when an overload is applied to the system, the first component to achieve 100% utilization will be the bottleneck component.

$\square$

8.2 FORCED FLOW LAW

Consider a system and that during an observation interval, T, C_0 system completions were counted, and C_i completions were counted for each resource i. The visit count of a resource, V_i, is the ratio of the number of completions at that resource to the number of system completions. The visit count to a resource i may also be described as the average number of visits to the resource i by each system-level request.

The forced flow law presents a relationship between system throughput, X_0, and the components' throughputs, $X_i, \forall i$. The system is required to be balanced, that is $A_0 = C_0$, over the observation period T. Consider the throughput of component i, that is $X_i = \frac{C_i}{T}$. Therefore, we have:

$$X_i = \frac{C_i}{T} = \frac{C_i}{T} \times \frac{C_0}{C_0},$$

$$X_i = \frac{C_i}{C_0} \times \frac{C_0}{T},$$

which leads to

$$X_i = V_i \times X_0. \tag{8.2.1}$$

Example 8.2.1. Suppose that when one (1) transaction is executed on a server (and consequently on the processor), two (2) disk drive accesses are carried out. If 5.6 transactions are computed on the server per second, what is the flow of the disk drive?

Consider $T = 1\,s$, so $X_{server} = 5.6\,tps$ and $V_{disk} = 2$; thus :

$$X_{disk} = V_{disk} \times X_{server} = 2 \times 5.6\,tps = 11.2\,tps.$$

$\square$

8.3 DEMAND LAW

The concept of a **service demand** (demanded time) is related to the set of requests a service makes to the system's pool of resources. The service demand denoted as D_i is defined as the total average time for carrying out a set of requests of a given class through a set of resources $\{i\}$. Several devices may be visited multiple times throughout the execution of the group of requests (a transaction). By definition, the service demand does not comprise queuing time since it is the sum of service times. Service demand is an essential notion in performance modeling.

The demanded time a transaction requires of a resource is the time that such a transaction requires its processing.

We know from the Utilization Law that

$$U_i = S_i \times X_i.$$

The Forced Flow Law defines

$$X_i = V_i \times X_0.$$

Hence, we conclude that:

$$U_i = S_i \times V_i \times X_0 = D_i \times X_0,$$

$$U_i = D_i \times X_0. \tag{8.3.1}$$

Thus, the service demand of a request (a transaction) to a resource i is

$$D_i = \frac{U_i}{X_0}, \tag{8.3.2}$$

where

$$D_i = S_i \times V_i. \tag{8.3.3}$$

That is, the time a transaction demands from resource i is the service time of component i (S_i) multiplied by the number of visits to the resource i during the execution of the transaction.

This law is of great importance since it allows estimating the time required by a transaction to be executed by a resource (total time demanded by the transaction) from its utilization (several monitoring tools provide this metric) and the system throughput X_0, a measure observable by the user since it is the "product" of the system.

It is also worth mentioning that components´ utilization (U_i) is directly proportional to the demand times (D_i), and since the system throughput (X_0) is considered in calculating the required demand times of all system components, the "bottleneck" component is (as well as when the utilizations are observed) the one with the longer time required by the transaction.

Example 8.3.1. Consider that a Web server was monitored for $10\,min$ and that the CPU (during this period) utilization was 90.2348%. The Web server log recorded $30,000$ ($C_0 = C_{WS}$) processed requests. What is the CPU (D_{CPU}) demand time for this class of transactions?

We know that $T = 10 \times 60\,s = 600\,s$ and $X_{WS} = X_0 = \frac{C_{WS}}{T} = \frac{30,000}{600} = 50\,rps$ (requests per second) Therefore:

$$D_{CPU} = \frac{U_{CPU}}{X_{WS}} = \frac{0.902348}{50} = 0.018047\,s$$

per request.

$\square$

Example 8.3.2. A system composed of five servers was monitored for four hours ($T = 4 \times 60 \times 60\,s = 14400\,s$) under operational conditions. In this period, the log registered $C_0 = 28978$ transactions processed. The servers´ utilizations were obtained over the period every $30\,s$. Hence a sample of 480 utilizations for each server was recorded. The average utilizations over the four hour period of each server were $\overline{U_{s_1}} = 0.3996$, $\overline{U_{s_2}} = 0.2389$, $\overline{U_{s_3}} = 0.2774$, $\overline{U_{s_4}} = 0.5253$, and $\overline{U_{s_5}} = 0.2598$, respectively. The mean time demanded of a typical transaction in each server may be estimated through

$$D_{s_i} = \frac{\overline{U_{s_i}}}{X_0},$$

since $X_0 = C_0/T = 28978\,trans./14400\,s = 2.0124\,tps$. The respective time demands of a transaction in each server are depicted in Table 8.1.

Table 8.1
Demands

Server	Demand (s)
Server 1	0.1986
Server 2	0.1187
Server 3	0.1378
Server 4	0.2610
Server 5	0.1291

Therefore, each typical transaction demanded the respective times of each specific server. Now, assume that a considerable demand increase is forecasted. It is expected that $C_0' = 60000$ transactions would be requested in the same four hours period. Thus, the expected throughput would be $X_0' = 60000/14400\,s = 4.1667\,tps$. The foreseen utilization of each server may be estimated through

$$U_{s_i}' = \lceil D_{s_i} \times X_0' \rceil,$$

since the maximal utilization is 1. Therefore (see Table 8.2),

Table 8.2
Utilization

Server	U_{si}'
Server 1	0.8274
Server 2	0.4947
Server 3	0.5743
Server 4	1
Server 5	0.5378

and Server 4 would reach 80% of utilization for a throughput of $X_0 = 3.065\,tps$, because $X_0 = 0.8/0.261$.

□

Example 8.3.3. A server was monitored for $T = 2h$ considering a specific workload. In this period, the average processor utilization was $U_{cpu} = 0.38$, and $C_0 = 374,356$ transactions were processed. Each transaction, on average, reads/writes $18,427.44$ bytes from/to the disk. The average time to read or write one sector (512 bytes) from/to the disk is 0.26 ms. The transaction throughput is

$$X_0 = \frac{C_0}{T} = \frac{374,356}{2 \times 60 \times 60\,s} = 51.99389tps.$$

The number of sectors read/written per transaction is

$$\frac{18,427.44\,bytes}{512\,bytes} = 35.9911\,sectors.$$

As the time to read/write one sector (512 bytes) to the disk is 0.00026 s, the time to read/write 35.9911 sectors is

$$D_{disk} = 0.00026\,s \times 35.9911\,sectors = 0.009358\,s = 9.358\,ms.$$

Therefore,

$$U_{disk} = D_{disk} \times X_0 = 0.009358\,s \times 51.99389tps = 0.486542.$$

And as $U_{cpu} = 0.38$, the bottleneck is the disk.

$\square$

8.4 LITTLE'S LAW

Little's Law deals with queuing systems at which items arrive at some rate. The items could be people, digital packets, requests, parts to assemble a product, instructions waiting to be executed in a processor, etc. The input flow of items enters the system, joins one or more queues, is somewhat processed, and exits the system in an output stream of departures. In most cases, service is the bottleneck that builds up the queue size. Therefore, usually, we have service processes with service times, but this is not required. When there is no service time, we assume only a waiting time. Hence, occasionally it is important to make a distinction between the number of items in the queue and the total number of items in the system, which are the number of items in the queue plus the items being served [241].

Consider the queue system depicted in Figure 8.3. Little's law relates the length of the queue, the response time, and the arrival rate. Thus, the only requirement for adopting this law is that the number of arrivals (A_0) is equal to the number of completions (C_0) in the observation period T.

This relation is:

$$N = \lambda \times R, \tag{8.4.1}$$

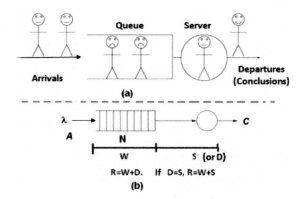

Figure 8.3 Finite Size System Queue (a) and Queue Representation (b).

where N is the number of items (transactions, people, packets) in the system, λ is the effective arrival rate at the system, and R is the response time (residence time). The response time, R, can be decomposed into the waiting time (W) and time the transaction demands (D) of the server (resource), that is:

$$N = \lambda \times (W + D). \tag{8.4.2}$$

Considering that the system has only one resource (a server); thus the number of visits to the server is $V = 1$, and we have $W = 0$; hence as $R = W + D$, and $D = V \times S$, we obtain $R = S$. Therefore, one obtains:

$$N = U = \lambda \times S, \tag{8.4.3}$$

which is simply the Utilization Law (see 8.1.1). Thus, it is worth stressing that Little's law applied to a single resource without queue provides its utilization.

Example 8.4.1. Consider that a bank organizes its clients to be serviced in a queue. This client row is shown in Figure 8.4 and was monitored for 8 hours. Every 30 minutes, the number of clients waiting to be served was counted. The sample obtained is in Table 8.3.

During a period of 8 hours, it was verified that the number of clients that arrived at the queue and those that were attended was approximately equal. The number of clients that arrived was $A_0 = 324$ customers. What is the average residence time of each client in this system (residence time)?

We know that $N = \lambda \times R$; therefore:

$$R = \frac{\overline{N}}{\lambda}.$$

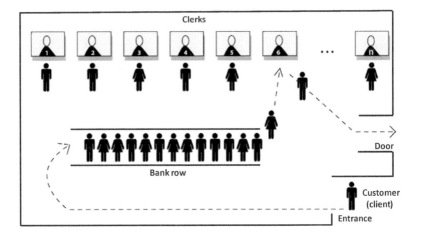

Figure 8.4 Bank Queue.

As

$$\overline{N} = \frac{\sum_{i=1}^{16} N_i}{16} = 11.2 \ clients.$$

The throughput (customers served per minute) is:

$$\lambda = \frac{A_0}{T} = \frac{324 \ customers}{8 \, h \times 60 \ minutes} = 0.675 \, cpm \ (customers \ per \ minute).$$

Given that the system is balanced ($A_0 \approx C_0$), we have that $X_0 \approx \lambda$, and we have:

Table 8.3
Number of clients in the system.

Sample Point	Count	Sample Point	Count
1	11	9	16
2	7	10	8
3	13	11	0
4	17	12	15
5	17	13	5
6	19	14	18
7	3	15	6
8	11	16	14

Table 8.4
Number of clients in the system and in the queue.

Sample j	1	2	3	4	5	6	7	8	9	10	11	12	13	14	15	16
N_q^j	10	8	13	10	18	8	9	11	16	8	13	16	10	11	14	9
N_j	12	11	16	12	20	11	12	14	19	11	16	19	13	14	17	11

$$R = \frac{\overline{N}}{\lambda} = \frac{11.2}{0.675} = 16,67 \ minutes.$$

That is, the mean time spent by a customer in the bank is approximately 16.67 minutes.

□

Example 8.4.2. Adopt the same bank-line system depicted in Example 8.4.1. Consider that the system was again monitored during 8 hours (T) and that every 30 minutes, the number of customers in the system (N) and in the queue (N_q) were recorded. These numbers are in Table 8.4. N is N_q plus the customers being served. The number of customers that arrived in the system was 120 (A_0).

The arrival rate in the period $T = 8 \times 60 \, minutes = 480 \, minutes$ is

$$\lambda_0 = \frac{A_0}{T} = \frac{120 \, customers}{480 \, minutes} = 0.25 \, cpm.$$

As the system is balanced, the system throughput is also $X_0 = 0.25 \, cpm$. The average number of customers in the system and in the queue during T were $\overline{N} = \sum_{j=1}^{16} N_j / 16 = 14.25$ and $\overline{N_q} = \sum_{j=1}^{16} N_q^j / 16 = 11.5$, respectively. Therefore, the residence time and the waiting time are

$$R = \frac{\overline{N}}{\lambda_0} = \frac{14.25}{0.25} = 57 \, minutes$$

and

$$W = \frac{\overline{N_q}}{\lambda_0} = \frac{11.5}{0.25} = 46 \, minutes.$$

As $R = W + S$, then the service time is

$$S = 57 - 46 = 11 \, minutes.$$

□

8.5 GENERAL RESPONSE TIME LAW

One method of computing the mean response time per transaction, R, for a system with many components is to apply Little's law to the entire system by considering each of its components. In this system, clients make requests to a distributed system with k nodes as depicted in Figure 8.5. Each request demands a transaction execution on the distributed nodes. Each node is a subsystem that has its processing units, storage devices, may have a console, etc. It is interesting to note that Little's law can be applied to any part of the system. The only requirement is a balanced workflow.

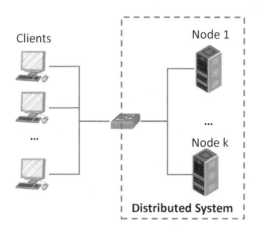

Figure 8.5 Multiple Resources System.

From Little's law we have:

$$N = X_0 \times R,$$

where N is the total number of transactions (or requests) in the distributed system, R is the system response time, and X_0 is the system throughput. Given that the number of transactions (requests) in the system is the sum of the number of transactions (requests) in each node, we have:

$$N = N_1 + N_2 + \ldots + N_k = \sum_{i=1}^{k} N_i.$$

Hence:

$$R = \frac{X_1}{X_0} \times R_1 + \frac{X_2}{X_0} \times R_2 + \ldots + \frac{X_k}{X_0} \times R_k = \sum_{i=1}^{k} \frac{X_i}{X_0} \times R_i =$$

$$V_1 \times R_1 + V_2 \times R_2 + \ldots + V_k \times R_k = \sum_{i=1}^{k} V_k \times R_i.$$

Thus:

$$R = \sum_{i=1}^{k} V_k \times R_i \qquad (8.5.1)$$

where

$$V_i = \frac{X_i}{X_0}. \qquad (8.5.2)$$

Example 8.5.1. Consider a balanced system composed of three subsystems $(ss_1, ss_2,$ and $ss_3)$. Each of these subsystems consists of a machine (S_i) and an input queue (Q_i). Samples of the row sizes of Q_1, Q_2, and Q_3 were collected every $18s$ for a period $T = 30\,min$ (1800 s). We obtained, therefore, three (3) samples with one hundred (100) measures each. A queue representation of such a system is depicted in Figure 8.6. The three samples were recorded as in Table 8.3. The average sizes of the respective queues were $\overline{N_1} = 20.862$, $\overline{N_2} = 8.123$, and $\overline{N_3} = 12.237$.

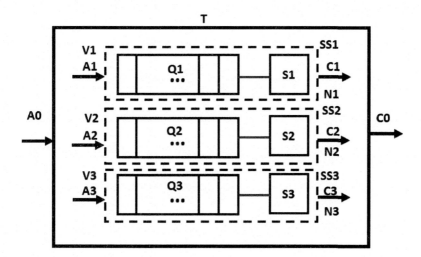

Figure 8.6 Multiple Resources System Model.

The number of transactions completed by $(ss_1, ss_2,$ and $ss_3)$ and by the system were $C_1 = 120$, $C_2 = 90$, $C_3 = 70$, and $C_0 = 210$, respectively. Therefore, the respective throughputs were:

$X_1 = \frac{120}{1800} = 0.0667\,tps$, $X_2 = \frac{90}{1800} = 0.05\,tps$, $X_3 = \frac{70}{1800} = 0.0389\,tps$, and $X_0 = \frac{210}{1800} = 0.1167\,tps$. Therefore, as $R = \frac{N}{X_0}$, we have:

$$R_1 = \frac{\overline{N_1}}{X_1} = 312.936\,s,$$

$$R_2 = \frac{\overline{N_2}}{X_2} = 162.451\,s,\,\text{and}$$

$$R_3 = \frac{\overline{N_3}}{X_3} = 314.653\,s.$$

We also know that $V_1 = \frac{X_1}{X_0}$, $V_2 = \frac{X_2}{X_0}$, and $V_3 = \frac{X_3}{X_0}$.

Thus:

$$V_1 = \frac{0.0667}{0.1167} = 0.5714,$$

$$V_2 = \frac{0.05}{0.1167} = 0.4286,\,\text{and}$$

$$V_3 = \frac{0.0389}{0.1167} = 0.3333.$$

As

$$R = \sum_{i=1}^{k} V_i \times R_i,$$

and $k = 3$, we have:

$$R = V_1 \times R_1 + V_2 \times R_2 + V_3 \times R_3;$$

hence, $R = 0.5714 \times 312.9368\,s + 0.4286 \times 162.451\,s + 0.3333 \times 314.6533\,s$.

Thus, the mean response time (mean residence time) of a transaction in the system was $R = 353.3273\,s$.

$\square$

8.6 INTERACTIVE RESPONSE TIME LAW

In an interactive system, users (clients) generate requests to a server or a set of servers such as a cloud-based system that responds to user machines. Then, after a certain period Z (which may represent the time the user thinks of the subsequent transactions to be executed), users send the next request. In this case, Little's law is applied to analyze the system in which we also consider the user (machine) performance behavior.

Consider a system with a single user and a server as depicted in Figure 8.7.a. The time interval between the instant the user sends a request and the instant the user gets the corresponding response is $R' = R + L_t + L_r$, where $R = D + W$ is the time to process the transaction on the server taking into account internal server waiting times (W), and D is the processing time transaction demanded from the server. L_t is the time to transmit the request, and L_r is the time to transmit the result. Since the user spends Z time units "thinking" to make the subsequent request, the period between two concurrent requests corresponds to $R' + Z$ (See Figure 8.8).

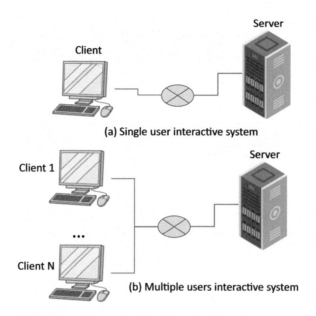

(a) Single user interactive system

(b) Multiple users interactive system

Figure 8.7   Interactive Systems.

If the system is monitored for a period T, the number of requests processed will be

$$\frac{T}{R' + Z}.$$

If we disregard the request transmission time, L_t, and then the result transmission time, L_r, we get

$$\frac{T}{R + Z}.$$

Consider now that we have N clients (with similar behavior) concurrently sending requests to the system (see Figure 8.7.b). Therefore, the total number of transactions processed in period T is

$$\frac{N \times T}{R + Z}.$$

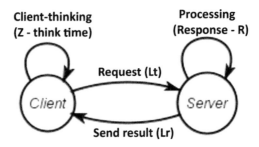

Figure 8.8 Interactive System – Transaction Cycle.

We know that the throughput is the ratio between the number of transactions processed and the period of observation (monitoring); therefore:

$$X = \frac{\frac{N \times T}{R+Z}}{T} = \frac{N \times T}{R+Z} \times \frac{1}{T} = \frac{N}{R+Z}.$$

Therefore, we have:

$$X = \frac{N}{R+Z} \qquad (8.6.1)$$

and

$$R = \frac{N}{X} - Z. \qquad (8.6.2)$$

If we disregard internal server waiting times (W), we obtain

$$X = \frac{N}{D+Z}. \qquad (8.6.3)$$

It is worth mentioning that if we assume $Z = 0$ in Equation 8.6.2, it reduces to Little's law.

Example 8.6.1. Consider the example shown in Figure 8.9. This system consists of two nodes (CN_1 and CN_2), a cloud manager (CM), and a communication system (links, routers, and switches). This system is used by users, N.

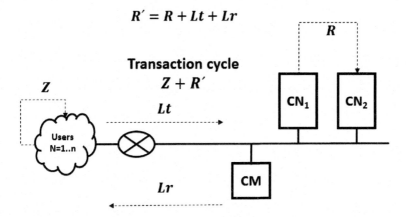

Figure 8.9   Tiny Private Cloud.

In our study, we considered only one user ($N = 1$). Counting on previous experiments, we adopted a think time (Z) equal to $4936.00\,ms$. We measured the transmission times of the requests, the processing at the nodes CN_1 and CN_2, and the transmission time of the results to the user. The system was monitored by $T = 505887.026\,ms$. During this period, $C_0 = 100$ requests (transactions) were processed. The measured values of D, L_t, and L_r were recorded in tables similar to Table 8.3. The mean values for D, L_t, and L_r were $99.974\,ms$, $7.886\,ms$, and $15.392\,ms$, respectively.

Since:

$$\overline{R} = \overline{L_t} + \overline{D} + \overline{L_r} =$$
$$\overline{R} = 7.886 + 99.974 + 15.392 = 123.252\,ms.$$

and as $\overline{Z} = 4935.619\,ms$ and $N = 1$,

we have:

$$\overline{X} = \frac{N}{\overline{R} + \overline{Z}} = \frac{1}{123.252 + 4935.61} = 197.7 \times 10^{-6}\,tpms.$$

If we consider $\overline{L_t} = 0$ and $\overline{L_r} = 0$; thus $\overline{R} = \overline{D}$. Hence,

$$\overline{X} = \frac{N}{\overline{D} + \overline{Z}} = \frac{1}{99.974 + 4935.61} = 198.6 \times 10^{-6}\,tpms.$$

If we also consider $\overline{Z} = 0$, then:

$$\overline{X} = \frac{N}{\overline{D}} = \frac{1}{99.974} = 10.0026 \times 10^{-3}\,tpms.$$

□

8.7 BOTTLENECK ANALYSIS AND BOUNDS

The Demand law shows that the demanded time of a transaction to a resource i is proportional to the utilization of this resource since $D_i = \frac{U_i}{X_0}$. Since X_0 is the system throughput, that is, it is used to calculate the demand for all the resources of the system, so the resource with the highest demand is the most demanded resource; hence the "bottleneck" of the system. This device is the primary component that bounds system performance. Therefore, priority should be given to identifying this resource to improve system performance. This is a critical step in improving overall system performance.

Let us look at two limiting scenarios:

- First, consider that each cloud node can completely execute a transaction initiated by a user; that is, the transaction is completely executed in only one resource.

- Then consider the opposite scenario, in which the complete transaction execution demands the use of every system resource.

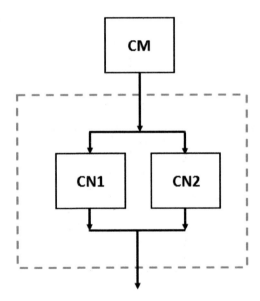

Figure 8.10   Tiny Private Cloud - Concurrent Execution.

We can represent these situations through a tiny cloud system composed of two physical nodes (CN_1 and CN_2)) and a cloud manager (CM). Consider also that nodes CN_1 and CN_2 have different performance capabilities. The CM has as the main function (in this constraint context) to be a load balancer, and the delays related to its function are incorporated into the nodes' delays.

Let us first consider the first scenario since any of the two nodes (CN_1 and CN_2) can execute their transactions separately. This scenario is represented by the information flow depicted in Figure 8.10.

The time demanded of node CN_1 related to a transaction execution is denoted by D_{CN_1}, and the demand for this transaction at node CN_2 is D_{CN_2}. Therefore, the system bottleneck is the CN_k, where $k = Max\{D_{CN_1}, D_{CN_2}\}$. Therefore the resource with the highest demand, $D_{max} = Max\{D_1, D_2\}$, is the "bottleneck" of the system.

Generalizing, for M components, we have:

$$k = arg\,Max_j^M\{D_j\}$$

is the resource with the highest demand ("bottleneck" of the system), and $D_{max} = Max_j^M\{D_j\}$. Hence,

$$X_0 = \frac{U_{CN_k}}{D_k} = \frac{U_{CN_k}}{D_{max}}.$$

As $Max(U_{CN_k}) = 1$, we have:

$$X_0 \leq \frac{1}{D_{max}}. \tag{8.7.1}$$

So:

$$R \geq \frac{N}{X_0} - Z = N \times D_{max} - Z.$$

Therefore:

$$R \geq N \times D_{max} - Z. \tag{8.7.2}$$

Let us now consider the second scenario. In this scenario, transaction processing requires every system resource, and the use of these resources is sequential. To illustrate this scenario, consider the infrastructure we have adopted (the tiny cloud composed of a cloud manager (CM) and two nodes (CN_1 and CN_2)) and the respective information flow depicted in Figure 8.11. We also consider that the delays related to the cloud manager are built into node delays.

From the General Law of Response Time, we know that:

$$R = \sum_{i=1}^{k} v_i \times R_i.$$

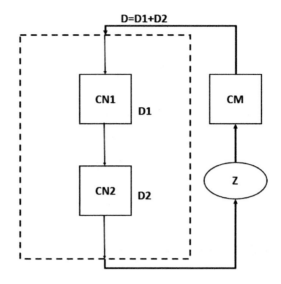

Figure 8.11 Tiny Private Cloud - Sequential Execution.

Applying it to the case of Figure 8.11, we have:

$$R = v_1 \times R_1 + v_2 \times R_2.$$

It is known that

$$R_i = W_i + S_i.$$

Thus:

$$R \geq v_1 \times S_1 + v_2 \times S_2.$$

As $D_i = v_i \times S_i$, then:

$$R \geq D_1 + D_2.$$

We denote

$$D = D_1 + D_2.$$

Generalizing for M co-actors, we have:

$$D = \sum_{i=1}^{M} D_i.$$

Therefore:

$$R \geq D = \sum_{i=1}^{M} D_i \qquad (8.7.3)$$

From the General Law of Response Time, the throughput can be expressed by:

$$X = \frac{N}{R+Z}.$$

If $N = 1$, then:

$$X = \frac{1}{R+Z}.$$

Considering that in order to execute the transaction entirely, every resource is used (in a sequential way), that is, $R = D$, we obtain:

$$X = \frac{1}{D+Z}.$$

If $N > 1$, then:

$$X = \frac{N}{R(N)+Z} \leq \frac{1}{D+Z},$$

since $R(N) \leq D$.

$X(N)$ and $R(N)$ are, respectively, the system throughput and the response time (residence time) of the system when N users are considered.

For $Z = 0$,

$$X(N) \leq \frac{N}{D}. \qquad (8.7.4)$$

From the General Law of Response Time, we have that the response time can be expressed by:

$$R = \frac{N}{X} - Z.$$

We know that $X_0 \leq \frac{1}{D_{max}}$;

therefore:

$$R \geq \frac{N}{X_0} - Z = N \times D_{max} - Z.$$

That is:

$$R \geq N \times D_{max} - Z. \tag{8.7.5}$$

Considering Inequation 8.7.1 and Inequation 8.7.4, we have:

$$X \leq Min(\frac{1}{D_{max}}, \frac{N}{D}). \tag{8.7.6}$$

We also have

$$R \geq N \times D_{max} - Z \tag{8.7.7}$$

and

$$R \geq D. \tag{8.7.8}$$

Therefore

$$R \geq Max(D, N \times D_{max} - Z). \tag{8.7.9}$$

For $Z = 0$, we have:

$$R \geq Max(D, N \times D_{max}). \tag{8.7.10}$$

The knee, where the two curves meet, is determined by:

$$Knee = \frac{D + Z}{D_{max}}. \tag{8.7.11}$$

If we consider $Z = 0$, we have:

$$Knee = \frac{D}{D_{max}}. \tag{8.7.12}$$

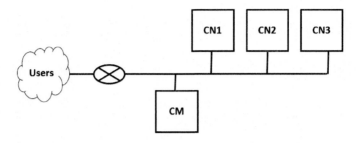

Figure 8.12   Four Nodes Private Cloud - CM, NC_1, NC_2, NC_3.

Example 8.7.1. Consider an example in which an application requests a service (execution of transactions) to the private cloud depicted in Figure 8.12. The respective services are hosted on the nodes NC_1, NC_2, and NC_3. This system was monitored for 30 min. The mean values of the respective transaction demands on each node are $D_{NC_1} = 38.990\,ms$, $D_{NC_2} = 32.991\,ms$, and $D_{NC_3} = 29.9902\,ms$. Therefore, $D_{max} = 38.990\,ms$ and $D = 38.990 + 32.991 + 29.9902 = 99.974\,ms$.

This experiment was carried out in two stages. First, we studied the system throughput concerning the number of users who requested the execution of transactions. In this step, we consider the following number of users: $N = 1, 2, 3, 4, 5$, and 6:

$$X_0 = \frac{1}{D_{max}},$$

and

$$X(N) = \frac{N}{D} = \frac{N}{\sum_{i=1}^{3} D_{NC_i}}.$$

The guaranteed throughput is provided by:

$$X \leq Min(\frac{1}{D_{max}}, \frac{N}{D}).$$

The "Knee" can be calculated by:

$$Knee = \frac{D}{D_{max}} = \frac{99.974}{36.990} = 2.703.$$

The system throughput and the respective asymptotic curves are shown in Figure 8.13.

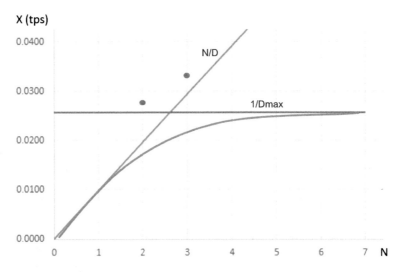

Figure 8.13 $X(N) = \frac{N}{D}$ and $X = \frac{1}{D_{max}}$ vs NC.

The red line shows the maximum throughput that the system can guarantee without considering communication time and the users´ interaction delay; that is, users request a service execution as soon as they receive a response from the previous request ($Z = 0$ – think time). Due to other delays, queuing, what is expected is that the actual limits follow the asymptote in green.

Keep in mind, however, that the system throughput may occasionally be higher than the maximum guaranteed throughput (red line); after all, the limit throughput takes into account D_{max} of the "parallel" system, since each node can execute the transactions alone. Again, the highest throughput is achieved when the fastest node executes the transaction. However, the transaction may be processed by a slower node. Therefore, the maximum guaranteed throughput should be estimated considering the slowest node. Hence, notice the two dots above the red line. The values of the blue dotted line (obtained for $N = 1, 2, 3, 4, 5$, and 6) that are above the red line values cannot be guaranteed.

The second stage of the study evaluates the behavior of the system response time as a function of the number of users requesting transaction executions. Here, we consider the following number of users: $N = 1, 2, 3, 4, 5$, and 6 and plot the graphs of these two functions:

$$R = D,$$

$$R = N \times D_{max},$$

where $D = \sum_{i=1}^{3} D_{NC_i}$, and $D_{max} = Max_{i=1}^{3}(D_{NC_i})$.

The guaranteed response time is provided by:

$$R \geq Max(D, N \times D_{max}).$$

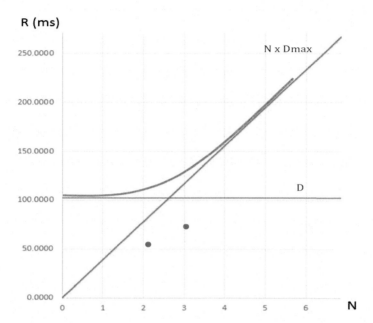

Figure 8.14 $R(N)$ vs NC.

Figure 8.14 shows the response time guaranteed by the system (if we disregard the communication) and that users request the execution of new transactions as soon as they receive the results from the previous transaction (think time – Z equal to zero). As shown for the throughput, due to other delays and queuing, the actual limits must follow an asymptote similar to the one depicted in green. Again, response times shorter than the guaranteed limit are possible since a transaction instance may be executed on nodes (resources) faster than the slowest one (Notice the red dots below the red curve). The slowest node is the system bottleneck for that class of transaction on the system.

□

Example 8.7.2. A computer system was monitored for $4 \times 10^4\,ms$ (T). There were 175000 transactions ($C_{server} = C_0$) processed by the server. Each transaction requires, on average, access to $60\,KB$. Assume disk sectors have 512 bytes; hence the mean number of sectors accessed per transaction (NS) is

$$NS = \frac{60 \times 1024\,bystes}{512\,bystes} = 120\,sectors.$$

If mean time to access (read and write) one sector of the disk is $0.008332\,ms$ ($S_{disk,1\,sector}$), then the time to access $60\,KB$ is

$$D_{disk} = NS \times S_{disk,1\,sector} = 120 \times 0.008332\,ms = 0.99984\,ms.$$

In the observation period, the processor utilization is 48% ($U_{server} = U_{cpu}$). The processor service demand is estimated by

$$D_{server} = \frac{U_{server}}{X_0},$$

where

$$X_0 = \frac{C_0}{T} = \frac{175000\,transactions}{600000\,ms} = 0.29167\,tpms.$$

Hence

$$D_{server} = \frac{U_{server}}{X_0} = \frac{0.48}{0.29167\,tpms} = 1.64571\,ms.$$

As $D_{server} > D_{disk}$, the server processor is the system bottleneck.

$\square$

EXERCISES

Exercise 1. A computational system was observed for $30\,s$. In this period, a web server handled 120 transactions. Each transaction process demands, on average, two accesses to a storage system. The mean service time at the storage system is $25\,ms$. What is the mean utilization of the storage system?

Exercise 2. A file server was monitored for $300 \times 10^3\,ms$ (T). The server processed 80000 transactions. Each transaction requires, on average, access (reads and writes) to $120\,KB$. Assume the disk sectors have 512 bytes, and the average time to access (reads and writes) one sector is $= 0.009\,ms$. During this observation period, the processor had utilization of 51%. **(a)** Estimate the processor service demand. **(b)** Calculate the disk utilization. **(c)** Which component is the "bottleneck" of this system?

Exercise 3. Consider an e-mail server that consists of one processor (CPU) and two disk drives (D_1 and D_2). Each typical transaction accesses the D_1 five times and accesses D_2 six times, as well as twelve accesses to the CPU. The service time of D_1 and D_2 is $25\,ms$ and $30\,ms$, respectively. The CPU service time is $12\,ms$. **(a)** What is the service demand of each device? **(b)** If D_1 utilization is 58%, what are the CPU and D_2 utilizations? **(c)** What is the maximum throughput of the system?

Exercise 4. A computational system was monitored for $3600\,s$. In this period, 5×10^3 requests were processed. What is the utilization of the disk if its mean service time was about $25\,ms$ and the disk was visited 3 times in every request?

Exercise 5. Consider a system composed of one processor and two disks (D_1 and D_2). This system is monitored during $3600\,s$. The processor's and the D_2's utilization were 30% and 58%, respectively. Each transaction executed by the system, on average, executes seven requests to D_1 and four requests to D_2. The mean service time at D_2 is $25\,ms$ and at D_1 is $20\,ms$. **(a)** Estimate the system throughput. **(b)** Calculate the utilization of D_1. **(c)** Compute the mean service demands at the processor, D_1, and D_2.

Exercise 6. A computational system was monitored for $3600\,s$. During this time, 10^4 transactions were executed, and 1.7×10^4 read/write requests were executed on a disk. The disk utilization was 40%. **(a)** What is the mean number of read-write requests per transaction on the disk? **(b)** What is the disk mean service time?

Exercise 7. A client-server system was observed for three hours. During the observation period, the average utilization of a specific disk was 45%. On average, each client request processing transaction makes three accesses to the disk, whose service time is $15\,10^{-3}\,s$. Assuming 140 clients, and the average think time being $8\,s$, calculate the average response time.

9 Discrete Time Markov Chain

This chapter introduces the concepts of the stochastic process and Markov chains. It focuses on the discrete-time Markov chain, DTMC, by discussing the respective Chapman-Kolmogorov equation and transient and steady-state solutions. The chapter also examines the concepts of mean recurrence time, mean first passage time, holding time, and mean time to absorption. These methods and concepts are illustrated by examples that enable the readers to gain understanding of each of these concepts.

Markov chains have been applied in many areas of science and engineering. For example, they have been widely adopted for performance and dependability evaluation of manufacturing, logistics, communication, computer systems, and so forth [172]. Markov chains have their name from the Russian mathematician Andrei Andreevich Markov. Markov was born on June 14th, 1856, in Ryazan, Russia, and died on July 20th, 1922, in Saint Petersburg [376].

In 1907, Markov began the study of an important type of change process, in which the outcome of an experiment can affect the outcome of the subsequent experiment. This type of process is now called a Markov chain [445]. Agner Karup Erlang applied Markovian techniques for studying telephone traffic planning problems for reliable service provisioning [130], and in 1931, Andrey Nikolaevich Kolmogorov, in his famous paper "Über die analytischen Methoden in der Wahrscheinlichkeitsrechnung" (Analytic Methods in Probability Theory) laid the foundations for the modern theory of Markov processes [216] [247].

The bibliography offers many books on Markov Chains [24, 52, 138, 325, 413, 437]. These books cover Markov chain theory and applications in different depths and styles. This chapter presents a concise overview of the Markov chain theory and discusses many modeling applications to the performance evaluation of systems.

9.1 STOCHASTIC PROCESSES

In classical physics, a primary role is played by the fundamental principle of scientific determinism: the system state at an instant t_1 may be deduced from the state of the system at an earlier time t_0. As a consequence of this principle, one obtains a primary method of analyzing systems: the state of a system at a given time may be deduced from a knowledge of its state at an earlier time.

For systems that obey probabilistic laws, a similar principle may enunciate the probability that the system will be in a given state at a given time t_2 may be deduced from a knowledge of its state at any earlier time t_1 [325]. Thus, stochastic processes may represent such systems. Thus, stochastic processes provide the foundation for modeling and quantitatively studying behaviors of systems that obey probabilistic laws.

A stochastic process is defined as a family of random variables $(\{X_i(t) : t \in T\})$ indexed through some parameter (t). Each random variable $(X_i(t))$ is defined on some probability space. The parameter t usually represents time, so $X_i(t)$ denotes the value assumed by the random variable at time t. T is called the parameter space and is a subset of $\mathbb{R}$.

If T is discrete, that is, $T = \{0, 1, 2, ...\}$, the process is classified as a discrete-(time) parameter stochastic process. On the other hand, if T is continuous, that is, $T = \{t : 0 \le t < \infty\}$, the process is a continuous-(time) parameter stochastic process.

Consider a stochastic process $\{X_i(t)\}$;the values assumed by its random variables $(X_i(t))$ define the stochastic process state. The set of all possible states define the state space of the process. The state space can be continuous or discrete. Figures 9.1, 9.2, 9.3, and 9.4 depict a Discrete-State-Space Discrete-Time, a Discrete-State-Space Continuous-Time, a Continuous-State-Space Discrete-Time, and a Continuous-State-Space Continuous-Time Process, respectively. Discrete state space stochastic processes are often called stochastic chains. Observe that in the Continuous-State-Space processes (Figures 9.3 and 9.4) the state values $(X_i(t) = x_i)$ are values in $\mathbb{R}$, whereas the state values of Discrete-State-Space processes (Figures 9.1 and 9.2) belong to $\mathbb{Z}$.

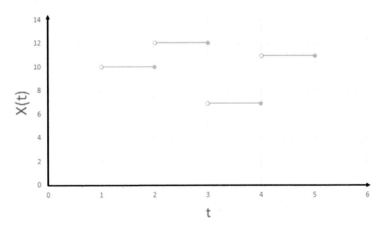

Figure 9.1 Discrete-State-Space Discrete-Time Process.

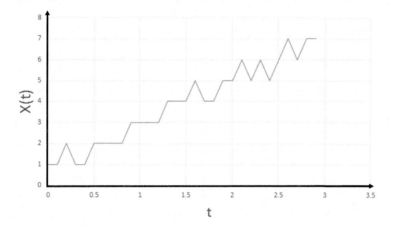

Figure 9.2   Discrete-State-Space Continuous-Time Process.

The complete probabilistic description of a stochastic process might be provided by the joint cumulative probability distribution function (CDF) of its random variables. Nevertheless, for arbitrary processes, obtaining such a probability distribution is often not feasible. Fortunately, for many of the stochastic processes we find in practice, there are relatively simple means to accomplish this task [72]. Thus, the joint probability distribution function of stochastic processes may be formally defined as:

Definition 9.1.1. Consider a stochastic process $\{X_i(t_i)\}$, $i = \{1,...,n\}$. Its the joint cumulative distribution function (CDF) is defined by:

$$F_{\mathbf{X(t)}}(\mathbf{x},\mathbf{t}) = P(X_1(t_1) \leq x_1, X_2(t_2) \leq x_2, \ ... \ , X_n(t_n) \leq x_n),$$

where $\mathbf{X(t)} = (X_1(t_1), X_2(t_2), \ ... \ X_n(t_n))$ is the stochastic variables´ vector, $\mathbf{t} = (t_1, t_2, \ ... \ t_n)$ is the parameter vector, and $\mathbf{x} = (x_1, x_2, \ ... \ x_n)$ is the state vector.

For a discrete-time stochastic process, the joint probability mass function (PMF) may be formally defined as follows:

Definition 9.1.2. Consider a discrete-time stochastic process $\{X_i(t_i)\}$, $i = \{1,...,n\}$. Its joint probability mass function (PMF) is defined by:

$$P_{\mathbf{X(t)}}(\mathbf{x},\mathbf{t}) = P(X_1(t_1) = x_1, \ X_2(t_2) = x_2, \ ... \ , \ X_n(t_n) = x_n),$$

where $\mathbf{X(t)} = (X_1(t_1), X_2(t_2), \ ... \ X_n(t_n))$ is the stochastic variables´ vector, $\mathbf{t} = (t_1, t_2, \ ... \ t_n)$ is the parameter vector, and $\mathbf{x} = (x_1, x_2, \ ... \ x_n)$ is the state vector.

For a discrete-time stochastic process, it is usually representing a random variable $X_i(t_i)$ by the simpler notation X_i, in which the index parameter is omitted. Therefore,

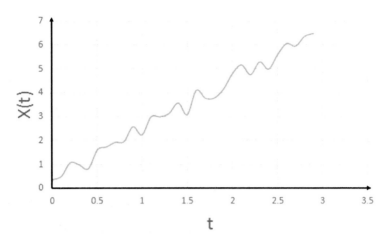

Figure 9.3   Continuous-State-Space Continuous-Time Process.

whenever the more straightforward representation may be adopted without confusion, we should favor it.

For a continuous-time stochastic process, the joint probability density function (PDF) may be formally defined as follows:

Definition 9.1.3. Consider a continuous-time stochastic process $\{X_i(t_i)\}$, $i = \{1,...,n\}$. Its joint probability density function (PDF) is defined by:

$$f_{\mathbf{X(t)}}(\mathbf{x},\mathbf{t}) = \frac{\partial F_{\mathbf{X}}(\mathbf{x},\mathbf{t})}{\partial t_1\, \partial t_2 ... \partial t_n},$$

where $\mathbf{X(t)} = (X_1(t_1), X_2(t_2),\ ...\ X_n(t_n))$ is the stochastic variables´ vector, $\mathbf{t} = (t_1, t_2,\ ...\ t_n)$ is the parameter vector, and $\mathbf{x} = (x_1, x_2,\ ...\ x_n)$ is the state vector.

In some models, the performance attributes we are interested in may depend on the time t at which the system is started. The evolution of a process that started at t_0 may be different from the evolution of that same process if it started at t_1 ($t_1 \neq t_0$). A process whose progress depends on the time at which it started its execution is said to be **nonstationary**. On the other hand, a stochastic process is said to be **stationary** when it is invariant under an arbitrary shift of the time origin [72, 325, 413, 437]. A stationary stochastic process is stationary if its joint distribution is invariant to shifts in time, that is:

$$P(\mathbf{X}(t_1) \leq \mathbf{x_1}) = P(\mathbf{X}(t_1 + \alpha) \leq \mathbf{x_1}).$$

At this point, we also define the homogeneity concept. An **homogeneous** process is defined when the actual time instances are not important for its evolution, but only

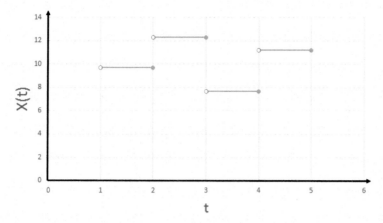

Figure 9.4 Continuous-State-Space Discrete-Time Process.

their relative differences. For instance, consider discrete-time discrete-state space stochastic process $\mathbf{X(t)}$, if

$$P(\mathbf{X(t_n)} = \mathbf{x_n} \,|\, \mathbf{X(t_{n-r})}) = \mathbf{x_{n-r}} =$$
$$P(\mathbf{X(t_m)} = \mathbf{x_m} \,|\, \mathbf{X(t_{m-r})}) = \mathbf{x_{m-r}},$$

then $\mathbf{X(t)}$ is homogeneous.

Consider a stochastic process $\{X_1(t), X_2(t), \dots, X_n(t)\}$ in which all its random variables are mutually independent (**independent process**); then:

$$F_{\mathbf{X(t)}}(\mathbf{x,t}) = P(X_1(t) \leq x_1, X_2(t) \leq x_2, \dots, X_n(t) \leq x_n) =$$

$$F_{X_1(t)}(x_1,t)\, F_{X_2(t)}(x_2,t) \,\dots\, F_{X_n(t)}(x_n,t) =$$

$$F_{\mathbf{X(t)}}(\mathbf{x,t}) = \prod_{i=1}^{n} F_{X_i(t)}(x_i,t)$$

is the respective joint cumulative distribution function.

A stochastic process is called a **Markov process** if its future reachable states $(\mathbf{X(t_n)} = \mathbf{x_n})$ depend only upon its current state $(\mathbf{X(t_{n-1})} = \mathbf{x_{n-1}})$. In other words, it means that the paths the process walked to the current state do not affect the chances of reaching its next feasible states (Memoryless property – Geometric random variable – see Section 5.1). More formally:

$$P(\mathbf{X(t_n)} = \mathbf{x_n} \,|\, \mathbf{X(t_1)} = \mathbf{x_1}, \mathbf{X(t_2)} = \mathbf{x_2}, \dots,$$

$$\mathbf{X(t_{n-1})} = \mathbf{x_{n-1}}) = P(\mathbf{X(t_n)} = \mathbf{x_n} \,|\, \mathbf{X(t_{n-1})} = \mathbf{x_{n-1}}), \qquad (9.1.1)$$

where $\mathbf{x_i}$ is the state vector at time instant $\mathbf{t_i}$.

A Markov process is a stochastic chain, and as the index parameter may be either discrete or continuous, a Markov process can be classified as either a Discrete Time Markov Chain (DTMC) or as a Continuous Time Markov Chain (CTMC).

9.2 CHAPMAN-KOLMOGOROV EQUATION

Consider a discrete-time discrete-state space process X, and two of its states, i and j (see Figure 9.5). The one-step state transition probabilities are denoted as:

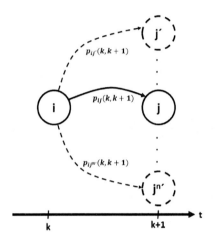

Figure 9.5 Transitions Between Two States.

$$p_{ij}(k,k+1) \equiv P(X_{k+1} = j \,|\, X_k = i),$$

for any discrete time instant $k = 0, 1, \ldots$ Besides, it is clear that $0 \le p_{ij}(k,k+1) \le 1$ and $\sum_{\forall j} p_{ij}(k,k+1) = 1$.

Let's extend the one-step state transition probabilities and consider n-step state transition probabilities, $n = 1, 2, \ldots$ The n-step transition probabilities are represented by:

$$p_{ij}(k,k+n) \equiv P(X_{k+n} = j \,|\, X_k = i). \qquad (9.2.1)$$

Now, consider reaching the state j after n time steps from the state i, taking into account the following intermediate states $v \in V$ reached at the instant u (see Figure 9.6). In other words, if we condition the event $[X_{k+n} = j \,|\, X_k = i]$ on $[X_u = v]$, and use the rule of total probability, we have:

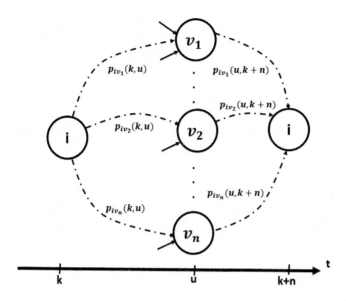

Figure 9.6 n-Steps Transition States.

$$p_{ij}(k,k+n) = \sum_{\forall v \in V} P(X_{k+n} = j \mid X_u = v, \, X_k = i) \times P(X_u = v \mid X_k = i). \quad (9.2.2)$$

By the memoryless property (random variables geometrically distributed – see Section 5.1):

$$P(X_{k+n} = j \mid X_u = v, \, X_k = i) = P(X_{k+n} = j \mid X_u = v) = p_{vj}(u,k+n).$$

Moreover, the second term in the sum in 9.2.2 is:

$$P(X_u = v \mid X_k = i) = p_{iv}(k,u).$$

Hence:

$$p_{ij}(k,k+n) = \sum_{\forall v \in V} p_{iv}(k,u) \times p_{vj}(u,k+n), \quad (9.2.3)$$

$k < u \le k+n$. The above equation is called the **Chapman-Kolmogorov equation**, and is a fundamental for the study of DTMCs. The Chapman-Kolmogorov equation may also be presented in matrix form:

$$\mathbf{P}(k,k+n) \equiv (p_{ij}(k,k+n)), \quad i,j = 0,1,2,...$$

Thus:

$$\mathbf{P}(k, k+n) = \mathbf{P}(k, u) \times \mathbf{P}(u, k+n).$$

Chosing $u = k + n - 1$, we have:

$$\mathbf{P}(k, k+n) = \mathbf{P}(k, k+n-1) \times \mathbf{P}(k+n-1, k+n). \tag{9.2.4}$$

Equation 9.2.4 is known as the **forward Chapman-Kolmogorov equation**. If we adopt $u = k + 1$, we have:

$$\mathbf{P}(k, k+n) = \mathbf{P}(k, k+1) \times \mathbf{P}(k+1, k+n). \tag{9.2.5}$$

The Equation 9.2.5 is known as the **backward Chapman-Kolmogorov equation**. Whenever the transition probability $p_{ij}(k, k+1)$ is independent of k for all $i, j \in X$, the Markov chain is said to be **homogeneous**. In simple terms, in homogeneous Markov chains, the probability of a state transition from i to j is always the same, regardless of the point in time transition occurs. In this case, we use the notation:

$$p_{ij} = P(X_{k+1} = j \mid X_k = i),$$

where p_{ij} is independent of k. As already mentioned, homogeneity is a form of stationarity that applies to transition probabilities only.

In simple terms, in homogeneous Markov chains, the probability of a state transition from i to j is always the same, regardless of the point in time when the transition occurs.

In a homogeneous Markov chain, the n-step transition probability $p_{ij}(k, k+n)$ may be concisely represented by p_{ij}^n. Therefore, by setting $u = k + m$ ($m < n$), Equation 9.2.3 may be expressed as:

$$p_{ij}(k, k+n) = \sum_{\forall v \in V} p_{iv}(k, k+m) \times p_{vj}(k+m, k+n) =$$

$$p_{ij}^n = \sum_{\forall v \in V} p_{iv}^m \times p_{vj}^{n-m}.$$

For $m = n - 1$, we have the forward Chapman-Kolmogorov equation for a homogeneous Markov chain:

$$p_{ij}^n = \sum_{\forall v \in V} p_{iv}^{n-1} \times p_{vj}. \tag{9.2.6}$$

In matrix form, we have:

$$\mathbf{P}(n) = \mathbf{P}(n-1) \times \mathbf{P}(1) = \qquad\qquad (9.2.7)$$

$$\mathbf{P}(n) = \mathbf{P}(n-1) \times \mathbf{P} =$$

$$\mathbf{P}^n = \mathbf{P}^{n-1} \times \mathbf{P},$$

where $\mathbf{P}(n) = \mathbf{P}^n \equiv (p_{ij}^n)$, and $\mathbf{P}$ is the one-step state **transition probability matrix**. From this point on, we will be interested only in the homogeneous Markov chain. Otherwise, we explicitly state it.

Example 9.2.1. Consider a computer system that may be functional (UP) or in failed (DOWN) state ($\mathscr{X} = \{UP, DOWN\}$). This system's state is checked every hour. If the system is in an UP state, the probability that it stays in that state in the next hour is α. On the other hand, if it is the *DOWN* state, the probability of staying in the *DOWN* state over the next hour is β.

The respective diagram of this DTMC is depicted in Figure 9.7, and its transition probability matrix is:

$$\mathbf{P} = \begin{pmatrix} \alpha & 1-\alpha \\ 1-\beta & \beta \end{pmatrix}$$

$$\mathbf{P} = \begin{pmatrix} 0.9 & 0.1 \\ 0.7 & 0.3 \end{pmatrix}$$

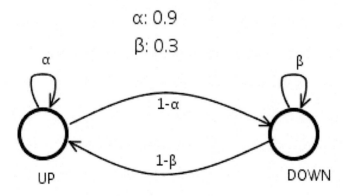

Figure 9.7 Two States DTMC.

The 4-step transition probability matrix is:

$$\mathbf{P}(4) = \mathbf{P}^4 = \begin{pmatrix} 0.875 & 0.125 \\ 0.874 & 0.126 \end{pmatrix}$$

Therefore, if the system is in the UP state at $n = 0$, then the probability of being in the UP state after 4 hours is 0.875. The probability of being in the $DOWN$ state is 0.125. If we consider that the system is in the $DOWN$ state at $n = 0$, then the probability of being in the UP state after 4 hours is 0.874, and the probability of being in the $DOWN$ state is 0.126.

□

Now, let us analyze the second example.

Example 9.2.2. A processor was monitored for a period $T = 3600\,s$. Samples of the processor's state were recorded. The processor's states are: B (Busy), I (Idle), and W (Waiting); hence the state space is $\mathscr{X} = \{B, I, W\}$. The time between samples (TBS) was $1\,s$. The DTMC diagram that depicts the transition between states is shown in Figure 9.8.

The transition probabilities are denoted by p_{BB}, p_{BW}, p_{BI}, p_{II}, p_{IW}, p_{IB}, p_{WW}, p_{WI}, and p_{WB}. The transition probability matrix, therefore, is:

$$\mathbf{P} = \begin{pmatrix} p_{BB} & p_{BI} & p_{BW} \\ p_{IB} & p_{II} & p_{IW} \\ p_{WB} & p_{WI} & p_{WW} \end{pmatrix}$$

The sample trace obtained is a sequence similar to this: $\{B, I, B, B, B, W, I, I, B, B, W, \dots\}$. Based on the sample, the state transition probabilities were estimated through:

$$\hat{p}_{ij} = \frac{\text{The total number of transitions from } i \text{ to } j}{\text{Number of occurrences of state } i}.$$

Table 9.1 presents the number of transitions from each state to each state observed in the sample. We also observed that each state was visited $\#B = 2200$, $\#I = 800$, and $\#W = 600$. Therefore, we could estimate the state transition probabilities (see Table 9.2).

pBB: 0.54091   pII: 0.30875   pWW: 0.33833
pBW: 0.18818   pIB: 0.19125   pWI: 0.16
pBI: 0.27091   pIW: 0.5   pWB: 0.50167

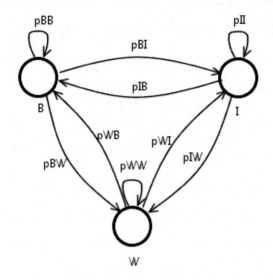

Figure 9.8   Processor´s State.

Table 9.1
State Transition Occurrences

Transitions	Transition Occurrences
$B \to B$	1190
$B \to W$	414
$B \to I$	596
$I \to I$	247
$I \to W$	153
$I \to B$	400
$W \to W$	203
$W \to I$	96
$W \to B$	301
Total	3600

Table 9.2
State Transition Probabilities

$\hat{p}_{ij}$	Values
$\hat{p}_{BB}$	0.54091
$\hat{p}_{BW}$	0.18818
$\hat{p}_{BI}$	0.27091
$\hat{p}_{II}$	0.30875
$\hat{p}_{IW}$	0.19125
$\hat{p}_{IB}$	0.5
$\hat{p}_{WW}$	0.33833
$\hat{p}_{WI}$	0.16
$\hat{p}_{WB}$	0.501667

Therefore, **P** is:

$$\mathbf{P} = \begin{pmatrix} 0.54091 & 0.27091 & 0.18818 \\ 0.5 & 0.30875 & 0.19125 \\ 0.50167 & 0.16 & 0.33833 \end{pmatrix}$$

The 3-step transition probability matrix is:

$$\mathbf{P}^3 = \begin{pmatrix} 0.5217 & 0.2567 & 0.2216 \\ 0.5217 & 0.2566 & 0.22175 \\ 0.5217 & 0.2534 & 0.2249 \end{pmatrix}$$

Thus, if the system is in state B state at $n = 0$, then the probability of being in the B, I, and W states are 0.5217, 0.2567, and 0.2216, respectively, after three steps. If the system is in state I at $n = 0$, then the probabilities of being in states B, I, and W states are 0.5217, 0.2566, and 0.22175, respectively, after 3 seconds. Finally, if the system is in state W at $n = 0$, the probability of being in the B, I, and W states, after three steps, are 0.5217, 0.2534, and 0.2249, respectively. $\quad\square$

9.3 TRANSIENT DISTRIBUTION

The probability of being in state j at step k may be represented by:

$$\pi_j(k) \equiv P(X_k = j). \qquad (9.3.1)$$

The **transient state probability vector** is denoted by:

$$\Pi(k) = (\pi_j(k)). \tag{9.3.2}$$

The dimension of a vector is equal to the dimension of the state space of the chain.

A DTMC is completely specified by its state space $\mathscr{X}$, the transition probability matrix $\mathbf{P}$, and initial state probability $\Pi(0) = (\pi_j(0))$ vector, that is $(\mathscr{X}, \mathbf{P}, \Pi(0))$. The probability of staying in state j after k steps can be calculated by conditioning $\mathbf{P}^k$ on the initial state $\Pi(0)$:

$$\Pi(k) = \Pi(0) \times \mathbf{P}^k. \tag{9.3.3}$$

The probability of being in state k, given that you are in state $k-1$, can also be obtained by multiplying the state vector $\Pi(k-1)$ and the transition probability $\mathbf{P}$, that is:

$$\Pi(k) = \Pi(k-1) \times \mathbf{P}, \tag{9.3.4}$$

since,

$$\Pi(1) = \Pi(0) \times \mathbf{P},$$

$$\Pi(2) = \Pi(1) \times \mathbf{P} = \Pi(0) \times \mathbf{P} \times \mathbf{P} = \Pi(0) \times \mathbf{P}^2.$$

Therefore:

$$\Pi(k) = \Pi(0) \times \mathbf{P} \times \ldots \times \mathbf{P} = \Pi(k) = \Pi(0) \times \mathbf{P}^k.$$

$$\Pi(k) = \Pi(0) \times \mathbf{P}^k. \tag{9.3.5}$$

Example 9.3.1. Example 9.2.2 evaluated a DTMC composed of three states that represented the processor´s states. Considering $\mathbf{P}^3$ and the initial state $\Pi(0) = (0,0,1)$, we can calculate the state vector at $k = 3$, that is, $\Pi(3)$ by applying Equation 9.3.3:

$$\Pi(3) = (0,0,1) \times \begin{pmatrix} 0.5217 & 0.2567 & 0.2216 \\ 0.5217 & 0.2566 & 0.22175 \\ 0.5217 & 0.2534 & 0.2249 \end{pmatrix} =$$

$$\Pi(3) = (0.5217, 0.2534, 0.22491).$$

$\square$

Now, let us consider another example and compute the transient solution.

Example 9.3.2. Figure 9.9 presents a DTMC with six (6) states and this initial state probability vector: $\Pi(0) = (1,0,0,0,0,0)$. The transition probability $\mathbf{P}$ is:

$$\mathbf{P} = \begin{pmatrix} 0 & p01 & 0 & p03 & 0 & 0 \\ p10 & 0 & p12 & 0 & p14 & 0 \\ 0 & 0 & 0 & 0 & 0 & p25 \\ 0 & 0 & 0 & p33 & 0 & 0 \\ 0 & 0 & 0 & 0 & 0 & 0 \\ 0 & 0 & p52 & 0 & 0 & 0 \end{pmatrix} =$$

$$\mathbf{P} = \begin{pmatrix} 0 & \frac{1}{2} & 0 & \frac{1}{2} & 0 & 0 \\ \frac{1}{2} & 0 & \frac{1}{4} & 0 & \frac{1}{4} & 0 \\ 0 & 0 & 0 & 0 & 0 & 1 \\ 0 & 0 & 0 & 1 & 0 & 0 \\ 0 & 0 & 0 & 0 & 0 & 0 \\ 0 & 0 & 1 & 0 & 0 & 0 \end{pmatrix}.$$

The state probability vector at $k = 0, 1, 2,$, and 3 are depicted in Table 9.3[1].

p01: 1/2   p12: 1/4   p14: 1/4   p25: 1
p10: 1/2   p03: 1/2   p33: 1   p52: 1

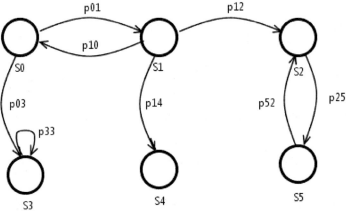

Figure 9.9   Six State DTMC.

---

[1]The notation adopted in the Mercury tool: $P\{s\}$, where s is the state name. The time step is implicitly specified; that is, during evaluation the analyst defines the time step of interest.

Table 9.3
State Probabilities

k	$\pi_{S0}(k)$	$\pi_{S1}(k)$	$\pi_{S2}(k)$	$\pi_{S3}(k)$	$\pi_{S4}(k)$	$\pi_{S5}(k)$
0	1	0	0	0	0	0
1	0	0.5	0	0.5	0	0
2	0.25	0	0.125	0.5	0.125	0
3	0	0.125	0	0.625	0.125	0.125

9.4 STEADY STATE DISTRIBUTION

In the previous section, we were interested in finding the probability of staying in a state i at a time instant k. In the transient analysis, we were interested in computing the probability of states considering a given finite number of steps. For many Discrete-Time Markov Chains (but not all), the rows of $\Pi(k)$ converge to a common steady probability vector when $k \to \infty$; that is, each component of the vector approaches a limiting value. When we have such a convergence, this probability vector is independent of the initial probability, and it is denoted by the **steady-state probability vector (stationary probability vector)**. In more detail, we know that (from Equation 9.3.3):

$$\Pi(k) = \Pi(0) \times \mathbf{P}^k.$$

If $\lim_{k \to \infty} \Pi(k) = \Pi$, then:

$$\Pi = \lim_{k \to \infty} \Pi(k) = \lim_{k \to \infty} \Pi(0) \times \mathbf{P}^k.$$

Nevertheless, if $\Pi = \lim_{k \to \infty} \Pi(k)$, we also have $\Pi = \lim_{k \to \infty} \Pi(k+1)$; hence :

$$\Pi = \lim_{k \to \infty} \Pi(k+1) = \lim_{k \to \infty} \Pi(0) \times \mathbf{P}^{k+1}$$

$$\Pi = \left(\lim_{k \to \infty} \Pi(0) \times \mathbf{P}^k \right) \times \mathbf{P}.$$

As $\lim_{k \to \infty} \Pi(0) \times \mathbf{P}^k = \Pi$, then:

$$\Pi = \Pi \times \mathbf{P}. \tag{9.4.1}$$

Hence, for finding the steady state solution (if there is one), we solve Equation 9.4.1, considering $\Pi \times \mathbb{1}^T = 1$ [2].

---

[2] $\mathbb{1}^T = (1_i)_{|\mathscr{X}|}$ is a column vector, $s_i \in \mathscr{X}$. $\mathscr{X}$ is the state space.

Example 9.4.1. Let us consider the DTMC of Example 9.2.2 and find the steady-state probability vector. The transition probability matrix of the DTMC is:

$$\mathbf{P} = \begin{pmatrix} 0.54091 & 0.27091 & 0.18818 \\ 0.5 & 0.30875 & 0.19125 \\ 0.50167 & 0.16 & 0.33833 \end{pmatrix}$$

We also have that $\pi_B + \pi_I + \pi_W = 1$, then

$$\Pi = \Pi \times \mathbf{P}.$$

$$(\pi_B, \pi_I, \pi_W) = (\pi_B, \pi_I, \pi_W) \times \begin{pmatrix} 0.54091 & 0.27091 & 0.18818 \\ 0.5 & 0.30875 & 0.19125 \\ 0.50167 & 0.16 & 0.33833 \end{pmatrix},$$

$$\pi_B + \pi_I + \pi_W = 1.$$

Solving this system of equations, we have the steady-state probabilities[3]:

$$(\pi_B, \pi_I, \pi_W) = (0.44279, 0.24565, 0.31156).$$

□

As mentioned above, not every Markov chain approaches a steady state. In order to study this subject in more depth, first we need to classify the states of a Markov chain into states that are visited infinitely often and states that are visited only a finite number of times. The following section discusses this subject.

Chapter 10 presents one direct method and one iterative method to calculate steady-state distributions.

9.5 CLASSIFICATION OF STATES, MEAN RECURRENCE TIME, AND MEAN FIRST PASSAGE TIME

This section presents a classification of states of DTMCs. This classification helps us evaluate if a DTMC has a steady-state probability vector. The section also presents a method for calculating the mean recurrence time and the mean first passage time.

Consider a DTMC specified by $MC = (\mathscr{X}, \mathbf{P}, \Pi(0))$, where $\mathscr{X}$ is the state space, $\mathbf{P}$ is the transition probability matrix, and $\Pi(0)$ is the initial state probability vector. A state j is **reachable** from a state i if $p_{ij}(k) > 0$, for any k [172]. The reachability of j from i is depicted by $i \to j$. If i is also reachable from i, $j \to i$, these two states are said to be **communicating**, denoted by $i \sim j$.

The communicating relation ($\sim$) is an equivalence relation [4], since it is:

---

[3] The notation adopted in Mercury tool: $P\{s\}$, where s is the state name.

[4] An equivalence relation is a binary relation that is **reflexive, symmetric**, and **transitive**. Hence, an equivalence relation provides a partition of a set into equivalence classes. Two elements $a, b \in S$ belong to the same equivalence class if and only if a and b are equivalent.

- **transitive** - if $i \sim j$, $j \sim k$, then $k \sim i$,

- **symmetric** - if $i \sim j$, then $j \sim i$, and

- **reflexive** - for $k = 0$, $p_{ii}(0) = 1$, so $i \rightarrow i$; thus $i \sim i$.

As $\sim$ is an equivalence relation, then the DTMC set of states, $\mathscr{X}$, is partitioned into state communicating classes. If every state of the DTMC belongs to the same state communicating class, the **DTMC** is said to be **irreducible**; otherwise the **DTMC** is named **reducible**. The state communicating classes are named according to the characteristic of their state members. These characteristics are discussed as follows.

The period $d_i \in \mathbb{N}$ of a state i is the Greatest Common Divisor (GCD) of those values k for which $p_{ii}(k) > 0$. If the period of a state i is $d_i = 1$, this state is defined as **aperiodic**, in which case, at every time step there is a non-zero probability of residing in state i. A state i is said to be **periodic** if its period is larger than one, that is $d_i > 1$.

For instance, consider the DTMC depicted in Figure 9.10. The chain is composed of six states. The probability of transitioning from state S_0 to S_1 and S_2 is 0.4 and 0.6, respectively. Every other probability of transitions depicted in this DTMC is one.

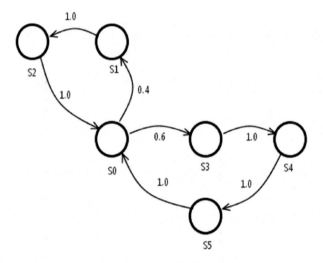

Figure 9.10   Six State DTMC – State Period of $p_{00}(k) > 0$ - $d_0 = 1$.

Table 9.4 presents the probability $p_{00}(k)$, for the respective number of steps $k = 1, 2, 3, 4$, and 5. The greatest common divisor of k from which $p_{00}(k) > 0$ is $GCD(3,4) = 1$, since 3 and 4 are the values of k such that $p_{00}(k) > 0$. Therefore, the period for $p_{00}(k) > 0$ is $d_0 = 1$, then the respective DTMC is aperiodic.

Table 9.4
Six State DTMC – Period of S_0

k	$p_{00}(k)$
1	0
2	0
3	0.4
4	0.6
5	0
$d_0 = GCM(3,4)$	1

Now, take into account the DTMC depicted in Figure 9.11. As in the previous chain, the other probability of transitions depicted are equal to one. Table 9.5 presents the probability $p_{00}(k)$, for the respective number of steps $k = 1, 2, 3, 4,$ and 5. The greatest common divisor of k from which $p_{00}(k) > 0$ is $GCD(2,4) = 2$, since 2 and 4 are the values of k such that $p_{00}(k) > 0$. Therefore, the period for $p_{00}(k) > 0$ is $d_0 = 2$, and then the respective DTMC is periodic.

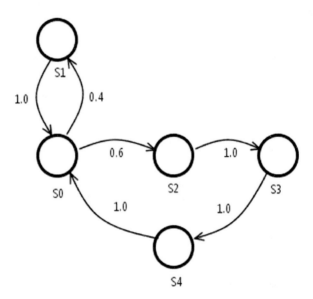

Figure 9.11 Five State DTMC – State Period for $p_{00}(k) > 0$ - $d_0 = 2$.

A state i is defined as **absorbing** if $\lim_{k \to \infty} p_{ij}(k) = 0$, $\forall j \in \mathscr{X}$, $i \neq j$. When a DTMC has only one absorbing state (j); the probability of reaching such a state is one, that is $\lim_{k \to \infty} p_{ij}(k) = 1$, for any k.

Table 9.5
Five State DTMC – Period of $p_{00}(k) > 0$

k	$p_{00}(k)$
1	0
2	0.4
3	0
4	0.76
5	0
$d_0 = GCM(2,4)$	2

Let T_{ij} denote the time a chain first reaches the state j given it started in state i (**first passage time**). If $j = i$, T_{ii} is named the **recurrence time**. Now, let $f_{ij}(k)$ be the probability that exactly k steps after leaving state i, state j is reached for the first time ($P(T_{ij} = k)$). Therefore, $f_{ii}(k)$ is the probability of two successive visits to state i after exactly k steps ($P(T_{ii} = k)$). The probability of ever returning to state i is denoted by f_{ii} and is given by:

$$f_{ii} = \sum_{k=1}^{\infty} f_{ii}(k), \tag{9.5.1}$$

where:

$$f_{ii}(k) = p_{ii}(k) - \sum_{l=1}^{k-1} f_{ii}(l) \times p_{ii}(k-l). \tag{9.5.2}$$

If $f_{ii} = 1$, then state i is **recurrent** [24, 138]. States i that $f_{ii} < 1$ are named **non-recurrent** or **transient**. The derivation of Equations 9.5.1 and 9.5.2 can be found in [413].

Example 9.5.1. Consider the DTMC presented in Figure 9.12. This chain is composed of three states, S_0, S_1, and S_2. The transition probability is:

$$\mathbf{P} = \begin{pmatrix} 0 & 1 & 0 \\ 0.6 & 0 & 0.4 \\ 0 & 0 & 1 \end{pmatrix}.$$

Table 9.6 presents $f_{S_0 S_0}(k)$, $f_{S_1 S_1}(k)$, $f_{S_2 S_2}(k)$, $f_{S_0 S_0}$, $f_{S_1 S_1}$, and $f_{S_2 S_2}$. As $f_{S_0 S_0} = f_{S_1 S_1} = 0.6$ and $f_{S_2 S_2} = 1$, then S_0 and S_1 are transient states and S_2 a recurrent state.

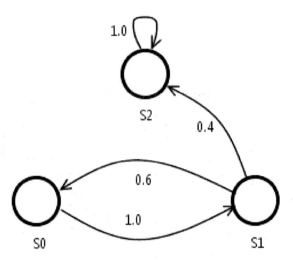

Figure 9.12 Probability of Ever Returning to State i.

The **mean first passage time** from i to j ($i \neq j$) may be obtained by:

$$mfpt_{ij} = \sum_{k=1}^{\infty} k \times f_{ij}(k). \tag{9.5.3}$$

For recurrent states (those states i that $f_{ii} = 1$), the **mean recurrence time** of state i may be obtained by:

$$mrt_i = \sum_{k=1}^{\infty} k \times f_{ii}(k). \tag{9.5.4}$$

The mean first passage time and mean recurrence time may also be iteratively calculated from:

$$\mathbf{M}^{k+1} = \mathbf{1} + \mathbf{P} \cdot (\mathbf{M}^k - \mathbf{DM}^k), \ \mathbf{M}^0 = \mathbf{1}, \tag{9.5.5}$$

where $\mathbf{1}$ denotes a square matrix whose components are all equal to 1, and $\mathbf{DM}^k$ is the diagonal matrix obtained from $\mathbf{M}^k$, that is, the ith diagonal element of $\mathbf{DM}^k$ is the ith diagonal element of $\mathbf{M}^k$ ($dm_{ii}^k = m_{ii}^k$). The diagonal elements of $\mathbf{M}^\infty$ are the mean recurrence times, and the off-diagonal elements are the mean first passage times. The derivation of Equation 9.5.5 can be obtained in [413].

$\square$

Table 9.6
The Probability of Ever Returning to State $i - f_{ii}$

State S_i	k	$f_{S_iS_i}(k)$	$p_{S_iS_i}(k)$
0	1	0	0
0	2	0.6	0.6
0	3	0	0
0	4	≈ 0	0.36
0	5	0	0
0	6	≈ 0	0.216
0	2k	≈ 0	-
0	2k+1	0	-
0	$f_{S_0S_0} =$	0.6	-
1	1	0	0
1	2	0.6	0.6
1	3	0	0
1	4	≈ 0	0.36
1	5	0	0
1	6	≈ 0	0.216
1	2k	≈ 0	-
1	2k+1	0	-
1	$f_{S_1S_1} =$	0.6	-
2	1	1	1
2	2	0	1
2	3	0	1
2	4	0	1
2	5	0	1
2	6	0	1
2	$f_{S_2S_2} =$	1	-

Example 9.5.2. Consider the DTMC shown in Figure 9.12 and compute mean recurrence times of each state and the mean first passage times of each state given it was in another state. Here, we have adopted the interactive approach presented by Equation 9.5.5. For computing $\mathbf{M}^1$, it is required to have $\mathbf{P}$, $\mathbf{M}$, $\mathbf{DM}$, and $\mathbf{1}$:

$$\mathbf{P} = \begin{pmatrix} 0 & 1 & 0 \\ 0.6 & 0 & 0.4 \\ 0 & 0 & 1 \end{pmatrix},$$

$$\mathbf{M}^0 = \begin{pmatrix} 1 & 1 & 1 \\ 1 & 1 & 1 \\ 1 & 1 & 1 \end{pmatrix},$$

$$\mathbf{DM}^0 = \begin{pmatrix} 1 & 0 & 0 \\ 0 & 1 & 0 \\ 0 & 0 & 1 \end{pmatrix},$$

$$\mathbf{M}^0 - \mathbf{DM}^0 = \begin{pmatrix} 0 & 1 & 1 \\ 1 & 0 & 1 \\ 1 & 1 & 0 \end{pmatrix},$$

$$\mathbf{P} \cdot (\mathbf{M}^0 - \mathbf{DM}^0) = \begin{pmatrix} 1 & 0 & 1 \\ 0.4 & 1 & 0.6 \\ 1 & 1 & 0 \end{pmatrix},$$

$$\mathbf{M}^1 = 1 + \mathbf{P} \cdot (\mathbf{M}^0 - \mathbf{DM}^0) = \begin{pmatrix} 2 & 1 & 2 \\ 1.4 & 2 & 1.6 \\ 2 & 2 & 1 \end{pmatrix}.$$

From $\mathbf{M}^1$, we can compute $\mathbf{M}^2$:

$$\mathbf{M}^2 = 1 + \mathbf{P} \cdot (\mathbf{M}^1 - \mathbf{DM}^1) = \begin{pmatrix} 2.4 & 1 & 2.6 \\ 1.8 & 2.4 & 2.2 \\ 3 & 3 & 1 \end{pmatrix}.$$

Recursively applying this process, we obtain, for instance, $\mathbf{M}^{80}$ and $\mathbf{M}^{81}$:

$$\mathbf{M}^{80} = 1 + \mathbf{P} \cdot (\mathbf{M}^{79} - \mathbf{DM}^{79}) = \begin{pmatrix} 33.6 & 1 & 5 \\ 33 & 33.6 & 4 \\ 81 & 81 & 1 \end{pmatrix},$$

$$\mathbf{M}^{81} = 1 + \mathbf{P} \cdot (\mathbf{M}^{80} - \mathbf{DM}^{80}) = \begin{pmatrix} 34 & 1 & 5 \\ 33.4 & 34 & 4 \\ 82 & 82 & 1 \end{pmatrix}.$$

Observing this pattern, we see that:

$$\mathbf{M}^\infty = \begin{pmatrix} \infty & 1 & 5 \\ \infty & \infty & 4 \\ \infty & \infty & 1 \end{pmatrix}.$$

Therefore, $mrt_{S_2} = 1$, $mfpt_{S_0 S_1} = 1$, $mfpt_{S_0 S_2} = 5$, and $mfpt_{S_1 S_2} = 4$. Observe that once you reach S_2, every next step you keep visiting S_2; hence $mrt_{S_2} = 1$. If you are in S_0, the mean first passage time to state S_1 is one, since in the next step you will surely reach S_1. Some components of $\mathbf{M}^\infty$ are infinite; this corresponds to the case where the respective metrics diverge when k approaches infinite.

A recurrent state i is classified as **recurrent positive** (or **recurrent non-null**) if the mrt_i is finite. On the other hand, if mrt_i is infinite, state i is classified as **recurrent null**. Figure 9.13 depicts a DTMC with some classes of states. States s_0, s_1, s_2, s_3, and s_4 are transients, state s_8 is recurrent and absorbing, and states s_5 and s_6 are recurrent, non-null, and periodic states. Figure 9.14 summarizes the classes of states discussed in this section.

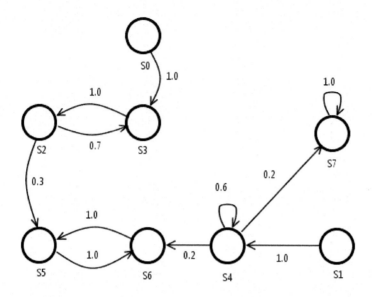

Figure 9.13 Transient and Recurrent States.

□

Example 9.5.3. Consider the DTMC depicted in Figure 9.15. This chain is composed of four states, named S_0, S_1, S_2, and S_3. The aim of this example is to apply the described methods for classifying the states. For this, we first compute f_{ii} for each state and check if $f_{ii} < 1$ (transient) or $f_{ii} = 1$ (recurrent). For recurrent states, we compute the mean recurrence time, mrt_i, to evaluate if they are null recurrent ($mrt_i \to \infty$) or non-null (positive) recurrent ($mrt_i < \infty$). The mean first passage time, $mfpt_{ij}$, is also provided. Finally, we also analyze if the recurrent states are periodic or aperiodic by computing the period for reaching each periodic state (Aperiodic states: $d_i = 1$. Periodic states - $d_i > 1$).

Table 9.7 presents $p_{ii}(k)$, $f_{ii}(k)$, and f_{ii} for each state of the chain. Using f_{ii}, we can state whether a state is transient (non-recurrent) or recurrent. As $f_{S_2 S_2}$ and $f_{S_3 S_3}$ are equal to one, S_2 and S_3 are recurrent. $f_{S_0 S_0}$ and $f_{S_1 S_1}$ are smaller than one, so they are transient states.

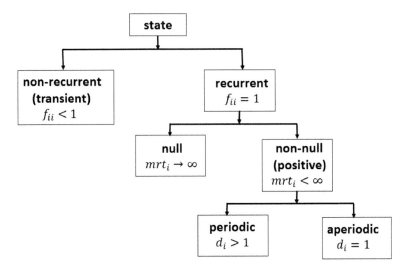

Figure 9.14 DTMC – State Classes.

Now, we calculate the mean recurrence time for the recurrent states. Besides, we also compute the mean first passage times. For estimating these metrics, we use Equation 9.5.5. In the following, we present some steps of this process and the respective results:

$$\mathbf{P} = \begin{pmatrix} 0 & 1 & 0 & 0 \\ 0 & 0.7 & 0.3 & 0 \\ 0 & 0 & 0 & 1 \\ 0 & 0 & 0.8 & 0.2 \end{pmatrix},$$

$$\mathbf{M}^0 = \begin{pmatrix} 1 & 1 & 1 & 1 \\ 1 & 1 & 1 & 1 \\ 1 & 1 & 1 & 1 \\ 1 & 1 & 1 & 1 \end{pmatrix},$$

$$\mathbf{DM}^0 = \begin{pmatrix} 1 & 0 & 0 & 0 \\ 0 & 1 & 0 & 0 \\ 0 & 0 & 1 & 0 \\ 0 & 0 & 0 & 1 \end{pmatrix},$$

$$\mathbf{M}^0 - \mathbf{DM}^0 = \begin{pmatrix} 0 & 1 & 1 & 1 \\ 1 & 0 & 1 & 1 \\ 1 & 1 & 0 & 1 \\ 1 & 1 & 1 & 0 \end{pmatrix},$$

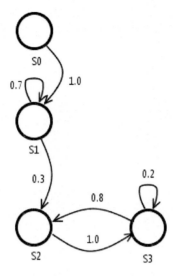

Figure 9.15   Classification of DTMC states – f_{ii}, mrt_i, and $mfpt_{ij}$.

$$\mathbf{P} \cdot (\mathbf{M^0} - \mathbf{DM^0}) = \begin{pmatrix} 1 & 0 & 1 & 1 \\ 1 & 0.3 & 0.7 & 1 \\ 1 & 1 & 1 & 0 \\ 1 & 1 & 0.2 & 0.8 \end{pmatrix},$$

$$\mathbf{M^1} = 1 + \mathbf{P} \cdot (\mathbf{M^0} - \mathbf{DM^0}) = \begin{pmatrix} 2 & 1 & 2 & 2 \\ 2 & 1.3 & 1.7 & 2 \\ 2 & 2 & 2 & 1 \\ 2 & 2 & 1.2 & 1.8 \end{pmatrix}.$$

From $\mathbf{M^1}$, we can compute $\mathbf{M^2}$:

$$\mathbf{M^2} = 1 + \mathbf{P} \cdot (\mathbf{M^1} - \mathbf{DM^1}) = \begin{pmatrix} 3 & 1 & 2.7 & 3 \\ 3 & 1.6 & 2.19 & 2.7 \\ 3 & 3 & 2.2 & 1 \\ 3 & 3 & 1.24 & 1.8 \end{pmatrix}.$$

Recursively applying this process, we obtain, for instance, $\mathbf{M^{99}}$ and $\mathbf{M^{100}}$:

$$\mathbf{M^{99}} = 1 + \mathbf{P} \cdot (\mathbf{M^{98}} - \mathbf{DM^{98}}) = \begin{pmatrix} 100 & 1 & 4.3333 & 5.3333 \\ 100 & 30.7 & 3.3333 & 4.3333 \\ 100 & 100 & 2.25 & 1 \\ 100 & 100 & 1.25 & 1.8 \end{pmatrix},$$

Table 9.7

f_{ii} – DTMC of Figure 9.15

State S_i	k	$f_{S_iS_i}(k)$	$p_{S_iS_i}(k)$
0	1	0	0
0	2	0	0
0	3	0	0
0	4	0	0
0	5	0	0
0	6	0	0
0	∞	0	0
0	$f_{S_0S_0} =$	0	-
1	1	0.7	0.7
1	2	0	0.49
1	3	0	0.343
1	4	0	0.2401
1	5	0	0.1681
1	6	0	0.1176
1	∞	0	-
1	$f_{S_1S_1} =$	0.7	-
2	1	0	0
2	2	0.8	0.8
2	3	0.16	0.16
2	4	0.03	0.67
2	5	0.01	0.2624
2	6	0	0.59
2	∞	0	-
2	$f_{S_2S_2} =$	1	-
3	1	0.2	0.2
3	2	0.8	0.84
3	3	0	0.328
3	4	0	0.7376
3	5	0	0.4099
3	6	0	0.6721
3	∞	0	-
3	$f_{S_3S_3} =$	1	-

$$\mathbf{M}^{100} = \mathbf{1} + \mathbf{P} \cdot (\mathbf{M}^{99} - \mathbf{DM}^{99}) = \begin{pmatrix} 101 & 1 & 4.3333 & 5.3333 \\ 101 & 31 & 3.3333 & 4.3333 \\ 101 & 101 & 2.25 & 1 \\ 101 & 101 & 1.25 & 1.8 \end{pmatrix}.$$

Observing this pattern, we see that:

$$\mathbf{M}^{\infty} = \begin{pmatrix} \infty & 1 & 4.3333 & 5.3333 \\ \infty & \infty & 3.3333 & 4.3333 \\ \infty & \infty & 2.25 & 1 \\ \infty & \infty & 1.25 & 1.8 \end{pmatrix}.$$

Therefore, $mrt_{S_2} = 2.25$ and $mrt_{S_3} = 1.8$. As both are not infinite, then S_2 and S_3 are non-null (positive) recurrent states. The mean first passage times are: $mfpt_{S_0S_2} = 4.3333$, $mfpt_{S_0S_3} = 5.3333$, $mfpt_{S_1S_2} = 3.3333$, $mfpt_{S_1S_3} = 4.3333$, $mfpt_{S_2S_3} = 1$, and $mfpt_{S_3S_2} = 1.25$.

Now, we calculate the period of the recurrent states S_2 and S_3 to verify if they are periodic or aperiodic. The respective information for estimating the periods of these states are depicted in Tables 9.8. As the period of batch states is one, $d_2 = d_3 = 1$, they are aperiodic states.

Table 9.8
Classification of a DTMC States – Period of $p_{22}(k) > 0$.

k	$p_{22}(k)$	$p_{33}(k)$
1	0	0.2
2	0.8	0.84
3	0.16	0.328
4	0.672	0.7376
5	0.2624	0.4099
6	0.5901	0.6721
$d_2 = GCM(2,3,4,5,6)$	1	-
$d_3 = GCM(1,2,3,4,5,6)$	-	1

□

It has been shown that in irreducible DTMCs, all states belong to one same class; that is, they are all transient, recurrent null, recurrent non-null, periodic or aperiodic [138]. An irreducible, recurrent non-null, aperiodic DTMC is defined as ergodic (**ergodic DTMC**) [52].

After having discussed the state classes, the following theorem states when a DTMC has one steady-state probability vector:

Theorem 9.5.1. *In an irreducible aperiodic Markov chain, the limits* $\Pi = \lim_{k \to \infty} \Pi(k)$ *exist and are independent of the initial state probability vector.*

The proof of this theorem can be found in [325].

For an irreducible, positive-recurrent DTMC, the mean recurrence time of state i may be obtained by:

$$mrt_i = \frac{1}{\pi_i}. \tag{9.5.6}$$

Equation 9.5.6 may be verified from Equation 9.5.5. Let us consider Equation 9.5.5 and adopt $\mathbf{M}$ for $\mathbf{M}^\infty$, since $\mathbf{M}^{k+1} = \mathbf{M}^k$ as $\lim k \to \infty$. We also know that for an irreducible, positive-recurrent DTMC, $mrt_i < \infty$ (mean recurrence times do not diverge) for everyone of its states. Hence, in such conditions, we may write:

$$\mathbf{M} = \mathbf{1} + \mathbf{P} \cdot (\mathbf{M} - \mathbf{DM}). \tag{9.5.7}$$

Multiplying both sides of Equation 9.5.7 by Π, we have:

$$\Pi \cdot \mathbf{M} = \Pi \cdot (\mathbf{1} + \mathbf{P} \cdot (\mathbf{M} - \mathbf{DM})) =$$

$$\Pi \cdot \mathbf{M} = \Pi \cdot \mathbf{1} + \Pi \cdot (\mathbf{P} \cdot (\mathbf{M} - \mathbf{DM})) =$$

$$\Pi \cdot \mathbf{M} = \Pi \cdot \mathbf{1} + \Pi \cdot \mathbf{P} \cdot \mathbf{M} - \Pi \cdot \mathbf{P} \cdot \mathbf{DM}).$$

As $\Pi \cdot \mathbf{P} = \Pi$, then:

$$\Pi \cdot \mathbf{M} = \Pi \cdot \mathbf{1} + \Pi \cdot \mathbf{M} - \Pi \cdot \mathbf{DM}.$$

Therefore:

$$\Pi \cdot \mathbf{1} = \Pi \cdot \mathbf{DM} =$$

$$\Pi \cdot \mathbf{DM} = \mathbf{1}$$

Multiplying both sides by $\mathbf{DM}^{-1}$, we have:

$$\Pi \cdot \mathbf{DM} \cdot \mathbf{DM}^{-1} = \mathbf{1} \cdot \mathbf{DM}^{-1}.$$

$$\Pi = \mathbf{1} \cdot \mathbf{DM}^{-1} = \frac{\mathbf{1}}{\mathbf{DM}}.$$

Hence:

$$\Pi = \frac{1}{DM}. \tag{9.5.8}$$

So,

$$\pi_i = \frac{1}{mrt_i}.$$

Example 9.5.4. Let us consider an irreducible, positive-recurrent DTMC depicted in Figure 9.8. Its transition probability matrix is:

$$\mathbf{P} = \begin{pmatrix} 0.54091 & 0.27091 & 0.18818 \\ 0.5 & 0.30875 & 0.19125 \\ 0.50167 & 0.16 & 0.33833 \end{pmatrix}$$

and we also know its steady-state probability vector (see Example 9.4.1):

$$(\pi_B, \pi_I, \pi_W) = (0.44279, 0.24565, 0.31156).$$

Therefore:

$$(mrt_B, mrt_I, mrt_W) = (\frac{1}{0.44279}, \frac{1}{0.24565}, \frac{1}{0.31156}).$$

$$(mrt_B, mrt_I, mrt_W) = (2.2584, 4.0708, 3.2097).$$

$\square$

9.6 HOLDING TIME (SOJOURN TIME OR RESIDENCE TIME)

In Markov chains, state transitions depend on the current state and neither on the history that led to the current state nor on time already spent in the current state.

If at some time step k the system is in the state i, at the time step $k + 1$, the system may remain in i, with probability p_{ii}, or leave it for any state j with probability $1 - p_{ii} = \sum_{\forall j, \ j \neq i} p_{ij}$. The number of consecutive time steps that a DTMC remains in i is called the holding time (h_i), sojourn time, or residence time of state i (see Figure 9.16).

One may see in Figure 9.16 that each state transition is a Bernoulli experiment with success (leaving state i) probability $1 - p_{ii}$. Hence, the holding time h_i of a state i is a geometrically distributed random variable with probability mass function:

$$P(h_i = k) = (1 - p_{ii}) \times p_{ii}^{k-1}, \ k \in \mathbb{N}.$$

Therefore, the **mean holding time** is:

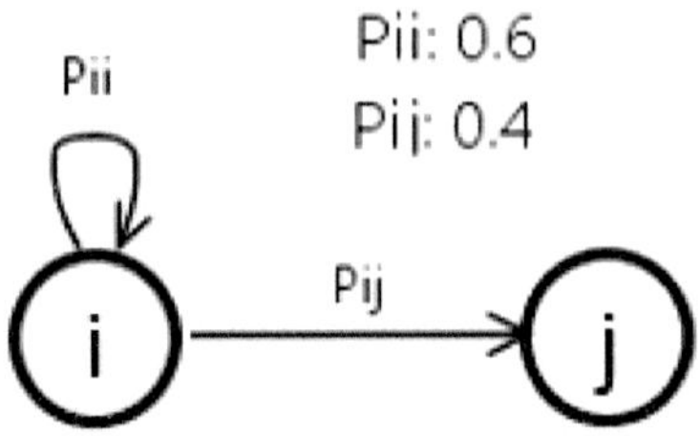

Figure 9.16 Holding Time, Sojourn Time, or Residence Time.

$$E(h_i) = \frac{1}{1 - p_{ii}}, \tag{9.6.1}$$

and the **variance of the holding time** is:

$$Var(h_i) = \frac{p_{ii}}{(1 - p_{ii})^2}. \tag{9.6.2}$$

The mean holding time of the state i is $\frac{1}{1-0.6} = 2.5$ steps and variance of the holding time is $\frac{0.6}{(1-0.6)^2} = 3.75$ steps.

Example 9.6.1. Consider the DTMC depicted in Figure 9.8. Each transition probability is presented in Table 9.2. From that table, we have $p_{BB} = 0.54091$, $p_{II} = 0.30875$, and $p_{WW} = 0.33833$. Hence, (using Formulas 9.6.1 and 9.6.2) the mean holding time of each state and the respective variances are:

$$E(h_B) = \frac{1}{1 - 0.54091} = 2.178222,$$

$$E(h_I) = \frac{1}{1 - 0.30875} = 1.446655,$$

$$E(h_W) = \frac{1}{1 - 0.33833} = 1.511327,$$

$$Var(h_B) = \frac{0.54091}{(1 - 0.54091)^2} = 2.56643,$$

$$Var(h_I) = \frac{0.30875}{(1 - 0.308756)^2} = 0.646155,$$

and

$$Var(h_W) = \frac{0.33833}{(1 - 0.33833)^2} = 0.772783.$$

$\square$

9.7 MEAN TIME TO ABSORPTION

This section presents a method to calculate the mean time to absorption of a DTMC [325], that is, the time steps the chain spends in non-recurrent states before reaching absorption states.

Consider a DTMC with state-space $\mathscr{X}$, and let T $(T \subset \mathscr{X})$ denote the set of non-recurrent states in the chain. Let $\mathbf{m}$ be a column vector whose components are $m_j \in T$. The mean time to absorption, given the chain is in state j, may be calculated by:

$$\mathbf{m} = \mathbf{N} \cdot \mathbf{1}, \tag{9.7.1}$$

where $\mathbf{1}$ is the column vector each of whose components are 1, and $\mathbf{N}$ (**fundamental matrix**) [325] is

$$\mathbf{N} = (\mathbf{I} - \mathbf{Q})^{-1}.$$

$\mathbf{Q}$ is a matrix that presents the transition probabilities of non-recurrent states to non-recurrent states, that is, from states in T to states in T. The reader may refer to [325] for a detailed deduction of Equation 9.7.1.

Example 9.7.1. Consider a DTMC depicted in Figure 9.17 composed of two transient and three recurrent states.

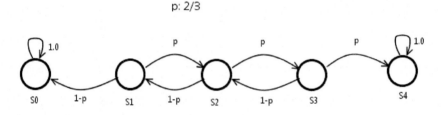

Figure 9.17 Mean Time to Absorption.

The transition probability is:

$$\mathbf{P}_{original} = \begin{pmatrix} 1 & 0 & 0 & 0 & 0 \\ 1-p & 0 & p & 0 & 0 \\ 0 & 1-p & 0 & p & 0 \\ 0 & 0 & 1-p & 0 & p \\ 0 & 0 & 0 & 0 & 1 \end{pmatrix}.$$

Let us re-organize $\mathbf{P}_{original}$ by placing all-absorbing states at the rightmost columns and the bottom lines of the matrix. Let us call this re-organized matrix $\mathbf{P}$.

$$
\mathbf{P} = \begin{array}{c} \\ S_1 \\ S_2 \\ S_3 \\ S_0 \\ S_4 \end{array}
\begin{array}{ccccc} S_1 & S_2 & S_3 & S_0 & S_4 \end{array}
\left(\begin{array}{ccccc}
0 & p & 0 & 1-p & 0 \\
1-p & 0 & p & 0 & 0 \\
0 & 1-p & 0 & 0 & p \\
0 & 0 & 0 & 1 & 0 \\
0 & 0 & 0 & 0 & 1
\end{array} \right)
$$

Hence, we have $\mathbf{Q}$ as the upper leftmost sub-matrix of $\mathbf{P}$:

$$
\mathbf{P} = \begin{array}{c} \\ \\ \\ S_0 \\ S_4 \end{array}
\left(\begin{array}{ccccc}
 & & & S_0 & S_4 \\
 & & & 1-p & 0 \\
 & \mathbf{Q} & & 0 & 0 \\
 & & & 0 & p \\
0 & 0 & 0 & 1 & 0 \\
0 & 0 & 0 & 0 & 1
\end{array} \right)
$$

The Q matrix is:

$$
\mathbf{Q} = \left(\begin{array}{ccc}
0 & p & 0 \\
1-p & 0 & p \\
0 & 1-p & 0
\end{array} \right).
$$

Now, we obtain $\mathbf{I} - \mathbf{Q}$:

$$
\mathbf{I} - \mathbf{Q} = \left(\begin{array}{ccc}
1 & 1-p & 0 \\
p-1 & 1 & -p \\
0 & p-1 & 1
\end{array} \right).
$$

Then, we can calculate $(\mathbf{I} - \mathbf{Q})^{-1}$:

$$
(\mathbf{I} - \mathbf{Q})^{-1} = \left(\begin{array}{ccc}
\frac{1-p+p^2}{1-2p+2p^2} & \frac{p}{1-2p+2p^2} & \frac{p^2}{1-2p+2p^2} \\
\frac{1-p}{1-2p+2p^2} & \frac{1}{1-2p+2p^2} & \frac{p}{1-2p+2p^2} \\
\frac{1-2p+p^2}{1-2p+2p^2} & \frac{1-p}{1-2p+2p^2} & \frac{1-p+p^2}{1-2p+2p^2}
\end{array} \right).
$$

For $p = \frac{3}{5}$, we have:

$$
\mathbf{N} = (\mathbf{I} - \mathbf{Q})^{-1} = \left(\begin{array}{ccc}
\frac{19}{13} & \frac{15}{13} & \frac{9}{13} \\
\frac{10}{13} & \frac{25}{13} & \frac{15}{13} \\
\frac{4}{13} & \frac{10}{13} & \frac{19}{13}
\end{array} \right).
$$

Thus, we can compute the mean time to absorption by $\mathbf{m} = \mathbf{N} \cdot \mathbf{1}$. Therefore:

$$\mathbf{m} = \begin{pmatrix} \frac{43}{13} \\ \frac{50}{13} \\ \frac{33}{13} \end{pmatrix} = \begin{pmatrix} 3.3077 \\ 3.8462 \\ 2.5385 \end{pmatrix},$$

that is, the *mtta* given the chain started from S_3 is 3.3077, the *mtta* given the chain started from S_4 is 3.8462, and the *mtta* given the chain started from S_5 is 2.5385.

□

9.8 SOME APPLICATIONS

This section presents applications of DTMC for performance analysis of systems. This first example concerns the performance and energy evaluation of a program procedure.

Example 9.8.1. Consider a program that supervises an embedded system. This program was written in C language and is composed of several procedures. Part of one of its procedures is presented in Code 10. This procedure is presented in the Atmel AT89S8252 microcontroller assembly language. The procedure might have been written initially either in C or assembly. Either way, the code presented is the object code generated by the compiler (assembler).

A basic block (*bb*) is a sequence of instructions bounded by control-flow instructions (in its beginning and at its end) and instruction without any other control-flow instructions within its set of instructions. Control-flow instructions are unconditional and conditional branches, procedures calls, procedure returns, software interruption calls, and interruption returns. Hence, when an instruction of a basic block is executed, the next instruction to be executed is within the basic block, unless it is the last instruction of the basic block. In such a case, the next instruction to be executed may be of a different basic block or an instruction of the same basic block. Therefore, the Code 10 is composed of three basic blocks, named here as **A**, **B**, and **C**. Basic block **A** is composed by the instruction presented from line 2 to line 14. Basic block **B** is composed by the instruction presented from line 15 to line 18. Moreover, the instructions that belong to basic block **C** are presented from line 19 to line 22. The basic blocks are also in the Pseudo-Code 11.

The energy consumption (*EC*), the number of cycles (*NC*), and the mean power consumption per cycle of each basic block are presented in Table 9.9. First, the number of cycles of each basic block is estimated by summing up the number of cycles of each instruction of the respective basic block. Likewise, the energy consumption of each basic block is obtained by summing the energy consumption of each instruction of the basic block. Finally, the mean power consumption per cycle is estimated by dividing the energy consumption of a basic block by its number of cycles, that is:

$$mppc(bb) = \frac{EC(bb)}{NC(bb)}.$$

Algorithm 10 Assembly Code

```
 1: CRC16:
 2:        push 0
 3:        push acc
 4:        ...
 5:        mov r0,#8
 6:        xrl 07,a
 7: loop1: clr
 8:        mov a,06
 9:        rlc a
10:        mov 06,a
11:        mov a,07
12:        rlc a
13:        mov 07,a
14:        jnc loop2
15:        ...
16:        xlr 06,#10h
17:        xlr 07,#21h
18: loop2: djnz ro loop1
19:        ...
20:        pop acc
21:        pop 0
22:        ret
```

Algorithm 11 Basic Blocks

```
1: CRC16:
2: loop1: Basic Block A
3:        jnc loop2
4:        Basic Block B
5: loop2: djnz ro loop1
6:        Basic Block C
7:        ret
```

Table 9.9
Energy Consumption, Number of Cycles, and Mean Power per Cycle

Basic Block	EC(nJ)	NC - Cycle Time = 1 μs	$mppc$ - mW
A	832.569	20	41.628
B	166.978	4	41.745
C	430.230	10	43.023

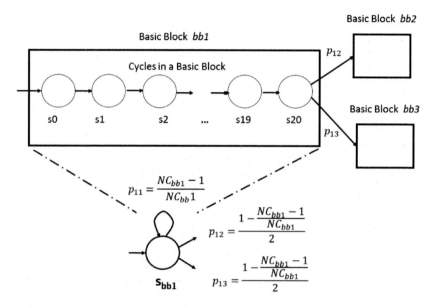

Figure 9.18 Basic Block Visit Probability.

The upper part of Figure 9.18 presents a sequence of transition within a basic block with 20 cycles (steps) – basic block 1 -$bb1$. After the 20th step, the processor executing the basic block leaves the basic block $bb1$ and reaches one of the basic blocks addressed in the control-flow instruction that closes $bb1$. It is worth stressing that the $bb1$ might be one of the $bb1$'s outgoing basic blocks. Hence, considering one $bb1$ execution (from its first instruction to the last), the processor stays in $bb1$ during 19 cycles (steps) out of 20 cycles. Therefore, during the period (execution of $bb1$), we may say that the frequency of visits to $bb1$ is

$$\frac{NC(bb1) - 1}{NC(bb1)},$$

Therefore, the probability of keeping visiting $bb1$ (p_{ii}) may be estimated from the above frequency. At the end of the block, the processor switches to one of the outgoing basic blocks. If the control-flow instruction is conditional, the probability of reaching each of the outgoing basic blocks is dependent on the processor's state (modified by the program execution), that depends on the data processing, or if the program reads the outside world, it depends on the data read from it. At any rate, we are not considering these aspects here. For simplicity, we assume each outgoing basic block has an equal probability of being reached by the processor, and so start its execution. Therefore, the probability of switching to an outgoing basic block of $bb1$ is estimated as:

$$p_{1j} = \frac{1 - \frac{NC(bb1) - 1}{NC(bb1)}}{NOGBB(bb1)},$$

where $NOGBB(bb1)$ is the number of outgoing basic blocks of the basic block $bb1$. The lower part of Figure 9.18 depicts a DTMC that represents a basic block with two outgoing arcs.

A DTMC that represents the subroutine is shown in Figure 9.19. We have, therefore, assumed that cycle times are geometrically distributed. The states **A**, **B**, and **C** represents the respective basic blocks depicted in Code 11. Besides these states, an additional absorbing state (**AS**) was included to represent the sub-routine end. When state **AS** is reached, it denotes the sub-routine's end of execution. The sub-routine's mean execution time (met) can; thus, be estimated by computing the mean time to absorption ($mtta$). The mean execution time computed was $met = 21.333\mu s$.

Let us consider that soon the sub-routine provides a result to its caller; it is called again infinitely often. For representing such behavior, the DTMC was modified by removing the absorbing state (**AS**) and connecting the state **C** to state **A** to represent the iteration mentioned above. As in the DTMC depicted in Figure 9.19, the absorbing state may be reached from state **B**, and since the new DTMC specifies a sub-routine that is called again infinitely often, that is, after its end it starts again, the probability of reaching state **AS** was transferred to the state **A**, that is, the first basic block of the sub-routine. The new DTMC is presented in Figure 9.20. This DTMC is recurrent, non-null (positive), and aperiodic, that is, ergodic. Therefore, the steady-state probability can be calculated. We assigned a reward function to each of its states for representing the mean power consumption per cycle in each state ($mppc$); hence the states have the following reward functions:

$$mppc(\mathbf{A}) = 41.628\ mW,$$

$$mppc(\mathbf{B}) = 41.745\ mW,$$

$$mppc(\mathbf{C}) = 43.023\ mW.$$

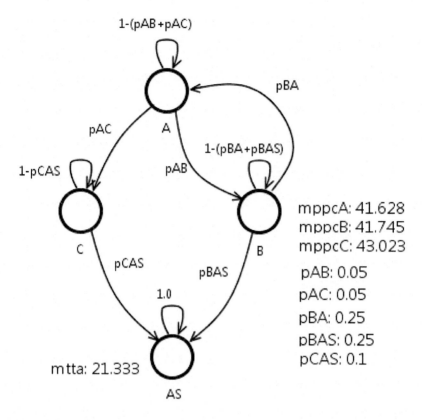

Figure 9.19 DTMC Representing the Sub-Routine Depicted in Code 10.

The mean energy consumption per execution (*MECPE*) of the sub-routine is estimated by:

$$MECPE = (\pi_{\mathbf{A}} \times mppc(\mathbf{A}) + \pi_{\mathbf{B}} \times mppc(\mathbf{B}) + \pi_{\mathbf{C}} \times mppc(\mathbf{C})) \times mtta.$$

The steady-state probabilities, the holding times, and the recurrence times of each state are presented in Table 9.10. The sub-routine's mean energy consumption per execution (*MECPE*) is estimated as 890.738 *nJ*.

☐

Example 9.8.2. Let us consider the irreducible, positive-recurrent aperiodic DTMC, that is, an ergodic DTMC, depicted in Figure 9.21. Its transition probability matrix is:

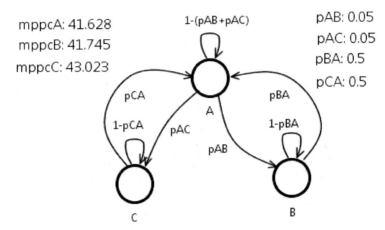

mppcA: 41.628
mppcB: 41.745
mppcC: 43.023

1-(pAB+pAC)

pAB: 0.05
pAC: 0.05
pBA: 0.5
pCA: 0.5

met= mtta: 21.333

MECPE: $(\pi_A \times mppc(\mathbf{A}) + \pi_B \times mppc(\mathbf{B}) + \pi_C \times mppc(\mathbf{C})) \times mtta$

MECPE = 890.738082

Figure 9.20   The DTMC Without Absorbing State.

Table 9.10
Energy Consumption, Number of Cycles, and Mean Power per Cycle

Metric	A	B	C
π	0.833	0.083	0.083
Holding time (μs)	10	2	2
Recurrence time (μs)	1.2	12	12

$$\mathbf{P} = \begin{pmatrix} 0.8 & 0.1 & 0.1 & 0 & 0 \\ 0 & 0.8 & 0 & 0 & 0.2 \\ 0 & 0 & 0.7 & 0.3 & 0 \\ 0.2 & 0 & 0.3 & 0.3 & 0.2 \\ 0.4 & 0 & 0 & 0 & 0.6 \end{pmatrix}.$$

The steady-state probability is computed by solving $\Pi = \Pi \cdot \mathbf{P}$. The steady-state probability vector is:

$$\Pi = (\pi_0, \pi_1, \pi_2, \pi_3, \pi_4) = (0.37, 0.18, 0.22, 0.09, 0.14).$$

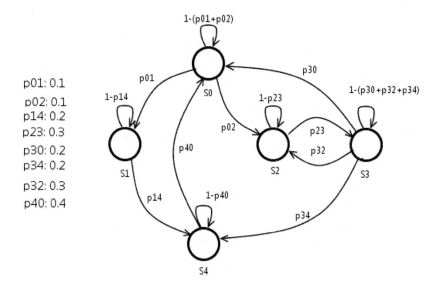

p01: 0.1
p02: 0.1
p14: 0.2
p23: 0.3
p30: 0.2
p34: 0.2
p32: 0.3
p40: 0.4

Figure 9.21 Ergodic DTMC.

As the DTMC is irreducible, positive-recurrent, the mean recurrence times of each state can be computed by Equation 9.5.6. Thus:

$$(mrt_0, mrt_1, mrt_2, mrt_3, mrt_4) = (2.71, 5.42, 4.64, 10.83, 7.22).$$

Now consider a time period T. The mean time spent (mts) by the chain in state i over the time period T is estimated by:

$$mts_i = \pi_i \times T. \tag{9.8.1}$$

Hence, considering $T = 100\ t.u.$[5] the mean times spent in each state of the chain depicted in Figure 9.21 are:

$$(mts_0, mts_1, mts_2, mts_3, mts_4) = (36.92, 18.46, 21.54, 9.23, 13.85).$$

The mean number of visits to state i between two successive visits to state j (v_{ij}) may be estimated by:

$$v_{ij} = \frac{\pi_i}{\pi_j}. \tag{9.8.2}$$

Therefore, the mean number of visits to states S_1, S_2, S_3, and S_4, between two successive visits to state S_0 are presented in Table 9.11.

---

[5]t.u. denotes time units.

Table 9.11

Mean Number of Visits to States Between Two Successive Visits to S_0

States j	v_{0j}
1	0.5
2	0.5833
3	0.25
4	0.375

☐

Example 9.8.3. Consider a computer server S. This server may be operational (O) or failed (F). The server's time to failure and time to repair are geometrically distributed. The mean time to failure (MTTF) is 1464 h, and the mean time to repair (MTTR) is 96 h. The server steady-state availability may be estimated from the DTMC depicted in Figure 9.22.

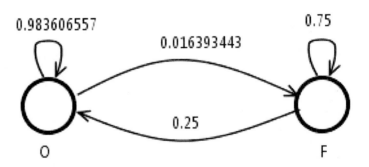

A: 0.9384615348

Figure 9.22 Server's State.

Let us consider a time step equal to 24 h; hence the mean time to failure and the mean time to repair expressed in time steps are:

$$MTTF = \frac{1464}{24} = 61,$$

$$MTTR = \frac{96}{24} = 4.$$

The probabilities of transitioning from O to F and from O to O in one time step are:

$$p_{OF} = \frac{1}{61} = 0.0164,$$

$$p_{OO} = 1 - \frac{1}{61} = 0.9836.$$

Likewise, the probabilities of transitioning from F to O and from F to F in one time step are:

$$p_{FO} = \frac{1}{4} = 0.25,$$

$$p_{FF} = 1 - \frac{1}{4} = 0.75.$$

The steady-state probability of each state is $\pi(O) = 0.9385$ and $\pi(F) = 0.0615$. Thus, the availability and the unavailability are:

$$A = PO = \pi(O) = 0.9385,$$

$$UA = PF = \pi(F) = 0.0615.$$

The holding time and the recurrence time of each state are depicted in Table 9.12.

Table 9.12
Holding Time and Recurrence Time

State i	Holding Time (steps)	Recurrence Time (steps)	Holding Time (h)	Recurrence Time (h)
O	61	1.0656	1464	25.5744
F	4	16.25	96	390

□

Example 9.8.4. Consider a small cooling system composed of two air conditioners. Both devices can be either operating or switched off, and they are controlled by a temperature managing system that keeps the environment temperature within predefined bounds. The system's state is defined by

$$s_i = (s_{d_1}, s_{d_2}),$$

where

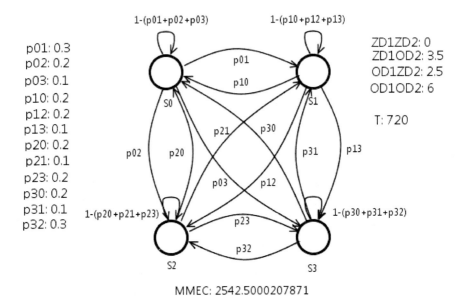

p01: 0.3
p02: 0.2
p03: 0.1
p10: 0.2
p12: 0.2
p13: 0.1
p20: 0.2
p21: 0.1
p23: 0.2
p30: 0.2
p31: 0.1
p32: 0.3

ZD1ZD2: 0
ZD1OD2: 3.5
OD1ZD2: 2.5
OD1OD2: 6

T: 720

MMEC: 2542.5000207871

Figure 9.23 DTMC Representing Two Air Conditioners.

$$s_{d_i} := \begin{cases} On & \text{if } d_i \text{ is operating} \\ Off & \text{if } d_i \text{ is switched off} \end{cases}$$

Consider, as in Example 9.2.2, that this system was monitored for a period T and its state was recorded every hour (time step $= 1h$) and the state transition probabilities were estimated, and the transition probability matrix is:

$$\mathbf{P} = \begin{pmatrix} 0.4 & 0.3 & 0.2 & 0.1 \\ 0.2 & 0.5 & 0.2 & 0.1 \\ 0.2 & 0.1 & 0.5 & 0.2 \\ 0.2 & 0.1 & 0.3 & 0.4 \end{pmatrix}.$$

For each state a reward function was defined assigning the average power consumption if the respective device is operating and zero if it is switched off. Hence, $R_{T(s_i)} = R_{P(d_1)} + R_{P(d_2)}$, where

$$R_{P(d_1)} := \begin{cases} 2500\ W & \text{if } d_1 \text{ is operating} \\ 0 & \text{if } d_1 \text{ is switched off} \end{cases}$$

and

$$R_{P(d_2)} := \begin{cases} 3500\ W & \text{if } d_2 \text{ is operating} \\ 0 & \text{if } d_2 \text{ is switched off.} \end{cases}$$

Since the chain is positive recurrent and aperiodic, the steady-state probability vector is

$$\Pi = (0.25, 0.25, 0.3125, 0.1875).$$

The holding time and the recurrence time of each state are shown in Table 9.13.

Table 9.13
Holding Time and Recurrence Time

State i	Holding Time (steps)	Recurrence Time (steps)
$s^\cdot0$	1.7	4
$s^\cdot1$	2	4
$s^\cdot2$	2	3.2
$s^\cdot3$	1.7	5.3

The mean energy consumption in a period T ($MMEC$) may be estimated by:

$$MMEC = \left(\sum_{\forall s_i} \pi(s_i) \times R_{T(s_i)} \right) \times T$$

$$MMEC = \left(\pi(s_0) \times R_{T(s_0)} + \pi(s_1) \times R_{T(s_1)} + \pi(s_2) \times R_{T(s_2)} + \pi(s_3) \times R_{T(s_3)} \right) \times T$$

where $T = 720\ h$ is the number of hours in a month. The estimated mean energy consumption per month is $MMEC = 2542.5\ kWh$.

$\square$

EXERCISES

Exercise 1. Explain what you understand by (**a**) nonstationary, (**b**) stationary, and (**c**) homogeneity.

Exercise 2. Describe the following concepts: (**a**) irreducible DTMC, (**b**) reducible DTMC, (**c**) aperiodic state, and (**d**) periodic state.

Exercise 3. Explain the following concepts: (**a**) recurrent state, (**b**) non-recurrent state, (**c**) recurrent null state, (**d**) recurrent non-null state, (**e**) mean first passage time, and (**f**) mean recurrence time.

Exercise 4. Give an example of **(a)** a stationary, homogeneous stochastic process, **(b)** a stationary, nonhomogeneous stochastic process, **(c)** a nonstationary, homogeneous stochastic process, and **(d)** a nonstationary, nonhomogeneous stochastic process.

For each case, state if the process is a discrete state or a continuous state process and if it is a discrete-time or a continuous-time process.

Exercise 5. What do you understand by an ergodic DTMC?

Exercise 6. A surveillance camera may be in an operational state (UP) or failed state (DOWN). This camera is checked every six hours. If the camera is in an UP state, the probability that it stays in that state in the next six hours is p_{uu}. On the other hand, if it is DOWN, the probability of staying DOWN over the next six-hours is p_{dd}. Assuming that the camera is operational at $t = 0$, what is the camera's probability to be operational at $t = 24\,h$. Consider $p_{uu} = 0.6$ and $p_{dd} = 0.3$.

Exercise 7. Consider the DTMC depicted in Figure 9.9. Assuming $\Pi(0) = (1,0,0,0,0,0)$, calculate $\Pi(k)$, for $k = 4,5,6$.

Exercise 8. Consider the DTMC shown in Figure 9.24. Compute mean recurrence times of each state and the mean first passage times of each state, given it was in another state.

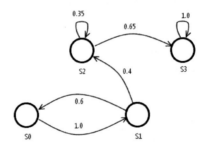

Figure 9.24   DTMC – Exercise 7.

Exercise 9. Classify the states of the DTMC depicted in Figure 9.24 according to the classes shown in Figure 9.14.

Exercise 10. Calculate the mean holding time and variance of the holding time of each state of the DTMC shown in Figure 9.24.

Exercise 11. Compute the mean time to absorption of the DTMC depicted in Figure 9.17. Assume $p = 3/4$.

Exercise 12. Take into account the DTMC depicted in Figure 10, and suppose $p_{AB} = 0.06$, $p_{AC} = 0.07$, $p_{BA} = 0.3$, $p_{BAS} = 0.2$, and $p_{CAS} = 0.15$. Compute its mean time to absorption.

Exercise 13. Consider the chain presented in Figure 9.21, and assume $p_{01} = 0.15$, $p_{02} = 0.08$, $p_{14} = 0.25$, $p_{23} = 0.32$, $p_{30} = 0.2$, $p_{34} = 0.15$, $p_{32} = 0.35$, and $p_{40} = 0.15$. Calculate: **(a)** the steady state probabilities of each state, **(b)** the mean recurrence time of each state, **(c)** and mean time spent in each state if a time period of observation $T = 200t.u.$.

Exercise 14. The transition probability matrix of a DTMC is given by

$$\mathbf{P} = \begin{pmatrix} 0 & 0 & 0 & 0 & 1 \\ 0 & 0 & 1 & 0 & 0 \\ 0 & 0 & 0 & 1 & 0 \\ 0 & 0.75 & 0.25 & 0 & 1 \\ 0.5 & 0 & 0.5 & 0 & 0 \end{pmatrix}.$$

Write the sample paths of length four that begin in state 1. What is the probability of being in each state after four steps given state 1 is the initial state?

Exercise 15. Compute the mean recurrence time of state 2 and the mean first passage time from state 1 to state 2 in DTMC that has

$$\mathbf{P} = \begin{pmatrix} 0.2 & 0.2 & 0.6 \\ 0.15 & 0.55 & 0.3 \\ 0.35 & 0.4 & 0.25 \end{pmatrix}.$$

10 Continuous Time Markov Chain

This chapter introduces the concept of continuous time Markov chain, CTMC, by discussing the respective Chapman-Kolmogorov equation, rate matrix, holding time, and transient and steady-state solutions. Some well-established numerical methods for calculating transient and steady-state solutions are introduced, as well as a specific method for computing moments of CTMC with absorbing states. Semi-Markovian chains are also briefly discussed. The chapter also examines the concepts of mean recurrence time, mean first passage time, holding time, and mean time to absorption. These methods and concepts are illustrated by examples that enable the readers to understand each of these concepts. Furthermore, the CTMC is applied to model and evaluate computer system performance problems.

In a DTMC, state changes may occur in specific time instants (steps). In continuous time Markov chain (CTMC), a state change may occur at any point in time. A CTMC is a continuous-time, discrete state-space stochastic process; that is, the state values are discrete, but parameter t has a continuous range over $[0, \infty)$. HOWEVER, for CTMC analysis, we can no longer use the transition probability matrix since a standard clock does not synchronize state transitions as in a DTMC.

Differently from DTMCs, in which interactions between states are specified regarding probabilities, in CTMCs, the interactions of the state are represented through the rates at which the state transitions occur.

10.1 RATE MATRIX

In a chain, the probability of transitioning from a state i to a state j depends not only up being in state i but also upon the period. In other words, let

$$p_{ij}(t, t + \triangle t) \tag{10.1.1}$$

be the probability for changing from state i, at time t, to state j, at time $t + \triangle t$. $p_{ij}(t, t + \triangle t)$ depends on state i and on $\triangle t$.

Now, let us consider that the time interval becomes small, that is, $\triangle t \to 0$, so $p_{ij}(t, t + \triangle t)$ also becomes small, $p_{ij}(t, t + \triangle t) \to 0$, for $i \neq j$. Therefore, the probability of remaining in state i increases, that is, $p_{ii}(t, t + \triangle t) \to 1$, as $\triangle t \to 0$. On the other hand, as $\triangle t$ becomes larger, $p_{ij}(t, t + \triangle t)$ increases.

Dividing the Expression 10.1.1 by $\triangle t$, we have

$$\frac{p_{ij}(t, t + \triangle t)}{\triangle t}, \ i \neq j.$$

This is a dimensional metric. It is a rate. It is the rate at which the chain changes from state i to state j. For supporting this idea, let us think of $p_{ij}(t, t + \triangle t)$ as a distance. Then

$$\frac{p_{ij}(t, t + \triangle t)}{\triangle t}$$

may be thought of as a speed. It would be an average speed at which the chain transitions from state i to state j.

Now, consider $\triangle t \to 0$; then:

$$q_{ij}(t) = \lim_{\triangle t \to 0} \frac{p_{ij}(t, t + \triangle t)}{\triangle t}, \quad i \neq j. \qquad (10.1.2)$$

$q_{ij}(t)$ is the instantaneous rate at which the chain changes from state i to state j. Hence, $q_{ij}(t)$ could be thought of as the instantaneous speed at which the chain transitions from i to j.

We know that

$$\sum_{\forall j, j \neq i} p_{ij}(t, t + \triangle t) + p_{ii}(t, t + \triangle t) = 1.$$

Hence:

$$\sum_{\forall j, j \neq i} p_{ij}(t, t + \triangle t) = 1 - p_{ii}(t, t + \triangle t). \qquad (10.1.3)$$

Now, divide both sides of Equation 10.1.3 by $\triangle t$.

$$\frac{\sum_{\forall j, j \neq i} p_{ij}(t, t + \triangle t)}{\triangle t} = \frac{1 - p_{ii}(t, t + \triangle t)}{\triangle t}.$$

Applying $\lim \triangle t \to 0$, we have:

$$\lim_{\triangle t \to 0} \frac{\sum_{\forall j, j \neq i} p_{ij}(t, t + \triangle t)}{\triangle t} = \lim_{\triangle t \to 0} \frac{1 - p_{ii}(t, t + \triangle t)}{\triangle t}.$$

Thus

$$\sum_{\forall j, j \neq i} \lim_{\triangle t \to 0} \frac{p_{ij}(t, t + \triangle t)}{\triangle t} = \lim_{\triangle t \to 0} \frac{1 - p_{ii}(t, t + \triangle t)}{\triangle t}. \qquad (10.1.4)$$

From 10.1.2, we know that

$$q_{ij}(t) = \lim_{\triangle t \to 0} \frac{p_{ij}(t, t + \triangle t)}{\triangle t}, \quad i \neq j,$$

so

$$\sum_{\forall j, j \neq i} \lim_{\triangle t \to 0} \frac{p_{ij}(t, t + \triangle t)}{\triangle t} = \sum_{\forall j, j \neq i} q_{ij}(t).$$

Therefore (from 10.1.4)

$$\sum_{\forall j, j \neq i} q_{ij}(t) = \lim_{\Delta t \to 0} \frac{1 - p_{ii}(t, t + \Delta t)}{\Delta t}.$$

Let us define

$$q_{ii}(t) = -\lim_{\Delta t \to 0} \frac{1 - p_{ii}(t, t + \Delta t)}{\Delta t},$$

as the state i's remaining rate. Therefore

$$\sum_{\forall j, j \neq i} q_{ij}(t) = -q_{ii}(t);$$

then

$$\sum_{\forall j, j \neq i} q_{ij}(t) + q_{ii}(t) = 0.$$

$$q_{ii}(t) = -\sum_{\forall j, j \neq i} q_{ij}(t). \tag{10.1.5}$$

Let $\mathbf{Q}(t)$ be a matrix whose element $q_{ij}(t)$ denotes the transition rate from state i to state j, and $q_{ii}(t)$ is the state i's remaining rate, that is

$$\mathbf{Q}(t) = \lim_{\Delta t \to 0} \frac{\mathbf{P}(t, t + \Delta t) - \mathbf{I}}{\Delta t},$$

where $\mathbf{P}(t, t + \Delta t)$ is the transition probability matrix and $\mathbf{I}$ is the identity matrix. $\mathbf{Q}(t)$ is defined as the **Infinitesimal Generator** or the **Rate Matrix**. For homogeneous chains, the transition rates $q_{ij}(t)$ and $q_{ii}(t)$ are independent of time. In this case, we can adopt $\mathbf{Q}$.

Example 10.1.1. A CTMC can be represented by a state-transition diagram in which the vertices represent states and the arcs between vertices i and j are labelled with the respective transition rates, that is, $\lambda_{ij}, i \neq j$. Consider a chain composed of three states, s_0, s_1, and s_2, and their transition rates, α, β, γ, and λ. The model transitions from s_0 to s_1 with rate α; from state s_1 the model transitions to state s_0 with rate β, and to state s_2 with rate γ. When in state s_2, the model transitions to state s_1 with rate λ. This chain is presented by its transition rate diagram depicted in Figure 10.1. The rate matrix, $\mathbf{Q}$ is

$$\mathbf{Q} = \begin{pmatrix} -\alpha & \alpha & 0 \\ \beta & -(\beta + \gamma) & \gamma \\ 0 & \lambda & -\lambda \end{pmatrix} = \begin{pmatrix} -20 & 20 & 0 \\ 10 & -35 & 25 \\ 0 & 15 & -15 \end{pmatrix}.$$

□

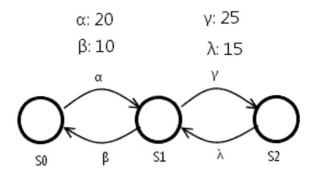

Figure 10.1   Three States CTMC.

10.2 CHAPMAN-KOLMOGOROV EQUATION

Similarly to the DTMC case (see 9.2.1), for the continuous time, discrete state-space process, our starting point is $p_{ij}(s,t) \equiv P(X(t) = j \mid X(s) = i)$, where $X(s) = i$ is the state of the process at the time instant s, and $X(t) = j$ is the state of the process at the time instant t. $p_{ij}(s,t)$ denotes the probability of reaching state j at time t, given the chain is in state i at time s, for nonhomogeneous chains [1].

For reaching state j at time t, given the chain is in state i at time s, the chain may transition from state i at time s to a state v_k at time u, and then reach state j at time t from the respective state v_k at time u. Therefore:

$$p_{ij}(s,t) = \sum_{\forall v_k} p_{iv_k}(s,u) \cdot p_{v_k j}(u,t). \qquad (10.2.1)$$

These transitions are depicted in Figure 10.2.

Now, let us consider the homogeneous case, and that $s = 0$, $u = t$, and that $t = t + \triangle t$ ($\triangle t > 0$). Hence, we have:

$$p_{ij}(0,t + \triangle t) = \sum_{\forall v_k} p_{iv_k}(0,t) \cdot p_{v_k j}(t,t + \triangle t).$$

Consider $p_{ij}(a,b) \equiv p_{ij}(b-a)$; hence :

$$p_{ij}(t + \triangle t) = \sum_{\forall v_k} p_{iv_k}(t) \cdot p_{v_k j}(\triangle t). \qquad (10.2.2)$$

Additionally, consider that the time interval $\triangle t$ is very small, that is, $\triangle t \to 0$, such that $p_{v_k j}(\triangle t) \to 0$. In other words, the probability of one transition occurring during this time interval is small. Hence, the probability that we observe multiple transitions during $\triangle t$ is negligible.

---

[1] In nonhomogeneous chains the transition probabilities are dependent on the time instants.

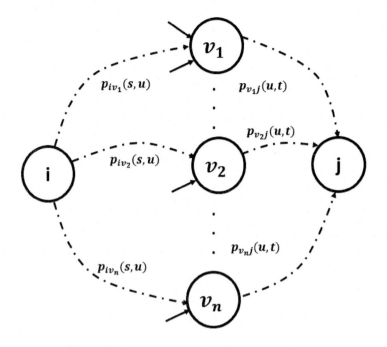

Figure 10.2 State Transitions.

We may re-write Equation 10.2.2 as:

$$p_{ij}(t + \triangle t) = \left(\sum_{\forall v_k, v_k \neq j} p_{iv_k}(t) \cdot p_{v_k j}(\triangle t) \right) + p_{ij}(t) \cdot p_{jj}(\triangle t) \qquad (10.2.3)$$

Now, subtract both sides of the Equation 10.2.3 by $p_{ij}(t)$, so we have:

$$p_{ij}(t + \triangle t) - p_{ij}(t) = \left(\left(\sum_{\forall v_k, v_k \neq j} p_{iv_k}(t) \cdot p_{v_k j}(\triangle t) \right) + p_{ij}(t) \cdot p_{jj}(\triangle t) \right) - p_{ij}(t),$$

and divide both sides by $\triangle t$. So, we have:

$$\frac{p_{ij}(t + \triangle t) - p_{ij}(t)}{\triangle t} = \frac{\left(\left(\sum_{\forall v_k, v_k \neq j} p_{iv_k}(t) \cdot p_{v_k j}(\triangle t) \right) + p_{ij}(t) \cdot p_{jj}(\triangle t) \right) - p_{ij}(t)}{\triangle t} =$$

$$\frac{\left(\sum_{\forall v_k, v_k \neq j} p_{iv_k}(t) \cdot p_{v_k j}(\triangle t) \right)}{\triangle t} + \frac{p_{ij}(t) \cdot p_{jj}(\triangle t) - p_{ij}(t)}{\triangle t}$$

Applying $\lim \triangle t \to 0$, we obtain:

$$\lim_{\triangle t \to 0} \frac{p_{ij}(t + \triangle t) - p_{ij}(t)}{\triangle t} =$$

$$\lim_{\triangle t \to 0} \frac{\left(\sum_{\forall v_k, v_k \neq j} p_{iv_k}(t) \cdot p_{v_k j}(\triangle t) \right)}{\triangle t} + \lim_{\triangle t \to 0} \frac{p_{ij}(t) \cdot p_{jj}(\triangle t) - p_{ij}(t)}{\triangle t}.$$

Therefore:

$$\frac{\partial p_{ij}(t)}{\partial t} = \sum_{\forall v_k, v_k \neq j} p_{iv_k}(t) \times \lim_{\triangle t \to 0} \frac{\left(p_{v_k j}(\triangle t) \right)}{\triangle t} + p_{ij}(t) \times \lim_{\triangle t \to 0} \frac{p_{jj}(\triangle t) - 1}{\triangle t} =$$

$$\sum_{\forall v_k, v_k \neq j} p_{iv_k}(t) \times q_{v_k j}(\triangle t) + p_{ij}(t) \times q_{jj}(\triangle t).$$

Thus:

$$\frac{\partial p_{ij}(t)}{\partial t} = \sum_{\forall v_k, v_k \neq j} p_{iv_k}(t) \times q_{v_k j}(\triangle t) + p_{ij}(t) \times q_{jj}(\triangle t). \qquad (10.2.4)$$

$$\frac{\partial p_{ij}(t)}{\partial t} = \sum_{\forall v_k} p_{iv_k}(t) \times q_{v_k j}(\triangle t), \qquad (10.2.5)$$

where

$$q_{v_k j}(\triangle t) = \lim_{\triangle t \to 0} \frac{p_{v_k j}(\triangle t)}{\triangle t}, \quad \forall v_k, v_k \neq j \qquad (10.2.6)$$

and

$$q_{jj}(\triangle t) = \lim_{\triangle t \to 0} \frac{p_{jj}(\triangle t) - 1}{\triangle t}. \qquad (10.2.7)$$

These quantities ($q_{v_k j}(\triangle t)$ and $q_{jj}(\triangle t)$) denote a transition rates. Equation 10.2.5 is named the **Chapman-Kolmogorov Forward Equations**. In matrix form, Equation 10.2.5 may be written as

$$\frac{\partial \mathbf{P}(t)}{\partial t} = \mathbf{P}(t) \cdot \mathbf{Q}(t). \qquad (10.2.8)$$

We know that in homogeneous Markov chains the transition rate matrix is independent of t, that is, $\mathbf{Q}(t) = \mathbf{Q}$; hence

$$\frac{d\mathbf{P}(t)}{dt} = \mathbf{P}(t) \cdot \mathbf{Q}. \qquad (10.2.9)$$

In a similar manner, we may derive the **Chapman-Kolmogorov Backward Equations**, which are

$$\frac{\partial p_{ij}(t)}{\partial t} = \sum_{\forall v_k} q_{iv_k}(\triangle t) \times p_{v_k j}(t). \tag{10.2.10}$$

In matrix form, the Equation 10.2.10 may be written as

$$\frac{\partial \mathbf{P}(t)}{\partial t} = \mathbf{Q}(t) \cdot \mathbf{P}(t). \tag{10.2.11}$$

And, for homogeneous Markov chains, we have

$$\frac{d p_{ij}(t)}{dt} = \sum_{\forall v_k} q_{iv_k} \times p_{v_k j}(t). \tag{10.2.12}$$

$$\frac{d\mathbf{P}(t)}{dt} = \mathbf{Q} \cdot \mathbf{P}(t). \tag{10.2.13}$$

We know that

$$\frac{\frac{df(x)}{dx}}{f(x)} = \frac{d \ln f(x)}{dx},$$

and thus

$$\frac{\frac{d\mathbf{P}(t)}{dt}}{\mathbf{P}(t)} = \frac{d \ln \mathbf{P}(t)}{dt}.$$

As (from Equation 10.2.13),

$$\mathbf{Q} = \frac{\frac{d\mathbf{P}(t)}{dt}}{\mathbf{P}(t)},$$

then

$$\mathbf{Q} = \frac{d \ln \mathbf{P}(t)}{dt}.$$

Integrating both sides, we have:

$$\int_0^t \frac{d \ln \mathbf{P}(t)}{dt} dt = \int_0^t \mathbf{Q} dt.$$

$$\ln \mathbf{P}(t) - \ln \mathbf{P}(0) = \mathbf{Q}t.$$

$$\ln \left(\frac{\mathbf{P}(t)}{\mathbf{P}(0)} \right) = \mathbf{Q}t.$$

Exponentiating both sides, we have:

$$e^{\ln \left(\frac{\mathbf{P}(t)}{\mathbf{P}(0)} \right)} = e^{\mathbf{Q}t}.$$

Thus

$$\frac{\mathbf{P}(t)}{\mathbf{P}(0)} = e^{\mathbf{Q}t}.$$

Therefore

$$\mathbf{P}(t) = \mathbf{P}(0)\, e^{\mathbf{Q}t}. \qquad (10.2.14)$$

For $\mathbf{P}(0) = \mathbf{I}$ and applying the Taylor-Maclaurin expansion (see Section 5.4), we have [313, 413]:

$$\mathbf{P}(t) = \mathbf{P}(0)\, e^{\mathbf{Q}t} = \mathbf{I} + \sum_{k=1}^{\infty} \frac{\mathbf{Q}t^k}{k!}. \qquad (10.2.15)$$

Unfortunately, the computation of the matrix exponential can be rather strenuous and unstable [283, 284, 413]. We shall consider this later. Nevertheless, let us compute such a solution for a tiny chain. Let's consider a CTMC depicted in Figure 10.3.

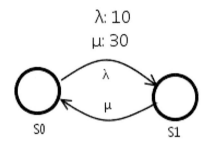

Figure 10.3 Two States CTMC.

Example 10.2.1. This chain is composed of only two states, s_0 and s_1. The rates are $\lambda = 30\, h_{-1}$ and $\mu = 30\, h_{-1}$; hence the rate matrix is

$$\mathbf{Q} = \begin{pmatrix} -\lambda & \lambda \\ \mu & -\mu \end{pmatrix} = \begin{pmatrix} -10 & 10 \\ 30 & -30 \end{pmatrix}$$

The probability matrices at $t = 0.01\, h$, $0.1\, h$, and $0.4\, h$, truncated at $k = 100$, are:

$$\mathbf{P}(0.01) = \begin{pmatrix} 0.91758 & 0.08242 \\ 0.24726 & 0.75274 \end{pmatrix}.$$

$$\mathbf{P}(0.1) = \begin{pmatrix} 0.754579 & 0.245421 \\ 0.736263 & 0.263737 \end{pmatrix}.$$

$$\mathbf{P}(0.4) = \begin{pmatrix} 0.75 & 0.25 \\ 0.75 & 0.25 \end{pmatrix}.$$

These matrices were computed using Mathematica 11 standard libraries with 20 decimal digit precision. If we adopt this approach (10.2.15) for computing $\mathbf{P}(t)$, for higher values of t, however, the results become unstable. For instance, for $t = 0.92$, the probability matrix has even negative values and values above one. The obtained matrix was:

$$\mathbf{P}(0.92) = \begin{pmatrix} -0.1875 & 1.1875 \\ 0.1875 & 0.8125 \end{pmatrix}.$$

Better solutions will be discussed later in this document.

$\square$

A state classification for CTMCs is similar to DTMCs without the notion of periodic/aperiodic states. A state i is **absorbing** if once reaching i, the process remains there, that is, $q_{ij} = 0$, for $j \neq i$. A state j is **reachable** from state i if $p_{ij}(t)$ for some $t > 0$. A CTMC is **irreducible** if every state is reachable from every other state [52, 437]. A state of a CTMC is said to be ergodic if it is positive recurrent. A CTMC is ergodic if all its states are ergodic.

Consider a CTMC specified by $(\mathscr{X}, \mathbf{Q})$, where $\mathscr{X}$ is its set of state and $\mathbf{Q}$ is the rate matrix. Let $\Pi(t)$ be a vector that represents the probability of being in each state of $\mathscr{X}$ at time t. The state probability vector has a dimension equal to the state space of the chain, that is,

$$\Pi(t) = (\pi_i(t))_{|\mathscr{X}|}.$$

$\pi_i(t)^2$ is the probability of being in state i at time t.

Now, let us consider the system of equations 10.2.8 and $\Pi(t)$. Therefore,

$$\frac{\partial \Pi(t)}{\partial t} = \Pi(t) \cdot \mathbf{Q}(t). \tag{10.2.16}$$

One may notice that $\Pi(t)$ might be considered one of the probability vectors of the matrix $\mathbf{P}(t)$. For homogeneous Markov chains (from 10.2.9), we have

$$\frac{d\Pi(t)}{dt} = \Pi(t) \cdot \mathbf{Q}, \tag{10.2.17}$$

that has the following solution:

$$\Pi(t) = \Pi(0)\, e^{\mathbf{Q}t} = \Pi(0) \left(\mathbf{I} + \sum_{k=1}^{\infty} \frac{\mathbf{Q}t^k}{k!} \right). \tag{10.2.18}$$

In many cases, however, the instantaneous behavior, $\Pi(t)$, of the Markov chain is more than we need. In many cases, we are often already satisfied when we can compute the steady-state probabilities , that is, $\Pi = \lim t \to \infty \Pi(t)$. Hence, let us take the

---

[2]The notation adopted in the Mercury tool is $P\{s\}$, where s is the state name. The time instant of interest, t, is specified during evaluation by the analyst.

system of differential equations presented in 10.2.17. If the steady-state distribution exists, then

$$\frac{d\Pi(t)}{dt} = 0.$$

Consequently, for calculating the steady-state probabilities we only need to solve the system :

$$\Pi \cdot \mathbf{Q} = 0, \quad \sum_{\forall i} \pi_i = 1. \tag{10.2.19}$$

Sections 10.4 and 10.5 present a set of methods for calculating the steady-state and transient distributions of Markov chains.

10.3 HOLDING TIMES

Let us consider the CTMC presented in Figure 10.4. This chain is composed of three states, named i, j_1, and j_2. The states j_1 and j_2 are absorbing states. Moreover, consider that the chain is in state i at $t = 0$. The transition rates are depicted by λ_{ij_1} and λ_{ij_2}. The infinitesimal generator $\mathbf{Q}$ is

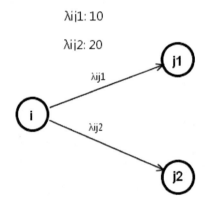

Figure 10.4 CTMC – Holding Time (Residence Time).

$$\mathbf{Q} = \begin{matrix} & \begin{matrix} i & \quad j_1 & \quad j_2 \end{matrix} \\ \begin{matrix} i \\ j_1 \\ j_2 \end{matrix} & \begin{pmatrix} -(\lambda_{j_1} + \lambda_{j_2}) & \lambda_{j_1} & \lambda_{j_1} \\ 0 & 0 & 0 \\ 0 & 0 & 0 \end{pmatrix} \end{matrix}.$$

Since

$$\frac{d\Pi(t)}{dt} = \Pi(t) \cdot \mathbf{Q} \quad (\text{see} 10.2.17),$$

we have:

$$\frac{d\pi_i(t)}{dt} = -(\lambda_{ij_1} + \lambda_{ij_2}) \cdot \pi_i(t),$$

and

$$\frac{d\pi_i(t)/dt}{\pi_i(t)} = -(\lambda_{ij_1} + \lambda_{ij_2}). \tag{10.3.1}$$

As

$$\frac{df(x)/dx}{f(x)} = \frac{d\ln f(x)}{dx},$$

thus

$$\frac{d\pi_i(t)/dt}{\pi_i(t)} = \frac{d\ln\pi_i(t)}{dt}. \tag{10.3.2}$$

Hence (from 10.3.1 and 10.3.2):

$$\frac{d\ln\pi_i(t)}{dt} = -(\lambda_{ij_1} + \lambda_{ij_2}).$$

Integrating both sides:

$$\int_0^t \frac{d\ln\pi_i(t)}{dt}dt = -\int_0^t (\lambda_{ij_1} + \lambda_{ij_2})dt.$$

$$\ln\pi_i(t) - \ln\pi_i(0) = -(\lambda_{ij_1} + \lambda_{ij_2})t.$$

If $\pi_i(0) = 1$, then:

$$\ln\pi_i(t) = -(\lambda_{ij_1} + \lambda_{ij_2})t.$$

Exponentiating both sides:

$$e^{\ln\pi_i(t)} = e^{-(\lambda_{ij_1} + \lambda_{ij_2})t}.$$

$$\pi_i(t) = e^{-(\lambda_{ij_1} + \lambda_{ij_2})t}. \tag{10.3.3}$$

Let T_i be the state i residence time (holding time or sojourn time). $\pi_i(t)$ ($F_i(t)$) is the state i probability distribution function.
As

$$\frac{dF_i(t)}{dt} = f_i(t),$$

hence

$$f_i(t) = \frac{d\pi_i(t)}{dt} = (\lambda_{ij_1} + \lambda_{ij_2})\, e^{-(\lambda_{ij_1} + \lambda_{ij_2})t}.$$

Since $E(T_i) = \int_0^\infty t \cdot f_i(t)\, dt$; hence :

$$E(T_i) = \int_0^\infty t \cdot (\lambda_{ij_1} + \lambda_{ij_2})\, e^{-(\lambda_{ij_1} + \lambda_{ij_2})t}\, dt.$$

$$E(T_i) = \frac{1}{\lambda_{ij_1} + \lambda_{ij_2}} = \frac{1}{-\lambda_{ii}},$$

where $\lambda_{ii} = -(\lambda_{ij_1} + \lambda_{ij_2})$.

Generalizing for n states, that is $\{i, j_1, j_2, \ldots, j_n\}$, we have:

$$E(T_i) = \frac{1}{\sum_{\forall j, j \neq i} \lambda_{ij}} = \frac{1}{-\lambda_{ii}},$$

where $\lambda_{ii} = -\sum_{\forall j, j \neq i} \lambda_{ij}$.

Considering the CTMC depicted in Figure 10.4, the holding time of state i is $h_i = \frac{1}{\lambda_{ij_1} + \lambda_{ij_2}} = \frac{1}{10+20} = 0.0333\, t.u..$[3]

Example 10.3.1. Let us consider the CTMC shown in Figure 10.1. This chain has three states, s_0, s_1, and s_2. The state transition rates are: $\alpha = 20$, $\beta = 10$, $\gamma = 25$, and $\lambda = 15$. The residence time of each state is:

$$h_{s_0} = \frac{1}{\alpha} = \frac{1}{20} = 0.05\, t.u.,$$

$$h_{s_1} = \frac{1}{\beta + \gamma} = \frac{1}{10 + 25} = 0.0286\, t.u., \text{ and}$$

$$h_{s_2} = \frac{1}{\lambda} = \frac{1}{15} = 0.0667\, t.u.$$

$\square$

10.4   STATIONARY ANALYSIS

There are two broad types of solutions in stationary numerical analysis: direct solution methods and iterative solution methods. Direct methods present a set of well-defined steps that lead to a system solution. However, the number of steps may be large and rounding errors may be significant in some instances. On the other hand, iterative methods begin with an initial approximation of the solution and iteratively proceed reaching closer solutions to the exact solution. However, it is important to

---

[3]t.u. denotes time units.

stress that iterative methods may require a very long time to converge or even do not converge to the exact solution.

This section introduces some methods to compute stationary distributions of homogeneous DTMCs and CTMCs. In particular, we present the Gauss elimination method (a direct method), the power method (iterative), and the Gauss-Seidel iterative method. Many other methods are thoroughly presented in [413].

The most straightforward approach for computing the stationary distribution of a DTMC is to let the chain evolve, step by step, until reaching its stationary distribution. Once the probability vector no longer changes from step n to step $n + 1$, that vector can be taken as the stationary probability distribution. This method is commonly named the **Power Method** and was introduced in Section 9.3 and 9.4. The power method may also be applied to evaluated CTMCs; first, however, the transition probability matrix ($\mathbf{P}$) should be obtained from the transition rate matrix ($\mathbf{Q}$). This process is depicted in the following. The subsequent steps for obtaining the CTMC´s stationary distribution are the same as presented for DTMCs.

Let us begin considering a finite ergodic DTMC. The stationary distribution can be computed by solving (9.4.1)

$$\Pi = \Pi \times \mathbf{P}, \tag{10.4.1}$$

$$\Pi \times \mathbb{1}^T = 1.$$

If we consider an ergodic CTMC, its steady-state distribution may be computed by solving the following system of equations (10.2.19):

$$\Pi \cdot \mathbf{Q} = 0, \tag{10.4.2}$$

$$\Pi \times \mathbb{1}^T = 1.$$

These two systems of equations may be presented in the same form; for instance, $\Pi \times \mathbf{P} = \Pi =$ may be presented as

$$\Pi \times \mathbf{P} - \Pi = \Pi - \Pi,$$

$$\Pi (\mathbf{P} - \mathbf{I}) = 0.$$

The reader should observe that $\mathbf{P} - \mathbf{I}$ has all the properties of the rate matrix. CTMCs, on the other hand, may be discretized. The discretization process is presented in Section 10.5.4.

Therefore, the numerical methods designed to compute the steady-state distribution of CTMCs may be used to compute the steady-state distributions of DTMCs and vice versa.

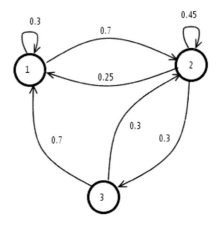

Figure 10.5   Transition Probability Matrix.

Example 10.4.1. Consider a DTMC depicted in Figure 10.5. Its transition probability matrix $\mathbf{P}$ is

$$
\begin{array}{c c c c}
 & 1 & 2 & 3 \\
\begin{array}{c} 1 \\ 2 \\ 3 \end{array} &
\left(\begin{array}{c c c}
0.3 & 0.7 & 0 \\
0.25 & 0.45 & 0.3 \\
0.7 & 0.3 & 0
\end{array} \right)
\end{array} \quad .
$$

Therefore, $\mathbf{P} - \mathbf{I}$ is

$$
\begin{array}{c c c c}
 & 1 & 2 & 3 \\
\begin{array}{c} 1 \\ 2 \\ 3 \end{array} &
\left(\begin{array}{c c c}
-0.7 & 0.7 & 0 \\
0.25 & -0.55 & 0.3 \\
0.7 & 0.3 & -1
\end{array} \right)
\end{array} \quad .
$$

□

Stochastic Matrix

A matrix $\mathbf{P} = (p_{ij})_{|n| \times |m|}$, $p_{ij} \in \mathbb{R}$ is said to be stochastic (**stochastic matrix**) if

1. $0 \le p_{ij} \le 1$, $\forall i, j$.

2. $\sum_{\forall j} p_{ij} = 1$, $\forall i$.

10.4.1   GAUSS ELIMINATION

This section applies the Gauss elimination method to find the steady-state distributions of Markov chains. The method is named Gauss elimination since it involves combining equations to eliminate unknowns. Although it is one of the earliest methods for solving linear equations, it is still one of the most important algorithms and the basis for solving linear equations on many software tools.

Consider a finite, irreducible, and ergodic CTMC with infinitesimal generator $\mathbf{Q}$. Computing the steady-state distribution of such a chain consists of solving the system

$$\Pi \cdot \mathbf{Q} = 0,$$

$$\Pi \times \mathbb{1}^T = 1.$$

It should also be highlighted that $\mathbf{Q}$ is weakly diagonal dominant, since q_{ii} is the sum of all a_{ij}, $\forall j$.

$\Pi \cdot \mathbf{Q} = 0$ has n linear equations in which the n unknowns are π_i, $i = 1, 2, \dots, n$. This system provides only $n - 1$ linearly independent equations, but $\Pi \times \mathbb{1}^T = 1$ provides the means for normalization. One alternative is substituting any equation of $\Pi \cdot \mathbf{Q} = 0$ by $\Pi \times \mathbb{1}^T = 1$. Another alternative is solving $\Pi \cdot \mathbf{Q} = 0$ and, at the end, applying a normalization step.

Let us consider a CTMC and its rate matrix $\mathbf{Q}$. The system described above may be rearranged and presented as

$$\mathbf{Q}^T \cdot \Pi^T = \mathbf{0}, \tag{10.4.3}$$

where $\mathbf{Q}^T$ is the transposed $\mathbf{Q}$ matrix, Π^T is the vector Π presented as a column vector, and $\mathbf{0}$ is a column vector with every element equal to 0. Now, substitute the last equation of System 10.4.3 by the Equation

$$\Pi \times \mathbb{1}^T = 1.$$

This new system of equations may be represented by

$$\mathbf{A} \cdot \Pi^T = \begin{pmatrix} \mathbf{0} \\ 1 \end{pmatrix}, \tag{10.4.4}$$

where $\mathbf{A}$ is the $\mathbf{Q}^T$ with the last row having been substituted by $(1, 1, 1)$, and the column vector

$$\begin{pmatrix} \mathbf{0} \\ 1 \end{pmatrix}$$

is a vector with $n - 1$ row elements equal to 0 and the last element row equal to 1. The augmented coefficient matrix, $\mathbf{C}$, of such a system is composed of matrix $\mathbf{A}$ appended by the column vector $\begin{pmatrix} \mathbf{0} \\ 1 \end{pmatrix}$, that is

$$\mathbf{C} = \mathbf{A} \,|\, \begin{pmatrix} \mathbf{0} \\ 1 \end{pmatrix}.$$

Therefore, the augmented matrix $\mathbf{C}$ is composed of n rows (E_i), each of which depicts the coefficient of each equation of the system 10.4.4.

$$C = \begin{pmatrix} E_1 \\ E_2 \\ \dots \\ E_n \end{pmatrix},$$

where $E_2 = ()$

Example 10.4.2. Consider the CTMC depicted in Figure 10.6.

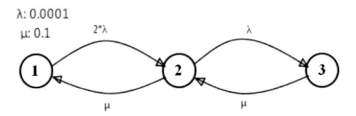

Figure 10.6   Gauss Elimination.

$$\mathbf{Q} = \begin{array}{c} \\ 1 \\ 2 \\ 3 \end{array} \begin{array}{ccc} 1 & 2 & 3 \\ \begin{pmatrix} -2\lambda & 2\lambda & 0 \\ \mu & -(\mu + \lambda) & \lambda \\ 0 & \mu & -\mu \end{pmatrix} \end{array} \quad .$$

The transposed matrix $\mathbf{Q}^T$ is

$$\mathbf{Q}^T = \begin{array}{c} \\ 1 \\ 2 \\ 3 \end{array} \begin{array}{ccc} 1 & 2 & 3 \\ \begin{pmatrix} -2\lambda & \mu & 0 \\ 2\lambda & -(\mu + \lambda) & \mu \\ 0 & \lambda & -\mu \end{pmatrix} \end{array} \quad .$$

The matrix $\mathbf{A}$ is obtained by substituting, for instance, the last row of $\mathbf{Q}^T$ by the coefficients of $\pi_0 + \pi_1 + \pi_2 = 1$, that is $(1, 1, 1)$:

$$\mathbf{A} = \begin{array}{c} \\ 1 \\ 2 \\ 3 \end{array} \begin{array}{ccc} 1 & 2 & 3 \\ \begin{pmatrix} -2\lambda & \mu & 0 \\ 2\lambda & -(\mu + \lambda) & \mu \\ 1 & 1 & 1 \end{pmatrix} \end{array} \quad .$$

Therefore, the system $\mathbf{A} \cdot \Pi^T = \begin{pmatrix} \mathbf{0} \\ 1 \end{pmatrix}$ is composed of three equations, E_1, E_2, and E_3, as shown below:

$$\begin{cases} -2\lambda\,\pi_1 + \mu\,\pi_2 + 0\,\pi_3 = 0, & (E_1) \\ 2\lambda\,\pi_1 + -(\mu+\lambda)\pi_2 + \mu\pi_3 = 0, & (E_2) \\ \pi_1 + \pi_2 + \pi_3 = 1. & (E_3) \end{cases}$$

This system is also represented in the augmented coefficient matrix, **C**, of the above system,

$$\begin{array}{c} \\ E_1: 1 \\ E_2: 2 \\ E_3: 3 \end{array} \begin{array}{cccc} 1 & 2 & 3 & 4 \\ \left(\begin{array}{ccc|c} -2\lambda & \mu & 0 & 0 \\ 2\lambda & -(\mu+\lambda) & \mu & 0 \\ 1 & 1 & 1 & 1 \end{array}\right) \end{array},$$

where each equation (E_1, E_2, and E_3) is represented in the respective row. □

Gaussian Elimination Algorithm

The Gaussian elimination method is composed of two phases, named the reduction and substitution phases. The reduction phase multiplies rows of **C** by scalars and subtracts rows from one another, aiming at obtaining an upper-triangular matrix. This method is shown in the Algorithm 12.

Algorithm 12 Gauss Elimination Applied to Markov Chains

1: **Input:** number of equation and unknowns, n, and the augmented coefficient matrix, **C**.
2: **Output:** steady-state distribution $\Pi = (\pi_1, \pi_2, ..., \pi_n)$.
3:
4: **Reduction Phase**
5: *For $i = 1,...,n-1$, do*
6:    *For $j = i,...,n$, do*
7:      $m_{j,i} = \frac{c_{j,i}}{c_{i,i}}$
8:      $E_j \leftarrow E_j - (m_{j,i}) \cdot E_i$ (Rewrite the row E_j.)
9:
10: **Substitution Phase**
11: $\pi_n = \frac{c_{n,n+1}}{c_{n,n}}$
12: *For $i = n-1,...,1$, do*
13:    $\pi_i = \frac{0-\sum_{j=i+1}^{n} c_{i,j}\cdot\pi_j}{c_{i,i}}$
14: *Output $(\pi_1, \pi_2, ..., \pi_n)$.*
15: *End*

This process starts by reading the augmented coefficient matrix, **C**, and the number of unknowns, n (Line 1). Then, the reduction phase proceeds by varying i from 1 to $n-1$ (Line 5) and j from $i+1$ to n (Line 6). Each jth equation is changed by subtracting it from $m_{j,i}$ times the ith equation (see Line 7 and 8). At the end of this process, an upper-triangular matrix is obtained. Now, the substitution phase is executed. It starts by computing the steady-state probability of the state n, that is, π_n, by dividing $c_{n,n+1}$ by $c_{n,n}$ (See Line 11). Afterward, the probabilities of the state $n - 1$ are obtained by subtracting 0 from $c_{i,j} \cdot \pi_j$ and dividing this partial result by $c_{i,i}$. The probabilities of the other states (State $n - 2$ to State 1) are calculated in similar fashion, as depicted in Line 13. When the substitution phase is concluded, the steady-state probability distribution is available (Line 14).

Example 10.4.3. Now we apply the method presented to calculate the steady-state distribution of the CTMC depicted in Example 10.4.2. The inputs are the number of unknowns, $n = 3$, and the augmented coefficient matrix, $\mathbf{C}$ (Line 1), which was already shown in the previous example. Let us assume the following values for the CTMC's parameters: $\lambda = 0.0001$ and $\mu = 0.1$. Considering these values, we have an augmented coefficient matrix, $\mathbf{C}$:

$$
\begin{array}{c}
E_1: \\
E_2: \\
E_3:
\end{array}
\begin{array}{c}
1 \\
2 \\
3
\end{array}
\left(
\begin{array}{ccc|c}
1 & 2 & 3 & 4 \\
-0.0002 & 0.1 & 0 & 0 \\
0.0002 & -0.1001 & 0.1 & 0 \\
1 & 1 & 1 & 1
\end{array}
\right) .
$$

The reduction phase aims at transforming the augmented coefficient matrix, $\mathbf{C}$, into an upper-triangular matrix. The first step in this process consists of transforming the element $c_{2,1}$ in zero. For accomplishing that, we have to define a value $m_{2,1}$ (Line 7) that multiplied by $\mathbf{C}$ matrix row E_1 and subtracted from the $\mathbf{C}$ row E_2 generates a new value for the element $c_{2,1}$, named $c'_{2,1}$, that is zero (Line 8).

Since $m_{2,1} = c_{2,1}/c_{1,1}$, then take $c_{1,1}$ and $c_{2,1}$. As $c_{1,1} = -0.0002$ and $c_{2,1} = 0.0002$, then $m_{2,1} = -1$. Now we compute $E'_2 = E_2 - m_{2,1} \cdot E_1$:

$$
E'_2 = (0.0002, \ -0.1001, \ 0.1, \ | \ 0) \ - \ (-1) \cdot (0.0002, \ -0.1001, \ 0.1, \ | \ 0).
$$

Hence

$$
E'_2 = (0, \ -0.1001, \ 0.1, \ | \ 0).
$$

Therefore, the augmented coefficient matrix, $\mathbf{C}$, is updated to

$$
\begin{array}{c}
E_1: \\
E_2: \\
E_3:
\end{array}
\begin{array}{c}
1 \\
2 \\
3
\end{array}
\left(
\begin{array}{ccc|c}
1 & 2 & 3 & 4 \\
-0.0002 & 0.1 & 0 & 0 \\
0 & -0.0001 & 0.1 & 0 \\
1 & 1 & 1 & 1
\end{array}
\right) .
$$

Now, we should obtain a new row E_3, named E'_3 in which the element $c_{3,1}$ is null. This is accomplished by $E'_3 = E_3 - m_{3,1} \cdot E_1$, where $m_{3,1} = c_{3,1}/c_{1,1}$. Thus, as $c_{3,1} = 1$ and $c_{1,1} = -0.0002$, $m_{3,1} = -5000$. Therefore, $E'_3 = E_3 - m_{3,1} \cdot E_1$:

$$E_3' = (1, \quad 1, \quad 1, \quad | \quad 1) - (-5000) \cdot (-0.0002, \quad 0.1, \quad 0, \quad | \quad 0) .$$

Thus

$$E_3' = (0, \quad 501, \quad 1, \quad | \quad 1).$$

Therefore, **C** is updated to

$$
\begin{array}{cccc}
 & 1 & 2 & 3 & 4 \\
\begin{array}{c} E_1: 1 \\ E_2: 2 \\ E_3: 3 \end{array} &
\left(\begin{array}{ccc|c}
-0.0002 & 0.1 & 0 & 0 \\
0 & -0.0001 & 0.1 & 0 \\
0 & 501 & 1 & 1
\end{array} \right)
\end{array} .
$$

Now, we calculate a new row E_3, called E_3'' in which the element $c_{3,2}$ is null. This is accomplished by $E_3'' = E_3 - m_{3,2} \cdot E_2$, where $m_{3,2} = c_{3,2}/c_{2,2}$. Thus, as $c_{3,2} = 501$ and $c_{2,2} = -0.0001$, $m_{3,1} = -5010000$. Therefore, $E_3'' = E_3 - m_{3,2} \cdot E_2$:

$$E_3'' = (0, \quad 501, \quad 1, \quad | \quad 1) - (-5010000) \cdot (0, \quad -0.0001, \quad 0.1, \quad | \quad 0) .$$

Thus

$$E_3'' = (0, \quad 0, \quad 501001, \quad | \quad 1).$$

Thus, **C** is updated to

$$
\begin{array}{cccc}
 & 1 & 2 & 3 & 4 \\
\begin{array}{c} E_1: 1 \\ E_2: 2 \\ E_3: 3 \end{array} &
\left(\begin{array}{ccc|c}
-0.0002 & 0.1 & 0 & 0 \\
0 & -0.0001 & 0.1 & 0 \\
0 & 0 & 501001 & 1
\end{array} \right)
\end{array} .
$$

At this point, the reduction phase is finished, and the substitution phase starts. The first step is calculating π_3 by $c_{3,4}/c_{3,3}$ (See Line 11). Thus $\pi_3 = \frac{1}{501001} = 1.996 \times 10^{-6}$. After that, π_2 and π_1 are respectively computed (Line 13), that is

$$\pi_2 = \frac{0 - (-0.0001 \times 1.996 \times 10^{-6})}{0.1} = 0.001996004, \quad \text{and}$$

$$\pi_1 = -\frac{0 - (0.1 \times 0.001996004)}{0.0002} = 0.998002.$$

Therefore

$$(\pi_1, \pi_2, \pi_3) = (0.998002, 0.001996004, 1.996 \times 10^{-6})^4.$$

$\square$

---

[4]The notation adopted in the Mercury tool is $P\{s\}$, where s is the state name.

10.4.2 GAUSS-SEIDEL METHOD

Iterative methods are seldom adopted for analyzing small dimension Markov chains since the time needed for reaching the required accuracy exceeds those of direct methods, such as Gaussian elimination. For large Markov chains, however, these methods are efficient concerning both storage and computation time.

Iterative solution methods are frequently obtained from the specification of a problem in the form $x = f(x)$ and then constructing the iterative process

$$x^{k+1} = f(x^k),$$

with some initial approximation x^0, where k refers to the iteration step of the respective approximation. In other words, the new iterate (x^{k+1}) is obtained by inserting the value at the previous iterate (x^k) into the right-hand side, that is $f(x^k)$. The most widely known iterative solutions are the Jacobi, the Gauss-Seidel, and successive overrelaxation methods [413].

Consider the system of linear equations depicted in 10.4.3

$$\mathbf{A} \cdot \Pi^T = \mathbf{0},$$

where $\mathbf{A}$ is the transposed rate matrix $(\mathbf{Q}^T)$. This system of equations is fully represented as

$$
\begin{cases}
-a_{1,1}\pi_1 + a_{1,2}\pi_2 + a_{1,3}\pi_3 + \ldots + a_{1,n-1}\pi_{n-1} + a_{1,n}\pi_n = 0, \\
a_{2,1}\pi_1 - a_{2,2}\pi_2 + a_{2,3}\pi_3 + \ldots + a_{2,n-1}\pi_{n-1} + a_{2,n}\pi_n = 0, \\
a_{3,1}\pi_1 + a_{3,2}\pi_2 - a_{3,3}\pi_3 + \ldots + a_{3,n-1}\pi_{n-1} + a_{3,n}\pi_n = 0, \\
\ldots \\
a_{n-1,1}\pi_1 + a_{n-1,2}\pi_2 + a_{n-1,3}\pi_3 + \ldots + a_{n-1,n-1}\pi_{n-1} - a_{n-1,n}\pi_n = 0, \\
a_{n,1}\pi_1 + a_{n,2}\pi_2 + a_{n,3}\pi_3 + \ldots + a_{n,n-1}\pi_{n-1} - a_{n,n}\pi_n = 0.
\end{cases}
$$

Moving all terms off-diagonal to the right-hand side of the equations we have

$$
\begin{cases}
a_{1,1}\pi_1 = a_{1,2}\pi_2 + a_{1,3}\pi_3 + \ldots + a_{1,n-1}\pi_{n-1} + a_{1,n}\pi_n, \\
a_{2,2}\pi_2 = a_{2,1}\pi_1 + a_{2,3}\pi_3 + \ldots + a_{2,n-1}\pi_{n-1} + a_{2,n}\pi_n, \\
a_{3,3}\pi_3 = a_{3,1}\pi_1 + a_{3,2}\pi_2 + \ldots + a_{3,n-1}\pi_{n-1} + a_{3,n}\pi_n, \\
\ldots \\
a_{n-1,n-1}\pi_{n-1} = a_{n-1,1}\pi_1 + a_{n-1,2}\pi_2 + \ldots + a_{n-1,n-1}\pi_{n-1} + a_{n-1,n}\pi_n, \\
a_{n,n}\pi_n = a_{n,1}\pi_1 + a_{n,2}\pi_2 + a_{n,3}\pi_3 + \ldots + a_{n,n-1}\pi_{n-1}.
\end{cases}
$$

The iterative process starts by assuming a first guess for Π, denoted by $\Pi^0 = (\pi_1^0, \pi_2^0, \ldots, \pi_n^0)$. Then, the next estimates $\Pi^{k+1} = (\pi_1^{k+1}, \pi_2^{k+1}, \ldots, \pi_n^{k+1})$ are computed through:

$$\pi_i^{k+1} = -\frac{1}{a_{i,i}} \left(\sum_{j<i} \pi_j^{k+1} a_{i,j} + \sum_{j>i} \pi_j^k a_{i,j} \right),$$

where we assume the order of computation from π_1^{k+1} to π_n^{k+1}.

One fundamental aspect to consider is knowing when convergence has occurred. Hence, it important to find the number of iterations, k, needed to satisfy a numerical precision ε. The numerical precision of the iterative process can be computed by $(\sum_{i=1}^{n} (\pi_i^{k+1} - \pi_i^k)^2)^{1/2}$.

Testing convergence at every iteration has its drawbacks. The numerical precision at each iterate may vary, and small values may be reached soon. Later, it may get larger and finally may steadily reduce. If the convergence criterion is reached soon, the result provided may be too far from the actual solution. One alternative to overcome this issue is testing not successive iterates but iterates spaced further apart, such as

$$\left(\sum_{i=1}^{n} (\pi_i^k - \pi_i^{k-m})^2 \right)^{1/2}.$$

For preventing underflow, it is advisable to check the magnitude of the elements and make those smaller than a certain threshold to zero.

Gauss-Seidel Algorithm

The Gauss-Seidel method (Algorithm 13) inputs the number of unknowns, n, the transposed rate matrix, $\mathbf{A}$, an initial guess for the probability distribution, $\Pi(0)$, and the maximal error, ε, (see Line 1). The algorithm outputs the distribution probability, Π.

When choosing an initial probability vector guess, it is tempting to choose a simple initial approximation, such as a vector in which every component is null expect for one element. Nevertheless, such approximations may not converge. An interesting alternative is to assign uniform random numbers distributed between 0 and 1 to components of the initial guess and normalize them to produce a probability vector [413].

From the initial probability distribution guess $(\Pi(0) = (\pi_1(0), \pi_2(0), \dots, \pi_n(0)))$, other approximations are computed through summing up products of off-diagonal elements of each matrix $\mathbf{A}$ row $(a_{i,j})$ times the respective probabilities $(\pi_j^{k+1}$ or $\pi_j^k)$, and dividing by the respective diagonal element of matrix $\mathbf{A}$ $(a_{i,i})$. This is implemented in Lines 12, 14, and 15. The result of each iteration may not be a probability vector; that is, the sum of the components of the computed vector $(\sum_{i=1}^{n} \pi_i)$ may not be one. This vector, however, may be normalized by dividing each component by the sum of the components, i.e, $\pi_i / \sum_{i=1}^{n} \pi_i$. This is implemented in Line 16 and 21. For each iteration (k), we compute $S_k = \sum_{i=1}^{n} \sqrt{(\pi_i^{k+1} - \pi_i^k)^2}$ (see Line 23 and 24). If S_k is smaller or equal to the maximal specified error, the iterations stop (Line 7) and a solution is provided (Line 27); otherwise the iterative process goes on.

Algorithm 13 Gauss-Seidel Method Applied to Markov Chains

1: **Input:** number of equation and unknowns, n, the transposed rate matrix, $\mathbf{A}$, an initial guess $\Pi(0) = (\pi_1(0), \pi_2(0), \ldots, \pi_n(0))$, and the maximal error ε.

2:

3: **Output:** steady-state distribution $\Pi = (\pi_1, \pi_2, \ldots, \pi_n)$.

4:

5: $k = 0$, $S_k = 0$, $Sum = 0$, $SS = 0$, $\Pi^k = (\pi_1^k, \pi_2^k, \ldots, \pi_n^k) = \Pi(0)$.

6:

7: While $S_k > \varepsilon$, do

8:     For $i = 1, \ldots, n$, do

9:         $\sigma = 0$

10:         For $j = 1, \ldots, n$, do

11:             If $j < i$, then

12:                 $\sigma = \sigma + \pi_j^{k+1} a_{i,j}$

13:             If $j > i$, then

14:                 $\sigma = \sigma + \pi_j^{k} a_{i,j}$

15:         $\pi_i^{k+1} = -\frac{\sigma}{a_{i,i}}$

16:         $Sum = \pi_i^{k+1}$

17:

18:     **Normalization**

19:

20:     For $i = 1, \ldots, n$, do

21:         $\pi_i^{k+1} = \pi_i^{k+1} / Sum$

22:         $s_i^{k+1} = (\pi_i^{k+1} - \pi_i^{k})^2$

23:         $SS = s_i^{k}$

24:     $S_{k+1} = \sqrt{SS}$

25:     $k = k + 1$

26:

27: $\Pi = \Pi^{k-1}$

28:

29: **Output** $\Pi = (\pi_1, \pi_2, \ldots, \pi_n)$.

30: *End*

Example 10.4.4. The DTMC depicted in Figure 10.7 has the following transition probability matrix:

$$\mathbf{P} = \begin{array}{c} \\ 1 \\ 2 \\ 3 \end{array} \begin{array}{c} \begin{array}{ccc} 1 & 2 & 3 \end{array} \\ \left(\begin{array}{ccc} 0.3 & 0.7 & 0 \\ 0.25 & 0.45 & 0.3 \\ 0.7 & 0.3 & 0 \end{array} \right) \end{array} \; .$$

The rate matrix, $\mathbf{Q}$, is obtained by $\mathbf{P} - \mathbf{I}$:

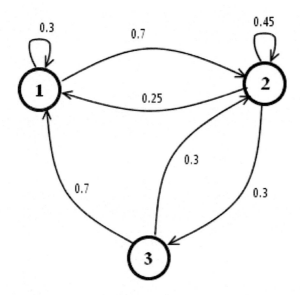

Figure 10.7 DTMC Analysis by Gauss-Seidel Method.

$$\mathbf{Q} = \begin{array}{c} \\ 1 \\ 2 \\ 3 \end{array} \begin{array}{ccc} 1 & 2 & 3 \\ \begin{pmatrix} -0.7 & 0.7 & 0 \\ 0.25 & -0.55 & 0.3 \\ 0.7 & 0.3 & -1 \end{pmatrix} \end{array},$$

and its transpose is

$$\mathbf{Q}^T = \begin{array}{c} \\ 1 \\ 2 \\ 3 \end{array} \begin{array}{ccc} 1 & 2 & 3 \\ \begin{pmatrix} -0.7 & 0.25 & 0.7 \\ 0.7 & -0.55 & 0.3 \\ 0 & 0.3 & -1 \end{pmatrix} \end{array}.$$

Let us assume the maximal error as $\varepsilon = 0.001$, and an initial guess equal to $\Pi^0 = (0.4, 0.3, 0.3)$. Hence, $\pi_1^0 = 0.4$, $\pi_2^0 = 0.3$, and $\pi_3^0 = 0.3$. Now, the next approximation can be obtained by

$$\pi_i^{k+1} = -\frac{1}{a_{i,i}} \left(\sum_{j<i} \pi_j^{k+1} a_{i,j} + \sum_{j>i} \pi_j^k a_{i,j} \right).$$

Therefore,

$$\pi_1^1 = -\frac{1}{-0.7}(0.25 \times 0.3 + 0.7 \times 0.3) = 0.4071,$$

$$\pi_2^1 = -\frac{1}{-0.55}(0.7 \times 0.4071 + 0.3 \times 0.3) = 0.6818,$$

$$\pi_3^1 = -\frac{1}{-1}(0 \times 0.4071 + 0.3 \times 0.3) = 0.2045.$$

Summing up π_1^1, π_2^1, and π_3^1 results 1.2935. Thus, normalization should be executed and it leads to

$$\pi_1^1 = \frac{0.4071}{1.2935} = 0.3148,$$

$$\pi_2^1 = \frac{0.6818}{1.2935} = 0.5271,$$

and

$$\pi_3^1 = \frac{0.2045}{1.2935} = 0.1581.$$

So $\Pi^1 = (0.3148, 0.5271, 0.1581)$. Thus,

$$S_1 = \sqrt{(0.3148 - 0.4)^2 + (0.5271 - 0.3)^2 + (0.1581 - 0.3)^2} = 0.3936.$$

As $S_1 > 0.001$, additional iterates are required.

At iterate $k = 5$, we get

$$\pi_1^5 = 0.3358,$$

$$\pi_2^5 = 0.5109,$$

$$\pi_3^5 = 0.1533,$$

and $S_5 < 0.001$. Therefore, the iterative process stops and $\Pi = (0.3358, 0.5109, 0.1533)$ is provided as the result.

$\square$

10.5 TRANSIENT ANALYSIS

We now turn our attention to the computation of transient distributions of homogeneous Markov chains. This section introduces the time interval subdivision numerical method, two algebraic methods to solve the differential equations, and the uniformization method.

As already mentioned, the numerical computation of the matrix exponential can be challenging and provide unstable results. We will discuss more stable approaches later on. First, however, we directly applied the approach presented in 10.2.18 to obtain the state probability distribution by applying

$$\Pi(t) = \Pi(0)\, e^{Qt} = \Pi(0) \left(I + \sum_{k=1}^{\infty} \frac{Qt^k}{k!} \right).$$

Example 10.5.1. Let us consider the CTMC depicted in Figure 10.1. This chain is composed of three states, s_0, s_1, and s_2, and let us assume that the probability vector at $t = 0$ is $\Pi(0) = (\pi_0(0) = 1, \pi_1(0) = 0)$. The transition rates, as already depicted earlier, are $\alpha = 20$, $\beta = 10$, $\gamma = 25$, and $\lambda = 15$. The rate matrix, as depicted in Example 10.1.1, is

$$Q = \begin{pmatrix} -20 & 20 & 0 \\ 10 & -35 & 25 \\ 0 & 15 & -15 \end{pmatrix}.$$

The probability distribution vectors at $t = 0.01\,h$, $0.1\,h$, and $1\,h$, truncated at $k = 100$, are

$$\Pi(0.01) = (\ 0.826561, \quad 0.15353, \quad 0.0199092\ ),$$

$$\Pi(0.1) = (\ 0.27072, \quad 0.331068, \quad 0.398212\ ),$$

and

$$\Pi(0.5) = (\ 0.157971, \quad 0.315816, \quad 0.526243\ ).$$

These probability vectors were computed using Mathematica 11 standard libraries with 20 decimal digit precision. Adopting this approach for computing $\Pi(t)$ for higher values of t is not advisable since results become unstable. For instance, the result obtained for $t = 0.74$ was

$$\Pi(0.74) = (\ -2.375, \quad -1.375, \quad 0.75\ ).$$

$\square$

10.5.1 INTERVAL SUBDIVISION

Moler and Van Loan [283, 284] discuss nineteen dubious ways to compute the exponential matrices. Attempting to calculate the exponential matrix directly is likely to yield unsatisfactory results since the process is mainly dependent on the norm of $\mathbf{Q}$ and on the t; that is, as the norm of $\mathbf{Q}$ or t becomes large the results become unstable (as seen above).

An alternative is to divide the interval $0 - t$ into subintervals $\triangle t_i = t_{i,e} - t_{i,b}$, compute the transient solution at the end of each interval $(t_{i,e})$, and use that solution as the starting point at the beginning $(t_{i+1,b})$ of the next interval, such as

$$\Pi_1(t_{1,e}) = \Pi(0)\, e^{\mathbf{Q}t_{1,e}} = \Pi(0) \left(I + \sum_{k=1}^{kr} \frac{\mathbf{Q}t_{1,e}^k}{k!} \right),$$

$$\Pi_2(t_{2,e}) = \Pi_1(t_{1,e})\, e^{\mathbf{Q}t_{2,e}} = \Pi_1(t_{1,e}) \left(I + \sum_{k=1}^{kr} \frac{\mathbf{Q}t_{2,e}^k}{k!} \right),$$

$$\Pi_3(t_{3,e}) = \Pi_2(t_{2,e})\, e^{\mathbf{Q}t_{3,e}t} = \Pi_2(t_{2,e}) \left(I + \sum_{k=1}^{kr} \frac{\mathbf{Q}t_{3,e}^k}{k!} \right),$$

$$\dots$$

$$\Pi_n(t_{n,e}) = \Pi_{n-1}(t_{n-1,e})\, e^{\mathbf{Q}t_{n,e}} = \Pi_{n-1}(t_{n-1,e}) \left(I + \sum_{k=1}^{kr} \frac{\mathbf{Q}t_{n,e}^k}{k!} \right),$$

where $t = \sum_{i=1}^{n} \triangle t_i$, and kr is the term at which the series were truncated.

This approach was applied to the CTMC analyzed in Example 10.5.1. In this case we adopted the following time sub-intervals: $\triangle t_1 = 0.2$, $\triangle t_2 = 0.2$, $\triangle t_3 = 0.15$, $\triangle t_4 = 0.15$, and $\triangle t_5 = 0.04$. This process was implemented in Mathematica using standard libraries with 20 decimal digit precision. The respective piece of code is depicted in Algorithm 14.

The probability vector at $t = 0.74\,h$ obtained is

$$\Pi(0.74) = \begin{pmatrix} 0.157896, & 0.31579, & 0.526315 \end{pmatrix}.$$

The reader may observe that the issue faced in Example 10.5.1 has been overcome.

10.5.2 FIRST ORDER DIFFERENTIAL LINEAR EQUATION

In this section, we algebraically solve a first-order differential equation system of a small CTMC. The aim is to illustrate how algebraic solutions may be obtained. Consider a CTMC shown in Figure 10.3. The rate matrix is also depicted in Example 10.2.1. Applying the Solution 10.2.17 to this chain results in the following system of differential equations:

$$\frac{d\Pi(t)}{dt} = \Pi(t) \cdot \mathbf{Q}.$$

Algorithm 14 Solving e^{Qt} considering subintervals $\triangle t_i$

1: $Q = \{\{-20, 20, 0\}, \{10, -35, 25\}, \{0, 15, -15\}\};$
2: $Id = IdentityMatrix[3];$
3: $Pi0 = \{1, 0, 0\};$
4: $\triangle t = 0.2;$
5: $Pi1 = N[Pi0.Sum[(MatrixPower[Q,k] * \triangle t^k)/k!, k, 1, 200] + Pi0.Id, 20]$
6: $\triangle t = 0.2;$
7: $Pi2 = N[Pi1.Sum[(MatrixPower[Q,k] * \triangle t^k)/k!, k, 1, 200] + Pi1.Id, 20]$
8: $\triangle t = 0.15;$
9: $Pi3 = N[Pi2.Sum[(MatrixPower[Q,k] * \triangle t^k)/k!, k, 1, 200] + Pi2.Id, 20]$
10: $\triangle t = 0.15;$
11: $Pi4 = N[Pi3.Sum[(MatrixPower[Q,k] * \triangle t^k)/k!, k, 1, 400] + Pi3.Id, 20]$
12: $\triangle t = 0.04;$
13: $Pi4 = N[Pi4.Sum[(MatrixPower[Q,k] * \triangle t^k)/k!, k, 1, 200] + Pi4.Id, 20]$

$$\left(\frac{d\pi_0(t)}{dt}, \frac{d\pi_1(t)}{dt}\right) = (\pi_0(t),\ \pi_1(t)) \cdot \begin{pmatrix} -\lambda & \lambda \\ \mu & -\mu \end{pmatrix}.$$

$$\frac{d\pi_0(t)}{dt} = -\lambda\, \pi_0(t) + \mu\, \pi_1(t), \tag{10.5.1}$$

$$\frac{d\pi_1(t)}{dt} = \lambda\, \pi_0(t) - \mu\, \pi_1(t). \tag{10.5.2}$$

As $\pi_0(t) + \pi_1(t) = 1$, then

$$\frac{d\pi_0(t)}{dt} = -\lambda\, \pi_0(t) + \mu\, (1 - \pi_0(t)).$$

$$\frac{d\pi_0(t)}{dt} = -\lambda\, \pi_0(t) + \mu - \mu\, \pi_0(t).$$

$$\frac{d\pi_0(t)}{dt} = -(\lambda + \mu)\, \pi_0(t) + \mu.$$

$$\frac{d\pi_0(t)}{dt} + (\lambda + \mu)\, \pi_0(t) = \mu.$$

Now consider a function $x(t)$ that

$$x(t)\,(\lambda + \mu) = \frac{dx(t)}{dt}. \tag{10.5.3}$$

Then

$$x(t) \cdot \frac{d\pi_0(t)}{dt} + x(t) \cdot (\lambda + \mu)\, \pi_0(t) = x(t) \cdot \mu. \tag{10.5.4}$$

As $x(t)(\lambda + \mu) = dx(t)/dt$, then:

$$x(t) \cdot \frac{d\pi_0(t)}{dt} + \frac{dx(t)}{dt}\pi_0(t) = x(t) \cdot \mu.$$

We know that

$$\frac{d(v(t)\,w(t))}{dt} = v(t)\frac{dw(t)}{dt} + \frac{dv(t)}{dt}w(t).$$

Thus

$$x(t) \cdot \frac{d\pi_0(t)}{dt} + \frac{dx(t)}{dt}\pi_0(t) = \frac{d(x(t)\,\pi_0(t))}{dt}.$$

Hence, considering 10.5.4, we have

$$\frac{d(x(t)\,\pi_0(t))}{dt} = x(t) \cdot \mu.$$

Integrating both sides

$$\int \frac{d(x(t)\,\pi_0(t))}{dt} = \int x(t) \cdot \mu.$$

$$x(t)\,\pi_0(t) + C = \int x(t) \cdot \mu.$$

Therefore

$$\pi_0(t) = \frac{\int x(t) \cdot \mu\; dt\; - C}{x(t)}. \qquad (10.5.5)$$

Let us make $A = -C$, so

$$\pi_0(t) = \frac{\int x(t) \cdot \mu\; dt\; + A}{x(t)}. \qquad (10.5.6)$$

As

$$\frac{dx(t)}{dt} = x(t)(\lambda + \mu), \qquad \text{(From 10.5.3),}$$

then

$$\frac{dx(t)/dt}{x(t)} = \lambda + \mu.$$

We also know that

$$\frac{dx(t)/dt}{x(t)} = \frac{d\ln x(t)}{dt}.$$

Hence

$$\frac{d\ln x(t)}{dt} = \lambda + \mu.$$

Integrating both sides:

$$\int \frac{d\ln x(t)}{dt} \, dt = \int (\lambda + \mu) \, dt.$$

$$\ln x(t) + K = (\lambda + \mu)t + R.$$

$$\ln x(t) = (\lambda + \mu)t + R - K.$$

Let us make $B = R - K$; then

$$\ln x(t) = (\lambda + \mu)t + B.$$

Exponentiating both sides

$$e^{\ln x(t)} = e^{(\lambda + \mu)t + B}$$

$$x(t) = e^B \, e^{(\lambda + \mu)t}$$

Let us define $D = e^B$; then

$$x(t) = D \, e^{(\lambda + \mu)t} \tag{10.5.7}$$

Applying the result above in 10.5.6, we have:

$$\pi_0(t) = \frac{\int D \, e^{(\lambda + \mu)t} \cdot \mu \, dt + A}{D \, e^{(\lambda + \mu)t}}.$$

Hence

$$\pi_0(t) = \frac{D \left(\mu \int e^{(\lambda + \mu)t} \, dt + A/D \right)}{D \, e^{(\lambda + \mu)t}}.$$

Let us make $E = A/D$

$$\pi_0(t) = \frac{\left(\mu \int e^{(\lambda + \mu)t} \, dt + E \right)}{e^{(\lambda + \mu)t}}.$$

As $\int e^{(\lambda + \mu)t} \, dt = e^{(\lambda + \mu)t}/(\lambda + \mu)$, then

$$\pi_0(t) = \frac{\left(\frac{\mu \, e^{(\lambda + \mu)t}}{\lambda + \mu} + E \right)}{e^{(\lambda + \mu)t}}.$$

Therefore

$$\pi_0(t) = \frac{\mu}{\lambda + \mu} + E\, e^{-(\lambda + \mu)t}.$$

As $\pi_0(0) = 1$, then

$$1 = \frac{\mu}{\lambda + \mu} + E\, e^{-(\lambda + \mu)t},$$

and then

$$E = \left(1 - \frac{\mu}{\lambda + \mu}\right) = \frac{\lambda}{\lambda + \mu}.$$

Hence

$$\pi_0(t) = \frac{\mu}{\lambda + \mu} + \frac{\lambda}{\lambda + \mu}\, e^{-(\lambda + \mu)t}. \tag{10.5.8}$$

As $\pi_0(t) + \pi_1(t) = 1$, then

$$\pi_1(t) = 1 - \left(\frac{\mu}{\lambda + \mu} + \frac{\lambda}{\lambda + \mu}\, e^{-(\lambda + \mu)t}\right).$$

$$\pi_1(t) = \frac{\lambda}{\lambda + \mu} - \frac{\lambda}{\lambda + \mu}\, e^{-(\lambda + \mu)t}. \tag{10.5.9}$$

Let us assign 10 and 30 to λ and μ, respectively. Figure 10.8 presents the probabilities $\pi_0(t)$ and $\pi_1(t)$ over the time range $(0, 0.4)$.

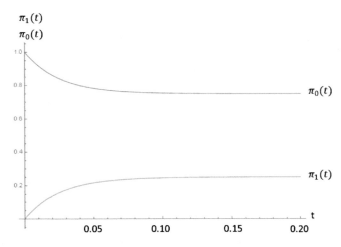

Figure 10.8 $\pi_0(t)$ and $\pi_1(t)$

10.5.3 SOLUTION THROUGH LAPLACE TRANSFORM

This section also illustrates how to obtain algebraic solutions to transient distributions of CTMCs. Here, we adopted the Laplace transform for obtaining the solution. Let us again consider the CTMC studied in the previous section. Now the transition solution to the differential system of equations formed by Equation 10.5.1 and 10.5.2 is provided via the Laplace transform.

Before starting solving the system of differential equations, however, let us summarize the five Laplace transformations adopted in this particular process. These transformations are depicted in Table 10.1, where a is constant and $f'(x)$ is the derivative of $f(x)$.

Table 10.1
Laplace Transformations

$f(x)$	$LT[f(x)]$
1	$1/s$
a	a/s
$a f(x)$	$a LT[f(t)]$
$f'(x)$	$s LT[f(x)] - f(0)$
e^{at}	$1/(s-a)$

Let us begin by taking into account Equation 10.5.2, that is

$$\frac{d\pi_1(t)}{dt} = \lambda \pi_0(t) - \mu \pi_1(t).$$

We also know that $\pi_1(0) = 0$, and that $\pi_0(t) = 1 - \pi_1(t)$. Therefore

$$\frac{d\pi_1(t)}{dt} = \lambda (1 - \pi_1(t)) - \mu \pi_1(t),$$

which leads to

$$\frac{d\pi_1(t)}{dt} = -(\lambda + \mu) \pi_1(t) + \lambda.$$

Now, let us apply the Laplace transform to both sides of the above equation.

$$LT[\frac{d\pi_1(t)}{dt}] = LT[-(\lambda + \mu) \pi_1(t) + \lambda].$$

Hence

$$LT[\frac{d\pi_1(t)}{dt}] = LT[-(\lambda + \mu) \pi_1(t)] + LT[\lambda].$$

As

$$LT\left[\frac{d\pi_1(t)}{dt}\right] = s\,LT\left[\pi_1(t)\right] - \pi_1(0),$$

and as $\pi_1(0) = 0$, then

$$LT\left[\frac{d\pi_1(t)}{dt}\right] = s\,LT\left[\pi_1(t)\right],$$

and

$$LT\left[-(\lambda + \mu)\,\pi_1(t)\right] = -(\lambda + \mu)\,LT\left[\pi_1(t)\right];$$

$$LT[\lambda] = \frac{\lambda}{s},$$

therefore

$$s\,LT\left[\pi_1(t)\right] = -(\lambda + \mu)\,LT\left[\pi_1(t)\right] + \frac{\lambda}{s}.$$

Thus,

$$LT\left[\pi_1(t)\right](s + \lambda + \mu) = \frac{\lambda}{s},$$

so

$$LT\left[\pi_1(t)\right] = \frac{\lambda}{s\,(s + \lambda + \mu)}.$$

Now, we apply the inverse Laplace transform (LT^{-1}) on both sides of the above equation.

$$LT^{-1}\left[LT\left[\pi_1(t)\right]\right] = LT^{-1}\left[\frac{\lambda}{s\,(s + \lambda + \mu)}\right]$$

$$\pi_1(t) = LT^{-1}\left[\frac{\lambda}{s\,(s + \lambda + \mu)}\right]. \tag{10.5.10}$$

Now, let us take

$$\frac{\lambda}{s\,(s + \lambda + \mu)}$$

and expand to obtain partial fractions:

$$\frac{\lambda}{s\,(s + \lambda + \mu)} = \frac{A}{s} + \frac{B}{s + \lambda + \mu}. \tag{10.5.11}$$

Hence

$$\lambda = A(s + \lambda + \mu) + B s$$

$$\lambda = A s + A \lambda + A \mu + B s$$

$$\lambda = (A + B) s + A(\lambda + \mu).$$

Therefore

$$\lambda = A(\lambda + \mu);$$

thus,

$$A = \frac{\lambda}{\lambda + \mu}.$$

and

$$0 = (A + B) s,$$

so

$$B = -\frac{\lambda}{\lambda + \mu}.$$

Considering Equation 10.5.10, we have

$$\pi_1(t) = LT^{-1}\left[\frac{\lambda}{s(s + \lambda + \mu)}\right].$$

As

$$LT^{-1}\left[\frac{\lambda}{s(s + \lambda + \mu)}\right] = LT\left[\frac{A}{s} + \frac{B}{s + \lambda + \mu}\right]$$

$$LT^{-1}\left[\frac{\lambda}{s(s + \lambda + \mu)}\right] = LT\left[\frac{A}{s}\right] + LT\left[\frac{B}{s + \lambda + \mu}\right]$$

then

$$LT^{-1}\left[\frac{\lambda}{s(s + \lambda + \mu)}\right] = LT\left[\frac{\lambda/(\lambda + \mu)}{s}\right] - LT\left[\frac{\lambda/(\lambda + \mu)}{s + \lambda + \mu}\right].$$

$$LT^{-1}\left[\frac{\lambda}{s(s + \lambda + \mu)}\right] = \frac{\lambda}{\lambda + \mu} LT\left[\frac{1}{s}\right] - \frac{\lambda}{\lambda + \mu} LT\left[\frac{1}{s + \lambda + \mu}\right].$$

Applying the first and the fifth inverse transformation depicted in Table 10.1, we have

$$\pi_1(t) = LT^{-1}\left[\frac{\lambda}{s(s + \lambda + \mu)}\right] = \frac{\lambda}{\lambda + \mu} - \frac{\lambda}{\lambda + \mu} e^{-(\lambda + \mu)t}.$$

Hence

$$\pi_1(t) = \frac{\lambda}{\lambda + \mu} - \frac{\lambda}{\lambda + \mu} \, e^{-(\lambda+\mu)t}. \qquad (10.5.12)$$

As $\pi_0(t) = 1 - \pi_1(t)$, then

$$\pi_0(t) = 1 - \left(\frac{\lambda}{\lambda + \mu} - \frac{\lambda}{\lambda + \mu} \, e^{-(\lambda+\mu)t} \right);$$

therefore

$$\pi_0(t) = \frac{\mu}{\lambda + \mu} + \frac{\lambda}{\lambda + \mu} \, e^{-(\lambda+\mu)t}. \qquad (10.5.13)$$

10.5.4 UNIFORMIZATION METHOD

We already know that calculating the CTMCs transient distributions consists of solving a first-order differential equation system. Many are the methods proposed for solving such systems. Among the numerical approaches, it is worth mentioning the Euler method, Runge-Kutta methods, and the uniformization method [413]. The uniformization method has attracted much attention when calculating transient probabilities of CTMCs since it often outperforms other numerical methods. The interested reader, however, is invited to [413, 414] for a detailed presentation of the method mentioned above and many other numerical approaches for calculating transient and steady-state distributions of Markov chains. Here, we introduce the uniformization method and apply it for computing the transient probabilities of a CTMC. The uniformization method has also been called discretization, randomization, and Jensen´s method [7, 172, 173].

Let us consider a finite CTMC with rate matrix $\mathbf{Q}$. Its steady-state distribution may be obtained from (10.2.19)

$$\Pi \cdot \mathbf{Q} = 0, \quad \sum_{\forall i} \pi_i = 1.$$

We may discretize the CTMC by multiplying the transition rate, $\mathbf{Q}$, by a time interval, $\triangle t$, that is smaller or equal to the shortest residence time of all states of the CTMC. Therefore,

$$\triangle t \leq \frac{1}{\max_{\forall i} |q_{ii}|},$$

where q_{ii} are the diagonal elements of $\mathbf{Q}$.

Hence, from Equation 10.2.19, we have

$$\Pi \cdot \mathbf{Q} \, \triangle t = 0.$$

Let us introduce some intuition about this process. As we mentioned in Section 10.1, we may think of probability as distance and rate as speed. Thus, multiplying a speed

(the transition rate from state i to j, q_{ij}) by a time interval ($\triangle t$) yields a distance, that is, the probability of transitioning from state i to state j, p_{ij} during the time interval $\triangle t$.

As the chosen $\triangle t$ is smaller or equal to the smallest state residence time of the entire CTMC, the probability of two transitions taking place in $\triangle t$ is small.

The description given above leads us to conclude that the elements of $\mathbf{Q} \triangle t$ are probabilities. Nevertheless, the reader should observe that the diagonal elements are negative. However, if we consider the identity matrix such that $\mathbf{Q} \triangle t + \mathbf{I}$, then

$$\mathbf{P} = \mathbf{Q} \triangle t + \mathbf{I}, \tag{10.5.14}$$

$$\Pi(\mathbf{Q} \triangle t + \mathbf{I})$$

$$\Pi \mathbf{Q} \triangle t + \Pi \mathbf{I} = \Pi \mathbf{Q} \triangle t + \Pi.$$

$$\Pi \mathbf{Q} \triangle t + \Pi = \Pi.$$

The reader should notice that the equation presented above is a stochastic matrix [5].

The steady-state probability vector of the CTMC, computed from $\Pi \cdot \mathbf{Q} = 0$, is identical to the vector obtained from the discretized chain calculated through

$$\Pi \mathbf{Q} \triangle t + \Pi = \Pi. \tag{10.5.15}$$

Therefore, the numerical methods used for computing the stationary distributions of DTMCs may be adopted to calculate the stationary distributions of CTMCs.

Example 10.5.2. Consider a CTMC depicted in Figure 10.9 and its rate matrix $\mathbf{Q}$.

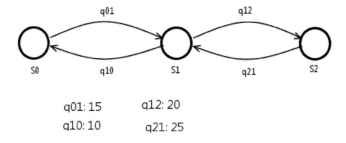

Figure 10.9 Three States CTMC.

---

[5]A stochastic matrix is a square matrix whose elements are nonnegative real numbers specifying probabilities.

$$\mathbf{Q} = \begin{pmatrix} -q_{01} & q_{01} & 0 \\ q_{10} & -(q_{10}+q_{12}) & q_{12} \\ 0 & q_{21} & -q_{21} \end{pmatrix} =$$

$$\begin{pmatrix} -15 & 15 & 0 \\ 10 & -30 & 20 \\ 0 & 25 & -25 \end{pmatrix}.$$

Let us make $\triangle t = 1/40$, then

$$\mathbf{P} = \mathbf{Q}\,\triangle t + \mathbf{I} = \begin{pmatrix} 1-q_{01}\triangle t & q_{01}\triangle t & 0 \\ q_{10}\triangle t & 1-(q_{10}+q_{12})\triangle t & q_{12}\triangle t \\ 0 & q_{21}\triangle t & 1-q_{21}\triangle t \end{pmatrix} =$$

$$\begin{pmatrix} 0.625 & 0.375 & 0 \\ 0.25 & 0.25 & 0.5 \\ 0 & 0.625 & 0.375 \end{pmatrix}.$$

Assuming $\Pi(0) = (1,0,0)$, then we can compute $\Pi(k)$. For $k = 2$, 4, 10, and 100, we have

$$\Pi(2) = (0.4844, 0.3281, 0.1875),$$

$$\Pi(4) = (0.3357, 0.3860, 0.2783),$$

$$\Pi(10) = (0.2723, 0.4049, 0.3229),$$

and

$$\Pi(100) = (0.2703, 0.4054, 0.3243).$$

Therefore, we may consider $\Pi(100) = (0.2703, 0.4054, 0.3243)$ to be the steady-state distribution of the CTMC.

□

Now, let us consider the two-state CTMC depicted in Figure 10.3. However, consider that the rate from state s_0 to state s_1 and th rated from state s_1 to state s_0 as q_{01} and q_{10}, respectively. The infinitesimal generator is

$$\mathbf{Q} = \begin{pmatrix} -q_{01} & q_{01} \\ q_{10} & -q_{10} \end{pmatrix} =$$

Assume a small time interval, $\triangle t \to 0$, adopted for discretizing, and let us define

$$q_i = \sum_{\forall j} q_{ij}$$

as the summation of transition rates leaving a state i. Therefore, for this CTMC, $q_0 = q_{01}$ and $q_1 = q_{10}$. The transition probability matrix is then

$$\mathbf{P} = \mathbf{Q} \, \triangle t + \mathbf{I} = \begin{pmatrix} 1 - q_0 \triangle t & q_0 \triangle t \\ q_1 \triangle t & 1 - q_1 \triangle t \end{pmatrix}.$$

To ensure that $0 \leq q_0 \triangle t \leq 1$ and $0 \leq q_1 \triangle t \leq 1$, it is required that the time interval $\triangle t$ satisfies $0 \leq \triangle t \leq q_0^{-1}$ and $0 \leq \triangle t \leq q_1^{-1}$.

Now, consider, for instance, that $q_0 > q_1$; thus a time interval $\triangle t$ that satisfies $0 \leq \triangle t \leq q_0^{-1}$ also satisfies $0 \leq \triangle t \leq q_1^{-1}$.

As above, to make sure that $0 \leq 1 - q_0 \triangle t \leq 1$ and $0 \leq 1 - q_1 \triangle t \leq 1$, it is also required that $0 \leq \triangle t \leq q_0^{-1}$. For instance, consider the following rate matrix and $\triangle t = 30$.

$$\mathbf{Q} = \begin{pmatrix} -10 & 10 \\ 20 & -20 \end{pmatrix},$$

so

$$\mathbf{P} = \mathbf{Q} \, \triangle t + \mathbf{I} = \begin{pmatrix} 1 - 1/3 & 1/3 \\ 2/3 & 1 - 2/3 \end{pmatrix} = \begin{pmatrix} 2/3 & 1/3 \\ 2/3 & 1/3 \end{pmatrix}.$$

Now, consider $\triangle t = 15$, and obtain $\mathbf{Q} \, \triangle t + \mathbf{I}$:

$$\begin{pmatrix} 1 - 10/15 & 10/15 \\ 20/15 & 120/15 \end{pmatrix} =$$

$$\begin{pmatrix} 1/3 & 2/3 \\ 4/3 & -1/3 \end{pmatrix}.$$

So, if we adopt $\triangle t = 15$ the conditions are not satisfied. The matrix $\mathbf{Q} \, \triangle t + \mathbf{I}$ would have negative values and values above one. Consequently, for $\mathbf{Q} \, \triangle t + \mathbf{I}$ being a stochastic matrix, the values assigned to $\triangle t$ are subject to

$$\triangle t \leq \frac{1}{\max_{\forall i} |q_i|},$$

where q_i are the diagonal elements of $\mathbf{Q}$.

From 10.2.18, we know that

$$\Pi(t) = \Pi(0) \, e^{\mathbf{Q}t} = \Pi(0) \left(\mathbf{I} + \sum_{k=1}^{\infty} \frac{\mathbf{Q}t^k}{k!} \right), \tag{10.5.16}$$

where $\Pi(0)$ is the state probability vector at $t = 0$. We also know (from 10.5.14) that the transition probability of discretized chains obtained from a CTMC is

$$\mathbf{P} = \frac{\mathbf{Q}}{\lambda} + \mathbf{I}, \tag{10.5.17}$$

where $\lambda = 1/\triangle t$, and $\triangle t \leq 1/\max_{\forall i} |q_i|$ ($\lambda = \max_{\forall i} |q_i|$). Therefore,

$$\mathbf{Q} = \lambda(\mathbf{P} - \mathbf{I}).\qquad(10.5.18)$$

Thus,

$$\Pi(t) = \Pi(0)\,e^{\mathbf{Q}t} = \Pi(0)\,e^{\lambda(\mathbf{P}-\mathbf{I})t} =$$

$$\Pi(0)\,e^{\lambda\mathbf{P}t} \cdot e^{-\lambda\mathbf{I}t} =$$

$$\Pi(0)\,e^{\lambda\mathbf{P}t} \cdot e^{-\lambda t}.$$

Hence

$$\Pi(t) = \Pi(0)\,e^{\mathbf{Q}t} = \Pi(0)\,e^{-\lambda t} \cdot e^{\lambda\mathbf{P}t}.\qquad(10.5.19)$$

Apply the Taylor-Maclaurin series (see Section 5.4) to expand $e^{\lambda\mathbf{P}t}$. Hence, we obtain

$$e^{\lambda\mathbf{P}t} = \sum_{k=0}^{\infty} \frac{\mathbf{P}^k(\lambda\,t)^k}{k!},$$

so

$$\Pi(t) = \Pi(0)\,e^{-\lambda t} \cdot \left(\sum_{k=0}^{\infty} \frac{\mathbf{P}^k(\lambda\,t)^k}{k!} \right).\qquad(10.5.20)$$

Rearranging, we have

$$\Pi(t) = \sum_{k=0}^{\infty} \Pi(0) \cdot \mathbf{P}^k \frac{(\lambda t)^k}{k!}\,e^{-\lambda t}.\qquad(10.5.21)$$

The term $\Pi(0) \cdot \mathbf{P}^k$ ($\hat{\Pi}(k)$) may be thought of as the vector that provides the probability distribution of the embedded DTMC after k steps. The term

$$\frac{(\lambda t)^k}{k!}\,e^{-\lambda t}$$

is the probability of k events occurring given by the Poisson distribution with rate λ over the interval $[0,t)$.

Let us denote

$$P(X = k) = \psi(\lambda t, k) = \frac{(\lambda t)^k}{k!}\,e^{-\lambda t}.$$

$\psi(\lambda t, k)$ can be interpreted as weights that, when multiplied with the distribution of the DTMC after k steps and summed over all possible number of steps, yields the transient distribution $\Pi(t)$.

Therefore, we may present 10.5.21 as

$$\Pi(t) = \sum_{k=0}^{\infty} \Pi(0) \cdot \mathbf{P}^k \, \psi(\lambda t, k). \tag{10.5.22}$$

Hence an iterative solution may be obtained by

$$\Pi(t) = \sum_{k=0}^{\infty} \psi(\lambda t, k) \, \hat{\Pi}(k), \tag{10.5.23}$$

where $\hat{\Pi}(k) = \hat{\Pi}(k-1) \cdot \mathbf{P}$, and $\hat{\Pi}(0) = \Pi(0)$.

The reader may wonder why we should use adopt 10.5.21 when we already had 10.5.16. It should be stressed, however, that $\mathbf{Q}$ contains both positive and negative elements, and this leads to unstable solutions, as we have already seen. Matrix $\mathbf{P}$, on the other hand, has only positive values lying in the range $[0, 1]$.

Now, let us deal with the infinite summation. We may obtain an approximation ($\tilde{\Pi}(t)$) solution by the truncated series, that is

$$\tilde{\Pi}(t) = \sum_{k=0}^{kr} \hat{\Pi}(k) \, \psi(\lambda t, k). \tag{10.5.24}$$

Let $\delta(t) = \Pi(t) - \tilde{\Pi}(t)$; thus, for a given t, we have

$$\|\delta(t)\| = \|\sum_{k=0}^{\infty} \Pi(0) \cdot \mathbf{P}^k \, \psi(\lambda t, k) - \sum_{k=0}^{kr} \hat{\Pi}(k) \, \psi(\lambda t, k)\| =$$

$$\|\sum_{k=kr+1}^{\infty} \hat{\Pi}(k) \, \psi(\lambda t, k)\|.$$

As each component of $\hat{\Pi}(k)$, $\hat{\pi}_i(k)$, lies within $[0, 1]$, then

$$\|\delta(t)\| = \|\sum_{k=kr+1}^{\infty} \hat{\Pi}(k) \, \psi(\lambda t, k)\| =$$

$$\|\sum_{k=kr+1}^{\infty} \hat{\Pi}(k) \, \frac{(\lambda t)^k}{k!} \, e^{-\lambda t}\|$$

$$\leq \sum_{k=kr+1}^{\infty} \frac{(\lambda t)^k}{k!} \, e^{-\lambda t}.$$

As

$$\sum_{k=0}^{\infty} \frac{(\lambda t)^k}{k!} \, e^{-\lambda t} = \sum_{k=0}^{kr} \frac{(\lambda t)^k}{k!} \, e^{-\lambda t} + \sum_{k=kr+1}^{\infty} \frac{(\lambda t)^k}{k!} \, e^{-\lambda t}.$$

Thus

$$1 = \sum_{k=0}^{kr} \frac{(\lambda t)^k}{k!} \, e^{-\lambda t} + \sum_{k=kr+1}^{\infty} \frac{(\lambda t)^k}{k!} \, e^{-\lambda t}.$$

$$\sum_{k=kr+1}^{\infty} \frac{(\lambda t)^k}{k!} \, e^{-\lambda t} = 1 - \sum_{k=0}^{kr} \frac{(\lambda t)^k}{k!} \, e^{-\lambda t}.$$

$$1 - \sum_{k=0}^{kr} \frac{(\lambda t)^k}{k!} \, e^{-\lambda t} \leq \varepsilon.$$

$$\sum_{k=0}^{kr} \frac{(\lambda t)^k}{k!} \, e^{-\lambda t} \geq 1 - \varepsilon.$$

Therefore

$$\sum_{k=0}^{kr} \frac{(\lambda t)^k}{k!} \geq (1 - \varepsilon) \, e^{\lambda t}.$$

Example 10.5.3. Consider the CTMC depicted in Example 10.5.2. Given $\Pi(0) = (1,0,0)$, calculate the transient distribution at $t = 0.1$, taking into account $\varepsilon \leq 10^{-4}$. The rate matrix of the CTMC is

$$\begin{pmatrix} -15 & 15 & 0 \\ 10 & -30 & 20 \\ 0 & 25 & -25 \end{pmatrix}.$$

Let us consider $\lambda = 40$ as the normalization rate ($\lambda \geq \max = 15, 25, 30$). Now we can obtain the number of terms at which the series may be truncated (kr).

$$(1 - \varepsilon) \, e^{\lambda t} = (1 - 10^{-4}) \, e^{40 \times 0.1} = 54.5927.$$

Thus, we have to find the minimal k, kr, that satisfies

$$\sum_{k=0}^{kr} \frac{(\lambda t)^k}{k!} \geq 54.5927.$$

Table 10.2 presents the set of values of $\sum_{k=0}^{kr} (\lambda t)^k / k!$. The reader may observe that, at $k = 13$, $\sum_{k=0}^{kr} (\lambda t)^k / k!$ is already larger than 54.5927, so we may truncate the summation at this term and satisfy the error requirement ($\varepsilon \leq 10^{-4}$).

Now, using 10.5.24, we can calculate

$$\tilde{\Pi}(t) = \sum_{k=0}^{11} \hat{\Pi}(k) \, \psi(40 \times 0.1, k),$$

Table 10.2

Values of $\sum_{k=0}^{kr}(\lambda t)^k/k!$

k	$(\lambda t)^k/k!$	$\sum_{k=0}^{kr}(\lambda t)^k/k!$
0	1	1
1	4	5
2	8	13
3	10.6667	23.6667
4	10.6667	21.3333
5	8.5333	42.8667
6	5.6889	48.5556
7	3.2508	51.8063
8	1.6254	53.4317
9	0.7224	54.1541
10	0.2890	54.4431
11	0.1051	54.5482
12	0.0350	54.5832
13	0.0108	54.5940

where

$$\hat{\Pi}(k) = \hat{\Pi}(k-1) \cdot \mathbf{P} = \hat{\Pi}(0) \cdot \mathbf{P}^k, \; \hat{\Pi}(0) = \Pi(0),$$

and

$$\psi(40 \times 0.1, k) = \frac{(40 \times 0.1)^k \, e^{40 \times 0.1}}{k!}.$$

Table 10.3 presents the evaluated values of $\psi(40 \times 0.1, k)$ and $\hat{\Pi}(k)$ for each k.

As

$$\tilde{\Pi}(t) = \sum_{k=0}^{kr} \hat{\Pi}(k) \, \psi(\lambda t, k),$$

hence

$$\tilde{\Pi}(0.1) = \sum_{k=0}^{13} \hat{\Pi}(k) \, \psi(40 \times 0.1, k).$$

$$\tilde{\Pi}(0.1) = (\hat{\pi}_0(0.1), \hat{\pi}_1(0.1), \hat{\pi}_2(0.1)).$$

$$\tilde{\Pi}(0.1) = (0.384788268, 0.373559978, 0.241575426).$$

□

Table 10.3

$\psi(40 \times 0.1, k)$ **and** $\hat{\Pi}(k)$

k	$\psi(40 \times 0.1,k)$	$\hat{\pi}_0(k)$	$\hat{\pi}_1(k)$	$\hat{\pi}_2(k)$
0	0.018315639	1	0	0
1	0.073262556	0.625	0.375	0
2	0.146525111	0.4844	0.3281	0.1875
3	0.195366815	0.384765625	0.380859375	0.234375
4	0.195366815	0.335693359	0.385986328	0.278320313
5	0.156293452	0.306304932	0.396331787	0.297363281
6	0.104195635	0.290523529	0.399799347	0.309677124
7	0.059540363	0.281527042	0.402444363	0.316028595
8	0.029770181	0.276565492	0.403701603	0.319732904
9	0.013231192	0.273778856	0.404470503	0.321750641
10	0.005292477	0.272229433	0.404878825	0.322891742
11	0.001924537	0.271363109	0.405113071	0.323523819
12	0.000641512	0.270880222	0.405241817	0.32387796
13	0.000197388	0.270610601	0.405314267	0.324075133

10.6 TIME TO ABSORPTION

Let us adopt a CTMC with $m+1$ states, whose states $1, 2, \ldots, m-1$ are transient states, m is an absorbing state, and the probability vector at time $t = 0$, $\Pi(0)$. Let us consider that $\pi_m(0) = 0$. The transient distribution may be obtained through 10.2.18 or by applying one of the methods presented in Section 10.5. This chain is depicted in Figure 10.10.

The probability of reaching the absorbing state by time t is

$$F_A(t) = \pi_m(t),$$

and the probability of staying in transient states by time t is

$$F_T(t) = 1 - F_A(t) = 1 - \pi_m(t).$$

We know that

$$f_A(t) = \frac{dF_A(t)}{dt} = -\frac{dF_T(t)}{dt}.$$

The mean time to reach the absorbing state (Mean Time to Absorption – MTTA) is

$$MTTA = E[T] = \int_0^\infty t\, f_A(t)\, dt = -\int_0^\infty \frac{dF_T(t)}{dt} t\, dt,$$

where T is the time to reach the absorption state.

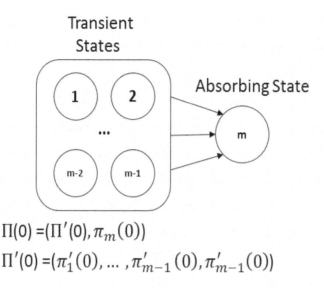

$$\Pi(0) = (\Pi'(0), \pi_m(0))$$
$$\Pi'(0) = (\pi'_1(0), \dots, \pi'_{m-1}(0), \pi'_{m-1}(0))$$

Figure 10.10   One Absorbing State CTMC.

Let

$$u = t \quad \text{and} \quad dv = \frac{d F_T(t)}{dt},$$

and integrating by parts [6], we have

$$du = dt, \quad v = F_T(t).$$

Thus,

$$MTTA = -\left(t F_T(t)\big|_0^\infty - \int_0^\infty F_T(t)\,dt \right) =$$

As $\lim_{t \to \infty} F_T(t) \to 0$, then

$$MTTA = \int_0^\infty F_T(t)\,dt = \int_0^\infty (1 - \pi_m(t))\,dt,$$

where $\pi_m(t)$ may computed by (10.2.18)

$$\Pi(t) = \Pi(0)\, e^{Qt} = \Pi(0) \left(I + \sum_{k=1}^\infty \frac{Qt^k}{k!} \right)$$

or by applying one of the methods depicted in Section 10.5.

---

[6] $\int u\,dv = uv - \int v\,du$

Example 10.6.1. The CTMC depicted in Figure 10.11 has two transient states (2 and 1) and one absorbing state (0). The transition rate from state 2 to state 1 is λ_2, and the transition rate from state 1 to state 0 is λ_1. The rate matrix is

$$\mathbf{Q} = \begin{pmatrix} -\lambda_2 & \lambda_2 & 0 \\ 0 & -\lambda_1 & \lambda_1 \\ 0 & 0 & 0 \end{pmatrix},$$

and the probability distribution at $t = 0$ is $\Pi(0) = (\pi_2(0), \pi_1(0), \pi_0(0)) = (1,0,0)$. Therefore, we have

$$\frac{d\,\Pi(t)}{dt} = \Pi(t)\mathbf{Q}, \ \Pi(0) = (1,0,0),$$

that yields

$$\begin{cases} \frac{d\pi_2(t)}{dt} = -\lambda_2\,\pi_2(t), \\ \frac{d\pi_1(t)}{dt} = \lambda_2\,\pi_2(t) - \lambda_1\,\pi_1(t), \\ \frac{d\pi_0(t)}{dt} = \lambda_1\,\pi_1(t), \\ \pi_2(0) = 1, \ \pi_1(0) = 0, \ \pi_0(0) = 1. \end{cases}$$

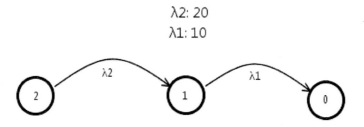

Figure 10.11   Two Transient and One Absorbing State CTMC.

Applying the method presented in Section 10.5.2 or in Section 10.5.3, we obtain the following algebraic expressions:

$$\pi_2(t) = e^{-\lambda_2 t},$$

$$\pi_1(t) = \frac{\lambda_2 \left(e^{-\lambda_1 t} - e^{-\lambda_2 t}\right)}{\lambda_1 - \lambda_2},$$

$$\pi_0(t) = 1 - \frac{\lambda_1}{\lambda_1 - \lambda_2}\,e^{-\lambda_2 t} + \frac{\lambda_2}{\lambda_1 - \lambda_2}\,e^{-\lambda_1 t}$$

Figure 10.12 plots the probability distributions $(\Pi(t))$ of the chain in the time interval $[0, 0.5]$ $t.u.$ [7] as well as the probability of not reaching the absorbing state (state 0) $F_T(t) = 1 - \pi_0(t)$. The reader should observe that $F_A(t) = \pi_0(t)$. $F_T(t)$ is a hypoexponential distribution with rates λ_1 and λ_2.

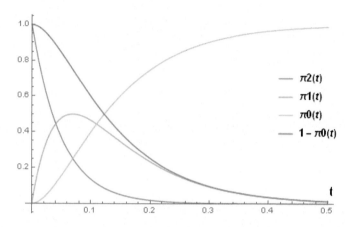

Figure 10.12 Probability Distributions $\Pi(t)$, $F_T(t)$, and $F_A(t)$ Over the Time Interval $[0, 0.5]$.

Integrating $1 - \pi_0(t)$ over $[0, \infty)$ yields the $MTTA$, that is

$$MTTA = \int_0^\infty (1 - \pi_0(t)) dt =$$

$$\int_0^\infty \left(\frac{\lambda_1}{\lambda_1 - \lambda_2} e^{-\lambda_2 t} - \frac{\lambda_2}{\lambda_1 - \lambda_2} e^{-\lambda_1 t} \right) dt = 0.15 \, t.u.$$

□

Example 10.6.2. The CTMC presented in Figure 10.13 is also composed of three states as in the previous example. The rate assigned to the transitions $(2, 1)$, $(1, 2)$, and $(1, 0)$ are λ_1, μ, and λ_2. The rate assigned to this transition is μ. Its rate matrix is

$$\mathbf{Q} = \begin{pmatrix} -\lambda_1 & \lambda_1 & 0 \\ \mu & -(\lambda_2 + \mu) & \lambda_2 \\ 0 & 0 & 0 \end{pmatrix},$$

The probability distribution at $t = 0$ is $\Pi(0) = (\pi_2(0), \pi_1(0), \pi_0(0)) = (1, 0, 0)$. Therefore, we have

---

[7] $t.u.$ stands for time unity.

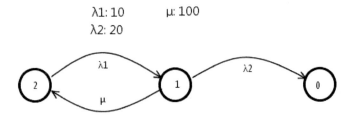

Figure 10.13 Another Two Transient and One Absorbing State CTMC.

$$\frac{d\,\Pi(t)}{dt} = \Pi(t)\mathbf{Q}, \ \ \Pi(0) = (1,0,0),$$

that yields

$$
\begin{cases}
\frac{d\pi_2(t)}{dt} = -\lambda_1\,\pi_2(t) + \mu\,\pi_1(t), \\
\frac{d\pi_1(t)}{dt} = \lambda_1\,\pi_2(t) - (\lambda_2 + \mu)\,\pi_1(t), \\
\frac{d\pi_0(t)}{dt} = \lambda_2\,\pi_1(t), \\
\pi_2(0) = 1, \ \pi_1(0) = 0, \ \pi_0(0) = 1.
\end{cases}
$$

The transient probability distributions over the time interval $[0,4]$ were computed using the Mercury tool [25, 26, 273, 274], and we adopted the uniformization method presented in Section 10.5.4.

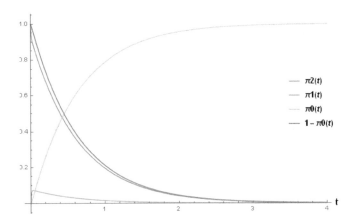

Figure 10.14 Probability Distributions $\Pi(t)$, $F_T(t)$, and $F_A(t)$ Over the Time Interval $[0, 0.5]$.

Figure 10.14 depicts the probability distributions $(\Pi(t))$ in the time interval $[0, 4]$ $t.u.$ as well as the probability of not reaching the absorbing state (state 0) $F_T(t) = 1 - \pi_0(t)$. The reader is reminded to observe that $F_A(t) = \pi_0(t)$. The MTTA was also numerically computed using the uniformization method (through the Mercury tool) by

$$MTTA = \int_0^\infty (1 - \pi_0(t)) \, dt = 0.65 \, t.u.$$

$\square$

10.6.1 METHOD BASED ON MOMENTS

Now we turn our attention to a method based on the moments of phase-type distributions. Phase-type distributions are an important class of distributions that can be seen as generalizations of the exponential distribution. For example, Erlang, hypoexponential, hyperexponential, and Cox distributions are well-known phase-type distributions. Nevertheless, the distribution of time to absorption of any CTMC with a single absorbing state can be thought of as a phase-type distribution [63, 132, 173, 180, 353].

Let us consider the chain depicted in Figure 10.10. This chain has m transient states and one absorbing state. The probability distribution at time $t = 0$ is denoted by

$$\Pi(0) = (\Pi'(0), \pi_m(0)), \qquad (10.6.1)$$

where $\Pi'(0)$ is the probability distribution of transient states at time $t = 0$, that is

$$\Pi'(0) = (\pi_1'(0), \pi_2'(0), \dots, \pi_{m-2}'(0), \pi_{m-1}'(0)). \qquad (10.6.2)$$

The infinitesimal generator of this chain may be represented by

$$Q = \begin{pmatrix} R & R^0 \\ 0 & 0 \end{pmatrix}, \qquad (10.6.3)$$

where R presents the transition rates among transient states, R^0 is a vector of rates from transient states to the absorbing state, and 0 is a null vector.

If the absorbing state is not the state m, the chain should be rearranged so that the absorbing states should be the last to obtain the infinitesimal generator in the above format.

The moments $E[X]^i]$ about the origin of a phase-type distribution are given by

$$E[X]^i] = (-1)^i \, i! \, \Pi'(0) \, R^{-i} \, 1.$$

1 is a vector whose elements are 1.

Therefore, the first moment about the origin of the time to reach the absorbing state (mean time to absorption) is denoted by

$$MTTA = E[X] = -\Pi'(0) \mathbf{R}^{-1} \mathbf{1}. \tag{10.6.4}$$

Now, multiply both sides by $\mathbf{R}$

$$MTTA \, \mathbf{R} = -\Pi'(0) \mathbf{R}^{-1} \mathbf{R} \, \mathbf{1}. \tag{10.6.5}$$

As

$$MTTA = \sum_{i=1}^{m-1} \tau_i = T \, \mathbf{1}, \tag{10.6.6}$$

where $T = (\tau_i)_{|S-1|}$ is a vector whose element, τ_i, is the mean time spent in each transient state. S is the set of states of the chain.

Hence

$$T \, \mathbf{1} \, \mathbf{R} = -\Pi'(0) \, \mathbf{1}. \tag{10.6.7}$$

$$T \, \mathbf{R} = -\Pi'(0). \tag{10.6.8}$$

Having T, we obtain the $MTTA$ (from 10.6.6).

Example 10.6.3. Here we compute the MTTA of the chain adopted in Example 10.6.1 by adopting the method presented in this section. The initial probability distribution of this chain is $\Pi(0) = (1,0,0)$. As we know, the rate matrix of that chain is

$$\mathbf{Q} = \begin{pmatrix} -\lambda_2 & \lambda_2 & 0 \\ 0 & -\lambda_1 & \lambda_1 \\ 0 & 0 & 0 \end{pmatrix}.$$

Thus, we have

$$\mathbf{R} = \begin{pmatrix} -\lambda_2 & \lambda_2 \\ 0 & -\lambda_1 \end{pmatrix},$$

$$\mathbf{R^0} = \begin{pmatrix} 0 \\ \lambda_1 \end{pmatrix},$$

and $\Pi'(0) = (1,0)$.

Applying 10.6.8 and 10.6.7, we have

$$T \, \mathbf{R} = -\Pi'(0).$$

$$(\tau_2, \tau_1) \begin{pmatrix} -\lambda_2 & \lambda_2 \\ 0 & -\lambda_1 \end{pmatrix} = \begin{pmatrix} -1 \\ 0 \end{pmatrix}$$

$$\begin{cases} -\lambda_2 \tau_2 = -1 \\ \lambda_2 \tau_2 - \lambda_1 \tau_1 = 0. \end{cases}$$

Assuming $\lambda_1 = 10$ and $\lambda_2 = 20$, we obtain

$$\tau_2 = \frac{1}{\lambda_2} = 0.05 t.u.,$$

$$\tau_1 = \frac{\lambda_2 \tau_2}{\lambda_1} = 0.1 t.u.$$

Then

$$MTTA = \tau_1 + \tau_2 = \frac{\lambda_1 + \lambda_2{}^2 \tau_2}{\lambda_1 \lambda_2} = \frac{3}{20} = 0.15 t.u.$$

$\square$

Example 10.6.4. In this example, we apply the method introduced in this section to compute the $MTTA$ of the CTMC presented in Example 10.6.2. The infinitesimal generator of the chain is

$$\mathbf{Q} = \begin{pmatrix} -\lambda_1 & \lambda_1 & 0 \\ \mu & -(\lambda_2 + \mu) & \lambda_2 \\ 0 & 0 & 0 \end{pmatrix};$$

thus

$$\mathbf{R} = \begin{pmatrix} -\lambda_1 & \lambda_1 \\ \mu & -(\lambda_2 + \mu) \end{pmatrix}.$$

As $\Pi(0) = (1,0,0)$, then $\Pi'(0) = (1,0)$. Hence,

$$T \mathbf{R} = -\Pi'(0).$$

Therefore

$$\begin{cases} -\lambda_1 \tau_2 + \mu \tau_1 = -1 \\ \lambda_1 \tau_2 - (\lambda_2 + \mu) \tau_1 = 0 \end{cases}$$

so,

$$\tau_1 = \frac{\lambda_1 \tau_2}{\mu} = 0.05 t.u.,$$

$$\tau_2 = \frac{(\lambda_2 + \mu)(\lambda_1 \tau_2)}{\lambda_1 \mu} = 0.6t.u.$$

Hence

$$MTTA = \tau_1 + \tau_2 = \frac{\lambda_1 \tau_2}{\mu} + \frac{(\lambda_2 + \mu)(\lambda_1 \tau_2)}{\lambda_1 \mu} = 0.65t.u.$$

$\square$

10.7 SEMI-MARKOV CHAIN

Now let us consider systems in which the times held in each state are neither exponentially distributed nor geometrically distributed. Such behavior may be expressed by semi-Markov chains (*SMC*) [172, 173, 223]. For example, an *SMC* may be represented by:

$$SMC = (\mathbf{P}, F(t)),$$

where $\mathbf{P}$ is the one-step probability matrix of the embedded DTMC and $F(t) = (F_i(t))$ is a vector that denotes the holding time probability distribution of each state i. This model has been named the semi-Markov chain. Therefore, at time instants in which there are transitions from states to states, the *SMC* acts as a DTMC, and the matrix $\mathbf{P}$ depicts such behavior. However, when entering in a state i, the model is held in that state according to the probability distribution $F_i(t)$.

For computing the steady-state distributions of an *SMC*, first the steady-state distribution of the embedded DTMC should be computed from $\mathbf{P}$, that is

$$\Theta = \Theta \mathbf{P}, \tag{10.7.1}$$

$$\sum_{\forall i} \theta_i = 1,$$

where $\Theta = (\theta_i)$.

The mean holding times of each state i are computed either by

$$mht_i = \int_0^\infty t f_i(t)dt \quad \text{or}$$

$$mht_i = \int_0^\infty F_i(t)dt,$$

where $f_i(t) = \frac{dF_i(t)}{dt}$.

It is worth mentioning that the steady-state probability distribution only requires the mean holding times, mht_i; thus if the mean values are available, the integration above is not needed.

The steady-state probability is then computed by

$$\pi_i = \frac{mht_i\,\theta_i}{\sum_{\forall j} mht_j\,\theta_j} \qquad \forall i. \tag{10.7.2}$$

It is important to stress that the embedded DTMC may not be aperiodic [223].

The **mean recurrence time** of the *SMC* can be computed by [223]

$$mrt_j = \frac{\sum_{i=1}^{N} mht_i\,\theta_i}{\theta_j}, \qquad 1 \le J \le N. \tag{10.7.3}$$

Example 10.7.1. Let us take into account an embedded system program composed of four basic blocks A, B, C, and D (see Example 9.8.1) as depicted below. Consider the times spent in each basic block are $21.3\,\mu s$, $8.5\,\mu s$, $12.6\,\mu s$, and $10.2\,\mu s$, and also assume the average powers of each basic block are $41.843\,mW$, $41.745\,mW$, $43.023\,mW$, and $42.852\,mW$, respectively.

Algorithm 15 Program Composed of Four Basic Blocks

1:	Basic Block A
2:	JNC 5
3:	Basic Block B
4:	JC 1
5:	Basic Block C
6:	JC 1
7:	Basic Block D
8:	JMP 1

The SMC depicted in Figure 10.15 represents the program described above. The model is composed of four states. The state i denotes the basic block i; state A represents the basic block A. The SMC is represented by its embedded DTMC and the mean holding time of each state. The mean holding time of each state is the respective time spent in each basic block. Table 10.4 depicts the mean holding time and the mean power assigned to each state.

According to a data flow analysis and considering the interface with environment, the following probability transition between basic blocks were inferred: $P_{A,B} = 0.7$, $P_{A,C} = 0.3$, $P_{B,A} = 0.6$, $P_{B,C} = 0.4$, $P_{C,A} = 0.7$, $P_{C,D} = 0.3$, and $P_{D,A} = 1$. The one-step probability matrix of the embedded DTMC is

$$\mathbf{P} = \begin{array}{c} \\ A \\ B \\ C \\ D \end{array} \begin{array}{c} \begin{array}{cccc} A & B & C & D \end{array} \\ \left(\begin{array}{cccc} 0 & 0.7 & 0.3 & 0 \\ 0.6 & 0 & 0.4 & 0 \\ 0.7 & 0 & 0 & 0.3 \\ 1 & 0 & 0 & 0 \end{array} \right) \end{array} .$$

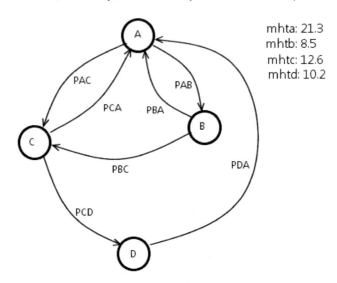

mhta: 21.3
mhtb: 8.5
mhtc: 12.6
mhtd: 10.2

Figure 10.15 SMC.

Table 10.4
Mean Holding Time and Mean Power

States i	mht_i (μs)	P_i (mW)
A	21.3	41.843
B	8.5	41.475
C	12.6	43.023
D	10.2	42.852

The steady-state probability distribution of the embedded DTMC was computed from 10.7.1.

$$\Theta = (\theta_A, \theta_B, \theta_C, \theta_D).$$

$$\Theta = (0.4075, 0.2852, 0.2363, 0.0709).$$

Using 10.7.2, the steady-state probability distribution of the SMC is estimated:

$$\Pi = (\pi_A, \pi_B, \pi_C, \pi_D).$$

$$\Pi = (0.5862, 0.1638, 0.2011, 0.0488).$$

We know that the energy consumed of a system with average power consumption P_{avg} in a time interval T is

$$E = \int_0^T P_{avg}\, dt = P_{avg} \times T.$$

Therefore, the average energy consumption in T related to being in state i is

$$E_i = P_i \times T \times \pi_i,$$

where P_i is average power consumption when in state i and π_i is the steady-state probability of being in state i. As the energy consumed in the time interval T is the summation of the energy consumed in each state, then

$$E = \sum_{i \in \{A,B,C,D\}} E_i = \sum_{i \in \{A,B,C,D\}} P_i \times T \times \pi_i,$$

and the average power consumption over the period T is estimated by

$$P_{avg} = \frac{E}{T}.$$

Now, estimate the consumed energy over one hour ($T = 3600\,s$). These results are depicted in Table 10.5. In addition, the mean recurrence time of each state is also presented in this table. For example, the mean recurrence time of the basic block D is the average execution time of one iteration of the program since after executing the basic block D, the program starts over again (an infinite loop).

Table 10.5

Energy, Power in $T = 3600\,s$, and Mean Recurrence Time (s)

States i	$E_i\ (J)$	$mrt_i\ (s)$
A	88.3092	36.3328
B	24.4516	51.9040
C	31.1532	62.6428
D	7.5357	208.8092
E (J)	151.4497	
$P_{avg}\ (mW)$	42.0694	

□

10.8 ADDITIONAL MODELING EXAMPLES

This section presents some additional examples where CTMCs have been adopted for estimating performance index. This section presents pure performance models. Availability, reliability, and performability models will be discussed in subsequent chapters.

10.8.1 ONLINE PROCESSING REQUEST CONTROL

Let us consider a piece of software that controls online processing requests from students in the student affairs department of a college. The internal department police are rigorous regarding providing the first feedback to students concerning their requests. For supporting such police, a processing request software sends alerts and downrates the internal quality index if more than three requests are made without the respective first feedback. Besides, it also blocks another control task until up to three requests are in the request queue. The queue is depicted in Figure 10.16.a.

Consider that the time between requests and the service time are both exponentially distributed with rates λ and μ, respectively. The CTMC presented in the Figure 10.16.b represents the control system. The chain state space is $\chi = \{0, 1, 2, 3\}$. Each state denotes the respective number of requests in the system, that is, 0, 1, 2 or 3 requests. Assume that the following rates: $\lambda = 0.2$ and $\mu = 0.4$ rpm (requests per minute).

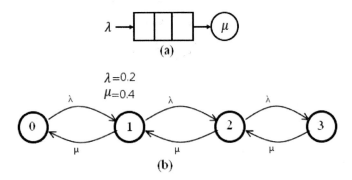

(a)

(b)

Figure 10.16 Online Processing Request Control.

The steady-state distribution is $\Pi = (\pi_0, \pi_1, \pi_2, \pi_3) = (0.5333, 0.2667, 0.1333, 0.0667)$. As $\lambda < \mu$ the system throughput is input rate less the discard rate. The discard rate is related to arrivals when the system is full, that is, it has three requests yet to be processed. Therefore, system throughput (tp) can be computed by the difference between the input rate (λ) and the discard rate (λ_d), that is, the non-discard rate (λ_{nd}).

$$tp = \lambda_{nd} = \lambda - \lambda_d,$$

where λ_d is the discard rate that is estimated calculated by multiplying the input rate (λ) by the probability of the system being full (π_3), that is, the probability of having discards.

$$\lambda_d = \lambda \times \pi_3.$$

Therefore, the discard rate and the actual throughput are

$$\lambda_d = 0.2 \times 0.0667 = 0.0133\,rpm,$$

$$tp = 0.2 - 0.2 \times 0.0667 = 0.1867\,rpm.$$

The average number of requests (*anr*) in the system is estimated by

$$anr = \sum_{i=1}^{3} i\,\pi_i = \pi_1 + 2 \times \pi_2 + 3 \times \pi_3$$

$$anr = 0.2667 + 2 \times 0.1333 + 3 \times 0.0667 = 0.7333.$$

The response time can be obtained through Little's law (see Equation 8.4.1), where

$$rt = \frac{anr}{tp} = \frac{0.7333}{0.1867} = 3.9286\,min.$$

10.8.2 TINY PRIVATE CLOUD SYSTEM

Consider a tiny private cloud system composed of five processing nodes and one node manager (see Figure 10.17) [94, 330]. Transaction requests arrive at the cloud manager (*CM*), which among other activities, distributes the request to the processing nodes. Each node was monitored throughout $600\,s$ (T). In this period, the cloud system received 1000 transaction requests and processed the same number of transactions (A_0 and C_0). It was observed that in the monitored period, the processing node 1 ($N1$) received 700 transaction requests (A_1) and processed roughly the same number of transactions (C_1). The average utilization processing node 1 over the monitored period was 65%. Each processing node has a controller (software) that manages the transactions sent to the respective node. Each node controller manages the transaction request queue, which stores transaction requests to the processing node. $N1$ has a queue that supports up to 10 requests.

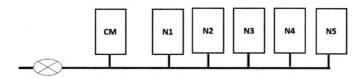

Figure 10.17   Tiny Private Cloud System.

In the monitored period, the cloud throughput (see 8.0.3) was, therefore

$$X_0 = \frac{C_0}{T} = \frac{1000}{600} = 1.6667\,tps.$$

The time each transaction demands from the processing node can be estimated by (8.3.1):

$$D_1 = \frac{U_1}{X_0} = \frac{0.65}{1.6667} = 0.39\,s.$$

Assume that the transaction demand time, named here service time (ST), and the time between arrivals (TBA) at $N1$ are exponentially distributed. Therefore, we can estimate the parameter (λ and μ) of both time distributions by

$$\mu = \frac{1}{D_1} = \frac{1}{0.39} = 2.5641\,tps.$$

and

$$\lambda = \frac{A_1}{T} = \frac{700}{600} = 1.1667 tps.$$

The CTMC in Figure 10.18 is a performance model that depicts the transaction arrivals and the transaction processing at $N1$. Each state name denotes the respective number of transactions in the node queue. The respective rates depict transactions' arrival and services executions, that is, λ and μ.

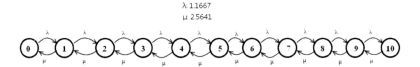

Figure 10.18   Node 1 CTMC Model.

The metrics we are interested in are the average number of transactions in the system ($ants$), the discard rate (dr), the throughput (tp), the response time (rt), and the node 1 utilization (u). These metrics are depicted by the following expressions and are computed using the CTMC's steady-state distribution.

$$ants = \sum_{i=1}^{10} i\,\pi_i = 1.1509\,transaction,$$

$$dr = \lambda \times \pi_{10} = 1.1667 \times 9.3412 \times 10^{-4} = 0.0011\,tps,$$

$$tp = \lambda - \lambda \times \pi_{10} = 1.1667 - 0.0011 = 1.1656 tps,$$

$$rt = \frac{\sum_{i=1}^{10} i\,\pi_i}{\lambda - \lambda \times \pi_{10}} = \frac{1.1509}{1.1656} = 0.9874\,s,$$

and

$$u = 1 - \pi_0 = 1 - 0.4629 = 0.5371.$$

Now, let us vary the node 1 input rate and analyze the metrics depicted above. The range of λ in this experiments was set to $[0.01\,tps,\ 2.56\,tps]$. We considered intermediate steps of $0.1\,tps$. These results are presented in Figure 10.19.

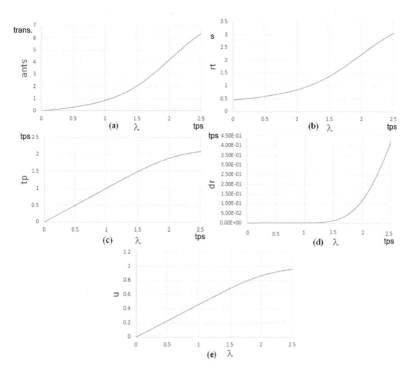

Figure 10.19 Metrics Values for $\lambda \in [0.01\,tps,\ 2.56\,tps]$.

One should observe in Figure 10.19.d the significant increase of the discard rate for values of $\lambda > 1.5\,tps$, since the probability of the queue being full ceases to be negligible. Observe the probability of the queue being full for different values of λ. For instance, for $\lambda = 1$, the probability that the queue is full is 0.03%. For $\lambda = 1.5$, the probability of the queue being full is 0.78%, and for $\lambda = 2.5$, the probability of the queue being full is 16.72%. We also already observe the tendency of reaching its maximum value, that is, 2.17 (see Figure 10.19.c).

10.8.3 TWO SERVERS WITH DIFFERENT PROCESSING RATES

Let us consider a computer system composed of two servers and a load balancer. The load balancer receives a request to process a transaction of a given type and assigns each request to one server. The load balancer manages a queue of size $q = 10$. We assume that the time between transaction processing requests and the time to process each transaction (in either server) are exponentially distributed. We also consider that the transaction processing request rate is defined as $\lambda = 100tps$ and the processing rates of Server 1 and Server 2 are $\mu_1 = 65tps$ and $\mu_2 = 45tps$. The load balancer processing time is considered to be negligible (or considered to be "inserted" in the servers´ processing time). We assume that when both servers are idle, and one request arrives, this request is assigned to Server 1. This system is depicted in Figure 10.20.

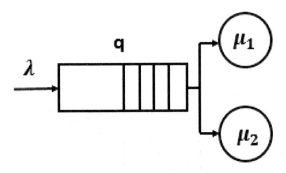

Figure 10.20 Two Servers with Different Processing Rates.

The CTMC that represents this system performance behavior is presented in Figure 10.21.

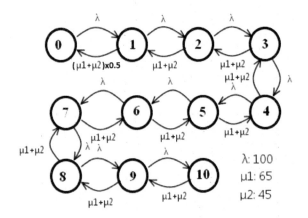

Figure 10.21 CTMC Representing the Two Server System with Different Processing Rates.

The state 0 denotes the state in which the system has no transaction to process. When one request arrives, the system transitions to state 1. In that state, two events are possible; that is, a new request may occur, which makes the system transition to the state 2, or the request may be served by Server 1, which transitions the system back to state 0. From state 2 on, the system has at least two requests to process, and these requests are evenly assigned to both servers. Therefore every transition from a state s to a state $s - 1$, $s \leq 2$, have rate $\mu_1 + \mu_2$.

The discard rate is estimated by

$$dr = \lambda \times \pi_{10},$$

and the system throughput through

$$tp = \lambda - \lambda \times \pi_{10} = \lambda(1 - \pi_{10}).$$

The average number of transactions in the system is calculated by

$$ants = \sum_{i=1}^{10} i\,\pi_i, \qquad \text{and}$$

the response time by

$$rt = \frac{\sum_{i=1}^{10} i\,\pi_i}{\lambda(1 - \pi_{10})}.$$

The average utilization of each server (probability of each server being busy - $i \in \{1,2\}$) is

$$u_i = \frac{1 - \pi_0}{2}.$$

The system utilization is estimated by

$$u = 1 - \pi_0.$$

The steady-state values of the above metrics are depicted in Table 10.6.

An experiment was executed by varying $\lambda \in [1\,tps, 190\,tps]$. The respective values of the metrics depicted above are presented in Figure 10.22.

Figure 10.22.a shows the discard rate as λ increases. The discard rate is very small for $\lambda < 100$. However, as λ approaches $110\,tps$, we notice that the discard rate becomes non-negligible and heavily increases for higher values of λ. The system throughput (see Figure 10.22.b) linearly increases with λ until λ approaches values around $110\,tps$. For higher values of λ, the system throughput stays steady at $110\,tps$. The number of transactions in the system ($ants$) increases with λ (see Figure 10.22.c). The reader may notice that up to λ values equal to $110\,tps$, the curve is concave up, and from then on (λ values higher than $110\,tps$) the curve is concave down but keeps increasing. It is also worth noting that from this point on, the discard rate also becomes very significant. Figure 10.22.d presents the residence time

Table 10.6
Results

Metrics	Values
dr	5.8024 tps
tp	94.1976 tps
ants	4.3699 trans.
rt	0.0464 s
u_1	0.4623
u_2	0.4623
u	0.9248

as a function of λ. The residence time begins equal to $0.0154s$ and increases with λ. Again, one should observe that for λ values up to $110tps$, the rt curve is concave up, and from then on (λ values higher than $110tps$), the rt curve is concave down but stays increasing. The rt does not increase sharply since the discard rate strongly increases for λ values higher than $110tps$, due to queue capacity. As the rt cannot increase beyond its maximal capacity, the residence time reduces its increase tendency. The utilization (U_i) of both servers – $i \in \{1,2\}$ - (probability of being used) increases with the values of λ (see Figure 10.22.e). Figure 10.22.f) shows the system utilization.

Now, let turn our attention to the actual queue size and the waiting time. The system starts queueing from state 3 since the system's requests represented by states 1 and 2 are directly assigned to the servers. Therefore, the state 3 denotes that 3 requests are in the system, but only one is in the queue. State 4 shows that two requests are being served and the other two are in the queue, and so on. Therefore, the average queue size is computed through

$$aqs = \sum_{i=ns+1}^{q} (i - ns)\,\pi_i, \qquad (10.8.1)$$

where ns is the number of servers and q is system capacity. In this particular case, $ns = 2$ and $q = 10$; hence :

$$aqs = \sum_{i=3}^{10} (i - 2)\,\pi_i$$

Considering $\lambda = 100tps$, and $\mu_1 = 65tps$ and $\mu_2 = 45tps$, we have $aqs = 2.6572$ transactions. If we vary λ in $[1tps, 190tps]$, we have the respective curve presented in Figure 10.23.a.

The waiting time is estimated using Little's law (as is done for calculating the residence time). Therefore

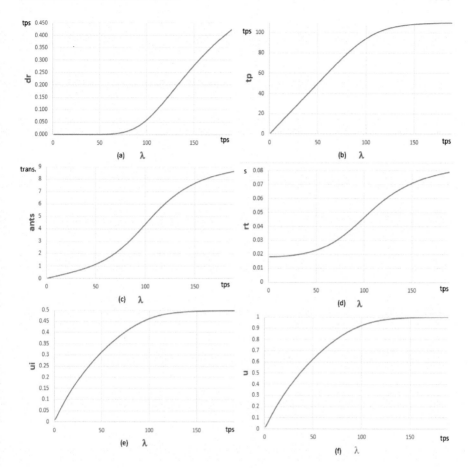

Figure 10.22   Metrics Values for $\lambda \in [1tps, 190tps]$.

$$wt = \frac{aqs}{tp}. \tag{10.8.2}$$

$$wt = \frac{\sum_{i=ns+1}^{q}(i-ns)\,\pi_i}{\lambda\,(1-\pi_q)}. \tag{10.8.3}$$

Hence, in this example, we have

$$wt = \frac{\sum_{i=3}^{10}(i-2)\,\pi_i}{\lambda\,(1-\pi_{10})}.$$

When considering $\lambda = 100tps$, and $\mu_1 = 65tps$ and $\mu_2 = 45tps$, the waiting time is $wt = 0.0282\,s$. The respective waiting times when we vary λ in $[1tps, 190tps]$ are depicted in the curve presented in Figure 10.23.b.

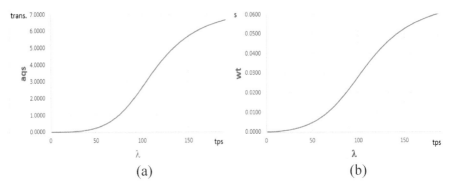

(a)   (b)

Figure 10.23   Queue Size and Waiting Time for $\lambda \in [1\,tps, 190\,tps]$.

10.8.4 $M/E/1/4$ QUEUE SYSTEM

Now consider a simple queue system composed of only one server. A request arrives at the system and is assigned to the server. The system capacity is four; that is, the maximal queue size is three. The time between requests (tbr) is exponentially distributed with rate $\lambda = 20\,tps$. However, the service time (st) obeys an Erlang distribution with four-phase ($\gamma = 4$) and the rate of each phase equal to $\mu_E = 160\,tps$. This queue is depicted in Figure 10.24.

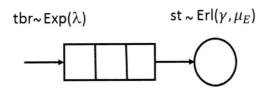

Figure 10.24 $M/E/1/4$.

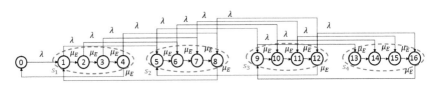

Figure 10.25 CTMC Representing the Queue $M/E/1/4$.

The CTMC depicting this system performance behavior is presented in Figure 10.25. The CTMC is composed of seventeen states ($\chi = \{0, 1, ... 15, 16\}$). State 0 denotes that no request is in the system. When one request arrives, represented by the rate λ, the system transitions to state 1. In that state, two events are possible: a new request arrival (for which the system transitions to state 5) and the server processing first phase (for which the system transitions to state 2). As the service time is distributed according to $Erl(\gamma = 5, \mu_E = 160 tps)$, the CTMC represents such distribution as sets of four sequential exponential phases. Therefore, the service times are denoted by four phases, each phase with a rate μ_E. When the request starts to be processed, the system transitions to state 2. In that state, again, two events are possible. They are: a new request arrives, making the system transition to state 6, or the processing of the first request advances one more phase, taking the system to state 3. In this state, a new request may also arrive. This event transitions the system to state 8. Another possible event is the execution of the last phase of the service, which transitions the system to state 0. The states 1, 2, 3, and 4 were grouped to form a "super-state" s_1. Similarly, states 5, 6, 7, and 8, states 9, 10, 11, and 12, and states 13, 14, 15, and 16 formed the "super-states" s_2, s_3, s_4, respectively. For keeping the service time "history", when the system is in one of the "sub-states" of each super-state, and one new request arrives, the system transitions from that particular sub-state (of the super-state) to the equivalent sub-state of the next super-state. For instance, if the system is in state 2 and a new request arrives, the system transitions to state 5, which is the second sub-state of the super-state s_2.

The super-state names represent the number of requests in the system, that is, s_1 depicts one request in the system, s_2 shows that two requests are in the system, and so on. Therefore, the average number of requests in the system is obtained through

$$ants = \sum_{j=1}^{4} j \times \sum_{i=1}^{4} \pi_{4(j-1)+i}.$$

This expression is equivalent to

$$ants = (\pi_1 + \pi_2 + \pi_3 + \pi_4) + 2 \times (\pi_5 + \pi_6 + \pi_6 + \pi_8) +$$
$$3 \times (\pi_9 + \pi_{10} + \pi_{11} + \pi_{12}) + 4 \times (\pi_{13} + \pi_{14} + \pi_{15} + \pi_{16}).$$

The utilization is obtained by

$$u = 1 - \pi_0.$$

The discard rate and the throughput are estimated by

$$dr = \lambda \times \sum_{i=13}^{16} \pi_i$$

and

$$tp = \lambda - dr = \lambda(1 - \sum_{i=13}^{16} \pi_i),$$

respectively. The response time is calculated through

$$rt = \frac{ants}{tp} = \frac{\sum_{j=1}^{4} j \times \sum_{i=1}^{4} \pi_{4(j-1)+i}}{\lambda(1 - \sum_{i=13}^{16} \pi_i)}.$$

The steady-state values of the above metrics are depicted in Table 10.6.

Table 10.7
Results

Metrics	Values
dr	0.2642 tps
tp	19.7358 tps
ants	0.7559 trans.
rt	0.0383 s
u	0.4934

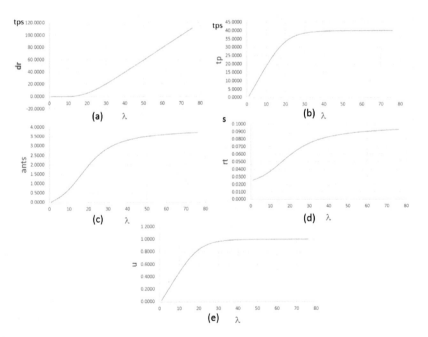

Figure 10.26   Metrics Values for $\lambda \in [1\,tps,\ 80\,tps]$ – Queue $M/E/1/4$.

Now, let us vary the rate of the time between request distributions and analyze the metrics depicted above. The range of λ in this experiments was set to $[1\,tps,\ 80\,tps]$.

Theses results are presented in Figure 10.26. The discard rate is very small for $\lambda < 15$. For $\lambda > 20$, however, the discard rate grows linearly with λ. Such a behavior is depicted in Figure 10.26.a. The throughput, on the other hand, grows almost linearly with λ values up to $20tps$. From that point on the throughput growth rate sharply reduces and remains steady at $40tps$, for $\lambda \leq 40tps$ (see Figure 10.26.b). The response time starts at $0.0254s$ for $\lambda = 1tps$ and increases. The curve $rt(\lambda)$ presents a positive concavity up to around $\lambda = 17tps$. From that point on, however, the growth rate reduces and the curve concavity becomes negative. This trend is also observed in the curve *ants* vs. λ. These two curves are presented in Figure 10.26.c and 10.26.d. The system utilization is presented in Figure 10.26.e.

The waiting time, queue size, and other metrics are also estimated accordingly, as already depicted in previous examples.

10.8.5 MOBILE APPLICATION OFFLOADING

Consider an IT company that plans to design a cloud infrastructure to provide offloading solutions for mobile applications. The developer expects that partitioning the application at the method level and distributing the methods on several servers would reduce the application′s execution time. In this example, we aim to estimate an application's mean execution time and calculate the probability of finishing the application execution by a specific time. This application (see Code 16) was partitioned into methods, and those methods were deployed and executed in particular virtual machines, and each virtual machine was executed in exclusive processors cores.

Algorithm 16 Application Code

```
1: root function
2:    a ← m1()
3:    b ← m2(a)
4:    c ← m3()
5:    return b,c
6: end function
```

A representative sample of the execution time of each method in each particular virtual machine was measured. In the exploratory data analysis, it was observed that exponential distributions well represent the execution times distributions, and that the respective mean execution times are $met_{m1} = 2800ms$, $met_{m2} = 3200ms$, and $met_{m3} = 3000ms$. Therefore, the distribution parameters are

$$\lambda_a = \frac{1}{met_{m1}} = \frac{1}{2800ms} = 3.5714 \times 10^{-4} \, ms^{-1},$$

$$\lambda_b = \frac{1}{met_{m2}} = \frac{1}{3200ms} = 3.125 \times 10^{-4} \, ms^{-1} \quad \text{and}$$

$$\lambda_c = \frac{1}{met_{m3}} = \frac{1}{3000\,ms} = 3.3333 \times 10^{-4}\,ms^{-1}.$$

The CTMC that represents the performance model is depicted in Figure 10.28. This CTMC might have been directly obtained or could be first expressed using a higher-level notation such as an automaton, in which individual sequential automatons are specified (Figure 10.27.a and 10.27.b) and later composed using a parallel operator (Figure 10.27.c) in order to generate the final automaton (Figure 10.27.d). The CTMC is then obtained from this automaton by assigning the respective rates related to each specific method execution.

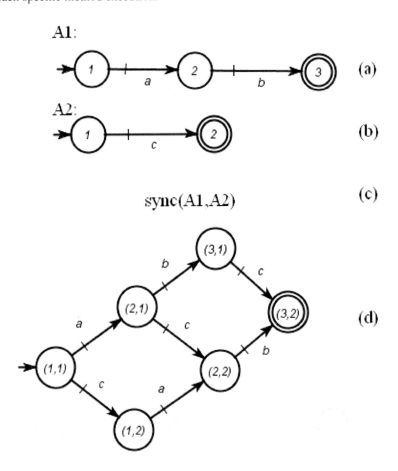

Figure 10.27 Automata Representation of the Application.

The rate matrix is

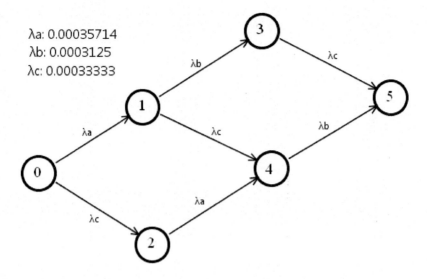

Figure 10.28   Performance Model – CTMC.

$$Q = \begin{pmatrix} -(\lambda_a+\lambda_c) & \lambda_a & \lambda_c & 0 & 0 & 0 \\ 0 & -(\lambda_b+\lambda_c) & 0 & \lambda_b & \lambda_c & 0 \\ 0 & 0 & -\lambda_a & 0 & \lambda_a & 0 \\ 0 & 0 & 0 & -\lambda_c & 0 & \lambda_c \\ 0 & 0 & 0 & 0 & -\lambda_b & \lambda_b \\ 0 & 0 & 0 & 0 & 0 & 0 \end{pmatrix}.$$

Thus, we have

$$R = \begin{pmatrix} -(\lambda_a+\lambda_c) & \lambda_a & \lambda_c & 0 & 0 \\ 0 & -(\lambda_b+\lambda_c) & 0 & \lambda_b & \lambda_c \\ 0 & 0 & -\lambda_a & 0 & \lambda_a \\ 0 & 0 & 0 & -\lambda_c & 0 \\ 0 & 0 & 0 & 0 & -\lambda_b \end{pmatrix}.$$

and $\Pi'(0) = (1,0,0,0,0)$.

The mean execution time (*met*) of the application can be calculated by 10.6.8, that is

$$met \times R = -\Pi'(0).$$

Hence *met* $= 6750.8348\,ms$.

Computing the probability of reaching the absorbing state (state 5) by time t $(\pi_6(t))$ allows us to estimate the cumulative distribution function of the execution time of the application ($F_{et}(t)$). This function is presented in Figure 10.29. We adopted the uniformization method (10.5.4) for obtaining the transient probabilities.

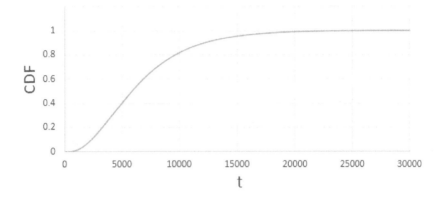

Figure 10.29 Cumulative Distribution Function – $F_{et}(t)$.

Using $F_{et}(t)$, we can calculate the probability of the execution time being larger or shorter than t, the probability that the execution time lies in a time interval, as well as many statistics. For example, we computed the probability of the execution time (tte) being shorter than $5100\,ms$, larger than $10200\,ms$, and lying within $(5100\,ms, 10200\,ms)$. These results are

$$P(et \leq 5100\,ms) = 0.4145932,$$

$$P(et > 10200\,ms) = 0.1754237,$$

and

$$P(5100 < et \leq 10200\,ms) = 0.4099831,$$

respectively.

10.8.6 QUEUE SYSTEM WITH MMPP ARRIVAL

Consider a system well represented by a one-server queue model with a capacity equal to k, whose service time is exponentially distributed. However, the arrival process is a Markov modulated Poisson process (MMPP), that is, a Poisson process with a time-varying arrival rate.

In this particular example (see Figure 10.30), the constant arrival rates are either λ_1 or λ_2. During a specified period, the arrival traffic sends requests at the rate λ_1. This period is exponentially distributed with rate β. After this period, the arrival traffic changes its behavior and starts sending arrival traffic at the rate λ_2, and keeps at this rate for a period exponentially distributed with the rate α. The system capacity considered in this example is 5.

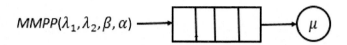

$$MMPP(\lambda_1, \lambda_2, \beta, \alpha)$$

Figure 10.30   System with MMPP Arrival Traffic.

The CTMC depicted in Figure 10.31 represents the performance behavior of such a system. The state names are represented by pairs, (i, j), where $i \in \{0, 1\}$ denotes states at which the arrival rates are λ_{i+1}, and $j \in \{0, 1, 2, 3, 4, 5\}$ denotes the number of requests in the system. Therefore, state $(0, 0)$ denotes that the arrival rate is λ_1 and that there is no request to be processed by the system. In this state, two events are possible: arrival at the rate λ_1 and the event that denotes a change in the arrival rate. This event, whose rate is β, is represented by the transition to the state $(1, 0)$. In state $(1, 0)$, two events again are possible: an arrival (at the rate λ_2) and the event that denotes a change in the arrival rate. This event is represented by the transition to the state $(1, 0)$ and has a rate α. If in state $(0, 0)$ and an arrival occurs (at λ_1), the system transitions to state $(0, 1)$. In this state, three events are possible: a service execution, whose rate is μ, a new arrival occurrence (represented by λ_1), or a change in the arrival rate (depicted by β). If the system is in state $(1, 0)$ and an arrival occurs (at λ_2), we have a transition to state $(1, 1)$. As in state $(0, 1)$, three events are possible in state $(1, 1)$: a service execution (μ), a new arrival occurrence (represented by λ_2), or a change in the arrival rate (depicted by α). A similar behavior is observed in states (i, j), where $i = \{0, 1\}$ and $j = \{2, 3, 4\}$. When in state $(0, 5)$ or $(1, 5)$, no other event arrival is allowed since the queue is full. Hence, depending on the system state, we may have a service execution or an arrival rate β or α.

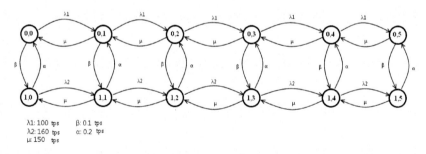

Figure 10.31   CTMC of a System with MMPP Arrival Traffic.

The discard rate can be calculated through this expression

$$dr = \lambda_1 \times \pi_{0,5} + \lambda_2 \times \pi_{1,5},$$

and the throughput can be computed through

$$tp = \sum_{i=0}^{1} \sum_{j=1}^{5} \pi_{i,j} \times \mu.$$

The average number of requests in the system is expressed by

$$ants = \sum_{i=0}^{1} \sum_{j=1}^{5} j\, \pi_{i,j},$$

and the average number of requests in the queue is denoted by

$$antq = \sum_{i=0}^{1} \sum_{j=2}^{5} (j-1)\, \pi_{i,j}.$$

The response and the waiting times can be obtained by

$$rt = \frac{\sum_{i=0}^{1} \sum_{j=1}^{5} j\, \pi_{i,j}}{\sum_{i=0}^{1} \sum_{j=1}^{5} \pi_{i,j} \times \mu},$$

and

$$wt = \frac{\sum_{i=0}^{1} \sum_{j=2}^{5} (j-1)\, \pi_{i,j}}{\sum_{i=0}^{1} \sum_{j=1}^{5} \pi_{i,j} \times \mu}.$$

Considering $\lambda_1 = 100\,tps$, $\lambda_2 = 160\,tps$, $\mu = 140\,tps$, $\beta = 0.02\,tps$, and $\alpha = 0.02\,tps$, the values of the metrics presented above are those depicted in Table 10.8.

Table 10.8
Results

metrics	values
dr	$21.20320\,tps$
tp	$108.8001\,tps$
$ants$	$2.2333\,trans.$
$antq$	$1.4562\,trans.$
rt	$20.53\,ms$
wt	$13.38\,ms$
u	0.7771

Figure 10.32 shows the discard rate curve versus α. In this experiment, the reader may observe the changes in the discard rates as the time spent in $(1, j)$ states changes. When the system spends more time in $(1, j)$ states, the discard rates are larger, since $\lambda_2 > \lambda_1$.

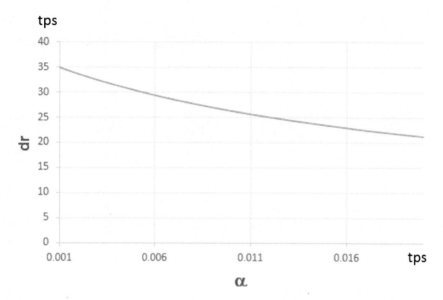

Figure 10.32 Discard Rate vs. α.

10.8.7 POISSON PROCESS AND TWO QUEUES

Consider a system composed of two servers each with it particular queue (see Figure 10.33). Each server (s_i) and its queue (q_i) is denoted as the sub-system ss_i. The arrival traffic is the Poisson process with rate λ. When a request (req) arrives, it is assigned to sub-system ss_1 with probability p and to sub-system s_2 with probability $1 - p$. The services times of both sub-systems are exponentially distributed with rate μ_1 and μ_2, respectively.

The CTMC depicted in Figure 10.34 is a performance model of this system. Its states are specified by pairs, (i, j), $i \in \{0, 1, 2, 3\}$, $j \in \{0, 1, 2, 3, 4\}$, where i and j denote the number of requests in the subsystem ss_1 and ss_2, respectively. Hence, for instance, state $(0, 0)$ denotes a system with no requests, and the state $(3, 4)$ represents a system with three requests in the subsystem ss_1 and four requests in the subsystem ss_2, where no other request is allowed in the system before at least one request is processed by one of the servers.

The discard rate is the probability of the system being full times the arrival rate, that is

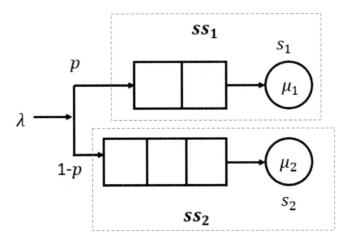

Figure 10.33 Poisson Process and Two Queues.

$$dr = \pi_{3,4} \times \lambda.$$

Therefore, the throughput is the arrival rate less the discard rate:

$$tp = \lambda - \pi_{3,4} \times \lambda.$$

So

$$tp = \lambda \left(1 - \pi_{3,4}\right).$$

The average number of requests in the system (*anrs*) is

$$anrs = \sum_{i=0}^{3} \sum_{j=0}^{4} (i+j)\, \pi_{i,j}.$$

The response time is calculated through

$$rt = \frac{anrs}{tp}.$$

Hence,

$$rt = \frac{\sum_{i=0}^{3} \sum_{j=0}^{4} (i+j)\, \pi_{i,j}}{\lambda \left(1 - \pi_{3,4}\right)}.$$

And the utilization of each server is

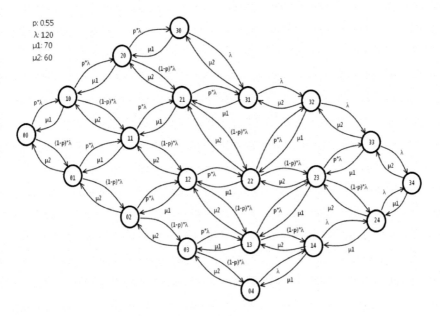

Figure 10.34   Performance Model.

$$u_1 = 1 - \sum_{j=0}^{4} \pi_{0,j}, \text{ and}$$

$$u_2 = 1 - \sum_{i=0}^{3} \pi_{i,0},$$

respectively.

Considering $\lambda = 120\,rps$[8], $p = 0.55$, $\mu_1 = 70\,rps$, and $\mu_2 = 60\,rps$, the values of the metrics presented above are depicted in Table 10.9.

Figure 10.35 presents the metrics (presented above) results for $\lambda \in (0, 500\,tps)$. It is important to stress the change in discard rate when λ approaches $100\,rps$ (Figure 10.35.a). For values o λ smaller than $100\,rps$, the discard rate is negligible, but from that point onwards the discard rate grows linearly with λ. An opposite behavior is observed for the system throughput (see Figure 10.35.b). For $\lambda < 100\,rps$ the throughput follows λ, but for values of $\lambda > 100\,rps$ the throughput derivative sharply reduces, and the throughput stays steady for $\lambda \leq 130\,rps$. The average number of request in the system to be processed grows with λ. The curve concavity of the

---

[8]rps – request per seconds

Table 10.9
Results

Metrics	Values
dr	$14.6836\,rps$
tp	$105.3164\,rps$
$anrs$	$3.2253\,req.$
rt	$30.6253\,ms$
u_1	0.8862
u_2	0.7214

curve is positive for values of λ up to around $100\,rps$. From that point on, however, the curve concavity becomes negative. This can be observed in Figure 10.35.c. A similar behavior is also noticed in curve $rt\,vs.\,\lambda$ (Figure 10.35.d). The utilization of both servers is depicted in Figure 10.35.e and Figure 10.35.f, respectively.

10.8.8 TWO STAGE TANDEM SYSTEM

Consider a computer system composed of two server subsystems. Transaction requests arrive at Server 1 subsystem according to a Poisson process with rate λ. Each subsystem may be processing one transaction, may have another request waiting in its arrival buffer, or may not have a request to be processed. When Server 1 finishes processing a request, it delivers it to be processed by Server Sub-system 2. This request only is accepted if there is an available position in Server Sub-system 2. Both service times (the time to process requests in each server) are exponentially distributed with rates μ_1 and μ_2, respectively. Figure 10.36 represents this system as two blocking tandem sub-systems (ss_1 and ss_2), each composed by a one-position-buffer and one server.

The CTMC depicted in Figure 10.37 is a performance model of the system depicted in Figure 10.36. As mentioned, each sub-system (ss_1 and ss_2) may have none, one or two requests. Hence, the system state may be specified by a pair $(i, j), i, j \in \{0, 1, 2\}$, where i and j are the number of requests in ss_1 and ss_2, respectively.

At states $(2, j), j \in \{0, 1, 2\}$, no other request is accepted in the system. Therefore, additional request arrivals are discarded. Therefore, the discard rate is expressed by

$$dr = \lambda \sum_{j=0}^{2} \pi_{2,j},$$

and the Server 1 throughput may be calculated either through

$$tp_{s_1} = \lambda \left(1 - \sum_{j=0}^{2} \pi_{2,j}\right)$$

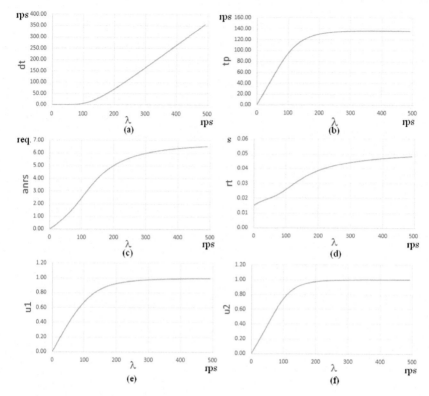

Figure 10.35 Performance Results.

or

$$tp_{s_1} = \sum_{i=1}^{2} \sum_{j=0}^{1} \pi_{i,j} \times \mu_{s_1}.$$

The Server 2 throughput may be obtained by

$$tp_{s_2} = \sum_{i=0}^{2} \sum_{j=1}^{2} \pi_{i,j} \times \mu_{s_2}.$$

The average number of requests in the system is estimated by

$$anrs = \sum_{i=1}^{2} \sum_{j=1}^{2} (i+j) \, \pi_{i,j},$$

and the average number of requests in Server Sub-system 1 and Server Sub-system 2 are estimated by

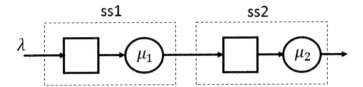

Figure 10.36 Two Stage Tandem System.

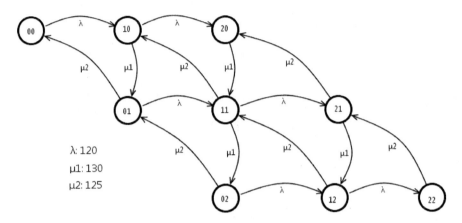

λ: 120
μ1: 130
μ2: 125

Figure 10.37 CTMC – Performance Model.

$$anrs_1 = \sum_{i=1}^{2}\sum_{j=0}^{2} i\,\pi_{i,j},$$

and

$$anrs_2 = \sum_{i=0}^{2}\sum_{j=1}^{2} j\,\pi_{i,j}.$$

The response time is calculated by summing up the response time of Server Sub-system 1 and of Server Sub-system 2, that is $rt = v_{s1} \times rt_{s_1} + v_{s2} \times rt_{s2}$ (see Equation 8.5.1); hence

$$rt = \frac{anrs_1}{tp_{s_1}} + \frac{anrs_2}{tp_{s_2}}.$$

$$rt = \frac{\sum_{i=1}^{2}\sum_{j=0}^{2} i\,\pi_{i,j}}{\sum_{i=1}^{2}\sum_{j=0}^{1} \pi_{i,j} \times \mu_{s_1}} + \frac{\sum_{i=0}^{2}\sum_{j=1}^{2} j\,\pi_{i,j}}{\sum_{i=0}^{2}\sum_{j=1}^{2} \pi_{i,j} \times \mu_{s_2}}.$$

where $v_{s1} = v_{s2} = 1$.

The utilization of each server is obtained by

$$u_{s_1} = \sum_{i=1}^{2} \sum_{j=0}^{2} \pi_{i,j}$$

and

$$u_{s_2} = \sum_{i=0}^{2} \sum_{j=1}^{2} \pi_{i,j},$$

respectively.

Considering $\lambda = 120\,rps$, $\mu_1 = 130\,rps$ and $\mu_2 = 125\,rps$, the values of the metrics presented above are depicted in Table 10.10.

Table 10.10
Results

Metrics	Values
dr	$47.5957\,rps$
tp_{s_1}, tp_{s_2}	$72.4043\,rps$
$anrs$	$1.9549\,req.$
rt	$27\,ms$
u_{s_1}	0.7329
u_{s_2}	0.5792

10.8.9   EVENT RECOMMENDATION MASHUP

Many applications on the Internet are made available in the form of web services, a concept that encompasses applications that are technology-neutral, loosely coupled, and support location transparency [324]. Communication employing well-established standards and protocols, such as XML and HTTP, makes web services an efficient but straightforward programming model, enabling almost seamless integration with third-party products. The composition of different web services is a trend in the development of web applications towards building added-value products, known as mashup services.

When deploying web services (composite or not), providers often commit service-level agreements (SLAs) with their customers, which include performance and dependability-related metrics [370], such as the mean response time and service reliability. As a composite web service may have complex application logic, it is non-trivial to check whether or not the composing service will meet its SLA. In this context, analytic approaches to determine the overall performance of composite web services have been proposed in the literature [261, 370].

This study uses an event recommendation application to demonstrate the applicability of CTMCs to analyze composite web services (mashups). Figure 10.38 depicts a UML activity diagram for such a service.

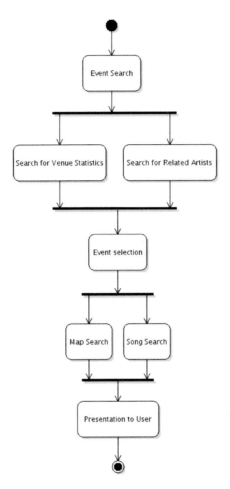

Figure 10.38   UML Activity Diagram for an Event Recommendation Mashup.

The UML diagram shows that the first activity is the search for events, which may employ the user location as input. The location may be manually provided or obtained by communicating with a GPS (Global Positioning System) application. After obtaining an event, the next step is based on concurrent calls to two different services: one searches for venue statistics, such as the average rating of previous events in that concert place; the other searches for similarities between the artists which will be present in the event and those preferred by the user. After obtaining the responses from those two services, the mashup selects the better event, based on the venue and artist criteria. Once the event is selected, the application searches for additional information that may be helpful for the user, namely the map indicating directions from his/her current place to the event venue and one sample song from the leading artist in that event. The last activity is the presentation of all gathered information to the user.

Based on the previously presented UML diagram, a continuous-time Markov chain (CTMC) was created to represent the presented mashup application, enabling the computation of the expected value for the response time of the overall composite service. The CTMC depicted in Figure 10.39 includes only the calls to external web services. The response times of activities "Event Selection" and "Presentation to User" – which are executed by its own mashup application – are not considered in this model.

Each state in the CTMC denotes that a request was sent to a given service. The transition rates are estimated as the inverse of the mean response time of the corresponding web service ($1/mrt_X$). The concurrent calls to the "Search for Venue Statistics" and "Search for Related Artists" services are represented in the state called "**Event Analysis**". Depending on the web service that first replies, the system transitions either to the state "**Venue Stats Finished**", with a rate of $1/mrt_{VS}$, or to "**Similar Artists Finished**", with a rate of $1/mrt_{SA}$. The system goes to the state "**Top Event Processing**" just after receiving the response of both the services, i.e., "Search for Venue Statistics" and "Search for Related Artists". The state "**Top Event Processing**" denotes the concurrent calls to "**Map Search**" and "**Song Search**". The system goes to a distinct state depending on the service that replies first. The transition to "**Map Search Finished**" occurs with a rate of $1/mrt_{MS}$ and to "**Song Search Finished**" with a rate of $1/mrt_{SS}$. After finishing both the services, the CTMC goes to state "**Complete**", which is an absorbing state that represents the end of composite web service execution. All response times are assumed to be exponentially distributed.

The CTMC depicted in Figure 10.39 enables the computation of the mean response time for this system as well as other metrics such as the probability of reaching the state complete by a given maximum time value. In addition, closed-form equations may also be found to compute the mean response time of this system, as seen in Equation 10.8.4.

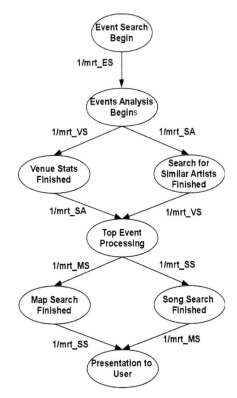

Figure 10.39 CTMC for the Composite Web Service.

$$
mrt_{sys} = mrt_{ES} + \left(mrt_{VS} + mrt_{SA} - \frac{1}{\dfrac{1}{mrt_{VS}} + \dfrac{1}{mrt_{SA}}} \right)
$$
$$
+ \left(mrt_{MS} + mrt_{SS} - \frac{1}{\dfrac{1}{mrt_{MS}} + \dfrac{1}{mrt_{SS}}} \right)
$$

(10.8.4)

Table 10.11 shows the input parameters employed for evaluating the response time metric using the CTMC of Figure 10.39. Considering those input parameters, the mean response time computed for this composite web service is 11.65 s. This value is estimated as the mean time to absorb this model since the state "Complete" is an absorbing state.

The response time CDF (cumulative distribution function) can be estimated by computing the transient probability of the system being in the state "Complete" for dis-

Table 10.11
Input Parameters and Numerical Result for the Composite Web Service CTMC

Service	Resp. time (s)
Event Search	3.01
Venue Stats	3.50
Similar Artists	3.56
Map Search	1.30
Song Search	2.95
Composite Service	**11.65**

tinct time values in a given range. Figure 10.40 depicts such a graph, indicating that by $30s$ there is almost 100% probability of having completed the composition execution. This is an example of an analytic result that may guide systems developers and administrators to establish expected SLA levels and tune their applications or infrastructure to meet that QoS attribute.

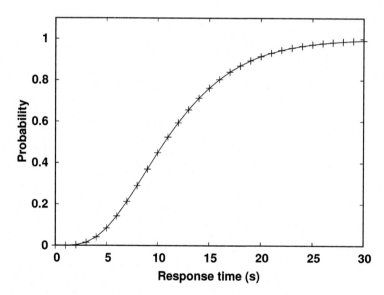

Figure 10.40   Estimation of Response Time CDF.

EXERCISES

Exercise 1. Concerning the exponential probability distribution, answer: a) Why is the exponential distribution widely adopted in performance and reliability modeling? b) Why is the exponential distribution the only memoryless continuous distribution? c) What is the relation between the exponential and the geometric distributions? d) What is the relation between the exponential and the Erlang distributions? d) What is the relation between the exponential and the hyperexponential distributions?

Exercise 2. What do you mean by Markovian properties? Explain in detail.

Exercise 3. Considering the CTMCs. Explain the following concepts: **(a)** Homogeneity and **(b)** Ergodicity.

Exercise 4. Explain what you understand by rate matrix.

Exercise 5. Comment on the main difficulties when solving

$$\mathbf{P}(t) = \mathbf{P}(0)\, e^{\mathbf{Q}t} = \mathbf{I} + \sum_{k=1}^{\infty} \frac{\mathbf{Q}t^k}{k!}.$$

Exercise 6. Draw the CTMC whose infinitesimal generators are given below:

$$\mathbf{Q} = \begin{pmatrix} -5 & 3 & 2 \\ 0 & -2 & 2 \\ 0 & 3 & -3 \end{pmatrix}.$$

Exercise 7. Calculate the steady-state probability of all states of the chain represented by the infinitesimal generator specified in the previous exercise.

Exercise 8. Consider the chain shown in Figure 10.16, and compute **(a)** the mean number of transactions in the system, **(b)** the discard rate, **(c)** throughput, **(d)** the probability of the system being full, **(e)** the utilization, **(f)** the response time, **(g)** the mean number of transactions in the queue, and **(h)** the mean waiting time. Assume $\lambda = 100\,tps$, $\mu = 110\,tps$, and $k = 20$.

Exercise 9. Now update the previous infrastructure to consider 3 identical servers. Propose a CTMC for this system and calculate the same metrics for the previous exercise, assuming the service rate of each server is $\mu_i = 110\,tps$ $(i = 1, 2, 3)$ and $\lambda = 320\,tps$.

Exercise 10. A mobile phone company has received numerous complaints about the unavailability of lines to answer phone calls in a particular geographic region (see Figure 10.41.I). The users observe the unavailability of lines through the "busy" signal, notice when they make calls and have no available channels. Therefore, the planning department decided to conduct a performance study. When studying the geographic region, it is observed that there is a single base station (**I**) that serves the telephone calls of the locality. The number of channels on the base station is 16. When a telephone connection is made, one channel is busy (it is unavailable for other calls as it is in use), so it remains until the connection is ended. The telephone company has a policy that aims to maintain the unavailability of lines (discard calls) below 1%. However, the information collected shows that users in the region have observed the unavailability of lines above this defined limit.

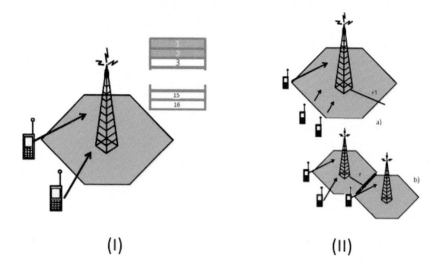

Figure 10.41   Geographic Region – Mobile Phone Cells.

In order to reduce the unavailability of lines, it was decided to install another base station (**II**) to serve the population of the region. As installing other base stations at a distance from the existing station reduces the number of users served by the already installed base station, it should reduce the unavailability of rows (see Figure 10.41.II).

A study was made of the call history of the region, and based on this study, it is estimated that the number of calls per hour per square kilometer is 80 ($\tau = \lambda/A = 80\,h^{-1}\,Km^{-2}$), where $A - \pi r^2$ is the circle area, and r its radius. Therefore, we have $\lambda = \pi r^2 \tau$ ($\lambda = \pi r^2\,80\,h^{-1}\,Km^{-2}$).

We assume that the time between calls is exponentially distributed. In this study, it was observed that the mean time of each connection is 90 seconds ($0.025\,h$, $\mu = 1/0.025\,h = 40h^{-1}$). We also considered that the call duration is exponentially distributed.

What should be the largest radius of the resized cell (delimited by the new base station positioning) so that the unavailability of lines stays within the established limit?

Exercise 11. A private cloud system composed of five processing nodes and one node manager (CM) (see Figure 10.18) processes transactions that arrive at the CM.

Transaction requests arrive at the CM, which distributes the request to the processing nodes. The arrival request rate was constant and equal to $\lambda = 1.5tps$. The constant service rate of each node was $\mu = 0.32tps$. The system has a queue of maximal size equal to $k = 20$. Propose a CTMC that represents this system, and estimate the average number of transactions in the system (*ants*), the discard rate (*dr*), the throughput (*tp*), the response time (*rt*), and utilization (*u*).

Exercise 12. A system composed of one server processes transactions at the client requests. A request arrives at the system and is assigned to the server. The system capacity is $k = 8$ (the maximal queue size is seven). The time between requests (*tbr*) is exponentially distributed with rate $\lambda = 25tps$. The service time (*st*) obeys an Erlang distribution with three-phase ($\gamma = 3$) and the rate of each phase is equal to $\mu_E = 150tps$. Queue model $M/E/1/k$ well describes this system. Propose a CTMC that represents this system, and estimate the average number of transactions in the system (*ants*), the discard rate (*dr*), the throughput (*tp*), the response time (*rt*), and the utilization (*u*).

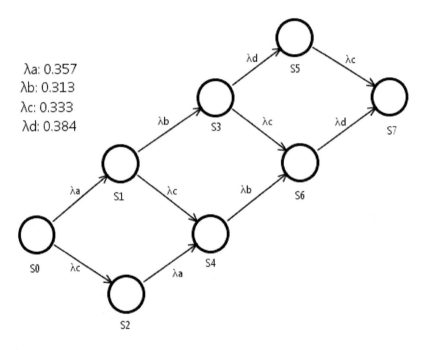

λa: 0.357
λb: 0.313
λc: 0.333
λd: 0.384

Figure 10.42 Performance Model.

Exercise 13. Consider the CTMC depicted in Figure 10.42 is a performance model of software system composed of four main functions (f_a, f_b, f_c, and f_d). The time to execute each of these functions is exponentially distributed and their means are $mtte_a = 2.8s$, $mtte_b = 3.2s$, $mtte_c = 3.0s$, and $mtte_d = 2.6s$. **(a)** Show the matrix Q,

(b) Show the matrix R (see Sub-section 10.6.1), **(c)** Use the method of **Moments of Phase-Type Distributions** (presented in Sub-section 10.6.1) to compute the mean time to execute the software system (mean time to absorption). **(d)** Plot the cumulative distribution of the time to execute the software system.

11 Basic Queueing Models

Queues are present in our everyday lives since they appear whenever there is competition for constrained resources. The ability to model and analyze systems of queues helps to minimize their response time and maximize the use of systems´ resources. This chapter presents a set of elementary queue systems. Such systems are characterized by symmetric structures, which allows evaluating the system performance by analytic solutions. On the one hand, these models represent very constrained systems; on the other hand, such models can describe and evaluate many practical performance problems. As these models are based on the Birth and Death process, first we introduce this model, which is considered further in the subsequent models introduced in this chapter.

First, however, let us explain some basic terms: the server(s) and the queue into which customers arrive constitute a service facility. Besides, it is common to refer to a queue and its server(s) as a queue. Moreover, when multiple service facilities are combined into a network of queues, the term node is commonly adopted to refer to a service facility.

11.1 THE BIRTH AND DEATH PROCESS

Consider an infinite capacity single queue system in which the time between arrivals and the service time are exponentially distributed. These arrivals can be seen as births, and the end of their service executions can be regarded as dead. Suppose, however, that the arrival rate changes at each arrival. Therefore, the rate of the first arrival is λ_0, the rate of the second arrival is λ_1, and so on. Likewise, the service rate also changes. Thus, μ_0 denotes the service rate of the first executed service, μ_1 is the service rate of the second service execution, and so on.

The queue facility is depicted in Figure 11.1.a and the respective CTMC is presented in Figure 11.1.b. The CTMC rate matrix is partially represented by

$$
\mathbf{Q} = \begin{array}{c} \\ 0 \\ 1 \\ 2 \\ 3 \\ \cdots \end{array}
\begin{array}{c}
\begin{array}{cccccc} 0 & 1 & 2 & 3 & 4 & \cdots \end{array} \\
\left(\begin{array}{cccccc}
-\lambda_0 & \lambda_0 & 0 & 0 & 0 & \cdots \\
\mu_1 & -(\lambda_1 + \mu_1) & \lambda_1 & 0 & 0 & \cdots \\
0 & \mu_2 & -(\lambda_2 + \mu_2) & \lambda_2 & 0 & \cdots \\
0 & 0 & \mu_3 & -(\lambda_3 + \mu_3) & \lambda_3 & \cdots \\
\cdots & \cdots & \cdots & \cdots & \cdots & \cdots
\end{array}\right)
\end{array}.
$$

Solving $\Pi \cdot \mathbf{Q} = 0$, we have

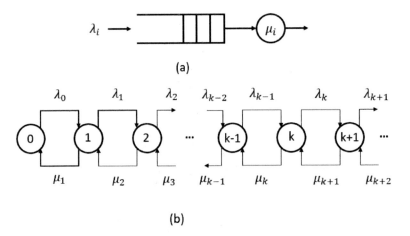

Figure 11.1 Birth and Death Process.

$$\begin{cases} \lambda_0 \pi_0 + \mu_1 \pi_1 = 0, & (E_1) \\ \lambda_0 \pi_0 - (\mu_1 + \lambda_1)\pi_1 + \mu_2\pi_2 = 0, & (E_2) \\ \lambda_1 \pi_1 - (\mu_2 + \lambda_2)\pi_2 + \mu_3\pi_3 = 0, & (E_3) \\ \quad \dots \end{cases}$$

Solving E_1, we have:

$$\pi_1 = \frac{\lambda_0}{\mu_1}\pi_0. \qquad (11.1.1)$$

Solving E_2, using Equation 11.1.1 , we have:

$$\pi_2 = \frac{\lambda_0\lambda_1}{\mu_1\mu_2}\pi_0. \qquad (11.1.2)$$

Solving E_3, using Equation 11.1.1 and 11.1.2 , we have:

$$\pi_3 = \frac{\lambda_0\lambda_1\lambda_2}{\mu_1\mu_2\mu_3}\pi_0. \qquad (11.1.3)$$

Therefore

$$\pi_k = \frac{\lambda_0\lambda_1\lambda_2...\lambda_{k-1}}{\mu_1\mu_2\mu_3...\mu_k}\pi_0. \qquad (11.1.4)$$

Hence

$$\pi_k = \pi_0 \prod_{i=0}^{k-1} \frac{\lambda_i}{\mu_{i+1}}, k \geq 1. \qquad (11.1.5)$$

As $\pi_0 + \sum_{k=1}^{\infty} \pi_k = 1$, then:

$$\pi_0 + \sum_{k=1}^{\infty} \pi_0 \prod_{i=0}^{k-1} \frac{\lambda_i}{\mu_{i+1}} = 1.$$

So

$$\pi_0 \left(1 + \sum_{k=1}^{\infty} \prod_{i=0}^{k-1} \frac{\lambda_i}{\mu_{i+1}}\right) = 1.$$

Hence

$$\pi_0 = \frac{1}{1 + \sum_{k=1}^{\infty} \prod_{i=0}^{k-1} \frac{\lambda_i}{\mu_{i+1}}}. \qquad (11.1.6)$$

This concludes the derivation of the steady-state solution, which is provided by the combination of 11.1.5 and 11.1.6. This solution is essential for evaluating simple queueing systems and is extensively adopted for finding the steady-state solution of the models depicted in this chapter. An additional remark should be made here about the existence of a steady-state solution. Such a solution is closely related to the sum[1]

$$1 + \sum_{k=1}^{\infty} \prod_{i=0}^{k-1} \frac{\lambda_i}{\mu_{i+1}}$$

If $\sum_{k=1}^{\infty} \prod_{i=0}^{k-1} \frac{\lambda_i}{\mu_{i+1}}$ diverges, the chain is either null recurrent or transient. It should be noticed, however, that if λ_i is smaller than μ_i the series converges and a steady-state solution is obtained. It can be seen that this situation arises whenever we have

$$\frac{\lambda_i}{\mu_i} < 1.$$

11.2 M/M/1 QUEUE

The simplest model derived from the formulation depicted in the previous section is a model in which all the arrival and service rates are the same for all states, that is, λ and μ, respectively. This model is named $M/M/1$ queue system (see Figure 11.2.a) and the respective CTMC is depicted in Figure 11.2.b.

Therefore, from 11.1.6, it follows that

$$\pi_0 = \frac{1}{1 + \sum_{k=1}^{\infty} \left(\frac{\lambda}{\mu}\right)^k}. \qquad (11.2.1)$$

For $\lambda < \mu$,

$$\sum_{k=1}^{\infty} \left(\frac{\lambda}{\mu}\right)^k = \frac{\lambda/\mu}{1 - \lambda/\mu}.$$

---

[1] See the denominator of 11.1.6.

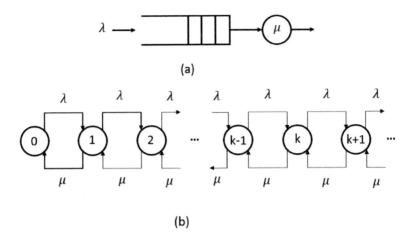

Figure 11.2 $M/M/1$ Queue System.

Thus

$$\pi_0 = \frac{1}{1 + \frac{\lambda/\mu}{1 - \lambda/\mu}}.$$

Therefore,

$$\pi_0 = 1 - \frac{\lambda}{\mu}. \tag{11.2.2}$$

Let us define $\rho = \lambda/\mu$ as the traffic intensity. Hence, we may also state

$$\pi_0 = 1 - \rho. \tag{11.2.3}$$

Utilization - The server utilization (for $\rho < 1$) is estimated by

$$u = 1 - \pi_0, \tag{11.2.4}$$

$$u = \rho = \frac{\lambda}{\mu}, \tag{11.2.5}$$

which is the time proportion the server is busy. When $\rho \geq 1$, however, the utilization is one, since $\pi_0 = 0$.

From 11.1.5, we have

$$\pi_k = \pi_0 (\frac{\lambda}{\mu})^k, \; k \geq 1. \tag{11.2.6}$$

From 11.2.3, we obtain

$$\pi_k = (1-\rho)(\frac{\lambda}{\mu})^k, \ k \geq 1. \tag{11.2.7}$$

And

$$\pi_k = (1-\rho)\rho^k, \ k \geq 1. \tag{11.2.8}$$

Throughput - The throughput is the departure rate of the server. If $\rho < 1$, the throughput is λ. However, if $\rho \geq 1$, the throughput is μ.

Mean System Size - Let N be the random variable that specifies the number of customers, clients, requests, or transactions in the system at a steady-state, and $E(N)$ be the expected value of N. The average number (of transactions, clients, requests) in the system at steady-state is estimated by

$$mss = E(N) = \sum_{k=0}^{\infty} k \, \pi_k.$$

Therefore

$$mss = \sum_{k=0}^{\infty} k(1-\rho)\rho^k.$$

$$mss = (1-\rho)\sum_{k=0}^{\infty} k\rho^k.$$

$$mss = (1-\rho)\rho \sum_{k=0}^{\infty} k\rho^{k-1}.$$

Hence

$$mss = (1-\rho)\rho \frac{\partial}{\partial \rho} \sum_{k=0}^{\infty} \rho^k. \tag{11.2.9}$$

Let us take

$$s_n = \sum_{k=0}^{n} \rho^k.$$

Hence

$$s_n = 1 + \rho + \rho^2 + \ldots + \rho^n. \tag{11.2.10}$$

Multiplying both sides by ρ leads to

$$\rho \, S_n = \rho + \rho^2 + \rho^3 + \ldots + \rho^{n+1}. \tag{11.2.11}$$

Subtracting 11.2.10 from 11.2.11, we have

$$s_n - \rho \, S_n = 1 - \rho^{n+1}.$$

Thus

$$s_n(1-\rho) = 1 - \rho^{n+1},$$

which leads to

$$s_n = \frac{1 - \rho^{n+1}}{(1-\rho)}.$$ (11.2.12)

If $n \to \infty$ and $\rho < 1$, then

$$s_\infty = \frac{1}{1-\rho}.$$

Therefore (from 11.2.9), we have

$$mss = (1-\rho)\rho \frac{\partial}{\partial\rho}(\frac{1}{1-\rho}).$$

Hence

$$mss = (1-\rho)\rho \frac{1}{(1-\rho)^2}.$$

$$mss = \frac{\rho}{1-\rho}.$$ (11.2.13)

Therefore

$$mss = \frac{\lambda/\mu}{1-\lambda/\mu}.$$ (11.2.14)

And

$$mss = \frac{\lambda}{\mu-\lambda}.$$ (11.2.15)

If $\rho \geq 1$, $mss \to \infty$.

Variance of the System Size - The variance of the number of customers, clients, requests, or transactions in the system is defined as

$$Var(N) = E(N^2) - E(N)^2.$$ (11.2.16)

Since

$$E(N^2) = \sum_{k=0}^{\infty} k^2 \pi_k,$$

and considering 11.2.8, we have

$$E(N^2) = \sum_{k=0}^{\infty} k^2 (1-\rho)\rho^k.$$

Thus

$$E(N^2) = (1-\rho)\rho \sum_{k=0}^{\infty} k^2 \rho^{k-1}.$$

Therefore

$$E(N^2) = (1-\rho)\rho \frac{\partial}{\partial \rho} \sum_{k=0}^{\infty} k\rho^k. \tag{11.2.17}$$

Let us take $\frac{\partial}{\partial \rho} \sum_{k=0}^{\infty} k\rho^k$, and define

$$x_n = \sum_{k=0}^{n} k\rho^k.$$

So

$$x_n = \rho + 2\rho^2 + 3\rho^3 + \dots + n\rho^n. \tag{11.2.18}$$

Now, multiplying both sides by ρ leads to

$$\rho x_n = \rho^2 + 2\rho^3 + 3\rho^4 + \dots + n\rho^{n+1}. \tag{11.2.19}$$

And subtracting 11.2.18 from 11.2.19, we have

$$x_n - \rho x_n = \rho \sum_{k=0}^{n} \rho^k.$$

Therefore

$$x_n = \frac{\rho}{1-\rho} \sum_{k=0}^{n} \rho^k. \tag{11.2.20}$$

From 11.2.12, we have that

$$\sum_{k=0}^{n} \rho^k = \frac{1-\rho^{n+1}}{(1-\rho)}.$$

Thus, considering 11.2.20, we have

$$x_n = \frac{\rho}{1-\rho} \frac{1-\rho^{n+1}}{(1-\rho)}.$$

If $\rho < 1$ and for $n \to \infty$, we obtain:

$$x_\infty = \sum_{k=0}^{\infty} k\rho^k = \frac{\rho}{(1-\rho)^2}.$$

Using the result above in 11.2.17 leads to

$$E(N^2] = (1-\rho)\rho \frac{\partial}{\partial \rho} \frac{\rho}{(1-\rho)^2}.$$

As

$$\frac{\partial}{\partial \rho} \frac{\rho}{(1-\rho)^2} = \frac{1}{(1-\rho)^2} + \frac{2\rho}{(1-\rho)^3},$$

hence

$$E(N^2] = \frac{\rho(1+\rho)}{(1-\rho)^2}.$$

Applying in 11.2.16, we have

$$Var(N) = \frac{\rho(1+\rho)}{(1-\rho)^2} - \left(\frac{\rho}{1-\rho}\right)^2,$$

since $E(N) = \rho/(1-\rho)$. Therefore,

$$Var(N) = \frac{\rho}{(1-\rho)^2}. \tag{11.2.21}$$

Mean Response Time - By using Little's law (see 8.4.1), the mean response time is calculated (for $\rho < 1$):

$$rt = \frac{mss}{tp}.$$

Since $tp = \lambda$, we have

$$rt = \frac{\lambda/(\mu - \lambda)}{\lambda}.$$

$$rt = \frac{1}{\mu - \lambda}. \tag{11.2.22}$$

For $\rho \geq 1$, the response time is infinity, because $mss \to \infty$. When $\lambda \to 0$, $rt \to 1/\mu$, since, in this state, the only delay expected by a customer is the service time.

Mean Queue Size - Let Q be a random variable that specifies the number of clients, customers, or transactions waiting in the queue at a steady state. The mean queue size is estimated by

$$mqs = \sum_{k=1}^{\infty} (k-1)\pi_k.$$

$$mqs = \sum_{k=1}^{\infty} k\pi_k - \sum_{k=1}^{\infty} \pi_k.$$

$$mqs = mss - \rho.$$

Thus

$$mqs = \frac{\rho}{1-\rho} - \rho.$$

$$mqs = \frac{\lambda}{\mu} \frac{\lambda}{\mu - \lambda}. \tag{11.2.23}$$

$$mqs = \frac{\lambda^2}{\mu(\mu - \lambda)}. \tag{11.2.24}$$

Mean Waiting Time - Applying Little´s law; we estimated the mean waiting time, since

$$mqs = tp \times wt.$$

Hence

$$wt = \frac{\lambda^2/(\mu(\mu - \lambda))}{\lambda}.$$

$$wt = \frac{\lambda}{\mu(\mu - \lambda)}. \tag{11.2.25}$$

Table 11.1 summarizes the metrics presented for the $M/M/1$ queue system. The second column depicts the expression of the metrics when the system is stable ($\lambda/\mu < 1$), whereas the third column presents the metrics when $\lambda/\mu \geq 1$ (instability).

Table 11.1
Metrics for $M/M/1$ Queue System

Metrics	$\lambda/\mu < 1$	$\lambda/\mu \geq 1$
Utilization	λ/μ	1
Throughput	λ	μ
Mean System Size	$\lambda/(\mu - \lambda)$	∞
Mean Response Time	$1/(\mu - \lambda)$	∞
Mean Queue Size	$(\lambda^2)/(\mu(\mu - \lambda))$	∞
Mean Waiting Time	$\lambda/(\mu(\mu - \lambda))$	∞

Example 11.2.1. Consider a single server computer system, where transactions arrive according to a Poisson distribution at the rate of $\lambda = 100$ transactions per minute (tpm). This implies that the interarrival times have an exponential distribution with the mean interarrival time of 0.01 minutes. Furthermore, the server has an exponential service time distribution with a service rate of 110 tpm. As we have exponential

interarrival and service times and a single server, a $M/M/1$ queue is a suitable model for representing the system performance.

Table 11.2
Results for $M/M/1$ System

Metrics	Values
Utilization	0.9091
Throughput	$100tpm$
Mean System Size	10.0000
Variance System Size	110.0000
Mean Response Time	$0.1000min$
Mean Queue Size	9.0909
Mean Waiting Time	$0.0909min$

As $\lambda/\mu = 100/110 < 1$, the system is stable. Table 11.2 depicts the values of the metrics depicted in this section.

Figure 11.3 depicts the values of the metrics for $\mu = 110tpm$ and $\lambda(1tpm, 109tpm)$. Figure 11.3.a and b shows that utilization and the throughput linearly increase with λ. *mss*, *mrt*, *mqs*, and *mwt* (Figures 11.3.c, d, e, and f) depicts small impacts for λ smaller than around $80tpm$. However, for greater values of λ, the metrics values are significantly affected.

$\square$

Example 11.2.2. Let us suppose there is a switch with processing capacity (pc) equal to $100Mbps$. Consider that the time between package (each package has 524 bytes) arrival is exponentially distributed with mean $6ms$ ($0.006s$) (mean time between arrivals – *mtba*). What is the switch utilization, the mean number of bytes in the system, and the mean time to process a package (mean response time)?

The package arrival rate[2] is calculated by inverting the mean time between package arrivals, that is

$$\lambda_{pps} = \frac{1}{mtba} = \frac{1}{0.006s} = 166.6667pps.$$

Converting this rate to bits per seconds (bps), we have:

$$\lambda_{bbs} = \lambda_{pps} \times 524bytes \times 1024bits = 89.4293 \times 10^6 bps = 89.4293Mbps.$$

The processing capacity is the service rate; hence $\mu = 100 \times 10^6 bps$. Let us assume μ is constant. The switch utilization is, then, estimated by

---

[2]pps - package per second.

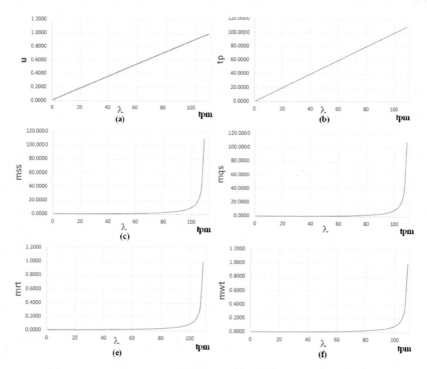

Figure 11.3 $M/M/1$ Results.

$$u = \frac{\lambda_{bps}}{\mu} = \frac{89.4293 \times 10^6 \, bps}{100 \times 10^6 \, bps} = 0.8943.$$

The mean system size (in bits) is

$$mss_b = \frac{\lambda}{\mu - \lambda} = \frac{89.4293 \times 10^6 \, bps}{100 \times 10^6 \, bps - 89.4293 \times 10^6 \, bps} = 8.4601 \, bits,$$

Converting to bytes, we have

$$mss_B = \frac{mss_b}{8} = 1.0575 \, bytes.$$

The mean response time to process a package is estimated by the time one bit stays in the system times the number of bits of a package, that is

$$mrt = \frac{1}{\mu - \lambda} \times 524 \, bytes \times 1024 \, bits.$$

Thus,

$$mrt = \frac{1}{100 \times 10^6\, bps - 89.4293 \times 10^6\, bps} \times 524\, bytes \times 1024\, bits.$$

$$mrt = 50.7608\, ms.$$

□

11.3 M/M/m QUEUE

This section extends the model introduced in the previous section by taking into account m similar servers instead of only one. This new model is named the $M/M/m$ queue system. The first and second M denote that the interarrival and service times are exponentially distributed. The interarrival rate is λ, and the service rate of each server is μ. m denotes the number of servers in the system.

Upon arrival, a request is processed by one available server. If all servers are busy, the request is queued until one server becomes free. As in the previous model, the system capacity is infinity; the queue may store an infinite number of requests. If the system has $n < m$ requests, the number of busy servers is n. On the other hand, if the system has $n \geq m$ requests, the number of busy servers is m.

This system can be represented by a birth-death chain in which the arrival rate is λ, and the service rate is $n\mu$ when the number of requests in the system is n, and $m\mu$, when the number of requests in the system is larger than $m - 1$. Figure 11.4 presents the queue system and the respective birth-death chain. The stability criterion is satisfied if $\lambda < m\mu$.

Let us assume that the system is in state 0 at time 0. The only possible event is an arrival. This event occurs with rate λ, and takes the system to state 1 (see Figure 11.4.b). In state 1, two events are possible, that is, the service execution, at rate μ, which takes the system back to the state 0, and a new arrival. The new arrival transitions the system to state 2. State 2 denotes a system with two requests to be processed. Again, two events are possible in this state: a new arrival, which takes the system to state 3, and a service execution. A new arrival occurs at the rate λ (as before), but the service rate is now 2μ since the system has two requests to be processed and has the m server (assuming $m \geq 2$). This process continues in the same fashion. The state m denotes a system with m requests. In this state, the service is executed at $m\mu$ since the system has m requests and m servers. If a new request arrives, the system is taken to state $m + 1$ ($m + 1$ requests in the system). In this state (and further states, i.e., $m + 2$, $m + 3$ ...), however, the service rate is not increased, as observed so far, because the number of servers is m. Hence, the service rate is $m\mu$. The same occurs for states $m + 2$, $m + 3$ ...

Using 11.1.5, we obtain the steady-state probability

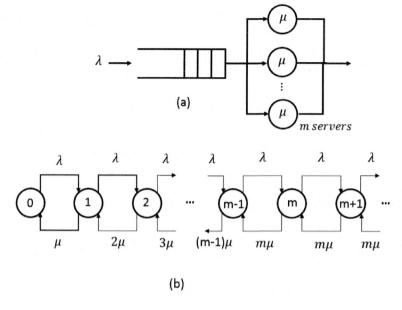

Figure 11.4 $M/M/m$ Queue System.

$$\pi_k = \begin{cases} \pi_0 \frac{(m\rho)^k}{k!}, & 0 \le k \le m-1, \\ \pi_0 \frac{m^m \rho^k}{m!}, & k \ge m, \end{cases} \qquad (11.3.1)$$

where

$$\rho = \frac{\lambda}{m\mu}, \qquad (11.3.2)$$

and $\rho < 1$ for the system to be stable.

Since $\pi_0 + \prod_{k=1}^{\infty} \pi_k = 1$ and considering 11.3.1, we get

$$\pi_0 = \left(\sum_{k=0}^{m-1} \frac{(m\rho)^k}{k!} + \frac{(m\rho)^m}{m!} \frac{1}{1-\rho} \right)^{-1}. \qquad (11.3.3)$$

Utilization - Let us define B as a random variable that represents the number of busy servers in a $M/M/m$ model. The mean number of busy servers is estimated by

$$E(B) = \sum_{k=0}^{m-1} k \pi_k + m \sum_{k=m}^{\infty} \pi_k.$$

From the equation above, we get

$$E(B) = m\rho. \tag{11.3.4}$$

It follows that an individual server utilization (for $\rho < 1$) is given by

$$u = \rho = \frac{E(B)}{m} = \frac{\lambda}{m\mu}. \tag{11.3.5}$$

If $\rho \geq 1, u = 1$.

Throughput - The system throughput is the system departure rate. If $\rho < 1$, the throughput is λ. However, if $\rho \geq 1$, the throughput is $m\mu$.

Mean System Size - Let N be the random variable that specifies the number of customers or transactions in the system at a steady-state. $E(N)$ defines the expected value of N. The mean number (of transactions, clients, requests) in the system at steady-state is estimated by

$$mss = E(N) = \sum_{k=0}^{\infty} k\, \pi_k,$$

when $\rho < 1$. Applying 11.3.3 and 11.3.1 in the equation presented above, we get

$$mss = m\rho + \rho \frac{(m\rho)^m}{m!} \frac{\pi_0}{(1-\rho)^2}. \tag{11.3.6}$$

If $\rho \geq 1, mss \to \infty$.

Mean Response Time - Considering Little's law, the mean response time is estimated ($mrt = mss/\lambda$); thus :

$$mss = \frac{m\rho + \rho \frac{(m\rho)^m}{m!} \frac{\pi_0}{(1-\rho)^2}}{\lambda}.$$

Hence

$$mrt = \frac{m}{\mu} + \frac{1}{\mu} \frac{(m\rho)^m}{m!} \frac{\pi_0}{(1-\rho)^2}, \quad \rho < 1. \tag{11.3.7}$$

If $\rho \geq 1, mrt \to \infty$.

Mean Queue Size - The mean queue size is estimated by $mqs = \sum_{k=m+1}^{\infty} k\, \pi_k$. Considering this, we obtain

$$mqs = \frac{\rho}{1-\rho} \frac{(m\rho)^m}{m!(1-\rho)} \pi_0, \quad \rho < 1. \tag{11.3.8}$$

For $\rho \geq 1, mqs \to \infty$.

Mean Waiting Time - Considering Little's law, the mean waiting time is estimated ($mwt = mqs/\lambda$); thus :

$$mwt = \frac{\frac{\rho}{1-\rho} \frac{(m\rho)^m}{m!(1-\rho)} \pi_0}{\lambda}, \quad \rho < 1.$$

Hence

$$mwt = \frac{1/\mu}{1-\rho} \frac{(m\rho)^m}{m!\,(1-\rho)} \pi_0, \quad \rho < 1. \qquad (11.3.9)$$

If $\rho \geq 1$, $mwt \to \infty$.

Queueing Probability Considering $\rho < 1$, the probability that a request does not find an idle server is estimated by

$$P_Q = \sum_{k=m}^{\infty} \pi_k,$$

which is

$$C = P_Q = \frac{(m\rho)^m}{m!} \frac{\pi_0}{1-\rho}. \qquad (11.3.10)$$

This expression is also known as the **Erlang C** formula after Agner Karup Erlang.

If $\rho \geq 1$, $P_Q = 1$.

Table 11.3 summarizes the metrics presented for the $M/M/m$ queue model.

Table 11.3
Metrics for $M/M/m$ Queue System

Metrics	$\lambda/m\mu < 1$	$\lambda/m\mu \geq 1$
Utilization	$u = \frac{\lambda}{m\mu}$	1
Throughput	λ	$m\mu$
Mean System Size	$m\rho + \rho \frac{(m\rho)^m}{m!} \frac{\pi_0}{(1-\rho)^2}$	∞
Mean Response Time	$\frac{m}{\mu} + \frac{1}{\mu} \frac{(m\rho)^m}{m!} \frac{\pi_0}{(1-\rho)^2}$	∞
Mean Queue Size	$\frac{\rho}{1-\rho} \frac{(m\rho)^m}{m!(1-\rho)}$	∞
Mean Waiting Time	$\frac{1/\mu}{1-\rho} \frac{(m\rho)^m}{m!(1-\rho)}$	∞
Erlang C	$\frac{(m\rho)^m}{m!} \frac{\pi_0}{1-\rho}$	

Example 11.3.1. A cluster of $m = 3$ equivalent servers hosts a specific service (S) used only by mobile customers in a local wireless area network. Upon a request arrival, the load balancer fairly distributes the transaction execution among the servers to keep the system well balanced. Let us assume that the service execution

rate is constant and equal to $\mu = 500tps$. We also consider that the typical time between the transaction of each mobile customer i is exponentially distributed with rate $\lambda_i = 20tps$. Figure 11.5 presents this infrastructure.

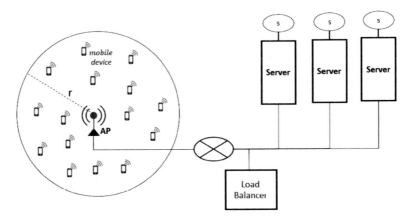

Figure 11.5 Mobile Devices and Server.

The geographical area in which the mobile customers can access the service hosted in the *server* is constrained by the access point (*AP*) coverability radius (*r*). The coverability area is thus $A = \pi r^2$. Let us define the customer density, *cd*, by the number of mobile customers (*n*) divided by the coverability area (*A*) that is

$$cd = \frac{n}{\pi r^2}. \tag{11.3.11}$$

The aggregate arrival request rate, λ, is estimated by the number of customers in the area times the customer request rate (λ_i); hence

$$\lambda = n\lambda_i. \tag{11.3.12}$$

Therefore, we define arrival request rate density (γ) as

$$\gamma = \frac{\lambda}{A} = \frac{\lambda}{\pi r^2} = \frac{n\lambda_i}{\pi r^2}. \tag{11.3.13}$$

Hence, for a given arrival request rate density and a specific radius, we can estimate the aggregate arrival request rate by

$$\lambda = \gamma \pi r^2. \tag{11.3.14}$$

Table 11.4 presents the values of *mss*, *mqs*, *mrt*, *mwt*, and the P_Q for a particular scenario in which the coverability radius is $r = 50m$ and $\gamma = 0.18tps/m^{23}$. The aggregate arrival request rate is $\lambda = 1413.7167tps$.

Table 11.4

Scenario: $\mu = 500tps$, $\gamma = 0.18tps/m2$, **and** $r = 50m$

Metrics	Values
Utilization	0.942
Throughput	$1413.7167tps$
Mean System Size	$17.463req$
Mean Response Time	$12.3528ms$
Mean Queue Size	$14.636req$
Mean Waiting Time	$10.3528ms$
Erlang C	0.4718

Let us now adopt the utilization formula presented in Table 11.3 for estimating the utilization against the coverability radius since the larger the radius, the larger the number of users, so the higher the arrival rate. Hence, we have

$$u = \frac{\lambda}{m\mu} = \frac{\pi\gamma r^2}{m\mu},$$

which leads to

$$r = \sqrt{\frac{u\,m\,\mu}{\pi\,\gamma}}. \tag{11.3.15}$$

Now let us vary the coverability radius, keep the other parameter values of the scenario described above and plot the utilization against the radius. Figure 11.6 shows this behavior.

If the infrastructure administrator intends to keep the system utilization below 80%, the radius should not be larger than $46.0659m$, since,

$$r \leq \sqrt{\frac{u\,m\,\mu}{\pi\,\gamma}} \tag{11.3.16}$$

$$r \leq \sqrt{\frac{0.8 \times 3 \times 500}{\pi \times 0.18}}$$

$$r \leq 46.0659m.$$

Considering a radius equal to $46.0659\,m$, Table 11.5 presents the values of mss, mqs, mrt, mwt, and the P_Q.

---

[3]tps/m^2 – transactions per second per square meter.

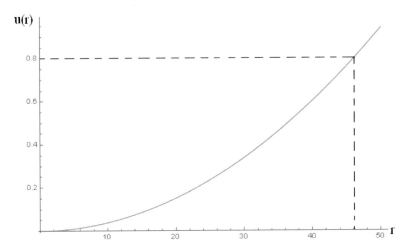

Figure 11.6   Utilization vs Radius.

Table 11.5

Scenario: $\mu = 500\,tps$, $\gamma = 0.18\,tps/m^2$, **and** $r = 46.0659\,m$

Metrics	Values
Utilization	0.8000
Throughput	$1200.0010\,tps$
Mean System Size	$4.9888\,req$
Mean Response Time	$4.1573\,ms$
Mean Queue Size	$2.5888\,req$
Mean Waiting Time	$2.1573\,ms$
Erlang C	0.3929

Now consider it is required to increase the coverability radius to $75\,m$. How many servers are required to provide the service, considering that utilization should not be higher than 80%?

Adopting Equation 11.3.15, we obtain m by

$$m_{min} = arg_{m\in\mathbb{N}} \min\{\frac{\pi \times \gamma \times r^2}{m \times \mu} \leq 0.8\}.$$

Therefore, solving

$$m_{min} = arg_{m\in\mathbb{N}} \min\{\frac{\pi \times 0.18 \times 75^2}{m \times 500} \leq 0.8\},$$

we obtain $m_{min} = 8$. Figure 11.7 presents the utilization for $m = \{7, 8, 9, 10, 11, 12\}$. For $m \leq 6$, the utilization is 1.

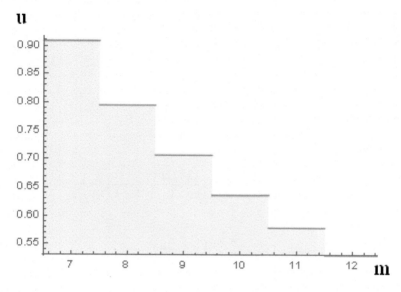

Figure 11.7   Utilization vs. Number of Servers – $\mu = 500tps$, $\gamma = 0.18tps/m^2$, and $r = 75m$.

$\square$

Example 11.3.2. In this example, we compare the response time of two $M/M/1$ systems with each arrival rate equal to $\lambda/2$ and service rate equal to μ with one $M/M/2$ system with arrival and service rates equal to λ and μ (for each server), respectively. These two systems are depicted in Figure 11.8.

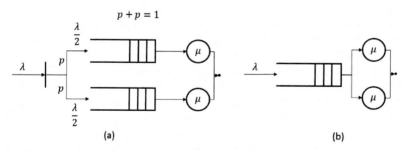

(a)   **(b)**

Figure 11.8   Two $M/M/1$ System vs. One $M/M/2$ System.

Let us consider the $M/M/2$ model. As the system parameters are λ, μ, and $m = 2$, and taking into account 11.3.6, we have

$$mss = m\rho + \rho\,\frac{(m\rho)^m}{m!}\,\frac{\pi_0}{(1-\rho)^2}.$$

$$mss_{M/M/2} = 2\frac{\lambda}{2\mu} + \frac{\lambda}{2\mu}\,\frac{(2\lambda/2\mu)^2}{2!}\,\frac{\pi_0}{(1-\lambda/2\mu)^2}.$$

From 11.3.3, we have

$$\pi_0 = \left(\sum_{k=0}^{1}\frac{(2\rho)^k}{k!} + \frac{(m\rho)^m}{m!}\,\frac{1}{1-\rho}\right)^{-1}.$$

Hence

$$\pi_0 = \left(\sum_{k=0}^{m-1}\frac{(m\lambda/2\mu)^k}{k!} + \frac{(2\lambda/2\mu)^2}{2!}\,\frac{1}{1-\lambda/2\mu}\right)^{-1}.$$

So

$$\pi_0 = \frac{1-\lambda/2\mu}{1+\lambda/2\mu}.$$

Therefore

$$mss_{M/M/2} = \frac{4\lambda\mu}{4\mu^2 - \lambda^2}.$$

As $mrt = mss/\lambda$, then

$$mrt_{M/M/2} = \frac{(4\lambda\mu)/(4\mu^2-\lambda^2)}{\lambda}.$$

Hence

$$mrt_{M/M/2} = \frac{4\mu}{4\mu^2 - \lambda^2}.$$

Now, let us analyze the system composed by two $M/M/1$ queue systems. From 11.2.15, we know that

$$mss = \frac{\lambda}{\mu - \lambda}.$$

Hence

$$mss_{Two\,M/M/1} = \frac{\lambda/2}{\mu - \lambda/2} + \frac{\lambda/2}{\mu - \lambda/2}.$$

So

$$mss_{Two\,M/M/1} = \frac{2\lambda}{2\mu - \lambda}.$$

Multiplying and dividing by $2\mu + \lambda$, we have

$$mss_{Two\,M/M/1} = \frac{4\mu}{4\mu^2 - \lambda}\left(\lambda + \frac{\lambda^2}{\mu}\right).$$

From 11.2.22, we have

$$rt = \frac{1}{\mu - \lambda}.$$

Thus

$$rt_{Two\,M/M/1} = \frac{1}{\mu - \lambda/2} = \frac{2}{2\mu - \lambda}.$$

Multiplying and dividing by $2\mu + \lambda$, we have

$$rt_{Two\,M/M/1} = \frac{4\mu + 2\lambda}{4\mu^2 - \lambda^2}.$$

Table 11.6 summarizes the *mss* and *mrt* for both systems.

Table 11.6
Comparing Two Independent $M/M/1$ and One $M/M/2$ System

Metrics	Two $M/M/1$	$M/M/2$
mss	$\frac{4\mu}{4\mu^2-\lambda}\left(\lambda + \frac{\lambda^2}{\mu}\right)$	$\frac{4\mu}{4\mu^2-\lambda^2}\lambda$
mrt	$\frac{4\mu+2\lambda}{4\mu^2-\lambda^2}$	$\frac{4\mu}{4\mu^2-\lambda^2}$

Therefore, it is clear that the mean system size and the mean response time of the $M/M/2$ are smaller than the respective metrics for two independent $M/M/1$ queues. □

11.4   M/M/∞ QUEUE

Now we consider a multi-server system that increases its capacity whenever more transaction are required to be served. In other words, a model with an infinite number of servers. Examples of such systems are self-service situations.

This model is named $M/M/\infty$. The arrival rate is constant and equal to λ. The service rate increases at each new request arrival. Thus, when the system has a k request, the service rate is $k\mu$ (for any k), and each request is immediately assigned to a server. Therefore, in such a system, there is **no queueing**; consequently, the **waiting time** is zero. Figure 11.9 presents the respective CTMC.

From 11.1.5, we obtain the steady-state probability of being in state k:

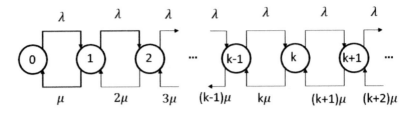

Figure 11.9 CTMC for $M/M/\infty$ System.

$$\pi_k = \frac{\lambda^k}{k\mu\,(k-1)\mu\ldots 2\mu\,\mu}\pi_0 = \frac{\lambda^k}{k!\,\mu^k}\pi_0.$$

Since $\pi_0 + \sum_{k=1}^{\infty}\pi_k = 1$, then

$$\pi_0 + \sum_{k=1}^{\infty}\frac{\lambda^k}{k!\,\mu^k}\pi_0 = 1.$$

Therefore

$$\pi_0\Big(1 + \sum_{k=1}^{\infty}\frac{\lambda^k}{k!\,\mu^k}\Big) = 1.$$

Hence

$$\pi_0 = \frac{1}{1 + \sum_{k=1}^{\infty}\frac{\lambda^k}{k!\,\mu^k}}.$$

Thus

$$\pi_0 = \frac{1}{1 + \sum_{k=1}^{\infty}\left(\frac{\lambda}{\mu}\right)^n\frac{1}{k!}} = e^{-\frac{\lambda}{\mu}}.$$

Therefore

$$\pi_k = \frac{\left(\frac{\lambda}{\mu}\right)^k}{k!}e^{-\frac{\lambda}{\mu}}, \tag{11.4.1}$$

which is the probability mass function of a Poisson random variable.

Mean System Size, Response Time, and Throughput – As a request will never wait to be served in an $M/M/\infty$ system, the mean time a request spends in the system (*mrt* – mean response time) to be processed is $1/\mu$. Therefore, the mean number of requests being processed in the system is estimated by the product of λ and $1/\mu$. This is also obtained by

$$mss = \sum_{k=1}^{\infty} k\, \pi_k.$$

$$mss = \sum_{k=1}^{\infty} k\, \frac{\left(\frac{\lambda}{\mu}\right)^k}{k!}\, e^{-\frac{\lambda}{\mu}}.$$

$$mss = e^{-\frac{\lambda}{\mu}} \sum_{k=1}^{\infty} k\, \frac{\left(\frac{\lambda}{\mu}\right)^k}{k!}.$$

$$mss = e^{-\frac{\lambda}{\mu}} \frac{\lambda}{\mu} \sum_{k=1}^{\infty} \frac{\left(\frac{\lambda}{\mu}\right)^{k-1}}{(k-1)!}.$$

As

$$\sum_{k=1}^{\infty} \frac{\left(\frac{\lambda}{\mu}\right)^{k-1}}{(k-1)!} = e^{\frac{\lambda}{\mu}},$$

we get

$$mss = \frac{\lambda}{\mu}. \tag{11.4.2}$$

As a request arrives it is promptly served; the **throughput** is λ. The mean response time may also be obtained from Little's law, that is, $mrt = \frac{mss}{\lambda}$, so

$$mrt = \frac{1}{\mu}. \tag{11.4.3}$$

Example 11.4.1. Consider a Cloud IaaS[4] provider, in which, at least theoretically, an infinite number of virtual machines could be provided. It means that, if the customers require, the IaaS provider can make available any number of virtual machines (VM). Let us also assume that each VM executes one software application (App) and that the time to set up the VM and to execute (execution time – et) the App is exponentially distributed with mean $1/\mu = 4.5\,min$. The time between customers' requests is also assumed to be exponentially distributed with mean $1/\lambda = 5\,min$. Figure 11.10 presents a concise view of the cloud provider data-center infrastructure. The cloud manager and load balancer request a new VM instance at each new customer request, which executes the App. After the App execution, the VM is finished.

Such a system may be well represented by a $M/M/\infty$ queue model. Figure 11.9 presents the respective CTMC that depicts this system queue. It is worth noting that at each new request, represented by a transition labeled with λ, the service rate increases by one since the number of VM instances was enhanced. This may be observed in transitions that denote a service execution. On the other hand, when one

---

[4] Infrastructure as a Service – IaaS.

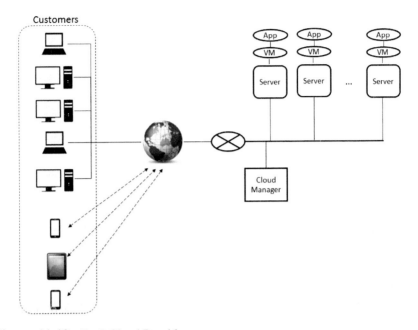

Figure 11.10 IaaS Cloud Provider.

service is executed (represented by the transition from a state k to a state $k-1$), the number of available VM is reduced because one VM instance was ended.

Using 11.4.2, the mean number of VM instances in the system is estimated:

$$mss = \frac{\lambda}{\mu}.$$

$$mss = \frac{1/5}{1/4.5} = 0.9.$$

The mean response time (11.4.3) is

$$mrt = \frac{1}{\mu} = \frac{1}{1/4.5} = 4.5\,min.$$

□

The probability of having more than five VMs instances active is estimated by using 11.4.1. Therefore

$$1 - \sum_{k=0}^{5} \pi_k = 1 - 0.99899 = 0.00101.$$

Table 11.7
π_k - **Probability of Having** $k\ VMs$ **Instances**

k	π_k
0	0.32919
1	0.36577
2	0.20321
3	0.07526
4	0.02091
5	0.00465

11.5 M/M/1k QUEUE

This section presents the $M/M/1/k$ queue model. As in the previous models, the arrival (λ) and the service (μ) rates are constant. However, the present model has only one server, and its capacity is limited to k transactions (customers, jobs, requests). Therefore, if the system has k transactions at a given moment and an additional request arrives, it is dropped because it cannot be queued due to the system capacity.

Discard Rate, Discard Probability, and Throughput – This queue is presented in Figure 11.11.a. Figure 11.11.b presents the respective CTMC of the $M/M/1/k$ queue. It is similar to the CTMC presented in Figure 11.2, but with finite (k) capacity. λ_d denotes the **discard rate**, which is estimated by

$$\lambda_d = \lambda\,\pi_k,$$

where π_k is the probability of having k transactions in the system (**discard probability** – p_d). λ_e is the **effective arrival rate**, that is, the arrival rate subtracted from the rate related to request lost (drops):

$$tp = \lambda_e = \lambda - \lambda_d,$$

$$tp = \lambda_e = \lambda\,(1 - \pi_k).$$

The effective arrival rate is equal to the system **throughput**. Finally, it is worth noting that the steady-state solution always exists, even for $\lambda \geq \mu$.

As mentioned, when k transaction requests are in the system, no other request is accepted since the model is in state k.

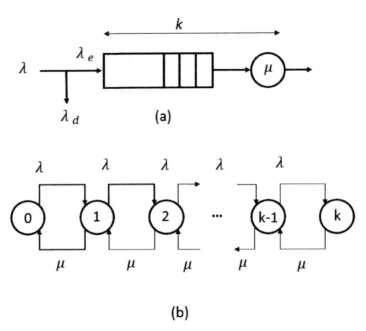

Figure 11.11 $M/M/1/k$ System.

Considering the CTMC depicted, the steady-state probability distribution can be computed. Using 11.1.5, the steady-state probability is estimated by

$$\pi_i = \pi_0 \prod_{j=0}^{i-1} \frac{\lambda}{\mu}, \quad 0 \le i \le k. \tag{11.5.1}$$

$$\pi_i = \pi_0 \left(\frac{\lambda}{\mu} \right)^i, \quad 0 \le i \le k. \tag{11.5.2}$$

The discard probability is estimated by

$$p_d = \pi_k = \pi_0 \left(\frac{\lambda}{\mu} \right)^k. \tag{11.5.3}$$

As $\rho = \lambda/\mu$, then from 11.5.2, we get

$$\pi_i = \pi_0 \rho^i, \quad 0 \le i \le k. \tag{11.5.4}$$

Thus

$$p_d = \pi_k = \pi_0 \rho^k. \tag{11.5.5}$$

As $\sum_{i=0}^{k} \pi_i = 1$, then

$$\sum_{i=0}^{k} \pi_0 \rho^i = \pi_0 \sum_{i=0}^{k} \rho^i = 1.$$

Thus

$$\pi_0 = \frac{1}{\sum_{i=0}^{k} \rho^i}.$$

Hence

$$\pi_0 = \begin{cases} \frac{1-\rho}{1-\rho^{k+1}} & \rho \neq 1, \\ \frac{1}{k+1} & \rho = 1. \end{cases}$$

Therefore, from 11.5.5, we obtain

$$p_d = \tag{11.5.6}$$

$$\begin{cases} \frac{1-\rho}{1-\rho^{k+1}} \rho^k & \rho \neq 1, \\ \frac{1}{k+1} \rho^k & \rho = 1. \end{cases}$$

Utilization - It should be highlighted that ρ is not the utilization. The utilization may be estimated by

$$u = 1 - \pi_0 = \tag{11.5.7}$$

$$\begin{cases} \frac{\rho(1-\rho^k)}{1-\rho^{k+1}} & \rho \neq 1, \\ \frac{k}{k+1} & \rho = 1. \end{cases}$$

It is worth mentioning that since ρ is allowed to become arbitrarily large, the utilization approaches 1 when $\rho \to \infty$. If, however, we require that $\rho < 1$, and as $k \to \infty$, the $M/M/1/k$ becomes similar to the stable case of the $M/M/1$ model, that is, ρ (in the $M/M/1$ model) approaches $1 - \pi_0$ (in $M/M/1/k$ model).

Mean System Size - The mean system size is estimated by summing up the products of the number of transactions (customers or requests) in the system multiplied by the probability of having that number of transactions in the system, that is

$$mss = \sum_{i=1}^{k} i\,\pi_i.$$

From the expression above, considering $\rho \neq 1$, we obtain ([413])

$$mss = \frac{\rho\left(1 - (k+1)\rho^k + k\rho^{k+1}\right)}{(1-\rho)(1-\rho^{k+1})}. \tag{11.5.8}$$

Mean Response Time - Using Little's law, the mean response time is obtained. Therefore

$$mrt = \frac{mss}{tp}, \quad \rho \neq 1.$$

$$mrt = \frac{\frac{\rho\left(1-(k+1)\rho^k+k\rho^{k+1}\right)}{(1-\rho)(1-\rho^{k+1})}}{\lambda(1-\pi_k)}, \quad \rho \neq 1. \tag{11.5.9}$$

Mean Queue Size and Mean Waiting Time - The **mean queue size** is estimated by summing up the products of the number of transactions (customers or requests) in the queue multiplied by the probability of having that number of transactions in the queue, that is

$$mqs = \sum_{i=2}^{k}(i-1)\,\pi_i. \tag{11.5.10}$$

From the expression above, we get

$$mqs = mss - \frac{\rho(1-\rho^k)}{1-\rho^{k+1}}, \quad \rho \neq 1. \tag{11.5.11}$$

And using the Little's law ($mwt = mqs/tp$), we obtain the **mean waiting time**:

$$mwt = \left(mss - \frac{\rho(1-\rho^k)}{1-\rho^{k+1}}\right)/(\lambda(1-\pi_k)), \quad \rho \neq 1. \tag{11.5.12}$$

Table 11.8 summarizes the metrics presented for $M/M/1/k$ queue system.

Table 11.8
Metrics for $M/M/1/k$ queue system for $\rho \neq 1$

Metrics	Values (for $\rho \neq 1$)
Utilization	$(\rho(1-\rho^k))/(1-\rho^{k+1})$
Discard probability	$\rho^i \frac{1-\rho}{1-\rho^{k+1}}$
Discard Rate	$\lambda\,\pi_k$
Throughput	$\lambda(1-\pi_k)$
Mean System Size	$\frac{\rho\left(1-(k+1)\rho^k+k\rho^{k+1}\right)}{(1-\rho)(1-\rho^{k+1})}$
Mean Response Time	$\frac{\rho\left(1-(k+1)\rho^k+k\rho^{k+1}\right)}{(1-\rho)(1-\rho^{k+1})}/(\lambda(1-\pi_k))$
Mean Queue Size	$mss - \frac{\rho(1-\rho^k)}{1-\rho^{k+1}}$
Mean Waiting Time	$(mss - \frac{\rho(1-\rho^k)}{1-\rho^{k+1}})/(\lambda(1-\pi_k))$

Example 11.5.1. Let us consider a system composed of one server, whose service rate is constant and equal to $20tps$. The maximal system capacity is 20 transactions. Hence, when the system has 20 transactions, and another request arrives, such a request is dropped. Assume the arrival traffic is a Poisson process with a rate λ. An experiment was executed, considering $\lambda \in (0, 30tps)$.

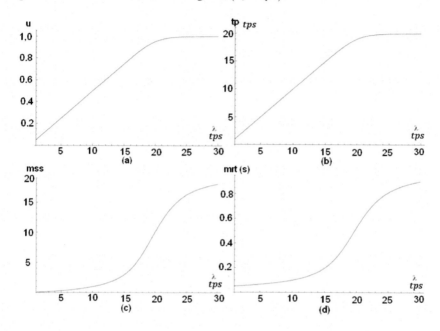

Figure 11.12   Experiment Results – Metrics: u, tp, mss, and mrt.

Figure 11.12 presents the utilization, the throughput, the mean system size, and the mean response time computed for $\lambda \in (0, 30tps)$. Figure 11.13 presents the probability distribution (probability of having -1, 2, 3, ... , 30″ transactions in the system) for $\lambda = 15tps$, $\lambda = 20tps$, and $\lambda = 30tps$.

It is important to highlight that $\pi_i < \pi_{i-1}$ for $\lambda < \mu$. For $\lambda = \mu$, $\pi_i = \pi'$ $\forall i$, and $\pi_i > \pi_{i-1}$ for $\lambda > \mu$. The drop probability may be observed in Figure 11.13 and is depicted by the respective π_{20}.

□

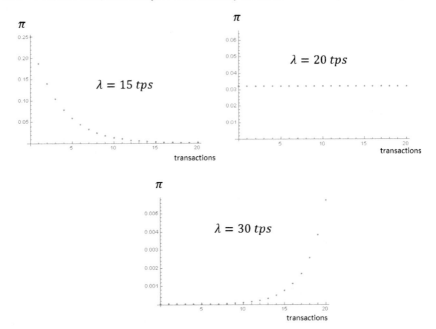

Figure 11.13 Probability Distribution for $\lambda = 15 tps$, $\lambda = 20 tps$, and $\lambda = 30 tps$.

11.6 M/M/mk QUEUE

This section presents the $M/M/m/k$ model. This model can be thought of as $M/M/m$ truncated at state k. Therefore, the time between arrivals is exponentially distributed as well as the service time. The system has m servers, and its capacity is k. Figure 11.14 presents the queue representation and the respective CTMC.

Let us assume that the number of servers is smaller than the system capacity, $m < k$. If the system is at state 0 and one request arrives, the system transitions to state 1. In state 1, two events are possible: a service execution, which leads the system back to the state 0, and a new request arrival, which takes the system to state 2. In state 2, two requests are in the system. As we have m servers (and let us assume $m \geq 2$), the transition connecting state 2 to state 1 is labeled with rate 2μ. A similar behavior continues up to state m. When a state $j > m$ is reached, the rates attached to the arcs that connect j to $j-1$ are $m\mu$ due to the maximal number of resources of the system.

As in the previous models, using 11.1.5, we have

$$\pi_i = \pi_0 \prod_{j=1}^{i} \frac{\lambda}{\mu}.$$

After some algebra, we obtain

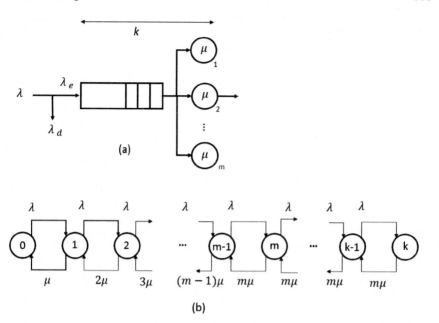

Figure 11.14 $M/M/m/k$ Queue System.

$$\pi_i = \tag{11.6.1}$$

$$\begin{cases} \frac{1}{i!}\left(\frac{\lambda}{\mu}\right)^i \pi_0 & 0 \le i < m, \\ \frac{1}{m^{i-m}m!}\left(\frac{\lambda}{\mu}\right)^i \pi_0 & m \le i \le k. \end{cases}$$

As $\sum_{i=0}^{k}\pi_i = 1$, we find

$$\pi_0 = \left(\sum_{i=0}^{m-1} \frac{1}{i!}\left(\frac{\lambda}{\mu}\right)^i + \sum_{i=m}^{k} \frac{1}{m^{i-m}m!}\left(\frac{\lambda}{\mu}\right)^i \right)^{-1}. \tag{11.6.2}$$

System Utilization - The probability that the system is being used (system utilization) is estimated by

$$u = \sum_{i=1}^{k}\pi_i = 1 - \pi_0. \tag{11.6.3}$$

$$u = \sum_{i=1}^{k}\pi_i = 1 - \left(\sum_{i=0}^{m-1} \frac{1}{i!}\left(\frac{\lambda}{\mu}\right)^i + \sum_{i=m}^{k} \frac{1}{m^{i-m}m!}\left(\frac{\lambda}{\mu}\right)^i \right)^{-1}. \tag{11.6.4}$$

Discard Probability, Discard Rate, and System Throughput - The probability of a request being dropped is the probability of the system bring full. Hence

$$p_d = \pi_k.$$

Thus, using 11.6.1 and 11.6.2, we find

$$p_d = \frac{1}{m^{k-m}m!} \left(\frac{\lambda}{\mu}\right)^k \left(\sum_{i=0}^{m-1} \frac{1}{i!} \left(\frac{\lambda}{\mu}\right)^i + \sum_{i=m}^{k} \frac{1}{m^{i-m}m!} \left(\frac{\lambda}{\mu}\right)^i\right)^{-1}. \qquad (11.6.5)$$

The **discard rate** is estimated by

$$\lambda_d = \pi_k \lambda. \qquad (11.6.6)$$

And the system **throughput** is estimated by

$$tp = \lambda(1 - \pi_k). \qquad (11.6.7)$$

The **Mean Queue Size and Mean System Size** - The mean queue size is estimated from

$$mqs = \sum_{i=m+1}^{k} (i - m)\pi_i.$$

Using 11.6.1 and the expression above, we obtain

$$mqs = \pi_0 \frac{(m\rho)^m \rho}{m!(1-\rho)^2} \left(1 - \rho^{k-m+1} - (1-\rho)(k-m+1)\rho^{k-m}\right), \qquad (11.6.8)$$

where $\rho = \lambda/m\mu$.

The mean system size can be computed from

$$mss = \sum_{i=1}^{k} i\,\pi_i = \sum_{i=1}^{m} i\,\pi_i + mqs.$$

Considering the expression above and 11.6.1, we get

$$mss = mqs + m - \sum_{i=0}^{m-1} (m-i)\frac{(\lambda/\mu)^i}{i!}\pi_0. \qquad (11.6.9)$$

Mean Waiting Time and Mean Response Time - Using Little's law, 11.6.9, and 11.6.7, we obtain the mean response time

$$mrt = \frac{mqs + m - \sum_{i=0}^{m-1}(m-i)\frac{(\lambda/\mu)^i}{i!}\pi_0}{\lambda(1 - \pi_k)}. \qquad (11.6.10)$$

Likewise, applying Little´s law, 11.6.8, and 11.6.7, we get the mean waiting time:

$$mwt = \frac{\pi_0 \frac{(m\rho)^m \rho}{m!(1-\rho)^2}\left(1 - \rho^{k-m+1} - (1-\rho)(k-m+1)\rho^{k-m}\right)}{\lambda(1-\pi_k)}. \qquad (11.6.11)$$

Example 11.6.1. Consider a set of multicore physical servers that provide virtual machines to customers, and assume that the maximal number of virtual machines that this set of servers could provide is $m = 20$. As in Example 11.4.1, suppose that each VM executes one software application (App) and that the time to set up the VM and to execute (execution time – et) the App is exponentially distributed with mean $1/mu = 4.5\,min$. The time between customers´ requests is also assumed to be exponentially distributed. At each customer request, a load balancer requests a new VM instance, executes the App, and finishes the VM instance. The maximal system capacity is 50; if 50 requests are in the system and another request arrives, it is not accepted.

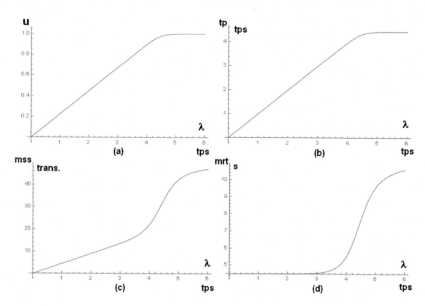

Figure 11.15 u, tp, mss, and mrt.

Figure 11.15 presents the metrics behavior as a function of the arrival rate λ. For these figures, we considered $\lambda \in (0, 6\,tps)$. The metrics considered are utilization (u), throughput (tp), mean system size (mss), and mean response time (mrt). The reader should notice that utilization (Figure 11.15.a) and throughput (Figure 11.15.b) linearly increase with the arrival rate. This behavior is observed for values of λ up to around $3.5\,tps$. After that, the metrics approach steady values. The mean system size (Figure 11.15.c) also presents a linear behavior for $\lambda < 3.5\,tps$. For values $\lambda \in (3.5, 4.5\,tps)$, the $mss(\lambda)$ derivative sharply increases. One should also observe the positive concavity of the curve. For higher values of λ, the curve concavity becomes negative, and the derivative markedly reduces its trend. The changes are even more acutely observed in the curve $mrt(\lambda)$. The mean response time is very small for $\lambda < 3tps$. For values of $\lambda \in (3, 4.5tps)$, the mrt significatively increases, and its concavity becomes positive. Nevertheless, for values of λ higher than $4.5tps$, the curve derivative reduces and its concavity becomes negative.

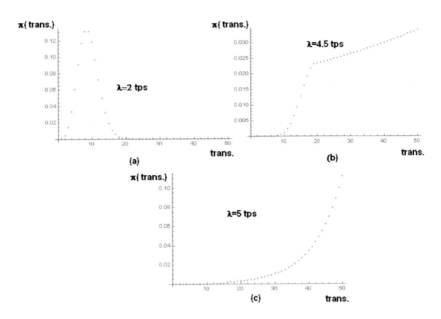

Figure 11.16 Distributions.

Table 11.9

Scenario: $\lambda = 2tps$, $\mu = 0.2222tps$, $m = 20$ **and** $k = 50$

Metrics	Values
Utilization	0.45
Throughput	$2tps$
Mean System Size	$9.0009\,trans.$
Mean Response Time	$4.5005\,s$
Mean Queue Size	$0.0009\,trans.$
Mean Waiting Time	$0.5\,ms$

Figure 11.16 presents the distributions of the number of transactions (state) in the system for $\lambda = 2tps$, $\lambda = 4.5tps$, and $\lambda = 5tps$. Table 11.9 presents the u, tp, mss,

mrt, *mqs*, and *mwt* for $\lambda = 2tps$. Table 11.10 depicts the *u*, *tp*, *mss*, *mrt*, *mqs*, and *mwt* for $\lambda = 6tps$.

Table 11.10
Scenario: $\lambda = 6tps$, $\mu = 0.2222tps$, $m = 20$ **and** $k = 50$

Metrics	Values
Utilization	0.9999
Throughput	$4.4444tps$
Mean System Size	$47.1437trans.$
Mean Response Time	$10.6074s$
Mean Queue Size	$27.1439trans.$
Mean Waiting Time	$6.10742s$

$\square$

11.7 M/M/m/m QUEUE

A particular case of the $M/M/m/k$ model is the $M/M/m/m$. In this model, the system capacity (*k*) equals the number of system servers (*m*), that is, $k = m$. Therefore, there is no queueing since it is automatically assigned to a server if a request is accepted. On the other hand, if the system is processing *m* transactions and a new request arrives, it is dropped since the system is full.

The CTMC shown in Figure 11.17 represents the $M/M/m/m$ queue system. The probability of having *m* transactions in the system (π_m) is the discard (loss or drop) probability of the system. Therefore, using 11.6.5, we obtain the **Erlang B** formula:

$$B(m, \lambda/\mu) = \pi_m = \frac{(\lambda/\mu)^m/m!}{\sum_{i=0}^{m}(\lambda/\mu)^i/i!}. \quad (11.7.1)$$

Example 11.7.1. In a mobile phone network, consider a micro-base station with 45 channels (m). Calls are assigned to channels until no channels are available. Then, whenever all channels are busy, a new call is blocked.

A statistical analysis of the call history of the region reveals that the number of calls per hour per square kilometer was 110,

$$\tau = \frac{\lambda}{A} = 110 \frac{calls}{h \times Km^2}.$$

Therefore,

$$\lambda = 110\pi r^2,$$

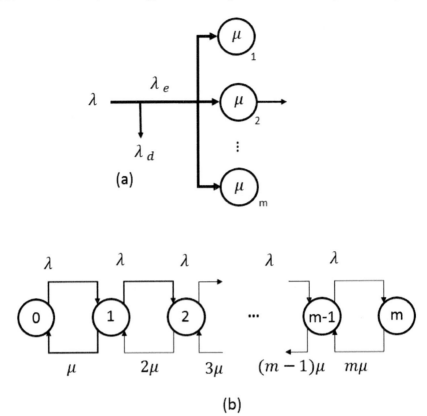

Figure 11.17 $M/M/m/m$ Queue.

where $A = \pi r^2$ is the area of the region, and $r = 2\,Km$ is the coverability radius related to the area. Hence, the arrival rate is $\lambda = 1382.3001\,cph^5$.

Let us assume that the time between calls is exponentially distributed. It was also observed that the average time of each connection is also is exponentially distributed with an average of $90\,s$, that is $0.025\,h$. Hence, we have

$$\mu = 1/0.025\,h = 40\,cph.$$

The probability of a call being rejected by the base station (block probability) is estimated using the Erlang B formula:

$$B(m, \lambda/\mu) = B(45, 1382.3001/40) = 1.4598\,\%.$$

□

---

[5] call per hour – cph

EXERCISES

Exercise 1. Service requests arrive at a web server according to a Poisson process with a mean interarrival time of $0.5\,s$. The web server is well represented by a single station and queue with infinite capacity. Consider the mean time to serve a request is exponentially distributed with mean $0.3\,s$. **(a)** What is the probability that one request occurs in the first second? **(b)** What is the mean number of requests in the system? **(c)** What is the mean number of requests in the queue? **(d)** What is the mean response time? **(e)** What is the mean waiting time? **(f)** What is the server utilization?

Exercise 2. Assume a system represented by $M/M/1/k$ queue. Represent the mean number of transactions in the system and the system throughput as a function of k, considering the arrival request is $\lambda = 0.5\mu, \lambda = \mu$, and $\lambda = 2\mu$, where the service rate is μ. Comment your findings.

Exercise 3. Let us consider a system composed of two subsystems, where each subsystem is a $M/M/1$ queue, where the arrival rate at each server is $\lambda = 1\,tps$, and the service rate is $\mu = 2\,tps$. Compute **(a)** the mean number of requests in the system, **(b)** the mean number of requests in the queue, **(c)** the mean response time, **(d)** the mean waiting time, and **(e)** the server utilization. Now, assume a system represented by $M/M/2$ queue with an arrival rate equal to $\lambda = 2\,tps$ and the service rate of each server equal to $\mu = 2\,tps$. Calculate **(f)** the mean number of requests in the system, **(g)** the mean number of requests in the queue, **(h)** the mean response time, **(i)** the mean waiting time, and **(j)** the server utilization. Comment upon the results.

Exercise 4. Assume a switch with processing capacity equal to $120\,Mbps$, and arrival traffic, where the mean time between package arrival is $4\,ms$. Consider that the time between package arrival is exponentially distributed and that the package sizes are 1024 bytes. Calculate **(a)** the switch utilization, **(b)** the mean number of bytes in the system, and **(c)** the mean time to process a package.

Exercise 5. Consider a system similar to one described in Example 11.3.1. Here, however, assume the arrival request rate density is $\gamma = 0.22\,tps/m^2$. Assume the single customer arrival rate is $\lambda_i = 20\,tps$, and the service execution rate of each server is $\mu = 500\,tps$. The system has three servers. **(a)** Find the maximal radius if the servers' utilization should be no greater than 85%. Considering the radius found, calculate **(b)** the mean number of requests in the system, **(c)** the mean number of requests in the queue, **(d)** the mean response time, and **(e)** the mean waiting time.

Exercise 6. Considering the previous exercise, obtain the minimum number of servers required if the coverability radius is defined as $70\,m$ and the maximal utilization is 85%.

Exercise 7. In a small call center with 20 attendants, the time between calls is exponentially distributed with an average of $18\,s$. Likewise, the call duration is also exponentially distributed with an average of $200\,s$. Next, calculate the probability of a customer waiting for an attendant.

Exercise 8. A Cloud IaaS provider with (theoretically) an infinite potential number of virtual machines (VMs) has a software application running upon each available VM. The time to execute each VM is exponentially distributed with a mean $480\,s$. The time between VMs' instantiation is also assumed to be exponentially distributed with a mean $540\,s$. Assume an $M/M/\infty$ well represents this system. Next, calculate the probability of having more than four VM instances.

Exercise 9. A set of servers provides virtual machines (VMs) to customers. The maximal number of simultaneous VMs that could be provided is $m = 30$. Assume each VM executes one software application and that the time to set up a VM and to execute the application is exponentially distributed with mean $540\,s$. The time between VMs instantiation requests is also assumed to be exponentially distributed with a mean $20\,s$. The maximal number of VM requests in the system is 40. If 40 requests are in the system and another request arrives, the new request is not accepted. Calculate **(a)** the system utilization, **(b)** the discard rate, **(c)** the system throughput, **(d)** the mean number of VMs requests in the system, and **(e)** the mean time a request waits for the VM instantiation to be executed.

Exercise 10. Consider a micro-base station with 60 channels of a mobile phone network in a specific geographic region. Phone calls are assigned to channels until all of them are busy. Whenever all channels are busy, new calls are rejected. The number of calls per hour per square kilometer is 120. Assume the station coverability area is a circle with a radius of $2.2\,Km$, and the service execution rate is constant and equal to $\mu = 48\,tps$. What is the probability of a call being rejected by the base station?

12 Petri Nets

This chapter introduces Petri Nets (PN), the background required to understand Stochastic Petri Nets (SPN). Nowadays, Petri nets refer to a family of models that share common features and were derived the Petri´s seminal work. More specifically, this chapter presents Place-Transition nets (PT). This model is often just called Petri nets [100] and is the basic untimed model on which the stochastic model is proposed. Therefore, before presenting SPN, place-transition nets are introduced. First, the basic definitions are presented with some basic models. Afterward, some behavioral and structural properties are discussed. Examples are also depicted and given to support the concepts considered [100, 295, 334, 385].

12.1 A GLANCE AT HISTORY

This section presents a summary and incomplete view of Petri net development over the years. Formally speaking, Petri nets were first introduced by Carl Adam Petri in his PhD dissertation, named "Kommunikation mit Automaten" defended in 1962 at the Science Faculty of Darmstadt Technical University [335]. The late 50s and early 60s saw the dawn of concurrency and parallelism in computer systems, not as much as an established research area yet, but as a prospect of exploiting parallelism in computer architectures and operating systems. Such a challenge required the definition of a foundation that could not only tackle the requirements intrinsic to the concurrency paradigm but also to extend the representative capacity of automata. Carl Adam Petri was the pioneer who first faced and succeeded in such an endeavor. His seminal model and a myriad of its extensions form what we now broadly call Petri nets.

Before, however, let us go back a few decades ago. Carl Adam Petri was born in Leipzig in 1926. On Petri´s 12th birthday, he received from his father two books on chemistry. Much later, Petri mentioned that the net´s graphical notation widespread in use nowadays was invented in August 1939 to memorize chemical processes, where circles were used for representing substances, squares for denoting reactions, and these objects were interconnected by arrows to denote inputs and output [59] [293]. In 1944, he joined the German army and became a prisoner in England until 1946. After being released, he stayed in England until 1949. When returned to Germany, he studied mathematics at Leibniz Universität Hannover until 1956. From 1959 until 1962 he worked at Universität Bonn and obtained his PhD degree from the Technische Universität Darmstadt under the supervision of Prof. Heinz Unger. His thesis has had an immense impact on the theory of concurrency and other topics of science and engineering. In his Turing Award acceptance speech in 1991, Robin Milner said: " Much of what I have been saying was already well understood in the sixties by Carl Adam Petri, who pioneered the scientific modeling of discrete concurrent systems. Petri's work has a secure place at the root of concurrency theory." [278].

Anatol W. Holt directed the translation into English of Petri´s PhD dissertation and named the nets as "Petri nets" [336]. In the late sixties, Petri´s work also came to the attention of Prof. Dennys and his group at MIT. There, Petri´s model was an object of significant research [386].

At this point, the Petri net model was not suitable for performance evaluation, since the concept of time had not been supported. To be precise, Petri´s model supported the concept of "logical time" (that captures causality), but not "Newtonian time". The first two proposals of including the time concept in Petri nets came out almost simultaneously. In January 1974, Merlin presented his PhD thesis in which assigned time to transitions as time intervals. This model was named Time Petri Nets [275, 276]. In February 1974, Ramchandani introduced Timed Petri Nets [350]. In this model, time duration was assigned to transitions. In 1977, Sifakis introduced Place-Time Petri net. In his model, Sifakis assigned time to places [383]. Many other models extended these three basic models [412, 480].

Symons, Natkin, and Molloy were the first to extend Petri nets with stochastic time [285, 286, 301, 302, 421]. They considered time as exponential random variables. These models have been widely adopted as high-level Markov chain automatic generation models as well as for discrete event simulation [256]. These models were named Stochastic Petri nets (SPN). In 1984, Marsan et al. proposed an extension to SPN by including, besides the timed transitions, immediate transitions [8]. This was named Generalized Stochastic Petri Nets (GSPN). Marsan and Chiola introduced Deterministic Stochastic Petri Nets (DSPN) in 1987 [257]. This model supported, besides exponentially distributed timed transitions and immediate ones, deterministic timed transitions. Many other timed stochastic extensions have been proposed [239] [153]. In this book, the term SPN is adopted to refer to the broad class of stochastic nets, instead of referring to the model proposed by Molloy or Natkin. When we use SPN to refer to those specific models, specific references are made.

12.2 BASIC DEFINITIONS

Place-transition nets are a direct bipartite multigraph that is usually defined through sets and matrices [385], by sets and relations [295] or by sets and bags (multisets) [334]. Here, we adopt the first two notations. Therefore, let us define the place-transition nets using the matrix notation.

Let $PN = (P, T, I, O, M_0)$ be a **Place-Transition net**, where

- P is the set of places. Places denote local states (conditions).

- T is the set of transitions. Transitions represent actions and events.

- $I = (i_{p,t})_{|P| \times |T|}$, $i_{p,t} \in \mathbb{N}$ is the input matrix. The input matrix represents the input relations of places to transitions.

- $O = (o_{p,t})_{|P| \times |T|}$, $o_{p,t} \in \mathbb{N}$ is the output matrix. The output matrix represents the output relations of places to transitions.

- $M_0 = (m_p)_{|P|}$, $m_p \in \mathbb{N}$ is the initial marking vector. This vector denotes the system initial state.

The **net structure** is represented by (P, T, I, O), whereas (N, M_0) is commonly called a **marked net**.

Graphically, places are represented by circles and transitions by rectangles (or squares). Transitions and place are connected through direct arcs. These arcs may have weights, represented by natural numbers graphed by the arcs to denote weights larger than one.

Let us adopt one simple example to illustrate the definition provided above. Consider an assembly system composed of several cells. One of its cells consists of two input buffers (*IB*1 and *IB*2), one output buffer (*OB*), and one assembling machine (*M*). In its present state, consider that *IB*1 and *IB*2 have two and three parts each, respectively. The task performed by the assembly stage comprises taking one part stored in *IB*1 and two parts stored in *IB*2 and assembling them to make another part. Once a new part is assembled, it is stored in *OB*. The assembly is performed by the machine *M*. Figure 12.1 depicts the assembly cell.

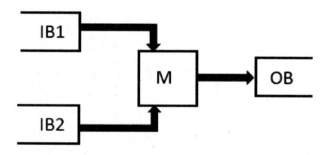

Figure 12.1   Assembly Cell.

The net depicted in Figure 12.2 denotes the assembly cell. Places p_0 and p_1 represent the input buffer *IB*1 and *IB*2, respectively. The number of tokens in each place represents the number of parts in each input buffer. Hence, the number of tokens in p_0 and p_1 are $m_{p_0} = 2$ $m_{p_1} = 3$. The output buffer *OB* is depicted by place p_4. A token in place p_3 represents that the machine is available for use. No token in p_3 represents that the machine is being used. One token in p_2 shows the cell is assembling a part. One token in *OB* denotes the cell has assembled one part. Transitions t_0 and t_1 represent the beginning and the end of the assembly process in the cell. Therefore, $P = \{p_0, p_1, p_2, p_3, p_4\}$, $T = \{t_0, t_1\}$, $M_0^T = (2, 3, 0, 1, 0)$,

$$I = \begin{array}{c} \\ p_0 \\ p_1 \\ p_2 \\ p_3 \\ p_4 \end{array} \overset{\begin{array}{cc} t_0 & t_1 \end{array}}{\left(\begin{array}{cc} 1 & 0 \\ 2 & 0 \\ 0 & 1 \\ 1 & 0 \\ 0 & 0 \end{array} \right)} \,,$$

and

$$O = \begin{array}{c} \\ p_0 \\ p_1 \\ p_2 \\ p_3 \\ p_4 \end{array} \overset{\begin{array}{cc} t_0 & t_1 \end{array}}{\left(\begin{array}{cc} 0 & 0 \\ 0 & 0 \\ 1 & 0 \\ 0 & 1 \\ 0 & 1 \end{array} \right)} \,.$$

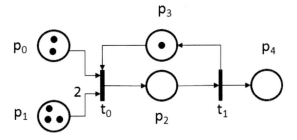

Figure 12.2 Place-Transition Net Representing the Assembly Cell.

Place-transition nets may also be defined by:

$PN = (P, T, F, W, M_0)$ defines a **Place-Transition net**, where

- P is the set of places. Places denote local states (conditions).

- T is the set of transitions. Transitions represent actions and events.

- $F \subseteq (P \times T) \cup (T \times P)$ is the set of arcs.

- $W : F \to \mathbb{N}$ is weight function.

- $M_0 = (m_p)_{|P|}$, $m_p \in \mathbb{N}$ is initial marking vector. This vector denotes the system initial state.

Hence, the net depicted in Figure 12.2 is depicted by the set of places, the set of transitions, the initial marking vector (as in the previous definition), and by the set of arcs

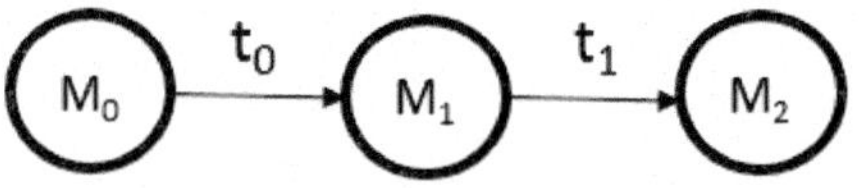

$$M_0^T = (2, 3, 0, 1, 0)$$
$$M_1^T = (1, 1, 1, 0, 0)$$
$$M_2^T = (1, 1, 0, 1, 1)$$

Figure 12.4 Reachability Graph of the Marked Net Presented in Figure 12.2

Reachability Graph - Consider a marked Petri net $N = (P, T, I, O, M_0)$. The reachability graph is defined by a pair $RG_N = (RS, A)$, where RS is the set of reachable markings of N (reachability set), and $A \subseteq RS \times T \times RS$.

Assume the marked net depicted in Figure 12.5.a. This net represents a system composed of customer's arrivals, a three slot queue, and a server. The net is composed of five places and three transitions, and the set of places is $P = \{p_0, p_1, p_2, p_3, p_4\}$, the set of transitions is $T = \{t_0, t_1, t_3\}$, the set of arcs is $F = \{(p_0, t_0), (t_0, p_0), (t_0, p_1), (p_2, t_0), (p_1, t_1), (t_1, p_2), (p_3, t_1), (t_1, p_4), (p_4, t_2), (t_2, p_3)\}$, and the weights of the arcs are $W(x, y) = 1, \forall (x, y) \in F, x, y \in P \cup T$. Customers's arrivals are represented by place p_0 and transition t_0. t_0 firing denotes the acceptance of a customer in the system. The queue is represented by places p_1, p_2, and transitions t_0 and t_1. A token in place p_1 represents a customer in the queue. The number of tokens in place p_2 denotes the number of available slots in the queue. A token in place p_3 states that the server is available. A token in place p_4 shows that a customer is being served (and the server is being used.). If the server is free (represented by a token in place p_3) and there is a customer in the queue (tokens in place p_1), the server may begin the service (firing transition t_2). When the server takes a customer from queue and begins the service, it also frees a slot in the queue. This is represented by restoring a token in place p_2. A token in place p_4 enables transition t_2. Transition t_2 denotes the event that represents the end of the service.

Figure 12.5.b depicts the respective reachability graph, which is composed of eight states. The reachability set is $RS = \{M_0, M_1, M_2, M_3, M_4, M_5, M_6, M_7\}$, where $M_0^T = (1.0, 3, 1, 0), M_1^T = (1, 1, 2, 1, 0), M_2^T = (1, 0, 3, 0, 1), M_3^T = (1, 2, 1, 1, 0), M_4^T = (1, 1, 2, 0, 1), M_5^T = (1, 3, 1, 0, 1, 0), M_6^T = (1, 2, 1, 0, 1), M_7^T = (1, 3, 0, 0, 1)$.

State Equation - Let's consider again the interleaving semantics. Assume a marked net $N = (P, T, I, O, M_0)$ and a sequence of firable transitions $\sigma = t_j t_a t_c$. Therefore, firing t_j, at M_0, leads to M_1:

$$M_1 = M_0 - I_{\bullet, t_j} + O_{\bullet, t_j},$$

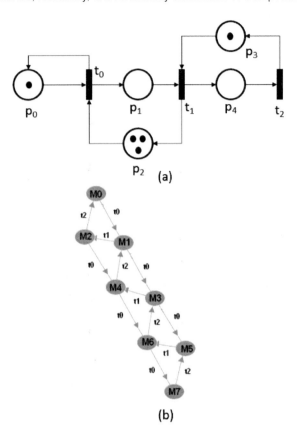

Figure 12.5   Marked Net and Its Reachability Graph.

$$M_1 = M_0 - I \times s^{t_j} + O \times s^{t_j},$$

where $s^{t_j} = (s_i)_{|T|}$ is a column vector, where $s_i = 1$ if $i = t_j$ and $s_i = 0$, for $i \neq t_j$. At M_1, transition t_a is enabled. Firing t_a, M_2 is reached. Hence

$$M_2 = M_1 - I \times s^{t_a} + O \times s^{t_a}.$$

$$M_2 = M_0 - I \times s^{t_j} + O \times s^{t_j} - I \times s^{t_a} + O \times s^{t_a}.$$

$$M_2 = M_0 + (O - I) \times (s^{t_j} + s^{t_a}).$$

M_2 enables t_c, and firing it, M_3 is reached. Thus

$$M_3 = M_2 - I \times s^{t_c} + O \times s^{t_c}.$$

$$M_3 = M_0 + (O - I) \times (s^{t_j} + s^{t_a} + s^{t_c}).$$

Hence

$$M_3 = M_0 + (O - I) \times \bar{s},$$

where $\bar{s} = s^{t_j} + s^{t_a} + s^{t_c}$.

Generalizing for any sequence σ, we get the **state equation** (also named fundamental equation):

$$M = M_0 + C \times \bar{s}, \tag{12.2.3}$$

where $\bar{s}$ is defined as the **characteristic vector** (or Parikh vector), and $C = O - I$ is named the **incidence matrix**. Therefore, it is clear that the incidence matrix, the set of places, and the set of transitions represent the net's structure.

Example 12.2.1. Let us consider the marked net, $N = (P, T, I, O, M_0)$, depicted in Figure 12.5, and take into account the firable sequence $\sigma = t_0 t_1 t_0 t_2$. Hence, $\bar{s}^T = (2, 1, 1)$. The incidence matrix is

$$
C = \begin{array}{c} \\ p_0 \\ p_1 \\ p_2 \\ p_3 \\ p_4 \end{array}
\begin{array}{ccc} t_0 & t_1 & t_2 \\ \left(\begin{array}{ccc} 0 & 0 & 0 \\ 1 & -1 & 0 \\ -1 & 1 & 0 \\ 0 & -1 & 1 \\ 0 & 1 & -1 \end{array}\right) \end{array}.
$$

The initial marking is $M_0^T = (1, 0, 3, 0)$. Therefore, firing the sequence σ, which is mapped to the state vector depicted above, we get

$$M = M_0 + C \times \bar{s}.$$

$$M^T = (1, 1, 2, 0)$$

$\square$

The adoption of the state equation is an interesting approach for analyzing marking reachability without recurring to individual transition firing (implemented by the Firing Rule 12.2.2). The state equation, however, has its drawbacks. The main issue is related to the mapping of sequences into a vector, since feasible and unfeasible sequences may be mapped into the same vector. Hence, a marking may be reached by firing a possible sequence, but may not be reached by another sequence, whose characteristic vector is equal to the one obtained from the feasible sequence.

For a marked net $N = (P, T, I, O, M_0)$, the set of markings obtained from the state equation is commonly named the Linearized Reachability Set (LRS_N). The set of reachable markings (RS_N) is a subset of the linearized reachable set (LRS_N), $RS_N \subseteq LRS_N$ [385].

Example 12.2.2. Now, consider, for instance, the marked net depicted in Figure 12.6. If we consider $M^T = (0,0,0,1)$ as a reachable marking and solve the state equation, we get the system:

$$M = M_0 + C \times \bar{s},$$

where $M_0^T = (1,0,0,0)$ and

$$
C = \begin{array}{c} \\ p_0 \\ p_1 \\ p_2 \\ p_3 \end{array}
\begin{pmatrix}
t_0 & t_1 \\
-1 & 0 \\
1 & -1 \\
-1 & 1 \\
0 & 1
\end{pmatrix}.
$$

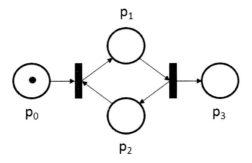

Figure 12.6   Marked Net.

Hence, one solution of this system is $\bar{s}^T = (1,1)$. Nevertheless, we easily see through the Rule 12.2.1 that neither sequence $\sigma_1 = t_0 t_1$ nor $\sigma_2 = t_1 t_0$ is firable.

□

Therefore, we see that the state equation fails in evaluating marking reachability, that is, for a marked net and given final marking, the solution of system $C \times \bar{s} = M - M_0$ does not imply a feasible sequence from M_0 to M. Nevertheless, we can use the state equation for checking **marking non-reachability**, since if no solution is obtained for the system $C \times \bar{s} = M - M_0$, we can assure that M is not reached from M_0. In other words, no sequence takes the net from marking M_0 to marking M.

A pair (p_i, t_j), $p_i \in P, t_j \in T$, is defined as a **self-loop**, if $t_j \in p_i^{\bullet}$ and if $p_i \in t_j^{\bullet}$. If a net has no self-loop (see Figure 12.7.a), it is said to be **Pure**, and otherwise **Impure**. It is worth stressing that, for pure nets, the incidence matrix do not precisely represent the net's structure, since the self-loop results in zero in matrix C. An impure net may be transformed into a pure net by removing the self-loop pairs through the insertion of pairs (p,t), in which $^{\bullet}p = \{t_j\}, t^{\bullet} = \{p_i\}$, and $p^{\bullet} = \{t\}$ and $^{\bullet}t = \{p\}$. Such pairs, (p,t), are named "dummy" pairs (see Figure 12.7.b).

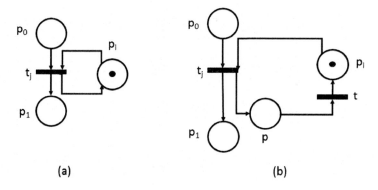

(a)   (b)

Figure 12.7   Self loop and a "Dummy" Pair

12.3 BASIC MODELS

This section presents five basic Petri nets. Every Petri net is built upon these basic fundamental models. The models are: sequencing, choice, merging, fork, and join.

Sequencing - The net depicted in Figure 12.8 represents the sequential composition of two activities, each specified by one transition. The activities are depicted by transitions t_0 and t_1. The initial system state is represented by the initial marking. The initial marking is $M_0^T = (1,0,0)$, that is, place p_0 has one token, and places p_1 and p_2 have no tokens.

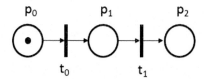

Figure 12.8   Sequencing.

At the initial marking, t_0 is enabled and t_1 is disabled. Firing t_0 changes the net marking to $M_1^T = (0,1,0)$. At M_1 the only transition enabled is t_1, and its firing leads to marking $M_2^T = (0,0,1)$. Hence, it is clear that t_1 may only be fired after firing t_0.

Choice - A choice between between activity´s execution is modeled by a net such as the one depicted in Figure 12.9. This net is composed of three places, $P = \{p_0, p_1, p_2\}$, and two transitions, $T = \{t_0, t_1\}$. The initial marking, $M_0^T = (1,0,0)$, enables both transitions. Any of these transitions; hence, may be fired. If, for instance, t_0 is fired, $M_1^T = (0,1,0)$ is reached. On the other hand, if, at M_1, t_1 is fired, the new marking is $M_2^T = (0,0,1)$.

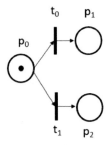

Figure 12.9 Choice.

Merging - This net depicts a context in which the execution of two or more activities fulfills a specific condition that may enable further activities. The net shown in Figure 12.10 depicts a case in which the execution of any of two activities, represented by transitions t_0 and t_1, accomplishes a specified condition.

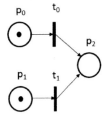

Figure 12.10 Merging.

At the initial marking, places p_0 and p_1 have one token each, whereas place p_2 has no token. In this marking, both transitions are enabled, and firing any removes one token of the transition's input place and stores one token in p_2.

Fork - The net depicted in Figure 12.11 allows us to represent parallel process generation. This net is composed of the set of places $P = \{p_0, p_1, p_2\}$ and one transition, t_0. The initial marking, $M_0^T = (1,0,0)$, enables transition t_0. Its firing removes one token from place p_0 and stores one token in p_1 and p_2. If p_1 and p_2 have transitions as output, these may be enabled in this new marking.

Join - The net presented in Figure 12.12 allows representing synchronization. The net is composed of a set of places, $P = \{p_0, p_1, p_2\}$, and one transition, t_0. Transition t_0 is only enabled when both of its input places (p_0 and p_1) have at least one token each. Firing t_0, which denotes the synchronization, removes one token of each input place and stores one token in p_2.

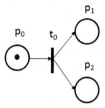

Figure 12.11   Fork.

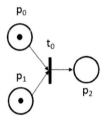

Figure 12.12   Join.

12.4   CONFLICT, CONCURRENCY, AND CONFUSION

Consider a marked net $N = (P, T, I, O, M_0)$ and a transition $t_j \in T$ enabled at marking M_0. Now, take into a account an enabled transition sequence σ_i in which $M_0[\sigma_i > M'$, where $M' < I_{t_j,\bullet}$, and $M'' \geq I_{t_j,\bullet}$ for any other reachable marking M'' in the sequence σ_i. The **enabling degree** of t_j at M_0, ED_{t_j,M_0}, is defined as $ED_{t_j,M_0} = \max_{\forall \sigma_i \in L(N,M')}(s_i^{t_j})$. $s_i^{t_j}$ is the t_j component of the characteristic vector $\overline{s_i}$ that represents the sequence σ_i. $L(N,M')$ is the set of all firable sequences of the marked net N to reach the final marking M'. This set is named the final **reachable language** of net N considering M'. In words, the enabling degree of a transition t_j at a marking M_0 is the number of its possible firings until reaching a marking M' in which t_j is not enabled.

Let us consider the marked net depicted in Figure 12.13. The enabling degree of t_0 at M_0 is

$$ED_{t_0,M_0} = \max_{\forall \sigma_i \in \{\sigma_0,\sigma_1,\sigma_2,\sigma_3\}} (2,1,1,0) = 2,$$

since the firable sequences from M_0 to markings in which t_0 is disabled are $\sigma_0 = t_0 t_0$, $\sigma_1 = t_0 t_1$, $\sigma_2 = t_1 t_0$ and $\sigma_3 = t_1 t_1$, where $s_0^{t_0} = 2$, $s_1^{t_0} = 1$, $s_2^{t_0} = 1$, and $s_3^{t_0} = 0$. The respective reachability graph is depicted in Figure 12.14.

Conflict - A transition $t_j \in T$ of a marked net $N = (P, T, I, O, M_0)$ is, at M_0, conflicting with another transition t if the enabling degree of t_j (ED_{t_j,M_0}) is higher than $ED_{t_j,M'}$,

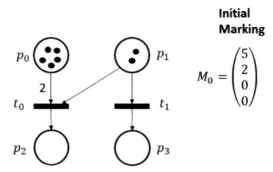

Figure 12.13   Enabling Degree.

where $M_0[t > M'$. In other words, t_j is in conflict with another transition, at marking M_0, if its enabling degree is reduced by the firing of any other transition.

If $t_j, t \in T$ have the behavior described above, they share at least one input place, that is, $^\bullet t_j \cap {}^\bullet t_j \neq \emptyset$. This structure is named **structural conflict**. The transitions t_0 and t_1, and t_a and t_b of the nets depicted in Figure 12.15 are in structural conflict, since $^\bullet t_0 = \{p_0\}$ and $^\bullet t_1 = \{p_0\}$, and $^\bullet t_a = \{p_a, p_b\}$ and $^\bullet t_b = \{p_a, p_b\}$.

The Figure 12.16 presents the nets´structures depicted in Figure 12.15 with different initial markings. Although the structures of these nets are in structural conflict, not all of them are in **effective conflict**, since, for instance, the nets shown in Figures 12.16.a, b, c, and e have only one transition enabled. Thus, in these nets, there is no effective conflict. On the other hand, the nets depicted in Figure 12.16.d and Figure 12.16.f are in effective conflict, since their marking enabled two transitions, and firing one of them, reduces the enabling degree of the other. The effective conflict is, therefore, dependent on the net structure and its marking. Chiola et al. [73] generalized the definition of conflict to *extended conflict* (EC), which allows us to partition the transitions into sub-sets named *extended conflict sets* - ECS. If two transitions are in effective conflict, they must be in the same ECS.

Concurrency - Consider two transition pairs, $t_0, t_2 \in T_1$ and $t_a, t_b \in T_2$ of the nets $N_1 = (P_1, T_1, I_1, O_1, M_0^1)$ and $N_2 = (P_2, T_2, I_2, O_2, M_0^2)$ depicted in Figure 12.17. These two pairs of transitions are enabled in the respective initial markings (M_0^1 and M_0^2). The firing of one transition of each pair, that is t_0 or t_2, and t_a or t_b does not affect the enabling degree of the respective transitions that were not fired. These pairs of transitions are defined as **concurrent**.

The reachability graph of N_1 is depicted in Figure 12.18. The enabling degree of both transitions, t_0 and t_2, is one at M_0, and firing either one does not affect the enabling degree of the other, since the ED_{t_2, M_1^1} and ED_{t_0, M_2^1} are also one.

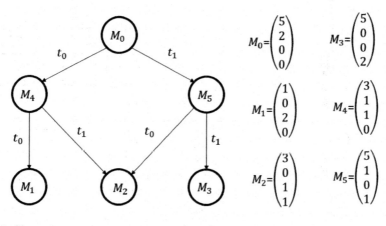

Markings

$$M_0 = \begin{pmatrix} 5 \\ 2 \\ 0 \\ 0 \end{pmatrix} \quad M_3 = \begin{pmatrix} 5 \\ 0 \\ 0 \\ 2 \end{pmatrix}$$

$$M_1 = \begin{pmatrix} 1 \\ 0 \\ 2 \\ 0 \end{pmatrix} \quad M_4 = \begin{pmatrix} 3 \\ 1 \\ 1 \\ 0 \end{pmatrix}$$

$$M_2 = \begin{pmatrix} 3 \\ 0 \\ 1 \\ 1 \end{pmatrix} \quad M_5 = \begin{pmatrix} 5 \\ 1 \\ 0 \\ 1 \end{pmatrix}$$

Firable sequences

$\sigma_0 = t_0 t_0$
$\sigma_1 = t_0 t_1$
$\sigma_2 = t_1 t_0$
$\sigma_3 = t_1 t_1$

Sequences and Markings

$M_0[\sigma_0 > M_1$
$M_0[\sigma_1 > M_2$
$M_0[\sigma_2 > M_2$
$M_0[\sigma_3 > M_3$

Figure 12.14 Reachability Graph.

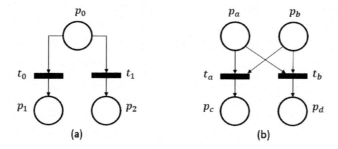

Figure 12.15 Structural Conflict.

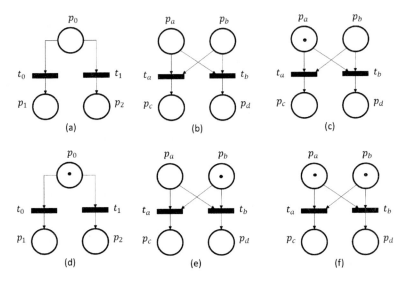

Figure 12.16 Effective Conflict.

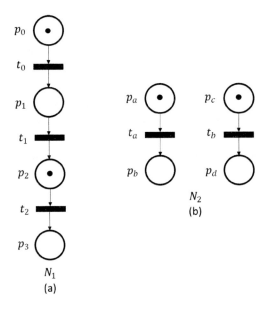

Figure 12.17 Concurrency.

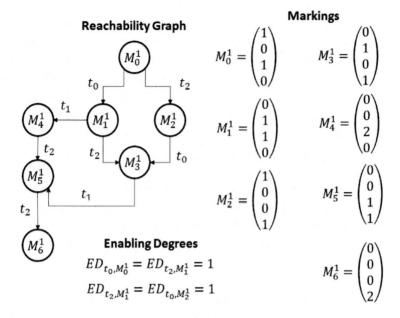

Figure 12.18   Reachability Graph of N_1 – Concurrent Transitions.

Figure 12.19 presents the reachability graph of the net N_2. At M_0, the eanbling degree of t_a and t_b is one, and firing either transition the enabling degree of the other is not affected.

Confusion - Now consider the net depicted in Figure 12.20.a. Transitions t_0 and t_1 are concurrent, since both are enabled at the initial marking and firing one of them does not affect the enabling degree of the other. Both transitions, however, are in conflict with t_2, because ${}^\bullet t_0 \cap {}^\bullet t_2 \neq \emptyset$, ${}^\bullet t_1 \cap {}^\bullet t_2 \neq \emptyset$, t_2 is enabled at the initial marking and its firing reduces the enabling degrees of t_0 and t_1. Actually, considering the initial marking depicted in Figure 12.20, firing t_2 disables t_0 and t_1. This relation is named **Symmetric Confusion**. Summarizing, this configuration denotes a symmetric confusion because two concurrent transitions (t_0 and t_1) that are in effective conflict with another transition (t_2).

Figure 12.21 presents the reachability graph of the net N_2 depicted in Figure 12.20.b. Transitions t_0 and t_2 are concurrent; hence their firing order would not affect the final markings reached. However, if t_2 is fired before t_0, M_2^2 is reached, and, although the enabling degree of t_0 in this new marking is the same as the initial marking ($ED_{t_0,M_2^2} = ED_{t_0,M_0^2} = 1$), now t_0 is in effective conflict with t_1. N_2 is in a configuration named **Asymmetric Confusion**.

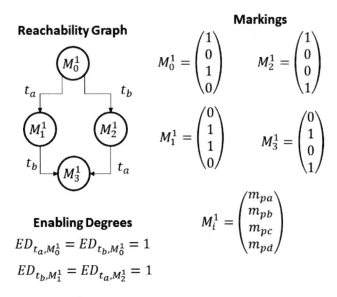

Figure 12.19 Reachability Graph of N_2 – Concurrent Transitions.

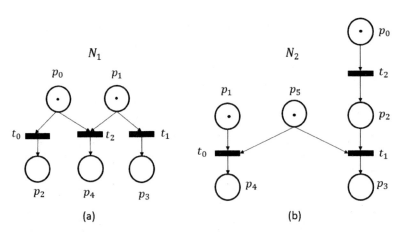

Figure 12.20 Symmetric (a) and Asymmetric (b) Confusion.

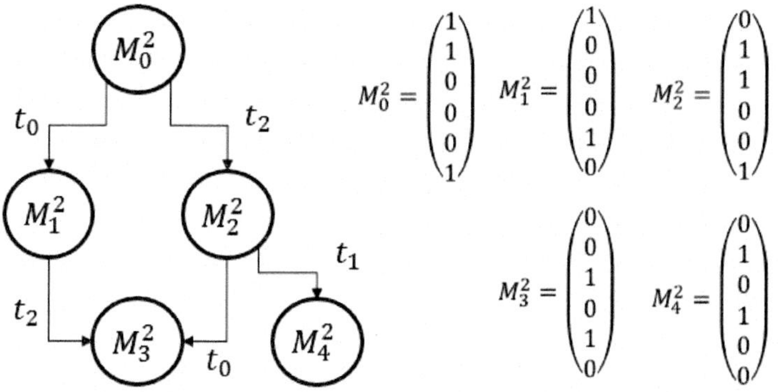

$$M_0^2 = \begin{pmatrix} 1 \\ 1 \\ 0 \\ 0 \\ 0 \\ 1 \end{pmatrix} \quad M_1^2 = \begin{pmatrix} 1 \\ 0 \\ 0 \\ 0 \\ 1 \\ 0 \end{pmatrix} \quad M_2^2 = \begin{pmatrix} 0 \\ 1 \\ 1 \\ 0 \\ 0 \\ 1 \end{pmatrix}$$

$$M_3^2 = \begin{pmatrix} 0 \\ 0 \\ 1 \\ 0 \\ 1 \\ 0 \end{pmatrix} \quad M_4^2 = \begin{pmatrix} 0 \\ 1 \\ 0 \\ 1 \\ 0 \\ 0 \end{pmatrix}$$

Figure 12.21   Reachability Graph – Asymmetric Confusion.

12.5   PETRI NETS SUBCLASSES

Petri nets are formal models. The primary objective of adopting a formalism (a formal model) is its capacity to represent systems neatly. However, a formal model also aims at property analysis or their verification. This will be introduced in subsequent sections. This section presents a classification of place-transition nets based on its structure. Figure 12.22 shows a diagram that illustrates the classes discussed here. Such a classification aims to depict reasonable structural restrictions which increase the decision power (property analysis) of models while not overly restricting modeling capacity [45, 99, 295, 334, 367].

State Machine - A state machine is a Petri net in which each transition has only one input place and only one output place. Consider a net $N = (P, T, F, W)$. N is classified as a state machine if $\bullet t_j = t_j^\bullet = 1$, $\forall t_j \in T$. The nets of Figure 12.23.a and b are state machines, but the net in Figure 12.23.c is not. The state machines subclass can model sequences, choices, and merging, but neither fork nor synchronization.

Marked Graph - A marked graph is a Petri net in which each place has one input transition and one output transition. A net $N = (P, T, F, W)$ is a marked graph if $\bullet p_j = p_j^\bullet = 1$, $\forall p_j \in P$. The nets of Figure 12.23.a and c are marked graphs, but not the net in Figure 12.23.b. The marked graph subclass can model sequences, forks (required to model concurrency), and joins (for synchronization), but neither choice nor merging.

Marked graphs are duals of state machines, since transitions have one input and one output in state machines, whereas places have one input and one output in marked graphs.

Free Choice - This subclass allows representing conflicts and merging as does state machines, and concurrency and synchronization as marked graphs, but in a more

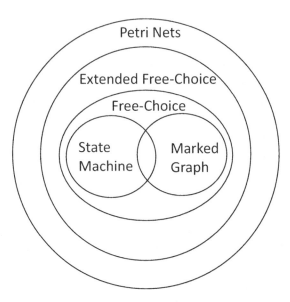

Figure 12.22 A Classification.

restricted manner than the general Petri net. Conflicts are allowed only when one place is input to several transitions. In a free-choice net, when one place is input to more than one transition, it is only the input place of such transitions. Therefore, when one of these transitions is enabled, all of them are also, since their enabling is only dependent on the marking on the shared input place. Consider a net $N = (P,T,F,W)$. N is classified as a free choice net if (1) $|p^\bullet| \leq 1$ or (2) $^\bullet(p^\bullet) = \{p\}$, $\forall p \in P$.

Therefore, the net depicted in Figure 12.24.a is free-choice, since $|p_0^\bullet| = 1$ and $|p_1^\bullet| = 0$. Likewise, the net depicted in Figure 12.24.b is also a free-choice, because $|p_0^\bullet| = |p_1^\bullet| = 1$ and $|p_2^\bullet| = |p_3^\bullet| = 0$. Considering the net depicted in Figure 12.24.c, we have: $|p_1^\bullet| = 1$, $|p_2^\bullet| = |p_3^\bullet| = 0$, and $|p_0^\bullet| = 2$. As $p_0^\bullet = \{t_0, t_1\}$, and $^\bullet t_0 = \{p_0, p_1\}$, so this net is not a free-choice. For the net presented in Figure 12.24.d, we have $|p_0^\bullet| = |p_1^\bullet| = 2$, $p_0^\bullet = \{t_0, t_1\}$, but $^\bullet t_0 = ^\bullet t_1 = \{p_0, p_1\}$. Hence, the model is a non-free-choice net. It should be stressed, however, that the transitions´ habilitation is only dependent on the same places. Therefore, when either transition is enabled, the other also is. This case is contemplated in the next definition.

Extended Free Choice - The last case discussed is interesting, because when one transition is enabled, the other also is (although more than one place of these transitions is input); hence we are also free to choose which transition to fire. Extended free-choice is a class of the nets that encompasses the configurations supported by the previous definition, but also includes cases such as the model of the Figure 12.24.d. A net $N = (P,T,F,W)$ is classified as extended free-choice if and only if $\forall p_i, p_j \in P$,

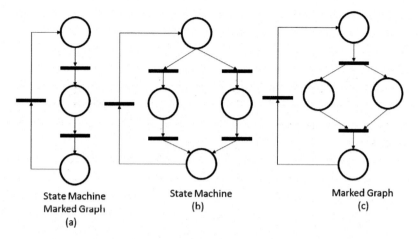

Figure 12.23 State Machines and Marked Graphs.

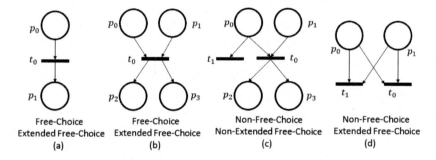

Figure 12.24 Free Choice and Extended Free-Choice.

if $p_i^\bullet \cap p_j^\bullet \neq \emptyset$, then $p_i^\bullet = p_j^\bullet$. The net depicted in Figure 12.24.a is obviously an extended free-choice net, since no pair of places has a shared output transition, that is, $p_0^\bullet \cap p_1^\bullet = \emptyset$. The net presented in Figure 12.24.b is also an extended free-choice, because the only pair of place where they share output transition is p_0 and p_1 ($p_0^\bullet \cap p_1^\bullet = \{t_0\}$), and in this case $p_0^\bullet = p_1^\bullet = \{t_0\}$. For the net shown in Figure 12.24.d, we have $p_0^\bullet \cap p_1^\bullet = \{t_0, t_1\}$, and $p_0^\bullet = p_1^\bullet = \{t_0, t_1\}$; thus it is an extended free-choice net. Finally, for the net depicted in Figure 12.24.c, we have $p_0^\bullet \cap p_1^\bullet \neq \emptyset$, but $p_0^\bullet \neq p_1^\bullet$ ($p_0^\bullet = \{t_0, t_1\}$ and $p_1^\bullet = \{t_0\}$). Hence, this net is not classified as extended free-choice.

Authors have also provided additional classes, such as **asymmetric choice** and **simple net**. The interested reader should, please, refer to [45, 367].

12.6 MODELING CLASSICAL PROBLEMS

This section adopts place-transition nets to model a set of classical problems that underlie many practical problems.

Parallel Processes - Let us take into account a parent process that creates two child processes. The parent process is only allowed to proceed with the execution of its subsequent tasks after both child processes have finished their executions. The net depicted in Figure 12.25 represents the processes creation, their execution, and their synchronization, which allows the parent process to execute its next operations.

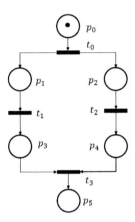

Figure 12.25 Parallel Processes.

A token in place p_0 shows a parent process enabled to create the child processes. The child process creation is represented by the firing of the transition t_0. Its firing removes one token from place p_0 and stores one token in places p_1 and p_2. The child process execution is denoted by the firing of transitions t_1 and t_2. Their firing removes tokens from their input places (p_1 and p_2) and stores tokens in the respective output places (p_3 and p_4). After firing both transitions, t_1 and t_2, the parent process is signaled, which is represented by the firing of transition t_3. Firing t_3 removes one token from places p_3 and p_4 and stores one token in place p_5.

Mutual Exclusion - Let us consider two infinite loop parallel processes. Each process has a critical and non-critical region. When in its critical region, the process accesses a shared resource. The shared resource is not accessed when the process is in the non-critical region.

The net depicted in Figure 12.26 represents these processes and the shared resource. One of the processes (Process 1) is represented by the set of places $P_1 = \{p_0, p_1, p_2\}$ and the set of transitions $T_1 = \{t_0, t_1, t_2\}$, and their arcs. Likewise, the other process (Process 2) is depicted by the set of places $P_2 = \{p_3, p_4, p_5\}$ and the set of transitions $T_2 = \{t_4, t_5, t_6\}$, and their arcs. The shared resource is represented by the place p_6.

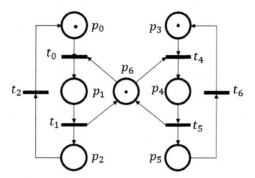

Figure 12.26 Mutual Exclusion.

The critical region of Process 1 is represented by $P_{cr1} = \{p_1\}$, $T_{cr1} = \{t_0, t_1\}$, and $F_{cr1} = \{(t_0, p_1), (p_1, t_1)\}$. Similarly, the critical region of Process 2 is denoted by $P_{cr2} = \{p_4\}$, $T_{cr2} = \{t_4, t_5\}$, and $F_{cr2} = \{(t_4, p_4), (p_4, t_5)\}$.

The initial marking shows that both processes are in their non-critical regions ($m_{p_0} = 1$ and $m_{p_3} = 1$), and, naturally, the shared resource is in no use ($m_{p_6} = 1$). Still in the initial marking, transitions t_0 and t_4 are enabled (they are in effective conflict). Their specific firings denote that the respective processes (Process 1 and Process 2) have entered in their critical regions. Therefore, firing t_0 removes one token from both p_0 and p_6 and stores one token p_1. This new making shows that the resource is not available any longer; hence Process 2 cannot enter its critical region until the resource being released. If instead of firing t_0, t_4 is fired, one token is removed from p_3 and p_6 and one token is stored in place p_4, which denotes Process 2 in its critical region. The end of each critical region is depicted by the firing of t_1 (critical region of Process 1) and t_5 (critical region of Process 2). Their firings remove a token either from p_1 or p_4 and stores one token either in p_2 or p_5, and in p_6. Tokens in p_2 and p_5 represent that Process 1 and Process 2 are in their non-critical regions, respectively. A token in place p_6 shows that the resource is again available for use.

Dataflow - The Figure 12.27.a shows a dataflow that represents the data dependencies of the expression that computes the horizontal distance of the projectile motion. In this case, the dataflow is depicted as a Direct Acyclic Graph (DAG), and the input, intermediate, and output data are represented by rectangles. The inputs are v_0 (initial velocity), θ (angle), 2, and g (acceleration due to gravity), and the output is the horizontal distance:

$$\frac{v_0^2 \sin 2\theta}{g}.$$

This DAG may be represented by the net depicted in Figure 12.27.b. The input, intermediate, and output values are specified by places and operations are denoted

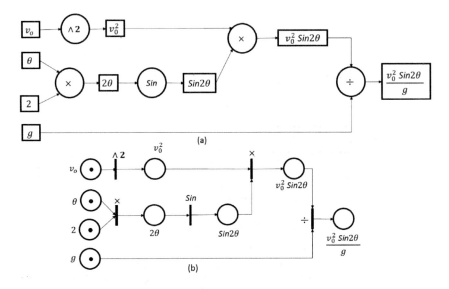

Figure 12.27 Dataflow.

by transitions. Therefore, v_0, θ, 2, g, v_0^2, 2θ, $\sin 2\theta$, $v_0^2 \sin 2\theta$, and $v_0^2 \sin 2\theta / g$) are depicted by places with the respective names. The operations, named $\times$, sin, $\wedge^2$, and $\div$, are represented by transitions. The initial marking shows that the input values are available. This is depicted by the tokens in places that represent the input at the initial marking. The initial marking enables a transition representing a multiplication and the transition denoting the square operation. These transitions are concurrent. Firing the transition that represents the multiplication removes tokens from θ and 2 and stores one token in 2θ. Firing $\wedge^2$ removes a token from v_0 and stores one token in v_0^2. A token in place 2θ enables transition sin. Its firing removes one token from 2θ and stores one token in $\sin 2\theta$. A token in $\sin 2\theta$ and one token in v_0^2 enables the second transition denoting a multiplication. Firing this transition removes one token of each input place and stores one token in place $v_0^2 \sin 2\theta$. Finally, transition $\div$ is enabled, and its firing removes tokens from $v_0^2 \sin 2\theta$ and g and stores one token in $v_0^2 \sin 2\theta / g$.

Pipelines – Consider a manufacturing system in which one of its stations is composed of three functional unities ($FU1$, $FU2$, and $FU3$) arranged in a pipeline, and has one input and one output buffer (Figure 12.28.a).

Figure 12.28.b is a net that represents the station depicted in Figure 12.28.a. The input and the output buffers are represented by places p_0 and p_7, respectively. Let us assume the number of items stored in the input buffer at its initial state is four. Hence, the initial marking of place p_0 is also four. Tokens in place p_1, p_3, and p_5 denotes that $FU1$, $FU2$, and $FU3$ are idle, respectively. A token in p_1 (denoting $FU1$ as idle) and tokens in p_0 (input buffer) enables t_0. The firing of t_0 denotes the

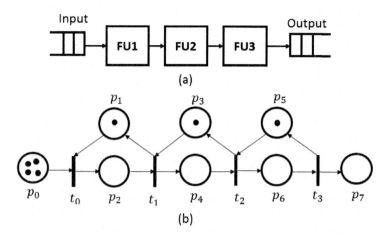

Figure 12.28 Pipeline

beginning of an operation by the FU. Firing t_0 removes a token from p_0 (takes one item from the input buffer) and the token from p_1, and stores one token in p_2, which denotes the processing of one item. The firing of t_1 represents the end of an operation in $FU1$ and the beginning of an operation in $FU2$. For firing t_1, a place p_3 must be marked (denoting the $FU2$ idle state). Its firing removes one token from p_2 and p_3 and stores one token in p_1 and p_4. This marking enables t_0 and t_2. Firing t_2 denotes the beginning of an operation in $FU3$ as already described for $FU1$ and $FU2$. When an item is processed by the three functional unities of the station, a token is stored in place p_7.

Synchronous Communication - Here a process ($||P$) is specified in process algebra FSP [252]. This process is composed of two parallel communicating sub-processes (P_A and P_B). The communication is synchronous; that is, they only communicate when both processes (P_A and P_B) are ready to perform the communication actions.

Algorithm 17 Synchronous Communication

1: $P_A = (pA1 \rightarrow com1 \rightarrow pA2 \rightarrow pA3 \rightarrow com2 \rightarrow P_A)$.
2: $P_B = (pB1 \rightarrow com1 \rightarrow pB2 \rightarrow com2 \rightarrow P_B)$.
3: $||P = (P_A||P_B)$.

Process P_A is a sequential process composed of actions $pA1$, $pA2$, and $pA3$ and two communication actions, $com1$ and $com2$. Process P_B is also a sequential process composed of actions $pB1$ and $pB2$, and two communication actions, $com1$ and $com2$. The communication action can only be executed when both processes are ready to perform the respective communication action. When the last communication action ($com2$) is executed, each process (P_A and P_B) starts itself over (Each process is recursive).

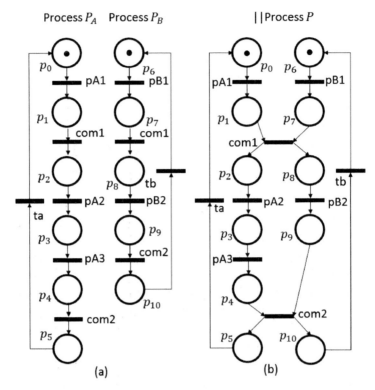

Figure 12.29   Synchronous Communication.

The nets depicted in Figure 12.29.a represent the process *PA* and *PB*, respectively. The actions of each specific process are represented by transitions labeled with the respective process´s action names. Recursion is represented by reversibility to the initial marking; after each net´s last transition firing, each net´s initial marking is reached again. For obtaining the process $||P$, transitions with the same name should be merged into one transition. Such a transition should have the original transitions´ input and output places as its respective input and output places. The net shown in Figure 12.29.b is the net that represents the process $||P$. The communication transitions are the only transitions that share the same names (*com*1 and *com*2); hence, $^{\bullet}com1 = \{p_1, p_7\}$, $com1^{\bullet} = \{p_2, p_8\}$, and $^{\bullet}com2 = \{p_4, p_9\}$, $com2^{\bullet} = \{p_5, p_{10}\}$.

The net´s (Figure 12.29.b) initial marking depicts the process in its initial state, that is, a state in which the action *pA*1 and *pB*1 are ready for execution. Likewise, the respective transition (*pA*1 and *pB*1) are enabled to fire. As they are concurrent, they can be fired in any order. After firing each, a token is stored in places p_1 and p_7. This marking enables *com*1, a transition that represents a synchronous communication. It should be stressed that such a transition may only be fired (communication occur) when both places have a token (process P_A and P_B are ready to communicate). Similarly, $com2$ can only fire when places p_4 and p_9 are marked (process P_A and P_B are again ready to communicate). After firing $com2$, the net is ready to reverse to its initial marking. The initial marking is reached back again by the firing of transitions t_a and t_b. Actually, these transitions (t_a and t_b) might be omitted. In such a case, places p_5 and p_{10} would be merged with places p_0 and p_6, respectively.

Send-Acknowledge Communication - Consider an application that requests a webservice execution and waits for a response to the query in order to process subsequent tasks. This system is shown in Figure 12.30.

This application sends a synchronous SOAP[1] request (1) to a server that has a web service enabled. The SOAP protocol aims at supporting the communication in heterogeneous systems. The request information (from the client operating platforms) is converted and sent to be processed at the server side (2). This is required since the client request may come from many different platforms (operating systems, languages). After processing the service (3), a response (to the client operating platform) is sent back to the client (4 and 5). Now the client can process the next tasks (6).

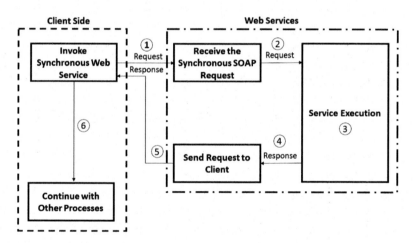

Figure 12.30 Synchronous Web-Service.

The Petri net depicted in Figure 12.31 is a model that represents the Synchronous Web-Service invocation depicted in Figure 12.30. The client side is represented by the set of places $P_{cs} = \{p_0, p_1, p_2, p_3\}$, the set of transitions $T_{cs} = \{t_0, t_1, t_2\}$, and the respective arcs. The service side is depicted by the set of places $P_{wss} = \{p_4, p_5, p_6, p_7\}$, the set of transitions $T_{wss} = \{t_3, t_4, t_5\}$, and their arcs. The web service invocation (service call) is represented by transition t_0 firing. The habilitation for invoking the service is represented by a token in place p_0. Firing t_0, removes one

---

[1]Simple Object Access Protocol

token from p_0 and stores one token in place p_1 and p_4. Transition t_1 denotes the reception of the result from the service execution. The client side waits until the service result (denoted by a token in place p_7) to proceed to the execution of next tasks. A token in place p_4 enables the web service execution. Here, we represent the reception of the SOAP request (t_3), the actual service execution (t_4), and the transmission of the result (t_5) to the client. These actions are denoted by transitions t_3, t_4, and t_5, respectively. As mentioned, one token in place p_4 enables t_3, and its firing enables t_4. Firing t_4, enables t_5, and its firing stores a token in place p_7. A token in p_7 and in p_1, enables t_1, and its firing removes one token from its input places and stores one token in p_2. Transition t_2 denotes a subsequent task in the client side.

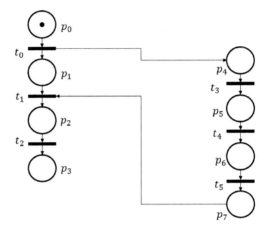

Figure 12.31   Petri net - Synchronous Web-Service.

Producer and Consumer Processes - Here we model a system composed of two concurrent processes (Figure 12.32). One of the processes (producer) produces an item and stores it in an infinite buffer (shared resource). After that, it resumes its initial state in order to produce and store a new item and so forth. The second process (consumer) takes an item from the buffer and uses it, and resumes its initial state again to consume and use other items.

Figure 12.33 presents a Petri net that models the system depicted in Figure 12.32. The producer process is represented by the set of places $P_p = \{p_0, p_1, p_2\}$, the set of transitions $T_p = \{t_0, t_1, t_2\}$ and their arcs. The consumer process is represented by the set of places $P_c = \{p_3, p_4, p_5\}$, the set of transitions $T_c = \{t_3, t_4, t_5\}$, and their respective arcs. The infinite buffer is represented by place p_6. The initial marking ($M_0^T = (1, 0, 0, 1, 0, 0, 0)$) enables transitions t_0. Its firing, which denotes the production of an item, removes a token from place p_0 and stores one token in place p_1. This new marking enables t_1, which denotes the storage of an item in the buffer. Firing t_1 removes one token from p_1 and stores one token in place p_2 and in place p_6. This new marking ($M_2^T = (0, 0, 1, 1, 0, 0, 1)$) enables transitions t_2, which takes the produ-

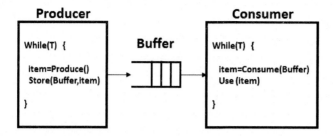

Figure 12.32   Producer-Consumer.

cer back to a marking that enables the production of a new item, and t_3. Firing t_3, which denotes the consumption of an item, takes one token from places p_3 and p_6, and stores a new token in place p_4. At this new marking, t_4 is enabled (it represents the use of an item). Its firing removes one token from p_4 and stores one token in p_5. At this marking, t_5 is enabled, and its firing takes the consumer back to a marking in which it is able to consume new items from the buffer.

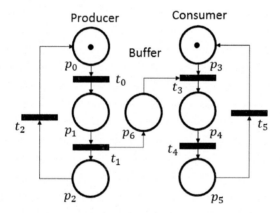

Figure 12.33   Producer-Consumer - Petri net.

Now let us consider a producer-consumer system with a bounded buffer. The net presented in Figure 12.34 is a model that represents such a system. The initial marking of place p_7 defines the maximal buffer size. In this specific case, we set it as five. One should note that the storage operation (represented by the firing of t_1) is dependent on the availability of tokens in p_7. If no token is in p_7, t_1 cannot be fired; that is, an item cannot be stored in the buffer. On the consumer side, when an item is taken from the buffer (represented by the firing of t_3), a token is removed from p_6 (representing the item removal) and p_3, and one token is stored in p_7 (a slot release of the buffer).

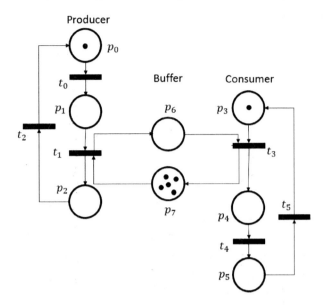

Figure 12.34 Producer-Consumer with Bounded Buffer.

Readers and Writers - Consider two classes of processes (readers and writers), each with two distinct regions, named Critical Regions (CR) and Non-Critical Region (NCR). When a reader process enters its critical region, it reads data from a shared resource, and, when in its non-critical region, it does not access the shared resource. When a writer is in its critical region, it changes the content of the shared resource, and when outside its critical region, the shared resource is not modified by the process. In this examples, both, writers and readers processes, execute their non-critical region, enter their respective critical region, access the shared resource (read or write), leave the critical region, and then start the process over again. When a writer enters its critical region, it is the only process that is granted access to the shared resource. On the other hand, when a reader enters its critical region, other readers can also have access to their critical region, but no writer can access their critical regions.

The net presented in Figure 12.35 is a model of this system. Writers' non-critical regions are depicted by the set of places $P_{wncr} = \{p_0, p_2\}$, the set of transitions $T_{wncr} = \{t_2\}$, and the arcs. Their critical regions are represented by the set of places $P_{wcr} = \{p_1\}$, the set of transitions $T_{wcr} = \{t_0, t_1\}$, and their arcs. Readers' non-critical regions are specified by the set of places $P_{rncr} = \{p_3, p_5\}$, the set of transitions $T_{rncr} = \{t_5\}$, and their arcs. Their critical regions are represented by the set of places $P_{rcr} = \{p_4\}$, the set of transitions $T_{rcr} = \{t_3, t_4\}$, and their arcs. In this example, we consider 4 readers and 2 writers. This is specified by the initial marking of p_0 and p_3. Hence, every process is in its non-critical region at the initial marking. Transitions t_0

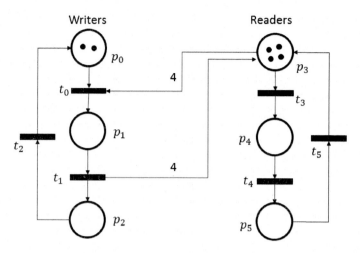

Figure 12.35 Readers-Writers.

and t_3 grants the access to the critical regions, whereas t_1 and t_4 firing denote that a process has left its critical region.

At the initial marking, readers and writers can access their critical regions. This is represented by the habilitation of transitions t_0 and t_3. If t_0 is fired (a writer has entered the critical region), no other process can access their critical region. This is properly represented since all tokens are removed from p_3; thus no reader is allowed to enter their critical region as well as no other writer since for firing t_0, p_3 must have four tokens. When the writer leaves its critical region (firing of t_1), four tokens are stored in p_3. This marking allows either the other writer or the readers to access their respective critical regions. If a reader has its access granted (denoted by the firing of t_3), no writer can access their critical regions, since less than four tokens are left in p_3. On the other hand, other readers can access their critical regions (concurrent access to a shared resource).

Dining Philosophers - Consider a system composed of concurrent processes, here named philosophers, that request shared distributed resources (called forks) to access their critical regions. Each philosopher may be "thinking" or "eating". The "eating" state denotes a philosopher in its critical region, whereas the "thinking" state specifies a philosopher in its non-critical region. The philosophers are sitting around a table sharing a common meal, and each philosopher shares a fork with its right and left neighbor as depicted in Figure 12.36. This system is the well known Dinning Philosophers problem. Let us consider that every philosopher is in its "thinking" state at the system initial state. After a while, each philosopher gets hungry and decides to eat the meal. For switching to its "eating" state, a philosopher must have granted access to its left and right forks. Having both forks, it changes to its "eating" state and stays in that state until it gets satisfied. When satisfied, it releases the forks and transitions back to its "thinking" state. Every philosopher should be able to think, eat, and the access to these states should be fair. This particular instance of the problem shown in Figure 12.36 shows a system composed of three philosophers.

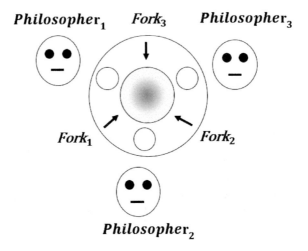

Figure 12.36 Dining Philosophers.

The net presented in Figure 12.37 models the system represented above. The distributed shared resources (forks: $fork_1$, $fork_2$, and $fork_3$) represent places f_1, f_2, and f_3, respectively. The *Philosopher*$_1$ is specified by the set of places $P_1 = \{p_0, p_1\}$, the set of transitions $T_1 = \{t_0, t_1\}$, and the respective arcs. The *Philosopher*$_2$ is represented by $P_2 = \{p_2, p_3\}$, $T_2 = \{t_2, t_3\}$, and the arcs. Finally, The *Philosopher*$_3$ is denoted by the set of places $P_3 = \{p_4, p_5\}$, the set of transitions $T_3 = \{t_4, t_5\}$, and their arcs. A token of places p_0, p_2, and p_4 shows that the respective philosopher is "thinking". Tokens in p_1, p_3, and p_5 depict a philosopher "eating". Tokens in places f_1, f_2, and f_3 shows that a specific fork is available.

The initial marking of the net presented in Figure 12.37 shows the three philosophers in "thinking" state, and, as expected, the three forks available for use. Thus, t_0, t_2, and t_4 are enabled. Consider that t_0 is fired. This firing removes tokens from p_0, f_1, and f_3, and stores a token in p_1. This new marking shows the *Philosopher*$_1$ eating while the others are thinking. No other philosopher can enter the critical region ("eating"), since *Fork*$_1$ and *Fork*$_3$ are in use. In this marking the only enabled transition is t_1, which denotes the philosopher has stopped eating. When t_1 is fired, a token is removed from p_1, and tokens are stored in p_0, f_1, and f_3. Now, the forks are again available, and the philosophers may access their critical regions.

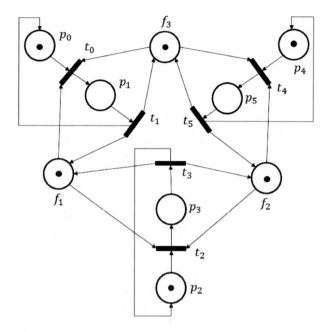

Figure 12.37   Dining Philosophers - a Model.

12.7 BEHAVIORAL PROPERTIES

This section presents a set of important qualitative properties. Qualitative properties can be classified as behavioral and structural properties. The structural properties are related to the structure of the net, whereas behavioral properties are related to both structure and its initial marking. This section introduces the behavioral properties. Structural properties are studied afterward.

Before presenting the behavioral properties, let us introduce the meaning of **verification**, **analysis**, and **validation** in this chapter [447].

Verification is the act of checking if a model has a stated property (a question). A verification technique may answer "yes, the model has the property" or "no, the model does not have the property". Nevertheless, some verification methods may fail either by not terminating or stating that a conclusive answer was not achieved. This class of verification methods, named one-sided, can answer "yes, the model has the property" or "can not state if the model has the property".

Analysis means finding answers to formal questions about the behavior of a model. The analysis differs from verification in the sense that the question may not necessarily be a "yes/no" question, or even in such a case, no priority is given to answering a "yes" or "no". For instance, an analysis question may be "What is the maximal number of transactions in the system?" or "What is the list of dead transitions?".

Moreover, for instance, if such a list is empty, we conclude the net is live[2].

Validation is the process of obtaining confidence that the model behaves as expected. The behavior of the model is compared with a specification or the expectation of the person who is validating the model. We may say that a model is never completely validated. On the other hand, if a validation process is successfully executed (considering a model and a set of scenarios), we gain confidence that the model represents the specification or the expectation we have. Nevertheless, if, in the future, we check the model against a new scenario, the model may not behave as expected.

Neither verification nor analysis guarantees the model behaves as expected. However, they support the evaluation of properties the model should hold, as, for instance, "There is no deadlock". They may also be useful for supporting validation, since knowing that a model has no deadlock may increase our reliance on the model.

12.7.1   BOUNDEDNESS

Consider a net $N = (P,T,I,O,M_0)$ and its reachability set RS. A place $p \in P$ is classified as bounded if $m_p \le k$, $k \in \mathbb{N}$, $\forall M \in RS$, $M = (m)_{|P|}$. If all places of a net are bounded, the net is bounded, that is, if $\exists k_i \in \mathbb{N}$, such that $m_{p_i} \le k_i$, $\forall p_i \in P$, N is bounded. For a bounded place, if $k = 1$, this place is classified as safe. If all places of a net are safe, the net is called safe.

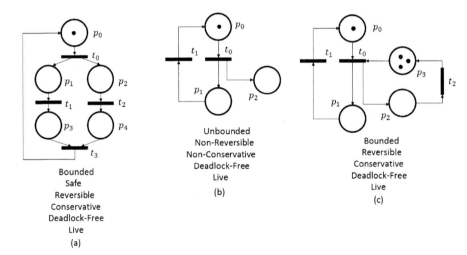

Figure 12.38   Some Models.

The net presented in Figure 12.38.a is bounded and safe since the maximal number of tokens each place stores is one. The net depicted in Figure 12.38.c is bounded, because places p_0 and p_1 stores at most one token, and places p_2 and p_3 have bounds

---

[2]This property will be presented later in this section.

equal to three. The net presented in Figure 12.38.b, however, is unbounded, since p_2 may store an infinite number of tokens.

12.7.2 REACHABILITY

For a net $N = (P,T,I,O,M_0)$, M is defined as reachable, if $M \in RS_N$, that is, if M belongs to the reachability set of of the net N. In other words, if M is reachable from M_0, there must exist a sequence $\sigma \in L(N)^3$, such that $M_0[\sigma > M$.

Consider the marked net in Figure 12.38.c, the marking $M_1^T = (0,1,2,1)$ is reachable, whereas $M_2^T = (0,2,2,1)$ is not reachable.

12.7.3 REVERSIBILITY

Let us take into account a net $N = (P,T,I,O,M_0)$. N is said to be reversible if for any reachable marking, it is always possible to reach M_0. More formally, N is classified as reversible if $\exists \sigma_j \in L(N)$, such that $M_i[\sigma_j > M_0, \forall M_i \in RS_N$.

The nets presented in Figure 12.38.a and c are reversible to their initial marking, and the net depicted in Figure 12.38.b is not.

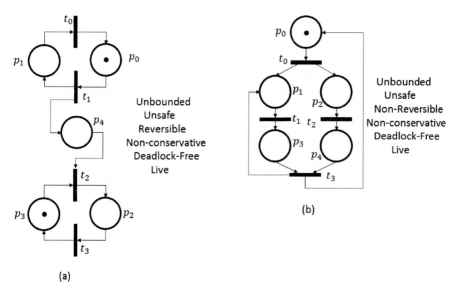

Figure 12.39 Other Models.

The net presented in Figure 12.39.a is reversible, whereas Figure 12.39.a is not.

In many models, the initial marking may not always be reachable. Even then, if there is a marking that is always reachable from any other reachable marking, the net is

---

[3] The Language ($L(N)$) of the net N is defined as the set of all firable sequences of marked net N.

also classified as reversible. Such marking is called **home-state**. Therefore, in this case we have: a net N is classified as reversible if $\exists M \in RS_N$ and $\exists \sigma_j \in L(N)$, such that $M_i[\sigma_j > M, \forall M_i \in RS_N$.

12.7.4 CONSERVATION

A net $N = (P,T,I,O,M_0)$ is defined as strictly conservative if for every reachable marking the summation of tokens of each marking stays constant, that is $\forall M \in RS_N$, $\sum_{\forall p \in P} m_p^0 = \sum_{\forall p \in P} m_p$, where $M_0 = (m_p^0)_{|P|}$ and $M = (m_p)_{|P|}$.

A net $N = (P,T,I,O,M_0)$ is defined as conservative if there is a vector weight of natural $(W = (w_p)_{|P|}, w_p \in \mathbb{N})$ such that $\forall M \in RS_N$, $\sum_{\forall p \in P} w_p \cdot m_p^0 = \sum_{\forall p \in P} w_p \cdot m_p$. In other words, a net is conservative if $\exists W$ such that $\forall M \in RS_N$ $W \cdot M_0 = W \cdot M$ where $W = (w_p)_{|P|}, w_p \in \mathbb{N}, M_0 = (m_p^0)_{|P|}$ and $M = (m_p)_{|P|}$.

The net presented Figure 12.38.a is conservative (but not strictly conservative), because for $W = (2,1,1,1,1)$, $W \cdot M = 2$, $\forall M \in RS$ (see Figure 12.40). The net depicted in Figure 12.38.c is strictly conservative, since for $W = (1,1,1,1,1)$, $W \cdot M = 4$, $\forall M \in RS$. The net shown in Figure 12.38.b, however, is not conservative, because $\nexists$ $W = (w_p)_{|P|}, w_p \in \mathbb{N}$ such that $W \cdot M$ is a constant value for every reachable marking of the net.

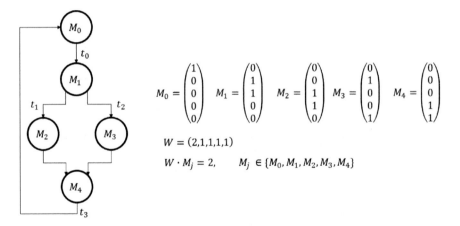

Figure 12.40 Conservation.

12.7.5 DEADLOCK FREEDOM

Consider a net $N = (P,T,I,O,M_0)$ and its reachability set RS. A reachable marking $M \in RS$ is said to be a deadlock if no transition is enabled at M, that is $\nexists t_j \in T$ such that $M \geq I_{\bullet,t_j}$.

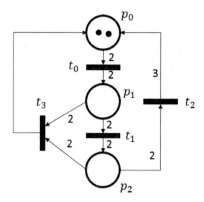

Figure 12.41   Deadlock.

None of the nets presented in Figure 12.38 and 12.39 have deadlocks. The net depicted in Figure 12.41 has a deadlock marking. Consider the enabled transition sequence $\sigma = t_0\ t_1 t_2 t_0\ t_1 t_2 t_0\ t_0 t_1 t_3$ at M_0; firing it leads to $M^T = (1,0,0)$, which is a deadlock.

12.7.6 LIVENESS

A transition $t \in T$ of a net $N = (P,T,I,O,M_0)$ is said to be dead if there is no marking in the set of reachable markings that enables it, that is if $\nexists M \in RS$ such that $M \geq I_{\bullet,t}$. The net N is classified as live if every transition can always be fired (not necessarily in every marking). In other words, $\forall M \in RS, \exists \sigma_i \in L(N), M_j[\sigma_i >$ and $t \in \sigma_i, \forall t \in T$.

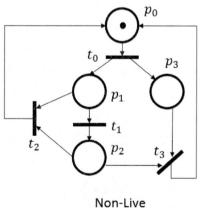

Non-Live
Deadlock Free

Figure 12.42   Non-Live Net.

Every net presented in Figure 12.38 and 12.39 is live, since they have no deadlocks and all their transitions are always firable. However, neither the net depicted in Figure 12.41 nor the net shown in Figure 12.42 are live. The former has a deadlock; hence no transition can be fired afterward; in the later, t_2 is never fired.

12.7.7 COVERABILITY

Consider a marked net $N = (P,T,I,O,M_0)$ and its reachability set RS. A marking M is said to be covered if $\exists M' \in RS$ such that $m'_p \geq m_p, \forall p \in P$, where $M = (m)_{|P|}$ and $M' = (m')_{|P|}$. For the net depicted in Figure 12.38.b, the marking $M_1^T = (2,0,0)$ is not covered, because $\nexists M \in RS$ such that $m_{p_0} \geq 2$. The marking $M_1^T = (1,0,100)$ is covered, since, for instance, the marking $M^T = (1,0,101) \in RS$.

There are many other properties such as Fairness, Persistence, and Synchronic Distance. The interested reader may refer to [101, 295, 334, 354, 358, 359, 391].

12.8 BEHAVIORAL PROPERTY ANALYSIS

The analysis of behavioral properties can, in general, be divided into three basic approaches: the coverability/reachability tree (or graph) method, the state equation method, and methods based on net reductions. Many advanced strategies have been proposed to cope with the constraints imposed by these methods. Among them, we can mention, for instance, the methods based on the stubborn set, persistent sets, symmetries, symbolic, BDDs, and many others. The interested reader is referred to [158, 447] for a first general view of such methods. This section introduces the basic approaches mentioned above.

12.8.1 COVERABILITY TREE

Consider a Petri net $N = (P,T,I,O,M_0)$, applying the transition enabling and firing rules, the net´s reachable marking can be obtained. For bounded nets, the reachability graph (or a tree) may be completed generated. Actually, applying such a method (even to bounded nets) is limited to net´s whose state space can be handled (memory and time) by the computer at hand. The computational complexity (state explosion problem) [447] constrains its application. For an unbounded net, however, the straight construction of the reachability graph/tree is not possible. In this case, a finite graph, known as coverability graph/tree, can be constructed [101, 205, 295, 334, 354].

Now consider a marked net $N = (P,T,I,O,M_0)$ and and enabled transition firing sequence σ such that $M_0[\sigma > M_1$, where $m_{p_j}^1 > m_{p_j}^0$ and $m_{p_i}^1 = m_{p_i}^0, p_j \neq p_i, \forall p_i \in P$, $M_1 = (m^1)_{|P|}$, and $M_0 = (m^0)_{|P|}$. In words, M_1 is larger than M_0 because p_j accumulates tokens $(m_{p_j}^1 > m_{p_j}^0)$. Now, let us consider that the firing sequence σ is not affected by the extra tokens stored in p_j, and that firing σ we reach M_2 $(M_1[\sigma > M_2)$ such that $m_{p_j}^2 > m_{p_j}^1$ and $m_{p_i}^2 = m_{p_i}^1, p_j \neq p_i, \forall p_i \in P, M_2 = (m^2)_{|P|}$, and $M_1 = (m^1)_{|P|}$. Then, let us take into account that such behavior continues indefinitely. Therefore, we can create an arbitrarily large number of tokens in p_j by firing the sequence σ over and over.

The infinite number of tokens in a place is represented by the symbol ω. This symbol has the following properties: $\omega + n = \omega$, $\omega - n = \omega$, $\omega > n$, and $\omega \geq \omega$, where $n \in \mathbb{R}$.

The coverability tree for a marked Petri net $N = (P, T, I, O, M_0)$ can be construct following the algorithm:

Algorithm 18 Coverability Tree

1: Label the initial marking M_0 as the root and tag it "new".
2: While "new" marking exists, do the following:
3:     Select a new marking M.
4:     If M is identical to a marking from the root to M, then tag M as "old", and go to another new
5:     marking.
6:     If no transition is enabled at M, tag M as "deadlock", and go to another new marking.
7:     While there is enabled transition at M, do the following for each enabled transition t:
8:         Obtain M' from the firing of t at M.
9:         On the path from the root to M' if there exists a marking M'' such that $m'_p \geq m''_p, \forall p \in P$,
10:         and $M' \neq M''$ (M'' is covered), then replace m'_p by ω for all places such that $m'_p > m''_p$.
11:         Introduce M' as a node, draw an arc with label t from M to M', and tag M' as "new".

Consider the net shown in Figure 12.43.a. Its coverability graph is depicted in Figure 12.43.b. As place p_1 stores an infinite number of tokens, the net is unbounded and non-conservative. It is also non-reversible and has a deadlock; hence it is non-live.

For bounded nets, the coverability tree (coverability graph) obtained is equal to the reachability tree (reachability graph). For instance, consider the net presented in Figure 12.42. As this net is bounded, its reachability set can be completely constructed; hence the coverability tree is the same as the reachability tree (see Figure 12.44). Analyzing the reachability tree, it is observed the net is bounded, conservative, and reversible, it has no deadlock, but it is not live, because t_2 is dead.

12.8.2 STATE EQUATION

As was discussed in Section 12.2, reachable markings are solutions to the state equation, but the opposite is not always true, since some solutions of the state equation may be spurious. As already mentioned, the main issue when applying transition sequences, σ, to the state equation, $M = M_0 + C \times \bar{s}$, is that the transitions that are part

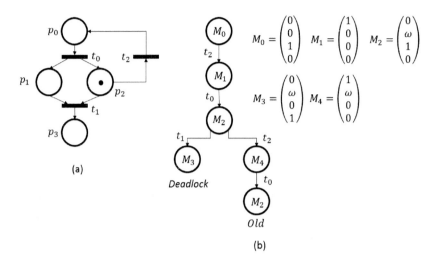

Figure 12.43 Coverability Tree

of the sequence σ are not evaluated, in intermediate marking, M_i , to check if they are enabled or not, $M_i \geq I_{\bullet,t_j}, t_j \in \sigma$ [4].

As presented, the set of markings obtained through the state equation is named the Linearized Reachability Set and is defined as

$$LRS = \{M = (m)_{|P|},\ m \in \mathbb{N}\ |\ \exists \bar{s} = (s)_{|T|},\ s \in \mathbb{N},\ such\ that\ M = M_0 + C \times \bar{s}.\} \tag{12.8.1}$$

As already stated, the $RS \subseteq LRS$, (see Figure 12.45); thus the solutions in $LRS - RS$ are spurious (see the example presented in Section 12.2). The state equation is a powerful tool for checking non-reachability based properties since it provides sufficient condition for attesting the non-reachability, but is only a necessary condition for reachability.

The description presented in 12.8.1 is suitable for incorporating the state equation for solving non-reachability as an integer programming problem. For instance, a sufficient condition for non-reachability of a marking $M \in RS$ consists of not finding a solution, $\bar{s} = (s)_{|T|},\ s \in \mathbb{N}$, to $C \times \bar{s} = M - M_0$.

Let us consider the net $N = (P,T,I,O,M_0)$ depicted in Figure 12.46. This net specifies two parallel processes, each of which with its critical region (p_2 and p_6, respectively). The access to the critical regions is only possible when two resources (tokens in p_8 and p_9) are available to each process. The mutual exclusion violation occurs if both places p_2 and p_6 are simultaneously marked. Therefore, if the marking

---

[4]Section 12.2 shows that the characteristic vector, $\bar{s}$, represents the transition sequence σ.

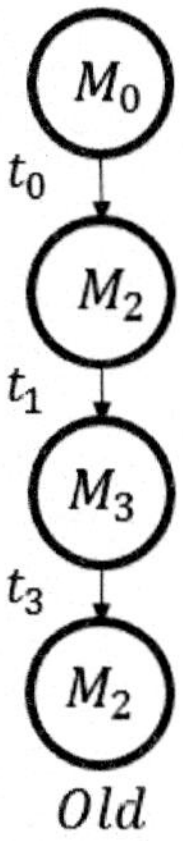

$$M_0 = \begin{pmatrix} 0 \\ 1 \\ 1 \\ 0 \end{pmatrix} \quad M_1 = \begin{pmatrix} 1 \\ 0 \\ 0 \\ 0 \end{pmatrix}$$

$$M_3 = \begin{pmatrix} 0 \\ 1 \\ 0 \\ 1 \end{pmatrix}$$

Figure 12.44 Coverability Tree $\equiv$ Reachability Tree – Net Depicted in Figure 12.42.

$M_1^T = (0,0,1,0,0,0,1,0,0,0)$ is reachable, both critical regions would be accessed at the same time (a mutual exclusion violation). It is possible to check if this marking is not accessible from the initial marking of the net by solving the state equation. As there is no solution to the system $C \times \bar{s} = M_1 - M_0$; hence a mutual exclusion violation due to reaching this marking is not possible.

Now, consider the net $N = (P.T, I, O, M_0)$ depicted in Figure 12.47.a. For the final marking $M^T = (0,1,0,0)$, we get the following system of equations (which was obtained from the state equation, that is $C \times \bar{s} = M - M_0$):

As the net incidence matrix is

$$C = \begin{array}{c} \\ p_0 \\ p_1 \\ p_2 \\ p_3 \end{array} \overset{\begin{array}{ccc} t_0 & t_1 & t_2 \end{array}}{\begin{pmatrix} 1 & -2 & 0 \\ -1 & 2 & 0 \\ 0 & -1 & 1 \\ 0 & 1 & -1 \end{pmatrix}},$$

hence

$$C \times \bar{s} = M - M_0,$$

where $\bar{s}^T = (s_0, s_1, s_2)$, $M^T - M_0^T = (-1, 1, 0, 0)$. Thus:

$$\begin{cases} s_0 - 2s_1 = -1, & (E_1) \\ -s_0 + 2s_1 = 1, & (E_2) \\ -s_1 + s_2 = 0, & (E_3) \\ s_1 - s_2 = 0, & (E_4) \end{cases}$$

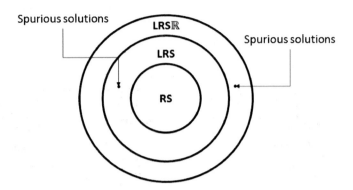

Figure 12.45 $RS \subseteq LRS \subseteq LRS\mathbb{R}$.

Many solutions are possible when solving the system considering $\bar{s} = (s)_{|T|}$, $s \in \mathbb{N}$. One such solution is $\bar{s} = (1,1,1)$, which states that firing t_0, t_1, and t_2 would lead to the final marking. Nevertheless, such a solution, actually, does not to reach M. It is a spurious solution. The reachability set of the net presented in Figure 12.47.a is $RS = \{\emptyset\}$.

Although positive integer linear programming is NP-complete, the non-reachability problem over integer ($\bar{s} = (s)_{|T|}$, $s \in \mathbb{Z}$) can be solved in polynomial time [373, 385]. We can further relax the solutions to the domain of reals ($\bar{s} = (s)_{|T|}$, $s \in \mathbb{R}$):

$$LRS\mathbb{R} = \{M = (m)_{|P|}, \; m \in \mathbb{N} \mid \exists \bar{s} = (s)_{|T|}, \; s \in \mathbb{R}, \; such \; that \; M = M_0 + C \times \bar{s}.\}$$
(12.8.2)

This relaxation introduces more spurious solutions (Figure 12.45), but allows us to use linear programming instead of integer programming, and this leads to polynomial time algorithms. For an in-depth study on the applications of linear algebraic and linear programming for the analysis of place-transition nets, the interested reader is referred to [385].

Now, let us take into account the net $N = (P.T,I,O,M_0)$ shown in Figure 12.47.b. For the final marking $M^T = (0,2,0,0)$, we get the following system of equations ($C \times \bar{s} = M - M_0$):

As incidence matrix is

$$C = \begin{array}{c} \\ p_0 \\ p_1 \\ p_2 \\ p_3 \end{array} \begin{array}{c} \begin{array}{ccc} t_0 & t_1 & t_2 \end{array} \\ \left(\begin{array}{ccc} 2 & -2 & 0 \\ -2 & 2 & 0 \\ 0 & -1 & 1 \\ 0 & 1 & -1 \end{array} \right) \end{array} \quad ;$$

thus

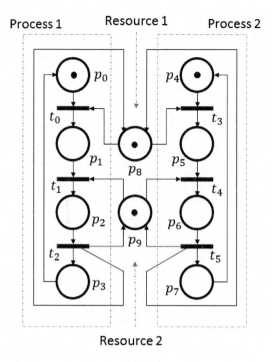

Process 1   Resource 1   Process 2

Resource 2

Figure 12.46   Mutual Exclusion Checking.

$$C \times \bar{s} = M - M_0,$$

where $\bar{s}^T = (s_0, s_1, s_2)$, $M^T - M_0^T = (-1, 1, 0, 0)$. Hence:

$$\begin{cases} 2s_0 - 2s_1 = -1, & (E_1) \\ -2s_0 + 2s_1 = 1, & (E_2) \\ -s_1 + s_2 = 0, & (E_3) \\ s_1 - s_2 = 0, & (E_4) \end{cases}$$

An infinite number of solutions are possible when solving the system of equation considering $\bar{s} = (s)_{|T|}$, $s \in \mathbb{R}$. One possible solution is $\bar{s} = (0.5, 1, 1)$, which states that firing $0.5 \times t_0$, t_1, and t_2 would lead to the final marking. Firing half a transition (t_0) does not make sense, however. Even then, such a solution, does not, actually, reach M, (it is spurious), since the reachability set of the net presented in Figure 12.47.b is also $RS = \{\emptyset\}$.

The major limitation of the analysis methods based on the state equation is related to spurious solutions. This limitation motivates the interest in techniques for removing such solutions from the set of solutions obtained. Strategies based on *traps, implicit*

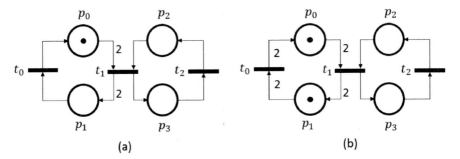

Figure 12.47   Spurious Solution.

places, and partially enabled firing sequences are some of such strategies. For more information, the reader is referred to as [385].

12.8.3 REDUCTIONS

Another very useful strategy for qualitative analysis is the transformation-based approach. Such transformations may be applied in the reachability graph or the nets. Transformation methods may be adopted for reducing the state space size, and; thus, alleviating the analysis methods complexity. Usually, these transformations are reductions that are applied to the models in order to obtain smaller models preserving qualitative properties of the original ones. The converse transformations are named refinements, which are useful in the synthesis process. Many reduction rules are available [44], but this section presents only a set of six primary reductions rules [158, 295]. The reductions rules presented in this section preserve safeness, boundedness, and liveness.

Fusion of Series Places (FSP) - Let us assume a net $N = (P, T, F, W, M_0)$, and consider the sub-net depicted in the left-hand side of Figure 12.48.a as part of N. N may be transformed into $N' = (P', T', F', W', M'_0)$ by merging p_0 and p_1 such that $P' = P - \{p_0, p_1\} \cup \{p_{01}\}$, $T' = T - \{t_0\}$, $F' = F - F_r$, $F_r = \{(t, p_0), (t, p_1), (p_1, t),$ $(p_0, t_0), (t_0, p_1)\} \cup \{(t, p_{01}), (p_{01}, t)\}$, $t \in {}^\bullet p_0 \cup {}^\bullet p_1 \cup p_1^\bullet$, $t \neq t_0, t_1$. $W'(f') = W(f)$, $\forall f' \in F' - F_r$, $W'(f') = 1$, $\forall f' \in F_r$, and $m'_{p01} = m_{p0} + m_{p1}$.

Fusion of Series Transitions (FST) - Let us consider a net $N = (P, T, F, W, M_0)$, and the sub-net depicted in the left-hand side of Figure 12.48.b as part of N. N may be transformed into $N' = (P', T', F', W', M'_0)$ by merging t_0 and t_1 such that $P' = P - \{p_0\}$, $T' = T - \{t_0, t_1\} \cup \{t_{01}\}$, $F' = F - F_r$, $F_r = \{(p, t_0), (t_0, p), (t_1, p),$ $(t_0, p_0), (p_0, t_1)\} \cup \{(p, t_{01}), (t_{01}, p)\}$, $p \in {}^\bullet t_0 \cup t_0^\bullet \cup t_1^\bullet$, $p \neq p_0, p_1$. $W'(f') = W(f)$, $\forall f' \in F' - F_r$, and $W'(f') = 1$, $\forall f' \in F_r$.

Fusion of Parallel Places (FPP) - Assume a net $N = (P, T, F, W, M_0)$, and consider the sub-net depicted in the left-hand side of Figure 12.48.c as part of N. N may be transformed into $N' = (P', T', F', W', M'_0)$ by merging p_0 and p_1 such that $P' =$

$P - \{p_0, p_1\} \cup \{p_{01}\}$, $T' = T$, $F' = F - F_r$, $F_r = \{(t_0, p_0), (t_0, p_1), (p_0, t_1), (p_1, t_1)\}$
$\cup \{(t_0, p_{01}), (p_{01}, t_1)\}$, $W'(f') = W(f)$, $\forall f' \in F' - F_r$, $W'(f') = 1$, $\forall f' \in F_r$, and
$m'_{p01} = m_{p0} + m_{p1}$.

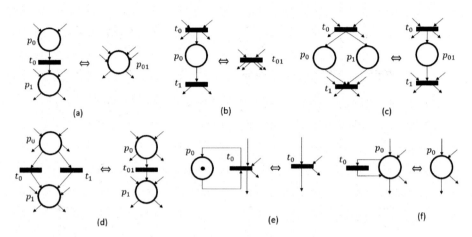

(a)   (b)   (c)

(d)   (e)   (f)

Figure 12.48   Reductions.

Fusion of Parallel Transitions (*FPT*) - Consider a net $N = (P, T, F, W, M_0)$ and the sub-net depicted in the left-hand side of Figure 12.48.d as part of N. N may be transformed into $N' = (P', T', F', W', M'_0)$ by merging t_0 and t_1 such that $P' = P$, $T' = T - \{t_0, t_1\} \cup \{t_{01}\}$, $F' = F - F_r$, $F_r = \{(p_0, t_0), (p_0, t_1), (t_0, p_1), (t_1, p_1)\} \cup \{(p_0, t_{01}), (t_{01}, p_1)\}$, $W'(f') = W(f)$, $\forall f' \in F' - F_r$, and $W'(f') = 1$, $\forall f' \in F_r$.

Elimination of Self-Loop Places (*ESLP*) - Consider a net $N = (P, T, F, W, M_0)$ and the sub-net depicted in the left-hand side of Figure 12.48.e as part of N. N may be transformed into $N' = (P', T', F', W', M'_0)$ by removing p_0 such that $P' = P - \{p_0\}$, $T' = T$, $F' = F - F_r$, $F_r = \{(p_0, t_0), (t_0, p_0)\}$ and $W'(f') = W(f)$, $\forall f' \in F' - F_r$.

Elimination of Self-Loop Transitions (*ESLT*) - Assume a net $N = (P, T, F, W, M_0)$ and the sub-net depicted in the left-hand side of Figure 12.48.f as part of N. N may be transformed into $N' = (P', T', F', W', M'_0)$ by removing t_0 such that $P' = P$, $T' = T - \{t_0\}$, $F' = F - F_r$, $F_r = \{(p_0, t_0), (t_0, p_0)\}$ and $W'(f') = W(f)$, $\forall f' \in F' - F_r$.

Consider the net depicted in Figure 12.49.a. By applying one Fusion of Series Places (*FSP*), two Fusion of Series Transitions, (*FST*) and one Fusion of Parallel Places (*FPP*), as depicted in the figure, the net presented in Figure 12.49.b is obtained. Now, two Fusion of Series Places may be applied, and so doing, the net depicted in Figure 12.49.c is generated. Merging two series transitions and eliminating a self-loop transition provides the net presented in Figure 12.49.d. Now, by eliminating a self-loop place, and then a self-loop transition (Figure 12.49.e.), the net presented in Figure 12.49.f is obtained. This net is live and bounded; hence the net presented in Figure 12.49.a also is.

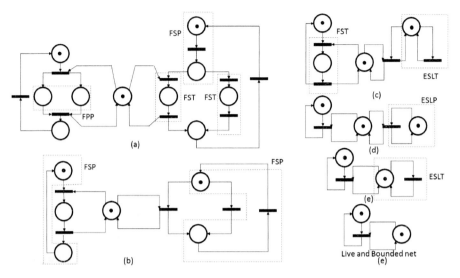

Figure 12.49 Applying Reductions.

12.9 STRUCTURAL PROPERTIES AND ANALYSIS

Many systems studied in engineering can be described by algebraic linear equations. It would be interesting if it were possible to model and analyze the dynamic behavior of Petri nets by equations completely. However, the non-deterministic nature inherent to Petri net models and the constraints of the solution as non-negative integers makes the use of such an approach somewhat limited. The behavior of net models is non-linear, but the so-called state equation represents an interesting linear relaxation. Nevertheless, the state equation may provide spurious solutions[5] [394].

Because of spurious solutions, this approach usually leads to semi-decision algorithms, or rather, it only provides necessary or sufficient conditions for the analysis of such behavioral properties as reachability, boundedness, liveness, and reversibility. Nevertheless, for certain property analysis, it permits a fast diagnosis without enumeration [394].

Spurious solutions can be removed using some other approaches, for instance, the inclusion of implicit places [393]. A place is defined as implicit if it can be removed without changing the behavior of the net [394]. The addition of implicit places generates a new model with identical behavior. The problem consists of where to insert the implicit places.

The structural properties discussed in this section express behavioral characteristics of nets as in the cases of behavioral properties. However, the behavioral features

---

[5]Markings (M^{st}) that are results of the state equation, but do not belong to the reachability set ($M^{st} \notin RS$).

of a net depicted by the behavioral properties were intrinsically related to the net's initial marking. Structural properties, on the other hand, are not associated with initial markings; they denote the possible behavior of a net disregarding its initial marking.

12.9.1 TRANSITION INVARIANTS

Considering a net $N = (P, T, I, O, M_0)$ and the state equation $M = M_0 + C \times \bar{s}$, if there exists a marking $M = M_0$; thus $C \times \bar{s} = 0$, a set of invariant laws (transition invariants - t-invariants). By solving this linear system of equations, the results obtained for the right annullers, $\bar{s} = (s_i)_{|T|}$, of the incidence matrix lead to a t-semiflow (a vector), and the right non-negative annullers of the incidence matrix provides a positive t-semiflow (vector).

Positive T-Semiflow: Let $\bar{s} \geq 0$ be a vector, such that $s_i \geq 0$. S is called a t-semiflow iff $C \times \bar{s} = 0$.

A positive t-semiflow represents the set of transitions (ST) that can be fired from M_0 back to M_0. The set of transition (ST) is the support of the t-semiflow. More formally:

Support of a Positive T-Semiflow: Let $\bar{s}$ be a positive t-semiflow, and ST be defined as the support of the t-semiflow $\bar{s}$, if $ST = \{t | s_t \geq 0\}$.

The positive t-semiflow support (ST) leads to a subnet (a part of N, a component of N) whose behavior is repetitive. Such a subnet is named a **repetitive component**.

Therefore, we have three interrelated (but distinct) concepts, that should, however, be clarified:

1. t-invariant is a law, a system of equations, $C \times \bar{s} = 0$, for a given net N.

2. positive t-semiflow is a vector, $\bar{s}$, that solves the system $C \times \bar{s} = 0$, $s_i \geq 0$.

3. a repetitive component is a subnet obtained from the t-semiflow support (ST) whose behavior is repetitive.

A t-semiflow is canonical if, and only if, the greatest common divisor of its non-null element is one. A generator set of t-semiflows, $\psi = \{\bar{s_1}, ..., \bar{s_n}\}$, is made of the least number of t-semiflows that will generate any t-semiflow. A **minimal positive t-semiflow** is a canonical semiflow whose support does not contain the support of any other positive t-semiflow. The t-semiflow generator of a net is finite and unique [392]. It is worth noting that any linear combination of semiflows is also a semiflow.

Consistency - A net $N = (P, T, I, O)$ is said to be **consistent** if all its transitions are support of positive t-semiflows, that is, the whole net is a repetitive component (the transitions are "covered" by positive t-semiflows). More formally, N is consistent if $\exists \ \bar{s} > 0$, where every $s_i > 0$, such that $C \times \bar{s} = 0$.

The net depicted in Figure 12.50.a is not consistent because its only minimal positive t-semiflow is $\bar{s}^T = (1, 1, 1, 0)$. Therefore, there is no set of positive t-semiflows that covers the transitions of the net. On the other hand, the net shown in Figure 12.50.b is consistent, since it has two minimal positive t-semiflows, and they cover all transitions of the net. The minimal positive t-semiflows are: $\overline{s_1}^T = (1,1,1,0)$ and $\overline{s_2}^T = (2,1,0,1)$. It is worth mentioning that $\overline{s_3}^T = \overline{s_1}^T + \overline{s_2}^T = (3,2,1,1)$ is also a positive t-semiflow as is any other flow obtained by linear combinations of others t-semiflows. Live nets are covered by positive t-semiflows[6], but a net covered by positive t-semiflows is not necessarily live. As a trivial example, consider a net with the structure of the model presented in Figure 12.50.b, but with initial marking $M_0^T = (0,0,0)$. This net is clearly not live, but covered positive t-semiflows.

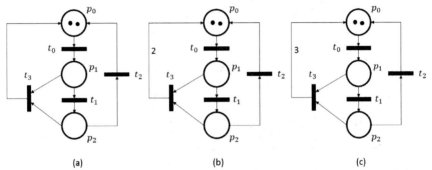

(a)   (b)   (c)

Consistency, Structural Repetitiveness, Structural Conservation, and Structural Boundedness.

Figure 12.50   Structural Properties.

Now consider the net $N = (P,T,I,O,M_0)$ and the state equation $M = M_0(p) + C \times \overline{s}$, if there exists a marking $M \geq M_0$; thus $C \times \overline{s} \geq 0$. This linear system of inequations is a set of **t-surinvariants** [184, 295, 384, 385]. Solving this linear system of inequations allows obtaining t-semiflows as well as positive t-semiflows. It is worth stressing two aspects: (1) these specific flows are solutions of the set of t-surinvariants, and (2) a t-surinvariant is not a t-invariant for $C \times \overline{s} > 0$.

Structural Repetitiveness - A net $N = (P,T,I,O)$ is said to be **structurally repetitive** if $\exists\ \overline{s} > 0$, where every $s_i > 0$, such that $C \times \overline{s} \geq 0$. A consistent net is also structurally repetitive, but not all repetitive nets are also consistent ($C \times \overline{s} > 0$).

The net shown in Figure 12.50.c is structurally repetitive, but not consistent, since the positive t-semiflow solutions of $C \times \overline{s} = 0$ do not cover transitions of the net. However, the transitions of the net are covered by positive t-semiflows which are solutions of $C \times \overline{s} \geq 0$ (t-surinvariant). The positive t-semiflows that are solutions of $C \times \overline{s} \geq 0$ are: $\overline{s_1}^T = (3,1,0,1)$, $\overline{s_2}^T = (2,1,0,1)$, $\overline{s_3}^T = (3,2,0,1)$, and $\overline{s_4}^T = (1,1,1,0)$. $\overline{s_4}$ is even a solution of $C \times \overline{s} = 0$ (t-invariant).

Since the net presented in Figure 12.50.b is consistent, it is also structurally repetitive. The net depicted in Figure 12.50.a is neither consistent nor structurally repetitive,

---

[6]The t-semiflows are obtained from $C \times \overline{s} = 0$ - t-invariant - or from $C \times \overline{s} \geq 0$ - t-surinvariant [184].

since $\nexists \ \bar{s} > 0$, where every $s_i > 0$, such that $C \times \bar{s} \geq 0$.

Therefore, it is worth summarizing that a live net is also structurally repetitive, that is, for a live net $\exists \ \bar{s} > 0$, where every $s_i > 0$, such that $C \times \bar{s} \geq 0$ (necessary condition), and it may also be consistent, i.e., there may $\exists \ \bar{s} > 0$, where every $s_i > 0$, such that $C \times \bar{s} = 0$.

12.9.2   PLACE INVARIANTS

A net $N = (P, T, I, O, M_0)$ is said to be conservative if the weighted sum of tokens is constant for any reachable marking $M \in RS_N$. Therefore

$$W \times M_0 = W \times M, \qquad \forall M \in RS_N.$$

As $M = M_0 + C \times \bar{s}$, then

$$W \times M_0 = W \times (M_0 + C \times \bar{s}), \qquad \forall M \in RS_N.$$

Thus,

$$W \times M_0 = W \times M_0 + W \times C \times \bar{s}.$$

Hence

$$W \times C \times \bar{s} = 0.$$

As $\exists \ \sigma \ L(N)$ that $M_0[\sigma > M$, then $\exists \ \bar{s} > 0$; thus

$$W \times C = 0.$$

It is worth noting that in the above linear system of equations there is no reference to the net's marking. Hence this system of equations is independent of markings. This system of linear equations is a set of invariant laws named p-invariants. By solving this linear system of equations, the results obtained for the left annullers, $W = (w_i)_{|P|}$, of the incidence matrix lead to a p-semiflow (a vector), and the left non-negative annullers of the incidence matrix provide a positive p-semiflow (vector).

P-Semiflow: Let $W \geq 0$ be a vector, such that $w_i \geq 0$. W is called a p-semiflow iff $W^T \times C = 0$.

A positive p-semiflow represents the set of places (SP) whose weighted sum stays constant. The set of places (SP) is the support of the t-semiflow. More formally:

Support of a P-Semiflow: Let W be a positive p-semiflow; SP is defined as the support of the p-semiflow W, if $SP = \{p | w_p \geq 0\}$.

The positive p-semiflow support (ST) leads to a subnet (a part of N, a component of N) whose weighted sum of tokens stays constant. Such a subnet is named a **conservative component**.

As for transitions, we have again three interrelated, but distinct, concepts, that should be highlighted:

1. p-invariant is a law, a system of equations, $W \times C = 0$, for a given net N.

2. positive p-semiflow is a vector, W, that solves the system $W \times C = 0$, $w_i \geq 0$.

3. a conservative component is a subnet obtained from the p-semiflow support (ST) whose weighted sum of tokens stays constant.

Nevertheless, it is common (in the literature) to refer to t-semiflows and p-semiflows as t-invariants and p-invariants, respectively, and whenever the context is clear, we may also adopt this.

A p-semiflow is canonical if, and only if, the greatest common divisor of its non-null elements is one. A generator set of a p-semiflow, $\omega = \{W_1, ..., W_m\}$ is made of the least number of them which will generate any p-semiflow. A positive p-semiflow is minimal if, and only if, it is canonical and its support does not contain the support of any other positive p-semiflow. The p-semiflow generator of a net is finite and unique. Any linear combination of semiflows is also a semiflow.

Structural Conservation - A net $N = (P, T, I, O)$ is said to be **structurally conservative** if $\exists$ W, where every $w_i > 0$, such that $W \times C = 0$. A structurally conservative net is conservative for any possible initial marking.

Neither the net shown in Figure 12.50.a nor the one presented in Figure 12.50.c have positive p-semiflows, so both are not structurally conservative. The net depicted in Figure 12.50.b is, however, structurally conservative, since positive p-semiflows cover all of its places. This net has one minimal positive p-semiflow: $W = (1, 1, 1)$. One should pay attention to the fact that if a net is structurally conservative, it is also conservative, but the contrary is not always true. As mentioned, the nets presented in Figure 12.50.a and Figure 12.50.c are not structurally conservative as the respectively marked nets are also not conservatives. However, if we consider $M_0^T = (1, 0, 0)$ as their initial marking, both marked nets become conservative, although they are not structurally conservatives.

Now consider the net $N = (P, T, I, O, M_0)$ and that $W \times M \leq W \times M_0$, $\forall M \in RS_N$. From this, $W \times C \leq 0$ is obtained. This linear system of inequations is a set of **p-subinvariants** [184, 295, 385]. Solving this linear system of inequations allows obtaining p-semiflows as well as positive p-semiflows. It is worth mentioning that these specific flows are solutions of the p-subinvariants, and that a p-subinvariant is not a p-invariant for $W \times C < 0$.

Structural Boundedness - A net $N = (P, T, I, O)$ is said to be **structurally bounded** if $\exists$ W, where every $w_i > 0$, such that $W \times C \leq 0$. A structurally conservative net is also structurally bounded, but not all structurally bounded nets are also structurally conservative ($W \times C < 0$).

The net presented in Figure 12.50.b is structurally conservative and hence also structurally bounded, since it is covered by positive p-semiflow ($W = (1, 1, 1)$). The net presented in Figure 12.50.a is not structurally conservative, since it has no positive p-semiflow that solves $W \times C = 0$. Nevertheless, it is structurally bounded because it has a positive p-semiflow that solves $W \times C \leq 0$ (p-subinvariant): $W = (1,1,1)$. The net shown in Figure 12.50.c is not structurally bounded (consequently not structurally conservative), since it has no positive p-semiflow that solves $W \times C \leq 0$.

The algorithm given below is a simple procedure to compute semiflow from the incidence matrix [392]. Here we considered it to calculate minimal p-semiflow.

Algorithm 19 Computation of Minimal p-semiflow

1: **Input**: Incidence matrix C, where $|P| = n$ and $|T| = m$.
2: **Output**: Set of minimal p-semiflow.
3: $A := C$, $W := I_n$, where I_n is an identity matrix of dimension n.
4: For $i := 1$ to m do:
5:   Add to the matrix $[A|W]$ all the rows that are a linear combination of pairs of rows of $[A|W]$ and which annul the ith column of A.
6:   Eliminate from $[A|W]$ the rows in which the ith column of A is non-null.
7: Remove from W all rows whose support is not minimal, and divide each by the g.c.d. of its non-null elements [392].

The rows of the matrix W are minimal p-semiflows of the net [392]. One of the problems with this kind of algorithm is the combinatory nature of the problem. Theoretically, an exponential number of semiflows may appear, since the linear programming problem considered is constrained to non-negative solutions. Actually, the semi-positive integer linear programming problem is NP-complete [385]. Nevertheless, for most practical examples, the complexity for finding a solution for these problems is polynomial and, for many cases, linear. In order to alleviate this situation, a series of heuristics is added to the basic algorithm which will help to control the combinatory explosion. Silva presents two alternative characterizations of non-minimal p-semiflows and how to consider them on the described algorithm in order to obtain only minimal p-semiflows [392]. The first one is based on their support and the other on the rank of some sub-matrixes of the original incidence matrix.

The algorithm presented is applied to the net depicted in Figure 12.51 to compute positive p-semiflows.
The incidence matrix of this net is

$$
C = \begin{array}{c} \\ p_0 \\ p_1 \\ p_2 \\ p_3 \\ p_4 \\ p_5 \\ p_6 \end{array}
\begin{array}{c} \begin{array}{cccc} t_0 & t_1 & t_2 & t_3 \end{array} \\
\left(\begin{array}{cccc}
-1 & 1 & 0 & 0 \\
1 & -1 & 0 & 0 \\
0 & 0 & -1 & 1 \\
0 & 0 & 1 & -1 \\
0 & -1 & 1 & 0 \\
0 & 0 & 0 & 0 \\
0 & 1 & -1 & 0
\end{array} \right) \end{array} .
$$

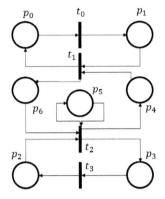

Figure 12.51 Positive p-semiflows.

Matrix A is a copy of matrix C. Appending the identity matrix (copied to W) to matrix A leads to

$$A|W = \begin{pmatrix} -1 & 1 & 0 & 0 & 1 & 0 & 0 & 0 & 0 & 0 & 0 \\ 1 & -1 & 0 & 0 & 0 & 1 & 0 & 0 & 0 & 0 & 0 \\ 0 & 0 & -1 & 1 & 0 & 0 & 1 & 0 & 0 & 0 & 0 \\ 0 & 0 & 1 & -1 & 0 & 0 & 0 & 1 & 0 & 0 & 0 \\ 0 & -1 & 1 & 0 & 0 & 0 & 0 & 0 & 1 & 0 & 0 \\ 0 & 0 & 0 & 0 & 0 & 0 & 0 & 0 & 0 & 1 & 0 \\ 0 & 1 & -1 & 0 & 0 & 0 & 0 & 0 & 0 & 0 & 1 \end{pmatrix}.$$

Now add to the matrix $[A|W]$ all the rows that are a linear combination of pairs of rows of $[A|W]$ and which annul the ith column of A. Hence summing the first and second rows results in

$$\begin{pmatrix} 0 & 0 & 0 & 0 & 1 & 1 & 0 & 0 & 0 & 0 & 0 \end{pmatrix}.$$

Add this row to the bottom of $[A|W]$ and remove the first and the second rows. This results in

$$A|W = \begin{pmatrix} 0 & 0 & -1 & 1 & 0 & 0 & 1 & 0 & 0 & 0 & 0 \\ 0 & 0 & 1 & -1 & 0 & 0 & 0 & 1 & 0 & 0 & 0 \\ 0 & -1 & 1 & 0 & 0 & 0 & 0 & 0 & 1 & 0 & 0 \\ 0 & 0 & 0 & 0 & 0 & 0 & 0 & 0 & 0 & 1 & 0 \\ 0 & 1 & -1 & 0 & 0 & 0 & 0 & 0 & 0 & 0 & 1 \\ 0 & 0 & 0 & 0 & 1 & 1 & 0 & 0 & 0 & 0 & 0 \end{pmatrix}.$$

Now, sum the third and fifth rows, add this new row to the bottom of $[A|W]$, and remove the third and fifth rows:

$$A|W = \begin{pmatrix} 0 & 0 & -1 & 1 & 0 & 0 & 1 & 0 & 0 & 0 & 0 \\ 0 & 0 & 1 & -1 & 0 & 0 & 0 & 1 & 0 & 0 & 0 \\ 0 & 0 & 0 & 0 & 0 & 0 & 0 & 0 & 0 & 1 & 0 \\ 0 & 0 & 0 & 0 & 1 & 1 & 0 & 0 & 0 & 0 & 0 \\ 0 & 0 & 0 & 0 & 0 & 0 & 0 & 0 & 1 & 0 & 1 \end{pmatrix} .$$

Finally, sums the first and second rows, add this new row to the bottom of $[A|W]$, and remove the first and second rows:

$$A|W = \begin{pmatrix} 0 & 0 & 0 & 0 & 0 & 0 & 0 & 0 & 0 & 1 & 0 \\ 0 & 0 & 0 & 0 & 1 & 1 & 0 & 0 & 0 & 0 & 0 \\ 0 & 0 & 0 & 0 & 0 & 0 & 0 & 0 & 1 & 0 & 1 \\ 0 & 0 & 0 & 0 & 0 & 0 & 1 & 1 & 0 & 0 & 0 \end{pmatrix} .$$

At this point, the matrix A is null, and the minimal positive p-semiflows are available in matrix W.

$$W = \begin{pmatrix} 0 & 0 & 0 & 0 & 0 & 1 & 0 \\ 1 & 1 & 0 & 0 & 0 & 0 & 0 \\ 0 & 0 & 0 & 0 & 1 & 0 & 1 \\ 0 & 0 & 1 & 1 & 0 & 0 & 0 \end{pmatrix} .$$

As columns one, three, five and six, of W, are linearly independent; thus the four rows are also linearly independent. Hence, the positive p-semiflows are minimal. They are: $W_1 = (0,0,0,0,0,1,0)$, $W_2 = (1,1,0,0,0,0,0)$, $W_3 = (0,0,0,0,1,0,1)$, and $W_4 = (0,0,1,1,0,0,0)$.

EXERCISES

Exercise 1. Consider the net N_1 presented in Figure 12.52, generate its reachability graph, and comment.

Exercise 2. What do you understand about conflict, concurrency, and confusion?

Exercise 3. Comment on the modeling capacity of the state machine, marked graph, free-choice, and extended free choice sub-classes.

Exercise 4. Can we use the state equation to analyze reachability? Comment.

Exercise 5. What is the characteristic vector?

Exercise 6. Present the input, output and incidence matrices of the net depicted in Figure 12.52.

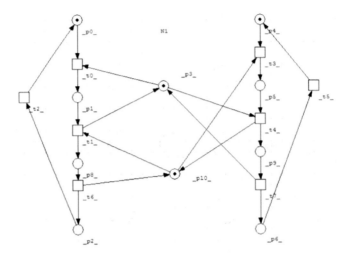

Figure 12.52   Net N_1.

Exercise 7. Consider the net depicted in Figure 12.26, **(a)** obtain the incidence matrix, **(b)** check if $M^T = (4,1,0,1,1,0) \in RS$, and **(c)** using the state equation, what can you tell about the reachability of M?

Exercise 8. Explain **(a)** place invariants, **(b)** transition invariants, **(c)** flows and semi-flows, and **(d)** repetitive and conservative components.

Exercise 9. What can you tell about **(a)** structural boundedness, **(b)** boundedness, **(c)** conservativeness, and **(d)** structural conservativeness?

Exercise 10. If a net is bounded, is it also structurally bounded? Explain.

Exercise 11. Explain the concepts of liveness, structural repetitiveness, and consistency.

Exercise 12. Can a net be live and not structurally repetitive? Comment.

Exercise 13. Are structural repetitiveness and reversibility equivalent? Comment.

Exercise 14. If for a given net $N = (P,T,I,O,M_0)$, $\exists \bar{s} \in \mathbb{N}_{|T|}^+$ such that $C \times \bar{s} = M - M_0$, can we state that M is reachable from M_0? Provide an argument that supports your answer.

Exercise 15. Calculate the minimal place and transition positive semi-flows of the net depicted in Figure 12.52. Interpret them.

Exercise 16. Analyze the net depicted in Figure 12.53, and state if it has the following properties: conservativeness, structural conservativeness, boundedness, structural boundedness, reversibility, and liveness.

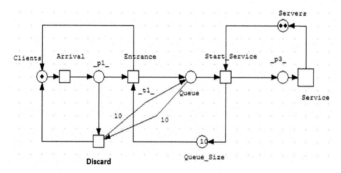

Figure 12.53 Net N_2.

13 Stochastic Petri Nets

This chapter introduces the stochastic Petri nets. Stochastic Petri nets is a term that denotes a family of stochastic models that is part of a larger family of behavioral models named Petri nets.

The first stochastic Petri net extensions were proposed independently by Symons, Natkin, and Molloy [421] [302] [285]. These models formed what was then named Stochastic Petri Nets (SPN). After, many other stochastic extensions were introduced. Marsan et al. extended the basic stochastic Petri nets by considering stochastic timed transitions and immediate transitions [8]. This model was named Generalized Stochastic Petri Nets (GSPN) [256]. Later on, Marsan and Chiola proposed an extension that also supported deterministic timed transitions [257], which was named Deterministic Stochastic Petri Nets (DSPN) [239]. Many other extensions followed, among them eDSPN [154] [153] and SRN [294].

In this book, the term SPN is adopted to describe stochastic timed Petri nets models in a broad sense. Here, the term SPN refers to a general model that encompasses the modeling capacity of the basic SPN model, GSPN, DSPN, and eDSPN. A broad definition of the SPN model is provided; as well specific instances and scenarios are also presented to highlight particular models.

This chapter first presents a definition of SPN. Concepts not yet introduced in the previous chapter are explained when describing the definition components. Afterward, a set of performance examples is presented to stress the modeling capacity of the model.

13.1 DEFINITION AND BASIC CONCEPTS

The Stochastic Petri net considered here is a very general stochastic extension of place-transition nets. Its modeling capacity is well beyond that presented by Symons, Natkin, and Molloy. The original SPN considered only exponential distributions. GSPNs adopted, besides exponential distributions, immediate transitions. These models shared the memoryless property also presented in untimed Petri nets since reachable marking is only dependent on the current Petri net marking.

The definition presented here takes into account any probability distribution [153]. Therefore, the memoryless property is not preserved unless for exponential and geometric distributions. Models that consider only memoryless distributions can be evaluated through numerical analysis as well as by simulation. However, if a net has probability distributions other than exponential and geometric, it can only be simulated. It is worth mentioning that when adopting non-memoryless distributions, some fundamental aspects of untimed Petri net are not preserved in the timed model since reachable markings would depend on the time spent on the current markings.

Stochastic Petri Nets - Let $SPN = (P,T,I,O,H,M_0,Atts)$ be a stochastic Petri net (SPN), where P,T,I,O, and M_0 are defined as for place-transition nets, that is, P is the set of places, T is the set of transitions, I is the input matrix, O is the output matrix, and M_0 is the initial marking. The set of transitions, T, is, however, divided into immediate transitions (T_{im}), timed exponentially distributed transitions (T_{exp}), deterministic timed transitions (T_{det}), and timed generically distributed transitions (T_g):

$$T = T_{im} \cup T_{exp} \cup T_{det} \cup T_g.$$

Immediate transitions are graphically represented by thin black rectangles, timed exponentially distributed are depicted by white rectangles, deterministic timed transitions are represented by thick black rectangles, and timed generically distributed gray rectangles denote transitions. Figure 13.1 presents a net in which these transition types are graphically represented. The set of immediate transitions is $T_{im} = \{t_0,t_1,t_4\}$, the set of deterministic transitions is $T_{det} = \{t_2\}$, the set of exponentially distributed transitions is $T_{exp} = \{t_3\}$, and the set of generically distributed transitions is $T_g = \{t_5\}$.

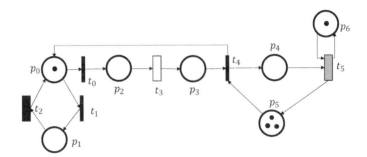

Figure 13.1 Graphical Notation of Transitions.

The matrices I and O represent the input and output arcs of transitions. These matrices, differently from place-transition nets, may be marking dependent; that is, the arc weights may be dependent on current marking:

$$I = (i_{p,t})_{|P| \times |T|}, \quad i_{p,t} : MD \times RS_{SPN} \to \mathbb{N},$$

and

$$O = (o_{p,t})_{|P| \times |T|}, \quad o_{p,t} : MD \times RS_{SPN} \to \mathbb{N},$$

where $MD = \{true, false\}$ is a set that specifies if the arc between p and t is marking dependent or not. If the arc is marking dependent, the arc weight is dependent on the current marking $M \in RS_{SPN}$, and RS_{SPN} is the reachability set of the net SPN. Otherwise, it is constant.

The net shown in Figure 13.2.a has one marking dependent arc. This model allows removing all tokens from place p_1 when at least one token is stored in place p_0. The input arc i_{p_1,t_0} is dependent on m_{p_1}. At the present marking, t_0 is enabled because $m_{p_0} \geq i_{p_0,t_0}$ and $m_{p_1} \geq i_{p_1,t_0}$, since $i_{p_0,t_0} = 1$ and $i_{p_1,t_0} = m_{p_1}$. Firing t_0, the marking depicted in Figure 13.2.b is reached. In this new marking t_0 is not enabled.

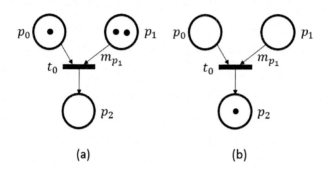

Figure 13.2   Marking Dependent Arc.

• $H = (h_{p,t})_{|P| \times |T|}$, $h_{p,t} : MD \times RS_{SPN} \rightarrow \mathbb{N}$, is a matrix of inhibitor arcs. These arcs may also be marking dependent, that is the arc weight may be dependent on current marking. $h_{p,t} : MD \times RS_{SPN} \rightarrow \mathbb{N}$, where $MD = \{true, false\}$ is a set that specifies if the arc between p and t is marking dependent or not. If the arc is marking dependent, the arc weight is dependent on the current marking $M \in RS_{SPN}$. Otherwise, it is constant.

An inhibitor arc $(h_{p,t})$ is a weighted arc from a place (p) to a transition (t), which inhibits (disables) the transition if $m_p \geq h_{p,t}$. Figure 13.3 presents four nets with inhibitor arcs. In Figure 13.3.a, transition t_0 is disabled, since $m_{p_1} \geq 3$. Likewise the transition t_0 in Figure 13.3.b is disabled. On the other hand, t_0 is enabled in Figure 13.3.c, and firing it, the new marking reached is depicted in Figure 13.3.d.

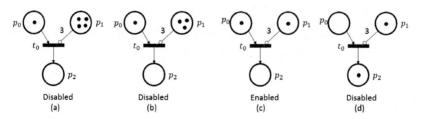

Figure 13.3   Inhibitor Arcs.

The inhibitor arcs depicted in Figure 13.4 are marking dependent. In Figure 13.4.a, transition t_0 is enabled because $m_{p_1} < 3$, since $2 \times m_{p_0} + 1 = 3$ ($m_{p_0} = 1$ and $m_{p_1} = 2$). In Figure 13.4.b, however, t_0 is disabled, since $m_{p_1} \geq 3$, since $2 \times m_{p_0} + 1 = 3$ ($m_{p_0} = 1$ and $m_{p_1} = 3$).

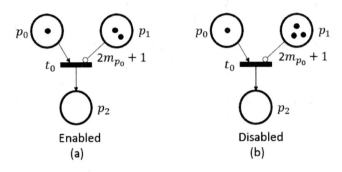

Figure 13.4   Marking Dependent Inhibitor Arc.

- $Atts = (\Pi, Dist, MDF, W, G, Policy, Concurrency)$ is the set of attributes assigned to transitions, where:

  ○ $\Pi : T \rightarrow \mathbb{N}$ is a function that assigns a firing priority on transitions. The larger the number, the higher is the firing priority. Figure 13.5 presents a subnet composed of two places and three immediate transitions. Considering the current marking ($M_0^T = (2,3)$), all three transitions are enabled. These transitions, however, have distinct priorities. Transition t_0 has priority $\pi(t_0) = 0$, transition t_1 has priority $\pi(t_1) = 1$, and t_2 has priority $\pi(t_2) = 2$. Therefore, in this marking the firable transition is t_2. A transition is firable if it is enabled and if it has the highest firing priority in the current marking. In firing t_2, two tokens are removed from p_1. Hence, the new marking is $M_1^T = (2,1)$. This marking enables t_0 and t_1. However, as $\pi(t_1) = 1$ and $\pi(t_0) = 0$, the firable transition is t_1. Its firing leads to marking $M_2^T = (1,0)$, which enables only t_0, and its firing reaches $M_3^T = (0,0)$.

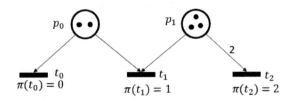

Figure 13.5   Priority.

Immediate transitions have higher priorities than timed transitions, and timed deterministic transitions have higher priorities than random timed transitions, that is,

$\pi(t_i) > \pi(t_j) > \pi(t_k)$, $t_i \in T_{im}$, $t_j \in T_{det}$, and $t_k \in T_{exp} \cup T_g$. The default transition type priorities are $\pi(t_i) = 2$, $t_i \in T_{im}$, $\pi(t_j) = 1$, $t_j \in T_{det}$, and $\pi(t_k) = 0$, $t_k \in T_{exp} \cup T_g$. Now, consider an $SPN = (P, T, I, O, H, M_0, Atts)$. If $\exists t_i \in T_{im}$ such that $\pi(t_i) = n$, then $\pi(t_j) < n$, $\forall t_j \in T_{det}$, and $\pi(t_k) < n$, $\forall t_j \in T_{exp} \cup T_g$. Likewise, if $\exists t_j \in T_{det}$ such that $\pi(t_j) = m$, then $\pi(t_k) < m$, $\forall t_k \in T_{exp} \cup T_g$.

Figure 13.6 presents a net in which t_0, t_1, and t_2 are enabled. t_0 is an immediate transition, t_1 is a timed deterministic transition, and t_2 is timed exponentially distributed transition. As immediate transitions have the highest priority, t_0 is the only firable transition. Its firing leads to marking $M_1^T = (0,1,1,1,0,0)$. At this marking, t_1 and t_2 are enabled. As the deterministic transition has higher firing priority than a stochastically distributed timed transition, t_1 is firable. Firing t_1 reaches $M_2^T = (0,0,1,1,1,0)$. At M_2, the only enabled transition is t_2, and its firing leads to $M_3^T = (0,0,0,1,1,1)$.

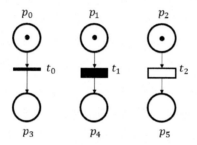

Figure 13.6 Priority over Distinct Transition Types.

Consider the net shown in Figure 12.20.b. This net is an asymmetric confusion. Transitions t_0 and t_2 are concurrent and t_0 is in conflict with t_1. As t_0 and t_2 are concurrent, their firing order would not affect the final marking. Nevertheless, if t_2 fires first, M_4 might be reached. On the other hand, this marking can not be reached if t_0 fires first. Such configurations (confusions) may be problematic for analysis. However, it may be overcome through different priority levels assigned to t_0 and t_2. For instance, if $\pi(t_0) > \pi(t_2)$, M_4 would not be reached.

○ $Dist : T_{exp} \cup T_g \rightarrow \mathscr{F}$ is a function that assigns a non-negative probability distribution function to random delay transitions. $\mathfrak{F}$ is the set of functions.

○ $MDF : T \rightarrow MD$ is a function that defines if the probability distribution functions assigned to delays of transitions are marking dependent or not. $MD = \{true, false\}$.

○ $W : T_{exp} \cup T_{det} \cup T_{im} \rightarrow \mathbb{R}^+$ is a function that assigns a non-negative real number to exponential, deterministic, and immediate transitions. For exponential transitions, these values correspond to the parameter values of the exponential distributions (rates). In case of deterministic transitions, they are the deterministic delays assigned to transitions. Moreover, in the case of immediate transitions, they denote the weights assigned to transitions.

Let us adopt the net depicted in Figure 13.7 to exemplify the assignment of the delay transition parameters introduced so far (Π, *Dist*, *MDF*, and *W*). These mappings are presented in Table 13.1.

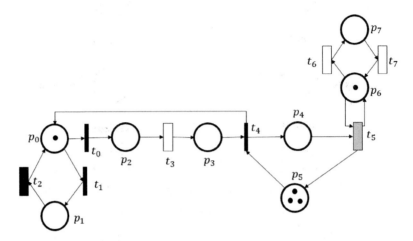

Figure 13.7 Delay and Priority Attribute Assignment.

Table 13.1
Delay and Priority Attributes

Transitions	Π	*Dist*	*MDF*	*W*
t_0	3		false	w_0
t_1	3		true	$w_{t_1,M} = f_1(m_{p_5}, wn_1)$
t_2	1		false	d_2
t_3	0	$1 - e^{-\lambda_3 t}$	false	λ_3
t_4	2		false	w_4
t_5	0	$N(\mu_5, \sigma_5)$	false	
t_6	0	$1 - e^{-\lambda_6 t}$	true	$\lambda_{t_6,M} = f_6(m_{p_4}, \lambda n_6)$
t_7	0	$1 - e^{-\lambda_7 t}$	false	λ_7

Transitions t_0, t_1, and t_4 are immediate transitions. t_0 and t_4 are non-marking-dependent and t_1 is marking dependent. The weights assigned to t_0 and t_4 are w_0 and w_4, whereas the weight assigned to t_1 is dependent on the number of tokens in p_5. In this case, the weight (w_1) is a non-negative value produced by the function

$f_1(m_{p_5}, wn_1)$, and wn_1 is a non-negative constant weight. Transitions t_3, t_6, and t_7 are timed exponentially distributed transitions. t_3 and t_7 are non-marking-dependent and t_6 is marking dependent. The rates assigned to t_3 and t_7 are λ_3 and λ_7, respectively, and their distribution functions are $1 - e^{-\lambda_3 t}$ and $1 - e^{-\lambda_7 t}$. The rate assigned to t_6 is dependent on the marking of p_4 (m_{p_4}). Hence, the rate assigned to t_6 is a non-negative value obtained from the evaluation of $f_6(m_{p_4}, \lambda n_6)$, where λn_6 is a non-negative constant rate. t_2 is a deterministic timed transition, and its delay is a positive constant real value d_2. Finally, transition t_5 is a non-exponential random timed transition ($t_5 \in T_g$), and its probability distribution is defined as $N(\mu_5, \sigma_5)$.[1]

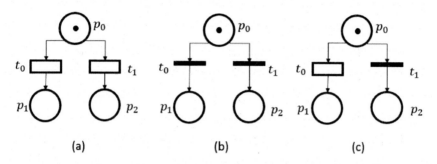

(a)   **(b)**   **(c)**

Figure 13.8 Conflicts.

Consider the random timed transitions t_0 and t_1 of the net depicted in Figure 13.8.a. These transitions are in conflict. The conflict resolution depends on the delays associated with transitions ($d_0 = 1/w_0$ and $d_1 = 1/w_1$, respectively), which is resolved through **race policy**. The race policy defines that when several random timed transitions are enabled (ES_M) in a given marking M, the transition with the shortest associated delay fires first, that is, t_i is the transition referred to by $i = \arg\min_{\forall j \in ES_M}\{d_j\}$. Now consider the immediate transitions t_0 and t_1 of the net depicted in Figure 13.8.b. These transitions are also in conflict. Their conflict resolution depends on the priority level and the weights associated with transitions (w_0 and w_1, respectively). When several immediate transitions are enabled in a given marking M (ES_M) at the highest priority level (FS_M – firable transition set.[2]), the transition with the highest firing probability (in that marking) fires first (**probabilistic choice**). The firing probability of transition $t_i \in ES_M$ is defined by

$$Prob_{t_i, M} = \frac{w_{t_i, M}}{\sum_{\forall t_j \in FS_M} w_{t_j, M}}. \tag{13.1.1}$$

The transitions t_0 and t_1 of the net shown in Figure 13.8.c, however, are not in conflict, since the immediate transition has the highest firing priority than the timed

---

[1] $f_{N(\mu_5, \sigma_5)}(t) = \frac{1}{\sigma_5 \sqrt{2\pi}} e^{-\frac{(t-\mu_5)^2}{2\sigma_5^2}}$ – normal density function.

[2] FS_M will be formally defined.

transition.

   ○ $G : T \twoheadrightarrow \mathbb{N}^{|P|}$ is a partial operator that assigns to transitions a guard expressions. The guards are evaluated by $GE : (T \twoheadrightarrow \mathbb{N}^{|P|}) \to \{true, false\}$ that results in true or false. The guard expressions are Boolean formulas composed of predicates specified regarding marking of places. A transition may only be enabled if its guard function is evaluated as true. It is worth noting that not every transition may be guarded.

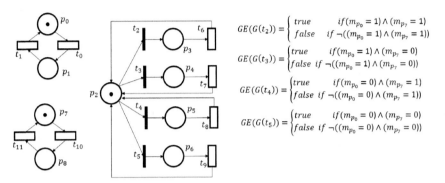

Figure 13.9   Guard Expressions.

Transitions t_2, t_3, t_4, and t_5 have guard expressions (see Figure 13.9). These guards are expressions that consider only the marking of places p_0, and p_7. They are $G(t_2) := [(m_{p_0} = 1) \wedge (m_{p_7} = 1)]$, $G(t_3) := [(m_{p_0} = 1) \wedge (m_{p_7} = 0)]$, $G(t_4) := [(m_{p_0} = 0) \wedge (m_{p_7} = 1)]$, and $G(t_5) := [(m_{p_0} = 0) \wedge (m_{p_7} = 0)]$.

As we know, the net presented in Figure 13.10.a is unbounded. This net can be made unbounded by including a place, p_1, that limits the number of tokens in p_0 as depicted in Figure 13.10.b. In this model the total number of tokens in p_0 and p_1 is $m_{p_0} + m_{p_1} = k$. If t_0 is a timed transition and t_1 is immediate, as shown in Figure 13.10.c the model is bounded, since t_1 has higher firing priority than t_0; hence when both transitions are enabled, t_1 will always fire before t_0. t_0 will only be firable when no token is stored in p_0. We can also use inhibitor arcs to make an unbounded net bounded. Hence, instead of adopting a place that limits the number of tokens in p_0 (as illustrated in Figure 13.10.b), an inhibitor arc from places p_0 to transition t_0 with a weight equal to k may be included (see Figure 13.10.d). In this net, t_0 is only enabled when $m_{p_0} \leq k$. Another alternative to make the net depicted in Figure 13.10.a bounded is including a guard expression in t_0 such that t_0 is only firable if the guard is evaluated as true. Thus, considering the guard $[m_{p_0} \leq k]$, t_0 is disabled when $m_{p_0} > k$ (see Figure 13.10.e).

An important issue that arises at every transition firing is concerned with the memory policy of transitions. The main concern is how to set the transition timers (time past since a transition became enabled) when a marking change occurs, possibly modi-

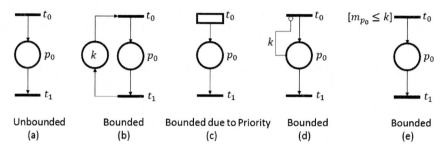

Figure 13.10 Boundedness.

fying the enabling of transitions. The memory policies assigned to transitions are: **restart** and **continue**.

○ *Policy* : $T \rightarrow \{prd, prs\}$, where *prd* denotes preemptive repeat different (restart), and *prs* is preemptive resume (continue). The timers of transitions with *prd* are discarded and new values are generated in the new marking. The timers of transitions with *prs* hold the present values.

After a transition firing, several scenarios should be carefully analyzed in the new marking:

1. the fired transition could become disabled or be still enabled (changing or not its enabling degree),

2. the previously enabled transitions could be kept enabled (changing or not its enabling degree) or could become disabled,

3. disabled transitions could become enabled.

These distinct behaviors give rise to different ways of keeping track of the past and may be implemented by associating *prd* or *prs* mechanisms to timed transitions.

Before continuing the explanation, let us introduce some concepts: the enabling rule, enabled and firable transition sets, and the firing rule.

Enabling Rule - Assume an $SPN = (P, T, I, O, H, M_0, Atts)$, a transition $t_i \in T$ and reachable marking $M \in RS_{SPN}$. t_i is enabled at M if

$$M \geq I_{\bullet, t_i} \wedge M < H_{\bullet, t_i} \wedge GE(G(t_i)) = true, \qquad (13.1.2)$$

where $I_{\bullet, t_j}$ is the column vector obtained from column t_j of matrix I, $H_{\bullet, t_i}$ is the column vector obtained from column t_j of matrix H, and $G(t_i)$ is the guard function of t_i .

Enabled Transition set (ET_M) and **Firable Transition set** (FT_M) in a marking M. Let N be a net and $M \in RS_N$ a reachable marking. The enabled transition set at M

is $ET_M = \{t_i | M \geq I_{\bullet,t_i} \wedge M < H_{\bullet,t_i} \wedge GE(G(t_i)) = true\}$. The firable transition set at M is the set of enabled transitions with the highest priority level among the enabled transitions, that is $FT_M = \{t_i | t_i \in ET_M \wedge \pi(t_i) = \max_{t_j \in ET_M} \{\pi(t_j)\}\}$.

Multiset of Firable Transition ($FTMS_M$) - The transitions' enabling in a marking M may be specified by a multiset over the firable set of transition FT_M. The multiset of firable transition in M is defined by $FTMS_M\{(t_i, no(t_i)) | t_i \in FT_M \wedge no : T \rightarrow ED_{\forall t_i \in T,M}\}$, where $no(t_i)$ denotes the multiplicity of transition t_i.

However, this notation is too heavy for being commonly adopted. A more common notation considers the explicit representation of the element multiplicity by writing the element the number of times equal its multiplicity. Hence the multiset $\{(t_0, 2), (t_1, 1), (t_2, 3)\}$ may be written as $\{t_0, t_0, t_1, t_2, t_2, t_2\}$.

Firable Rule - Consider a $SPN = (P, T, I, O, H, M_0, Atts)$, and a firable transition $t_i \in FT_M$ in the reachable marking $M \in RS_{SPN}$. Firing t_i leads to marking $M' \in RS_{SPN}$ ($M[t_i > M')$ and M' is obtained by

$$M' = M - I_{\bullet,t_j} + O_{\bullet,t_j}, \tag{13.1.3}$$

where $I_{\bullet,t_j}$ is the column vector obtained from column t_j of matrix I, and $O_{\bullet,t_j}$ is the column vector obtained from column t_j of matrix O.

Now, let us consider the net presented in Figure 13.11, and assume that the memory policies of all transitions are *prd*. The set of enabled transitions at marking M_0 is $ET_M = \{t_0, t_1, t_4\}$. Let us assume that t_0 is fired; then the next marking is $M_1^T = (0, 1, 0, 1, 0)$. In M_1, the enabled transitions are t_2 and t_4. t_1, which was enabled at M_0, is disabled at M_1. When, in the future, t_1 becomes enabled again, a new time will be sampled from its probability distribution and assigned to its timer, since its memory policy is *prd* (restart). Likewise, a time is sampled from the probability distribution of t_2 and assigned to its timer. t_4 was enabled at M_0 and is still enabled at M_1. However, as its memory policy is also *prd*, in M_1 a new time is sampled from its probability distribution and assigned to its timer. If, however, the memory policy of t_0, t_1, and t_4 were defined as *prs* (continue), the timer value of t_1 would be kept and used the next time t_1 becomes enabled; as well the timer value of t_4 would also be kept and used in M_2. Yet, if the memory policy of t_0, t_1 were *prd* (restart) and if the memory policy of t_4 were defined as *prs* (continue), in the future, when t_1 becomes enabled again, a new time would be sampled from the t_1 probability distribution and assigned to its timer, and a timer value of t_4 would be kept and used in M_2.

These different behaviors are summarized in three alternatives:

1. **Resampling** – At each transition firing, the timers of each of the timed transitions are discarded (**restart** – *prd*). No memory of the past is recorded. After discarding all timers' values, for those transitions that are enabled in the new marking, new values are sampled from the respective transitions' probability distributions and assigned to each specific timer.

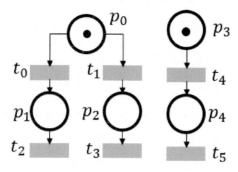

Figure 13.11 Memory Policies.

2. **Enabling memory** - At each transition firing, the timers of all the timed transitions that are disabled are restarted (**restart** – *prd*), and the timers of all the timed transitions that are not disabled hold their present value (**continue** – *prs*).

3. **Age memory** - At each transition firing, the timers of all the timed transitions hold their present values (**continue** – *prs*).

Special attention must be observed to the timing semantics of timed transitions with enabling degree larger than one. Consider the transition t_0 in Figure 13.12.a, which has the enabling degree equal to three ($ED_{t_0,M_0} = 3$). From queueing network terminology, different semantics may be assigned to stations of a queue system: **single server**, **infinite server**, and **k-server** semantics. It is worth mentioning, however, that the memoryless characteristics of exponential probability distributions make the distinction among the three policies irrelevant for nets that only consider exponentially distributed delays. Indeed, reseting or not reseting the timer (restart or continue – *prd* or *prs*) of a transition does not change its remaining firing time probability distribution (F_{rmf_i}).

○ *Concurrency* : $T - T_{im} \rightarrow \{sss, iss\}$ is a function that assigns to each timed transition a timing semantics, where *sss* denotes single server semantics and *iss* is infinite server semantics.

Let us assume the memory policy assigned to t_0 and t_1 is *prd*, their concurrency policy are *sss*, and that both have the same priority firing. In the initial marking (M_0), both transitions are firable ($ET_{M_0} = \{t_0, t_1\}$). In the simulation process, at the initial time ($t = 0$ – global time), a sample is obtained from both distribution functions ($F_{t_0}(t) = 1 - e^{-\lambda_0 t}$ and $F_{t_1}(t) = 1 - e^{-\lambda_1 t}$) and assigned to each transition delay variable (v_{t_0} and v_{t_1}), that is, $v_{t_0} := d_0^1$, $d_0^1 \leftarrow F_{t_0}(t)$, and $v_{t_1} := d_1^1$, $d_1^1 \leftarrow F_{t_1}(t)$. The values of v_{t_0} and v_{t_1} are assigned to variables that represent the remaining firing time of each transition (rft_{t_0} and rft_{t_1}); hence $rft_{t_0} := d_0^1$ and

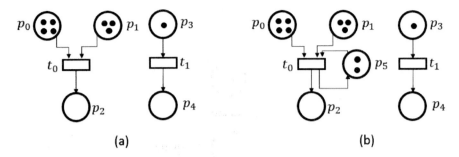

Figure 13.12   Server Policies.

$rft_{t_1} := d_1^1$. The minimal of these values defines the transition that should be fired; thus $t_k \leftarrow \arg rft_{min} = \min_{\forall t_i \in ET_{M_0}} \{rft_{t_i}\}$. Let us consider that $d_0^1 < d_1^1$, so the transition to fired is t_0. Firing t_0 leads to marking $M_1^T = (3,2,1,1,0)$, and the global time is updated to $t = 0 + rft_{min} = d_0^1$ (0 was the previous value of t). As in M_1 both transitions are again firable, and since the memory policies of both are *prd*, new samples must be obtained from $F_{t_0}(t)$ and $F_{t_1}(t)$. Consider that the obtained values were d_0^2 and d_1^2, respectively. Assuming $d_1^2 < d_0^2$, t_1 is the transition to be fired, and its firing leads to $M_2^T = (3,2,1,0,1)$ and $t = d_0^1 + d_1^2$. Now, the only firable transition is t_0. As in the previous markings, a new delay is obtained from $F_{t_0}(t)$, d_0^3. As t_0 is the only enabled transition, it is fired. The new marking is $M_3^T = (2,1,2,0,1)$, and the global time is updated to $t = d_0^1 + d_1^2 + d_0^3$. In M_3, again, the only firable transition is t_0. A new delay is obtained from its probability distribution, d_0^4. Firing t_1 reaches marking $M_4^T = (1,0,3,0,1)$ and the final global time of this first run ($\sigma_1 = t_0 t_1 t_0 t_0$) is $t = d_0^1 + d_1^2 + d_0^3 + d_0^4$. Obviously, when executing subsequent runs, different global times will be obtained. Therefore, in order to obtain the estimate of the average global time, many runs should be executed. However, this is the subject of Chapter 14.

Now, let us consider that the concurrency policy of t_0 is *iss* and that its memory policy is *prs* as well as consider that t_1 has the same attributes adopted in the case studied above, that is *sss* and *prd*. The simulation process begins at the time $t := 0$ (initial global time) and the marking presented in Figure 13.12.a. The enabling degree of t_0 is $ED_{t_0,M_0} = 3$. Since its concurrency policy is *iss* and $ED_{t_0,M_0} > 1$, t_0 is three times concurrently enabled. As the concurrency policy assigned to t_1 is *sss*, only one enabling is considered, even if its enabling degree was higher than one. In this specific marking, $ED_{t_1,M_0} = 1$. Therefore, the multiset of firable transitions is $FTMS_{M_0} = \{t_0,t_0,t_0,t_1\}$. For each transition enabling, a delay is sampled from the respective distribution functions ($F_{t_0}(t) = 1 - e^{-\lambda_0 t}$ and $F_{t_1}(t) = 1 - e^{-\lambda_1 t}$) and assigned to the delay variables ($v_{t_0}^1$, $v_{t_0}^2$, $v_{t_0}^3$, and v_{t_1}). Let us assume that the sampled delays are d_0^1, d_0^2, d_0^3, and d_1^1. The values of $v_{t_0}^1$, $v_{t_0}^2$, $v_{t_0}^3$ and v_{t_1} are assigned to variables that represent the remaining firing time of each transition enabling, that is $rft_{t_0}^1$, $rft_{t_0}^2$, $rft_{t_0}^3$ and rft_{t_1}. Therefore, $rft_{t_0}^1 := d_0^1$, $rft_{t_0}^2 := d_0^2$, $rft_{t_0}^3 := d_0^3$ and

$rft_{t_1} := d_1^1$. The minimal of these values specify the transition that should be fired; hence $t_k \leftarrow \arg rft_{min} = \min_{\forall t_i \in FT_{M_0}}\{rft_{t_i}\}$. It is worth noting that t_0 is considered three times, whereas t_1 is only once. Hence, if their probability distribution were the same, the chances of firing t_0 would be higher than firing t_1. Let us consider that d_0^2 is the shortest delay, so the transition to be fired is t_0. Firing t_0 leads to marking $M_1^T = (3,2,1,1,0)$, and the global time is updated to $t := 0 + rft_{min} = d_0^2$.

In M_1, the multiset of firable transitions is $FTMS_{M_1} = \{t_0, t_0, t_1\}$ (the enabling degree of t_0 was reduced to $ED_{t_0, M_0} = 2$). As the concurrency and memory policies of t_0 are *isss* and *prs*, and of t_1 are *prd*, the $rft_{t_0}^1 := d_0^1 - rft_{min}^{M_0}$, $rft_{t_0}^2 := d_0^3 - rft_{min}^{M_0}$ ($rft_{min}^{M_0}$ was the minimal remaining firing time in M_0 - in M_0, $rft_{min}^{M_0} = d_0^2$). For t_1, a new delay (d_1^2) is sampled from the distribution function and assigned to v_{t_1}, which is then assigned to rft_{t_1}. The shortest remaining firing time is $rft_{min} := \min_{\forall t_i \in \{t_0, t_0, t_1\}}$ $\{d_0^1 - rft_{min}^{M_0}, d_0^3 - rft_{min}^{M_0}, d_1^2\}$. Considering that $d_0^1 - rft_{min}^{M_0}$ is the shortest delay, t_0 fires. The new marking is $M_5^T = (2,1,2,1,0)$, and the global time is $t := d_0^2 + d_0^1 - rft_{min}^{M_0} = d_0^2 + d_0^1 - d_0^2 = d_0^1$.

In M_5, the multiset of firable transitions is $FTMS_{M_5} = \{t_0, t_1\}$. Hence, as in M_1, $rft_{t_0} := d_0^3 - rft_{min}^{M_0} - rft_{min}^{M_1} = d_0^3 - d_0^2 - d_0^1 - rft_{min}^{M_0} = d_0^3 - d_0^2 - d_0^1 - d_0^2 = d_0^3 - 2 \times d_0^2 - d_0^1$, and a new delay ($d_1^3$) is sampled from the distribution function and assigned to v_{t_1}. Therefore, $rft_{min} := \min_{\forall t_i \in \{t_0, t_1\}} \{d_0^3 - 2 \times d_0^2 - d_0^1, d_1^3\}$. If $d_1^3 < d_0^3 - 2 \times d_0^2 - d_0^1$, t_1 fires, M_3 is reached, and the global time is updated to $t := d_0^1 + d_1^3$. In M_3, the only enabled transition is t_0, and its remaining firing time was adjusted to $rft_{t_0}^1 := d_0^3 - 2 \times d_0^2 - d_0^1 - rft_{min}^{M_5} = d_0^3 - 2 \times d_0^2 - d_0^1 - d_1^3$. Firing t_0, M_4 is reached, and the global time is updated to $t := d_0^1 + d_1^3 + d_0^3 - 2 \times d_0^2 - d_0^1 - d_1^3 = d_0^3 - 2 \times d_0^2$.

The transition t_0 of the net shown in Figure 13.12.b has its highest enabling degree constrained to 2 due to the marking of place p_5. Hence, its enabling degree at M_0 is $ED_{t_0, M_0} = 2$. In marking $M_j^T = (2,1,2,1,0,2)$, its enabling degree is $ED_{t_0, M_j} = 1$ because of $m_{p_1}^j = 1$. Therefore, the number of tokens in p_5, $m_{p_5} = k$, restrains the infinite server semantics to k-server semantics (*kss*).

Table 13.2 summarizes the most important points regarding the server policy presented so far. More details will discussed later on. The key aspect of concern here is understanding the impact of server policy on the firing probability of transitions. The overview presented in this table is related to the net's initial marking and global time equal $t = 0$. The enabled and the firable transition sets at M_0 are $ET_{M_0} = \{t_0, t_1\}$ and $FT_{M_i} = \{t_0, t_1\}$, respectively. *sss* and *iss* are studied considering the net presented in Figure 13.12.a, whereas *kss* is assessed considering the model depicted in Figure 13.12.b.

The enabling degree of t_0 in these particular *sss* and *iss* instances is three. In any case, the enabling degree of t_1 is one. In the *sss* case, one delay sample was obtained from each time distributions, that is from $F_{t_0}(t)$ and $F_{t_1}(t)$. It is important stressing that although $ED_{t_0, M_0} = 3$, its server policy is *sss*; thus only one transition

Table 13.2
Server Policy

Policy	ED_{t_j, M_i}	rft_{t_j}
sss	$ED_{t_0, M_0} = 3,\ ED_{t_1, M_0} = 1$	$rft_{t_0} = d_0^1,\ rft_{t_1} = d_1^1$
iss	$ED_{t_0, M_0} = 3,\ ED_{t_1, M_0} = 1$	$rft_{t_0}^1 = d_0^1,\ rft_{t_0}^2 = d_0^2,\ rft_{t_0}^3 = d_0^3,\ rft_{t_1} = d_1^1$
kss	$ED_{t_0, M_0} = 2,\ ED_{t_1, M_0} = 1$	$rft_{t_0}^1 = d_0^1,\ rft_{t_0}^2 = d_0^2,\ rft_{t_1} = d_1^1$

enabling is considered at a time. In the *iss* case, however, three delays are sampled from $F_{t_0}(t)$ and one is obtained from $F_{t_1}(t)$, since the server policy assigned to t_0 is *iss*. In the *kss* case, the enabling degree of t_0 is restrained to $ED_{t_0, M_0} = 2$. Hence, in this scenario, only two delays are sampled from $F_{t_0}(t)$. One should notice that when deciding which transition should be fired in one marking (in any of these three cases: *sss*, *iss*, and *kss*), the minimal remaining firing time should first be obtained, $rft_{min} = \min_{\forall t_i \in FT_{M_0}} \{rft_{t_i}\}$. The transition that provides the shortest remaining firing time is the one that must be fired. Hence, in *iss* and *kss* the chances of firing t_0 are higher than in *sss*.

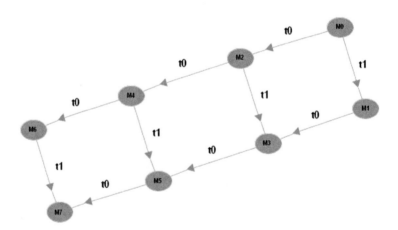

Figure 13.13 Reachability Graph of Nets Shown in Figure 13.12.

Now, let us look at the reachability graphs of the nets depicted in Figure 13.12.a and Figure 13.12.b. These reachability graphs are , and their structure is presented in Figure 13.13. Each respective marking is, however, different, since the number of places in each net is not the same. For the net depicted in Figure 13.12.a, the set of reachable markings is $RS = \{M_0, M_1, M_2, M_3, M_4, M_5, M_6, M_7\}$, where $M_0^T = \{4, 3, 0, 1, 0\}$, $M_1^T = \{4, 3, 0, 0, 1\}$, $M_2^T = \{3, 2, 1, 1, 0\}$, $M_3^T = \{3, 2, 1, 0, 1\}$, $M_4^T = \{2, 1, 2, 1, 0\}$,

$M_5^T = \{2,1,2,0,1\}$, $M_6^T = \{1,0,3,1,0\}$, and $M_7^T = \{1,0,3,0,1\}$. For the net depicted in Figure 13.12.b, the respective markings are $M_0^T = \{4,3,0,1,0,2\}$, $M_1^T = \{4,3,0,0,1,2\}$, $M_2^T = \{3,2,1,1,0,2\}$, $M_3^T = \{3,2,1,0,1,2\}$, $M_4^T = \{2,1,2,1,0,2\}$, $M_5^T = \{2,1,2,0,1,2\}$, $M_6^T = \{1,0,3,1,0,2\}$, and $M_7^T = \{1,0,3,0,1,2\}$.

As the parameters of the probability distributions $F_{t_0}(t)$ and $F_{t_1}(t)$ are λ_0 and λ_1, and considering sss as the transitions' server policies, the respective CTMC can be obtained by assigning the respective rate (λ_0 and λ_1) to the reachability graph arcs depicting the firing of each specific transition. Figure 13.14.a shows this CTMC.

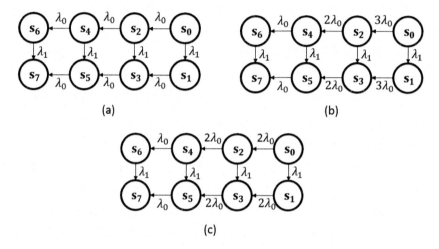

(a)   (b)

(c)

Figure 13.14   CTMCs Obtained From Nets Shown in Figure 13.12.

Now, consider that iss is assigned to transition t_0. Its enabling degrees in each reachable marking are: $ED_{t_0,M_0} = ED_{t_0,M_1} = 3$, $ED_{t_0,M_2} = ED_{t_0,M_3} = 2$, and $ED_{t_0,M_4} = ED_{t_0,M_5} = 1$. The rates assigned to each arc ($M[t_0 > M'$) that represents the firing of t_0 is the enabling degree of t_0 in M multiplied by λ_0, since $Concurrency(t_0) = iss$. To the arcs representing the firing of t_1, the rate assigned is just λ_1 because $Concurrency(t_1) = sss$. This CTMC is shown in Figure 13.14.b.

For the net depicted in Figure 13.12, when considering $Concurrency(t_0) = iss$ and $Concurrency(t_0) = sss$, the respective CTMC is the one shown in Figure 13.14.c, because place p_5 restrains the maximal enabling degree of t_0 to two.

13.1.1   A COMMENT ABOUT THE MODEL PRESENTED

The SPN definition presented corresponds to a quite complex stochastic process, since the net supports generally distributed transitions. Such a model is sometimes called *Generally Distributed Timed Transitions Stochastic Petri Nets* (**GDTT-SPN**)

[9]. When all transitions in a net are timed exponentially distributed, the model co-incides with the SPN models proposed by Molly and Natkin. If besides the exponentially distributed timed transitions, immediate transitions are also supported, the model matches the **GSPN**. If timed deterministic transitions are also supported, the nets correspond to a **DSPN**. If marking dependent arcs, rates and weights are part of the model, the net equates an **eDSPN** or a **SRN**. The SPN discussed in the rest of this chapter supports exponentially distributed timed and immediate transitions, marking dependent arcs, rates, and weights. This class of nets allows modeling phase-type exponential distributions (poly-exponential distributions) and can be numerically analyzed and simulated. If non-memoryless distributions are considered, the models´ evaluation is supported only by simulation. Simulation is discussed in Chapter 14.

13.2 MAPPING SPN TO CTMC

In this section, we introduce the process of obtaining the CTMCs underlying SPNs composed of exponentially distributed timed and immediate transitions. First of all, however, it is worthwhile to remind that the term (performance) evaluation is applied to denote processes of calculating performance measures, and it encompasses closed-form solutions, numerical analysis, and simulation. Moreover, when the term analysis is used, the reader should bear in mind that we refer to numerical analysis.

It is also important to highlight that steady-state solution analysis is only possible if a net is bounded, reversible (not necessarily to the initial marking), and deadlock free. A steady state solution may, however, be performed through simulation for unbounded and non-reversible nets. A bounded SPN generates a finite reachability graph. If we consider only exponentially distributed timed and immediate transitions, a CTMC can be obtained from the reachability graph. This Markov chain is often referred to as the *underlying* or the *embedded* CTMC of the SPN [173]. Therefore, this SPN can be evaluated through the embedded CTMC. This section focuses on the construction of the underlying CTMC from the SPN. A set of small examples is depicted to illustrate the construction of the embedded CTMCs from SPNs. The SPN analysis is, in general, composed of the following tasks:

1. generation of the net reachability graph,

2. generation of the CTMC from the net´s reachability graph,

3. numerical evaluation of the CTMC, and

4. computation of SPN metrics from the CTMC results.

The first task consists of generating the net´s reachability graph. From the reachability graph, the respective CTMC should be obtained and analyzed. The steady state or transient solution should be computed depending on the measures of interest and on the net´s qualitative properties (a transient analysis solution can be obtained for the net with deadlock, for instance). Afterward, the SPN measures should be derived from the state solution calculated from the CTMC. The SPNs can also be evaluated through simulation (5 in Figure 13.15). Analysis or simulation has its advantages and drawbacks [52]. The main concern related to numerical analysis is the state space size since this could be immense or infinite. Therefore, even for bounded nets, such an approach may not be an option due to memory constraints. The main general concern related to simulation is the time for obtaining a solution with the desired confidence and error. Therefore, the modeler/analyst should carefully ponder aspects such as metrics of interest, the model's qualitative properties, resource constraints, and possible approximations and decide which alternative is the best to be conducted. Figure 13.15 summarizes the primary tasks required for evaluating an SPN.

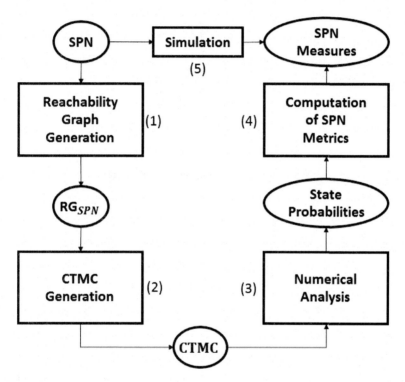

Figure 13.15 SPN Evaluation: Main Tasks.

As a first example, consider the net presented in Figure 13.16.a. This net has six places and six exponentially distributed timed transitions. No other transition type is considered. All transition priority is equal to one, no transition is guarded, and the arcs and the transition rates are not marking dependent. This model is equivalent to the SPN proposed by Natking and Molloy. The rate of each transition t_i is equal to λ_i. The net's reachability graph is presented in Figure 13.16.b as well as the marking vectors.

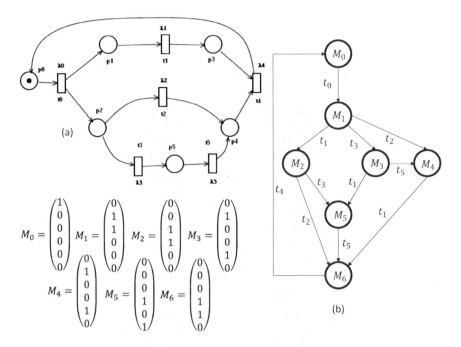

Figure 13.16 SPN and Its Reachability Graph - Only Exponentially Distributed Timed Transitions.

The respective CTMC is obtained from the reachability graph. Each net marking is mapped to a CTMC state, and arcs in the CTMC represent the reachability graph arcs. The rate of each arc of the CTMC is the individual transition rate of the reachability graph. Figure 13.17 presents the CTMC of the net shown in Figure 13.16.

The next two examples aims at highlighting the differences between *sss* and *iss* when generating a CTMC from an SPN. Initially, we take into account a net in which only *sss* is adopted. Figure 13.18.a presents a net composed of two places and two exponentially distributed timed transitions. The server policies of both transitions are *sss*. These transitions have no guard expression, their priority is equal to one and their rates, λ_0 and λ_1, respectively, are not marking dependent.

In this initial marking, $M_0^T = (2,0)$, the only firable transition is t_0. Firing t_0 leads to $M_1^T = (1,1)$, which enables t_0 and t_1. If t_1 is fired, the M_0 is reached back. On the other hand, if t_1 fires $M_2^T = (0,2)$ is reached. At M_2, the only firable transition is t_1, and firing it, leads back to M_1. The rechability graph of this net is shown in Figure 13.18.b. The CTMC is obtained from the reachability graph, where each marking is mapped to a state and each reachability graph arcs is mapped to an arc in the CTMC. The rate assigned to each arc (of the CTMC) is the respective rate assigned to each

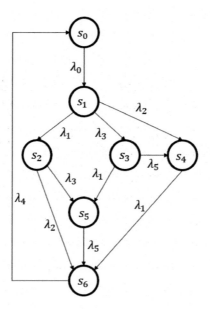

Figure 13.17 CTMC Obtained From Net of Figure 13.16.a

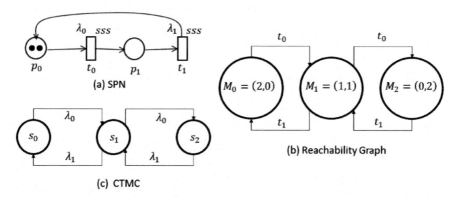

Figure 13.18 Single Server Semantics.

transition fired represented in each reachability graph arc. The CTMC is depicted in Figure 13.18.c.

The structure of the net presented in Figure 13.19.a is equal to the structure of the net presented in Figure 13.18.a. The only difference between these nets is the server semantics of transition t_1. The server semantics of t_1 in the net presented in Figure 13.19.a is *iss*.

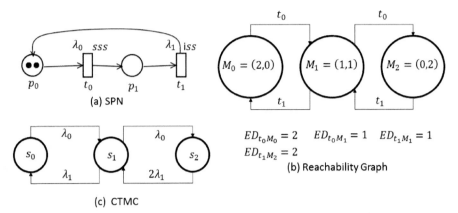

Figure 13.19 Single Server and Infinite Server Semantics.

The reachability graph of the net shown in Figure 13.19.a is also equal to the reachability graph of the net depicted in Figure 13.18.a. However, as the server semantics of transition t_1 is *iss*, its enabling degree in each marking should be considered for generating the respective CTMC. The respective rates (in the CTMC) related to transition t_0 are obtained as in the previous examples, since its server semantics is *sss*. For t_1, nevertheless, the transition rate should be multiplied by its enabling degree in each marking. Hence, the rate assigned to the arcs connecting s_2 to s_1 is $ED_{t_1,M_2} \times \lambda_1 = 2 \times \lambda_1$. Likewise, in marking M_1, the rate assigned to the arcs connecting s_1 to s_0 is $ED_{t_1,M_1} \times \lambda_1 = \lambda_1$. The CTMC is presented in Figure 13.19.c. The infinitesimal generator $\mathbf{Q}$ (rate matrix) is

$$
\mathbf{Q} = \begin{array}{c} 0 \\ 1 \\ 2 \end{array}
\begin{array}{ccc}
 & 0 \qquad\quad 1 \qquad\quad 2 & \\
\left(\begin{array}{ccc}
-\lambda_0 & \lambda_0 & 0 \\
\lambda_1 & -(\lambda_0 + \lambda_1) & \lambda_0 \\
0 & 2\lambda_1 & -2\lambda_1
\end{array}\right) &
\end{array} \quad .
$$

Consider a marking of an SPN with immediate transitions (a GSPN). If an immediate transition is enabled, only immediate transitions are firable, because they have higher priority than timed transitions. A marking in which an immediate transition is firable is named a **vanishing marking**. No delay is spent in a vanishing marking. Markings in which timed transitions are firable are named **tangible markings**. The set of reachable markings, RS, is; thus, composed of the vanishing marking set, VS, and of the tangible marking set, TS, that is $RS = VS \cup TS$. For obtaining the CTMC from an SPN with immediate transitions, the vanishing markings should be removed from the reachability graph. Two different processes can be applied: *elimination on the fly* and *post-elimination* [78]. Elimination on the fly is efficient concerning memory requirements because vanishing markings are not stored at all. However, these memory savings have to be traded with an additional time cost. In post-elimination, the complete reachability graph is stored during generation. Once the reachability graph is generated, it is transformed into a CTMC by removing the vanishing markings. For a detailed description of such processes, the reader may refer to [78] [52] [173] [256].

Now, let us take into account the net depicted in Figure 13.20. This net is composed of four places, three exponentially distributed timed transitions, and two immediate transitions. All timed transitions have single server semantics (*sss*), their priorities are equal, the immediate transitions also have the same priority, no transition has guards, and their parameters are not marking dependent. Their rates and weights are: λ_0, λ_3, λ_4, ω_1, and ω_2.

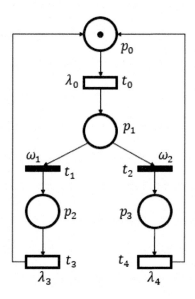

Figure 13.20   GSPN.

In the initial marking ($M_0^T = (1,0,0,0)$), the only firable transition is t_0. Firing t_0 leads to marking $M_1^T = (0,1,0,0)$. In M_1, the firable transitions are t_1 and t_2. These are immediate transitions. In M_1, either t_1 or t_2 can fire. If t_1 is fired, M_2 is reached ($M_2^T = (0,0,1,0)$). At M_2, t_3 can fire, and its firing takes the net back to M_0. If, in M_1, t_4 is fired, M_3 is reached ($M_3^T = (0,0,0,1)$). At M_3, t_4 can fire, and its firing leads to M_0. The net's reachability graph is depicted in Figure 13.21.a; its $TS = \{M_0, M_2, M_3\}$ and $VS = \{M_1\}$.

Figure 13.21.b shows the transitions' rates and weights were assigned to the respective transition firings. In the case of vanishing markings (M_1), the selection of which transition should be fired is based on priorities and weights. The set of enabled transitions at the highest priority level (firable transition set) should be first found, and

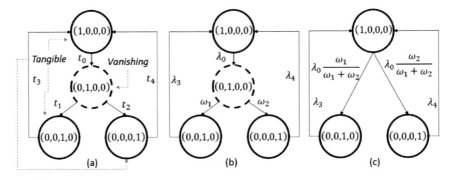

Figure 13.21 Reachability Graph, Vanishing and Tangible Markings, and CTMC.

if it has more than one transition, the selection is made considering the probability calculated through expression 13.1.1, which takes into account the transition weights and all firable transitions at M. Hence, the probability also considers non-conflicting transitions at M. From the modeler point of view, it may be hard to specify the transition´s weight considering the reachable marking of the whole net [9]. However, if no confusion is present in the net, the normalization of weights can be done only among transitions that belong to the same ECS [258], and the modeler can assign different priorities to transitions in different ECS. In this particular example, the probability of firing t_1 is $\omega_1/(\omega_1 + \omega_2)$, and the probability of firing t_2 is $\omega_2/(\omega_1 + \omega_2)$. The vanishing marking should be removed in order to obtain the Markov chain (see Figure 13.21.c). The Markov chain is obtained by removing the vanishing marking, and connecting the tangible marking M_0 to the tangible markings M_2 and M_3. The rate assigned to the arc (M_0, M_2) is the product between λ_0 and $\omega_1/(\omega_1 + \omega_2)$. Likewise, the rate assigned to the arc (M_0, M_3) is the product between λ_0 and $\omega_2/(\omega_1 + \omega_2)$.

The net shown in Figure 13.22 is composed of four places, two exponentially distributed timed transitions, and one immediate transition. The priority levels of the timed transitions are the same, the net has no guarded transition, and the server semantics of the both timed transitions is sss. The rate assigned to t_0 is λ_0, and the rate assigned to t_2 depends on the marking in place p_2 according to:

$$\lambda_2 := \begin{cases} \lambda, & \text{if } m_{p_2} = 1 \\ \frac{\lambda}{2}, & \text{otherwise.} \end{cases}$$

In the initial marking, only t_0 is enabled, and its firing takes the net to M_1 ($M_1^T = (0,1,0,2)$). At M_1, t_1 is the only enabled transition. Firing t_1 leads to M_2 ($M_2^T = (1,0,1,1)$), which enables t_0 and t_2. If t_2 fires, the net reaches the initial marking again. If t_0 is fired, the new marking is M_3 ($M_3^T = (0,1,1,1)$), which enables t_1. Firing t_1 takes the model to the marking M_4 ($M_4^T = (1,0,2,0)$). In this marking t_0 and t_2 are firables. If t_2 is fired, M_2 is reached. However, if t_0 fires, the next marking

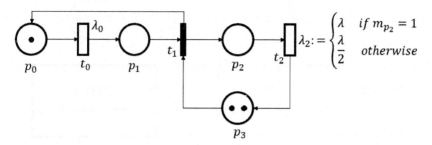

Figure 13.22   Marking Dependent Transition Rate.

is M_5 ($M_5^T = (0,1,2,0)$), which only enables t_2, whose firing takes the net to marking M_3. The reachability graph is presented in Figure 13.23.

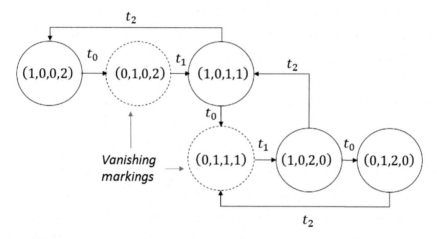

Figure 13.23   Reachability Graph of the Net Depicted in Figure 13.22

Markings M_1 and M_3 are vanishing markings, since they enable t_0; thus the time spent in them is zero. For obtaining the respective CTMC, the transitions' rates and weight should be assigned to arcs that represent the firing of each respective transitions. The rate assigned to t_0 is constant (λ_0 – non-marking dependent), but the rate assigned to t_2 depends on the number of tokens in place p_2, as mentioned above. Hence, the rate assigned to t_2 firing depends on the current marking. In M_1, $\lambda_2 = \lambda$, but in M_4 and M_5, $\lambda_2 = \lambda/2$.

The CTMC may then be generated. As there is only one immediate transition, when t_1 is firable, only it can be fired (there is no conflict); hence the probability of firing

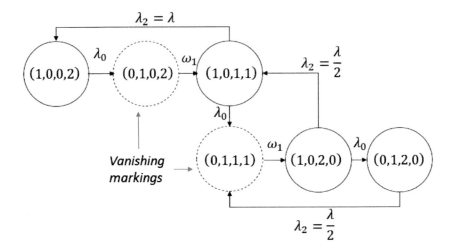

Figure 13.24   Vanishing and Tangible Markings.

t_1 such markings (M_1 and M_3) is one. Therefore, removing the vanishing markings generates the CTMC depicted in Figure 13.25. The rates between arcs (M_0, M_2) and (M_2, M_4) are $\lambda_0 \times \omega_0/\omega_0 = \lambda_0$. The CTMC is shown in Figure 13.25.

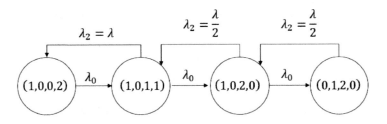

Figure 13.25   CTMC Obtained from the Net Depicted in Figure 13.22.

13.3 PERFORMANCE MODELING WITH SPN

This section presents several performance models. These examples aim to show how systems can be represented as well as support the analyst in modeling similar or more complex problems guided by the fundamental modeling constructs introduced here.

13.3.1 $M/M/1/K$ QUEUE SYSTEM

This section shows how to model through SPN an $M/M/1/k$ queue system. The reader should bear in mind that CTMC can model such a system well (see Chapters 10 and 11). Nevertheless, it important to observe the basic structures adopted to represent such a system.

The $M/M/1/k$ queue system is composed of a finite queue and one station (see Section 11.5). The interarrival and the service times are both exponentially distributed with parameters λ and μ, respectively. Figure 13.26.a shows this system queue again. The SPN depicted in Figure 13.26.b represents this system. The net is composed of two places (p_0 and p_1), and two exponentially distributed timed transitions (t_0 and t_1). Both transitions have the same firing priority levels, $\pi(t_0) = \pi(t_1) = 1$, their server semantics are sss, their rates are constant and equal to λ and μ, respectively, and they do not have guard expressions.

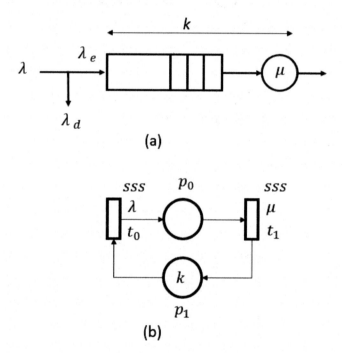

(a)

(b)

Figure 13.26 $M/M/1/k$ System and the Respective SPN.

In the initial marking, $M_0^T = (0,k)$, t_0 is the only enabled transition. M_0 shows that arrival is the only event possible, denoted by the enabling of t_0 and that no customer (or transaction) is in the system. This is represented by the number of tokens in p_1 ($m_{p_1} = 0$). In this marking, the system has k available positions, which is represented by the marking of place p_2, $m_{p_2} = k$. Firing t_0 leads to M_1 ($M_1^T = (1, k-1)$).

The token in place p_1 shows that one customer (or transaction) is in the system. The number of tokens in p_2 was reduced by one, which denotes the number of available positions in the system is now $k - 1$. M_1 enables both transitions. Since both have equal firing priority, any may be fired. If t_1 is fired, which represents a service execution, the initial marking, M_0, is reached again. If, on the other hand, t_0 is fired, a new marking is reached, M_2. In this new marking the number of tokens in p_1 is two. This represents two customers or transactions in the system. The number of available positions in the system is now $k - 2$. When the number of customers or transaction in the system is k, represented by $m_{p_1} = k$, there is no available position in the system, $m_{p_2} = 0$. Hence, no arrival is any longer possible, since t_0 is not enabled. The only possible event is the service execution (t_1 is enabled). In this marking, a new arrival would be dropped (discarded). If t_1 is fired, however, one position would be available in the system, because $m_{p_2} = 1$. The net's reachability graph is isomorphic to the CTMC depicted in Figure 11.11.b. It is worth stressing that changing the system's maximal capacity (number of positions) does not change the net structure. The only required change is the marking of place p_2. This is a clear advantage for adopting SPN instead of CTMC, particularly when k is large. This advantage is not particularly significant in this specific model ($M/M/1/k$) since the closed-form solution is available. However, this feature is relevant when the model's structure does not help to derive closed-form solutions.

The mean number of customers/transactions (**mean system size** – mss in the system can be estimated by

$$mss = \sum_{i=1}^{k} i \times \pi(m_{p_0} = i),$$ (13.3.1)

where $\pi(m_{p_0} = i)$ is the probability of place p_0 having i tokens. $\pi(m_{p_0} = i)$ is computed by

$$\pi(m_{p_0} = i) = \sum_{\forall M \in MS_i} \pi(M),$$ (13.3.2)

where MS_i is the set of markings in which place p_0 has i tokens. The notation adopted in Mercury for $\pi(m_{p_0} = i)$ is $P\{\#p_0 = i\}$. # represents the number of tokens in a place.[3]

The metric 13.3.1, mss, may be specified in Mercury notation by

$$mss = E\{\#p_0\},$$ (13.3.3)

which denotes the expected number of tokens in place p_0.

The **throughput** is estimated by the effective arrival rate (λ_e):

$$tp = \lambda_e = \lambda - \lambda_d,$$

---

[3]The notation adopted in Mercury is based on the notation proposed in TimeNet and GreatSPN [166, 428].

where λ_d is the **discard rate**, which is estimated by

$$\lambda_d = \pi(m_{p_0} = k) \times \lambda. \qquad (13.3.4)$$

In Mercury notation:

$$\lambda_d = P\{\#p_0 = k\} \times \lambda.$$

Therefore:

$$tp = \lambda \times (1 - \pi(m_{p_0} = k)). \qquad (13.3.5)$$

In Mercury notation:

$$tp = \lambda \times (1 - P\{\#p_0 = k\}).$$

The throughput can also be estimated by

$$tp = \pi(m_{p_0} > 0) \times \mu, \qquad (13.3.6)$$

that is, the probability of having tokens in the system times the service rate.

The **mean response time** (residence time) is estimated through Little's law. Therefore,

$$mrt = ass/tp = \frac{\sum_{i=1}^{k} i \times (\sum_{\forall M \in MS_i} \pi(M))}{\lambda \times (1 - P\{\#p_0 = k\})},$$

where MS_i is the set of markings in which place p_0 has i tokens.
In Mercury notation:

$$mrt = \frac{E\{\#p_0\}}{\lambda \times (1 - P\{\#p_0 = k\})}. \qquad (13.3.7)$$

The utilization is the probability that the system is busy; hence

$$u = \pi(m_{p_0} > 0). \qquad (13.3.8)$$

In Mercury notation, we have

$$u = P\{\#p_0 > 0\}.$$

From Equation 11.5.10, we know that the **mean queue size** may be estimated by

$$mqs = \sum_{i=2}^{k} (i-1) \pi_i.$$

Thus,

$$mqs = \sum_{i=2}^{k} i\,\pi_i - \sum_{i=2}^{k} \pi_i$$

$$mqs = \sum_{i=1}^{k} i\,\pi_i - \sum_{i=2}^{k} \pi_i - \pi_1$$

$$mqs = \sum_{i=1}^{k} i\,\pi_i - \sum_{i=1}^{k} \pi_i.$$

$$mqs = mss - u.$$

Hence, in Mercury notation, we have

$$mqs = E\{\#p_0\} - P\{\#p_0 > 0\}. \tag{13.3.9}$$

The **mean waiting time** is estimated through Little's law, $mqs = tp \times mwt$; thus:

$$mwt = \frac{mqs}{tp}$$

$$mwt = \frac{mss - u}{tp}$$

$$mwt = \frac{mss - u}{tp}.$$

The mean waiting time may be expressed in Mercury notation by

$$mwt = \frac{E\{\#p_0\} - P\{\#p_0 > 0\}}{\lambda \times (1 - P\{\#p_0 = k\})}. \tag{13.3.10}$$

Example 13.3.1. Consider a system composed of one server with a constant service rate equal to $\mu = 10\,tps$, and with the maximal capacity of $k = 20$ transactions. Assume the arrival traffic is a Poisson process with rate λ. The mean system size (mss) and the mean queue size (mqs) considering $\lambda \in [2, 33\,tps]$ is depicted in Figure 13.27.a. Both measures are very small for values of λ up to about $\lambda = 5\,tps$. For values in the interval $[2, 10\,tps)$ the curves' concavities are positive, and their growths are significant for $\lambda \in (5, 10\,tps)$. For values of λ above $10\,tps$, both curve concavities chance and become negative. The trends are also reduced, and each approaches a constant value.

Figure 13.27.b presents the mean response time (mean system time), mrt, and the mean waiting time, mwt, for the arrival traffic rate (λ) in the interval $[2, 33\,tps]$. The shapes of both curves are similar to those of mss and mqs.

The utilization (u) and the discard probability are presented in Figure 13.28, considering the arrival traffic rate (λ) in the interval $[2, 100\,tps]$. The utilization steadily

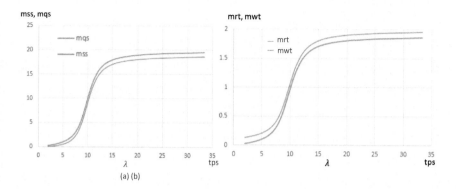

Figure 13.27 mss, mqs, mrt, $mwt \times \lambda$.

grows for values of λ up to $10tps$, when it reaches 1. The discard probability is very small for $\lambda < 10tps$. For higher values of λ, however, dp sharply increases.

The throughput (tp) and the discard rate (dr) curves are presented in Figure 13.29. The values of λ considered were in the interval $[2, 33tps]$. The throughput has an almost linear increase in the interval $[2, 10tps)$. For values of λ higher than $10tps$, $tp = 10tps$. Considering values of $\lambda \in [2, 10tps)$, the discard rate is negligible. For higher values of λ, the discard rate steadily increases with λ.

$\square$

13.3.2 MODULATED TRAFFIC

This section presents a modulated workload traffic applied to a queue system with one server and capacity k. The model presented is simple, but the same idea may be adopted for more complex modulation and traffic bursts. As the system is composed of a queue system with one server and capacity k, the model introduced in the previous section is adopted (other infrastructures could also be considered). However, the traffic arrival is modified in order to represent traffic modulation. In the example introduced here, requests are either arriving (active period) at a rate λ or not arriving (silent period).

Figure 13.30 presents two equivalent models that represents this modulated traffic arrival. The net depicted in Figure 13.30.a represents the active traffic arrival period by a token in place p_3, since t_0 is enabled while there is a token in p_3 and tokens in p_0. The net stays in that sub-marking ($m_{p_3} = 1$) until t_2 fires. The time assigned to t_2 is equal to the active time period, at. When it fires, a token is removed from p_3, and one token is stored in p_2. This new marking disables t_0, and no request arrives until t_3 fires. The time assigned to t_3 is equal to the silent time period (st). When t_3 fires, a new active period begins, and new requests are allowed to arrive. The model presented in Figure 13.30.b uses a self-loop instead of adopting an inhibitor arc. As

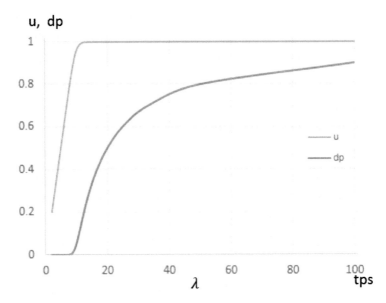

u, dp

Figure 13.28 $u, dp \times \lambda$.

the system infrastructure was already introduced in the previous section, the metrics expressions of these models are also the same as presented in Section 13.3.1.

Example 13.3.2. Consider a queue system of capacity $k = 20$ composed of one server with the service time exponential distributed with rate $\mu = 10tptu$ [4]. The request arrival is a one-off process with active periods exponentially distributed with expected value equal to $5t.u.$ and silent periods exponentially distributed with expected value equal to $2t.u.$. When the traffic is on (active period), the arrival obeys a Poisson process with rate $\lambda = 8tptu$. The steady-state values of the metrics are presented in Table 13.3.

Figure 13.31 presents the mean system size as a function of the silent period (inactive period). Here, the silent period was considered in the interval $st \in [0.01t.u., 1t.u.]$ and all other parameters were kept constant. The figures show that the mean system size decreases as the silent period increases. □

13.3.3 $M/M/M/K$ QUEUE SYSTEM

This section presents two equivalent SPNs that represent a $M/M/m/k$ queue system. Again, the section aims to provide the basic modeling structures adopted to represent this and more complex systems. The two models are presented in Figure 13.32.

---
[4]tptu - transaction per time unity.

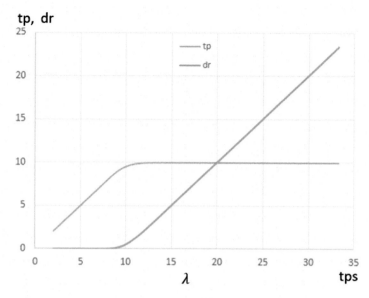

Figure 13.29 $tp, dr \times \lambda$.

Table 13.3
Results – Queue System with Modulated Traffic

Measure	Value
mss	$2.2526\,trans.$
mqs	$1.6817\,trans.$
dp	6.6818×10^{-4}
dr	$0.0053\,tptu$
tp	$7.9947\,tptu$
mrt	$0.2818\,t.u.$
mwt	$0.2104\,t.u.$
u	0.5709

However, let us first discuss the net presented in Figure 13.32.a. This net is very much similar to the net that represents the $M/M/1/k$ system, shown in Figure 13.26. There are two main differences that should be stressed: the self-loop represented by place p_2 and transition t_1, and the server semantics of transition t_1 that now is *iss*. The number of tokens in place p_2 represents the number of stations (processors) of the system. The server semantics $(k - server)$ is modeled using the structure introduced in the net shown in Figure 13.12, and the respective embedded Markov chain is similar to the one presented in Figure 11.14.

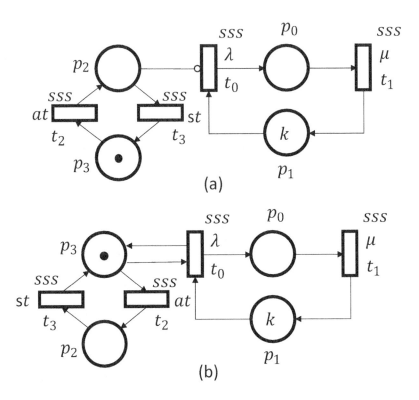

Figure 13.30 Modulated Traffic.

The mean system size is estimated by

$$mss = E\{\#p_1\}. \tag{13.3.11}$$

Taking the CTMC presented in 11.14 into account, the mean queue size may be estimated by

$$mqs = \sum_{i=m}^{k} (i-m)\,\pi_i,$$

where π_i is the probability of being in marking (state) i. π_i is also equal to the probability of place p_1 having i tokens, $P\{\#p_1 = i\}$. Hence

$$mqs = \sum_{i=1}^{k} (i-m)\,\pi_i - \sum_{i=1}^{m-1} (i-m)\,\pi_i.$$

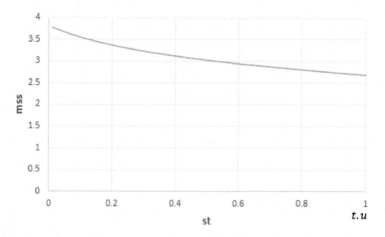

Figure 13.31 Mean System Size × Silent Period – Modulated Traffic.

$$mqs = \sum_{i=1}^{k} i\,\pi_i - m\sum_{i=1}^{k} \pi_i - \sum_{i=1}^{m-1} i\,\pi_i + m\sum_{i=1}^{m-1} \pi_i.$$

$$mqs = \sum_{i=1}^{k} i\,\pi_i - m\sum_{i=m}^{k} \pi_i - \sum_{i=1}^{m-1} i\,\pi_i.$$

Considering the SPN depicted in Figure 13.32.a, and using the Mercury-like notation, we have

$$mqs = E\{\#p_1\} - m \times P\{\#p_1 \geq m\} - \sum_{i=1}^{m-1} i \times P\{\#p_1 = i\}. \tag{13.3.12}$$

The discard probability is estimated by

$$dp = P\{\#p_1 = k\}, \tag{13.3.13}$$

and the discard rate is

$$dr = \lambda \times P\{\#p_1 = k\}, \tag{13.3.14}$$

where λ is the arrival rate, and $P\{\#p_1 = k\}$ is the probability of a full system. As the throughput is estimated by $tp = \lambda - dr$, then

$$tp = \lambda(1 - P\{\#p_1 = k\}). \tag{13.3.15}$$

The mean system time (*mst* – mean response time) and the mean waiting time (*mwt*) are estimated through Little's law; hence :

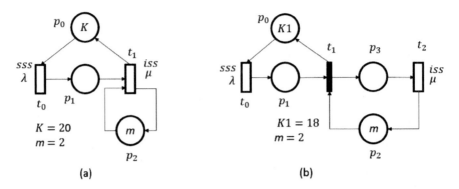

Figure 13.32 SPNs for $M/M/m/k$ Queue System.

$$mst = \frac{mss}{tp}.$$

$$mst = \frac{E\{\#p_1\}}{\lambda(1 - P\{\#p_1 = k\})}. \tag{13.3.16}$$

$$mwt = \frac{mqs}{tp}.$$

$$mwt = \frac{E\{\#p_1\} - m \times P\{\#p_1 \geq m\} - \sum_{i=1}^{m-1} i \times P\{\#p_1 = i\}}{\lambda(1 - P\{\#p_1 = k\})}. \tag{13.3.17}$$

The utilization may be estimated by

$$u = P\{\#p_1 \geq m\} + \frac{\sum_{i=1}^{m-1} P\{\#p_1 = i\}}{m}, \tag{13.3.18}$$

where m is the number of stations or processors.

Now let us consider the net depicted in Figure 13.32.b. This net represents the system in two parts: queue and stations. The system capacity is the number of tokens of place p_0 plus the number of tokens of place p_0 at the initial marking, $k = k_1 + m$. The number of tokens in p_1 denotes the number of transactions in the queue, and the number of tokens in p_3 is the number of transactions being served. Transition t_1 is immediate; hence as soon as a token is stored in p_1 and if there is a token in p_2, t_1 is fired. As in the previous model, the server semantics of t_2 is *iss*. The mean system size is estimated by

$$mss = E\{\#p_1\} + E\{\#p_3\}. \tag{13.3.19}$$

The mean queue size is estimated by

$$mqs = E\{\#p_1\}. \tag{13.3.20}$$

The discard probability is estimated by

$$dp = P\{(\#p_1 = k) \wedge (\#p_3 = m)\}^5, \tag{13.3.21}$$

and the discard rate is

$$dr = \lambda \times P\{(\#p_1 = k) \wedge (\#p_3 = m)\}, \tag{13.3.22}$$

where λ is the arrival rate, and $P\{(\#p_1 = k) \wedge (\#p_3 = m)\}$ is the probability of a full system.

As the throughput is estimated by $tp = \lambda - dr$, then

$$tp = \lambda(1 - P\{(\#p_1 = k) \wedge (\#p_3 = m)\}). \tag{13.3.23}$$

The mean system time is estimated by $mst = mss/tp$:

$$mst = \frac{E\{\#p_1\} + E\{\#p_3\}}{\lambda(1 - P\{(\#p_1 = k) \wedge (\#p_3 = m)\})}. \tag{13.3.24}$$

The mean waiting time is estimated by $mwt = mqs/tp$:

$$mwt = \frac{E\{\#p_1\}}{\lambda(1 - P\{(\#p_1 = k) \wedge (\#p_3 = m)\})}. \tag{13.3.25}$$

The utilization may be estimated by

$$u = \frac{E\{\#p_3\}}{m}. \tag{13.3.26}$$

Example 13.3.3. A server was monitored for $600s$ under a specific workload. In this period, 4800 transactions were executed in the system, and the processor's average utilization was 0.8. The time between transactions' arrival was exponentially distributed with rate $\lambda = 8tps$. The mean time the processor spends processing a transaction may be estimated through the demand law (8.3.1), which states that

$$D_{trans,cpu} = \frac{U_{cpu}}{X_{system}},$$

---

[5] In Mercury $\wedge$ is represented by *AND* and $\vee$ by *OR*.

where U_{cpu} is the average processor utilization, and X_{system} is the observed throughput. Therefore, $D_{trans,cpu} = 0.1\,s$, since $X_{system} = 4800trans./600\,s = 8tps$, and $U_{cpu} = 0.8$. Considering the time to process a transaction is exponentially distributed, the service rate may be estimated by

$$\mu = \frac{1}{D_{trans,cpu}} = 10tps.$$

Now, consider that instead of one server, the system is composed of two identical servers and that transactions requests are equally assigned to each server. The system also has one queue with a capacity of storing 18 transaction requests. Assuming the description given, the following metrics should be estimated: mss, mqs, dp, dr, tp, mst, mwt, and u. Both models presented provide the same results. These results are presented in Table 13.4.

Table 13.4
Results - $M/M/2/20$ **SPN**

Measure	Value
mss	$0.95238\,trans.$
mqs	$0.15238\,trans.$
dp	9.42439×10^{-9}
dr	$7.53951 \times 10^{-8}\,tps$
tp	$\approx 8tps$
mst	$0.11905\,s$
mwt	$0.01905\,s$
u	≈ 0.4

$\square$

13.3.4 QUEUE SYSTEM WITH DISTINCT CLASSES OF STATIONS

This section presents an SPN that represents a queue system with distinct classes of stations (processors). The basic modeling structures aim at supporting the reader to acquire the skill to represent this and similar classes of systems. In this specific case, a system with two classes of stations is considered (Class a and Class b), and each class has m_a and m_b stations, respectively. One shared queue (queue capacity $= k > 0$) stores the requests, which are then assigned to the particular class of stations with probability pr_a and pr_b. This queue system is depicted in Figure 13.33. The time between request arrivals follows an exponential distribution with rate λ, and the service times of each station class also obey exponential distributions with rates μ_a (Class a) and μ_b (Class b).

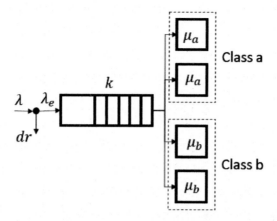

Figure 13.33 Queue System with Two Classes of Stations.

At the initial marking of the net depicted in Figure 13.34, the only enabled transition is t_0, which its firing denotes as a transaction request. This transition is enabled as long as there are tokens in p_0. The number of tokens in p_0 denotes the number of available positions in the input queue. When t_0 fires, one token is removed from p_0 (this represents that one less position is available in the queue), and one token is stored in p_1. Tokens in p_1 represent requests waiting to be processed. If tokens are in p_1 and $m_{p_3} > 0$ and $m_{p_5} > 0$ (stations of each class are available), t_1 and t_2 are firable. One should bear in mid that immediate transitions have higher priorities than timed ones. Hence, even if t_0 is enabled, it is not firable. The probability of firing t_1 and t_2 is calculated from their weights (ω_1 and ω_2), where $pr_1 = \omega_1/(\omega_1 + \omega_2)$ and $pr_2 = \omega_2/(\omega_1 + \omega_2)$. Let us consider that t_1 is fired. Its firing, removes one token from p_1 and p_3, and stores one token in p_0 (a new position is made available in the queue) and one token in p_2. The token in p_2 denotes that one transaction is being executed in one station of *Class a*. The firing of t_1 removed one token from p_3, which represents that less one station (processor) is available for processing new arrivals. The token in p_2 enables t_3. The firing of t_3 represents the transaction processing. This firing, removes one token from p_2 (a transactions was processed) and stores one token in p_3, which denotes that one station of *Class a* is made available. When at least one token is p_1 and $m_{p_3} > 0$ and $m_{p_5} > 0$, if instead of t_1, t_2 is fired a similar process is executed. The only difference is that *Class b* stations are used. The server semantics of t_3 and t_4 are *iss* for implementing *k-server* semantics, since more than one station may be available for processing. The server semantics of t_0 is *sss*.

The SPN shown in Figure 13.35 is equivalent to the model presented in Figure 13.34. This new model, uses guard expressions assigned to transitions t_0, t_1, and t_2, instead of places, for limiting the number of tokens in places p_1, p_2, and p_4. The guard expression $\#p_1 < k$ prevents the firing of t_0 when $m_{p_1} = k$. Likewise, the guards of t_1 ($\#p_2 < m_1$) and t_2 ($\#p_4 < m_2$) disable each of these transitions when $m_{p_2} = m_1$

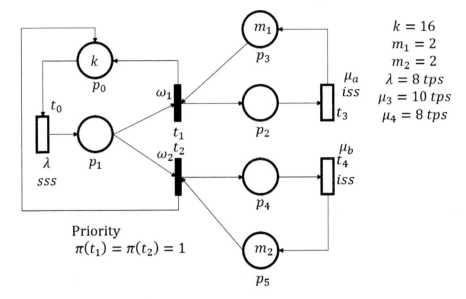

Figure 13.34   A Model for the System with Distinct Classes of Stations.

and $m_{p_4} = m_2$, respectively. The names of places and transitions in the net depicted in Figure 13.35 are the same as the equivalent places and transitions of the net in Figure 13.34. This way, the metric expressions presented in the following works for both models.

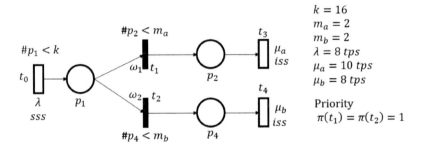

Figure 13.35   A Second Model for the System with Distinct Classes of Stations.

The mean system size (*mss*) and the mean queue size (*mqs*) measures may be estimated through the following expressions:

$$mss = E\{\#p_1\} + E\{\#p_2\} + E\{\#p_4\} \tag{13.3.27}$$

and

$$mqs = E\{\#p_1\}. \tag{13.3.28}$$

The discard probability and the discard rate may be estimated by

$$dp = P\{(\#p_1 + \#p_2 + \#p_4) = (k + s_1 + s_2)\} \tag{13.3.29}$$

and

$$dr = P\{(\#p_1 + \#p_2 + \#p_4) = (k + s_1 + s_2)\} \times \lambda. \tag{13.3.30}$$

These metrics may also be estimated by

$$dp = P\{(\#p_1 = k) \wedge (\#p_2 = s_1) \wedge (\#p_4 = s_2)\} \tag{13.3.31}$$

and

$$dr = P\{(\#p_1 = k) \wedge (\#p_2 = s_1) \wedge (\#p_4 = s_2)\} \times \lambda. \tag{13.3.32}$$

The throughput may be estimated by the difference between the arrival rate and the discard rate ($tp = \lambda - dr$); hence the throughput can be computed from

$$tp = \lambda \times (1 - P\{(\#p_1 + \#p_2 + \#p_4) = (k + s_1 + s_2)\}). \tag{13.3.33}$$

The throughput may also be computed from the summation throughputs of each class of stations. The throughput of the *Class a* station may be estimated by

$$tp_a = \sum_{i=1}^{m_a} P\{\#p_2 = i\} \times i \times \mu_a.$$

Likewise, the throughput of the *Class b* station may be estimated by

$$tp_b = \sum_{i=1}^{m_b} P\{\#p_4 = i\} \times i \times \mu_b.$$

Therefore

$$tp = \sum_{i=1}^{m_a} P\{\#p_2 = i\} \times i \times \mu_a + \sum_{i=1}^{m_b} P\{\#p_4 = i\} \times i \times \mu_b. \tag{13.3.34}$$

The mean response time (or mean system time) may be estimated by $mrt = mss/tp$; thus:

$$mrt = \frac{E\{\#p_1\} + E\{\#p_2\} + E\{\#p_4\}}{\lambda \times (1 - P\{(\#p_1 + \#p_2 + \#p_4) = (k + m_1 + m_2)\})}, \qquad (13.3.35)$$

and the mean waiting time may be computed through:

$$mwt = \frac{E\{\#p_1\}}{\lambda \times (1 - P\{(\#p_1 + \#p_2 + \#p_4) = (k + m_1 + m_2)\})}. \qquad (13.3.36)$$

The utilization of stations or processors of each class may be computed using these expressions:

$$u_a = \frac{E\{\#p_2\}}{m_a}, \qquad (13.3.37)$$

$$u_b = \frac{E\{\#p_4\}}{m_b}. \qquad (13.3.38)$$

Example 13.3.4. Let us consider a system composed of two classes of servers, each class having two servers, and one shared input queue. This system is well represented by the model shown in Figure 13.34. Assuming the arrival rate $\lambda = 8\,tps$, the queue maximal capacity $k = 16$, and the service rates of each class as $\mu_a = 4\,tps$ and $\mu_b = 2\,tps$, provide the respective results of the measures mss, mqs, tp, mrt, mwt, u_a, and u_b, taking into account the probability assignment to each processor class is the same.

Table 13.5
Results – System with Distinct Classes of Stations

Measure	Value
mss	$3.52453\,trans.$
mqs	$0.78196\,trans.$
tp	$7.9984\,tps$
mrt	$0.44065\,s$
mwt	$0.09776\,s$
u_a	0.62831
u_b	0.74297

Figure 13.36 shows how the utilization varies with $\omega_0 \in [0.5, 3.8]$. In this experiment, ω_1 was considered constant and equal to 1. Figure 13.36 also presents the transaction to station assignment probability as function of the transitions weights.

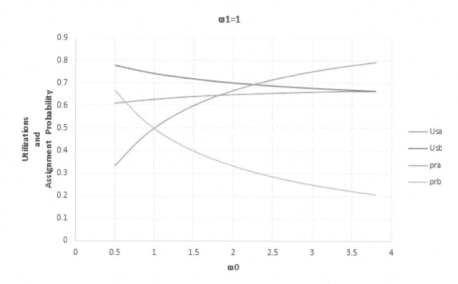

Figure 13.36 u_a, u_b, pr_a and $pr_b \times \omega_0$.

☐

13.3.5 QUEUE SYSTEM WITH BREAKDOWN

This section presents a model for queues with failures. As an example, let us consider the $M/M/m/k$ queue system represented in Section 13.3.3. In that system, servers were considered failure-free. Now, however, let us assume the servers may fail. The new model is depicted in Figure 13.37. Transition t_0 firing denotes a request, and the firing of t_1 represents the service execution. The number of requests in the system (represented by the number of tokens in p_1) is limited to the queue capacity (k_q) and the number of available (non-failed) servers (m_{p_2} – in Mercury notation: #p_2). The system capacity is $k = k_q + m$. This is specified by the guard expression assigned to transition t_0, which is #$p_1 < (k_q + \#p_2)$. In this particular example, failures and repairs are both exponentially distributed with rate λ_f and μ_r, respectively. Servers' failures and repairs are denoted by the firing of transitions t_3 and t_4, respectively.

We also consider that all servers (m) are available at the initial marking ($m_{p_2}^0 = m$). Therefore, servers may fail. As mentioned, a failure (represented by t_3 firing), removes one token from p_3 and stores one token in p_3. As m servers may be operational (at initial marking), the concurrent server failures are represented by the semantics assigned to t_3 (*iss*). Repairs are represented by the t_4 firing. In this specific

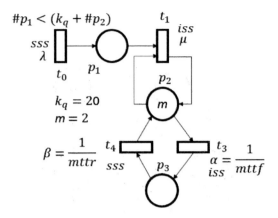

Figure 13.37 $M/M/m/k$ Queue System with Breakdown.

example, only one repair team is considered. Hence the server semantics assigned to t_4 is sss. The reader should bear in mind that server failures reduce the maximal enabling degree of t_1 (because it removes tokens from p_2); hence affecting the system throughput and other related performance measures. Repairs, on the other hand, increase the maximal enabling degree of transition t_1, since tokens are added to p_2.

Example 13.3.5. Let us consider a system composed of m servers of one class. The service time is exponentially distributed with rate $\mu = 10\,tps$. The arrival rate is constant and equal to $\lambda = 9.8039\,tps$, and the failure rate is also constant and equal to $\lambda_f = 3.47222 \times 10^{-7}$ failures per second. An experiment was conducted for $mttr \in (1000\,s, 15000\,s)$. The mean system size ($mss$) and the discard rate ($dr$) are depicted in Figure 13.38. The reader can observe that the mean system size increases with the $mttr$. The discard rate also increases with the $mttr$, since the longer the $mttr$, the longer the servers' unavailability (see Figure 13.39). Here, the unavailability ($ua = 1 - a$) is presented in numbers of nines ($\#9s = -\log ua$ - a is the availability). The availability may be calculated through

$$a = P\{\#p_2 > 0\}. \tag{13.3.39}$$

□

13.3.6 QUEUE SYSTEM WITH PRIORITY

This section presents an SPN that represents a queue system with two classes of stations and different priorities for assigning requests to the station classes. The system is composed of one shared input queue with capacity k_q, and m_a stations of *Class a*, and m_b stations of *Class b* (Figure 13.40.a). The SPN that represents this system is depicted in Figure 13.40.b. The net initial marking shows the system with no

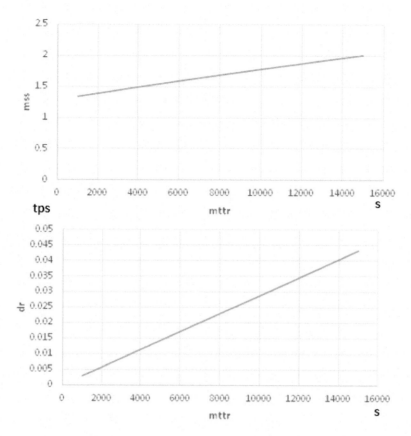

Figure 13.38 $M/M/m/k$ Queue System with Breakdown – *mss* and *dr* × *mttr*.

transaction request. Thus, the only firable transition is t_0, which denotes a request arrival. t_0 is enabled because its guard expression is evaluated as true, since $m_{p_1} > k_q$ ($\#p_1 > k_q$).

When t_0 fires, one token is stored in p_1. Tokens in p_1 may enable t_1 and t_2. These transitions would be enabled if $m_{p_2} > m_a$ and $m_{p_4} > m_b$ ($(\#p_1 > m_a)$ and $(\#p_4 > m_b)$ in Mercury notation), respectively. If these conditions are satisfied, their respective guard expressions are evaluated as true. Let us assume that both transitions are enabled. As the firing priority of t_2 is higher than the firing priority of t_1, only t_2 is firable. Firing t_2, removes one token from p_1 and stores one token in p_4. In this new marking, either t_0 or t_4 may fire. If t_4 fires (it denotes a *Class b* service execution), the token is removed from p_4, and the net gets back to its initial marking.

Now consider the marking $m_{p_1} = n$ ($0 < n < k_q, n \in \mathbb{Z}$), $m_{p_4} = m_b$, and $m_{p_2} = 0$. This marking enables only t_1. Its firing removes a token from p_1 and stores one token in p_2. In this new marking both t_0 and t_3 are enabled. If t_3 is fired (a *Class a* service

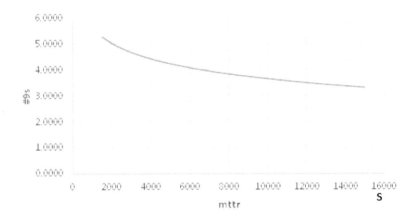

Figure 13.39 $M/M/m/k$ Queue System with Breakdown – *Unvailabiliy* (in number of 9s) × *mttr*.

execution), one token is removed from p_2. The performance metrics expressions are the same as those presented in Section 13.3.4, since places and transitions of the SPN introduced here have the same names as the models depicted there.

It is worth stressing that *Class b* services have priority over the *Class a* services, and that this service execution priority is specified in the net through the firing priorities assigned to t_1 and t_2.

Example 13.3.6. Let us consider a system composed of two classes of servers like the one depicted in Example 13.3.4. The system is composed of four processors, each class having two servers, and one shared input queue. This system is specified by the model shown in Figure 13.40. Let us assume the arrival rate $\lambda = 8\,tps$, the queue maximal capacity $k = 16$, and the service rates of each class as $\mu_a = 4\,tps$ and $\mu_b = 2\,tps$. The transaction assignment priorities are $\pi(t_1) = 1$ (*Class a* assignment priority) and $\pi(t_2) = 2$ (*Class b* assignment priority) for each processor class, respectively. The mean system size, the mean queue size, the average throughput, the mean response time, the mean waiting time, and the processor utilization are provided in Table 13.6. It is important to highlight the processors´ utilization in comparison with the results of the Example 13.3.4. *Class b* servers have higher utilization than *Class a* servers.

□

13.3.7 OPEN TANDEM QUEUE SYSTEM WITH BLOCKING

This section presents an SPN for an open tandem queueing network with two $M/M/1/k$ nodes (N_1 and N_2). Each node has one server and one input bounded

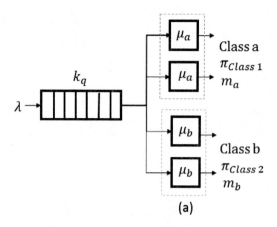

(a)

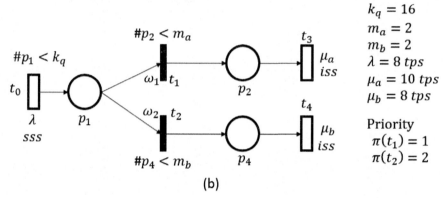

(b)

Figure 13.40 Queue System with Priority.

Table 13.6
Results – System with Distinct Classes of Stations and Different Assignment Priorities

Measure	Value
mss	$3.65176\,trans.$
mqs	$0.81940\,trans.$
tp	$7.99832\,tps$
mrt	$0.45657\,s$
mwt	$0.10245\,s$
u_a	0.58340
u_b	0.83278

queue (see Figure 13.41.a). Each node is capable of holding k_1 and k_2 jobs, respectively. Transaction requests arrive at node N_1 according to a Poisson process with rate λ. When Server 1 finishes processing a request, it delivers it to be processed by N_2. This request only is accepted if there is an available position in N_2's queue. If no position is available in N_2, Server 1 is blocked, and it stays blocked until a position in node N_2 becomes available. The service times of each server are exponentially distributed with rates μ_1 and μ_2, respectively. Figure 13.41.b represents the queue system. A CTMC model was presented in Example 10.8.8 for the case $k_1 = k_2 = 2$.

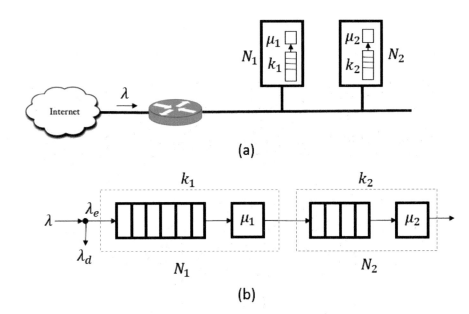

Figure 13.41 Open Two Nodes Tandem Queue System.

The net depicted in Figure 13.42 is a performance model of the system described in Figure 13.41. Transition t_0 represents the arrival process. Its server semantics is *sss* and the respective rate is λ. The capacity of N_1 is represented by the initial number of tokens in place p_1 ($m_{p_1}^0 = k_1$). The number of tokens in p_0 denotes the number of transaction requests in node N_1. The service rate of node N_1 is assigned to transition t_1 (μ_1). Likewise, the capacity of N_2 is specified by the initial number of tokens in place p_3 ($m_{p_3}^0 = k_2$), the number of tokens in p_2 depicts the number of requests in node N_2, and the node N_2 service rate is assigned to transition t_2 (μ_2). The server semantics of t_1 and t_2 are also *sss*.

The discard rate ($dr = \lambda_d$) is computed by the product of the probability of node N_1 being full ($P\{\#p_0 = k_1\}$) and the arrival rate (λ); thus

$$dr = P\{\#p_0 = k_1\} \times \lambda. \tag{13.3.40}$$

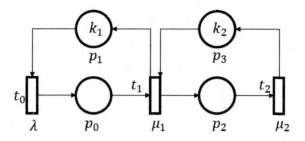

Figure 13.42 SPN for the Tandem Queue System.

The discard probability is equal to the probability of node N_1 being full

$$dp = P\{\#p_0 = k_1\}. \tag{13.3.41}$$

The node N_1 throughput can be estimated either by the difference between the arrival rate (λ) and the discard rate (dr), that is $tp_{N_1} = \lambda_e = \lambda - \lambda_d$, which is

$$tp_{N_1} = \lambda(1 - P\{\#p_0 = k_1\}) \tag{13.3.42}$$

or by multiplying the probability of t_1 being enabled by its rate (μ_1)

$$tp_{N_1} = P\{\#p_0 > 0\} \times \mu_1. \tag{13.3.43}$$

The node N_2 throughput can be computed by the product of the probability of t_2 being enabled by its rate (μ_2)

$$tp_{N_2} = P\{\#p_2 > 0\} \times \mu_2. \tag{13.3.44}$$

The mean number of requests in N_1 and N_2 is

$$mnr_{N_1} = E\{\#p_0\} \tag{13.3.45}$$

and

$$mnr_{N_2} = E\{\#p_2\}, \tag{13.3.46}$$

respectively.

Hence, the mean number of requests in the system (mss – mean system size) is estimated by

$$mss = mnr_{N_1} + mnr_{N_2}.$$

$$mss = E\{\#p_0\} + E\{\#p_2\}. \tag{13.3.47}$$

The mean response time of node N_1 and N_2 is

$$mrt_{N_1} = \frac{mnr_{N_1}}{tp_{N_1}} = \frac{E\{\#p_0\}}{P\{\#p_0 > 0\} \times \mu_1} = \frac{E\{\#p_0\}}{\lambda(1 - P\{\#p_0 = k_1\})}. \tag{13.3.48}$$

and

$$mrt_{N_2} = \frac{mnr_{N_2}}{tp_{N_2}} = \frac{E\{\#p_2\}}{P\{\#p_2 > 0\} \times \mu_2}. \tag{13.3.49}$$

Therefore, the system mean response time is tallied by

$$mrt = mrt_{N_1} + mrt_{N_2},$$

which can be expressed either by

$$mrt = \frac{E\{\#p_0\}}{P\{\#p_0 > 0\} \times \mu_1} + \frac{E\{\#p_2\}}{P\{\#p_2 > 0\} \times \mu_2} \tag{13.3.50}$$

or

$$mrt = \frac{E\{\#p_0\}}{\lambda(1 - P\{\#p_0 = k_1\})} + \frac{E\{\#p_2\}}{P\{\#p_2 > 0\} \times \mu_2}. \tag{13.3.51}$$

Let us consider a configuration in which $k_1 = 30$, $k_2 = 20$, $\mu_1 = 0.1 tps$ and $\mu_2 = 0.125 tps$. The CTMC generated from SPN has 651 states. Table 13.7 presents the evaluation results of the metrics described above for $\lambda \in \{0.05 tps, 0.0625 tps, 0.2 tps\}$.

Table 13.7
Results – Configuration: $k_1 = 30$, $k_2 = 20$, $\mu_1 = 0.1 tps$, $\mu_2 = 0.125 tps$.

Measure	$\lambda = 0.05 tps$	$\lambda = 0.0625 tps$	$\lambda = 0.2 tps$
dr (tps)	2.4531×10^{-11}	1.7792×10^{-8}	1.0023×10^{-1}
tp_{N1} (tps)	5.0000×10^{-2}	6.2500×10^{-2}	9.9767×10^{-2}
tp_{N2} (tps)	5.0000×10^{-2}	6.2501×10^{-2}	9.9768×10^{-2}
mss (trans.)	1.6667	2.6667	32.8109
mrt (s)	8.3335×10^{-2}	1.6667×10^{-1}	3.2802

The results presented in Column 2 of Table 13.7 are pretty much close to the open tandem queueing network without blocking (infinite queues), since in this case $\lambda < \mu_1$, $\lambda < \mu_2$, and k_1 and k_2 are relatively large, which makes the discard rate very small ($dr = 2.4531 \times 10^{-11}$).

Now, consider a configuration in which $k_1 = 3$ and $k_2 = 2$. Table 13.8 shows the evaluation results of the metrics for the same values of λ. The CTMC generated (from the SPN) for this configuration has only 12 states; thus it could be easily represented directly though CTMC. For the previous configuration, however, it would be much more challenging.

Table 13.8

Results – Configuration: $k_1 = 3$, $k_2 = 2$, $\mu_1 = 0.1\,tps$, $\mu_2 = 0.125\,tps$

Measure	$\lambda = 0.05\,tps$	$\lambda = 0.0625\,tps$	$\lambda = 0.2\,tps$
dr (tps)	4.3254×10^{-3}	9.0601×10^{-3}	1.2697×10^{-1}
tp_{N1} (tps)	4.5675×10^{-2}	5.3440×10^{-2}	7.3028×10^{-2}
tp_{N2} (tps)	4.5675×10^{-2}	5.3440×10^{-2}	7.3028×10^{-2}
mss (trans.)	1.3247	1.6985	3.3410
mrt (s)	6.6030×10^{-2}	1.0180×10^{-1}	3.0566×10^{-1}

13.3.8 MODELING PHASE-TYPE DISTRIBUTIONS

One of the reasons for adopting exponential distribution for modeling performance of systems is the mathematical tractability that flows from the memoryless property of this distribution [413]. Nevertheless, on many occasions, this is not enough to overcome the need to model systems that are not well represented by an exponential distribution. This leads us to explore more general distributions that can represent such systems while keeping some tractability of the exponential distributions [305]. A phase-type distribution (also called polyexponential or expolynominal distributions) is a probability distribution constructed by phases of exponential distributions. These distributions were introduced in Chapter 2. This section presents a set of SPN that represent some specific phase-type distributions. Here, the specific distributions considered are Erlang, hypoexponential, hyperexponential, Cox-1, and Cox-2 distributions.

Phase-type distribution is very useful for representing empirical distributions based on their expectation and variance [102]. Table 13.9 shows which phase-type distribution may represent the empirical distributions based on the inverse of the coefficient of variation ($1/CV$).

Consider that a resource was monitored during a period. A sample of the time demanded for a specific transaction to be executed in that resource was registered. This sample provides an empirical distribution ($F_E(t)$) of the time required to execute that type of transaction (T) in the monitored resource. The sample mean (first moment about the origin - $\overline{T}$) and its variance (second central moment - $Var(T)$) can be used to obtain the respective parameters of the equivalent phase-type distribution obtained according to the Table 13.9, since $SD(T) = Var(T)^{1/2}$, and $CV(T) = SD(T)/\overline{T}$. The

Table 13.9
Fitting Empirical Distributions to Phase-Type Distribution Based on Moments

Cases	$n = (1/CV)^2$	Distributions
Case 1	$n = 1$	Exponential
Case 2	$n \in \mathbb{Z}, n > 1$	Erlang or Cox-1
Case 3	$n \in \mathbb{R}, n \notin \mathbb{Z}, n > 1$	Hypoexponential or Cox-1
Case 4	$n < 1$	Hyperexponential or Cox-2

respective phase-type distribution parameters can be obtained by matching the algebraic expressions of the mean (E_{pt}), and the standard deviation (SD_{pt})[6], that is

$$E_{pt} = \overline{T}$$

and

$$SD_{pt} = SD(T).$$

In general, many phase-type distributions may be obtained for each specific case. The models presented here, however, aim at reducing the number of phases of each model.

13.3.8.1 Erlang Distribution

This section presents an SPN that represents the time of transaction or service specified by an Erlang distribution ($Erl(\gamma, \lambda)$), where γ is the number of phases and λ is the rate. The Erlang distribution may be specified by γ sequential phases of exponential distributions, each phase having rate λ_i. Its cumulative distribution function is

$$F_{Erl}(t) = 1 - \sum_{i=0}^{\gamma-1} \frac{e^{-\lambda t}(\lambda t)^i}{i!}, \quad t \geq 0 \; \gamma = 1, 2, \dots \tag{13.3.52}$$

where

$$E_{Erl} = \frac{\gamma}{\lambda} \tag{13.3.53}$$

and

$$Var_{Erl} = \frac{\gamma}{\lambda^2}. \tag{13.3.54}$$

---

[6] *pt* denotes Erlang, hypoexponential, hyperexponential, Cox-1, and Cox-2.

An empirical distribution can be approximated by an Erlang distribution when the coefficient of variation is smaller than one, and its inverse is an integer (Case 2 depicted in Table 13.9). The Erlang parameters can be estimated by matching

$$E_{Erl} = \overline{T}$$

and

$$Var_{Erl} = SD(T)^2.$$

Hence, Erlang distribution parameters are estimated by:

$$\gamma = \left(\frac{\overline{T}}{SD(T)} \right)^2 \tag{13.3.55}$$

$$\lambda = \frac{\gamma}{\overline{T}} = \frac{\overline{T}}{SD(T)^2}. \tag{13.3.56}$$

Figure 13.43.a presents a generically distributed timed transition that is later specified by a an Erlang distribution with γ phase and rate λ. The Erlang distribution is represented by the net depicted in Figure 13.43.b. The places p_0 and p_1 of the net of Figure 13.43.a are also represented in the model shown in Figure 13.43.b. The generic transition is refined by transition t_0, t_1, and t_2, places p_2 and p_2, and their respective arcs. It is important to stress the weight (γ) assigned to the arcs (t_0, p_2) and (p_3, t_2). The server semantics of transition t_1 is sss, and its rate is λ. Thus, its respective delay is $1/\lambda$. This net is a generic model that could be simplified or modified when modeling specific problems or systems.

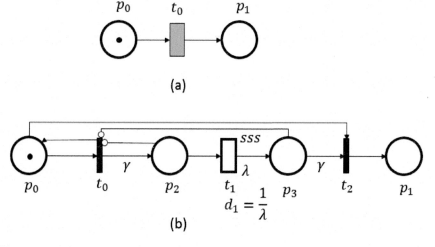

Figure 13.43   SPN for Erlang Distribution with γ Phases and Rate equal to λ.

When a token is stored in place p_0, it enables t_0. Firing t_0 removes one token from p_0, stores one token back in place p_0, and stores γ tokens in p_2. Storing back a token in place p_0 allows correctly representing firing policies (**race policy**) when conflicting activities are enabled, since the subnet is kept enabled until its completion. Such a strategy is adopted for all phase-type models represented in the subsequent sections. Tokens in p_2 and p_3 disable t_0. In this marking, only t_1 is enabled. Its enabling degree is γ. Hence, it fires γ times. After these firings, γ tokens are stored in p_3. This new marking enables t_2, since $m_{p_0} = 1$ and $m_{p_0} = \gamma$. Firing t_2 removes one token from p_0 and γ tokens from p_2, and stores one token in p_1. Considering the initial marking, the time for one token to reach place p_1 is distributed according to an Erlang distribution with γ phase and rate λ.

The time to process a request in a server was measured during an observation period, and a sample was recorded. The mean time to process and the respective standard deviation were estimated based on that sample. The estimates were $\overline{T} = 40\,ms$, $SD(T) = 20\,ms$. Since $1/CV = 2$, the Erlang distribution with 4 phases and rate $0.1\,tpms$ is suitable to represent the time to process such requests, because

$$\gamma = \left(\frac{\overline{T}}{SD(T)} \right)^2 = \left(\frac{40\,ms}{20\,ms} \right)^2 = 4,$$

and

$$\lambda = \frac{\overline{T}}{SD(T)^2} = \frac{40\,ms}{400\,ms^2} = 0.1\,tpms.$$

The net depicted above may represent this distribution by setting $\gamma = 4$ and $\lambda = 0.1\,tpms$. Using the Mercury tool, the time for a token to reach place p_1 (from the initial marking – $M_0^T = (1,0,0,0)$) was computed as well as the probability of place p_1 having one token up to time t. This measures were calculated through numerical transient analysis (uniformization method – see Section 10.5.4). The mean time to absorption ($mtta$) was $40\,ms$.. Figure 13.44 shows the probability distribution of the time to absorption, that is the time a token takes to reach place p_1. From this distribution we can compute, for instance, the probability of a token reaching place p_1 by $t = 50\,ms$, which is 0.735. The median time to absorption can also be easily obtained, $mdta = 36.72\,ms$ (see Section 3.2) and other order statistics.

Now, let us consider an $M/E/1/k$ queue system depicted in Figure 13.45.a. The net presented in Figure 13.45.b is a high-level representation of the queue system, in which the service time is denoted by the generic transition t_2. This net is similar to the one described in Section 13.3.1. A refined model from this "abstract" model is represented by the SPN shown in Figure 13.45.c. The Poisson traffic arrival is represented by transition t_1 firing. Transition t_1 is only enabled if the system is not full, which is represented by tokens p_1. If no token is present in p_1, the system is full. Place p_2 represents the queue, and the token in p_2 depicts the number of requests waiting to be served. The generic transition t_2 (in gray) is refined places p_3, p_4, and p_5, transitions t_2, t_3, and t_4, and their arcs. This subnet is slightly different from the

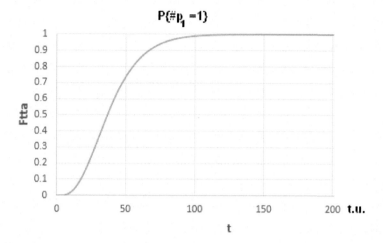

Figure 13.44 Distribution of the Time for a Token to Teach Place p_1 – Erlang Model.

one depicted in Figure 13.43, since the arc (t_0, p_0) (Figure 13.43) was substituted by place p_5 and its arcs. Therefore, during this subnet "firing", a token is kept in place p_5, which denotes a transaction being served. The server semantics of all timed transition of the net shown in Figure 13.45.c are *sss*.

The utilization is tallied by the probability of the system not being empty:

$$u = P\{(\#p_2 + \#p_5) > 0\}. \tag{13.3.57}$$

The number of transaction in the system may be estimated by

$$mss = E\{\#p_2\} + E\{\#p_5\}. \tag{13.3.58}$$

From Equation 13.3.9, the mean queue size is estimated:

$$mqs = E\{\#p_2\} + E\{\#p_5\} - P\{(\#p_2 + \#p_5) > 0\}. \tag{13.3.59}$$

The discard probability (block probability) is estimated by the probability of the system being full:

$$dp = P\{(\#p_2 + \#p_5) = k\}. \tag{13.3.60}$$

The discard rate is computed by multiplying the discard probability (dp) by the arrival rate (λ):

$$dr = P\{(\#p_2 + \#p_5) = k\} \times \lambda. \tag{13.3.61}$$

The throughput may be estimated either by the difference between the arrival rate (λ) and the discard rate (dr), which may be specified by

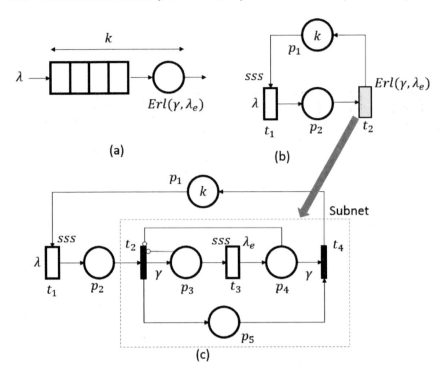

Figure 13.45 SPN Representing an $M/E/1/k$ Queue System.

$$tp = \lambda \times (1 - P\{(\#p_2 + \#p_5) = k\}),$$ (13.3.62)

or by

$$tp = \frac{P\{\#p_3 > 0\} \times \mu_e}{\gamma}.$$ (13.3.63)

It should be stressed that for each transaction service, t_3 is fired γ times; hence $P\{\#p_3\} \times \mu_e$ must be divided by γ in order to obtain the throughput. Using Little's law, Equation 13.3.59 and the throughput, the mean response time (residence time) is obtained, which is represented by

$$mrt = \frac{E\{\#p_2\} + E\{\#p_5\}}{\lambda \times (1 - P\{(\#p_2 + \#p_5) = k\})}$$ (13.3.64)

or by

$$mrt = \frac{E\{\#p_2\} + E\{\#p_5\}}{\frac{P\{\#p_3 > 0\} \times \mu_e}{\gamma}}.$$ (13.3.65)

Likewise, using Little's law, Equation 13.3.59 and the throughput, the mean waiting time may be estimated, which may be represented by

$$mwt = \frac{E\{\#p_2\} + E\{\#p_5\} - P\{(\#p_2 + \#p_5) > 0\}}{\lambda \times (1 - P\{(\#p_2 + \#p_5) = k\})} \tag{13.3.66}$$

or by

$$mwt = \frac{E\{\#p_2\} + E\{\#p_5\} - P\{(\#p_2 + \#p_5) > 0\}}{\frac{P\{\#p_3 > 0\} \times \mu_e}{\gamma}}. \tag{13.3.67}$$

Consider a queue system $M/E/1/k$ with arrival rate $\lambda = 8\,tps$, and the service time specified by an Erlang distribution with $\gamma = 4$ phase and each phase with rate $\mu_e = 40\,tps$. Assume the system capacity is 20. The performance measures presented above are shown in Table 13.10.

Table 13.10
Results – $M/E/1/20$ SPN

Measure	Value
mss	$2.7822\,trans.$
mqs	$1.9824\,trans.$
dp	2.2006×10^{-4}
dr	$0.0018\,tps$
tp	$7.9982\,tps$
mst	$0.3479\,s$
mwt	$0.2479\,s$
u	0.7998

13.3.8.2 Hypoexponential Distribution

This section presents a model that represents the Case 3 depicted in Table 13.9. The SPN presented here specifies a hypoexponential distribution (he) with three parameters, $Hypoexp(\gamma, \lambda_1, \lambda_2)$ [102]. The hypoexponential distribution parameters can be estimated by matching

$$E_{he} = \overline{T}$$

and

$$Var_{he} = SD(T)^2.$$

Thus, hypoexponential distribution parameters are estimated by:

$$\gamma \in \left[\left(\frac{\overline{T}}{SD(T)} \right)^2 - 1, \left(\frac{\overline{T}}{SD(T)} \right)^2 \right), \quad \gamma \in \mathbb{Z}. \tag{13.3.68}$$

$\lambda_1 = 1/d_1$, and

$$d_1 = \frac{\overline{T} \mp \sqrt{\gamma(\gamma+1)\,SD(T)^2 - \gamma \overline{T}^2}}{\gamma+1}. \tag{13.3.69}$$

$\lambda_2 = 1/d_2$, and

$$d_2 = \frac{\gamma \overline{T} \pm \sqrt{\gamma(\gamma+1)\,SD(T)^2 - \gamma \overline{T}^2}}{\gamma(\gamma+1)}. \tag{13.3.70}$$

The proposed SPN is similar to the SPN that represents an Erlang distribution. Figure 13.46.a presents a generically distributed timed transition that is refined by the SPN shown in Figure 13.46.b, which represents a hypoexponential distribution. The places p_0 and p_1 of the net of Figure 13.46.a are also represented in the model shown in Figure 13.46.b. The generic transition is refined by transition t_0, t_1, and t_2, places p_2 and p_2, and their respective arcs. It is worth highlighting the weight (γ) assigned to the arcs (t_0, p_2) and (p_3, t_2). The server semantics of transitions t_0 and t_1 are *sss*, and their rates are λ_1 and λ_2, respectively. Hence, their specific delays are $d_1 = 1/\lambda_1$ and $d_2 = 1/\lambda_2$. As in the previous case, this model is also generic, and it should/could be modified or simplified when representing specific systems or problems. The net behavior is similar to the net that represents the Erlang distribution.

The time to execute a program in a computer system was monitored, and a sample with n measures was recorded. The mean time to execute that program and the respective standard deviation were estimated based on the sample. The estimates were $\overline{T} = 40\,ms$, $SD(T) = 21\,ms$. Since $1/CV = 1.9048$, the hypoexponential distribution is suitable to represent the time to execute the program. The distribution parameters are $\gamma = 3$, $\lambda_1 = 0.22448\,tpms$, and $0.0844\,tpms$.

The net depicted in Figure 13.46.b represents this distribution by setting its parameters to $\gamma = 3$ and $\lambda_1 = 0.22448\,tpms$ and $\lambda_2 = 0.0844\,tpms$. The transient probability of place p_1 having one token (absorbing marking) was computed using the Mercury tool. The mean time to absorption (*mtta*) was $40\,ms$. Figure 13.47 shows the probability distribution for a token reaching place p_1 by time t. From the distribution, $P\{\#p_1 = 1, t = 50\,ms\} = 0.733$[7] was obtained. The median time to absorption was also calculated, $mdta = 36.25\,ms$.

13.3.8.3 Hyperexponential Distribution

The hyperexponential distribution can be adopted to approximate empirical distributions with a coefficient of variation larger than one ($1/CV < 1$ - Case 4). The hyperexponential distribution (*He*) may be specified by k parallel phases of exponential

---

[7]Mercury-like notation.

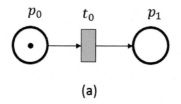

(a)

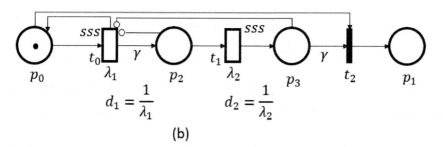

(b)

Figure 13.46 SPN for Hypoexponential Distribution with γ Phases, and Rates Equal to λ_1 and λ_2.

distributions, each phase having rate λ_i, and the probability of taking the phase i is specified by α_i ($\sum_{i=1}^{k} \alpha_i = 1$):

$$F_{He}(t) = \sum_{i=1}^{k} \alpha_i (1 - e^{-\lambda_i t}), \quad t \geq 0. \tag{13.3.71}$$

For a two-phase hyperexponential distribution, the cumulative distribution is

$$F_{He}(t) = \alpha_1 (1 - e^{-\lambda_1 t}) + \alpha_2 (1 - e^{-\lambda_2 t}), \quad t \geq 0, \; \alpha_1 + \alpha_2 = 1. \tag{13.3.72}$$

$$F_{He}(t) = 1 - \alpha_1 e^{-\lambda_1 t} - \alpha_2 e^{-\lambda_2 t}, \quad t \geq 0, \; \alpha_1 + \alpha_2 = 1. \tag{13.3.73}$$

Its expected value is estimated by

$$E_{He} = \frac{\alpha_1}{\lambda_1} + \frac{\alpha_2}{\lambda_2} \tag{13.3.74}$$

and the variance expression is

$$Var_{He} = 2 \left(\frac{\alpha_1}{(\lambda_1)^2} + \frac{\alpha_2}{(\lambda_2)^2} \right) - \left(\frac{\alpha_1}{\lambda_1} + \frac{\alpha_2}{\lambda_2} \right)^2 \tag{13.3.75}$$

For representing an empirical distribution with mean $\overline{T}$ and standard deviation $SD(T)$ (Case 4 - $1/CV < 1$), the two-phases hyperexponential distribution parameters can be estimated by matching

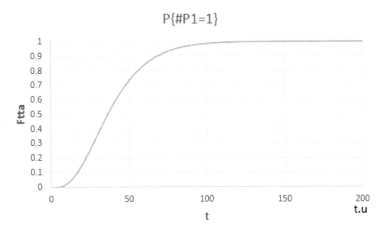

Figure 13.47 Distribution of the Time for a Token to Reach Place p_1 - Hypoexponential Model.

$$E_{He} = \overline{T}$$

and

$$Var_{He} = SD(T)^2.$$

Hence, the hyperexponential distribution parameters are estimated by:

$$\lambda_1 = \frac{1}{\overline{T}} \left(1 - \sqrt{\frac{\alpha_2}{\alpha_1} \frac{CV^2 - 1}{2}} \right)^{-1}. \tag{13.3.76}$$

$$\lambda_2 = \frac{1}{\overline{T}} \left(1 + \sqrt{\frac{\alpha_1}{\alpha_2} \frac{CV^2 - 1}{2}} \right)^{-1}. \tag{13.3.77}$$

The parameters α_1 and α_2 can be any values that satisfy

$$\alpha_1 + \alpha_2 = 1 \tag{13.3.78}$$

and

$$\sqrt{\frac{\alpha_2}{\alpha_1} \frac{CV^2 - 1}{2}} < 1 \tag{13.3.79}$$

since $\lambda_1 > 0$.

Therefore, the mean delays of each phase are

$$d_1 = \frac{1}{\lambda_1}$$

and

$$d_2 = \frac{1}{\lambda_2}.$$

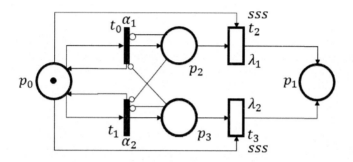

Figure 13.48   SPN for a Two-Phases Hyperexponential Distribution.

Now, consider again the time to execute a program in a computer system. As in the previous example, a sample with n measures was recorded. The mean time to execute the program and the respective standard deviation were $40\,ms$ and $60\,ms$, respectively. Hence, since $1/CV < 1$, then the hyperexponential distribution is suitable for representing the empirical distribution when considering the first moment about the origin and the second central moment. Hence, by matching

$$\frac{\alpha_1}{\lambda_1} + \frac{\alpha_2}{\lambda_2} = 40\,ms$$

and

$$2\left(\frac{\alpha_1}{(\lambda_1)^2} + \frac{\alpha_2}{(\lambda_2)^2}\right) - \left(\frac{\alpha_1}{\lambda_1} + \frac{\alpha_2}{\lambda_2}\right)^2 = (60\,ms)^2,$$

for $\alpha_1 = 0.4$ and $\alpha_2 = 1 - \alpha_1 = 0.6$, we obtain

$$\lambda_1 = 0.7873$$

and

$$\lambda_1 = 0.0152.$$

Hence

$$d_1 = \frac{1}{\lambda_1} = 1.2702\,ms,$$

and

$$d_2 = \frac{1}{\lambda_2} = 65.8199\,ms.$$

Let us assume an $M/He/1/k$ queue system, where the arrival rate is λ and the service time is specified by a two-phase hyperexponential distribution, $He(\alpha_1, \alpha_2, \mu_1, \mu_2)$. The SPN depicted in Figure 13.49.a is composed of two places and two transitions. Transition t_0 represents arrivals. Arrival is only accepted if the system is not full. The system capacity is limited by the number of tokens in p_1. The service is represented by the transition t_1, which is specified by a generically distributed transition (in gray). The number of requests in the system is represented by the number of tokens in place p_0. As the service time is distributed according to a hyperexponential distribution with parameters α_1, α_2, μ_1, and μ_2, t_2, transition t_1 is refined by the sub-net shown in the net depicted in Figure 13.49.b. The mean system size is then computed through

$$mss = E\{\#p_0\}. \tag{13.3.80}$$

The throughput may be estimated either by

$$tp = P\{\#p_2 > 0\} \times \mu_1 + P\{\#p_3 > 0\} \times \mu_2. \tag{13.3.81}$$

or by

$$tp = \lambda - dr = \lambda\left(1 - P\{\#p_0 = k\}\right) \tag{13.3.82}$$

where the discard rate is

$$dr = \lambda \times P\{\#p_0 = k\} \tag{13.3.83}$$

and the discard probability is

$$dp = P\{\#p_0 = k\}. \tag{13.3.84}$$

The mean response time (mean residence time, mean system time) is estimated through Little´s law. Thus

$$mst = \frac{E\{\#p_0\}}{P\{\#p_2 > 0\} \times \mu_1 + P\{\#p_3 > 0\} \times \mu_2}. \tag{13.3.85}$$

The mean queue size is estimated through

$$mqs = E\{\#p_0\} - P\{\#p_0 > 0\}, \tag{13.3.86}$$

and the mean waiting time is computed by

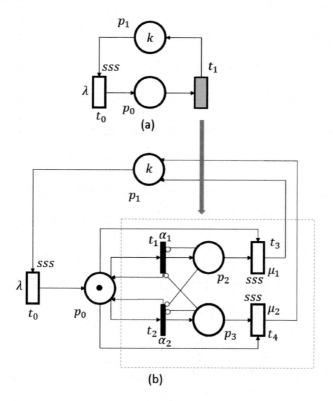

Figure 13.49 SPN for an $M/He/1/k$ Queue System.

$$mwt = \frac{E\{\#p_0\} - P\{\#p_0 > 0\}}{P\{\#p_2 > 0\} \times \mu_1 + P\{\#p_3 > 0\} \times \mu_2}. \qquad (13.3.87)$$

Consider a queue system $M/He/1/k$ with system capacity equal to 20, arrival rate $\lambda = 8\,tps$, and the service time specified by a two-phase hyperexponential distribution, $He(\alpha_1, \alpha_2, \mu_1, \mu_2)$, where $\lambda = 8\,tps$ $\alpha_1 = 0.4$, $\alpha_2 = 0.6$, $\mu_1 = 314.9193\,tps$, and $\mu_2 = 6.0772\,tps$. The values of the performance measures presented above are shown in Table 13.11.

Figure 13.50 presents the mean system size (mss), the discard rate (dr), the mean system time (mst), and the utilization (u) for $\lambda \in (8.3\,tps, 100\,tps)$. The shape of the mss and mst ((a) and (c)) are very similar, and sharply increase with λ up to around to $13\,tps$. From then on, the increase rates are reduced and approach their maximal values. The utilization ((d)), when considering the arrival rate $\lambda = 8.3\,tps$, is about 0.8 and increases with λ. When λ approaches $13\,tps$, utilization reaches values around 0.99. Figure 13.50.c shows the discard rate.

Table 13.11
Results – $M/He/1/20$ **SPN**

Measure	Value
mss	$5.8115\,trans.$
mqs	$4.2291\,trans.$
dp	0.0111
dr	$0.0885\,tps$
tp	$7.9115\,tps$
mst	$0.7346\,s$
mwt	$0.5346\,s$
u	0.7912

13.3.8.4 Cox-1 Distribution

The power of phase-type distributions lies in the fact that they are dense in the class of all non-negative distribution functions [174]. Practically speaking, this means that a phase-type distribution with a sufficient number of phases can approximate any non-negative distribution arbitrarily closely. A combination of exponential phases was proposed by Cox to cover all distributions with rational Laplace transforms [83]. These distributions are named after him. The γ-phase Cox distribution presented in Figure 13.51 has 2γ parameters.

In many practical cases, however, it is common for researchers to match the first central moment about the origin (mean) and the second central moment (variance). Therefore, there are two Cox distributions (named here Cox-1 and Cox-2) that should be stressed, since they support modeling empirical distributions in which $CV \leq 1$ or $CV > 1$.

An empirical distribution with $CV \leq 1$ can be approximated by a Cox-1 distribution presented in Figure 13.52 (Cases 2 and 3 depicted in Table 13.9).
The Cox-1 distribution parameters can be estimated by matching

$$E_{C1} = \overline{T} \tag{13.3.88}$$

and

$$Var_{C1} = SD(T)^2, \tag{13.3.89}$$

where

$$E_{C1} = \frac{(\gamma - 1)\,\omega + 1}{\lambda}, \tag{13.3.90}$$

and

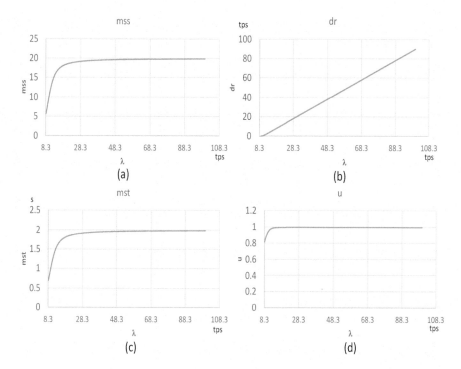

Figure 13.50 Mean System Size, Discard Rate, Mean System Time and Utilization *vs* λ.

$$Var_{C1} = \frac{-(\gamma-1)^2 \omega^2 + \gamma(\gamma-1)\omega + 1}{\lambda^2}. \qquad (13.3.91)$$

As the coefficient of variation is $CV = SD(T)/\overline{T}$, then

$$CV = \frac{\lambda \sqrt{\frac{(\gamma-1)\omega(\gamma(\omega-1)-\omega)-1}{\lambda^2}}}{(\gamma-1)\omega+1} \qquad (13.3.92)$$

and

$$CV^2 = \frac{(\gamma-1)\omega(\gamma(\omega-1)-\omega)-1}{((\gamma-1)\omega+1)^2}. \qquad (13.3.93)$$

It is worth noting that when $CV = 1$, the Cox-1 model is reduced to the exponential case.

From Equations 13.3.88 and 13.3.89, the parameters of the Cox-1 distribution are obtained:

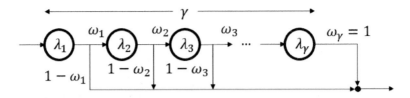

Figure 13.51 A γ-phase Cox Distribution.

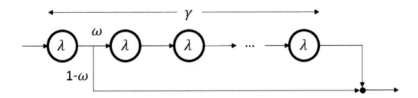

Figure 13.52 A Cox-1 Distribution.

$$\gamma = \left\lceil \frac{1}{CV^2} \right\rceil, \tag{13.3.94}$$

$$\omega = 1 - \frac{2\gamma CV^2 + (\gamma - 2) - \sqrt{\gamma^2 + 4 - 4\gamma CV^2}}{2(CV^2 + 1)(\gamma - 1)}, \tag{13.3.95}$$

and

$$\lambda = \frac{\gamma - (1 - \omega)(\gamma - 1)}{\overline{T}}. \tag{13.3.96}$$

The SPN shown in Figure 13.53.a presents a generic transition (in gray) that is refined by the subnet depicted in Figure 13.53.b, which represents a Cox-1 distributions. A token in p_0 enables t_0, and its firing leads to a marking in which a token is stored in p_2. This new marking disables t_0, because there is an inhibitor arc between p_2 and t_0. A token in p_2 enables t_1 and t_2. In order to guarantee that these transitions have firing probability equal to $1 - \omega$ and ω, respectively, these two transitions should be the only firable transitions, as they are in this specific case. In a larger net, priority may be adopted to constrain the firing of immediate transitions. As a matter of fact, the immediate transition firing of all phase-type nets should consider such a restriction. Therefore, if t_1 fires, one tokens is removed from places p_0 and p_2, and one token is stored in p_1. If, on the other hand, t_2 fires, one token is taken from p_2 and γ tokens are added to p_3. This marking enables t_3 and keeps t_0 disabled. The transition t_3 server semantics is *sss*. After firing t_3 γ times, the number of tokens in p_4 is γ. One token in p_0 and γ tokens in p_4 enables t_4, and its firing removes one token from p_0 and γ tokens from p_4, and stores one token in place p_1.

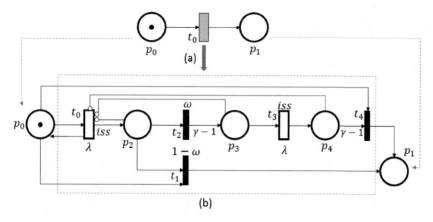

Figure 13.53 SPN Representing a Cox-1 Distribution.

Consider a computer system in charge of processing a variety of transactions was monitored for a period. A sample of the transaction´s execution time was recorded. Its average and standard deviation were $100\,ms$ and $60\,ms$, respectively. As $CV = 0.6$, the Cox-1 distribution is a suitable model for representing such an empirical distribution according to the method adopted here (see Table 13.9). Therefore, the distribution parameters may be estimated by applying Equations 13.3.94, 13.3.95, and 13.3.96. The respective parameters are: $\gamma = 3$, $\omega = 0.9607$, and $\lambda = 0.029214$ $(d = 1/\lambda = 34.23\,ms)$ The distribution function curve can be obtained by plotting the probability of having one token in place p_1 at time t (time to absorption – abs), given the initial marking is $M_0^T = (1,0,0,0,0)$. Figure 13.54 presents the respective curve $(F_{abs} \times t)$, considering $t \in [0, 350\,ms)$. These probabilities were calculated by applying the uniformization method in the Mercury tool. The probability that the execution time of a transaction being shorter than $150\,ms$ is 0.81965. It should be stressed, however, that such a probability is not equal to the probability computed through the empirical distribution since the phase-type and the empirical distributions are only equivalent regarding the first two moments.

Now, let us present an SPN that represents the $M/Cox1/1/k$ queue system (Figure 13.55.a). The model shown in Figure 13.55.b is a net with a generic transition (in gray). This model is refined by the net depicted in Figure 13.55.c.

Using the net presented in Figure 13.55.c, the performance measure is specified. The mean system size is computed through the metrics

$$mss = E\{\#p_0\}. \tag{13.3.97}$$

The discard probability and the discard rate can be estimated by

$$dp = P\{\#p_0 = k\} \tag{13.3.98}$$

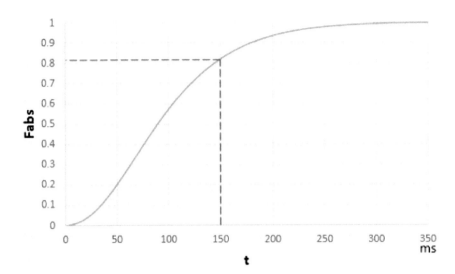

Figure 13.54 Probabilities of Absorption - Cox-1 Distribution.

and

$$dr = \lambda \times P\{\#p_0 = k\}, \qquad (13.3.99)$$

respectively. Therefore, the throughput can be estimated by

$$tp = \lambda \times (1 - P\{\#p_0 = k\}). \qquad (13.3.100)$$

The throughput can also be estimated by

$$tp = P\{(\#p_0 > 0) \wedge (\#p_2 = 0) \wedge (\#p_3 = 0) \wedge (\#p_4 = 0)\} \times \mu \qquad (13.3.101)$$

or

$$tp = \frac{P\{\#p_3 > 0\} \times \mu}{\gamma - 1}. \qquad (13.3.102)$$

Applying Little´s law, the response time is estimated, $rt = mss/tp$.

$$rt = \frac{E\{\#p_0\}}{\lambda \times (1 - P\{\#p_0 = k\})}. \qquad (13.3.103)$$

The mean queue size is estimated by

$$mqs = E\{\#p_0\} - P\{\#p_0 > 0\}, \qquad (13.3.104)$$

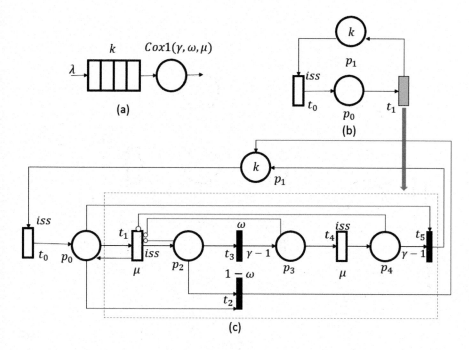

Figure 13.55 $M/Cox1/1/k$ Queue System – SPN.

and applying Little´s law, the waiting time is estimated, $mwt = mqs/tp$.

$$mwt = \frac{E\{\#p_0\} - P\{\#p_0 > 0\}}{\lambda \times (1 - P\{\#p_0 = k\})}. \tag{13.3.105}$$

Now consider a system in which the mean service time is $100\,ms$, the service time standard deviation is $60\,ms$, the mean arrival time is equal to $mat = 1/\lambda = 105\,ms$, and the system capacity $k = 20$. Assuming theses parameter values, the performance measures presented above are:

13.3.8.5 Cox-2 Distribution

An empirical distribution with $CV > 1$ can be approximated by a Cox-2 distribution presented in Figure 13.56.a (Case 4 depicted in Table 13.9). This section presents an SPN for representing the Cox-2 distribution (Figure 13.56.b).
The Cox-2 distribution mean (E_{C2}), variance (Var_{C2}), and the squared coefficient of variation (CV^2) are

$$E_{C2} = \frac{\mu_1 \omega + \mu_2}{\mu_1 \mu_2}, \tag{13.3.106}$$

Table 13.12

Results – $M/Cox1/1/20$ **SPN**

Measure	Value
mss	$7.6787\,trans.$
mqs	$6.74095\,trans.$
dp	0.01536
dr	$0.14633\,tps$
tp	$9.37748\,tps$
mst	$0.818845\,s$
mwt	$0.718852\,s$
u	0.93775

$$Var_{C2} = \frac{\mu_2^2 + 2\mu_1^2\omega - \mu_1^2\omega^2}{\mu_1^2\mu_2^2}, \qquad (13.3.107)$$

and

$$CV^2 = \frac{\mu_2^2 + 2\omega\mu_1^2 - \omega^2\mu_1^2}{(\omega\mu_1 + \mu_2)^2}. \qquad (13.3.108)$$

The Cox-2 distribution parameters can be estimated by matching the empirical mean and variance to the respective statistics of the Cox-2 distribution. As the Cox-2 statistics have three parameters, and the matching considers only two equations, an infinite number of solutions are possible. One particular solution for this system is

$$\mu_1 = \frac{2}{\overline{T}}, \qquad (13.3.109)$$

$$\mu_2 = \frac{1}{\overline{T} \times CV^2}, \qquad (13.3.110)$$

and

$$\omega = \frac{1}{2CV^2}. \qquad (13.3.111)$$

The SPN shown in Figure 13.53.b represents Cox-2 distributions. A token in p_0 enables t_0, and its firing leads to a marking in which a token is stored in p_2. This new marking disables t_1, because there is an inhibitor arc between p_2 and t_1. A token in p_2 enables t_2 and t_3. As in the previous model, these transitions have firing probability equal to $1 - \omega$ and ω, respectively. In a model in which other immediate transitions are also enabled, priority should be adopted to restrain the firing of immediate transitions. In this marking, if t_2 fires, one token is removed from places p_0 and p_2, and one tokens is stored in p_1. On the other hand, if t_3 fires, one token is taken from p_2

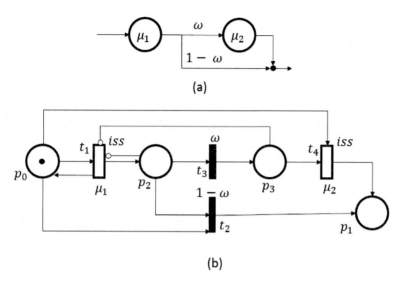

(a)

(b)

Figure 13.56 A Cox-2 Distribution.

and one token is added to p_3. This marking enables t_4 and keeps t_1 disabled. The transition t_3 server semantics is *sss*. Firing t_3, removes one token from p_0 and p_3, and stores one token in p_1.

As in the previous model, let us assume that a system which processes a class of transactions was monitored for a period. A sample of the transaction's execution time was recorded, and its average and standard deviation were $100\,ms$ and $150\,ms$, respectively. As $CV = 1.5$, the Cox-2 distribution is a model of choice for representing such an empirical distribution based on the moment matching method adopted here (see Table 13.9). Hence, the distribution parameters may be estimated by applying Equations 13.3.109, 13.3.110, and 13.3.111. The respective parameters are: $\mu_1 = 1/50\,tps$ ($d_1 = 1/\mu_1 = 50\,ms$), $\mu_2 = 2/450\,tps$ ($d_2 = 1/\mu_2 = 225\,ms$), and $\omega = 2/9$. The distribution function can be obtained by plotting the probability of having one token in place p_1 at time t (time to absorbtion – *abs*), given the initial marking is $M_0^T = (1,0,0,0)$. Figure 13.57 presents the respective curve ($F_{abs} \times t$), taking into account the range $t \in [0, 900\,ms]$. These probabilities were calculated by applying the uniformization method, and the Mercury tool. The probability that the transaction execution time is shorter than $150\,ms$ is 0.81782. As mentioned in the previous model, it is important to stress that this probability function is not equal to the empirical probability distribution, because the phase-type and the empirical distributions are only equivalent in terms of means and variances.

Figure 13.58 presents an SPN that represents the queue system $M/Cox2/1/k$. Figure 13.58.a is a model in which the Cox-2 distribution is denoted by the generic transition t_1 (in gray). This transition is refined by the subnet depicted in Figure 13.58.b

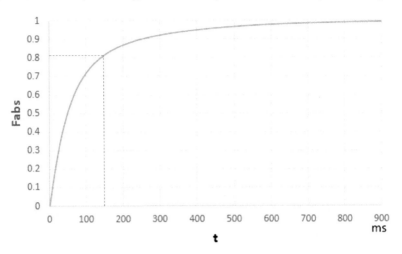

Figure 13.57 Probabilities of Absorption – Cox-2 Distribution.

(dotted line). In this model, the server semantics of all timed transitions are sss. The arrival rate (assigned to t_0) is λ, and the system capacity is specified by k (marking assigned to p_1). From the net shown in Figure 13.58.b, the performance measures are calculated. The respective metrics expressions are shown below.

The mean system size (mss) and the mean queue size (mqs) are represented by:

$$mss = E\{\#p_0\} \tag{13.3.112}$$

and

$$mqs = E\{\#p_0\} - P\{\#p_0 > 0\}. \tag{13.3.113}$$

The discard (block) probability (dp), the discard rate (dr), and the throughput (tp) are denoted by

$$dp = P\{\#p_0 = k\}, \tag{13.3.114}$$

$$,dr = \lambda \times P\{\#p_0 = k\} \tag{13.3.115}$$

and

$$tp = \lambda \times (1 - P\{\#p_0 = k\}). \tag{13.3.116}$$

The mean response time (rt) and the mean waiting time mwt are represented by

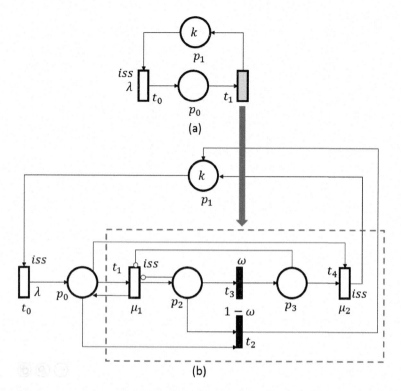

Figure 13.58 $M/Cox2/1/k$ Queue System – SPN.

$$rt = \frac{E\{\#p_0\}}{\lambda \times (1 - P\{\#p_0 = k\})} \qquad (13.3.117)$$

and

$$mwt = rt = \frac{E\{\#p_0\} - P\{\#p_0 > 0\}}{\lambda \times (1 - P\{\#p_0 = k\})}. \qquad (13.3.118)$$

A set of experiments was conducted considering the SPN shown in Figure 13.58.b. This experiment adopted $\lambda \in (9 \times 10^{-3} tps$, $20 \times 10^{-3} tps$), $k = 20$, $\mu_1 = 1/50\,tps$, $\mu_2 = 2/450\,tps$, and $\omega = 2/9$. Figure 13.59 shows the throughput and the discard rate as functions of the arrival rate. The throughput curve shows that stays steady for $\lambda > 13 \times 10^{-3} tps$. On the other hand, the discard rate, which was small for small values of λ, increases with λ, and equals the throughput by $\lambda = 20 \times 10^{-3} tps$, and keeps such a trend for higher values of λ.

The mean system size, the mean queue size, the response time, and the mean waiting time also increase with λ as shown in Figure 13.60 and Figure 13.61.

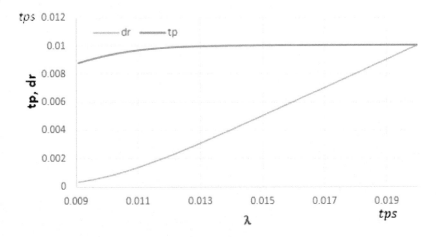

Figure 13.59   Throughput and Discard Rate × Arrival Rate – Cox-2 Distribution.

13.3.9   MODELING MEMORY POLICIES AND PHASE-TYPE DISTRIBUTIONS

The previous sections shown how SPN models could represent activities with generically distributed durations. These activities were represented by subnets that approximate the desired delay distributions. This section shows how to adapt such models to specify firing and memory policies, and outlines the importance of representing the preemptions of activities [166].

Consider a case where two conflicting activities (A_1 and A_2) are enabled. Let us also consider that the time to execute each activity is distributed according to $Exp(\mu)$ and $Hypoexp(\gamma, \lambda_1, \lambda_2)$, respectively. The SPN depicted in Figure 13.62.a shows a net that specifies these two conflicting activities. Transition t_0 represents A_2 and t_1 represents A_1. A token in p_0 enables both t_0 and t_1. As t_0 is a generically distributed transition, the standard numerical analysis is only possible if t_0 is refined by a phase-type distribution (it could be simulated, but this is the subject of the next chapter). In order to correctly implement the race policy between t_0 and t_1 (Figure 13.62.a), the refined models (Figure 13.62.b or Figure 13.62.c) must stores a token back in p_0 when t_0 (in Figure 13.62.b or Figure 13.62.c) is fired, since the race between t_0 and t_1 (Figure 13.62.a) should take into account the delay of the related t_0 and t_1 (Figure 13.62.a) and not only one phase of the hypoexponential distribution. The phase-type models (in these cases, the subnets surrounded by dashed rectangle) are slightly modified to consider the subtleties of the firing and memory policies. The SPN depicted in Figure 13.62.b was modified by assigning a guard function to transition t_2 ($\#p_0 > 0$). This net models the conflicting activities taking into account *age memory* policy.

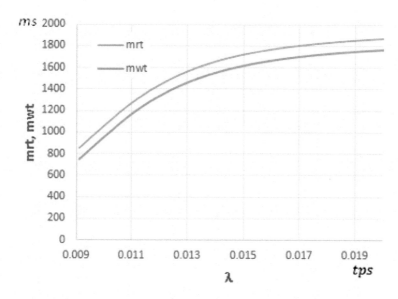

Figure 13.60   Mean System Size and Mean Queue Size × Arrival Rate - Cox-2 Distribution.

Let us carefully observe the model´s behavior. Consider a token is stored in p_0. This marking enables t_0 and t_1. Assume t_0 wins the race against t_1 and fires. Its firing removes one token from p_0, stores γ tokens in p_3, and stores one token back in p_0. It is very important to stress that the race between transitions that represent activities should consider the delays of all transitions of the hypoexponential subnet and not only the delay assigned to t_0. This is the reason for storing the token back in p_0. The token is only definitely removed from p_0 when either t_1 fires or all transitions of a hypoexponetial subnet are fired. Again, the token stays in p_0, and after a delay (in this case, considering $Hypoexp(\gamma, \lambda_1, \lambda_2)$), it is instantaneously fired. This instantaneous firing is "simulated" by keeping the token in p_0 when t_0 is fired and by removing the token from p_0 when t_3 fires. Now, assume t_0 is fired. Such a firing removes the token from p_0. As there is no token in p_0, the guard function assigned to t_2 disables t_2. When a token is stored again in p_0, the hypoexponential subnet resumes its enabling from the previous "counting" (age memory).

The phase-type model depicted in Figure 13.62.c was modified by adding two guarded immediate transitions (t_4 and t_5). These transitions are guarded by the functions $(\#p_0 = 0) \wedge (\#p_3 > 0)$ and $(\#p_0 = 0) \wedge (\#p_4 > 0)$, respectively. Therefore, when t_1 fires and removes the token from p_0, all tokens are flushed from p_3 and p_4. Hence, when a token is stored again in p_0, hypoexponential subnet enabling is started anew. This SPN represents the *enabling memory* policy.

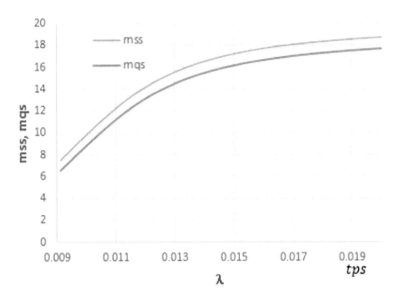

Figure 13.61 Mean Response Time and Mean Waiting Time × Arrival Rate - Cox-2 distribution

Example 13.3.7. Let us consider a computational system that serves clients'requests. This system is represented by a queue model that depicts the requests (*req*), a queue (p_1), its capacity ($m_{p_0} = k$), the processor (*cpu* − *idle* and *cpu* − *busy*), and the *service*. A token in *cpu* − *idle* represents the cpu in an idle state. The mean time between requests (*mtbr*) is assigned to transition *req*, and the mean service time (*mst*) is assigned to transition *service*. A first model is shown in Figure 13.63. This model consider all delay as exponentially distributed. This model is similar to the net shown in Figure 13.32.b if the number of processors is one ($m_{cpu−idle} + m_{cpu−busy} = 1$).

In this model, however, the processor may be periodically interrupted. The mean time between interruptions (*mtbi*) is assigned to transition *int*. The mean interruption service time (*mist*) is assigned to the transition that represents the interruption service (*is*). Places p_3, p_4, p_5, and p_6, and transitions t_1, t_2, t_3, and t_4 specify the interruption mechanism. When an interruption controller requests the processor´s service, a token is stored in place p_3. The processor may be in an idle state (token in *cpu* − *idle*) or may be processing a client´s request (*cpu* − *busy*). In either state, the processor is interrupted to process the interruption service. This is accomplished by the firing of either t_1 or t_2. After firing these transitions, a token is stored in p_4. A token in p_4 enables the interruption *is*, which denotes the interruption service. Its firing represents interruption service execution. If when the processor was interrupted, it was in the idle state (by firing t_2), a token was also stored in p_6. This is adopted to specify

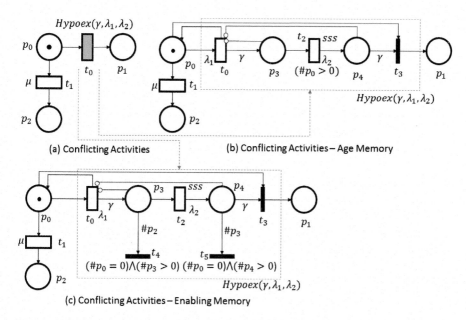

Figure 13.62 Conflicting Activities – Memory Policies.

if the processor was or was not processing a client request. After processing the interruption service (denoted by the firing of transition is), a token is stored in place p_5. A token in this place enables either t_3 or t_4, depending on the state the processor was in before being interrupted (idle or busy). When either of these transitions fire, the processor resumes its state before the interruption. The priority of transitions t_1, t_2, t_3, and t_4 is two ($\pi(t_i) = 2$, $i = \{1, 2, 3, 4\}$), whereas the priority of transition t_0 is one ($\pi(t_0) = 1$). The weight assigned to all immediate transitions are equal to one ($\omega(t_i = 1)$, $\forall t_i \in Tim.$). The processor utilization is estimated by

$$u = 1 - P\{\#cpu - idle = 1\}. \tag{13.3.119}$$

Let us assume the mean time between requests as $mtbr = 140\,ms$, the system capacity as $k = 20$, the mean service time as $mst = 100\,ms$, and the mean interruption service time as $mist = 5\,ms$. An experiment was performed by taking into account the mean time between interruptions in the interval $mtbi \in (100\,ms, 400\,ms)$. Figure 13.66 (blue) shows the cpu utilization calculated for these parameter values.

Now, let us assume the service time is distributed according to hypoexponential distribution $Hypoex(\gamma, \lambda_1, \lambda_2)$, $\gamma = 4$, $\lambda_1 = 0.0644\,tpms$, and $\lambda_2 = 0.04735\,tpms$ (the mean service time is $mst = 100\,ms$ and standard deviation of the service time is $sd(st) = 45\,ms.$). A second model is proposed in Figure 13.64. This model represents the service time specified by the hypoexponential distribution with age memory

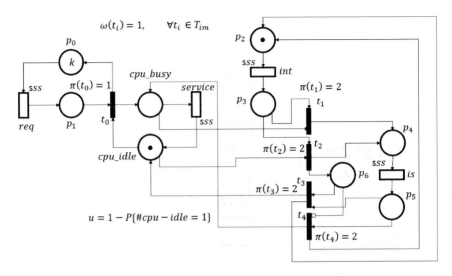

Figure 13.63   CPU Interruption.

policy. In this model, when the processor is interrupted, the service time "counting" is kept in the subnet that represents the hypoexponential distribution, which is resumed as soon as the interruption finishes. An experiment was performed considering the mean time between interruptions in the interval $mtbi \in 100\,ms,\ 400\,ms)$. Figure 13.66 (orange) depicts the CPU utilization for these parameter values.

A third model is shown in Figure 13.65. This model also considers the same hypoexponential distribution, but adopts the enabling memory policy. Therefore, whenever the processor is interrupted, the service time counting is discarded (see transitions t_8 and t_9, its guards, and input arcs weights), and when the interruption finishes the "firing" of the hypoexponential subnet starts anew. The guard functions of transition t_8 and t_9 are $(\#cpu - busy = 1) \wedge (\#p_6 > 0)$ and $(\#cpu - busy = 1) \wedge (\#p_7 > 0)$, respectively. The arc weights of the arcs (p_6, t_8) and (p_7, t_9) are $\#p_6$ and $\#p_7$.

As in the previous cases, an experiment was conducted by taking into account the mean time between interruptions in the interval $mtbi \in (100\,ms,\ 400\,ms)$. Figure 13.66 (green) shows the CPU utilization calculated for these parameter values. The utilization obtained when considering the enabling memory is higher than when adopting age memory, since the hypoexponential subnet "counting" is restarted whenever the interruption service finishes.

□

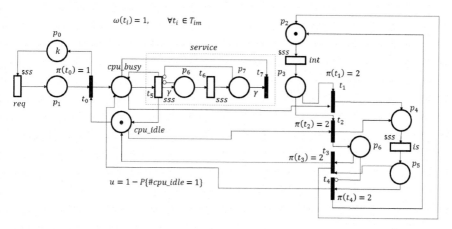

Figure 13.64 CPU Interruption – Hypoexponential Service Time Distribution –
Age Memory.

13.3.10 PROBABILITY DISTRIBUTION OF SPNS WITH ABSORBING MARKINGS

This section studies the probability distribution of SPNs with absorbing markings. Assume a model representing the time to execute a set of programs (T) in hardware infrastructure composed of n processors. The model proposed supports the computation of the mean time to execute the programs, the particular median time, and other order statistics such as interquartile range, and plots the cumulative distribution function [6, 318, 355].

Let us consider an example to illustrate the process and the respective model. In this example, we have a hardware infrastructure composed of n processors. The software system is represented by four programs ($Prog_1$, $Prog_2$, $Prog_3$, and $Prog_4$). The time to execute each program taking into account one processor is specified by the respective probability distributions $Exp(\lambda_1)$, $Erl(\gamma, \lambda_2)$, $Cox2(\omega_{31}, \omega_{32}, \lambda_{31}, \lambda_{32})$, and $Exp(\lambda_4)$:

Table 13.13
Distributions Parameters

Distributions	Parameters
$Exp(\lambda_1)$	$\lambda_1 = 5 \times 10^{-3}\,tpms$
$Erl(\gamma, \lambda_2)$	$\gamma = 16, \lambda_2 = 80 \times 10^{-3}\,tpms$
$Cox2(\omega_{31}, \omega_{32}, \lambda_{31}, \lambda_{32})$	$\omega_{31} = 0.29586, \omega_{32} = 0.70414, \lambda_{31} = 13.33 \times 10^{-3}\,tpms, \lambda_{32} = 3.94 \times 10^{-3}\,tpms$
$Exp(\lambda_4)$	$\lambda_4 = 6.67 \times 10^{-3}\,tpms$

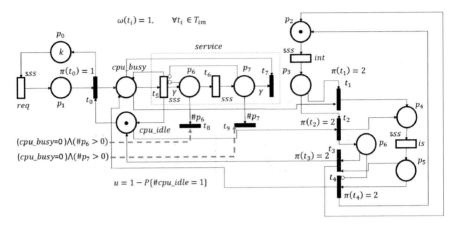

Figure 13.65 CPU Interruption – Hypoexponential Service Time Distribution – Enabling Memory.

A high-level SPN is shown in Figure 13.67. The gray transitions represent the time to execute each program. The respective time distributions are shown beside each transition. A refined SPN is obtained by using the phase-type SPNs for representing each high-level transition (in gray) and the processors´ allocations. The refined SPN is presented in Figure 13.68. The number of processors is specified by the number of tokens in place cpu ($\#cpu = n$).

The time to execute the programs is calculated by computing the time to reach the absorption marking. The SPN shown in Figure 13.68 has only one absorption marking, and this marking is reached for representing the end of the programs´ execution. The execution time distribution probability can be numerically estimated by calculating the probability of the token reaching place p_{19} by t in a time range $t \in (0, t')$, considering $P\{\#p_{19} = 1, t'\} \to 1$. Figure 13.69 shows the execution time probability distribution when considering n processors. The mean time to execute ($MTTE$) the programs and the respective median times ($MedTTE$) are presented in Table 13.14.

Table 13.14
Mean and Median Time to Execute the Programs

# Processors	$MTTE$ (ms)	$MedTTE$ (ms)
$n = 1$	700,00	635.10
$n = 2$	429.54	369.80
$n = 3$	363.55	295.00
$n = 4$	346.66	277.30

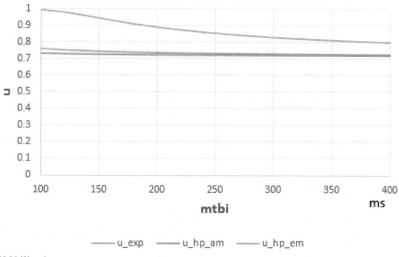

CPU Utilization.

Figure 13.66 Exponential and Hypoexponential Distributions – Enabling and Age Memory.

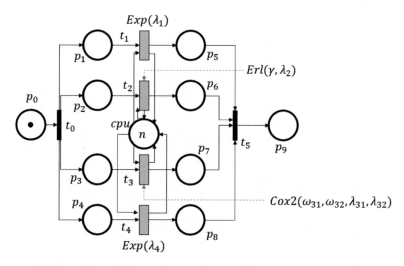

Figure 13.67 A High-Level SPN for Computing the Time to Execute a Set of Programs (T).

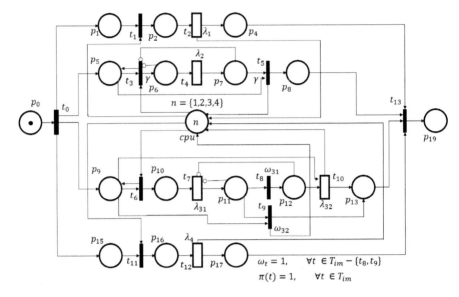

Figure 13.68 An SPN for Computing the Time to Execute a Set of Programs (T).

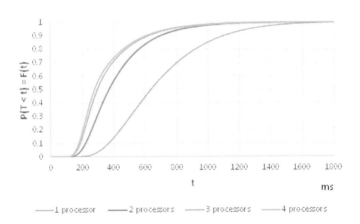

Figure 13.69 Distributions of T Considering n Processors.

EXERCISES

Exercise 1. Considering conflict resolution, explain (**a**) race policy, and (**b**) probabilistic choice.

Exercise 2. With respect to memory policies assigned to timed transitions, describe the mechanisms (**a**) restart, and (**b**) continue.

Exercise 3. Explain the following concepts: (**a**) preemptive repeat different (*prd*), and (**b**) preemptive resume (*prs*).

Exercise 4. Describe with the support of examples the following concepts: (**a**) resampling, (**b**) enabling memory, and (**c**) age memory.

Exercise 5. Considering the server semantics, describe (**a**) single server semantics, (**b**) infinite server semantics, and (**d**) k-server semantics.

Exercise 6. Explain, using examples, what one understands by (**a**) a vanishing marking, and (**b**) a tangible marking.

Exercise 7. Using examples, (a) describe the effect of assigning *SSS* or *ISS* to a timed transition when performing the numerical analysis. (b) If a modeling tool only supports assigning *SSS* and *ISS* to timed transitions, how can one model *KSS* semantics in such a tool?

Exercise 8. Describe the concepts of (a) enabling transition set and (b) firable transition multiset. Shows examples.

Exercise 9. Considering the evaluation alternatives depicted in Figure 13.15, explain the context in which one should choose either numerical analysis or simulation. Also explain the context in which one adopts analytic models. What are the pros and cons of each alternative? Explain.

Exercise 10. Answer and justify your response. (**a**) Why is it essential to check whether the SPNs are bounded before generating the embedded CTMC? (**b**) What do you mean by confusion? How do you solve it?

Exercise 11. Consider the SPN of Figure 13.70. (**a**) Using pencil and paper, generate the reachability graph and the embedded CTMC. (**b**) Using pencil and paper, calculate $E\{\#p_2\}$, $E\{\#p_4\}$, and the throughput of transitions t_1 and t_2. Assume all transitions have single server semantics and the same priority level. The delays of timed transitions are: $w(t_0) = 10s$, $w(t_1) = 5s$, $w(t_2) = 10s$, and $w(t_3) = 8s$. The weights of the immediate transition are equal to one.

Exercise 12. Considering the SPN that represents the queue system $M/M/2/20$ (Figure 13.71), perform the stationary analysis by varying the parameter *tba* in the interval $[0.11s, 0.13s]$ and draw the curves of the respective metrics as a function of the *tba* values: (**a**) utilization of servers, (**b**) throughput, (**c**) mean system size, (**d**) response time, (**e**) discard probability, and (**f**) discard rate.

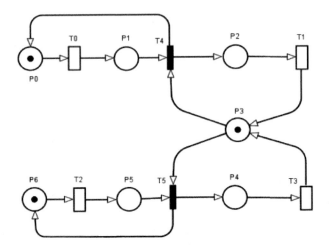

Figure 13.70 This SPN is a GSPN.

Exercise 13. Propose an SPN model that represents a queue $M/M/2/20$ (use the SPN depicted in Figure 13.71 as the starting point.) in which the server may fail and be repaired. Assume the time to failure and the time to repair are exponentially distributed with averages equal to $MTTF = 1400\,h$ and $MTTF = 40\,h$, respectively. Evaluate the impact of the failure and the repair activity on the metrics analyzed in Exercise 12.

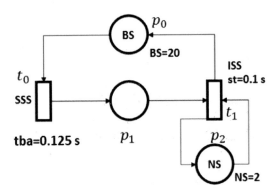

Figure 13.71 SPN representing $M/M/2/20$ Queue System.

Exercise 14. Extend the SPN proposed in Exercise 13 to consider a Markov modulated Poisson process (MMPP). Assume the time between silence periods is exponentially distributed with a rate of $0.1 s^{-1}$, and the silence period is exponentially distributed with a rate of $0.5 s^{-1}$. Evaluate the metrics analyzed in Exercise 12.

Exercise 15. Propose a variant of the SPN depicted in Figure 13.40, but adopt inhibitor arcs instead of guard expressions. Assuming the parameter values shown in Figure 13.40, calculate: (a) the discard probability and the discard rate, (b) the system throughput, (c) the mean number of transactions in the system, (d) the mean queue size, (e) the mean response time, and (f) the mean waiting time.

Exercise 16. Propose an SPN that represents a queue system with one servers, and capacity equal to thirty. Assume the arrival time is distributed according to $Exp(\lambda)$, where $\lambda = 0.1 tpms$, and the service time obeys $Erl(\gamma, \mu)$, where $\lambda = 0.1 tpms$, $\gamma = 2$, and $\mu = 0.2222 tpms$. Conduct a numerical analysis and calculate **(a)** the discard rate, **(b)** the throughput, **(c)** the mean system size, **(d)** the mean queue size, **(e)**, the mean response time, and **(f)** the mean waiting time.

Exercise 17. Extend the SPN proposed in Exercise 16 to consider server failures and repairs. Assume the time to failure and the time to repair are exponentially distributed with averages equal to $MTTF = 800h$ and $MTTF = 10h$, respectively. Evaluate the impact of the failure and the repair activity on the metrics analyzed in Exercise 16. Besides, calculate (a) the mean number of transactions lost due to downtime in one month, calculate (b) the mean number of transactions lost in a month due to discarding, and (c) calculate the total number of transactions lost in a month due to downtime and discarding.

Exercise 18. Propose an SPN model for the problem depicted in Exercise 9 of Chapter 10 and calculate the largest radius of the resized cell (delimited by the new base station positioning) so that the unavailability of lines stays below 1%.

Exercise 19. Propose an SPN for the Tandem Queue System depicted in Figure 13.72. Let us consider a configuration in which $k_1 = 30$, $k_2 = 20$, $k_3 = 10$, $\mu_1 = 0.1 tps$, $\mu_2 = 0.125 tps$, $\mu_3 = 0.12 tps$ and $w = 0.65$. Calculate discards probability, discard rate, the effective arrival rate, the system throughput, the mean system size, the mean response time, and each resource utilization for $\lambda \in \{0.05 tps, 0.0625 tps, 0.2 tps\}$, presents the evaluation results, and comment on the findings.

Exercise 20. A queue system is specified by transaction arrival requests represented by a Poisson process with rate λ, the system capacity specified as $K = 100$, and service time (st) is specified by the mean service time, $mst = 90 ms$, and its standard deviation, $sd_{st} = 150 ms$. The system has only one server. Propose an SPN model using exponential phase-type distributions to calculate: (a) mss, (b) dp, (c) dr, (d) throughput, (e) mrt, and (f) processor utilization u. Assume λ ($10 tpms, 15 tpms$).

Exercise 21. A queue system is specified by the time between transaction arrival specified by an exponential distribution with rate λ. The system capacity is specified as $K = 80$, and service time (st) is specified by the mean service time, $mst = 100 ms$,

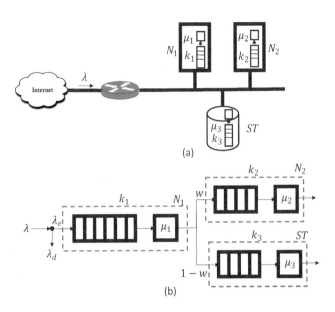

Figure 13.72   Three Nodes Tandem Queue System.

and its standard deviation, $sd_{st} = 50\,ms$. The system has only one server. Propose an SPN model using exponential phase-type distributions to calculate: (a) mss, (b) dp, (c) dr, (d) throughput, (e) mrt, and (f) the processor utilization u. Consider $mtba = 1/\lambda \in (90\,ms, 110\,ms)$.

Exercise 22. Assume the high-level SPN model shown in Figure 13.67. The hardware infrastructure is composed of n processors. The software system is represented by four functions (f_1, f_2, f_3, and f_4). The time to execute each function i (tte_{f_i}) in one processor is specified by the respective probability distributions:

- $tte_{f_1} \sim Erl(\gamma, \lambda_1)$,

- $tte_{f_2} \sim Cox2(\omega_{21}, \omega_{22}, \lambda_{21}, \lambda_{22})$,

- $tte_{f_3} \sim Exp(\lambda_3)$, and

- $tte_{f_4} \sim Exp(\lambda_4)$,

where $\gamma = 15$, $\lambda_1 = 50 \times 10^{-3}\,tpms$; $\omega_{31} = 0.31$, $\omega_{32} = 0.69$, $\lambda_{21} = 15 \times 10^{-3}\,tpms$, $\lambda_{22} = 4 \times 10^{-3}\,tpms$; $\lambda_3 = 7 \times 10^{-3}\,tpms$, and $\lambda_4 = 8 \times 10^{-3}\,tpms$.

Considering the scenarios in which the number of processors $n \in \{1, 2, 3, 4\}$, obtain (a) the system execution time cumulative distribution probability by solving the SPN via transient analysis; (b) the mean time to execute ($MTTE$) the software system, and the median times ($MedTTE$) considering the number of processors specified.

14 Stochastic Simulation

The objective of this chapter is twofold. First, the set of basic functionalities of a stochastic discrete event simulation framework is introduced, discussed, and illustrated. Second, a set of performance models is shown to represent stochastic simulation models' application for representing computational systems. In other words, this chapter aims to study the fundamentals of stochastic simulation, its methods, and apply them to solve performance and dependability problems.

The structure of the chapter is the following:

1. Introduction,

2. Discrete Event Simulation: an Overview,

3. Random Variate Generation,

4. Output Analysis – Steady-State Simulation, and

5. Output Analysis – Transient Simulation.

14.1 INTRODUCTION

Analytic or numerical methods can solve the models addressed in the previous chapters. Although the class of models presented is extensive, there are those that cannot be represented and solved with the techniques introduced. These models, however, can be evaluated using simulation.

There are many simulation strategies described in the literature. Nevertheless, they may fall into these distinct classes: *static simulation* vs. dynamic simulation, *time-driven simulation* vs. *event-driven simulation, deterministic simulation* vs. *stochastic simulation*, and *continuous simulation* vs. *discrete simulation*. Static simulation is adopted for representing systems in which time does not play a role or describing a system at a particular time, whereas dynamic simulation is used to evaluate a system that evolves. Time-driven simulations advance time with fixed time steps, then afterward the state variables are updated. The time step should be small enough to capture every event of interest in the system. This might imply a very small time step, which may lead to unacceptable computational times. In the event-driven simulation, the simulation time advances according to the next event chosen in the simulation process. Such a process will be described later in the chapter. The deterministic simulation considers models that do not contain any random variable; the output is determined once the input quantities and the model relations are defined. On the other hand, Stochastic simulation adopts models that have at least one random variable. Continuous simulation relies upon continuous models for representing systems, whereas discrete simulation is supported by discrete models [190], [191], [76], [364], [360],

[62], [479], [72], [188], [413], [173], [74]. For performance studies, discrete event simulation is the most adopted strategy. Considering the classes mentioned above, *discrete event simulation* (DES) is classified as event-driven, dynamic, stochastic, and discrete. Discrete event simulation is the subject studied in this chapter.

14.1.1 MONTE CARLO SIMULATION

Before presenting discrete event simulation, however, a brief introduction to *Monte Carlo simulation* is given, since DES evolved from it. Monte Carlo simulation relies on repeated random sampling and is adopted to evaluate probabilistic phenomena that do not change characteristics over time or non-probabilistic expressions using probabilistic methods. In order to conduct a Monte Carlo simulation, the analyst should:

1. Define a model,

2. Define the input parameters,

3. Generate random input data,

4. Apply the input data to the model, and

5. Analyze the output.

Example 14.1.1. Numerical Integration

As an example, let us find the area bounded by $y = 9 - x^2$ and $y = 0$ depicted in Figure 14.1. The first step is defining a model to be simulated. In order to obtain the model, we need to define the range of integration, and the maximum value of y (y_{max}) in the range of integration. In this particular case, the range in $x \in (-3,3)$ and $y_{max} = 9$. Hence, let us envelope $y = 9 - x^2$ and $y = 0$ by the rectangle: $x = -3, x = 3$, $y = 0$, and $y = 9$ (see Figure 14.1). Our model that estimates the area A_f is

$$\tilde{A}_f = \left(\frac{\sum_{k=1}^{n} C(x_k, y_k)}{n} \right) \times A_r,$$

$$C(x_k, y_k) = \begin{cases} 1 & \text{if } x_k^2 + y_k \leq 9, \\ 0 & \text{otherwise,} \end{cases}$$

$$x_k = 6 \times U(0,1) - 3,$$

and

$$y_k = 9 \times U(0,1),$$

where $U(0,1)$ is a function that generates a random number in the interval $[0,1]$, and $A_r = 9 \times 6 = 54$ is the area of the rectangle that envelopes the area we intend to estimated (A_f).

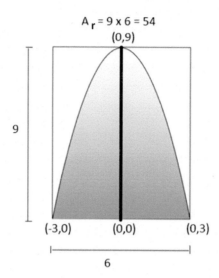

Figure 14.1   Numerical Integration Using Monte Carlo Simulation.

The reasoning for estimating A_f through the model presented is the following: first, we generate uniform random pairs (x_k, y_i) in the respective intervals $[-3, 3]$ and $[0, 9]$, and check if the points (x_k, y_k) are within or outside the interested region (area of interest). If a point is within the region, $C(x_k, y_k) = 1$; otherwise , $C(x_k, y_k) = 0$. By generating a large number (n) of pairs (x_k, y_k), the ratio $\sum_{k=1}^{n} C(x_k, y_k)/n$ is an estimation of the ratio A_f/A_r, which multiplied by A_r, results in an estimation of A_f.

The input parameters consist of pairs of numbers uniformly generated in the interval $[0, 1]$. The third step consists of generating n pairs (u_x, u_y) (points), where u_x, u_y are obtained from $U(0, 1)$. The n pairs are then applied to the model (fourth step), which are then counted to total the number of points within the region of interest $(\sum_{k=1}^{n} C(x_k, y_k)/n)$. The area is then estimated by $\tilde{A}_f$. The area can be easily calculated through a spreadsheet or using or your program language of choice. A straightforward implementation of this process is shown in Mathematica code 20.

Line 4 specifies the area of the rectangle that envelops the region of interest. The number of points to be simulated is defined in Line 5. The uniformly generated numbers are defined in Lines 7 and 8. The model is specified from Line 9 to Line 15. This code was executed for $n = 30,000$ points, and the estimated area was $\tilde{A}_f = 36.0162$, whereas the exact result is $A_f = \int_{-3}^{3}(9 - x^2)dx = 36$.

The second version of this program is shown below. In this version, the program ends its execution when the specified maximal error is obtained, or the maximal number of points is generated. Besides the point estimate, the respective confidence interval is also provided.

Algorithm 20 Numerical Integration

```
1:  ClearAll;
2:  c = 0;
3:  Cxy = 0;
4:  Ar = 54;
5:  n = 30000;
6:  For[i = 0, i < n, i++,
7:      x = RandomReal[-3, 3];
8:      y = RandomReal[0, 9];
9:      If[x² + y <= 9,
10:         c = 1,
11:         c = 0
12:     ];
13:     Cxy = Cxy + c;
14: ]
15: Af = N[(Cxy*Ar)/n];
16: Print["Area=", Af];
17: Quit
```

The confidence level is specified by setting the variable p to the appropriate level. The maximal error allowed is specified in variable e. The critical value of z is obtained through Line 4. The areas (computed during the process) are stored in a list (Line 13). These areas are used to estimate the error. The actual error is computed from Line 17 to Line 19. The standard deviation is only calculated for iterations larger than 30. If the required maximal error is obtained, the loop is ended and the results provided, that is, the point estimate, the respective confidence interval, the error obtained, and the number of points generated. In case the error margin has not been obtained, $i = n$; otherwise, it provides the number of points at which the maximal error was achieved.

Executing the program, these results were obtained: Area $= 36.0837$, Confidence Interval $= (36.0737, 36.0937)$, Error $= 0.00999997$, Confidence Level $= 95\%$, i= 25818 (number of points generated). Other executions, provide distinct results. It is worth mentioning that many improvements may be applied to the code presented in order to improve its performance and precision. These will be discussed later on in the chapter.

$\square$

Example 14.1.2. Estimating π

A similar strategy is adopted to estimate the number π. Here, we present one program that estimates the number π. The first step in estimating the number π consists of conceiving a model to simulate π. Consider the quarter circle of radius $r = 1$ depicted in Figure 14.2.

The area of the quarter circle is

Algorithm 21 Numerical Integration with Confidence

1: ClearAll;
2: l = –˝; i = 0; c = 0; s = 100; Cxy = 0; Ac = 0;
3: e = 0.01; p = 0.975; Ar = 54; n = 30000;
4: z = InverseCDF[NormalDistribution[0, 1], p];
5: While[i < n,
6:    i++;
7:    x = RandomReal[-3, 3];
8:    y = RandomReal[0, 9];
9:    If[x^2 + y <= 9,
10:      c = 1, c = 0];
11:    Cxy = Cxy + c;
12:    Ac = N[(Cxy*Ar)/i];
13:    AppendTo[l, Ac];
14:    If[i > 30,
15:      s = StandardDeviation[l]
16:    ];
17:    If[((z*s)/Sqrt[i]) < e,
18:      Break[]];
19:    ]
20: Print["Area=", Ac];
21: Print["Confidence Interval=(", Ac - ((z*s)/Sqrt[i]), " , ", Ac + ((z*s)/Sqrt[i]), ")"];
22: Print["Error=", (z*s)/Sqrt[i]];
23: Print["Confidence Level=", 100 - 200*(1 - p), "
24: Print["i=", i];

$$A_{QC} = \frac{\pi r^2}{4}.$$

Therefore,

$$\pi = \frac{4 \times A_{QC}}{r^2}.$$

As $r^2 = 1$, then

$$\pi = 4 \times A_{QC}.$$

Now, if we compute the area of the quarter circle using the method already depicted in the previous example, and obtain its estimate $A_{QC}^{\sim}$, then the estimate of π is

$$\tilde{\pi} = 4 \times A_{QC}^{\sim},$$

where the area of the quarter circle is estimated by

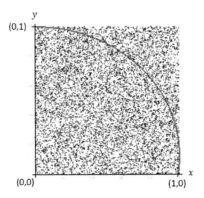

Figure 14.2 Quarter Circle of Radius 1.

$$A_{\widetilde{QC}} = \frac{\sum_{k=1}^{n} C_k(i,j)}{n} \times A_R = \frac{\sum_{k=1}^{n} C_k(i,j)}{n},$$

since the area of the square of side 1 is 1. $C_k(i,j)$ counts the number of points within the quarter circle. It is specified by

$$C_k(i,j) = \begin{cases} 1 & \text{if } d(i,j) \leq 1, \\ 0 & \text{otherwise,} \end{cases}$$

where $d(i,j) = d(u_i, u_i) = \sqrt{u_i^2 + u_j^2}$. u_i and u_j are numbers uniformly generated in the interval $[0,1]$. Therefore, our simulation model is

$$\tilde{\pi} = 4 \times \frac{\sum_{k=1}^{n} C_k(i,j)}{n}.$$

The first program that simulates π is depicted below:
The code was executed for generating 1,000,000 points (n). An estimate obtained was 3.14281. Figure 14.2 shows 30,000 points plotted on the plan (blue dots).   □

Example 14.1.3. Average Flow Rate

A manufacturing company is required to evaluate the design of a piston pump. Each product must pump $0.2\,ml/s$ (flow rate). A simulation project was set to estimate the mean flow rate over $10,000$ pumps, given the specified variations in piston diameter (d), stroke length (l), and the stroke frequency f (see Figure 14.3). Ideally, the pump flow rate across 10,000 pumps will have a standard deviation smaller or equal to $3.33 \times 10^{-3}\,ml/s$.

Algorithm 22 Estimating π

```
1:  ClearAll;
2:  cij = 0;
3:  Cxy = 0;
4:  pi = 0;
5:  n = 1,000,000;
6:  For[i = 0, i < n, i++,
7:      x = RandomReal[0, 1];
8:      y = RandomReal[0, 1];
9:      dij = Sqrt[x² + y²];
10:     If[dij <= 1,
11:         cij = 1,
12:         cij = 0
13:     ];
14:     Cxy = Cxy + cij;
15:     ];
16:     pi = N[(Cxy*4)/n];
17:     Print["π̃", pi];
18:     Quit;
```

The first step is to define a model that represents the flow rate. The flow rate (fr) can be estimated by

$$fr = \pi \times \left(\frac{d}{2}\right)^2 \times l \times f.$$

The input parameters are the diameter (d), the stroke length (l), and the stoke frequency (f). Considering the historical data of the company facility, the parameter distributions are:

Table 14.1
Input Variable Distributions[1]

Input Variable	Distribution
d	$N(0.1\,cm, 0.003\,cm)$
l	$N(3.5\,cm, 0.15\,cm)$
f	$N(0.5\,rps, 0.002833\,rps)$

The simulation program that evaluates the flow rate is presented in 23. This simulation generates 10,000 samples of d, l, and f, which represent 10,000 pumps according to the distributions that fit the historical data. This data is generated in Lines

---

[1]Methods for random variate are discussed later in this chapter.

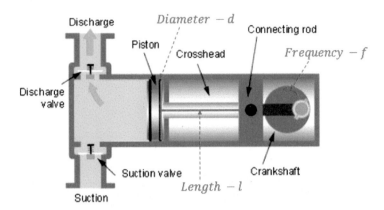

Figure 14.3   Piston Pump.

4, 5, and 6. The data is then applied to the model specified in Line 7, which computes 10,000 flow rates. The flow rates are stored in the list fr. The mean flow rate (mfr) and the respective standard deviation ($SD(fr)$) are computed in Lines 8 and 9. The 95% confidence intervals for the mean (cim) and standard deviation ($cisd$) are calculated in Lines 10 and 11. Table 14.2 shows the results obtained in one simulation. The confidence interval for the standard deviation is $(1.0016 \times 10^{-3}, 1.02976 \times 10^{-3})$. The standard deviation specified is well above the estimate; hence we may state that the facility operates according to the manufacturing requirements.

Table 14.2
Simulation Result

Metrics	Values (ml/s)
mfr	13.7699×10^{-3}
$SD(fr)$	1.0155×10^{-3}
cim	$(11.7794 \times 10^{-3}, 15.7605 \times 10^{-3})$
$cisd$	$(1.0016 \times 10^{-3}, 1.02976 \times 10^{-3})$

□

Algorithm 23 Estimating the Flow Rate
1: ClearAll;
2: n = 10000;
3: fr = −″;
4: d = RandomVariate[NormalDistribution[0.1, 0.003], n];
5: l = RandomVariate[NormalDistribution[3.5, 0.15], n];
6: f = RandomVariate[NormalDistribution[0.5, 0.002833], n];
7: fr = N[$\left(\frac{d}{2}\right)^2$*l*f*$\pi$];
8: m = Mean[fr];
9: sd = StandardDeviation[fr];
10: cim = StudentTCI[m, sd, Length[fr], ConfidenceLevel → .95];
11: cisd = Sqrt[VarianceCI[fr, ConfidenceLevel → .95]];
12: Print["Mean=", m, ";", " Mean˙CI=", cim, ";", " SD=", sd, ";", " SD˙CI=", cisd]
13: Quit;

14.2 DISCRETE EVENT SIMULATION: AN OVERVIEW

This section presents an overview of discrete event simulation (DES) and describes its essential functions. As in Monte Carlo simulation, DES relies upon random variate generation. In addition, however, the simulation of events is guided by a discrete event model representing the system being simulated. In this chapter, the discrete event simulation model adopted is Stochastic Petri nets.

A discrete event model could be coded and simulated using programming languages, and the metrics of interest could also be evaluated using such languages. For example, Appendix E presents a workload simulator for the CTMC depicted in Figure 24.31, which is also equivalent to the SPN shown in Figure 24.36. The Code 54 simulates online bookstore transactions depicted in the Flowchart 24.24. Such an implementation strategy is similar to the Monte Carlo approach depicted in the previous section, in which the model, the metrics of interest, and the stop criteria are coded as one entity. After the program is executed, an output is yielded, presenting the simulation result. However, it is important to emphasize that these systems are dynamic since their states evolve with time.

Figure 14.4 shows the main macro-activities and data structures usually implemented in a discrete event simulator. The aim here is to provide an overview of the event scheduling mechanism. The details related to random variate generation and output analysis are presented in later sections.

To explain this mechanism, let us estimate the utilization of a $G/G/1$ queue system (Figure 14.5).a. The SPN depicted in Figure 14.5.b is a performance model of this system. The traffic arrival is represented by the transition a, and the service is specified by the transition s. The server semantics of both transitions is sss. The number of tokens in place q represents the number of items (transactions, people, etc.) to be processed. The SPN marking vector of this model has only one component, that is, $M = (m_q)$, where $|(m_q)| = 1$. $M(t) = (m_q(t))$ represents the SPN marking at instant

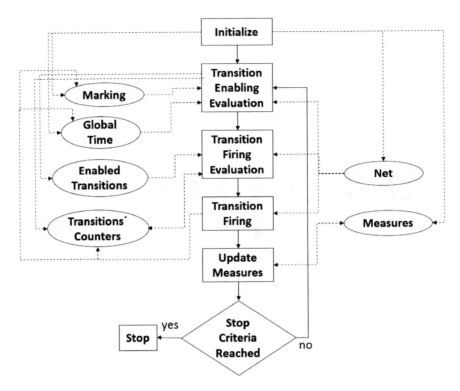

Figure 14.4 Discrete Event Simulation – Event Scheduling.

t. Hence, $m_q = i$ denotes that place q has exactly i tokens. Likewise, $m_q(t) = i$ denotes that place q has exactly i tokens at the instant t. Such a marking may also be represented in Mercury-like notation, that is, $\#q = i$ ($\#q(t) = i$ - the time-dependent version). The time distribution of transition a is $G_a(t)$ whereas the time distribution of transition s is $G_s(t)$. The probability of having i tokens in place q ($P(\#q = i)$[2]) by time instant t is estimated by

$$P(\#q = i)(t) = \hat{\pi}_i(t) = \frac{tsm_i(t)}{t}, \qquad (14.2.1)$$

where $tsm_i(t)$ is the total time the model (SPN) spent with i tokens in place q up to instant t. If the time interval $(0,t)$ is very long, and $P(\#q = i)(t)$ approaches a steady values ($\hat{\pi}_i$), if such a solution exists (a balanced system - arrivals are slower than services), $P(\#q = i)(t) \approx P(\#q = i)$, which represents the steady-state probability of having i tokens in place q.

---

[2]Mercury-like notation.

The mean number of tokens in place q by the time t $(E(\#q)(t))^3$ is defined by

$$E(\#q)(t) = \frac{\sum_{i=0}^{k} tsm_i(t) \times i}{t}, \qquad (14.2.2)$$

where k is the maximal number of tokens in place q by instant t. If the interval $(0,t)$ is long enough to $E(\#q)(t)$ to approach a steady value $E(\#q)$ (if such a solution exists), $E(\#q)$ represents the steady-state mean number of tokens in place q.

The system utilization by time instant t may be estimated through

$$u(t) = 1 - \frac{tsm_0(t)}{t},$$

where $tsm_0(t)$ is the overall time spent in marking $M_0(t)$ $(m_q^0(t) = 0$, which is also denoted by $\#q(t) = 0$) by the time t. This marking $(\#q(t) = 0)$ denotes a state in which the system is idle by the instant t over the time interval $(0,t)$. If the time interval $(0,t)$ is long enough so that $u(t)$ approaches a constant values u (if such a solution exists), u represents the steady-state utilization. Whenever clear, (t) is omitted from the following explanation in the interest of clarity.

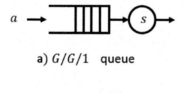

a) $G/G/1$ queue

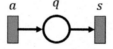

b) SPN representing the $G/G/1$ queue

Figure 14.5 $G/G/1$ Queue System.

The simulation process starts by initializing the global time variable (t) to $t = 0$, $tsm_0 = 0$, $u = 0$, and by defining the initial marking $M = M_0$ of the net. For this net, $M_0 = (0)$. In this marking, the set of enabled transition is $ET_{M_0} = \{a\}$ (see the enabling rule specified in 13.1.2), since transition s is disabled. As we have no immediate transitions in this net, the multiset of firable transitions is also the set

---

[3] Mercury-like notation.

$FT_{M_0} = \{a\}$ (see the multiset of firable transition)[4]. For all firable transitions, create a clock variable (y_i). In this marking, y_a was created. A random variate, v_a^1 [5], is generated according $G_a(t)$ and assigned to y_a, $y_a = v_a^1$. Now, given the current marking, $M = M_0$, look at current values of all clock variables (in this case, there is only one clock variable, y_a) and get the smallest clock value, $\min_{\forall t_i \in FT_{M_0}} \{y_i\} = v_a^1$, and find the respective transition, $e = \arg\min_{\forall t_i \in FT_{M_0}} \{y_i\} = \arg\{v_a^1\} = a$. At this point, the chosen transition should be fired (see the firing rule 13.1.3). Firing a, leads to $M_1 = (1)$. The time spent in M defines the time between transitions' firing. In this case ($M = M_0$), it is $y^* = y_a = v_a^1$. Now, the global time variable t is updated to $t = t + y^* = 0 + v_a = v_a^1$, the overall time spent in M_0 is updated to $tsm_0 = v_a^1$ as well as the utilization is changed to $u = 1 - v_a^1 / v_a^1 = 0$.

The clock variable of every fireable transition should now also be updated. Here, in general, we have to consider the memory policy of transitions, that is, *age memory*, *enabling memory*, and *resampling* (see in Section 13.1.). In this case, let us assume the *enabling memory* to both transitions. Therefore, there are two cases to consider:

1. $y_i' = y_i - y^*$, if $t_i \in FT_M \wedge t_i \neq e \wedge t_i \in FT_{M'}$, where $M[e > M'$,

2. $y_i = v_i$, where $v_i \sim G_{t_i}(t)$ if $t_i \in FT_{M'} \wedge (t_i = e \vee t_i \in FT_M)$, where $M[e > M'$.

In words, (first case) the clock variable of a transition t_i at the next marking (M'), y_i', which was also firable at M, but it was not the one fired ($e \neq t_i$) is calculated just subtracting its value from the time spent in the previous state (y^*), that i $y_i' = y_i - y^*$. The second case covers two additional circumstances: **I)** the case in which the fired transition at M (e) is also firable at M', and **II)** transitions that were firable at M, but are firable at M'. In both cases, a new value should be sampled from the respective time distribution $G_{t_i}(t)$.

At this point, we may highlight some differences between the *enabling memory* (considered in this example), *resampling*, and *age memory*. For transitions with *resampling*, at each new marking M', new clock values should be sampled and assigned to each firable transition clock variable; thus disregarding the past at each new marking.

Transitions with *age memory* should be considered distinct situations. When such a transition (t_i) becomes enabled in a marking M, we should consider the respective enabling degree, $ED_{t_i,M}$. One clock variable is created for each transition enabling ($y_{t_i,j}$) - j is the respective enabling - and one value is sampled from $G_{t_i}(t)$, and assigned to the respective clock variable (related to each enabling). If a transition fires (e) (related to a specific enabling. Remember that multiple enabling is allowed), the clock variable for all other transition or transition enabling that were not the one fired

---

[4]In this specific example, all multiset of firable transitions are sets, since the server semantics of both transitions are *sss*.

[5]The superscript in v_x^i, that is, i, is just to represent the value instance generated. In this particular case, it was the first - 1 - sample assigned to y_a

(t was fired, but a different enabling.) is subtracted from the time spend in M, that is y^*. We will come back to this later.

Let us come back to the example being studied. At marking $M_1 = (1)$, a and s are enabled and firable, $ET_{M_1} = \{a, s\}$ and $FT_{M_1} = \{a, s\}$. Therefore, the respective clock values should be sampled from their time distributions, since $a = e$ at M_0 and $s \notin FT_{M_0}$. Hence, $v_a^2 \sim G_a(t)$ and $v_s^1 \sim G_s(t)$. Thus, $y_a = v_a^2$ and $y_s = v_s^1$. Now, the simulator has to decide which transition should be fired. This transition is obtained from

$$e = \arg \min_{\forall t_i \in FT_{M_1}} \{y_i\}.$$

Thus

$$e = \arg \min \{v_a^2, v_s^1\}.$$

Assume $v_a^2 < v_s^1$, then $y^* = \min\{v_a^2, v_s^1\} = v_a^2$ and $e = \arg \min\{v_a^2\} = a$. Hence, the global time variable t is updated to $t = t + y^* = v_a = v_a^1 + v_a^2$. The transition $e = a$ is fired (see the firing rule 13.1.3). Its firing leads the net to marking $M_2 = (2)$. Now, the metrics should be updated. As current marking was M_1, the time spent in marking M_0, tsm_0 does not change. The utilization is updated to

$$u = 1 - \frac{tsm_0}{t} = 1 - \frac{v_a^1}{v_a^1 + v_a^2}.$$

Now, the simulator should find which transitions are enabled. In marking M_2, a and s are enabled. Both transitions are also firable ($ET_{M_2} = \{a, s\}$ and $FT_{M_2} = \{a, s\}$). As the memory policy is *enabling memory* (remember that the server semantics of a and s are *sss*) and considering that $e = a$ and $s \in FT_{M_1}$, then the clock variable of s should be updated by $y_s = y_s - y^* = v_s^1 - v_a^2$, and the a new sample should be obtained from $G_a(t)$ (v_a^3) and assigned to y_a. The similarly described simulation process continues until the stop criteria have been reached for each metric being evaluated. The stop criteria will be discussed later in this chapter.

It is worth noting, however, the case in which the firing semantics of transition s is *iss*. In such a case, the simulation proceeds in a slightly different manner. In this new marking (M_2), a and s are enabled, but s has two enabling (its firing degree is 2). Therefore, the firable transitions are better represented by a multiset than a set. In such a case, consider FT_{M_2} as multiset; hence, $FT_{M_2} = \{a, s, s\}$. Thus, the transition s, now, has two clock variables, y_s^i, $i = \{1, 2\}$. One of its enabling is still related to the previous marking since s was firable at that marking, but it was not fired at that marking. As in the case of *sss*, the clock variable of s should be updated to $y_s^1 = y_s - y^*$. However, the second transition s enabling is new; that is, it concerns the new marking (M_2), which increased the transition s enabling degree. For this enabling a new sample should be obtained from $G_s(t)$ and assigned to y_s^2. Therefore, in marking M_2, three clock variables' values should be looked at to define the shortest value, which defines the transition that must be fired; that is, $y^* = \min\{y_a, y_s^1 y_s^2\}$. It must be mentioned that the chances of firing the transition s are now higher than when considering the sss firing policy because two clock values are assigned to transition s and only one to transition a. More details about the memory policies and the firing semantics are provided later in this section.

Table 14.3 summarizes the simulation process for 7 transition firings. In this case, the simulated sequence was $seq = a \to s \to a \to a \to s \to s \to a$. The table's second column shows the variables' values in the initial marking. The initial marking was $M_0 = (0)$ (line 2), as mentioned above. As already described, the only firable transition in M_0 is a (line 10), which is shown in the set of firable transitions of the second column. A random variate was generated from $G_a(t)$ ($va_1 = 109.7491$) and assigned to y_a (lines 14 and 18). As a is the only firable transition, $y^* = min\{va_1\} = 109.7491$ (lines 22 and 6). Hence, time spent in M_0 is $tsm_0 = 109.7491$ (line 24). Firing a takes the system to marking M_1 (third column), and the global time is updated to $t = 0 + 109.7491 = 109.7491$ (line 8, column 3). Therefore, the utilization is updated to $u = 1 - tsm_0/t = 1 - 109.7491/109.7491 = 0$ (line 23, column 2).

Table 14.3
Simulation Steps - Time is Represented in $t.u.$ (time unity)

Current marking	M	M	M	M	M	M	M
	0	1	0	1	2	1	0
Next marking	M[e>M'	M[e>M'	M[e>M'	M[e>M'	M[e>M'	M[e>M'	M[e>M'
	1	0	1	2	1	0	
Sojourn time at M	y*	y*	y*	y*	y*	y*	y*
	109.7491	71.3786	19.8768	92.0716	23.5619	67.5335	7.42608
Global time	t	t	t	t	t	t	t
	0	109.7491	181.1277	201.0046	293.0761	316.6381	384.1715
Scheduled transition	e	e	e	e	e	e	e
	a	s	a	a	s	s	a
Set of firable transitions	FT(M)	FT(M)	FT(M)	FT(M)	FT(M)	FT(M)	FT(M)
	a	a,s	a	a,s	a,s	a,s	a
Random variate generated for a	va	va	va	va	va	va	va
	109.7491	91.2554		92.0716	98.5215		
Random variate generated for s	vs	vs	vs	vs	vs	vs	vs
		71.3786		115.6335		67.5335	
Remaining time of a	ya	ya	ya	ya	ya	ya	ya
	109.7491	91.2554	19.8768	92.0716	98.5215	74.9596	7.4261
Remaining time of s	ys	ys	ys	ys	ys	ys	ys
		71.3786		115.6335	23.56192	67.53348	
Minimal remaining time	y_{min}	y_{min}	y_{min}	y_{min}	y_{min}	y_{min}	y_{min}
	109.7491	71.3786	19.8768	92.0716	23.5619	67.5335	7.4261
Utilization	0	0.3941	0.3551	0.557705	0.5906	0.6626	0.6500
tsm_0	109.7491	109.7491	129.626	129.626	129.626	129.626	137.0521

In marking M_1, the firable set is $\{a, s\}$ (line 12, column 3). As shown earlier, a clock variate is sampled from $G_a(t)$ and $G_s(t)$ and assigned to y_a and y_s, respectively. Here these values are 91.2554 and 71.3786 (lines 18 and 20, column 3). As $y_s < y_a$, then $y_{min} = 71.3786$ (line 22, column 3), and $e = s$ (line 10, column 3). Hence, $y^* = 71.3786$ (lines 6, column 3). Firing $e = s$ takes the net back to marking M_0. The subsequent changes occur according to the process described. Table 14.3 shows this process up to 7 transition firings. The respective utilization obtained over time can be read in the columns of Line 23 and in Figure 14.6.

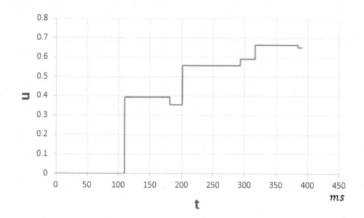

Figure 14.6 Utilization $\times$ t.

Now, let us give some more details about the memory policy. Consider the net depicted in Figure 14.7. The server semantics of all transitions but t_0 are *sss*. The server semantics of t_0 is *iss*. At the initial marking, $M_0^T = (2,0,1,0,0,1,0)$, the enabling degree of t_0 is 2 ($ED_{M_0}(t_0) = 2$). The enabling degree of all other transitions is 1 ($ED_{M_0}(t_i) = 1, t_i \neq t_0$). The set of enabled transition in M_0 is $ET_{M_0} = \{t_0, t_1, t_2, t_3\}$, and the multiset of firable transitions is $FT_{M_0} = \{t_0, t_0, t_1, t_2, t_3\}$. It is important the highlight that t_0 has two enabling. Also consider the initial global time as $t = 0$.

For each element of FT_{M_0}, one clock variable is created, that is $y_{t_0}^1$, $y_{t_0}^2$, y_{t_1}, y_{t_2}, and y_{t_3}. $y_{t_0}^1$, $y_{t_0}^2$ is clock variable of the first and the second enabling of t_0, respectively. In the simulation process, a time value is sampled from each time distribution assigned to each transitions, that is, $v_{t_0}^1$, $v_{t_0}^2$, $v_{t_1}^1$, $v_{t_2}^1$, and $v_{t_3}^1$. These values are assigned to the respective clock variable created. Hence, $y_{t_0}^1 = v_{t_0}^1$, $y_{t_0}^2 = v_{t_0}^2$, $y_{t_1} = v_{t_1}^1$, $y_{t_2} = v_{t_2}^1$, and $y_{t_3} = v_{t_3}^1$.

Let us take into account two different cases. First, consider the case in which $v_{t_0}^2$ is the smallest of these values. Thus, $y_{min} = \min\{ y_{t_0}^1, y_{t_0}^2, y_{t_1}, y_{t_2}, y_{t_3} \} = v_{t_0}^2, y^* = v_{t_0}^2$, and $e = \arg\{v_{t_0}^2\} = t_0$. Firing t_0 takes the net to marking M_1, that is $M_0[t_0 > M_1$, where $M_1^T = (1,1,1,0,0,1,0)$. The global time is updated to $t = 0 + y^* = v_{t_0}^2$. At M_1, the enabling degree of every transition is one, $ED_{M_1}(t_i) = 1, \forall t_i \in ET_{M_1}$, the set of enabled transition is $ET_{M_1} = \{t_0, t_1, t_2, t_3\}$, and the multiset of firable transition is $FT_{M_1} = \{t_0, t_1, t_2, t_3\}$.

When M_1 is reached, the transitions' clock variable must be updated. Hence,

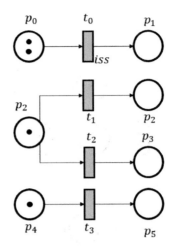

Figure 14.7 Memory Policy.

$$y_{t_0^1} = v_{t_0}^1 - y^* = v_{t_0}^1 - v_{t_0}^2,$$

$$y_{t_1} = v_{t_1}^1 - y^* = v_{t_1}^1 - v_{t_0}^2,$$

$$y_{t_2} = v_{t_2}^1 - y^* = v_{t_2}^1 - v_{t_0}^2,$$

and

$$y_{t_3} = v_{t_3}^1 - y^* = v_{t_3}^1 - v_{t_0}^2,$$

if either *enabling memory* or *age memory* are adopted. Now, let us take into account a second case. Consider $v_{t_1}^1$ is the smallest value. Thus, $y_{min} = \min_{t_i \in ET_{M_0}} \{y_{t_i}\} = v_{t_1}^1$, and $e = \arg v_{t_1}^1 = t_1$. Firing t_1 takes the net to marking M_2, that is $M_0[t_1 > M_2$, where $M_2^T = (2,0,0,1,0,1,0)$. In M_2, the set of enabled transitions is $ET_{M_2} = \{t_0, t_3\}$ and the multiset of firable transitions is $FT_{M_2} = \{t_0, t_0, t_3\}$. The global time is updated to $t = 0 + v_{t_1}^1 = v_{t_1}^1$, and the clock variables should also be updated. Here we have two different situations to consider. If the memory policy adopted is *enabling memory*, then the clock values are lost for all transitions that lost their enabling. Thus, as t_2 is no longer enabled, its clock variable is destroyed (or its value is lost). For transitions still enabled in M_2, their clock variables are updated as in the previous case. Thus,

$$y_{t_0^1} = v_{t_0}^1 - y^* = v_{t_0}^1 - v_{t_1}^1,$$

$$y_{t_0^2} = v_{t_0}^2 - y^* = v_{t_0}^2 - v_{t_1}^1,$$

and

$$y_{t_3} = v_{t_3}^1 - y^* = v_{t_3}^1 - v_{t_1}^1.$$

If *age memory* is adopted, the clock variables of every transition is subtracted from $v_{t_1}^1$, even for those that lose their enabling. Hence, $y_{t_2} = v_{t_2}^1 - v_{t_1}^1$, and this value is considered when t_2 becomes enabled again in the future.

In *resampling memory*, the clock variable of all enabled transitions is sampled again from their respective distribution probability at every new marking.

Example 14.2.1. Let us consider the net depicted in Figure 14.5. Now, however, assume the time between arrivals and the service time are exponentially distributed with rate λ ($Exp(\lambda)$) and normally distributed with mean μ and standard deviation σ ($N(\mu, \sigma)$), respectively. The mean system size is estimated by

$$mss = E\{\#q\}. \tag{14.2.3}$$

The throughput is estimated using

$$tp = P\{\#q > 0\} \times \frac{1}{\mu}, \tag{14.2.4}$$

and the response time is estimated through

$$rt = \frac{E\{\#q\}}{P\{\#q > 0\} \times \frac{1}{\mu}}. \tag{14.2.5}$$

Assume $\mu = 90\,ms$, $\sigma = 20\,ms$, and $\lambda = 0.01\,tpms$. The net was simulated using the Mercury tool, considering the maximal relative error of 5% and a confidence interval of 95%. The corresponding point estimation of that simulation related to the metrics above is presented in Table 14.4.

Table 14.4
Simulation Result – Queue $E/N/1$

Metrics	Values
u	0.9005
mss	5.2731
tp	$0.0100\,tpms$
rt	$527.0197\,ms$

Stop criteria based on error and confidence interval will be discussed later in this chapter.

$\square$

14.3 RANDOM VARIATE GENERATION

This section introduces a set of methods for stochastic random variate generation. First, however, let us be clear about the terms random number and random variate. Values in the range $[0, 1]$ generated from distribution functions other than uniform are usually called random variate. On the other hand, random variates in the range $[0, 1]$ generated from uniform distribution are called random numbers. Therefore, the term random number generation refers to a random variate generation of uniformly distributed values in the interval $[0, 1]$.

In this section, five basic methods for generating random variates are introduced. They are:

- Inversion transform,

- Convolution,

- Composition,

- Characterization, and

- Acceptance-Rejection.

Accuracy, speed, memory use, and simplicity are aspects to be considered when selecting an appropriate generator. The *accuracy* refers to how exactly the distribution of variates generated is to the adopted distribution. *Speed* concerns the computing time required to generate a variate. *Memory use* is related to the memory requirement of the generator. Moreover, *simplicity* refers to how simple the method is to be implemented. Figure 14.8 presents a guideline for supporting choosing a generator considering the aspects mentioned above.

14.3.1 PSEUDO-RANDOM NUMBER GENERATION

Stochastic simulation is deeply based on sequences of random variates. As random variate generation methods usually require strategies for generating random numbers, we begin the section by introducing random number generation. It is also important to be aware of the trade-off between accuracy, speed, and memory usage of the methods since they are intensively used throughout the whole simulation process.

As the "random number" generation strategy is intrinsically based on some procedure, these methods could not generate true randomness. Therefore, rigorously speaking, the values generated from such methods are indeed pseudo-random values. Pseudo-random generation methods can, however, perform well. The key aspects to weigh are the quality of "random numbers" and the computational effort required to generate large quantities of such numbers. These aspects should never be underestimated.

One of the most useful strategies for generating the random numbers is through deterministic procedures that produce sequences of independent identically distributed

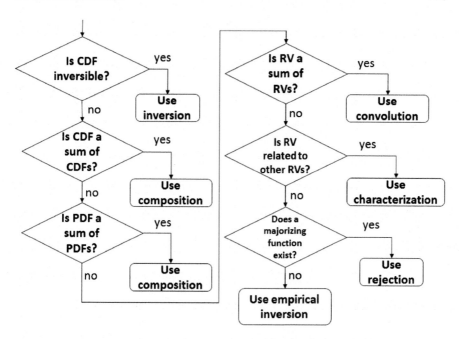

Figure 14.8 A Guide for Deciding the Random Generation Method.

(*iid*) random numbers in the range $[0, 1]$. Such sequences are composed of pseudo-random numbers produced by a pseudo-random number generator. A pseudo-random number generator aims to produce sequences of numbers in the interval $[0, 1]$ that imitate numbers produced from the uniform distribution $U[0, 1]$. Besides, the pseudo-random number generator should be fast since millions of numbers may be required during a simulation. As the generator produces a pseudo-random number (since the algorithms are deterministic), the sequence (period) starts over after a quantity of generated numbers. Therefore, to replicate true randomness, the period should be very long. An additional interesting property is only achieved due to the deterministic nature of the pseudo-random number generation: replicability. Considering a starting point (a seed), generating the same sequence of numbers should be possible. This feature allows replicating simulations. However, if a different sequence is required, change the seed. In this text, the term random number refers to a pseudo-random number. Whenever the context requires, however, we may explicitly mention pseudo-random numbers.

A pseudo-random number generator may be formally defined by the structure $\mathfrak{G} = (S, s_0, f, U, o)$ [191], where S is a finite set of states, $s_0 \in S$ is the initial state (seed), $f : S \to S$ is the next state function, U is the interval $[0, 1]$, and $o : S \to U$ is the output function. The state of the generator evolves from s_0 according to $s_i = f(s_{i-1})$, where $i = 1, 2, 3, \ldots$ At each state, $s_i \in S$, the output function generates a pseudo-random number $u_i \in U$. Indeed, the generator must eventually revisit a state previously seen, that is, $s_j = s_i$ for some $j > i \geq 0$.

There are many methods available for the generation of random numbers. It is worth mentioning the Tausworthe method [424], among the so-called digital methods, Fibonacci-based methods [188], congruential methods, and strategies that adopt a combination of other methods. The interested reader may refer to Jerry Banks Simulations Handbook, and Press et al. Numerical Recipes for a good number of methods [190] [316].

One of the most widely used techniques for generating random numbers is the linear congruential method (*LCM*) [234]. This method generates a sequence of pseudorandom numbers calculated with a discontinuous piecewise linear equation. In *LCM*, the state at step i is an integer s_i, and the transition between states is defined by

$$s_{i+1} = (a \times s_i + c) \mod m, \quad i = 0, 1, 2, \ldots \tag{14.3.1}$$

The initial state $s_0 \in S$ is called seed, $a > 0$ is named multiplier, c is an additive constant, and $m > 0$ is the modulus (a large prime number is recommended). If $c \neq 0$, the generator is called *mixed congruential method*. When $c = 0$, the generator is called *multiplicative congruential method*. The method consists of multiplying $s_{i-1} \in S$ by a, adding c (when $c \neq 0$), dividing this partial result by m, and taking the remainder of this division. The remainder is the new state $s_i \in S$. The output function takes s_i and produces u_i by dividing s_i/m; hence

$$u_i = \frac{s_i}{m}, \quad i = 0, 1, 2, \ldots \tag{14.3.2}$$

The above recurrence must eventually repeat itself, with a period no greater than m.

Example 14.3.1. For instance consider this toy generator $s_{i+1} = 5 \times s_i + 1 \mod 17$, and a seed equal to 3. Table 14.5 shows the number generated. After the last number, the sequences repeat.

□

Several authors advocated combining different generators to obtain a composite generator that behaves better than a component alone [316]. On the other hand, you should be cautious of overengineered generators that cause wasteful use of resources. Indeed, Law and Kelton give an example where combination makes things worse [208].

Example 14.3.2. Let us illustrate the use of the combination to generate pseudorandom numbers. Consider the generator just introduced above. Now, however, the multiplier, instead of being a constant value (5), it is also obtained from another generator. Hence, we have

Table 14.5
Pseudo-Random Numbers Generated from s_{i+1}
$s_{i+1} = 5 \times s_i + 1 \mod 17$ with seed 3. $u_i = s_i/17$.

i	s_i	u_i	i	s_i	u_i
0	3	0.1765	8	5	0.2941
1	16	0.9412	9	9	0.5294
2	13	0.7647	10	12	0.7059
3	15	0.8824	11	10	0.5882
4	8	0.4706	12	0	0.0000
5	7	0.4118	13	1	0.0588
6	2	0.1176	14	6	0.3529
7	11	0.6471	15	14	0.8235

$$s_{i+1} = (z_{j+1} \times s_i + c) \mod m, \quad i = 0, 1, 2, \ldots \quad (14.3.3)$$

where

$$z_{j+1} = (a \times z_j + d) \mod n, \quad j = 0, 1, 2, \ldots \quad (14.3.4)$$

$$u_i = \frac{s_i}{m}, \quad i = 0, 1, 2, \ldots \quad (14.3.5)$$

Table 14.6 shows a snapshot of the set of numbers generated.

Table 14.6
Two Pseudo-Random Numbers
Generated from $s_{i+1} = (z_{j+1} \times s_i + 1) \mod 19$ and $z_{j+1} = (5 \times z_j + 1) \mod 17$ with seeds $s_0 = 11$ and $z_0 = 1$, respectively.

j, i	z_j	s_i	u_i	j, i	z_j	s_i	u_i
1	6	10	0.5263	9	2	3	0.1579
2	14	8	0.4211	10	11	15	0.7895
3	13	6	0.3158	11	5	0	0.0000
4	16	2	0.1053	12	9	1	0.0526
5	13	8	0.4211	13	12	13	0.6842
6	15	7	0.3684	14	10	17	0.8947
7	8	0	0.0000	15	0	1	0.0526
8	7	1	0.0526	16	1	2	0.1053

□

Example 14.3.3. Let us consider another pseudo-random number generator specified by

$$s_{i+1} = 16,087 \times s_i \quad \text{mod} \quad 4294966441, \qquad (14.3.6)$$

$$u_i = \frac{s_i}{4294966441}. \qquad (14.3.7)$$

and the seed $s_0 = 23000009$. Table 14.7 shows a snapshot of the set of numbers generated. The multiplier, the modulus, and the seed are considered prime numbers. For many practical examples, the period of this generator may be considered very long to allow mimic true randomness since the modulus is 4294966441.

Table 14.7

Pseudo-Random Numbers

Generated from $s_{i+1} = 16,087 \times s_i$ mod 4294966441 with seed 23000009. $u_i = s_i/4294966441$

i	u_i	i	u_i
1	0.1476	8	0.8406
2	0.7926	9	0.9768
3	0.0888	10	0.1532
4	0.2508	11	0.7629
5	0.9252	12	0.3293
6	0.4552	13	0.2476
7	0.1829	14	0.0515

□

14.3.2 INVERSE TRANSFORM METHOD

Assume a non-negative random variable X with cumulative distribution function $F_X(x)$, and a uniformly distributed random variable defined in the range $[0,1]$. Figure 14.9 plots the cumulative distribution function of both variables. The cumulative distribution function $F_U(u)$ is plotted on the left-hand side of the cartesian plan, whereas $F_X(x)$ is shown on the right-hand side. Consider a random variate u_i in the range $[0,1]$, and take $F_U(u_i)$, which, by the way, is u_i (hence, we can avoid this step.)[6]. As $F_X(x_i) = F_U(u_i) = u_i$, x_i can be obtained from $x_i = F^{-1}(u_i)$.

Therefore, for using this method, the cumulative distribution function inverse must be known. The steps for generating a random variate are

---

[6]It was shown only for didactic purpose

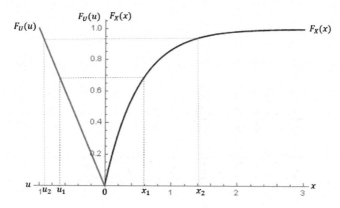

Figure 14.9 Inverse Transformation.

1. Generate a random number $u_i \in [0, 1]$, and

2. Obtain $x_i = F^{-1}(u_i)$ as a realization of X.

Example 14.3.4. Now, let us generate a random variate from a random variable, X, distributed according to an **exponential distribution** with rate $\lambda = 0.5$. As

$$u = F_U(u) = F_X(x),$$

then

$$u = 1 - \exp^{-\lambda x}.$$

Hence

$$1 - u = \exp^{-\lambda x}.$$

Thus

$$\ln(1 - u) = \ln(\exp^{-\lambda x}) = -\lambda x.$$

As u was generated from $U[0, 1]$, $1 - u$ is also distributed according $U[0, 1]$. Hence

$$\ln(u) = -\lambda x.$$

Therefore

$$x = -\frac{\ln(u)}{\lambda}. \tag{14.3.8}$$

Hence, for this particular case in which $F_X(x) = 1 - \exp^{-0.5x}$,

$$x = -2 \times \ln(u).$$

If $u = 0.55$, then $x = 1.195674$.

□

The inverse transform technique is quite general and can be adopted, for instance, to sample from a **discrete random variable distributions**. Consider a discrete random variable X that can take n different values $a_1 < a_2 < ... < a_n$ with the corresponding probability $p_1, p_2, ..., p_n$. Figure 14.10 presents the cumulative distribution function of X (considering $n = 3$).

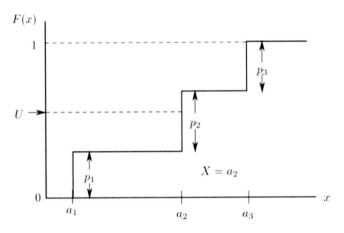

Figure 14.10 Inverse Transformation – Discrete Random Variable.

Therefore, the steps for generating a random variate sampled from F_X are:

1. Generate a random number $u \in [0, 1]$, and

2. Obtain the random variate according to

$$X = \begin{cases} a_1, & \text{if } 0 \le u \le p_1 \\ a_2, & \text{if } 0 < u \le p_1 + p_2 \\ ... & ... \\ a_n, & \text{if } 0 < u \le p_1 + p_1 + ... + p_n \end{cases}$$

Example 14.3.5. Let us consider Y a non-negative discrete random variable and its probability function

$$P_Y(y) = \begin{cases} 0.2, & y=1 \\ 0.3, & y=4 \\ 0.5, & y=6 \end{cases}$$

Since $F_Y(j) = \sum_{y=0}^{j} P_Y(y)$, then

$$F_Y(y) = \begin{cases} 0, & \text{if } 0 \le y < 1 \\ 0.2, & \text{if } 1 \le y < 4 \\ 0.5, & \text{if } 4 \le y < 6 \\ 1, & \text{if } y \ge 6 \end{cases}$$

Random variate samples obtained from $F_Y(y)$ can be obtained using this simple Mathematica program:

Algorithm 24 Discrete Random Variate Generation

1: u = RandomVariate[UniformDistribution[–0, 1ˆ]];
2: Which[u ≤ 0.2, y = 1, (u > 0.2) && (u ≤ 0.5), y = 4, u > 0.5, y = 6]

□

If the modeler cannot find a theoretical distribution to represent the data, adopting the **empirical distribution** of the data may be an alternative. Hence, random samples may be obtained from the empirical distribution. Let us assume a system's response time was measured, and a sample X of size n was recorded. Also, consider the sample was sorted in ascending order. This ordered sample is represented in the second column of Table 14.8. The empirical distribution (see the third column) can be computed by

$$F(x_i) = \frac{i}{n+1}.$$

Table 14.8
Empirical Distribution

i	x_i	$F(x_i)$	$F(x_{i+1})$
0	0	0	$F(v_1)$
1	v_1	$F(v_1)$	$F(v_2)$
2	v_2	$F(v_2)$	$F(v_3)$
...	...	...	...
n	v_n	$F(v_n)$	1

Figure 14.11 shows the empirical distribution of the sample X. For generating a random variate from the empirical distribution, $F(x_i)$, obtain a random number $u \in [0,1]$ and verify to which interval it belongs ($u \in I_i$) in the set of intervals $\{I_i\}$, where

$$I_1 = [0, F(v_1)),$$

$$I_2 = [F(v_1), F(v_2)),$$

$$\dots$$

$$I_n = [F(v_n), 1)],$$

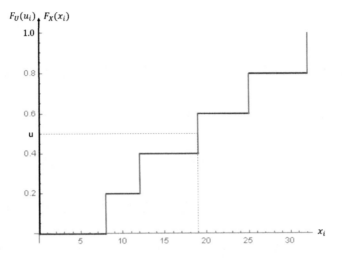

Figure 14.11 Empirical Distribution.

As there is no intersection between any of these sets, u belongs to only one of them. Therefore, the random variate is obtained according to

$$X = \begin{cases} v_1, & \text{if } u \in I_1 \\ v_j, & \text{if } u \in I_j, \ j = 2, ..., n-1 \\ v_n, & \text{if } u \in I_n \end{cases}$$

The Program 25 reads a sample from the spreadsheet file, obtains the respective empirical cumulative distribution ECD, plots the respective ECD, and generates a ten random variate based on ECD.

Example 14.3.6. Now, assume that the empirical distribution of the response time is presented in Table 14.9. The second column gives the ordered sample measured. The third column presents the cumulative distribution function, and the fourth column shows the cumulative distribution for the subsequent element of the ordered sample.

Now, assume $u = 0.8032$ was generated; then the respective random variate obtained from the empirical distribution is $X = 54.7$, since $u \in (0.7273, 0.8182]$ (see the third and fourth column of line 8 of Table 14.9).

□

Algorithm 25 Random variate generation based on ECD

1: ClearAll;
2: m = 10;
3: data = Flatten[Import["sse.xlsx"]];
4: ECD = EmpiricalDistribution[data];
5: max = Max[data];
6: Plot[CDF[ECD , x], x, 0, max, PlotStyle $->$ Blue]
7: For[i = 1, i <= m, i++,
8:    n = RandomVariate[ECD];
9:    Print["Number ", i, ": ", n];
10:]
11: Quit

Table 14.9

An Example of an Empirical Distribution

i	x_i	$F(x_i)$	$F(x_{i+1})$
0	0	0	0.0909
1	15.4	0.0909	0.1818
2	18.9	0.1818	0.2727
3	20.1	0.2727	0.3636
4	24.5	0.3636	0.4545
5	29.3	0.4545	0.5455
6	33.9	0.5455	0.6364
7	48.2	0.6364	0.7273
8	54.7	0.7273	0.8182
9	72.0	0.8182	0.9091
10	86.1	0.9091	1

If the data measured (sample) is believed to come from a continuous distribution (although not known), then it makes sense to interpolate between the observed data points to fill in the gaps [190]. A straightforward method involves applying linear interpolation between each pair of data points. Therefore, for each consecutive points $(x_i, F(x_i))$ and $(x_{i+1}, F(x_{i+1}))$, find the slope (a_i) and the intercept (b_i) of the respective line $(y = ax + b)$, and if $u \in I_i$ (see in Table 14.10), then obtain the random variate by

$$x = \frac{u - b}{a}.$$

Thus, by applying this method to the empirical distribution presented in Table 14.9, the respective slopes (a_i) and the intercepts (b_i) of each line (i) are computed (see

Table 14.10
Empirical Distribution with Linear Interpolation

i	x_i	$F(x_i)$	$F(x_{i+1})$	$a_i = (F(x_{i+1}) - F(x_i))/(x_{i+1} - x_i)$	$b_i = F(x_i) - a_i x_i$
0	0	0	$F(v_1)$		
1	v_1	$F(v_1)$	$F(v_2)$	$(F(x_1) - F(x_0))/(x_1 - x_0)$	$F(x_1) - a_1 x_1$
2	v_2	$F(v_2)$	$F(v_3)$	$(F(x_2) - F(x_1))/(x_2 - x_1)$	$F(x_2) - a_2 x_2$
...	...	...	...	...	...
n	v_n	$F(v_n)$	1	$(F(x_n) - F(x_{n-1}))/(x_n - x_{n-1})$	$F(x_n) - a_n x_n$

columns 5 and 6 of Table 14.11). Once the uniformly generated random number, u, is obtained, and found to belong to a given interval $(F(x_i), F(x_{i+1})]$, the random variate is obtained from $x_i = (u - b_i)/a_i$. Table 14.11 summarizes this process and presents the respective result for $u = 0.8032$.

Table 14.11
An Example of an Empirical Distribution with Interpolation

i	x_i	$F(x_i)$	$F(x_{i+1})$	a_i	b_i
0	0	0	0.0909		
1	15.4	0.0909	0.1818	0.005903	0.0
2	18.9	0.1818	0.2727	0.025974	-0.30909
3	20.1	0.2727	0.3636	0.075758	-1.25
4	24.5	0.3636	0.4545	0.020661	-0.14256
5	29.3	0.4545	0.5455	0.018939	-0.10038
6	33.9	0.5455	0.6364	0.019763	-0.12451
7	48.2	0.6364	0.7273	0.006357	0.32994
8	54.7	0.7273	0.8182	0.013986	-0.03776
9	72.0	0.8182	0.9091	0.005255	0.43983
10	86.1	0.9091	1	0.006447	0.353965

Hence, considering $u = 0.8032$, $x_i = (0.8032 - (-0.03776))/0.013986 = 60.1288$, since $u \in (0.7273, 0.8182]$ (see the third and fourth column of line 8 of Table 14.11).

A random variate from many distributions can be generated using the inverse transformation method. Here, a list of some is presented.

Dagun Distribution

CDF:

$$F(x) = \left(\left(\frac{x}{b} \right)^{-a} + 1 \right)^{-p}, \ x \geq 0.$$

Random variate generation:

$$x = b((1-u)^{-1/p} - 1)^{\frac{1}{a}}, \ u \in [0,1].$$

Laplace Distribution
CDF:

$$F(x) = 1 - \frac{e^{-x}}{2}, \ x \geq 0.$$

Random variate generation:

$$x = \begin{cases} \ln(2u), & 0 \leq u \leq 1/2, \\ -\ln(2(1-u)), & 1/2 > u \leq 1. \end{cases}$$

Uniform Distribution in $[a,b]$
CDF:

$$F(x) = \frac{x-a}{b-a}, \ x \in [a,b].$$

Random variate generation:

$$x = a(1-u) + bu, \ u \in [0,1].$$

Logistic Distribution
CDF:

$$F(x) = \frac{1}{1 + e^{-\frac{x-\mu}{\beta}}}, \ x \in (-\infty, \infty).$$

Random variate generation:

$$x = \mu - \beta \ln(\frac{1}{u} - 1), \ u \in [0,1].$$

Pareto Distribution
CDF:

$$F(x) = 1 - \left(\frac{k}{x}\right)^{\alpha}, \ x \geq k.$$

Random variate generation:

$$x = \frac{k}{u^{\frac{1}{\alpha}}}, \ u \in [0,1].$$

Triangular Distribution
CDF:

$$F(x) = \begin{cases} \frac{(x-a)^2}{(b-a)(c-a)}, & a \leq x \leq c, \\ 1 - \frac{(b-x)^2}{(b-a)(b-c)}, & c < x \leq b. \end{cases}$$

Random variate generation:

$$
x = \begin{cases} a + \sqrt{(b-a)(c-a)u}, & 0 \le u \le \frac{c-a}{b-a}, \\ b - \sqrt{(b-a)(b-c)(1-u)}, & \frac{c-a}{b-a} < u \le 1. \end{cases}
$$

Bernoulli Distribution

CDF:

$$
F(x) = \begin{cases} 0, & x < 0, \\ 1 - p, & 0 \le x < 1. \\ 1, & x \ge 1. \end{cases}
$$

Random variate generation:

$$
x = \begin{cases} 1, & u < p, \\ 0, & u \ge p. \end{cases}
$$

Geometric Distribution

CDF:

$$
F(x) = 1 - (1 - p)^x, \ x \in \{1, 2, 3, ...\}.
$$

Random variate generation:

$$
x = \left\lceil \frac{\ln u}{\ln(1-p)} \right\rceil, \ u \in [0, 1].
$$

Gumbel Distribution (Extreme Value Type I Distribution)

CDF:

$$
F(x) = 1 - e^{-e^{\frac{x-\mu}{\sigma}}}.
$$

Random variate generation:

$$
x = \mu + \sigma \ln(\ln(u)), \ u \in [0, 1].
$$

Weibull Distribution

CDF:

$$
F(x) = 1 - e^{-\left(\frac{x}{\beta}\right)^{\alpha}}, \ x \ge 0.
$$

Random variate generation:

$$
x = \beta(-\ln(u))^{\frac{1}{\alpha}}, \ u \in [0, 1].
$$

Cauchy Distribution

CDF:

$$
F(x) = \frac{\tan^{-1}\left(\frac{x-a}{b}\right)}{\pi} + \frac{1}{2}, \ x \in (-\infty, \infty).
$$

Random variate generation:

$$x = a + b\tan\left(\pi\left(u - \frac{1}{2}\right)\right), \ u \in [0, 1].$$

Rayleigh Distribution

CDF:

$$F(x) = 1 - e^{-\frac{x^2}{2\sigma^2}}, \ x \in (-\infty, \infty).$$

Random variate generation:

$$x = \sigma\sqrt{-\log\left((1 - u)^2\right)}, \ u \in [0, 1].$$

14.3.3 CONVOLUTION METHOD

The probability distribution of a sum of random variables may be obtained through the convolution of the distributions of the random variables. The random variate method, however, does not compute the convolution of the distributions. What is important here is that the relation to other variates (that are part of the sum) is more easily computed.

Therefore, if the random variable X can be expressed as a sum of n random variables $\sum_{i=1}^{n} Y_i$, where the variate of Y_i can be easily generated. The random variate x (from X) can be obtained by generating n random variate $y_i s$ (from $Y_i s$), and then summing them.

Notice the difference between composition and convolution. The former technique is used when the pdf or CDF can be expressed as a sum of other pdfs or CDFs. The latter technique is used when the random variable itself can be expressed as a sum of other random variables.

An **Erlang random variable** X with parameters γ (shape or phases) and λ (rate) is a sum of γ independent exponential variables Y_i with rate λ. The random variates of $Y_i s$ may be obtained using the inverse transformation method (see Section 14.3.2):

$$y_i = -\frac{\ln(u_i)}{\lambda}.$$

Hence the random variate of X may be obtained by

$$x = \sum_{i=1}^{\gamma} y_i. \tag{14.3.9}$$

$$x = \sum_{i=1}^{\gamma} -\frac{\ln(u_i)}{\lambda}.$$

$$x = -\frac{1}{\lambda} \sum_{i=1}^{\gamma} \ln(u_i).$$

736 Performance, Reliability, and Availability Evaluation of Computational Systems

$$x = -\frac{1}{\lambda} \ln\left(\prod_{i=1}^{n} u_i\right). \tag{14.3.10}$$

Example 14.3.7. Consider a random variable X distributed according to a Erlang distribution with shape 4 and rate 10. A random variate of X can be obtained by first generating u_1, u_2, u_3, and u_4 (assume $u_1 = 0.3820$, $u_2 = 0.4496$, $u_3 = 0.8797$, and $u_4 = 0.9676$), then calculating

$$y_1 = -\frac{\ln(0.382)}{10} = 0.0962,$$

$$y_2 = -\frac{\ln(0.4496)}{10} = 0.0799,$$

$$y_3 = -\frac{\ln(0.8797)}{10} = 0.0128,$$

and

$$y_4 = -\frac{\ln(0.9676)}{10} = 0.0033.$$

The random variate x is then obtained by summing up y_1, y_2, y_3, and y_4:

$$x = 0.0962 + 0.0799 + 0.0128 + 0.0033 = 0.1923.$$

It could also be directly obtained from Equation 14.3.10, that is

$$x = -\frac{1}{\lambda} \ln\left(\prod_{i=1}^{n} u_i\right).$$

$$x = -\frac{1}{10} \ln(0.382 \times 0.4496 \times 0.8797 \times 0.9676) = 0.1923.$$

$\square$

The probability distribution of the number of successes in a sequence of n independent Bernoulli experiments with constant parameter p is equal to the **binomial probability distribution** with parameters n and p. Therefore, a binomial variate (x) with parameters n and p is a sum of n independent Bernoulli variates (y_i) with success probability p, that is

$$x = \sum_{i=1}^{n} y_i,$$

where $y_i \sim B(1,p)$[7].

---

[7] Bernoulli with parameter p.

Example 14.3.8. Consider a random variable X distributed according to a binomial distribution with parameters $n = 10$ and $p = 0.8$ ($B(n, p)$). A random variate can be obtained by first generating 10 uniform random numbers in the interval $[0, 1]$, u_i, $i = 1, 2, \ldots 10$, then obtaining 10 Bernoulli random variates, y_1, $i = 1, 2, \ldots 10$, and summing them up. Table 14.12 presents the Bernoulli variates obtained. Summing them, we have $X = \sum_{i=1}^{10} y_i = 7$.

Table 14.12
Bernoulli Random Variates

i	u_i	y_i	i	u_i	y_i
1	0.62395	1	6	0.81652	0
2	0.40367	1	7	0.97629	0
3	0.61223	1	8	0.68538	1
4	0.54418	1	9	0.72665	1
5	0.97345	0	10	0.39546	1

□

The sum of n geometric variates, y_i, is a **Pascal variate**. Therefore, as

$$y_i = \left\lceil \frac{\ln u_i}{\ln(1 - p)} \right\rceil, \; u_i \in [0, 1],$$

x may be obtained by

$$x = \sum_{i=1}^{n} y_i.$$

$$x = \sum_{i=1}^{n} \left\lceil \frac{\ln u_i}{\ln(1 - p)} \right\rceil, \; u_i \in [0, 1]. \tag{14.3.11}$$

Example 14.3.9. Consider a random variable X distributed according to a Pascal distribution with parameters $n = 10$ and $p = 0.2$. A random variate can be obtained by first generating 10 uniform random numbers in the interval $[0, 1]$, $u_i, i = 1, 2, \ldots 10$, then obtaining 10 geometric random variates, y_1, $i = 1, 2, \ldots 10$, and summing them up. Table 14.13 presents the geometric variates obtained. Summing them, we have $X = \sum_{i=1}^{10} y_i = 52$.

□

It is worth mentioning that the convolution method may be applied to generate random variates of χ^2 and normal distributions. These variates can be generated through the convolution method, since the χ^2 distribution with n degrees of freedom is a sum

Table 14.13
Geometric Random Variates

i	u_i	y_i	i	u_i	y_i
1	0.360546	5	6	0.610431	3
2	0.294894	6	7	0.528581	3
3	0.676748	2	8	0.521714	3
4	0.379192	5	9	0.351756	5
5	0.019990	18	10	0.776666	2

of squares of n standard normal variates, the sum of a large number of variates (from any distribution) has a normal distribution, and normal variates may be obtained by adding an appropriate number of $U[0,1]$ variates.

14.3.4 COMPOSITION METHOD

This method can be applied if either the CDF or PDF of X may be represented by the weighted sum of other CDFs or PDFs. Hence, suppose that either form can represent the distribution function, $F_X(x)$, or the density function, $f_X(x)$, of random variable X:

1. $F_X(x) = \sum_{i=1}^{n} \alpha_i F_{X_i}(x)$,

2. $f_X(x) = \sum_{i=1}^{n} \alpha_i f_{X_i}(x)$,

where $\sum_{i=1}^{n} \alpha_i = 1$. If random variates of X_i can be generated, a random variate of X can be obtained applying this method.

Notice the difference between convolution and composition. The latter is adopted when the PDF or CDF can be represented as a sum of other PDFs or CDFs. The former may be applied when the random variable itself can be specified as a sum of other random variables.

Let us consider a three-phase **hyperexponential distribution** to illustrate the composition method. Assume X is a random variable and

$$F(x) = \alpha_1(1 - e^{-\lambda_1 x}) + \alpha_2(1 - e^{-\lambda_2 x}) + (1 - \alpha_1 - \alpha_2)(1 - e^{-\lambda_3 x})$$

is its CDF. Random variates for X can be generated as follows:

1. Generate a uniform random number $u \in [0,1]$.

2. Evaluate the indicator functions 1_1, 1_2, and 1_3 by considering

$$\phi(u) = \begin{cases} 1, & \text{if } 0 \le u \le \alpha_1, \\ 2, & \text{if } \alpha_1 < u \le \alpha_1 + \alpha_2, \\ 3, & \text{if } u > \alpha_1 + \alpha_2. \end{cases}$$

where

$$1_1 = \begin{cases} 0, & \text{if } \phi(u) \neq 1, \\ 1, & \text{if } \phi(u) = 1. \end{cases}$$

$$1_2 = \begin{cases} 0, & \text{if } \phi(u) \neq 2, \\ 1, & \text{if } \phi(u) = 2. \end{cases}$$

$$1_3 = \begin{cases} 0, & \text{if } \phi(u) \neq 3, \\ 1, & \text{if } \phi(u) = 3. \end{cases}$$

3. Obtain the variate using

$$x = 1_1 \times \left(-\frac{\ln u}{\lambda_1}\right) + 1_2 \times \left(-\frac{\ln u}{\lambda_2}\right) + 1_3 \times \left(-\frac{\ln u}{\lambda_3}\right).$$

Example 14.3.10. Now consider a random variable X distributed according to $F(x) = 0.2(1 - e^{-50x}) + 0.3(1 - e^{-100x}) + 0.5(1 - e^{-150x})$. A random variate can be obtained by first generating one uniform random number in the interval $[0,1]$ (Let us assume u was 0.42), evaluating $\phi(u)$ (in this case, $\phi(0.42) = 2$), and the indicator functions, that is $1_1 = 0$, $1_2 = 1$, and $1_3 = 0$, and finally obtaining the random variate $x = -\ln 0.42/100 = 0.01204$.

□

14.3.5 ACCEPTANCE-REJECTION METHOD

Sometimes the probability density function $f(x)$ of a random variable is readily available, whereas the respective cumulative distribution function $F(x)$ is difficult or even impossible. One example is the normally distributed random variable. In such cases, the acceptance-rejection method is an alternative.

Consider a random variable X and its density function $f(x)$ defined on the interval $[a,b]$. Also assume another function $g(x)$, such that $g(x) \geq f(x)$, $\forall x \in [a,b]$. $g(x)$ is named a majoring function of $f(x)$, and it is clearly not unique. Owing to the complex shape of $f(x)$, the simplest majoring function is a rectangle. Hence, consider

$$g(x) = \begin{cases} c, & x \in [a,b], \\ 0, & otherwise, \end{cases}$$

where $f(x) \leq c$, $\forall x \in [a,b]$. It is usual to choose $c = \max f(x)$, $\forall x \in [a,b]$. The process consists of generating two uniformly distributed random numbers, (u_1 and u_2), and then obtaining a point (x',y') through $x' = a + (b-a)u_1$ ($x' \leftarrow U[a,b]$), and $y' = u_2 \times c$ ($y' \leftarrow U[0,c]$). If $y' \leq f(x')$, accept x'; otherwise, reject it.

In other words, generate a point (u_1, u_2), and use this point to obtain another point (x',y'). The point (x',y') is uniformly distributed over a rectangle defined by base

(b, a) and height c. If (x', y') is below the function $f(x)$, accept x' as a random variate that satisfies the density $f(x)$; otherwise reject it and repeat the process. More formally:

1. Generate $x' \leftarrow U[a, b]$ and $y' \leftarrow U[0, c]$,

2. Obtain $f(x')$,

3. If $y' \leq f(x')$, accept x' as a random variate of $f(x)$; otherwise reject it, and repeat from Step 1.

As an example (see Figure 14.12), consider

$$g(x) = \begin{cases} 0.4, & 0 \leq x \leq 5, \\ 0, & otherwise. \end{cases}$$

Assume X has a **Pert distribution**, and its density function is

$$f(x) = \frac{(b-x)^{\frac{4(b-m)}{b-a}} (x-a)^{\frac{4(m-a)}{b-a}}}{(b-a)^5 B\left(\frac{4(m-a)}{b-a} + 1, \frac{4(b-m)}{b-a} + 1\right)},$$

where

$$B\left(\frac{4(m-a)}{b-a} + 1, \frac{4(b-m)}{b-a} + 1\right)$$

is a Beta function, $[a, b]$ is the domain of $f(x)$, and m is its mode.

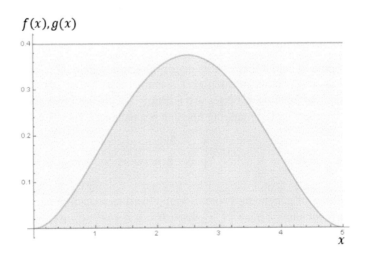

Figure 14.12 Acceptance-Rejection Method.

The Mathematica Program 26 generates random variates obtained from the Pert distribution by applying the acceptance-rejection method. The value of c $(g(x) = c$ – the majoring function) was defined to major $Pert(a, b, m)$, $a = 0$, $b = 5$, and $m = 2.5$. If other parameter values are adopted, c should be re-defined.

Algorithm 26 Pert Random Variate Generation

1: ClearAll;
2: i = 0;
3: a = 0;
4: b = 5;
5: m = 2.5;
6: c = 0.4;
7: While[True,
8:   x = RandomVariate[UniformDistribution[a, b]];
9:   y = RandomVariate[UniformDistribution[0, c]];
10:   $\text{fx} = \text{N}\left[\dfrac{(b-x)^{\frac{4(b-m)}{b-a}}(x-a)^{\frac{4(m-a)}{b-a}}}{(b-a)^5 B\left(\frac{4(m-a)}{b-a}+1, \frac{4(b-m)}{b-a}+1\right)}\right];$
11:   If[y <= fx,
12:     Print[x];
13:     Break[],
14:     Continue[]
15:   ]
16:]
17: Quit

As a second an example, consider

$$g(x) = \begin{cases} 1.55, & 0 \leq x \leq 1, \\ 0, & otherwise. \end{cases}$$

Assume X has a **beta distribution** (defined over $[0, 1]$), and its density function is

$$f(x) = \frac{x^{\alpha-1}(1-x)^{\beta-1}}{B(\alpha, \beta)},$$

where α and β are the shape parameters. The Mathematica Program 27 generates a random variate obtained from a beta distribution by applying the acceptance-rejection method. The value of c $(g(x) = c)$ was chosen to major $Beta(\alpha, \beta)$, $\alpha = 0$ and $\beta = 5$. If other parameter values are chosen, c should be re-defined.

Now, consider a random variable X distributed according to a **triangular distribution**; its density function is

$$f(x) = \begin{cases} \frac{2(x-a)}{(b-a)(m-a)} & a \leq x \leq m \\ \frac{2(b-x)}{(b-a)(b-m)} & m < x \leq b \end{cases},$$

Algorithm 27 Beta Random Variate Generation

1: ClearAll;
2: i = 0;
3: $\alpha = 0$;
4: $\beta = 5$;
5: c = 1.55;
6: While[True,
7:    x = RandomVariate[UniformDistribution[0, 1]];
8:    y = RandomVariate[UniformDistribution[0, c]];
9:    fx = N $\left[\dfrac{x^{\alpha-1}(1-x)^{\beta-1}}{B(\alpha,\beta)} \right]$;
10:   If[y <= fx,
11:      Print[x];
12:      Break[],
13:      Continue[];
14:   ]
15:]
16: Quit

---

where $a = 2$, $b = 6$, and $m = 4$, and the majoring function defined by

$$g(x) = \begin{cases} 0.5, & 2 \leq x \leq 6, \\ 0, & \textit{otherwise.} \end{cases}$$

The Mathematica Program 28 generates a random variate obtained from a triangular distribution by adopting the acceptance-rejection technique. The value of c ($g(x) = c$) was defined by a major triangular density defined in the interval $[2,6]$ with mode $m = 4$.

14.3.6 CHARACTERIZATION

The set of procedures in this class does not adopt one general strategy. Hence, what is presented in this section is not strictly one method but a set of specific methods that are often based on transformation and relation between random variables. In this section, a few examples of such procedures are introduced.

The Box-Muller method [58] generates pairs of **standard, normally distributed random variates**, given f uniformly distributed random numbers. Box and Muller show that if u_1 and u_2 are uniformly distributed, then

$$x_1 = \cos(2\pi \times u_1) \sqrt{-\ln u_2},$$

and

$$x_2 = \sin(2\pi \times u_1) \sqrt{-\ln u_2}$$

Algorithm 28 Triangular Random Variate Generation

1: ClearAll;
2: a = 2;
3: b = 6;
4: m = 4;
5: c = 0.5;
6: While[True,
7:    x = RandomVariate[UniformDistribution[a, b]];
8:    y = RandomVariate[UniformDistribution[0, c]];
9:    If[x <= m,
10:       fx = N[$\frac{2(x-a)}{(b-a)(m-a)}$],
11:       fx = N[$\frac{2(b-x)}{(b-a)(b-m)}$];
12:    ]
13:    If[y <= fx,
14:       Print[x];
15:       Break[],
16:       Continue[]
17:    ]
18:]
19: Quit;

are standard normal random variates, that is Z or $N(0, 1)$. **Normal random variates** following $N(\mu, \sigma)$ may obtained by setting

$$y_1 = \mu + x_1\,\sigma,$$

and

$$y_2 = \mu + x_2\,\sigma.$$

If only one variate, y_1 is needed each time, there is a waste of resource since y_2 is not used. Nevertheless, if many variates are required (which is common), the subsequent variate required uses the variate already computed. Such a policy improves the random variate generator performance.

Let y be a normal random variate generated from $N(\mu, \sigma)$; then a **lognormal random variate**, z, from $LN(\mu, \sigma)$ is obtained by $z = e^y$.

The Mathematica Program 29 generates two normally distributed ($N(\mu, \sigma)$) random variates (y_1 and y_2) and one variate distributed according to a $Log(\mu, \sigma)$ (z_1). In this program, μ and σ were set to 2 and 0.5, respectively.

An alternative that avoids the computation of sines and cosines is based on polar coordinates. This method calculates two uniformly distributed variates, $v_1 = 2u_1 - 1$ and $v_2 = 2u_2 - 1$, on the interval $(-1, 1)$. If $r < 1$, then $y_1 = v_1\rho$ and $y_2 = v_2\rho$, where $\rho = \sqrt{-\ln(r)/r}$ and $r = v_1^2 + v_2^2$.

Algorithm 29 Normal and Lognormal Random Variate Generation

1: ClearAll;
2: $\mu = 2$;
3: $\sigma = 0.5$;
4: u1 = RandomVariate[UniformDistribution[0, 1]];
5: u2 = RandomVariate[UniformDistribution[0, 1]];
6: x1 = Cos[2*Pi*u1]*Sqrt[-(Log[u2])];
7: x2 = Sin[2*Pi*u1]*Sqrt[-(Log[u2])];
8: y1 = μ + u1*σ;
9: y2 = μ + u2*σ;
10: z1 = e^{y1};
11: Quit;

If the interarrival times are exponentially distributed with rate λ, the number of arrivals in the interval T has a **Poisson distribution** with parameter λT. Hence, a Poisson variate can be generated by obtaining exponential variates until their sum exceeds T, that is $\sum_{i=1}^{n} \leq T$. The number of variates generated (n) is a Poisson variate.

The Mathematica Program 30 generates a Poisson variate distributed according to a $P(\lambda T)$. In this program, λ and T were set to 0.01 and 200, respectively.

Algorithm 30 Poisson Random Variate Generation

1: ClearAll;
2: n = 0;
3: $\lambda = 0.01$;
4: st = 0;
5: T = 200;
6: While[True,
7:   n++;
8:   x = RandomVariate[ExponentialDistribution[λ]];
9:   $st = st + x$;
10:   If[st <= T,
11:     Continue[],
12:     Break[]
13:   ];
14:]
15: Print[n];
16: Quit;

A **chi-squared** random variate with k degrees of freedom ($\chi^2(k)$) is equal to this gamma variate $\gamma(k/2, 2)$. Besides, if k is an even number, the χ^2 random variate with

k degrees of freedom can be obtained from the respective Erlang distribution, that is $Erl(k/2, 2)$.

The **Student's t** random variable with k degrees of freedom has the same distribution of the ratio $Z/\sqrt{Y/k}$, where Z is a standard normal variate and Y is a $\chi^2(k)$ random variable independent of Z. Therefore, a Student's t random variate can be generated using the relation between standard normal and $\chi^2(k)$ variates. Program 31 explores this relation and generates a random variate based on a Student's t with k degrees of freedom ($t(k)$).

Algorithm 31 Student's t Random Variate Generation

1: ClearAll;
2: k = 20;
3: z = RandomVariate[NormalDistribution[0, 1]];
4: y = RandomVariate[ChiSquareDistribution[k]];
5: x = z/Sqrt[y/k];
6: Print[x];
7: Quit;

14.4 OUTPUT ANALYSIS

So far we have seen how to generate sequences of random variates considering input parameters and discrete event models. When simulating a model, each execution or run of the experiment produces a single result such as the number of transactions in the system, response time, utilization, number of requests lost. Therefore, the output data of a simulation can be thought of as an estimate of some quantity of interest θ.

A point estimate of θ, denoted by $\widehat{\theta}$, is a number that estimates θ based on samples. A confidence interval estimate of θ is a range of values defined by $[\widehat{\theta} - \varepsilon_1, \widehat{\theta} + \varepsilon_2]$ that states that if the model simulation is repeated n times, it will generate $n/100\%$ intervals that will cover the true value θ given the simulation model that actually represents the system.

First, however, let us characterize the different types of simulations based on whether we are interested in the steady-state or a transient behavior of a system. Steady-state simulation has also been called stationary or non-terminating simulation, whereas transient simulation has also been named terminating simulation. In either case, the output data are used to estimate parameters or even the distribution functions themselves.

Non-terminating simulation studies the steady-state behavior of a system. In such a simulation, there is no obvious or natural point to stop (time instant, for instance), since we are interested in the system's behavior as $t \to \infty$. Therefore, looking at this aspect only, the longer the simulation, the better. Nevertheless, practical considerations (simulation time) limit this. Therefore, strategies should be adopted to "detect" the stationary behavior and stop the simulation process. Thus, a difficulty lies in defining a good stopping rule. This is the subject of study of Section 14.4.2.

Transient simulation studies aim at estimating metrics at a specific time instant. Therefore, the simulation result is related to the specified time instant. As a simulation sequence (run) is a random path, the estimate at a specific time instant varies from one run to another. Hence, one should look at strategies to allow estimating average point measures and confidence. This is the subject of analysis of Section 14.4.1.

The simplest and most common estimation is related to executions of independent and identically distributed random variables X_1, X_2, ..., X_n. Let us consider θ as the mean of a distribution. A point estimate of θ, $\widehat{\theta}$, based on n samples, is computed by

$$\widehat{\theta} = \overline{X} = \frac{1}{n}\sum_{i=1}^{n} X_i. \tag{14.4.1}$$

The interval the contains θ with some level of confidence is estimated by

$$P\left(\widehat{\theta} - Z_{\frac{\alpha}{2}}\sqrt{\frac{\sigma^2}{n}} \le \theta \le \widehat{\theta} + Z_{\frac{\alpha}{2}}\sqrt{\frac{\sigma^2}{n}}\right) = 1 - \alpha, \tag{14.4.2}$$

where σ^2 may be replaced by the sample variance S^2, since $S^2 \to \sigma^2$ as $n \to \infty$. Thus,

$$P\left(\widehat{\theta} - Z_{\frac{\alpha}{2}}\sqrt{\frac{S^2}{n}} \le \theta \le \widehat{\theta} + Z_{\frac{\alpha}{2}}\sqrt{\frac{S^2}{n}}\right) \approx 1 - \alpha. \tag{14.4.3}$$

This interval can also be approximated by

$$P\left(\widehat{\theta} - t_{n'-1,\frac{\alpha}{2}}\sqrt{\frac{S^2}{n}} \le \theta \le \widehat{\theta} + t_{n'-1,\frac{\alpha}{2}}\sqrt{\frac{S^2}{n}}\right) \approx 1 - \alpha, \tag{14.4.4}$$

where

$$t_{n'-1,\frac{\alpha}{2}}\frac{S}{\sqrt{n}} \le \varepsilon.$$

Hence

$$\left(t_{n'-1,\frac{\alpha}{2}}\frac{S}{\sqrt{n}}\right)^2 \le \varepsilon^2.$$

Therefore, the number of samples still required is

$$n \ge \left(t_{n'-1,\frac{\alpha}{2}} \times \frac{S}{\varepsilon}\right)^2, \tag{14.4.5}$$

where ε is the absolute precision error required, and n' is the current sample size.

Before discussing how to obtain accurate simulation results, it is important to high-light the difference between the performance figures obtained from the model and those measured from the system. The concern here is to obtain accurate results from the model, assuming the model represents the system. Our aim is not to evaluate how accurately the model predicts system performance. This is the concern of model val-idation. Therefore, it is important to stress that if the data considered as a model's parameters are not accurate, the simulation will not provide accurate predictions.

In this context, two key issues should be carefully analyzed to support accurate sim-ulation results:

1. removal of initialization bias, and

2. ensuring enough output data have been obtained to achieve precise estimates.

Removal of initialization bias is usually tackled by evaluating warm-up periods and initial condition settings. Ensuring enough output data have been obtained is often addressed through long runs and multiple replications.

14.4.1 TRANSIENT SIMULATION

As already mentioned, terminating simulation evaluates a system that starts in a par-ticular state and then ends after a specified period or when a predetermined condition is reached. Now, consider a model in a specified initial state, execute a terminating simulation, and record the number of transactions in the system (θ – a random vari-able) at time t_j, $\theta_1(t_j)$. Then, change the random generator seeds of the random variables, taking into account the same net's initial state, and execute a new simula-tion run, and obtain a new number of transactions in the system at t, $\theta_2(t)$. If such a process is simulated n times (n runs), a sample $\Theta(t_j) = \{\ \theta_1(t_j),\ \theta_2(t_j),\ ...,\ \theta_n(t_j)\}$. Figure 14.13 shows a set of runs of one replication. Then, obtain the average of $\theta_i(t_j)$ that compose the replication k at t_j, so that

$$\widehat{\theta}^k(t_j) = \frac{1}{n}\sum_{i=1}^{n}\theta_i(t_j).\tag{14.4.6}$$

If we are interested in p time instants, that is $\{t_1, t_2, ...t_p\}$, we need to compute $\widehat{\theta}^k(t_j), \forall t_j \in \{t_1, t_2, ...t_p\}$ for each run.

Figure 14.14 shows the estimate of $\theta^k(t)$ for the kth replication, which is represented by $\widehat{\theta}^k(t)$ for each t of interest.

Now, consider that we have m replications, where each replication has n runs. There-fore, for $t = t_j$, considering m replications, we have

$$\widehat{\Theta}(t_j) = \{\widehat{\theta}^1(t_j), \widehat{\theta}^2(t_j), ...\widehat{\theta}^m(t_j)\},$$

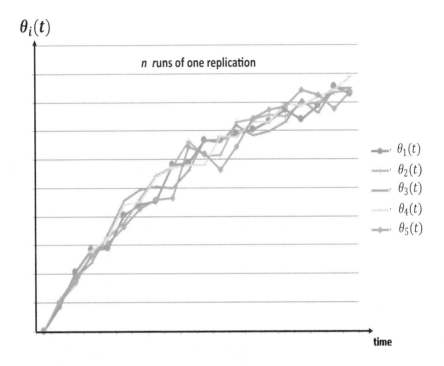

Figure 14.13 n Runs of One Replication.

for each t_j of interest. More formally:

$$\widehat{\theta}(t_j) = \frac{1}{m}\sum_{k=1}^{m}\widehat{\theta}^k(t_j),\tag{14.4.7}$$

is the estimate of θ at t_j for m replications , that is $k \in \{1, 2, \dots k \dots m\}$, where m is the number of replications. It is worth stressing once again that each replication k is composed of n runs, and in each run we may be interested in p time instants, that is $\{t_1, t_2, \dots t_p\}$.

Figure 14.15 shows the point estimate for each k replications of a total of m for each time instant of interest $t_j \in \{t_1, t_2, \dots t_p\}$.

Figure 14.16 shows the point estimate of $\theta(t)$ calculated from the replications for each time instant of interest $t_j \in \{t_1, t_2, \dots t_p\}$, where $\widehat{\theta}(t) = E(\theta(t))$ is an unbiased estimator of $\theta(t)$.

$\widehat{\theta}^k(t)$

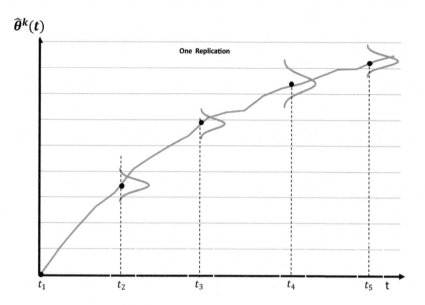

Figure 14.14 $\widehat{\theta}^k(t)$ for the kth Replication.

The variance of $\widehat{\theta}^k(t_j)$ is

$$Var(\widehat{\theta}^k(t_j)) = \frac{1}{m-1} \sum_{k=1}^{m} (\widehat{\theta}^i(t_j) - \widehat{\theta}(t_j))^2,$$

and the standard deviation of $\widehat{\theta}^k(t_j)$ is

$$SD(\widehat{\theta}^k(t_j)) = \sqrt{Var(\widehat{\theta}^k(t_j)}.$$

The confidence interval estimate of $\theta(t_j)$ is computed by

$$\widehat{\theta}(t_j) \pm t_{m-1,1-\alpha/2} \frac{SD(\widehat{\theta}^k(t_j))}{\sqrt{m}}. \qquad (14.4.8)$$

In other words, the replications (each composed of n runs) are conducted until required simulation time, t. If we are interested in a measure only at a specific time instant (t), each replication (k) produces only one measure, $\widehat{\theta}^k(t)$. However, if we

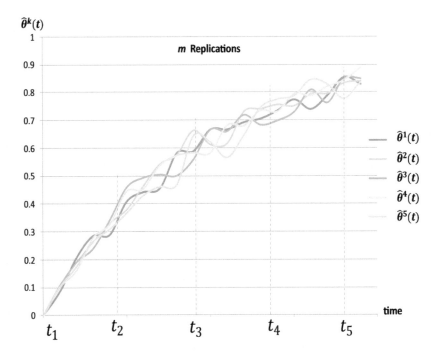

Figure 14.15 $\widehat{\theta}^k(t)$ for m Replications.

are interested in a set of points in the range $t \in [0, t']$, we need to estimate $\theta(t)$ values, $(\widehat{\theta}(t))$ for all time instants of interest in $t \in [0, t']$ (see Figure 14.16).

This method is called **Independent Replication Simulation**, where each replication is composed of n runs. It is worth mentioning that a replication may be composed of only one run. Independent replication strategy usually starts setting an initial number of replications to begin the simulation process. A small initial number of replications may be insufficient so that additional replications may be required. On the other hand, too much time may be wasted on unnecessary simulation runs if the number of replications initially defined is too large. A good practice is setting a reasonably small initial number of replications (m_0), such as thirty. In general, this is sufficient to have statistical confidence for estimating the additional number of replications needed to achieve the absolute precision error (ε) at t:

$$m \geq \left(t_{m_0 - 1, 1 - \frac{\alpha}{2}} \times \frac{SD(\widehat{\theta}^k(t))}{\varepsilon} \right)^2, \tag{14.4.9}$$

$$\widehat{\boldsymbol{\theta}}(\boldsymbol{t})$$

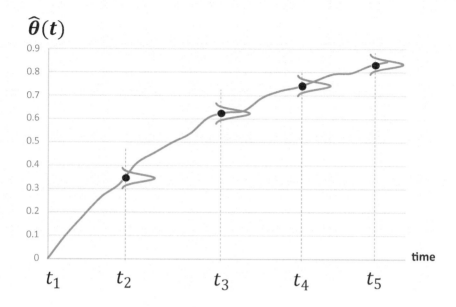

Figure 14.16 $\widehat{\theta}(t)$ - The Point Estimation Considering m Replications.

where ε is the absolute precision error required, and m_0 is the initial number of replications.

The relative precision error is specified by

$$\%\varepsilon = \frac{\varepsilon \times 100}{\widehat{\theta}(t)}, \tag{14.4.10}$$

which is the percentage deviation of the confidence interval about the mean. The number of replications required to achieve the relative precision error ($\%\varepsilon$) may be estimated by

$$m \geq \left(\frac{t_{m_0-1,1-\frac{\alpha}{2}} \, SD(\widehat{\theta}^k(t)) \, 100}{\%\varepsilon \, \widehat{\theta}(t)} \right)^2, \tag{14.4.11}$$

where $\widehat{\theta}^k(t)$ is the point estimate of $\theta(t)$ related to the kth replication.

Some Additional Details

Let us assume we have a discrete event model, such as an SPN, and consider we are interested in conducting a transient simulation of this model to estimate some metrics at the instant $t = 265t.u.$. Let us again take into account the model depicted in Figure 14.5.b. Also consider that transition a is distributed according to $N(\mu_a, \sigma_a)$, $\mu_a = 60t.u.$ and $\sigma_a = 30t.u.$, and that transition s is distributed according to $N(\mu_s, \sigma_s)$, $\mu_s = 100t.u.$ and $\sigma_a = 20t.u.$. Let us consider two particular metrics of interest, which are the utilization and the mean number of tokens in place q at the instant t. As already mentioned earlier, for this SPN, the utilization can be calculated by

$$u(t) = 1 - \frac{tsm_0}{t},$$

where tsm_0 is the period in the time interval $(0, t)$ in which no token was stored in place q, $m_q = \#q = 0$ (also see in the cell specified by column 1 and row 12 of Table 14.14). For this model, the mean number of tokens in place q at the instant t may be estimated by

$$E(m_q) = E(\#q) = frac \sum_{i=0}^{ss} i \times tsm_i t \tag{14.4.12}$$

where ss is the maximal number of tokens in the place q reached up to time t, and tsm_i (see Column 2 of Table 14.15) is the duration over the time interval $(0, t)$ in which place q stored i tokens. This metrics is depicted in column 4 of Table 14.15.

Adopting the enabling memory policy, consider that the following transition sequence $\langle a \rightarrow a \rightarrow a \rightarrow s \rightarrow a \rightarrow a \rightarrow s \rangle$ was fired, and that each respective transition was fired at the instants $\langle 83.34t.u. \rightarrow 22.48t.u. \rightarrow 63.09t.u. \rightarrow 10.12t.u. \rightarrow 47.97t.u. \rightarrow 16.21t.u. \rightarrow 26.28t.u. \rangle$.

The detailed simulation is represented in Table 14.14 and Table 14.15. These tables show only one run; the subsequent runs are similarly simulated to generate a replication. After that, other replications are simulated until the stop criteria at $t = 265t.u.$ is reached.

The initial state is defined by marking $M = (m_q) = \#q = 0$ and global time $t = 0$. In Table 14.14, the initial state may be observed in the second column and second row; and in the first column, cell block Global Time, $t = 0$. At this marking $(M = (m_q) = (0))$, only one transition is enabled, so that the set of enabled transitions is $ET_M = \{a\}$. Then, a random variate is generated for this transition according to the probability distribution assigned to transition a. As already mentioned, the probability distribution assigned to the delay of transition a was $N(\mu_a, \sigma_a)$, $\mu_a = 60t.u.$ and $\sigma_a = 30t.u.$. The random variate generated was $v_a = 83.34$ (see column $= 2$, row $= 14$). This value is also assigned to variable y_a; hence $y_a = v_a = 83.34$ (see column $= 2$, row $= 18$). This value is stored in a list. A second set that contains the set of enabled transitions at M (ET_M) and their respective generated delay is called the set of firable transitions at state (M, t), $FT_{(M,t)}$. The set of transitions that

Table 14.14

One Simulation Run that Aims at Estimating $U(t)$ and $E(\#q)(t)$, $t = 265\,t.u.$

Current marking	M	M	M	M	M	M	M
	0	1	2	2	3	3	4
Next marking	M[e>M'	M[e>M'	M[e>M'	M[e>M'	M[e>M'	M[e>M'	M[e>M'
	1	2	2	3	3	4	3
Sojourn time at M	y^*	y^*	y^*	y^*	y^*	y^*	y^*
	83.34	22.48	63.09	10.12	47.97	16.21	26.28
Global time t	t	t	t	t	t	t	t
0	83.34	105.82	168.91	179.03	227.00	243.21	269.49
Scheduled transition	e	e	e	e	e	e	e
	a	a	a	s	a	a	s
Set of firable transitions	FT(M)	FT(M)	FT(M)	FT(M)	FT(M)	FT(M)	FT(M)
	a	a,s	a,s	a,s	a,s	a,s	a,s
Random variate generated for a	va	va	va	va	va	va	va
	83.34	22.48	63.09	58.09		16.21	37.65
Random variate generated for s	vs	vs	vs	vs	vs	vs	vs
		95.69			90.46		
Remaining time of a	ya	ya	ya	ya	ya	ya	ya
	83.34	22.48	63.09	58.09	47.97	16.21	37.65
Remaining time of s	ys	ys	ys	ys	ys	ys	ys
		95.69	73.21	10.12	90.46	42.49	26.28
Minimal remaining time	y_{min}	y_{min}	y_{min}	y_{min}	y_{min}	y_{min}	y_{min}
	83.34	22.48	63.09	10.12	47.97	16.21	26.28
Utilization(t) $= 1 - (tsm_0/t)$	0.000	0.788	0.493	0.466	0.367	0.343	0.309
tsm_0	83.34	83.34	83.34	83.34	83.34	83.34	83.34

belong to $FT_{(M,t)}$ are shown in the table at the cell specified by column = 2 and row = 12. In that cell, we see $FT_{M,t}\{a,\}$. From the set of firable transitions at state (M,t), we find the transition with the shortest delay. As the list has only one component $(a, 83.34\,t.u.)$, the shortest delay is $83.34\,t.u.$, and the respective transition is a. The shortest delay found is then assigned to variable $y_{min} = 83.34\,t.u.$. This is depicted in column = 2 row = 22. As the shortest delay is assigned to transition a, this transition is the scheduled transition to be fired, which is shown in the table at the cell specified by column = 2 and row = 10. Therefore, firing transition a from state $(M = (0), t = 0$, the model reached a new state specified by marking $M = (1)$ (see the cell specified by column = 2 and row = 4), which is obtained by applying the Petri nets firing rule, and the global time t, which is updated to $83.34\,t.u.$. Such a value was calculated by summing up the previous global time (t=0) to the y_{min}; hence the new t is $t = 0\,y_{min} = 83.34\,t.u.$ (see the cell specified by column = 2 and row = 8). Therefore, the new state reached is $(M = (1), t = 83.34\,t.u.)$. This new marking is shown in the cell specified by column = 2 and row = 4. Such value is also copied to the cell specified by column = 3 and row = 2.

At this point of the simulation process, the set of metrics of interest should be updated. Considering the utilization, no token was stored in place q in the interval $(0, 83.34\,t.u.)$; thus $tsm_0 = 83.34\,t.u.$, which leads $u(83.34\,t.u.) = 1 - 83.34/83.34 = 0$. This partial results is depicted in the cell specified by column 2 and row 23 of Table 14.14. As there was no tokens in place q in the interval $(0, 83.34\,t.u.)$, the mean number of tokens in place q at the instant $83.34\,t.u.$ is zero.

At the state $(M,t) = ((1), 83.34t.u..$, represented by the cells specified by column 3 and row 2, and the instant specified by the cell depicted in column 2 and row 8, the two transitions are enabled, that is the enabling set of transitions is $ET = \{a, s\}$. Therefore, a token in place q enables transition s, and transition a is always enabled because it has neither input places nor guard a expression that disables the transition. As the simulation policy adopted is *enabling memory* and all transitions have single server semantics *(sss)*, neither transition a nor transition s may not have simultaneous enabling of themselves, that is, neither a nor s may not have auto-concurrent firing. The term auto-concurrency here is applied to express a state in which one SPN transition has two or more firings "running" simultaneously. On these grounds, we have two new transitions enabling in this state. In more detail, transition s just became enabled, and transition a was the one which was fired and since its server semantics is *sss*, there was no auto-concurrent firing. Hence, its enabling is new. As both transitions have new enabling (they became enabled in this new state), the random variate for each of them should be generated according to their time probability specifications. Using their respective probability specifications, one new variate was generated for each transition, which are $v_a = 22.48t.u.$ (column 3 and row 14) and $v_s = 95.69t.u.$ (column 3 and row 16). As both transitions have the same priority, both are firable as is shown in the]cell specified by column 3 and row 12, that is $FT_{M,t}\{a, s\}$. These variables' values are copied to variables y_a and y_s, respectively. Hence, $y_a = 22.48t.u.$ and $y_s = 95.69t.u.$. Now, we find the shortest delay among y_a and y_s, and assigns it to y_{mim}; thus $y_{min} = 22.48t.u.$ (in column 3 and row 22.). Consequently, the scheduled transition to fire is a (see cell specified by column $= 3$ and row $= 10$) since it is the one that provided the shortest delay. Firing again transition a, the model reaches the marking $M = (m_q) = \#q = 2$ (see cell specified by column 3 and row 4; which is also copied in the cell specified by column 4 and row 2.). The global time is then updated to $t = 105.82t.u.$, which was obtained by summing up the previous global time $(83.34t.u.)$ and $y*$ $(y* = y_{min} = 22.48t.u.)$.

At this point, the set of metrics should be updated again. Considering the interval $(0, 105.82t.u.)$, the duration that place q had no token was $tsm_0 = 83.34t.u.$. Hence, the utilization is $u(105.82t.u.) = 1 = 1 - 83.34/105.82$; thus $u(105.82t.u.) = 0.788$. Considering the period $(0, 105.82t.u.)$, the duration that the place had one token was $tsm_1 = 22.48t.u.$; hence the mean number of tokens in place q at the instant $105.82t.u.$ is $E(m_q) = E(\#q) = 0 \times 83.34 + 1 \times 22.48 = 22.48$. We may see this value in Table 14.15 by summing up the value of the cell specified by column 3 and row 2 to the value of the cell specified by column 3 and row 3.

This process goes on, as shown in Table 14.14 and Table 14.15 and according to the process already described in Section 14.2. However, it is worth mentioning that the chances of a run (the firing of a transition sequence) finishing exactly at $t = 265t.u.$ are tiny because it is based on the transition whose delays are random variables. In other words, it is an event-driven simulation and not a time-driven simulation. Therefore, each transient run should stop when the global time is higher or equal to the time of interest. There are some possible approaches to handle this. Polynomial interpolation and regression models are some alternatives (see Section 6.7).

Table 14.15
Mean Number of Transactions in the System at t - Time is Represented in t.u.

$\#q = i$	tsm_i	$i \times tsm_i$	$E(\#q) = (\sum_{i=0}^{4} i \times tsm_i)/(t)$	t
0	83.34	0	1.73	269.49
1	22.48	22.48		
2	73.21	146.42		
3	64.18	192.54		
4	26.28	105.12		

Figure 14.17 depicts four runs (j) of one replication (replication r). Each run j finishes when the global time is equal to or larger than t'. An intermediate instant was also depicted in Figure 14.17, t_i. In this figure, we observe the time instants when each run s finished. We also show the instants (related to each run j) when the respective events occurred and then reached the condition $t \geq t'$. This may observed for t' and t_i.

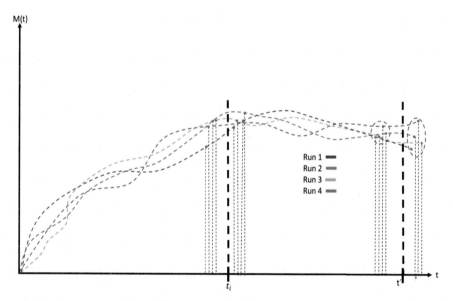

Figure 14.17 Runs of One Replication up the Instant t'.

Figure 14.18 zooms in at the instant t' and shows the four runs, their $t_j'^{-}$ and $t_j'^{+}$ (j is the run) and $t_j'^{-} < t'$ and $t_j'^{+} \geq t'$, and the respective metric values for each run j, that is $M_j(t'^{-})$ and $M_j(t'^{+})$. Therefore, for each run j, we have two points, which are $(t_j'^{-}, M_j(t'^{-}))$ and $(t_j'^{+}, M_j(t'^{+}))$. One possible simple approach to estimate $M(t')$ at t'

for run j is by using these two points to obtain a line equation and then getting $M(t')$ at t'. Hence, using the line equation

$$y = ax + b \tag{14.4.13}$$

and the two points, that is $(t_j'^-, M_j(t'^-))$ and $(t_j'^+, M_j(t'^+))$, we obtain a and b, where

$$a = \frac{M_j(t'^+) - M_j(t'^-)}{t_j'^+ - t_j'^-}, \tag{14.4.14}$$

and

$$b = M_j(t'^-) - \frac{M_j(t'^+) - M_j(t'^-)}{t_j'^+ - t_j'^-} t_j'^-. \tag{14.4.15}$$

Thus, the estimate of $\mu(t)$ in run j is

$$M_j(t') = \frac{M_j(t'^+) - M_j(t'^-)}{t_j'^+, - t_j'^-} t' + \tag{14.4.16}$$

$$M_j(t'^-) - \frac{M_j(t'^+) - M_j(t'^-)}{t_j'^+ - t_j'^-} t_j'^-,$$

which is the point estimate of M at t' provided by the run j.

Thus, considering an rth replication with k runs, the point estimate of the metric at t' ($\mu(t)$) is provided by

$$M^r(t') = \frac{\sum_{j=1}^{k} M_j(t')}{k}. \tag{14.4.17}$$

Now, using m replications, the point estimate for M at t' is calculated by

$$M(t') = \frac{\sum_{r=1}^{m} M^r(t')}{r}, \tag{14.4.18}$$

and the standard deviation of the means is estimated by

$$SD_{M^r(t')} = \left(\frac{\sum_{r=1}^{m} (M^r(t') - M(t'))^2}{m-1} \right)^{\frac{1}{2}}. \tag{14.4.19}$$

The using Equation 6.1.9 we compute the confidence interval for $M(t')$ taking into account m replications.

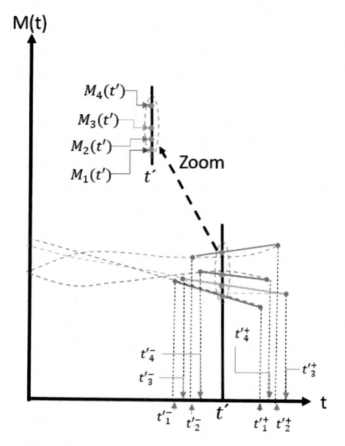

Figure 14.18 Zoom in the Runs at the Instant t'.

$$\mu(t) \in \left(M(t') - t_{\frac{\alpha}{2},m-1} \times \frac{SD_{M^r(t')}}{\sqrt{m}} , M(t') + t_{\frac{\alpha}{2},m-1} \times \frac{SD_{M^r(t')}}{\sqrt{m}} \right), \qquad (14.4.20)$$

where $M(t')$ is the point replication mean, m is the number of replications, $SD_{M^r(t')}$ is the standard deviation of the replication r means, $t_{\alpha/2,m-1}$ is the t value obtained when Student's t-distribution with $m-1$ is the degree of freedom, and α is the degree of significance.

A similar approach consists of calculating the mean values of all t'^-_j and t'^+_j for the j runs as well as the mean values of all $M_j(t'^-)$ and $M_j(t'^+)$, that is

$$t'_m = \frac{\sum_{j=1}^{k} t'^-_j}{k}$$

and

$$t'_M = \frac{\sum_{j=1}^{k} t'^{+}_j}{k},$$

and

$$M_m(t') = \frac{\sum_{j=1}^{k} M_j(t'^{-})}{k}$$

and

$$M_M(t') = \frac{\sum_{j=1}^{k} M_j(t'^{+})}{k}.$$

Hence, we have two points representing the averages of the k runs, that is $(t'_m, M_m(t'))$ and $(t'_M, M_M(t'))$. Figure 14.19 illustrates how these two points are estimated. Figure 14.20 zooms in on the region around the point and shows the segment of line connecting both.

After estimating a and b of Function 14.4.13, we may estimate of $\mu(t')$ by

$$M^r(t') = \frac{M_M(t') - M_m(t')}{t'_M, - t'_m} t' + \qquad (14.4.21)$$

$$M_m(t') - \frac{M_M(t') - M_m(t')}{t'_M - t'_m} t'_m,$$

which is the point estimate of M at t' provided by the replication r. Now, using m replications, the point estimate for M at t' is calculated by Equation 14.4.18, that is

$$M(t') = \frac{\sum_{r=1}^{m} M^r(t')}{r},$$

and the standard deviation of the means is estimated by Equation 14.4.19, which is replicated below

$$SD_{M^r(t')} = \left(\frac{\sum_{r=1}^{m} (M^r(t') - M(t'))^2}{m-1} \right)^{\frac{1}{2}}.$$

The confidence interval for $M(t')$ taking into account m replications may be estimated using Equation 14.4.20, which is also depicted below.

$$\mu(t) \in \left(M(t') - t_{\frac{\alpha}{2}, m-1} \times \frac{SD_{M^r(t')}}{\sqrt{m}}, M(t') + t_{\frac{\alpha}{2}, m-1} \times \frac{SD_{M^r(t')}}{\sqrt{m}} \right).$$

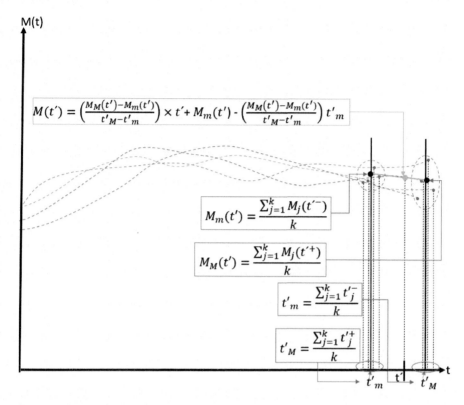

Figure 14.19 The Mean Points Before and After t', and the Line Segment Connecting the Central Points.

Some Examples

Example 14.4.1. For instance, consider a model was simulated and metrics $(\theta(t))$ were recorded at time $19\,ms$. In this simulation process, m_0 was set to 5 (initial number of replications)[8]. Each run was defined as 10. However, the values of each run are not shown. Besides the $\widehat{\theta}(19\,ms)$, $\widehat{\theta}(t)$ $t \in \{1,5,10,15\,ms\}$ were also recorded. The five initial replications are presented in Table 14.16. The value of the metrics related to each replication is presented in Columns 2 to 6, respectively. The first column shows the 6 time instants. Columns 7 and 8 show the mean and the standard deviation at each time instant of the first 5 replications. Column 9 depicts the number of additional replications required to achieve an absolute precision error of $\varepsilon \leq 0.08$ at each $t \in \{1,5,10,15\,ms\}$, considering a degree of confidence of 95%. Likewise, Column 10 presents the number of replications still needed to achieve a

---

[8]This initial number of replications may be larger; however 5 was adopted to fit the sample to the page width.

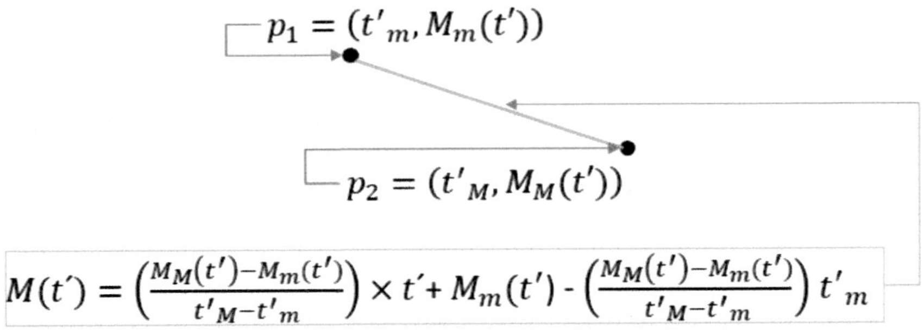

$$p_1 = (t'_m, M_m(t'))$$

$$p_2 = (t'_M, M_M(t'))$$

$$M(t') = \left(\frac{M_M(t') - M_m(t')}{t'_M - t'_m}\right) \times t' + M_m(t') - \left(\frac{M_M(t') - M_m(t')}{t'_M - t'_m}\right) t'_m$$

Figure 14.20   Zoom in on the Average Line and at t'.

relative precision error of $\%\varepsilon \leq 1\%$. $\widehat{\Theta}(t) = \{\widehat{\theta}_1(t), \widehat{\theta}_2(t), \widehat{\theta}_3(t), \widehat{\theta}_4(t), \widehat{\theta}_5(t)\}$ and $t_{4,0.975} = 2.776445$.

Table 14.16
Number of Replications - $\varepsilon \leq 0.08$ and $\%\varepsilon \leq 1\%$

t	$\widehat{\theta}^1(t)$	$\widehat{\theta}^2(t)$	$\widehat{\theta}^3(t)$	$\widehat{\theta}^4(t)$	$\widehat{\theta}^5(t)$	$\widehat{\theta}(t)$	$SD(\widehat{\theta}^i(t))$	m_ε	$m_{\%\varepsilon}$
1	0.086285	0.108027	0.106435	0.102558	0.100831	0.100827	0.008628	9	565
5	0.406266	0.378123	0.457188	0.442969	0.364181	0.409745	0.040133	195	740
10	0.665352	0.612222	0.665416	0.581027	0.620418	0.628887	0.036414	160	259
15	0.772107	0.751114	0.728639	0.792973	0.785325	0.766032	0.026247	83	91
19	0.827555	0.839775	0.848594	0.887920	0.835205	0.847810	0.023681	68	61

Considering the time instant $t = 19\,ms$, the number of additional replications to achieve $\varepsilon \leq 0.08$ and $\%\varepsilon \leq 1\%$ are $m_\varepsilon = 68$ and $m_{\%\varepsilon} = 61$, respectively. Hence, taking into account the initial number of replications, the total number of replications are $m_{\varepsilon,total} = 72$ and $m_{\%\varepsilon,total} = 66$. The number of replications to achieve the precision error required of other time instants are shown in columns m_ε and $m_{\%\varepsilon}$. □

Now, assume the SPN shown in Figure 14.5. This net has two random variables, AT (arrival time) and ST (service time). These random variables are assigned to transitions a (arrival) and s (service), respectively. $AT \sim G_1(t)$ and $ST \sim G_2(t)$. In Mercury, the measure is $mnts(t) = E\{\#q\}$.

Simulating n replications generates a sample $X(t) = \{m_q^i(t)\}$, where $|X(t)| = n$, where $m_q^i(t)$ is the marking of place q in replication i at time instant t. The mean number of transactions in the system ($mnts(t)$) measured at time instant t, specified in Mercury-like notation, is specified by taking the mean number of tokens in place q [9], that is

$$mnts(t) = E\{\#q(t)\}. \qquad (14.4.22)$$

$$mnts(t) = E\{\#q(t)\} = \overline{X(t)},$$

where

$$\overline{X(t)} = \frac{\sum_{i=1}^{n} m_q^i(t)}{n}.$$

The confidence interval is estimated by

$$\overline{X(t)} \pm t_{n-1,1-\alpha/2} \frac{SD(X(t))}{\sqrt{n}},$$

where $SD(X(t))$ is the standard deviation of $X(t)$.

The estimation of the utilization at t is specified in Mercury-like notation by

$$u(t) = P\{\#q(t) > 0\}.$$

$P\{\#q(t) > 0\}$ denotes the probability of the place q having at least one token at time instant t. In order to estimate this metric, an indicator function should be defined in which

$$1_{\#q>0^i(t)} = \begin{cases} 1 & m_q(t) > 0 \\ 0 & m_q(t) = 0, \end{cases}$$

where i is the replication. Simulating n replications generates a sample $X(t) = \{1_{\#q>0^i(t)}\}$, where $|X(t)| = n$. The point estimate of the utilization is obtained by

$$u(t) = P\{\#q(t) > 0\} = \overline{X(t)},$$

where

$$\overline{X(t)} = \frac{\sum_{i=1}^{n} 1_{\#q>0^i(t)}}{n},$$

where n is the total number of replications. The confidence interval is estimated by

$$\overline{X(t)} \pm t_{n-1,1-\alpha/2} \frac{SD(X(t))}{\sqrt{n}},$$

where $SD(X(t))$ is the standard deviation of $X(t)$.

The probability estimate of having j transactions (tokens) in the system at t, $P(m_q(t) = j)$, is specified in Mercury-like notation by

---

[9] In the Mercury tool, the time is not explicitly represented. The time instant is specified when the transient simulation is selected.

$$P\{\#q(t) = j\}. \tag{14.4.23}$$

In order to estimate this metric, an indicator function was defined in which

$$1_{\#q^i(t)=j} = \begin{cases} 1 & m_q(t) = j \\ 0 & m_q(t) = 0 \end{cases},$$

where i is the replication. Simulating n replications generates a sample $X(t) = \{1_{\#q^i(t)=j}\}$, where $|X(t)| = n$. The point estimate of the utilization is obtained by

$$P\{\#q(t) = j\} = \overline{X(t)},$$

where

$$\overline{X(t)} = \frac{\sum_{i=1}^{n} 1_{\#q^i(t)=j}}{n},$$

where n is the total number of replications. The confidence interval is estimated by

$$\overline{X(t)} \pm t_{n-1,1-\alpha/2} \frac{SD(X(t))}{\sqrt{n}},$$

where $SD(X(t))$ is the standard deviation of $X(t)$.

The throughput point estimate at t may be computed by

$$tp(t) = \frac{\sum_{i=0}^{n}\sum_{j>0} \pi_j^i(t)}{n} \times \frac{1}{E\{ST\}}, \tag{14.4.24}$$

where $\pi_j^i(t)$ is the probability estimate obtained in the replication i of having j transactions in the system at t. $\pi_j^i(t)$ is specified in Mercury notation by the expression presented in 14.4.23. The confidence interval is computed as in the previous metrics.

The response time may be estimated through Little's law, that is

$$mrt = \frac{mnts}{tp},$$

where $mnts$ is specified by Expression 14.4.22 and tp is computed through Expression 14.4.24. The confidence interval is estimated as previously shown.

Example 14.4.2. Now, let us assume the SPN shown in Figure 14.21. This net has two random variables, AT (arrival time) and ST (service time). These random variables are assigned to transitions a (arrival) and s (service), respectively. $AT \sim Exp(\lambda)$ and $ST \sim Erl(\gamma, \mu)$, where $\lambda = 0.1\,tpms$, $\gamma = 2$, and $\mu = 0.2222\,tpms$

A transient simulation was performed, and the mean number of transactions in the system (mean system size – mss)was obtained in the range $t \in [0, 2000\,ms]$. Figure 14.22 shows the respective curve and the confidence interval (dotted lines). These results were obtained considering a degree of confidence of 95% and a relative error

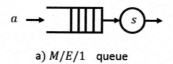

a) $M/E/1$ queue

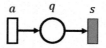

b) SPN representing the $M/E/1$ queue

Figure 14.21 $M/E/1$ Queue System.

of 5%. The point estimate and the confidence interval obtained in this simulation for mss at $t = 2000\,ms$ were $mss = 7.6417$, and $(7.4209, 7.8625)$, respectively. The error in the range $t \in [0, 2000\,ms]$ is plotted in Figure 14.23. Table 14.17 shows the point estimates and the respective confidence intervals for u, tp, mss, and mrt at $t = 2000\,ms$. These measures specified in Mercury notation are

$$u = P\{\#q > 0\},$$

$$tp = \frac{1}{mat},$$

$$mss = E\{\#q\},$$

and

$$mrt = E\{\#q\} \times mat.$$

Table 14.17
Utilization, Systems Size, and Response Time at $t = 2000\,ms$

Measure	mean	ci_{max}	ci_{min}
$u(t)$	0.9424	0.9338	0.9511
$mss(t)$	5.9336	5.6536	6.2137
$mrt(t)$ (ms)	59.3361	56.5356	62.1367

□

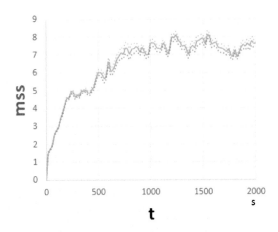

Figure 14.22 $M/E/1$ Queue System – Mean System Size (mss).

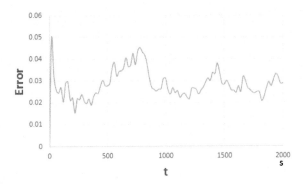

Figure 14.23 $M/E/1$ Queue System – mss Error.

Example 14.4.3. In this example we compute the cumulative distribution function, the median time to absorption, and the mean time to absorbtion of a net with absorbing marking. In this example, we have four concurrent programs ($Prog_A$, $Prog_B$, $Prog_C$, and $Prog_D$) that are executed in a hardware infrastructure with np processors. The SPN for computing these figures is a net with an absorbing marking. The absorbing marking is only reached when all the programs were executed. The median time and the mean time to execute the programs is estimated by calculating mean time to absorption and median time to absorption ($mtta$, $medtta$)[10]. Figure 14.24 depicts the model. $Prog_A$ is represented by the sets $\{p_1, p_2, p_3\}$, $\{t_1, t_2\}$, their respective arcs and annotations. Likewise, $Prog_B$, $Prog_C$, and $Prog_D$ are depicted by $\{p_4, p_5\}$, $\{t_3, t_4\}$; $\{p_6, p_7, p_8\}$, $\{t_5, t_6\}$; $\{p_9, p_{10}, p_{11}\}$, $\{t_7, t_8\}$ and their respective arcs and annotations.

---

[10]$mtta$ – mean time to absorption. $medtta$ – median time to absorption.

The number of processors (np) in the hardware infrastructure is specified by the initial number of token in place p_{12}. The processors' allocation to execute a program is specified by the arcs between p_{12} and t_1, t_5 and t_7, respectively. The execution of program $Prog_B$ is only possible after the execution of program $Prog_A$ (observe the arc between p_3 and t_3). When a program is finished, the respective processor is deallocated. The deallocation is represented by the arcs between t_2, t_4, t_6, and t_8; and p_{12}. The time to execute each program is represented by their execution time distributions, that is $Tr_A(a,b,c)^{11}$, $Erl_B(k,\lambda_B)$, $Exp(\lambda_C)$, and $Exp(\lambda_D)$. The time to start the programs is represented by the distribution assigned to transition t_0, which is $Exp(\lambda)$. Table 14.18 presents the respective distributions' parameters. As mentioned, the SPN representing has one absorbing marking, that is, when all programs are executed, one token is stored in place p_{13}. Using transient simulation, the system probability distribution and the respective moments may be estimated either by

1. **computing the absorption probability**, $P\{\#p_{13}(t) = 1\}$, in the range $t \in [0,t']$, where t' is large, such that $P\{\#p_{13}(t') = 1\} \to 1$ or

2. **computing the time to absorption** (tta) from the initial marking multiple times until getting the mean time to absorption ($mtta$) is computed by calculating the time to absorption (tta) through independent replication, where $TTAS = \{tta_i\}$ is the sample of time to absorption and tta_i is the time to absorption obtained in i replications. The cumulative probability distribution, the respective density function can be plotted using the computed sample $TTAS = \{tta_i\}$ and the respective statistics and moments.

Table 14.18
Distributions Parameters

Transitions	Distributions	Parameters
t_0	$Exp(\lambda)$	$\lambda = 10.00\,tpms$
t_2	$Tr_A(a,b,c)$	$a = 100\,ms, b = 190\,ms, c = 150\,ms$
t_4	$Erl_B(k,\lambda_B)$	$k = 4, \lambda_B = 26.667 \times 10^{-3}\,tpms$
t_6	$Exp_C(\lambda_C)$	$\lambda_C = 10.00 \times 10^{-3}\,tpms$
t_8	$Exp_D(\lambda_D)$	$\lambda_D = 5.00 \times 10^{-3}\,tpms$

Figure 14.25 and Figure 14.26 present the cumulative distribution and the density functions of the time to execute the programs taking into account the hardware infrastructure with $np = \{1,2,3\}$ processors. The median and the mean time to execute the programs ($medtta$ and $mtta$, respectively) are presented in Table 14.19.

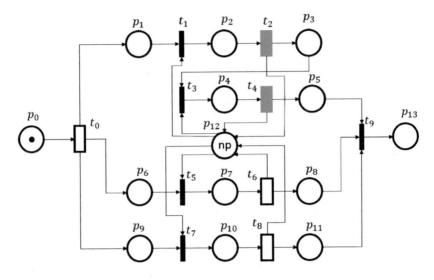

Figure 14.24 Parallel Activities and Shared Resource.

Table 14.19
Median and Mean Time to Execute the Programs with np Processors

np	$medtta$	$mtta$
1	$995.20\,ms$	$1047.45\,ms$
2	$739.96\,ms$	$787.96\,ms$
3	$707.36\,ms$	$754.68\,ms$

□

14.4.2 STEADY-STATE SIMULATION

In steady-state simulation (also called non-terminating or stationary simulation), the aim is estimating parameters of a stationary distribution. This process is distinct from terminating simulation because the estimate is only reached after the transient period, and we do not know the length of the transient phase. Many strategies have been applied to estimate point and confidence intervals of steady-state system parameters [208] [190] [191].

The point estimate of the mean measure θ is calculated by

---

[11] Triangular distribution. a is the minimal, b is the maximal, and c is the mode.

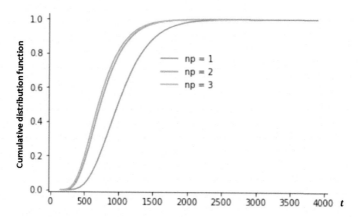

Figure 14.25 Cumulative Distribution Functions.

$$\widehat{\theta} = \lim_{n \to \infty} \frac{\sum_{i=1}^{n} \theta_i}{n}, \qquad (14.4.25)$$

where n is the number of observations.

As in the transient simulation, the method of independent replications can be, in principle, applied. However, since the transient phase must be disregarded, and many replications are required, such an approach is inefficient.

Long Run - The fundamental difference between steady-state simulation and transient simulation is that, in the former, the transient phase should not affect the result, and as the transient length is unknown, this is an issue to be overcome. An attempt is to obtain the required statistics from a single long run until the measure values seem to approach a steady value. A basic guideline is, therefore, to simulate long enough so that the effects of the transient period become negligible. Hence, a first aspect to be faced is the estimation of the length of the run, so that the transient effects do not affect the statistics. Here, the challenge is to identify an index n for truncating the observations.

$$\widehat{\theta} = \frac{\sum_{i=1}^{n} \theta_i}{n}. \qquad (14.4.26)$$

The confidence interval estimate of θ is computed by

$$\widehat{\theta} \pm t_{n-1,1-\alpha/2} \frac{SD(\theta_i)}{\sqrt{n}}. \qquad (14.4.27)$$

For large n, the Student's t-distribution approaches the standard normal; then the confidence interval may also be estimated by

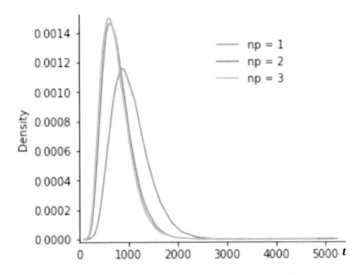

Figure 14.26 Density Functions.

$$\widehat{\theta} \pm z_{1-\alpha/2}\frac{SD(\theta_i)}{\sqrt{n}}. \qquad (14.4.28)$$

Obviously, this is not an efficient method.

Intelligent Initialization - Intelligent initialization (also known as expert initialization) consists of specifying an initial state that is closer to the steady-state conditions. This usually means setting a work-in-progress into the model at the beginning of a run, for example, the number of transactions or clients.

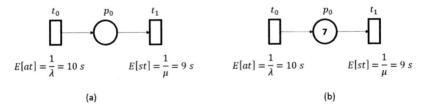

Figure 14.27 Intelligent Initialization.

For instance, consider an SPN that represents an $M/M/1$ queue system (see Figure 14.27.a), where the mean arrival time is $E(at) = 10\,s$, and the mean service time is $E(st) = 9\,s$. This model was simulated (using Mercury) for estimating the mean system size, *mss*, at steady state, considering that the system was empty at the beginning of the simulation. The sample size required for obtaining the steady-state estimate, considering 95% of confidence and a relative precision error smaller than 1% was 24×10^3. The point estimate was $mss = 8.36trans$. Afterward, the system size was set to 7 at the beginning of the simulation (see Figure 14.27.b), and the steady-state simulation was performed again. The mean system size estimated was obtained with a sample size of 13×10^3. The point estimate of the mean system size was $mss = 8.90trans$.

Transient Period Removal - The transient period (warm-up period) may also be removed from the run. Therefore, the length of the transient period should also be estimated. An elementary method to handle the transient effects is merely removing the first k observations. Therefore, the point estimate of the measure θ is obtained by

$$\widehat{\theta} = \frac{\sum_{i=k+1}^{n} \theta_i}{n-k}. \tag{14.4.29}$$

Many methods have been proposed for identifying the warm-up period, among them, graphical methods (slope, moving average, CUSUM), heuristics methods, and strategies based on regression [190, 191, 208, 361].

The linear regression strategy uses the least-squares method to determine if the slope coefficient approaches zero (steady state). The slopes are computed in a sliding window of measures over the sets of measures. This process should continue until the slope becomes smaller than a given threshold. Then, the set of measures up to that specific window should be disregarded from the steady state measure estimation. This process is illustrated in the pseudo-code 32. This routine (TR) receives, as parameters, the model (M), the run length (n), the sliding windows size (w), and the slope threshold (st). The process starts by simulating a run of size n, and assigning the sample to the ordered set os (line 4). The elements, $e_i = (i, \theta_i)$, of this set are pairs in which θ_i is the simulated measure at the observation i. The set os is ordered using i. Considering this sample, $n + 1 - w$ slopes are computed by taking into account w measures, where w is the number of elements of a sliding window applied to the ordered set (line 5). The first of these slopes is calculated considering the elements $e_1, ..., e_w$. The second slope is computed taking into account the elements $e_2, ..., e_{w+1}$. The subsequent slopes are likewise computed. The last $n + 1 - w$ slopes are not computed since the number of elements is smaller than the windows size w. If one slope is smaller than a slope threshold, st, the process stops (line 8) and the elements $e_0, ..., e_i$ are removed from the sample in order to compute the steady-state measures (line 11). If no slope is smaller than the threshold, more samples should be simulated and appended to the ordered set os (line 4), and the steps already described are executed again. When this process finishes, the simulated measures without the transient period are provided to the caller routine (line 12). Banks et al.'s [190] rule of thumb recommends a run-length of at least ten times the length of the warm-up period.

Table 14.20 presents a sample obtained from a simulation. This table shows only the first 32 measures, θ_i. Columns 1 and 4 present the number of each observation. Columns 2 and 5 show the measures. Figure 14.28 shows the simulated measures and

---

Algorithm 32 Transient Removal

1: TR(M,n,w,st)
2: os=∅;
3: While(T) {
4:     Simulate(os);
5:     For(i=0, i=n+1-w,i++) {
6:         s=Slope(os,i,n,w);
7:         If s < st
8:             Break;
9:     }
10: }
11: Remove(os,i);
12: Return(os);

---

their respective observations. The slopes computed considering a sliding window (w) of size 10 are presented in Columns 3 and 6. A slope threshold was defined as $st = 0.01$. Assuming this threshold, the transient period was defined as $[0, 29]$, since the slope computed considering the sliding windows $\{(19, 0.8523), ..., (29, 0.9623)\}$ is the first slope that is smaller than 0.01 ($s = 0.0086$). The slope values are also presented in Figure 14.29.

Table 14.20

Samples and Slopes - $w = 10$

i	θ_i	$slope_i$	i	θ_i	$slope_i$	i	θ_i	$slope_i$
0	0		11	0.6419	0.0568	22	0.8917	0.0208
1	0.1035		12	0.7019	0.0516	23	0.9205	0.0206
2	0.1556		13	0.7428	0.0457	24	0.9127	0.0202
3	0.2627		14	0.7366	0.0399	25	0.9140	0.0180
4	0.3401		15	0.7937	0.0367	26	0.9310	0.0181
5	0.3684		16	0.7195	0.0275	27	0.9388	0.0132
6	0.5128		17	0.7954	0.0265	28	0.9454	0.0108
7	0.4931		18	0.8105	0.0225	29	0.9623	0.0086
8	0.5897		19	0.8523	0.0228	30	0.9378	0.0062
9	0.5984		20	0.8768	0.0223	31	0.9696	0.0058
10	0.6374	0.0646	21	0.9215	0.0052	32	0.9719	0.0057

Batch Means Method - The batch means method is applied considering samples obtained from a single long run (see Figure 14.30). Let us assume a single long run of size l ($\theta_1, \theta_2, ... \theta_l$) divided into several parts (batches), each having a length n. This method can also be applied in conjunction with warm-up period removal, a

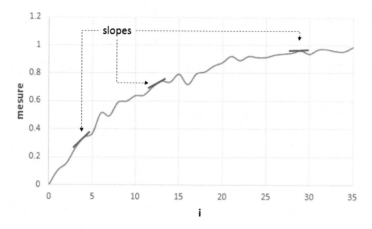

Figure 14.28   Simulated Measure (θ) × i.

period in which no data are collected. Thus, assume that θ_1, θ_2, ..., θ_k are removed from the original sample; hence the remaining samples are θ_{k+1}, ..., θ_l, where the number of samples (m) is specified by

$$m = \left\lfloor \frac{N}{n} \right\rfloor, \tag{14.4.30}$$

where $N = l - k$.

Therefore, the first batch ($j = 1$) consists of the set $\{\theta_{k+1}, \theta_{k+2}, ... \theta_{k+n}\}$. The second batch ($j = 2$) is formed by the samples $\{\theta_{k+n+1}, \theta_{k+n+2}, ... \theta_{k+2n}\}$. The subsequent batches are likewise formed. Hence, generalizing for any j, we have $\{\theta_{k+1+(j-1)n}, \theta_{k+2+(j-1)n}, ... \theta_{k+j\times n}\}$. For each batch, j, its mean ($\overline{\theta_j}$) is calculated and then treated as an individual observation.

$$\overline{\theta_j} = \frac{\sum_{i=k+1+(j-1)n}^{k+j\times n} \theta_i}{n}, \quad j = 1,2,...,m. \tag{14.4.31}$$

The unbiased point estimator of θ ($\widehat{\theta}$) is defined by the mean of the batch means.

$$\widehat{\theta} = \overline{\overline{\theta}} = \frac{\sum_{i=1}^{m} \overline{\theta_i}}{m}. \tag{14.4.32}$$

The standard deviation of the batch means is

$$SD(\overline{\theta}) = \sqrt{\frac{\sum_{i=1}^{m}(\overline{\theta_i} - \overline{\overline{\theta}})^2}{m-1}}. \tag{14.4.33}$$

The confidence interval estimate of θ is computed by

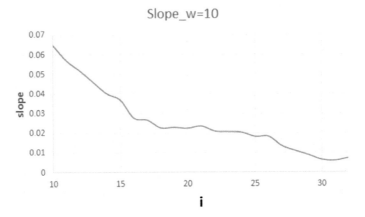

Figure 14.29 Slope(θ) $\times$ i.

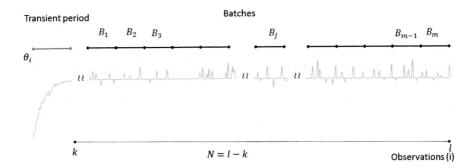

Figure 14.30 Batch Means Method: $\theta_i \times i$

$$\widehat{\theta} \pm t_{m-1,1-\alpha/2} \frac{SD(\overline{\theta})}{\sqrt{m}}. \tag{14.4.34}$$

The batch means method usually starts setting an initial length to the run (l_0), which is then divided into batches ($m_0 = l_0/n$), where n is the batch size. A good practice is setting a reasonably small initial number of batches, such as twenty. In general, this is enough to have statistical confidence for estimating the additional number of batches needed to achieve the absolute precision error (ε). The required number of batches is estimated by

$$m \geq \left(t_{m_0-1,1-\frac{\alpha}{2}} \times \frac{SD(\overline{\theta})}{\varepsilon} \right)^2, \tag{14.4.35}$$

where ε is the absolute precision error required, and m_0 is the initial number of batches estimated.

The relative precision error is specified by

$$\%\varepsilon = \frac{\varepsilon \times 100}{\widehat{\theta}}. \qquad (14.4.36)$$

Therefore, the number of batches required to achieve the relative precision error ($\%\varepsilon$) may be estimated by

$$m \geq \left(\frac{t_{m_0-1,1-\frac{\alpha}{2}} \times SD(\overline{\theta}) \times 100}{\%\varepsilon \times \widehat{\theta}} \right)^2. \qquad (14.4.37)$$

Algorithm 33 shortly summarizes the main steps for computing steady state measures via the batch means method. First, simulate the model to estimate a measure (θ) and obtain m_0 batches of size n (line 1). Then, remove the transient period k from the sample Θ (line 2). Considering this sample, estimate the number of batches required to obtain the measure θ taking into account the specified maximal error (ε_0), the degree of significance (α), and the initial number of batches specified m_0 (line 3). Afterward, the main loop is executed. Its first step is to simulate m batches, and estimate the measure – point estimate and confidence interval of θ – (line 5). Line 6 verifies if that the estimate violates the specified maximal error and the degree of confidence. If the estimate does not violate the criteria, the point and confidence measures are provided (lines 7 and 10). If the specified maximal error or the confidence interval were not achieved, a new number of batches is estimated (line 8), and the model is simulated again (line 5).

Algorithm 33 Batch Means

1: $\Theta \leftarrow$ Simulate(m_0,θ);
2: $\Theta \leftarrow$ Remove(Θ,k);
3: m $\leftarrow$ PredictNB($\alpha,\varepsilon_0,\Theta,m_0$);
4: While (T) {
5:       $\Theta \leftarrow$ Simulate(m,θ);
6:       If (($\varepsilon \leq \varepsilon_0$) and ($1-\alpha \leq cd$))
7:             Break;
8:       m $\leftarrow$ PredictNB($\alpha,\varepsilon_0,\Theta,m$);
9: }
10: Print($\widehat{\theta},\theta_{ci}$);
11: End;

Example 14.4.4. Let us assume a model was simulated and an initial run of a measure was generated. The length of the initial run was $l_0 = 399$. From this run, a transient period of size $k = 53$ was removed. Hence, the size of the run without the transient part is $N = l_0 - k = 346$. Assume the batch size was defined as $n = 10$. Then, the run was divided into $m_0 = \lfloor N/n \rfloor = \lfloor 346/10 \rfloor = 34$ batches. The mean of each batch was computed $(\overline{\theta_j})$. Considering them, the mean of means was calculated, $\overline{\overline{\theta}} = 1.01678$, and the standard deviation of the means was $SD(\overline{\theta}) = 0.01755$. Since for $\alpha = 5\%$, $t_{m_0-1,1-\frac{\alpha}{2}} = t_{33,0.975} = 2.03452$, and taking into account $\varepsilon \leq 0.01$, the required additional number of batches to reach the steady state measure estimate is $m = 13$ (applying inequation 14.4.35). Therefore, the total number of batches is $m_0 + m = 34 + 13 = 47$, and the complete run length is $l_0 + m \times n = 399 + 13 \times 10 = 529$.

□

It is worth mentioning that the computation applied to the method of independent replication and batch means is essentially the same. Nevertheless, the batch means method reduces the waste related to the number of samples discarded (when applying the method of independent replication to steady state simulation) since only k samples are removed (one transient period). If independent replication is applied to steady state simulation, the transient period of each replication ought to be removed. It is also important to stress that the confidence interval width is inversely proportional to $\sqrt{m \times n}$ (see Equation 14.4.34)[12]. This width may be reduced by increasing either or both the number of batches and the batch size. However, the batch size should be reasonably large (let us say, at least 30) for obtaining a small correlation between batches.

Autocorrelation Between Batches - One way to find a suitable batch size (n) is to compute the correlation of successive batch means, considering different batch sizes. The aim is to identify the interval between observations that provides small correlation.

Let us assume two random variables X and Y. The variance of their sum is

$$Var(X+Y) = Var(X) + Var(Y) + 2Cov(X,Y),$$

where $Cov(X,Y)$ is defined by

$$Cov(X,Y) = E((X - E(X)) \times (Y - E(Y))),$$

which is

$$Cov(X,Y) = E(XY) - E(X)E(Y).$$

If X and Y are discrete, $Cov(X,Y)$ is computed by

$$Cov(X,Y) = \frac{1}{n}\sum_{i=1}^{n}(x_i - E(X))(y_i - E(Y)).$$

If X and Y are independent, then $E(XY) = E(X)E(Y)$; hence

$$Cov(X,Y) = 0.$$

---

[12] m is the number of batches and n is the batch size.

Therefore, if X and Y independent,

$$Var(X+Y) = Var(X) + Var(Y).$$

It is worth noting that $Cov(X,Y) = 0$ does not imply independence, but two independent random variables have $Cov(X,Y) = 0$.

Correlation is defined as

$$Corr(X,Y) = \frac{Cov(X,Y)}{SD(X)\,SD(Y)},$$

where $Corr(X,Y) \in [-1,1]$. In words, similar to covariance, the correlation is a measure of the linear relationship between random variables. Correlation, however, is dimensionless, whereas covariance has a dimension. If X and Y have $Corr(X,Y) = 1$, they have a perfect direct linear relationship. On the other hand, if they have $Corr(X,Y) = -1$, they have a perfect inverse linear relationship. Values in the open interval $(-1,1)$ indicate the degree of linear relationship between the variables.

The covariance of two samples X and Y is computed by

$$Cov(X,Y) = \frac{1}{n-1} \sum_{i=1}^{n} (x_i - E(X))(y_i - E(Y)).$$

Now consider a set of observations obtained from a simulation long run (number of observations $-N$). Then, divide this set into batches of size n. The number of batches is, therefore, $m = N/n$. Afterward, compute the mean of each batch i ($\overline{x_i}$). Therefore, each mean is the average of n observations. For instance, $\overline{x_1}$ is the mean of observations $x_1, x_2,...,x_n$. $\overline{x_2}$ is the mean of observations $x_{n+1}, x_{n+2},...,x_{2n}$, and so forth (see Figure 14.31). The distance between the first element considered in the first mean and the first element considered in the second mean is the lag, which corresponds with the batch size. Then, outline two sub-samples, $\overline{X_i}$ and $\overline{X_{i+1}}$ generated from the batch means, where $\overline{X_i} = \{\,\overline{x_1}, \overline{x_2}, \overline{x_3}, \overline{x_4}, ...\,\}$, and $\overline{X_i}$ and $= \{\,\overline{x_2}, \overline{x_3}, \overline{x_4}, \overline{x_5}, ...\,\}$. The batch size is the lag between the two samples.

The covariance and the correlation between these two sub-samples, $Cov(\overline{X_i}, \overline{X_{i+1}})$, and

$$AC = Corr(\overline{X_i}, \overline{X_{i+1}}) \tag{14.4.38}$$

are named autocovariance and autocorrelation (serial correlation or lagged correlation), since the elements considered come from the same original sample. The smaller the covariance and the correlation, the smaller the linear relation between the batches. These statistics may initially be calculated considering a small lag ($-n-$ batch size); then the process should be repeated for larger lags until reaching a small correlation. When such a correlation is reached, the batch size is defined.

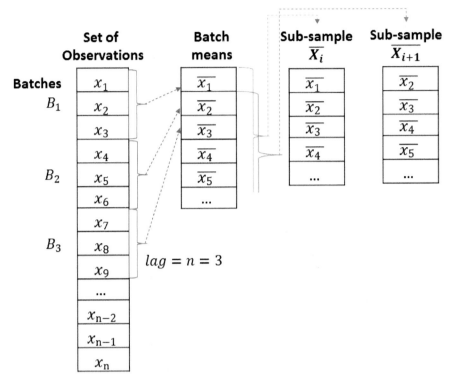

Figure 14.31 Autocorrelation Between Batches.

Example 14.4.5. Consider the net presented in Example 14.4.2 (Figure 14.21). This net was simulated (using Mercury) for obtaining steady state measure, considering the batch means method and transient period removal. The measures considered were the mean system size (mss) and the mean response time (mrt), utilization (u), and throughput (tp). As already shown, the arrival time (AT) is a random variable distributed according to $Exp(\lambda)$, where $\lambda = 0.1\,tpms$, and the service time (ST) is also a random variable that follows an Erlang distribution with 2 phases and rate $\mu = 0.2222\,tpms$. The utilization (u), throughput (tp), mean system size (mss), and mean response time (mrt) are specified by the following expressions:

$$u = P\{\#q > 0\},$$

$$tp = \frac{1}{mat},$$

$$mss = E\{\#q\},$$

and

$$mrt = E\{\#q\} \times mat.$$

The net was simulated, and the steady state measures were computed considering 1% of maximal relative precision error and 95% confidence. The throughput point estimate is $0.1\,tpms$. Table 14.21 depicts the point estimates and the respective confidence intervals for utilization (u), mean system size (mss), and mean response time (mrt).

Table 14.21
Utilization, Systems Size, and Response Time – Steady State Measures

Measure	mean	ci_{max}	ci_{min}
u	0.9026	0.9021	0.9031
mss	7.2332	7.1631	7.3033
mrt (ms)	72.3318	71.6306	73.0330

□

14.5 ADDITIONAL MODELING EXAMPLES

In this chapter, we have already introduced an SPN model for the $G/G/1$ queue system. In this section three other simple SPN models are introduced.

14.5.1 G/G/M QUEUE SYSTEM

This section presents an SPNs that represent a $G/G/m$ queue system (see Figure 14.32). This net is very similar to the net that represents the $M/M/m/k$ queue system discussed in Section 13.3.3. In this model, differently from the SPN shown in Figure 14.5, we split the customers being served from those waiting to be served. The queue is represented by place p_1, whereas marking of place p_3 represents the customers being served. The arrival traffic is represented by transition t_1, the service is specified by the transition t_2, and the number of tokens in place p_2 represents the number of stations of the system. The server semantics ($k - server$) is specified using the structure shown in Figure 13.12. The immediate transition t_3 is only enabled when at least one token is stored in p_1 (customer waiting to be served) and at least one token is stored in places p_2 (station available). As the time between arrivals and the service time are generically distributed, the transitions t_1 and t_2 are represented by generic timed transitions (gray). The firing semantics of t_{is} is single server semantics, whereas the semantics of t_2 is infinite server semantics.

The mean system size is estimated by

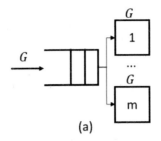

(a)

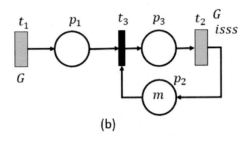

(b)

Figure 14.32 $G/G/m$ queue system

$$mss = E\{\#p_1\} + E\{\#p_3\}. \qquad (14.5.1)$$

The mean queue size may be estimated by

$$mqs = E\{\#p_1\}.$$

Assuming the arrival rate is λ, the system (residence, response) time and the waiting time may be respectively calculated using

$$mst = \frac{mss}{\lambda}.$$

$$mwt = \frac{mqs}{\lambda}.$$

The system utilization can be estimated by

$$u = \frac{P\{\#p_3 > 0\}}{m},$$

where m is the number of stations (servers).

Now, consider the time between arrivals (tba) is distributed according to an Erlang distribution with parameters $\lambda = 4.7619 \times 10^2\, tpms$ and $\gamma = 2$. Assume the service time (st) is distributed according to a normal distribution with parameters $\mu = 4\,ms$ $\sigma = 1\,ms$. This system was simulated using the Mercury tool taking into account a degree of confidence of 95% and a relative error of 5%. The results are shown in Table 14.22.

Table 14.22
Results – Steady State Measures
Point Estimate ($\hat{\theta}$) and Confidence Intervals ($\theta_{min}, \theta_{max}$).

Metrics	$\hat{\theta}$	θ_{min}	θ_{max}
mss	6.2924	6.0347	6.5500
$mst\ (ms)$	26.4280	25.3459	27.5101
u	0.8243	0.8214	0.8274
mqs	5.3423	5.0850	5.5997
$mwt\ (ms)$	22.4378	21.3571	23.5186
$tp\ (tpms)$	0.2061	0.2053	0.2068
$ar\ (tpms)$	0.2381	0.2381	0.2381

Varying the mean time between arrivals ($mtba$) in the interval $(4.01\,ms, 4.36\,ms)$ the mean system times obtained are shown in Figure 14.33

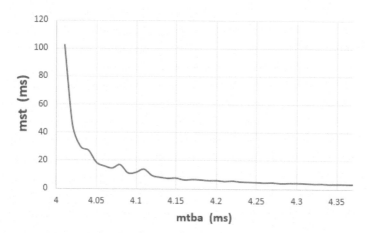

Figure 14.33 $G/G/m$ Queue System - $mst \times mat$.

14.5.2 G/G/M QUEUE SYSTEM WITH BREAKDOWN

This section presents a model for a $G/G/m$ queue system with failures. Let us assume the $G/G/m$ queue system represented in the previous example (see Section 14.5.1). In that system, servers were considered failure-free. Now, we consider the servers may fail. The new model is depicted in Figure 14.34. The queue is depicted by place p_1, and the number of tokens in place p_3 denotes the customers being served (as well as the number of busy servers). The arrival process is depicted by transition t_1, the service is represented by the transition t_2, and the number of tokens in place p_2 specifies the number of servers available and idle in the system. The transition t_3 is enabled when at least one token is in p_1 and one token is in places p_2. The times assigned to t_1 and t_2 are generically distributed; hence they are represented by generic timed transitions. Transitions t_4 and t_6 represent a server failure, and transition t_5 depicts a server repair. In this specific case, t_4, t_5, and t_6 transitions are timed exponential. The firing semantics of t_1 and t_5 are single server (*sss*), and the other transitions' firing semantics is infinite server (*iss*). Transition t_4 represents a server failure when the server is idle, whereas t_6 denotes a server failure when the server is busy. The number of tokens in place p_4 represents the unavailable servers.

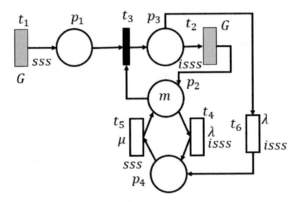

Figure 14.34 $G/G/m$ Queue System with Failure.

The performance measures considered are the same as in the previous example. Nevertheless, it is worth mentioning that now failures affect the results of those measures. Besides, the system availability and downtime may also be computed. The system steady-state unavailability (see Chapter 16) may be calculated using

$$UA = P\{\#p_4 = m\},$$

where m is the number of servers. The system availability can be estimated by

$$A = 1 - P\{\#p_4 = m\}.$$

The system downtime in the period T can be estimated by

$$DT = UA \times T = P\{\#p_4 = m\} \times T.$$

Let us assume a system with only one server ($m = 1$), the time between arrivals (tba) is distributed according to an Erlang distribution with parameters $\lambda = 4.7619 \times 10^2 \, tpms$ and $\gamma = 2$, and the service time (st) is distributed according to a normal distribution with parameters $\mu = 4 \, ms$ $\sigma = 1 \, ms$. Besides, consider the mean time to failure is $1500 \, h$ and the mean time to system repair is $48 \, h$. Simulating the model considering a degree of confidence of 95% and a relative error of 5%, the results shown in the upper part ($m = 1$) of the Table 14.23 are obtained. The lower part of the table ($m = 2$) depicts the simulation results when considering 2 servers. The estimated downtime was considered for a period of one year ($T = 8760 \, h$).

Table 14.23
Simulation Results - Steady State Measures

Point Estimate ($\hat{\theta}$) and Confidence Intervals ($\theta_{min}, \theta_{max}$).

Measures	$\hat{\theta}$	θ_{min}	θ_{max}
$m = 1$			
mss	32.9214	32.1921	33.6506
mst (ms)	138.2696	135.2069	141.3325
U	0.9368	0.935	0.9385
mqs	31.971	31.2417	32.7002
mwt (ms)	134.2780	131.2153	137.3408
A	0.9680	0.9675	0.9684
DT (h)	280.5251	276.5903	284.4600
$m = 2$			
mss	1.1636	1.1556	1.1716
mst (ms)	4.8871	4.8536	4.9205
U	0.0431	0.0427	0.0434
mqs	0.2130	0.2051	0.2209
mwt (ms)	0.8946	0.8613	0.9278
A	0.9974	0.9973	0.9976
DT (h)	22.3891	21.2847	23.4934

14.5.3 PLANNING MOBILE CLOUD INFRASTRUCTURES

This section presents an additional application for the models introduced in this chapter. Mobile Cloud Computing (MCC) is a successful solution for prolonging the battery life of mobile devices and reducing the execution time of mobile applications. Whenever an onerous task is encountered on the smartphone, it is offloaded to powerful remote servers for execution. Once the execution on the remote server finishes, the result is returned to the device, and execution continues normally. Usually, the remote side is a virtual machine on the cloud running the same operating system as the aided mobile device. MCC is limited to CPU code offloading.

General purpose computing on GPU (GPGPU) enables the possibility of optimizing the execution time of many parallel applications thanks to their large number of cores compared to the general CPUs. Imagine a typical smartphone being able to run the latest GPU-powered photo editor or to perform GPU-accelerated virus scanning, all thanks to the cloud system. This section presents a summarized view of real case study with SPN models to represent and evaluate parallel processes running on GPUs. A detailed description of such a study can be found in [17, 67, 81, 341, 387–389]. The main aim was of defining a proper GPU configuration is to satisfy the user's quality of service (QoS) requirements while reducing the design costs. Figure 14.35 depicts the basic structure of a process by using SPN representation.

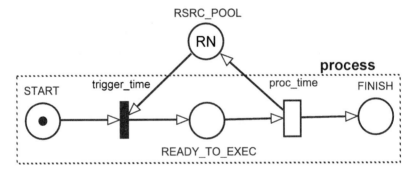

Figure 14.35 Basic SPN Representation of a Method-Call Execution.

The SPN process is composed of three **places** – *START*, READY_ TO_EXEC, and FINISH – and two **transitions** – trigger_time and proc_time. In addition, the marking of place RSRC_POOL represents the number of current available resources (Resources Number, RN). A marking in place START is the initial condition of the process, which contains tokens representing the input to be processed. The transition trigger_time is an immediate transition. The tokens move from START to READY_TO_EXEC place by firing trigger_time transition, which causes one resource from RSRC_POOL to be consumed at a time and the number of available resources to be decreased. Next, the execution is triggered by the proc_time transition, and when it finishes, the resource token comes back to the RSRC_POOL place. The transition proc_time follows an exponential distribution and represents the average processing time of the task being analyzed. Other distributions may also be considered (see Section 13.3.8 and Section 13.3.10). The place FINISH_r represents the completion of process execution.

Using the proposed parallel SPN model one can calculate the task execution, the cumulative distribution function (CDF), and many other statistics. A performance SPN model to represent parallel processes running in a set of GPU cores was proposed based on the basic SPN model. Figure 14.36 depicts the corresponding SPN with n parallel processes. The proposed SPN model has one place SYSTEM_INACTIVE that represents the local state before the parallel processes are called for execution. The model also has a final place, FINISH, and transitions that represent the task and events, which are meant to represent each separate process.

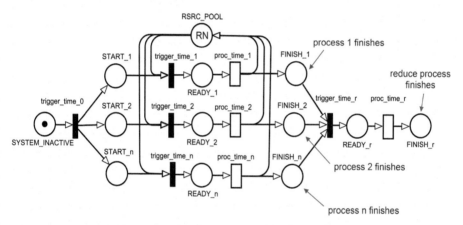

Figure 14.36 Basic SPN Representation of Parallel Method-Call.

A benchmark application from NVIDIA's samples was executed in a g2.2xlarge Amazon instance and execution times were measured. The mean execution time computed was 5.48 ms, considering a sample of 100 runs. The authors then divided the execution time by the number of CUDA[13] cores in order to obtain the execution time per core (EtpC) and feed the SPN model. In the absence of Amazon GPU instances with fewer CUDA cores, they defined four other types with 98, 256, 512, and 1024 cores, assuming they use the same GPU model as the real one. Then, they used the previously measured execution time per core to estimate the probabilities for each of the defined instances.

---

[13]CUDA is a parallel computing model developed by NVIDIA for general computing on graphical processing units.

The SPN was simulated considering a 90% a degree of confidence and a relative error of 5%. Figure 14.37 shows the transient simulation results considering a GPU with 98, 256, 512, 1024, and 1536 cores. If the user requires her task to finish before $4.5\,ms$, with a probability higher than 95% even the less powerful instance would satisfy her needs. If the desired execution time was less than or equal to $2.5\,ms$, the probability of the less powerful instance drops to 76%, and maybe another instance is better in this case.

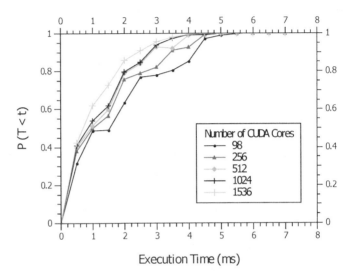

Figure 14.37 *CDF* Line Plot Considering Parameters from Amazon EC2 Instance.

EXERCISES

Exercise 1. What are the differences between Monte Carlo and discrete event simulation?

Exercise 2. Write a program that calculates the area bounded by $y = 16 - x^2$ and $y = 0$.

Exercise 3. Simulate the problem of rolling three dice until five dots appear on all three. Calculate the probability that this will take at least 25 throws.

Exercise 4. Consider a linear congruent pseudo-random number generator has a multiplier of five, an additive constant of three, and a modulus of sixteen. **(a)** What is the period of this generator? **(b)** Using $s_0 = 3$, generate the complete period of pseudo-random random numbers in the interval $[0, 1]$.

Exercise 5. Explain the inverse of generating random variates.

Exercise 6. Write a program that generates pseudo-random variates according to an Erlang distribution with four phases and a rate equal to 0.01.

Exercise 7. What are the reasons for choosing between transient and steady-state simulation?

Exercise 8. Is the method of independent replication suitable for steady-state simulation? Explain it.

Exercise 9. Describe the batch means method.

Exercise 10. Propose an SPN that represents a queue system with one servers, and capacity equal to thirty. Assume the arrival time is distributed according $Exp(\lambda)$, where $\lambda = 0.1\,tpms$, and the service time obeys $Erl(\gamma, \mu)$, where $\lambda = 0.1\,tpms$, $\gamma = 2$, and $\mu = 0.2222\,tpms$. Simulate the model and calculate **(a)** the discard rate, **(b)** the throughput, **(c)** the mean system size, **(d)** the mean queue size, **(e)**, the mean response time, and **(f)** the mean waiting time. Assume the 95% degree of confidence and a relative error of 5%.

Exercise 11. Use the SPN proposed in the previous exercise, and conduct an experiment considering $\lambda \in [0.05, 0.2]$. Simulate the SPN, and plot the figures of the mean system size, the mean response time, and the discard rate as a function of λ. Consider the 95% degree of confidence and a relative error of 5%.

Exercise 12. Propose an SPN that represents a queue system depicted in Exercise 10, but with an infinite queue. Simulate the SPN, and compute **(a)** the throughput, **(b)** the mean system size, **(c)** the mean queue size, **(d)**, the mean response time, and **(e)** the mean waiting time. Assume the 95% degree of confidence and a relative error of 5%.

Exercise 13. Simulate the SPN proposed in Exercise 18 of Chapter 13 and estimate the largest radius of the resized cell (delimited by the new base station positioning), so that the unavailability of lines stays below 1%. Assume the 95% degree of confidence and a relative error of 1%.

Bibliography

1. 3DMark - Technical Guide. Updated September 18, 2020.

2. J. A. Abraham, "An Improved Algorithm for Network Reliability," in IEEE Transactions on Reliability, vol. R-28, no. 1, pp. 58-61, April 1979. doi: 10.1109/TR.1979.5220476

3. Anderson, T. W., and D. A. Darling. "Asymptotic Theory of Certain 'Goodness of Fit' Criteria Based on Stochastic Processes." The Annals of Mathematical Statistics, vol. 23, no. 2, pp. 193–212, 1952.

4. Anderson, T. W., and D. A. Darling. "A Test of Goodness of Fit." Journal of the American Statistical Association, vol. 49, no. 268, pp. 765–769, 1954.

5. Automotive Engineering Council. http://aecouncil.com/ Retrieved at 5/10/2021.

6. Francisco Airton Silva, Sokol Kosta, Matheus Rodrigues, Danilo Oliveira, Teresa Maciel, Alessandro Mei, and Paulo Maciel. Mobile Cloud Performance Evaluation Using Stochastic Models. IEEE Transactions on Mobile Computing. 2018. ISSN: 1536-1233.

7. A. Jensen. Markov chains as an aid in the study of Markov processes. Skand. Aktuarietidskrift, 3:87–91, 1953.

8. Ajmone Marsan, Marco and Conte, Gianni and Balbo, Gianfranco. A Class of Generalized Stochastic Petri Nets for the Performance Evaluation of Multiprocessor Systems. ACM Trans. Comput. Syst. 1984. Vol: 2. n:2. pages: 93–122. issn:0734-2071. ACM.

9. Ajmone Marsan, M. and Bobbio, A. and Donatelli, S. Petri nets in performance analysis: An introduction. Lectures on Petri Nets I: Basic Models: Advances in Petri Nets. Springer Berlin Heidelberg. isbn: 978-3-540-49442-3. pages:211–256. 1998

10. Akhmedjanov, F. M.. Reliability databases: State-of-the-art and perspectives. Denmark. Forskningscenter Risoe. Risoe-R No. 1235(EN) 2001.

11. Algirdas Avizienis. 1967. Design of fault-tolerant computers. Causes and symptoms of logic faults in digital systems. In Proceedings of the November 14-16, 1967, fall joint computer conference (AFIPS '67 (Fall)). Association for Computing Machinery, New York, NY, USA, 733–743. DOI:https://doi.org/10.1145/1465611.1465708

12. Mukhtar M. Ali. Stochastic Ordering and Kurtosis Measure. Journal of the American Statistical Association. Vol.:69. Number: 346. Pages:543-545, Taylor & Francis. 1974.

13. Virgilio A. F. Almeida and Jussara M. Almeida. 2011. Internet Workloads: Measurement, Characterization, and Modeling. IEEE Internet Computing 15, 2 (March 2011), 15–18. DOI:https://doi.org/10.1109/MIC.2011.43

14. H. H. Amer and E. J. McCluskey, "Calculation of Coverage Parameter," in IEEE Transactions on Reliability, vol. R-36, no. 2, pp. 194-198, June 1987. doi: 10.1109/TR.1987.5222338

15. P. Ameri, N. Schlitter, J. Meyer and A. Streit, "NoWog: A Workload Generator for Database Performance Benchmarking," 2016 IEEE 14th Intl Conf on Dependable, Autonomic and Secure Computing, 14th Intl Conf on Pervasive Intelligence and Computing, 2nd Intl Conf on Big Data Intelligence and Computing and Cyber Science and Technology Congress(DASC/PiCom/DataCom/CyberSciTech), Auckland, 2016, pp. 666-673, doi: 10.1109/DASC-PICom-DataCom-CyberSciTec.2016.120.

16. Anselone, P. M. Persistence of an Effect of a Success in a Bernoulli Sequence. Journal of the Society for Industrial and Applied Mathematics. 1960, Vol. Vol. 8, No. 2.

17. Araujo, Camila and Silva, F and Costa, Igor and Vaz, Fabiano and Kosta, Sokol and Maciel, Paulo. Supporting availability evaluation in MCC-based mHealth planning. Electronics Letters. Vol: 52. Number:20. pp:1663–1665. IET. 2016.

18. Eltton Araujo, Paulo Pereira, Jamilson Dantas, and Paulo Maciel. Dependability Impact in the Smart Solar Power Systems: An Analysis of Smart Buildings. ENERGIES (BASEL). 2020. ISSN: 1996-1073

19. J. Arlat, Y. Crouzet and J. -. Laprie, "Fault injection for dependability validation of fault-tolerant computing systems," [1989] The Nineteenth International Symposium on Fault-Tolerant Computing. Digest of Papers, Chicago, IL, USA, 1989, pp. 348-355, doi: 10.1109/FTCS.1989.105591.

20. J. Arlat et al., "Fault injection for dependability validation: a methodology and some applications," in IEEE Transactions on Software Engineering, vol. 16, no. 2, pp. 166-182, Feb. 1990, doi: 10.1109/32.44380.

21. M. F. Arlitt and C. L. Williamson, "Internet web servers: Workload characterization and performance implications," IEEE/ACM Transactions on Networking (ToN), vol. 5, no. 5, pp. 631–645, 1997.

22. T. F. Arnold, "The Concept of Coverage and Its Effect on the Reliability Model of a Repairable System," in IEEE Transactions on Computers, vol. C-22, no. 3, pp. 251-254, March 1973. doi: 10.1109/T-C.1973.223703

23. Arrhenius, Svante. "Über die Reaktionsgeschwindigkeit bei der Inversion von Rohrzucker durch Säuren" Zeitschrift für Physikalische Chemie, vol. 4U, no. 1, 1889, pp. 226-248. https://doi.org/10.1515/zpch-1889-0416

24. R. B. Ash, Basic Probability Theory, Wiley, New York, 1970.

25. Bruno Silva, Paulo Maciel, Eduardo Tavares, Carlos Araujo, Gustavo Callou, Erica Souza, Nelson Rosa, Manish Marwah, Ratnesh Sharma, Tom Christian and J. Paulo Pires. ASTRO: A Tool for Dependability Evaluation of Data Center Infrastructures. In: IEEE International Conference on Systems, Man, and Cybernetics, 2010, Istanbul. IEEE Proceeding of SMC, 2010.

26. Bruno Silva, Paulo Maciel, Gustavo Callou, Eduardo Tavares, Jair Figueiredo, Erica Sousa, Carlos Araujo, Fábio Magnani and Francisco Neves. ASTRO: An Integrated Environment for Dependability and Sustainability Evaluation. Sustainable Computing, Informatics and Systems. Elsevier. 2012. ISSN: 2210-5379.

27. AUERBACH STANDARD EDP REPORTS 1 - An Analytic Reference Service for the Electronic Data Processing Field. Prepared, Edited and Published by AUERBACH Corporation. Philadelphia, Penna. Vol. 1. 1962.

28. A. Avizienis, Fault-tolerance: The survival attribute of digital systems, in Proceedings of the IEEE, vol. 66, no. 10, pp. 1109-1125, Oct. 1978, doi: 10.1109/PROC.1978.11107.

29. Avizienis, A. Toward Systematic Design of Fault-Tolerant Systems. IEEE Computer. 1997 , Vol. Vol. 30, no. 4.

30. Avizienis A., Laprie J. C., Randell B.. Fundamental Concepts of Computer System Dependability. IARP/IEEE-RAS Workshop on Robot Robots in Human Environments – Seoul, Korea, May 21-22, 2001

31. Avizienis A., Laprie J. C., Randell B.. UCLA CSD Report no. 010028 LAAS Report no. 01-145 Newcastle University Report no. CS-TR-739. 2001

32. D. Avresky, J. Arlat, J. -. Laprie and Y. Crouzet, "Fault injection for formal testing of fault tolerance," in IEEE Transactions on Reliability, vol. 45, no. 3, pp. 443-455, Sept. 1996, doi: 10.1109/24.537015.

33. Backblaze Hard Drive Data and Stats. https://www.backblaze.com/b2/hard-drive-test-data.html. Retrieved on 5/11/2021.

34. Bahga, A. and Madisetti, V.K. Synthetic workload generation for cloud computing applications. Journal of Software Engineering and Applications, 4(07), p.396. 2011.

35. Radu Banabic and George Candea. 2012. Fast black-box testing of system re-covery code. In Proceedings of the 7th ACM european conference on Computer Systems (EuroSys '12). Association for Computing Machinery, New York, NY, USA, 281–294. DOI:https://doi.org/10.1145/2168836.2168865

36. Barabady, J., & Kumar, U. (2007). Availability allocation through importance measures. International Journal of Quality and Reliability Management, 24(6), 643–657.

37. Barlow, Richard E. s.l., Mathematical reliability theory: from the beginning to the present time. Proceedings of the Third International Conference on Math-ematical Methods In Reliability, Methodology And Practice, 2002.

38. Gely P. Basharin, Amy N. Langville, Valeriy A. Naumov. The life and work of A.A. Markov. Linear Algebra and its Applications. Volume 386. 2004. Pages 3-26. ISSN 0024-3795. https://doi.org/10.1016/j.laa.2003.12.041.

39. Board of Directors of the American Institute of Electrical Engineers. Answers to Questions Relative to High Tension Transmission. s.l. : IEEE, September 26, 1902.

40. Benard, A. and Bos-Levenbach, E. C. (1953): Het uitzetten van waarnemin-gen op waarschijnlijkheids-papier. Statistica Neerlandica, Vol. 7 pp. 163-173. English translation by Schop, R. (2001): The Plotting of Observations on Prob-ability Paper. Report SP 30 of the Statistical Department of the Mathematics Centrum, Amsterdam. http://www.barringer1.com/wa.htm

41. Benso, Alfredo and Prinetto, Paolo. Fault Injection Techniques and Tools for Embedded Systems Reliability Evaluation. isbn: 1441953914. Springer Pub-lishing Company, Incorporated. 2010.

42. Bernard, A. and Bos-Levenbach, E.J. The plotting of observations on probability-paper. Stichting Mathematisch Centrum. Statistische Afdeling. Stichting Mathematisch Centrum. 1955.

43. Bernstein, S.. "Sur l'extension du théorème limite du calcul des probabilités aux sommes de quantités dépendantes." Mathematische Annalen 97 (1927): 1-59. ¡http://eudml.org/doc/182666¿.

44. G.Berthelot. Checking Properties of Nets Using Transformations. Advances in Petri Nets, vol 222, Lecture Notes in Computer Science, Springer Verlag, Edited by G. Rozenberg, pp 19-40, 1986.

45. E. Best, Structure Theory of Petri Nets: the Free Choice Hiatus, LNCS vol. 254, Springer Verlag, 1987

46. Birnbaum, Z. W., J. D. Esary and S. C. Saunders. Multi-component systems and structures and their reliability. Technometrics. 1961, Vol. 3 (1).

47. Birnbaum, Z. W.: On the importance of different components in a multi-component system. Technical Report Number 54, May 20th, 1968, University of Washington. Contract N-onr-477(38).

48. Birnbaum, Z. W.: On the importance of different components in a multi-component system. In: Krishnaiah, P. R. (ed.) Multivariate Analysis–II, pp. 581–592. Academic Press (1969)

49. Wallace R. Blischke, D. N. Prabhakar Murthy, [ed.]. Case Studies in Reliability and Maintenance. Hoboken: John Wiley & Sons, 2003. p. 661.

50. Joseph K. Blitzstein, Jessica Hwang. Introduction to Probability, Chapman & Hall/CRC Texts in Statistical Science. 596 Pages. Published 2014 by Chapman And Hall/CRC. ISBN-13: 978-1-4665-7557-8. ISBN: 1-4665-7557-3

51. Richard Blum. Professional Assembly Language. Wiley Publishing, Inc. ISBN: 0-7645-7901-0. 2005

52. Bolch, G., Greiner, S., Meer, H., Trivedi, K. S. Queueing Networks and Markov Chains - Modeling and Performance Evaluation with Computer Science Applications. John Wiley & Sons. 2006.

53. Jan Lodewijk Bonebakker Findin.g representative workloads for computer system design. PhD Thesis. Sun Microsystems, Inc., USA. 2007

54. George Boole. An Investigation of the Laws of Thought. 1854. Project Gutenberg's. Release Date: July 19, 2017.

55. J.-Y. Le Boudec, Performance Evaluation of Computer and Communication Systems. EPFL Press, Lausanne, Switzerland. 2010.

56. W. G. Bouricius, W. C. Carter, D. C. Jessep, P. R. Schneider and A. B. Wadia, "Reliability Modeling for Fault-Tolerant Computers," in IEEE Transactions on Computers, vol. C-20, no. 11, pp. 1306-1311, Nov. 1971. doi: 10.1109/T-C.1971.223132

57. Box, G. E. P., and D. R. Cox. "An Analysis of Transformations." Journal of the Royal Statistical Society. Series B (Methodological), vol. 26, no. 2, 1964, pp. 211–252. JSTOR, www.jstor.org/stable/2984418.

58. Box, G. E. P.; Muller, Mervin E. A Note on the Generation of Random Normal Deviates. Ann. Math. Statist. 29 (1958), no. 2, 610–611.

59. Wilfried Brauer and Wolfgang Reisig. Carl Adam Petri and "Petri Nets". Fundamental Concepts in Computer Science. 3:129–139. 2007

60. J. Brilhante, B. Silva, P. Maciel and A. Zimmermann, "EucaBomber 2.0: A tool for dependability tests in eucalyptus cloud infrastructures considering VM life-cycle," 2014 IEEE International Conference on Systems, Man, and Cybernetics (SMC), 2014, pp. 2669-2674, doi: 10.1109/SMC.2014.6974330.

61. W. Buchholz, "A synthetic job for measuring system performance," in IBM Systems Journal, vol. 8, no. 4, pp. 309-318, 1969, doi: 10.1147/sj.84.0309.

62. Bucklew, James. Introduction to Rare Event Simulation. isbn.: 1441918930. Springer. 2010.

63. Buzacott, J. A. Markov approach to finding failure times of repairable systems. IEEE Transactions on Reliability, Volume 19, issue 4, pages: 128-134. 1970

64. G. Callou, E. Sousa, Maciel, and F. Magnani, "A formal approach to the quantification of sustainability and dependability metrics on data center infrastructures," in *Proceedings of DEVS*. San Diego, CA, USA: SCS, 2011, pp. 274–281

65. G. Callou, P. Maciel, F. Magnani, J. Figueiredo, E. Sousa, E. Tavares, B. Silva, F. Neves, and C. Araujo, "Estimating sustainability impact, total cost of ownership and dependability metrics on data center infrastructures," in *Sustainable Systems and Technology (ISSST), 2011 IEEE International Symposium on*, May 2011, pp. 1 –6

66. Calzarossa, Maria Carla; Della Vedova Marco L.; Massari, Luisa; Petcu, Dana; Tabash, Momin I. M.; Workloads in the Clouds. Book chapter in Principles of Performance and Reliability Modeling and Evaluation: Essays in Honor of Kishor Trivedi on his 70th Birthday. Pages:525-550. ISBN: 978-3-319-30599-8. Springer International Publishing. 2016.

67. Campos, Eliomar and Matos, Rubens and Maciel, Paulo and Costa, Igor and Silva, Francisco Airton and Souza, Francisco. Performance evaluation of virtual machines instantiation in a private cloud. 2015 IEEE World Congress on Services. pp: 319–326. IEEE. 2015

68. HP Capacity Advisor 7.4 User Guide. HP Part Number: T8670-90054. Published in September 2014.

69. J. Carreira, H. Madeira and J. G. Silva, "Xception: a technique for the experimental evaluation of dependability in modern computers," in IEEE Transactions on Software Engineering, vol. 24, no. 2, pp. 125-136, Feb. 1998, doi: 10.1109/32.666826.

70. J. V. Carreira, D. Costa and J. G. Silva, "Fault injection spot-checks computer system dependability," in IEEE Spectrum, vol. 36, no. 8, pp. 50-55, Aug. 1999, doi: 10.1109/6.780999.

71. Cassady, C. R., Pohl, E. A., & Jin, S. (2004). Managing availability improvement efforts with importance measures and optimization. IMA Journal of Management Math, 15(2), 161–174.

72. Cassandras, Christos G., Lafortune, Stéphane. Introduction to Discrete Event Systems. SBN 978-0-387-68612-7. Springer-Verlag. 2008.

73. Giovanni Chiola and Marco Ajmone Marsan, Gianfranco Balbo and Gianni Conte. Generalized stochastic Petri nets: A definition at the net level and its implications. IEEE Transactions on Software Engineering. Vol.: 19. pages: 89-107. 1993.

74. Choi, Byoung Kyu and Kang, Donghun. Modeling and Simulation of Discrete Event Systems. isbn.: 111838699X. Wiley Publishing. 2013.

75. G. Choi, R. Iyer and V. Carreno, "FOCUS: an experimental environment for validation of fault-tolerant systems-case study of a jet-engine controller," Proceedings 1989 IEEE International Conference on Computer Design: VLSI in Computers and Processors, Cambridge, MA, USA, 1989, pp. 561-564, doi: 10.1109/ICCD.1989.63428.

76. Chung, Christopher A., Simulation Modeling Handbook: A Practical Approach. isbn.:0849312418. CRC Press, Inc. 2003.

77. Church, R. M. (1979). How to look at data: A review of John W. Tukey's Exploratory Data Analysis. Journal of the Experimental Analysis of Behavior, 31(3), 433–440.

78. Ciardo, Gianfranco and Muppala, Jogesh and Trivedi, Kishor S., On the Solution of GSPN Reward Models. Performance Evaluation. Vol:12. number:4. issn:0166-531. Elsevier. 1991.

79. Clark, Christopher and Fraser, Keir and Hand, Steven and Hansen, Jacob Gorm and Jul, Eric and Limpach, Christian and Pratt, Ian and Warfield, Andrew. Live migration of virtual machines. Proceedings of the 2nd conference on Symposium on Networked Systems Design & Implementation - Volume 2. NSDI'05. pp.: 273–286. USENIX Association. 2005

80. W. G. Cochran, "The Chi-Square Test of Goodness of Fit," Annals of Mathematical Statistics, Vol. 23, No. 3, 1952, pp. 315-345. doi:10.1214/aoms/1177729380

81. Costa, Igor and Araujo, Jean and Dantas, Jamilson and Campos, Eliomar and Silva, Francisco Airton and Maciel, Paulo. Availability Evaluation and Sensitivity Analysis of a Mobile Backend-as-a-service Platform. Journal on Quality and Reliability Engineering International. Vol: 32. Number:7, pp: 2191–2205

82. Cotroneo, Domenico, L. Simone, Pietro Liguori and R. Natella. "ProFIPy: Programmable Software Fault Injection as-a-Service." 50th Annual IEEE/IFIP International Conference on Dependable Systems and Networks (DSN). 364-372. 2020.

83. Cox, D. . A use of complex probabilities in the theory of stochastic processes. Mathematical Proceedings of the Cambridge Philosophical Society, 51(2), 313-319. 1955. doi:10.1017/S0305004100030231

84. Cramèr, H. "On the Composition of Elementary Errors". Scandinavian Actuarial Journal. (1): 13–74. 1928

85. Yves Crouzet, Karama Kanoun. System Dependability: Characterization and Benchmarking. A.Hurson, S.Sedigh. Advances in Computers. Special issue: Dependable and Secure Systems Engineering, Elsevier, pp.93-139, 2012, 978-0-12-396525-7.

86. M. Curiel and A. Pont, "Workload Generators for Web-Based Systems: Characteristics, Current Status, and Challenges," in IEEE Communications Surveys & Tutorials, vol. 20, no. 2, pp. 1526-1546, Second quarter 2018, doi: 10.1109/COMST.2018.2798641.

87. H. J. Curnow, B. A. Wichmann, A synthetic benchmark, The Computer Journal, Volume 19, Issue 1, 1976, Pages 43–49, https://doi.org/10.1093/comjnl/19.1.43

88. Sidney J. Cutler,Fred Ederer. Maximum utilization of the life table method in analyzing survival. Journal of Chronic Diseases. Volume 8, Issue 6, Pages 699-712 Elsevier. December 1958.

89. Edward W. Czeck and Zary Z. Segall and Daniel P. Siewiorek. Software implemented fault Insertion: An (FTMP) Example. Technical Report CMU-CS-87-101. Carnegie Mellon University. January 1987.

90. Dâmaso, A., Rosa, N., & Maciel, P. (2017). Integrated Evaluation of Reliability and Power Consumption of Wireless Sensor Networks. Sensors (Basel, Switzerland), 17(11), 2547. doi:10.3390/s17112547

91. Julien Danjou. Serious Python.Publisher: William Pollock. ISBN-13: 978-1-59327-878-6. 2020

92. Dantas, Jamilson and Matos, Rubens and Araujo, Jean and Maciel, Paulo. An availability model for eucalyptus platform: An analysis of warm-standby replication mechanism. Systems, Man, and Cybernetics (SMC), 2012 IEEE International Conference on. pp.: 1664–1669. IEEE. 2012.

93. Dantas, Jamilson and Matos, Rubens and Araujo, Jean and Maciel, Paulo. Eucalyptus-based private clouds: availability modeling and comparison to the cost of a public cloud. Computing. Vol.: 97. number: 11. pp.:1121–1140. Springer. 2015

94. Jamilson Dantas, Rubens Matos, Carlos Melo and Paulo Maciel. Cloud Infrastructure Planning: Models Considering an Optimization Method, Cost and Performance Requirements. International Journal of Grid and Utility Computing. 2020. ISSN: 1741-8488 (Online). ISSN: 1741-847X (Print).

95. Jamilson Dantas, Rubens Matos, Jean Teixeira, Eltton Tullyo and Paulo Maciel. Estimating Capacity-Oriented Availability in Cloud Systems. International Journal of Computational Science and Engineering. 2020. ISSN: 1742-7193 (Online). ISSN: 1742-7185 (Print).

96. Davison, A. C. and Hinkley, D. V., Bootstrap Methods and Their Application, Cambridge University Press, New York, NY, USA, 2013.

97. B. Silva and Paulo Romero Martins Maciel and Eduardo Tavares and Armin Zimmermann.Dependability Models for Designing Disaster Tolerant Cloud Computing Systems. The Third International Workshop on Dependability of Clouds, Data Centers and Virtual Machine Technology (DCDV). 2013

98. Denning, P. J., Buzen, J. P. The Operational Analysis of Queueing Network Models. Acm Computing Surveys, 10, 3, 225-261, September 01, 1978.

99. Desel, Jörg and Esparza, Javier, Free Choice Petri Nets, 1995, isbn: 0-521-46519-2, Cambridge University Press.

100. Desel, Jörg. Basic linear algebraic techniques for place/transition nets. Lectures on Petri Nets I: Basic Models: Advances in Petri Nets. Springer Berlin Heidelberg. pages:257–308. isbn:978-3-540-49442-3. 1998.

101. Desel, Jörg, W. Reisig. Place/Transition nets. Lectures on Petri Nets I: Basic Models: Advances in Petri Nets. Springer Berlin Heidelberg. pages:122–173. isbn:978-3-540-49442-3. 1998.

102. Desrochers, A.A. and Al-Jaar, R.Y., Applications of Petri Nets in Manufacturing Systems: Modeling, Control, and Performance Analysis, IEEE Press. 1995.

103. Dhillon, B. S. (Balbir S.),. Applied Reliability and Quality: fundamentals, methods and applications. London : Springer-Verlag, 2007.

104. DiCiccio, Thomas J.; Efron, Bradley. Bootstrap confidence intervals. Statist. Sci. 11 (1996), no. 3, 189–228. doi:10.1214/ss/1032280214. https://projecteuclid.org/euclid.ss/1032280214

105. J. Dickinson, G. S. Chakraborti, Nonparametric Statistical Inference, Marcel Dekker, Inc., Fourth Edition, 2003.

106. Dienes, P. The Taylor series: an introduction to the theory of functions of a complex variable. Dover, 1957. "An unabridged and unaltered republication of the 1st edition [1931] with errata incorporated into the text."

107. J. J. Dongarra, C. B. Moler, J. R. Bunch, and G. W. Stewart. LINPACK Users' Guide.1979. Pages: 364

108. Dongarra, J.J., Luszczek, P. and Petitet, A. (2003), The LINPACK Benchmark: past, present and future. Concurrency Computat.: Pract. Exper., 15: 803-820. doi:10.1002/cpe.728

109. Development and Evaluation of a Fault-Tolerant Multiprocessor Computer, Vol III, FTMP Test and Evaluation Charles Stark Draper Laboratories, 1983. NASA Contract Report 166073.

110. https://linux.die.net/man/1/dstat. Retrieved at 8/6/2020.

111. http://linuxadministrative.blogspot.com/2014/06/dstat-command-examples.html. Retrieved at 8/7/2020.

112. Dubrova, Elena. Fault-Tolerant Design. ISBN:1461421128. Springer Publishing Company. 2013.

113. Jeff Duntemann. Assembly Language Step-by-Step - Programming with Linux. Third Edition. ISBN: 978-0-470-49702-9. Wiley Publishing. 2009.

114. J. A. Duraes and H. S. Madeira, "Emulation of Software Faults: A Field Data Study and a Practical Approach," in IEEE Transactions on Software Engineering, vol. 32, no. 11, pp. 849-867, Nov. 2006, doi: 10.1109/TSE.2006.113.

115. Ebeling, C.E., An Introduction to Reliability and Maintainability Engineering, ISBN: 9781577666257, second edition, 2010. Waveland

116. L. Eeckhout, H. Vandierendonck and K. De Bosschere, "Designing computer architecture research workloads," in Computer, vol. 36, no. 2, pp. 65-71, Feb. 2003, doi: 10.1109/MC.2003.1178050.

117. L. Eeckhout and K. Hoste, "Microarchitecture-Independent Workload Characterization" in IEEE Micro, vol. 27, no. 03, pp. 63-72, 2007. doi: 10.1109/MM.2007.56.

118. Efron, Bradley and Hastie, Trevor. Computer Age Statistical Inference: Algorithms, Evidence, and Data Science. isbn: 1107149894. Cambridge University Press. 2016.

119. Efron, B. Bootstrap Methods: Another Look at the Jackknife. Ann. Statist. 7 (1979), no. 1, 1–26. doi:10.1214/aos/1176344552. https://projecteuclid.org/euclid.aos/1176344552

120. Efron, Bradley. "Nonparametric Estimates of Standard Error: The Jackknife, the Bootstrap and Other Methods." Biometrika 68, no. 3 (1981): 589-99. doi:10.2307/2335441.

121. Efron, Bradley, and Robert J. Tibshirani. An introduction to the bootstrap. CRC press, 1994.

122. Paul Ellgen. Thermodynamics and Chemical Equilibrium. 2021. Retrieved July 14, 2021, from https://chem.libretexts.org/@go/page/151654

123. Elsayed, E. A. (1996). Reliability engineering. Reading, Mass: Addison Wesley Longman.

124. Elsayed A. Elsayed. Accelerated Life Testing. Book chapter. Pages: 415-428. In Handbook of Reliability Engineering. ISBN: 978-1-85233-453-6. DOI: 10.1007/b97414. Springer-Verlag. 2003.

125. Edited by G. Somasundaram and A. Shrivastava. Information Storage and Management. John Wiley & Sons. ISBN: 978-0-470-61833-2, 2010.

126. Enderton, Herbert B. Elements of Set Theory. ISBN:978-0-12-238440-0. Copyright 1977 Elsevier Inc. All rights reserved 1977.

127. Electronic Parts - Reliability Data 2014. Prepared by Quanterion Solutions Incorporated for Reliability Information Analysis Center. ISBN-13: 978-1-933904-66-5. 2014.

128. Epstein, Benjamin and Sobel, Milton. Life Testing. Journal of the American Statistical Association. Sep. 1953, Vol. Vol. 48, No. 263.

129. Ericson, Clifton. Fault Tree Analysis - A History. Proceedings of the 17th International Systems Safety Conference. 17th International Systems Safety Conference, 1999.

130. A. K. Erlang. Principal Works of A. K. Erlang - The Theory of Probabilities and Telephone Conversations. First published in Nyt Tidsskrift for Matematik B. 1909, Vol. Vol 2

131. Principal Works of A. K. Erlang - The Theory of Probabilities and Telephone Conversations. First published in Nyt Tidsskrift for Matematik B. 1909, Vol. Vol 20.

132. Eva Ishay. Fitting Phase-Type Distributions to Data from a Telephone Call Center. Research Thesis. HAIFA, October 2002

133. Brian S. Everitt, Sabine Landau, and Morven Leese. Cluster Analysis (5th. ed.). Wiley Publishing. 2011.

134. Fanban - Open Source Performance and Load Testing Tool. http://faban.org/. Retrieved at 9/23/2020.

135. L. Feinbube, L. Pirl, P. Tröger and A. Polze, "Software Fault Injection Campaign Generation for Cloud Infrastructures," 2017 IEEE International Conference on Software Quality, Reliability and Security Companion (QRS-C), Prague, Czech Republic, 2017, pp. 622-623, doi: 10.1109/QRS-C.2017.119.

136. Feitelson, Dror G. Workload Modeling for Computer Systems Performance Evaluation. isbn:1107078237. Cambridge University Press. 2015

137. Feitelson D.G. (2002) Workload Modeling for Performance Evaluation. In: Calzarossa M.C., Tucci S. (eds) Performance Evaluation of Complex Systems: Techniques and Tools. Performance 2002. Lecture Notes in Computer Science, vol 2459. Springer, Berlin, Heidelberg. https://doi.org/10.1007/3-540-45798-4˙6

138. W. Feller, An Introduction to Probability Theory and Its Applications, Vols. I, II, Wiley, New York, 1968.

139. Domenico Ferrari. 1984. On the foundations of artificial workload design. SIGMETRICS Perform. Eval. Rev. 12, 3 (August 1984), 8–14. DOI:https://doi.org/10.1145/1031382.809309

140. J. Jair Figueiredo, Paulo Maciel, Gustavo Callou, Eduardo Tavares, Erica Sousa and Bruno Silva. Estimating Reliability Importance and Total Cost of Acquisition for Data Center Power Infrastructures. In: Proceedings of the 2011 IEEE International Conference on Systems, Man, and Cybernetics (IEEE SMC 2011). Anchorage, Alaska, USA, 2011.

141. Jason Fink, Matt Sherer, Kurt Wall. Linux Performance Tuning and Capacity Planning. Sams, Indianapolis, Indiana, 46290 USA. ISBN: 0-672-32081-9. 2002

142. Ronald Aylmer Sir Fisher. On a Distribution Yielding the Error Functions of Several Well Known Statistics. Proceedings International Mathematical Congress, Toronto. 2, pp. 805-813. 1924.

143. K. Florek, J. Łukaszewicz, J. Perkal, Hugo Steinhaus, S. Zubrzycki Colloquium Mathematicum 2, 282-285 DOI: 10.4064/cm-2-3-4-282-285. 1951

144. P. Folkesson, S. Svensson and J. Karlsson, "A comparison of simulation-based and scan chain implemented fault injection," Digest of Papers. Twenty-Eighth Annual International Symposium on Fault-Tolerant Computing (Cat. No.98CB36224), Munich, Germany, 1998, pp. 284-293, doi: 10.1109/FTCS.1998.689479.

145. Catherine Forbes, Merran Evans, Nicholas Hastings, Brian Peacock. Statistical Distributions. John Wiley & Sons, Inc. ISBN: 978-0-470-39063-4. 2011.

146. L. Fratta and U. Montanari, "A Boolean algebra method for computing the terminal reliability in a communication network," in IEEE Transactions on Circuit Theory, vol. 20, no. 3, pp. 203-211, May 1973. doi: 10.1109/TCT.1973.1083657

147. H. E. S. Galindo, W. M. Santos, P. R. M. Maciel, B. Silva, S. M. L. Galdino and J. P. Pires, "Synthetic workload generation for capacity planning of virtual server environments," 2009 IEEE International Conference on Systems, Man and Cybernetics, San Antonio, TX, 2009, pp. 2837-2842, doi: 10.1109/IC-SMC.2009.5346600.

148. Hugo Galindo, Erico Guedes, Paulo Maciel, Bruno Silva and Sérgio Galdino. WGCap: a synthetic trace generation tool for capacity planning of virtual server environments. In: IEEE International Conference on Systems, Man, and Cybernetics, 2010, Istanbul. IEEE Proceeding of SMC, 2010.

149. Gan, F. F., and K. J. Koehler. "Goodness-of-Fit Tests Based on P-P Probability Plots." Technometrics 32, no. 3 (1990): 289-303. doi:10.2307/1269106.

150. Gareth James, Daniela Witten, Trevor Hastie, and Robert Tibshirani. An Introduction to Statistical Learning: with Applications in R. Springer Publishing Company, Incorporated. 2014.

151. Jean-Claude Geffroy,Gilles Motet. Design of dependable computing systems. ISBN:1-4020-0437-0. 2002. Kluwer Academic Publishers

152. Silva, B. and Maciel, P. and Brilhante, J. and Zimmermann, A. GeoClouds Modcs: A performability evaluation tool for disaster tolerant IaaS clouds. Systems Conference (SysCon), 2014 8th Annual IEEE. pp.: 116-122. doi: 10.1109/SysCon.2014.6819245. 2014

153. German, Reinhard. Performance Analysis of Communication Systems with Non-Markovian Stochastic Petri Nets. 2000. isbn:0471492582. John Wiley & Sons, Inc. New York, NY, USA.

154. Reinhard German and Christoph Lindemann. Analysis of stochastic Petri nets by the method of supplementary variables. Performance Evaluation. Volume: 20, number: 1, pages: 317-335. issn: 0166-5316. 1994

155. Garth A. Gibson. Redundant Disk Arrays: Reliable, Parallel Secondary Storage. Thesis Ph.D. Thesis in Computer Science. University of California, Berkeley, April. 1991.

156. Gil, Daniel, Juan Carlos Baraza, Joaquin Gracia, and Pedro Joaquin Gil. "VHDL simulation-based fault injection techniques." In Fault injection techniques and tools for embedded systems reliability evaluation, pp. 159-176. Springer, Boston, MA, 2003.

157. Gilbreath, J., "A High-Level Language Benchmark," Byte, vol. 6, no. 9, September 1981, pp. 180–198.

158. Girault, Claude and Valk, Rudiger, Petri Nets for Systems Engineering: A Guide to Modeling, Verification, and Applications, isbn:3642074472, Springer Publishing Company, Incorporated, 2010.

159. Gnedenko, Igor A. Ushakov. Probabilistic Reliability Engineering. s.l. : Wiley-Interscience, 1995.

160. Demis Gomes, Guto Leoni, Djamel Sadok, Glauco Gonçalves, Patricia Endo, and Paulo Maciel. 2020. Temperature variation impact on estimating costs and most critical components in a cloud data centre. Int. J. Comput. Appl. Technol. 62, 4 (2020), 361–374. DOI:https://doi.org/10.1504/ijcat.2020.107426.

161. Anatoliy Gorbenko, Vyacheslav Kharchenko, Alexander Romanovsky. On composing Dependable Web Services using undependable web components. Int. J. Simulation and Process Modelling. Nos. 1/2, 2007, Vol. Vol. 3.

162. Tarun Goyal, Ajit Singh, Aakanksha Agrawal. Cloudsim: a simulator for cloud computing infrastructure and modeling, Procedia Engineering, Volume 38, 2012, Pages 3566-3572, ISSN 1877-7058, https://doi.org/10.1016/j.proeng.2012.06.412.

163. Gravette, M. A., & Barker, K. (2014). Achieved availability importance measures for enhancing reliability centered maintenance decisions. Journal of Risk and Reliability, 229(1), 62–72.

164. Gray, G. (1985). Why Do Computers Stop and What Can Be Done About It?. Tandem TR 85.7.

165. Franklin A. Graybill (Author), Hariharan K. Iyer. Regression Analysis: Concepts and Applications. ISBN-13: 978-0534198695. ISBN-10: 0534198694. Duxbury. 1994.

166. Chiola, G. and Franceschinis, G. and Gaeta, R. and Ribaudo, M. GreatSPN 1.7: Graphical Editor and Analyzer for Timed and Stochastic Petri Nets. Perform. Evaluation. Vol: 25. number:1-2. pages:47-68. isssn:0166-5316. Elsevier. 1995

167. Grinstead, Charles Miller, and James Laurie Snell. Introduction to probability. American Mathematical Soc., 2012.

168. Grottke, M., Matias, R., Trivedi, K. (2008). The fundamentals of software aging. In IEEE International Conference on Software Reliability Engineering Workshops.

169. Almir Guimarães, Paulo Maciel, Rivalino Matias, Bruno Silva, and Bruno Nogueira. An analytic approach for optimization of computer network design considering the integration of the communication and power infrastructures. International Journal of Network Management. 2021. ISSN: 1099-1190

170. Haas, Peter J. Stochastic Petri Nets: Modelling, Stability, Simulation. Springer, New York. pages:85–445, year: 2002. isbn: 978-0-387-21552-5, doi:10.1007/0-387-21552-2ˇ9.

171. (Godfrey Harold. A Course of Pure Mathematics. Third Edition. Cambridge at the University Press. 1921. ps.: The Project Gutenberg EBook. Release Date: February 5, 2012.

172. Boudewijn R. Haverkort. Markovian Models for Performance and Dependability Evaluation. Lectures on Formal Methods and Performance Analysis, Springer, 2001

173. Boudewijn R. Haverkort. Performance of Computer Communication Systems: A Model-Based Approach. John Wiley & Sons, Inc. New York, NY, USA, 1998.

174. Harchol-Balter, M. Performance Modeling and Design of Computer Systems: Queueing Theory in Action. Cambridge: Cambridge University Press. 2013 doi:10.1017/CBO9781139226424

175. Heath, Thomas, History of Ancient Greek Mathematics. Vol I. Oxford Press. 1921.

176. B. Herington, D. & Jacquot. The HP Virtual Server Environment: Making the Adaptive Enterprise Vision a Reality in your Data Center. Prentice-Hall, 2006.

177. Herzog, Ulrich. Formal Methods for Performance Evaluation. Book chapter. pp: 1-37. Formal Methods for Performance Evaluation. Lectures on Formal Methods and Performance Analysis. Springer Berlin Heidelberg. Editors:Brinksma, Ed, Hermanns, Holger, Katoen, Joost-Pieter, ISBN: 978-3-540-44667-5. 2001.

178. Hogg, R. V., Tanis, E. A., Probability and statistical inference, New York, Macmillan, 1977.

179. András Horváth, Marco Paolieri, Lorenzo Ridi, Enrico Vicario. Transient analysis of non-Markovian models using stochastic state classes. Performance Evaluation. North-Holland. Volume: 69. Issue: 7-8. Pages: 315-335. 2012.

180. Horváth, Gábor". Moment Matching-Based Distribution Fitting with Generalized Hyper-Erlang Distributions, Springer Berlin Heidelberg, Analytic and Stochastic Modeling Techniques and Applications: 20th International Conference, ASMTA 2013, Ghent, Belgium, July 8-10, 2013. Proceedings

181. Mei-Chen Hsueh, T. K. Tsai and R. K. Iyer, "Fault injection techniques and tools," in Computer, vol. 30, no. 4, pp. 75-82, April 1997, doi: 10.1109/2.585157.

182. https://linux.die.net/man/1/httperf. Retrieved at 10/3/2020.

183. Hu, Tao and Guo, Minyi and Guo, Song and Ozaki, Hirokazu and Zheng, Long and Ota, Kaoru and Dong, Mianxiong. MTTF of composite web services. Parallel and Distributed Processing with Applications (ISPA), 2010 International Symposium on. pp.: 130–137. IEEE. 2010.

184. P. H. Starke and S. Roch. INA - Integrated Net Analyzer - Version 2.2. Humbolt Universität zu Berlin - Institut für Informatik. 1999.

185. Intel Distribution for LINPACK Benchmark. https://software.intel.com/content/www/us/en /develop/documentation/mkl-linux-developer-guide/top/intel-math-kernel-library-benchmarks//intel-distribution-for-linpack-benchmark/ /overview-of-the-intel-distribution-for-linpack-benchmark.html. Retrieved at 9/8/2020.

186. ITIC 2020 Global Server Hardware, Server OS Reliability Report. Information Technology Intelligence Consulting Corp. February/March2020

187. B. Silva and Paulo Romero Martins Maciel and Armin Zimmermann. Performability Models for Designing Disaster Tolerant Infrastructure-as-a-Service Cloud. The 8th International Conference for Internet Technology and Secured Transactions (ICITST). 2013.

188. Jain, R., The art of computer systems performance analysis: Techniques for experimental design, measurement, simulation, and modeling. New York: Wiley. 1991.

189. Jean Araujo, Rubens Matos, Verônica Conceição, Gabriel Alves and Paulo Maciel. Impact of Capacity and Discharging Rate on Battery Lifetime: A Stochastic Model to Support Mobile Device Autonomy Planning Pervasive and Mobile Computing. Journal Pervasive and Mobile Computing. 2017. Online ISSN 1574-1192. Print ISSN 1574-1192.

190. Banks, Jerry, John S. Carson, and Barry L. Nelson. 1996. Discrete-event system simulation. Prentice-Hall. 4th Edition. isbn.: 10: 0131446797. 2004.

191. Edited by Jerry Banks. Handbook of Simulation: principles, methodology, advances, applications, and practice; John Wiley and Sons, Inc. isbn: 0471134031. 1998.

192. E. Jenn, J. Arlat, M. Rimen, J. Ohlsson and J. Karlsson, "Fault injection into VHDL models: the MEFISTO tool," Proceedings of IEEE 24th International Symposium on Fault-Tolerant Computing, Austin, TX, USA, 1994, pp. 66-75, doi: 10.1109/FTCS.1994.315656.

193. Arnulf Jentzen and Peter Kloeden. Taylor Approximations for Stochastic Partial Differential Equations. Series: CBMS-NSF Regional Conference Series in Applied Mathematics 83. Publisher: SIAM. ISBN: 9781611972009. 2011

194. Hao Jiang and Constantinos Dovrolis. 2005. Why is the internet traffic bursty in short time scales? SIGMETRICS Perform. Eval. Rev. 33, 1 (June 2005), 241–252. DOI:https://doi.org/10.1145/1071690.1064240

195. Joanes, D. N., and C. A. Gill. "Comparing Measures of Sample Skewness and Kurtosis." Journal of the Royal Statistical Society. Series D (The Statistician), vol. 47, no. 1, 1998, pp. 183–189.

196. Johnson SC. Hierarchical clustering schemes. Psychometrika. 1967 Sep;32(3):241-54. doi: 10.1007/BF02289588. PMID: 5234703.

197. Johnson, Mark E., Gary L. Tietjen, and Richard J. Beckman. "A New Family of Probability Distributions With Applications to Monte Carlo Studies." Journal of the American Statistical Association 75, no. 370 (1980): 276-79. doi:10.2307/2287446.

198. Johnson, Barry W. Design &Amp; Analysis of Fault-Tolerant Digital Systems. ISBN: 0-201-07570-9. Addison-Wesley Longman Publishing Co., Inc. 1988

199. Pallavi Joshi, Haryadi S. Gunawi, and Koushik Sen. 2011. PREFAIL: a programmable tool for multiple-failure injection. In Proceedings of the 2011 ACM international conference on Object-oriented programming systems languages and applications (OOPSLA '11). ACM, New York, NY, USA, 171–188. DOI:https://doi.org/10.1145/2048066.2048082

200. Juhás, Gabriel and Lehocki, Fedor and Lorenz, Robert. Semantics of Petri Nets: A Comparison. Proceedings of the 39th Conference on Winter Simulation: 40 Years! The Best is Yet to Come. Washington D.C. 2007. isbn: 1-4244-1306-0. page: 617–628. IEEE Press.

201. Joseph Juran, A. Blanton Godfrey. Juran's Quality Handbook. Fifth Edition. ISBN 0-07-034003-X. McGraw-Hill. 1998

202. G. A. Kanawati, N. A. Kanawati and J. A. Abraham, "FERRARI: a flexible software-based fault and error injection system," in IEEE Transactions on Computers, vol. 44, no. 2, pp. 248-260, Feb. 1995, doi: 10.1109/12.364536

203. E. L. Kaplan and Paul Meier. Nonparametric Estimation from Incomplete Observations. Journal of the American Statistical Association, Vol. 53, No. 282 (Jun. 1958), pp. 457-481

204. Kailash C. Kapur and Michael Pecht. 2014. Reliability Engineering (1st. ed.). Wiley Publishing.

205. Richard M. Karp and Raymond E. Miller, Parallel program schemat, Journal of Computer and System Sciences, vol.: 3, number: 2, year:1969, issn:0022-0000.

206. Kaufman, L. and P. Rousseeuw. Finding Groups in Data: An Introduction to Cluster Analysis. John Wiley. isbn: 978-0-47187876-6. doi: 10.1002/9780470316801. 1990.

207. W R Keesee. A METHOD OF DETERMINING A CONFIDENCE INTERVAL FOR AVAILABILITY. NAVAL MISSILE CENTER POINT MUGU CA. DEFENSE TECHNICAL INFORMATION CENTER. Accession Number: AD0617716. 09 July 1965.

208. Law, A. M. and W. D. Kelton (1991). Simulation Modeling and Analysis, second edition. McGraw-Hill, New York.

209. M. Khatiwada, R. K. Budhathoki and A. Mahanti, "Characterizing Mobile Web Traffic: A Case Study of an Academic Web Server," 2019 Twelfth International Conference on Mobile Computing and Ubiquitous Network (ICMU), Kathmandu, Nepal, 2019, pp. 1-6, doi: 10.23919/ICMU48249.2019.9006650.

210. https://www.iec.ch/si/binary.htm. Retrieved at 5/2/2020.

211. Kim, Dong Seong and Machida, Fumio and Trivedi, Kishor S. Availability Modeling and Analysis of a Virtualized System. Proceedings of the 2009 15th IEEE Pacific Rim International Symposium on Dependable Computing. PRDC '09. isbn:978-0-7695-3849-5. doi: 10.1109/PRDC.2009.64. IEEE Computer Society. 2009.

212. Kim, Dong Seong and Machida, Fumio and Trivedi, Kishor S. Availability modeling and analysis of a virtualized system. Dependable Computing, 2009. PRDC'09. 15th IEEE Pacific Rim International Symposium on. pp.: 365–371. IEEE, 2009.

213. Kimball, E. Harvey Fletcher and Henry Eyring: Men of Faith and Science. Dialogue: A Journal of Mormon Thought, 15(3), 74-86. 1982.

214. Ronald S. King. Cluster Analysis and Data Mining: An Introduction. Mercury Learning & Information, Dulles, VA, USA. 2014.

215. Anil K. Jain and Richard C. Dubes. Algorithms for clustering data. Prentice-Hall, Inc., USA. 1988.

216. Andrey Nikolaevich Kolmogorov. Kolmogoroff, A. Über die analytischen Methoden in der Wahrscheinlichkeitsrechnung (in German) Mathematische Annalen. Springer-Verlag, 1931.

217. Maha Kooli, Alberto Bosio, Pascal Benoit, Lionel Torres. Software testing and software fault injection. DTIS: Design and Technology of Integrated Systems in Nanoscale Era, Apr 2015, Naples, Italy.

218. Israel Koren, C. Mani Krishna. Fault-Tolerant Systems. Morgan Kaufmann Publishers Inc. 2007. ISBN: 10: 0-12-088568-9

219. G. Kotsis, K. Krithivasan and S. V. Raghavan, "Generative workload models of Internet traffic," Proceedings of ICICS, 1997 International Conference on Information, Communications and Signal Processing. Theme: Trends in Information Systems Engineering and Wireless Multimedia Communications (Cat., Singapore, 1997, pp. 152-156 vol.1, doi: 10.1109/ICICS.1997.647077.

220. Kotz, Samuel, and Saralees Nadarajah. Extreme value distributions: theory and applications. World Scientific, 2000.

221. K. Krishnamoorthy. Handbook of Statistical Distributions with Applications. Chapman & Hall/CRC. ISBN 1-58488-635-8. 206.

222. A. N. Kolmogorov, Sulla determinazione empirica di una legge di distribuzione, Giornale dell'Istituto Italiano degli Attuari, 4:83–91, 1933.

223. V. G. Kulkarni. Introduction to Modeling and Analysis of Stochastic Systems. Springer. 2011. ISBN:978-1-4419-1771-3.

224. Zuo, Way Kuo and Ming J. Optimal Reliability Modeling - Principles and Applications. s.l. : Wiley, 2003. p. 544.

225. Kuo, Way and Zhu, Xiaoyan. Importance Measures in Reliability, Risk, and Optimization: Principles and Applications. 2012. ISBN: 111999344X, 9781119993445. Wiley Publishing

226. Lance, G., & Williams, W.T. A General Theory of Classificatory Sorting Strategies: Hierarchical Systems. Comput. J., 9, 373-380. 1967.

227. Laprie, J.C. Dependable Computing and Fault Tolerance: Concepts and terminology. Proc. 15th IEEE Int. Symp. on Fault-Tolerant Computing. 1985.

228. J.C. Laprie. Dependability: Basic Concepts and Terminology. s.l. : Springer-Verlag., 1992.

229. Jerald F. Lawless. Statistical Models and Methods for Lifetime Data, Second Edition. First published:13 November 2002 Print ISBN:9780471372158 —Online ISBN:9781118033005 —DOI:10.1002/9781118033005. 2003 John Wiley & Sons

230. Lawless, J. F. Statistical models and methods for lifetime data. Hoboken, N.J: Wiley-Interscience. 2003.

231. M. Le and Y. Tamir, "Fault Injection in Virtualized Systems—Challenges and Applications," in IEEE Transactions on Dependable and Secure Computing, vol. 12, no. 3, pp. 284-297, 1 May-June 2015, doi: 10.1109/TDSC.2014.2334300.

232. Lee, Elisa T. and Wang, John Wenyu. Statistical Methods for Survival Data Analysis. isbn: 1118095022. 4th edition. Wiley Publishing. 2013.

233. Leemis Lawrence M. Reliability - Probabilistic Models and Statistical Methods. Second Edition. isbn: 978-0-692-00027-4

234. Lehmer, D. H., Proceedings 2nd Symposium on Largescale. Digital Calculating Machinery, Cambridge, Harvard University Press, pp. 141-146, 1951.

235. Lehn, M., Triebel, T., Rehner, R. et al. On synthetic workloads for multiplayer online games: a methodology for generating representative shooter game workloads. Multimedia Systems 20, 609–620 (2014). https://doi.org/10.1007/s00530-014-0359-z

236. Leithold, Louis, and Louis Leithold. The calculus 7th Edition. New York: HarperCollins College Pub. 1996.

237. Lewis, Byron C., and Albert E. Crews. "The Evolution of Benchmarking as a Computer Performance Evaluation Technique." MIS Quarterly, vol. 9, no. 1, 1985, pp. 7–16. JSTOR

238. Lilja, D. (2000). Measuring Computer Performance: A Practitioner's Guide. Cambridge: Cambridge University Press. doi:10.1017/CBO9780511612398

239. C. Lindemann. Performance Modelling with Deterministic and Stochastic Petri Nets. John Wiley and Sons. 1998.

240. https://people.sc.fsu.edu/~jburkardt/c_src/linpack_bench/linpack_bench.c. Retrieved at 10/10/2020.

241. John D. C. Little. Little's Law as Viewed on Its 50th Anniversary. Oper. Res. 59, 3. May 2011. 536–549. DOI:https://doi.org/10.1287/opre.1110.0940

242. https://www.netlib.org/benchmark/livermorec. Retrieved at 10/18/2020.

243. Roy Longbottom. Roy Longbottom's PC Benchmark Collection. http://www.roylongbottom.org.uk/. Retrieved at 9/8/2020.

244. Lyu, Michael R. Software Fault Tolerance. John Wiley & Sons, Inc. ISBN: 0471950688. New York, NY, USA. 1995.

245. Machida, F. and Andrade, E. and Kim, D.S. and Trivedi, K.S. Candy: Component-based Availability Modeling Framework for Cloud Service Management Using SysML. Reliable Distributed Systems (SRDS), 2011 30th IEEE Symposium on. pp.: 209–218. IEEE. 2011.

246. Paulo Maciel, Kishor Trivedi, Rivalino Matias and Dong Kim. Dependability Modeling. In: Performance and Dependability in Service Computing: Concepts, Techniques and Research Directions ed. Hershey, Pennsylvania: IGI Global, 2011.

247. P. Maciel, K. S. Trivedi, R. Matias, and D. S. Kim, "Dependability modeling," in Performance and Dependability in Service Computing: Concepts, Techniques and Research Directions. Hershey: IGI Global, 2011.

248. Maciel, Paulo; Dantas, Jamilson; Melo, Carlos; Pereira, Paulo; Oliveira, Felipe; Araujo, Jean; Matos, Rubens; A survey on reliability and availability modeling of edge, fog, and cloud computing, Journal of Reliable Intelligent Environments pages:2199-4676, Springer. 09/18/2021 , 10.1007/s40860-021-00154-1

249. MacQueen, James. Some methods for classification and analysis of multivariate observations. Proceedings of the fifth Berkeley symposium on mathematical statistics and probability. Vol. 1. No. 14. 1967.

250. Madeira H., Rela M., Moreira F., Silva J.G. (1994) RIFLE: A general purpose pin-level fault injector. In: Echtle K., Hammer D., Powell D. (eds) Dependable Computing — EDCC-1. EDCC 1994. Lecture Notes in Computer Science, vol 852. Springer, Berlin, Heidelberg. https://doi.org/10.1007/3-540-58426-9´132

251. H. Madeira, D. Costa and M. Vieira, "On the emulation of software faults by software fault injection," Proceeding International Conference on Dependable Systems and Networks. DSN 2000, New York, NY, USA, 2000, pp. 417-426, doi: 10.1109/ICDSN.2000.857571.

252. Magee, Jeff and Kramer, Jeff, Concurrency: State Models &Amp; Java Programs, 1999, isbn:0-471-98710-7, John Wiley & Sons, Inc., New York, NY, USA.

253. J. A. Manion, R. E. Huie, R. D. Levin, D. R. Burgess Jr., V. L. Orkin, W. Tsang, W. S. McGivern, J. W. Hudgens, V. D. Knyazev, D. B. Atkinson, E. Chai, A. M. Tereza, C.-Y. Lin, T. C. Allison, W. G. Mallard, F. Westley, J. T. Herron, R. F. Hampson, and D. H. Frizzell, NIST Chemical Kinetics Database, NIST Standard Reference Database 17, Version 7.0 (Web Version), Release 1.6.8, Data version 2015.09, National Institute of Standards and Technology, Gaithersburg, Maryland, 20899-8320. Web address: https://kinetics.nist.gov/

254. Mann, Nancy R., and Frank E. Grubbs. "Chi-Square Approximations for Exponential Parameters, Prediction Intervals and Beta Percentiles." Journal of the American Statistical Association 69, no. 347 (1974): 654-61. doi:10.2307/2285996.

255. Marsaglia, G., & Marsaglia, J. Evaluating the Anderson-Darling Distribution. Journal of Statistical Software. 2004.

256. Marsan, Marco Ajmone and Balbo, G. and Conte, Gianni and Donatelli, S. and Franceschinis, G. Modelling with generalized stochastic Petri nets. isbn:9780471930594, Wiley. 1995

257. M. Ajmone Marsan and G. Chiola. On Petri Nets with deterministic and exponentially distributed firing times. In G. Rozenberg, editor, Adv. in Petri Nets 1987, Lecture Notes in Computer Science 266, pages 132–145. Springer-Verlag, 1987.

258. M. Ajmone Marsan, G. Balbo, A. Bobbio, G. Chiola, G. Conte, and A. Cumani. The effect of execution policies on the semantics and analysis of stochastic Petri nets. IEEE Transactions on Software Engineering, pages:832-846. SE-15:832-846, 1989

259. Mathis, Matthew and Semke, Jeffrey and Mahdavi, Jamshid and Ott, Teunis. The macroscopic behavior of the TCP congestion avoidance algorithm. SIG-COMM Comput. Commun. Rev. pp.: 67–82. Vol: 27. no: 3. issn:0146-4833. doi:10.1145/263932.264023. ACM. 1997.

260. Rubens Matos, Paulo Maciel, Fumio Machida, Dong Seong Kim, Kishor Trivedi. Sensitivity Analysis of Server Virtualized System Availability. IEEE Transaction on Reliability. Volume 61, Number 4, Pages 994-1006. Published on December 2012. ISSN: 0018-9529.

261. MATOS, R. S.; MACIEL, P. R.; SILVA, R. M. Qos-driven optimization of composite web services: an approach based on grasp and analytic models. International Journal of Web and Grid Services, v. 9, n. 3, p. 304–321, 2013.

262. R. Matos, E. C. Andrade and P. Maciel, "Evaluation of a disaster recovery solution through fault injection experiments," 2014 IEEE International Conference on Systems, Man, and Cybernetics (SMC), San Diego, CA, USA, 2014, pp. 2675-2680, doi: 10.1109/SMC.2014.6974331.

263. Rubens Matos, Jean Araujo, Danilo Oliveira, Paulo Maciel and Kishor Trivedi. Sensitivity Analysis of a Hierarchical Model of Mobile Cloud Computing. Elsevier Journal Simulation Modelling Practice and Theory. Volume 50, January 2015, Pages 151–164. ISSN: 1569-190X.

264. Rubens Matos, Jamilson Dantas, Jean Araujo, Kishor S. Trivedi, and Paulo Maciel. Redundant Eucalyptus Private Clouds: Availability Modeling and Sensitivity Analysis. Journal of Grid Computing. 2016. Online ISSN 1572-9184. Print ISSN 1570-7873.

265. Rubens Matos, Jamilson Dantas, Eltton Araujo, and Paulo Maciel. Bottleneck detection in cloud computing performance and dependability: Sensitivity rankings for hierarchical models. Journal of Network and Systems Management (JONS). 2020. ISSN: 1064-7570.

266. Philippe Maurine, Karim Tobich, Thomas Ordas, Pierre Yvan Liardet. Yet Another Fault Injection Technique: by Forward Body Biasing Injection. YACC'2012: Yet Another Conference on Cryptography, Sep 2012, Porquerolles Island, France.

267. Michael P. McLaughlin. Compendium of Common Probability Distributions. Compendium of Common Probability Distributions Second Edition, v2.7. Copyright 2014 by Michael P. McLaughlin. All rights reserved. Second printing, with corrections.

268. McMahon, F H. The Livermore Fortran Kernels: A computer test of the numerical performance range. United States: N. p., 1986.

269. Meeker, W. Q., & Escobar, L. A. Statistical methods for reliability data. New York: Wiley. 1998.

270. Rosangela Melo, Maria Clara Bezerra, Jamilson Dantas, Rubens Matos, Ivanildo José de Melo Filho, Aline Santana Oliveira, Fábio Feliciano and Paulo Maciel. Sensitivity Analysis Techniques Applied in Video Streaming Service on Eucalyptus Cloud Environments. Journal of Information Systems Engineering & Management. 2018. ISSN: 2468-4376 (Online).

271. Melo, Carlos; Araujo, Jean; Dantas, Jamilson; Pereira, Paulo; Maciel, Paulo. A model-based approach for planning blockchain service provisioning. Computing. Springer. A10.1007/s00607-021-00956-4. 05/23/2021.

272. Carlos Melo, Paulo Pereira, Jamilson Dantas, and Paulo Maciel. Distributed Application Provisioning over Ethereum based private and permissioned Blockchain: Availability modeling, capacity, and costs planning. The Journal of Supercomputing. 2021. ISSN: 1573-0484.

273. Paulo Maciel, Rubens Matos, Bruno Silva, Jair Figueiredo, Danilo Oliveira, Iure Fé, Ronierison Maciel, and Jamilson Dantas. Mercury: Performance and Dependability Evaluation of Systems with Exponential, Expolynomial and General Distributions. , In: The 22nd IEEE Pacific Rim International Symposium on Dependable Computing (PRDC 2017). January 22-25, 2017. Christchurch, New Zealand.

274. Bruno Silva, Rubens Matos, Gustavo Callou, Jair Figueiredo, Danilo Oliveira, João Ferreira, Jamilson Dantas, Aleciano Lobo Junior, Vandi Alves and Paulo Maciel. Mercury: An Integrated Environment for Performance and Dependability Evaluation of General Systems. In: Proceedings of Industrial Track at 45th Dependable Systems and Networks Conference (DSN-2015). June 22 – 25, 2015. Rio de Janeiro, RJ, Brazil.

275. Philip M. Merlin. A Study of the Recoverability of Computing Systems. Ph.D. thesis, University of California, Irvine. January 1974.

276. Philip M. Merlin and David J. Farber. Recoverability of Communication Protocols–Implications of a Theoretical Study. IEEE Transactions on Communications, vol. 24, no. 9:1036 – 1043, September 1976

277. Mike Julian. Practical Monitoring: Effective Strategies for the Real World. ISBN-10: 1491957352. O'Reilly Media. 2017

278. Milner, Robin. Elements of Interaction: Turing Award Lecture. Commun. ACM. Volume: 36. Number:1. Pages: 78–89 Jan. 1993. ISSN:0001-0782. New York, NY, USA

279. Silvio Misera, Heinrich Theodor Vierhaus, and Andre Sieber. 2007. Fault Injection Techniques and their Accelerated Simulation in SystemC. Proceedings of the 10th Euromicro Conference on Digital System Design Architectures, Methods and Tools (DSD '07). IEEE Computer Society, USA, 587–595.

280. von Mises, R. E. Wahrscheinlichkeit, Statistik und Wahrheit. Julius Springer.1928.

281. Mark L. Mitchell, Alex Samuel, Jeffrey Oldham. Advanced Linux Programming. ISBN-10: 0735710430. New Riders Publishing. 2001

282. Mobley, R. Keith, Lindley R. Higgins, and Darrin J. Wikoff. Maintenance Engineering Handbook. New York: McGraw-Hill, 2008.

283. Cleve Moler and Charles Van Loan, Nineteen Dubious Ways to Compute the Exponential of a Matrix, SIAM REVIEW, Vols. 20, Issue 4, 1978.

284. Cleve Moler and Charles Van Loan, Nineteen Dubious Ways to Compute the Exponential of a Matrix, Twenty-Five Years Later, SIAM REVIEW, Vols. 45,Issue 1, 2003.

285. On the Integration of Delay and Throughput Measures in Distributed Processing Models. Ph.D. thesis. UCLA. Los Angeles. USA.

286. Molloy, M. K. Performance Analysis Using Stochastic Petri Nets. IEEE Trans. Comput. Vol. 31. n:9. 1982. ISSN: 0018-9340. IEEE Computer Society.

287. Montgomery, D. C., Runger, G. C., Applied statistics and probability, for engineers, Hoboken, NJ: Wiley., Addison-Wesley, Reading, Massachusetts, 2007.

288. Douglas C Montgomery; Elizabeth A Peck; G Geoffrey Vining. Introduction to linear regression analysis. Fifth Edition. John Wiley & Sons, Inc. ISBN 978-0-470-54281-1. 2012.

289. Moore, Edward F. Gedanken-Experiments on Sequential Machines. The Journal of Symbolic Logic. Mar. 1958, Vols. Vol. 23, No. 1, Association for Symbolic Logic.

290. E.F. Moore, C.E. Shannon. Reliable circuits using less reliable relays. Journal of the Franklin Institute.Volume 262. Issue 3. 1956. Pages 191-208. ISSN 0016-0032.

291. Les Cottrell, Warren Matthews and Connie Logg. Tutorial on Internet Monitoring and PingER at SLAC. http://www.slac.stanford.edu/comp/net/wanmon/tutorial.html. 1996.

292. David Mosberger and Tai Jin. Httperf—a tool for measuring web server performance. SIGMETRICS Perform. Eval. Rev. 26, 3 (Dec. 1998), 31–37. DOI:https://doi.org/10.1145/306225.306235

293. Silva, Manuel. 50 years after the Ph.D. thesis of Carl Adam Petri: A perspective. IFAC Proceedings Volumes 45, no. 29 (2012): 13-20.

294. Jogesh K. Muppala and Gianfranco Ciardo and Kishor S. Trivedi. Stochastic Reward Nets for Reliability Prediction. Communications in Reliability, Maintainability and Serviceability. Pages: 9-20. 1994.

295. T. Murata. Petri Nets: Properties, Analysis and Applications. Proc. IEEE. April. no. 4. year:1989. pages:541-580

296. https://www.nagios.com/. Retrieved at 5/19/2020.

297. NASCIMENTO, Rilson Oscar Do; Mark Wong; MACIEL, P. R. M. DBT-5: A Fair Usage Open-Source TPC-E Implementation for Performance Evaluation of Computer Systems. DOI.: 10.6084/m9.figshare.13123280. In: WPerformance – 2007, 2007, Rio de Janeiro. DO XXVII CONGRESSO DA SBC, 2007.

298. Nascimento, R., Maciel, P. DBT-5: An Open-Source TPC-E Implementation for Global Performance Measurement of Computer Systems. Computing and Informatics, 29 (5), 719-740. 1335-9150. DOI: 10.6084/m9.figshare.13123319. 2010

299. Pablo Pessoa do Nascimento, Paulo Pereira, Jr Marco Mialaret, Isac Ferreira, Paulo Maciel, A methodology for selecting hardware performance counters for supporting non-intrusive diagnostic of flood DDoS attacks on web servers, Computers & Security,Volume 110,ISSN 0167-4048, https://doi.org/10.1016/j.cose.2021.102434. 2021.

300. Roberto Natella, Domenico Cotroneo, and Henrique S. Madeira. 2016. Assessing Dependability with Software Fault Injection: A Survey. ACM Comput. Surv. 48, 3, Article 44 (February 2016), 55 pages. DOI:https://doi.org/10.1145/2841425

301. Natkin, G.F.S. Matrix Product Form Solution For Closed Synchronized Queuing Networks. Petri Nets and Performance Models. 1990. IEEE Computer Society.

302. Les Reseaux de Petri Stochastiques et leur Application a l'Evaluation des Systém Informatiques. PhD thesis. CNAM. Paris

303. http://www.netresec.com/?page=NetworkMiner. Retrieved at 5/19/2020.

304. Neumann, J. V. Probabilistic logics and the synthesis of reliable organisms from unreliable components. Annals of Mathematics Studies. CE Shannon and McCarthy, 1956, Vol. 34, AutomataStudies.

305. M. F. Neuts, Matrix-Geometric Solutions in Stochastic Models: An Algorithmic Approach. Dover, 1981.

306. Bob Neveln. Linux Assembly Language Programming. Publisher(s): Prentice-Hall. ISBN: 0130879401. 2000

307. https://linux.die.net/man/8/ngrep. Retrieved at 5/19/2020.

308. Ningfang Mi, Qi Zhang, Alma Riska, Evgenia Smirni, Erik Riedel, Performance impacts of autocorrelated flows in multi-tiered systems, Performance Evaluation, Volume 64, Issues 9–12, 2007, Pages 1082-1101, ISSN 0166-5316, https://doi.org/10.1016/j.peva.2007.06.016.

309. Nita, Mihaela-Catalina, Florin Pop, M. Mocanu and V. Cristea. "FIM-SIM: Fault Injection Module for CloudSim Based on Statistical Distributions." Journal of telecommunications and information technology 4. 2014.

310. http://nmon.sourceforge.net/pmwiki.php. Retrieved at 5/19/2020.

311. NOGUEIRA, Meuse; MACIEL, P. R. M. . A Retargetable Environment for Power-Aware Code Evaluation: An Approach Based on Coloured Petri Net.In: Power and Timing Modeling, Optimization and Simulation (PATMOS), 2005, Leuven. Lecture Notes in Computer Science, 2005.

312. NOGUEIRA, Meuse; VASCONCELOS NETO, Silvino; MACIEL, P. R. M.; LIMA, Ricardo Massa Ferreira; BARRETO, Raimundo. Embedded Systems' Software Performance and Energy Consumption by Probabilistic Modeling: An Approach Based on Coloured Petri Nets.In: Application and Theory of Petri Nets and Other Models of Concurrency, 2006, Turku. Lectures Notes in Computer Science – Proceedings of the Application and Theory of Petri Nets and Other Concurrency Models. Heidelberg, Germany: Springer Verlag, 2006.

313. J. R. Norris, Markov Chains, Vols. Cambridge University Press, 1997.

314. Nonelectronic Parts Reliability Data (NPRD-2016). Quanterion Solutions Incorporated . ISBN-13: 978-1-933904-76-4. 2016.

315. https://linux.die.net/man/5/ntp.conf. Retrieved at 5/14/2020.

316. William H. and Teukolsky, Saul A. and Vetterling, William T. and Flannery, Brian P. Numerical Recipes 3rd Edition: The Art of Scientific Computing. isbn:0521880688. Cambridge University Press. 2007

317. Mohammed S. Obaidat and Noureddine A. Boudriga. 2010. Fundamentals of Performance Evaluation of Computer and Telecommunications Systems. Wiley-Interscience, USA.

318. Danilo Oliveira, Nelson Rosa, André Brinkmann and Paulo Maciel. Performability Evaluation and Optimization of Workflow Applications in Cloud Environments. Journal of Grid Computing. 2019. ISSN: 1572-9184 (Online).

319. O'NEILL, M. The Genuine Sieve of Eratosthenes. Journal of Functional Programming, 19(1), 95-106. 2009. doi:10.1017/S0956796808007004

320. OREDA Offshore Reliability Data Handbook. 4th Edition. Publisher: Høvik. Norway. 2002.

321. OREDA. Offshore & Onshore Reliability Data. https://www.oreda.com/. Retrieved at 5/5/2021.

322. Diego Perez-Palacin, José Merseguer, and Raffaela Mirandola. 2012. Analysis of bursty workload-aware self-adaptive systems. In Proceedings of the 3rd ACM/SPEC International Conference on Performance Engineering (ICPE '12). Association for Computing Machinery, New York, NY, USA, 75–84. DOI:https://doi.org/10.1145/2188286.2188300

323. Diego Perez-Palacin, Raffaela Mirandola, José Merseguer, Accurate modeling and efficient QoS analysis of scalable, adaptive systems under bursty workload, Journal of Systems and Software, Volume 130, 2017, Pages 24-41, ISSN 0164-1212, https://doi.org/10.1016/j.jss.2017.05.022.

324. Papazoglou, M. P.. Service-oriented computing: Concepts, characteristics and directions. Proceedings of the Fourth International Conference on Web Information Systems Engineering. WISE '03, pages 3–12, Washington, DC, USA. IEEE Computer Society. 2003.

325. Emanuel Parzen. Stochastic Processes. Dover Publications Inc. 1962.

326. PCMark - Technical Guide. Updated September 10, 2020.

327. Karl Pearson F.R.S., X. On the criterion that a given system of deviations from the probable in the case of a correlated system of variables is such that it can be reasonably supposed to have arisen from random sampling, Philosophical Magazine Series 5, Vol. 50 , Iss. 302,1900

328. Witold Pedrycz. Knowledge-Based Clustering: From Data to Information Granules. Wiley-Interscience, USA. 2005.

329. Pelluri, Sudha and Keerti Bangari. "Synthetic Workload Generation in Cloud". International Journal of Research in Engineering and Technology 04. 2015. 56-66.

330. Paulo Pereira, Jean Araujo, Jamilson Dantas, Matheus Torquato, Carlos Melo and Paulo Maciel. Stochastic Performance Model for Web-Server Capacity Planning in Fog Computing. The Journal of Supercomputing. 2020. ISSN: 1573-0484 (Online). ISSN: 0920-8542 (Print).

331. Pereira, Paulo; Melo, Carlos; Araujo, Jean; Dantas, Jamilson; Santos, Vinícius; Maciel, Paulo; Availability model for edge-fog-cloud continuum: an evaluation of an end-to-end infrastructure of intelligent traffic management service; The Journal of Supercomputing; 1573-0484; 10.1007/s11227-021-04033-7. 09/03/2021.

332. Paulo Pereira, Carlos Melo, Jean Araujo, and Paulo Maciel. Analytic Models for Availability Evaluation of Edge and Fog Computing Nodes. The Journal of Supercomputing. 2021. ISSN: 1573-0484.

333. https://docs.microsoft.com/en-us/windows-server/administration/windows-commands/perfmon. Retrieved at 5/19/2020.

334. Peterson, James Lyle. Petri Net Theory and the Modeling of Systems. isbn:0136619835. 1981. Prentice-Hall PTR. Upper Saddle River, NJ, USA

335. Carl Adam Petri. Kommunikation mit Automaten. Schriften des Rheinisch-Westfälischen Institutes für Instrumentelle Mathematik an der Universität Bonn Nr. 2, 1962

336. Communication with Automata. New York: Griffiss Air Force Base, Technical Report, RADC TR-65-377-vol-1-suppl-1 Applied Data Research, Princeton, NJ, Contract AF 30(602)-3324, 1966

337. Editor: Hoang Pham. Handbook of Reliability Engineering. ISBN: 978-1-85233-453-6. DOI: 10.1007/b97414. Springer-Verlag. 2003.

338. Phone Arena - Phone News, Reviews and Specs. http://www.phonearena.com/. 2019. Online. Accessed 20-May-2019.

339. Pierce, W. H. Failure-tolerant computer design. New York: Academic Press, 1965. ISBN:978-1-4832-3179-2.

340. Pietrantuono, R.; Russo, S. Software Qual J (2019). https://doi.org/10.1007/s11219-019-09448-3, Springer US Print ISSN 0963-9314, Online ISSN 1573-1367. 2019

341. T. F. da Silva Pinheiro, F. A. Silva, I. Fe, S. Kosta, and P. Maciel. Performance prediction for supporting mobile applications' offloading. The Journal of Supercomputing, 74(8):4060–4103, Aug 2018.

342. Plackett, R. L. "Karl Pearson and the Chi-Squared Test." International Statistical Review / Revue Internationale De Statistique 51, no. 1 (1983): 59-72. doi:10.2307/1402731.

343. Pólya, G., Über den zentralen Grenzwertsatz der Wahrscheinlichkeitsrechnung und das Momentenproblem, Mathematische Zeitschrif, vol.: 8, 171-181, 1920

344. R. E. Barlow and F. Proschan. Mathematical Theory of Reliability. New York: John Wiley, 1967. SIAM series in applied mathematics.

345. J. D. Esary and F. Proschan. A Reliability Bound for Systems of Maintained, Interdependent Components. Journal of the American Statistical Association. 1970, Vol. Vol. 65, No. 329.

346. R. E. Barlow and F. Proschan. Proschan, R. E. Barlow and F. Statistical Theory of Reliability and Life Testing: Probability Models. New York. : Holt, Rinehart and Winston, 1975. Holt, Rinehart and Winston, New York, 1975.

347. Semyon G. Rabinovich. Evaluating Measurement Accuracy. Springer. ISBN 978-1-4419-1455-2. DOI 10.1007/978-1-4419-1456-9. 2010

348. Bharat Rajaram. Technical White Paper: Understanding Functional Safety FIT Base Failure Rate Estimates per IEC 62380 and SN 29500. Texas Instruments. June 2020

349. Kandethody M. Ramachandran and Ramachandran Tsokos and Chris P. Tsokos, Mathematical Statistics with Applications, Elsevier Academic Press, ISBN 13: 978-0-12-374848-5. 2009

350. C. Ramchandani. Analysis of Asynchronous Concurrent Systems by Timed Petri Nets. Technical Report: TR-120, Massachusetts Institute of Technology, Cambridge, MA, USA, February 1974.

351. Dunn-Rankin, Peter, Gerald A. Knezek, Susan R. Wallace, and Shuqiang Zhang. Scaling methods. Mahwah, N.J. USA. Lawrence Erlbaum Associates, 2004.

352. Rausand, M., System Reliability Theory: Models, Statistical Methods, and Applications. ISBN: 9780471471332. Wiley Series in Probability. Wiley. 2004.

353. Philipp Reinecke, Levente Bodrog, and Alexandra Danilkina. Phase-Type Distributions. Resilience Assessment and Evaluation of Computing Systems, Springer Berlin Heidelberg, 2012

354. W. Reisig. On the Semantics of Petri Nets. pp.:347-372. In Formal Models in Programming. Edited by E.J. Neuhold and G. Chroust. Proceedings of the IFIP TC2 Working Conference on The Role of Abstract Models in Information Process. Vienna. Austria. January-February. 1985. isbn: 0444878882.

355. Renata Pedrosa, Jamilson Dantas, Gabriel Alves, and Paulo Maciel. Analysis of a Performability Model for the BRT System. International Journal of Data Mining, Modelling and Management. 2018. ISSN Online 1759-1171 and ISSN print: 1759-1163

356. Alvin C. Rencher and G. Bruce Schaalje. Linear models in statistics. Second Edition. Wiley. ISBN 978-0-471-75498-5. 2008.

357. Richard L. Burden and J. Douglas Faires. Numerical Analysis, Ninth Edition. ISBN-13: 978-0-538-73351-9. Brooks/Cole, Cengage Learning. 2011.

358. *Lecture Notes on Petri Nets I: Basic Models.*Lecture Notes in Computer Science - Advances in Petri Nets, Springer-Verlag, Edited by W. Reisig and G. Rozenberg. 1998.

359. *Lecture Notes on Petri Nets II: Applications.* Lecture Notes in Computer Science - Advances in Petri Nets, Springer-Verlag, Edited by W. Reisig and G. Rozenberg. 1998.

360. Ripley, Brian D. Stochastic Simulation. isbn.: 0-471-81884-4. John Wiley & Sons, Inc. 1987

361. Robinson, Stewart.Simulation: The Practice of Model Development and Use.isbn:0470847727. John Wiley & Sons, Inc. 2004. USA.

362. Manuel Rodríguez, Frédéric Salles, Jean-Charles Fabre, and Jean Arlat. 1999. "MAFALDA: Microkernel Assessment by Fault Injection and Design Aid". In Proceedings of the Third European Dependable Computing Conference on Dependable Computing (EDCC-3). Springer-Verlag, Berlin, Heidelberg, 143–160.

363. Fabrizio Romano, Dusty Phillips, Rick van Hattem. Python: Journey from Novice to Expert. Packt Publishing. ISBN: 9781787122567. 2016.

364. Ross, Sheldon M.Simulation, Fourth Edition. isbn.: 0125980639.Academic Press, Inc. 2006.

365. Sheldon M. Ross. Introduction to Probability and Statistics for Engineers and Scientists. Elsevier Academic Press. ISBN 13: 978-0-12-370483-2. 2009.

366. Cisco Catalyst 3750 Data Sheet. http://tinyurl.com/38krjm. October. 2013.

367. G. Rozenberg, P. S. Thiagarajan, Petri Nets: Basic Notions, Structure, Behaviour, LNCS vol. 424, Springer Verlag, 1986

368. E. M. Salgueiro, P. R. F. Cunha, P. R. M. Maciel, J. A. S. Monteiro and R. J. P. B. Salgueiro, "Defining bandwidth constraints with cooperative games," 2009 International Conference on Ultra Modern Telecommunications & Workshops, St. Petersburg, Russia, 2009, pp. 1-8, doi: 10.1109/ICUMT.2009.5345534.

369. https://www.sisoftware.co.uk/2019/07/18/sisoftware-sandra-20-20-2020-released/ Retrieved at 9/19/2020.

370. Sato, N. and Trivedi, K. S.Stochastic modeling of composite web services for closed-form analysis of their performance and reliability bottlenecks. Proceedings of the 5th international conference on Service-Oriented Computing. ICSOC '07, pages 107–118, Berlin, Heidelberg. Springer-Verlag.. 2007.

371. Schaffer, Simon. Babbage's Intelligence: Calculating Engines and the Factory System. Critical Inquiry. The University of Chicago Press, 1994, Vol. 21, No. 1.

372. Schmidt Klaus. High Availability and Disaster Recovery: Concepts, Design, Implementation. isbn: 3642063799, 9783642063794. Springer Publishing Company, Incorporated. 2010.

373. Schrijver, Alexander, Theory of Linear and Integer Programming, John Wiley & Sons, Inc., isbn:0-471-90854-1, New York, NY, USA, 1986.

374. Z. Segall et al., "FIAT-fault injection-based automated testing environment," [1988] The Eighteenth International Symposium on Fault-Tolerant Computing. Digest of Papers, Tokyo, Japan, 1988, pp. 102-107, doi: 10.1109/FTCS.1988.5306.

375. Z. Segall et al., "FIAT - Fault injection-based automated testing environment," Twenty-Fifth International Symposium on Fault-Tolerant Computing, 1995, ' Highlights from Twenty-Five Years'., Pasadena, CA, USA, 1995, pp. 394-, doi: 10.1109/FTCSH.1995.532663.

376. Eugene Seneta. Markov and the Creation of the Markov Chains. School of Mathematics and Statistics, University of Sydney, NSW 2006, Australia

377. Seongwoo Woo. Reliability Design of Mechanical Systems. Second Edition. ISBN 978-981-13-7235-3. Springer Nature Singapore Pte Ltd. 2017.

378. Woo, Seongwoo. Reliability Design of Mechanical Systems: a Guide for Mechanical and Civil Engineers (Second edition.). Springer. 2020

379. Shannon, C. E. A Mathematical Theory of Communication. The Bell System Technical Journal. July, October, 1948, Vols. pp. 379–423, 623–656, Vol. 27.

380. Shetti, N. M. (2003). Heisenbugs and Bohrbugs: Why are they different?DCS/LCSR Technical Reports, Department of Computer Science, Rutgers, The State University of New Jersey.

381. Martin L. Shooman. Reliability of Computer Systems and Networks: Fault Tolerance, Analysis, and Design. 2002 John Wiley & Sons, Inc. ISBN: 0-471-29342-3

382. Ellen Siever, Stephen Figgins, Robert Love, and Arnold Robbins. Linux in a Nutshell, Sixth Edition. O'Reilly Media, Inc. ISBN: 978-0-596-15448-6. 2009

383. J. Sifakis. Use of Petri nets for Performance Evaluation. 3rd Intl. Symposium on Modeling and Evaluation, IFIP, North-Holland, pages 75–93, 1977.

384. Sifakis, Joseph, Structural properties of Petri nets, Mathematical Foundations of Computer Science, Springer Berlin Heidelberg, pp 474–483, 1978.

385. Silva, Manuel; Terue, Enrique; and Colom, José Manuel.Linear algebraic and linear programming techniques for the analysis of place/transition net systems. Lectures on Petri Nets I: Basic Models: Advances in Petri Nets. Springer Berlin Heidelberg. isbn:978-3-540-49442-3. pages: 309–373. 1998.

386. Manuel Silva.50 years after the Ph.D. thesis of Carl Adam Petri: A perspective. WODES. 2012.

387. F. A. Silva and M. Rodrigues and P. Maciel and S. Kosta and A. Mei. Planning Mobile Cloud Infrastructures Using Stochastic Petri Nets and Graphic Processing Units. 2015 IEEE 7th International Conference on Cloud Computing Technology and Science (CloudCom). DOI: 10.1109/CloudCom.2015.46. 2015

388. Silva, Francisco Airton and Zaicaner, Germano and Quesado, Eder and Dornelas, Matheus and Silva, Bruno and Maciel, Paulo. Benchmark applications used in mobile cloud computing research: a systematic mapping study. The Journal of Supercomputing. Vol.:72, number: 4. pp:1431–1452. Springer. 2016

389. Silva, Francisco Airton and Kosta, Sokol and Rodrigues, Matheus and Oliveira, Danilo and Maciel, Teresa and Mei, Alessandro and Maciel, Paulo. Mobile cloud performance evaluation using stochastic models. IEEE Transactions on Mobile Computing. Vol: 17. Number: 5. pp:1134–1147. IEEE. 2017

390. Bruno Silva, Rubens Matos, Eduardo Tavares, Armin Zimmerman and Paulo Maciel. Sensitivity Analysis of an Availability Model for Disaster Tolerant Cloud Computing System. International Journal of Network Management. 2018. ISSN: 1099-1190 (Online).

391. D. Leu, M. Silva, J. Colom, T. Murata. *Interrelationships among Various Concepts of Fairness for Petri Nets.* Proceedings of the 31st Midwest Symposium on Circuits and Systems. IEEE Computer Society Press,1988.

392. J.M.Colom, M.Silva. Convex Geometry and Semiflows in P/T Nets. A Comparative Study of Algorithms for Computation of Minimal P-Semiflows. Lecture Notes in Computer Science, vol-483, p. 79-112, Springer-Verlag, Edited by G. Rozenberg 1990.

393. J.M.Colom,M.Silva. Improving the Linearly Based Characterization of P/T Nets. Lecture Notes in Computer Science, vol-483, p. 113-145, Springer-Verlag, Edited by G. Rozenberg, 1990.

394. F.Dicesare, G. Harhalakis, J.M. Proth, M. Silva, F.B. Vernadat. Practice of Petri Nets in Manufacturing. Chapman and Hall, 1993.

395. Y. Choi, J. Silvester and H. Kim, "Analyzing and Modeling Workload Characteristics in a Multiservice IP Network," in IEEE Internet Computing, vol. 15, no. 2, pp. 35-42, March-April 2011, doi: 10.1109/MIC.2010.153.

396. Richard Simard and Pierre L'Ecuyer. Computing the Two-Sided Kolmogorov-Smirnov Distribution. Journal of Statistical Software.Vol. 39, number: 11. 2011. ISSN:1548-7660. Pages:1–18. DOI:10.18637/jss.v039.i11

397. Dandamudi, Sivarama P. Guide to Assembly Language Programming in Linux. ISBN 978-0-387-26171-3. Springer. 2005.

398. Service Level Agreement - MegaPath Business Access and Value-Added Services. http://tinyurl.com/cwdeebt. October. 2012.

399. J. G. Smith and H. E. Oldham, "Laser testing of integrated circuits," in IEEE Journal of Solid-State Circuits, vol. 12, no. 3, pp. 247-252, June 1977, doi: 10.1109/JSSC.1977.1050886.

400. Alan Jay Smith. 2007. Workloads (creation and use). Commun. ACM 50, 11 (November 2007), 45–50. DOI:https://doi.org/10.1145/1297797.1297821

401. Smith David J., Reliability, Maintainability and Risk - Practical methods for engineers. Eighth edition 2011. ISBN:978-0-08-096902-2

402. Smith David J., Reliability, Maintainability and Risk - Practical methods for engineers. Ninth edition 2017. ISBN:978-0-08-102010-4

403. Sneath, Peter HA. "The application of computers to taxonomy." Microbiology 17.1 (1957): 201-226.

404. https://www.iana.org/assignments/service-names-port-numbers/service-names-port-numbers.xhtml. Retrieved at 5/18/2020.

405. https://www.solarwinds.com/network-performance-monitor. Retrieved at 5/19/2020.

406. Hbrekke, Solfrid; Hauge, Stein; Xie, Lin; Lundteigen, Mary Ann. Failure rates of safety-critical equipment based on inventory attributes. Safety and Reliability – Safe Societies in a Changing World. Proceedings of ESREL 2018, June 17-21, 2018, Trondheim, Norway, 2419-2426

407. R. Souza, G. Callou, K. Camboin, J. Ferreira and P. Maciel, "The Effects of Temperature Variation on Data Center IT Systems," 2013 IEEE International Conference on Systems, Man, and Cybernetics, 2013, pp. 2354-2359, doi: 10.1109/SMC.2013.402.

408. D. Souza, R. Matos, J. Araujo, V. Alves and P. Maciel, "EucaBomber: Experimental Evaluation of Availability in Eucalyptus Private Clouds," 2013 IEEE International Conference on Systems, Man, and Cybernetics, Manchester, UK, 2013, pp. 4080-4085, doi: 10.1109/SMC.2013.696.

409. Souza, D., Rúbens de Souza Matos Júnior, J. Araujo, Vandi Alves and P. Maciel. "A Tool for Automatic Dependability Test in Eucalyptus Cloud Computing Infrastructures." Comput. Inf. Sci. 6 (2013): 57-67.

410. https://www.spec.org/30th/timeline.html. Retrieved at 9/19/2020.

411. SR-332 Issue 4. https://telecom-info.njdepot.ericsson.net/site-cgi/ido/docs.cgi?ID=SEARCH&DOCUMENT=SR-332. Retrieved at 5/7/2021.

412. Peter H. Starke. Remarks on Timed Nets. Petri Net Newsletter, 27:37–47, August 1987.

413. Stewart, William J., Probability, Markov chains, queues and simulation. Published by Princeton University Press. 2009.

414. Stewart, William J., Introduction to the Numerical Solution of Markov Chains. Published by Princeton University Press. 1994.

415. Stewart, James. Essential calculus: early transcendentals. Belmont, CA: Thomson Higher Education. 2007.

416. Stott, H. G. Time-Limit Relays and Duplication of Electrical Apparatus to Secure Reliability of Services at New York. s.l. : IEEE, 1905.

417. Gilbert Strang. Calculus. MIT. Publisher: Wellesley-Cambridge Press. ISBN 13: 9780961408824. 1991.

418. Stuart, H. R. Time-Limit Relays and Duplication of Electrical Apparatus to Secure Reliability of Services at Pittsburg. s.l. : IEEE, June 1905.

419. Rai, Suresh, Malathi Veeraraghavan, and Kishor S. Trivedi. "A survey of efficient reliability computation using disjoint products approach." Networks 25, no. 3 (1995): 147-163.

420. Cisco Systems: Switch dependability parameters. http://tinyurl.com/cr9nssu. October. 2012.

421. Symons F. J. W., Modelling and Analysis of Communication Protocols using Numerical Petri Nets, Ph.D Thesis, University of Essex, also Dept of Elec. Eng. Science Telecommunications Systems Group Report No. 152, May 1978.

422. http://man7.org/linux/man-pages/man2/syscalls.2.html. Retrieved at 5/1/2020.

423. https://github.com/sysstat/sysstat. Retrieved at 5/4/2020.

424. Tausworthe, Robert C. Random numbers generated by linear recurrence modulo two. Math. Comp. 19, 201–209, 1965.

425. Telcordia-Bellcore SR-332. http://www.t-cubed.com/faq telc.htm. Retrieved at 5/7/2021.

426. https://www.tcpdump.org/. Retrieved at 5/19/2020.

427. S. J. Einhorn and F. B. Thiess. "Intermittence as a stochastic process". S. J. Einhorn and F. B. Thiess, "Intermittence as a stNYU-RCA Working Conference on Theory of Reliability. Ardsley-on-Hudson, N. Y., 1957.

428. German, Reinhard and Kelling, Christian and Zimmermann, Armin and Hommel, Günter. TimeNET: A Toolkit for Evaluating non-Markovian Stochastic Petri Nets. Perform. Evaluation. Vol: 25. number:1-2. pages:69-87. isssn:0166-5316. Elsevier. 1995

429. Tobias, P. A., & Trindade, D. C. (2012). Applied reliability. Boca Raton, FL: CRC/Taylor & Francis.

430. Matheus D'Eça Torquato, Marco Vieira and Paulo Maciel. A Model for Availability and Security Risk Evaluation for Systems with VMM Rejuvenation enabled by VM Migration Scheduling. IEEE Access. 2019. ISSN: 2169-3536 (Online).

431. Matheus D'Eça Torquato and Paulo Maciel. Availability and Reliability Modeling of VM Migration as Rejuvenation on a System under Varying Workload. Software Quality Journal. 2019. ISSN: 1573-1367 (Online).

432. Torquato, Matheus; Maciel, Paulo; Vieira, Marco; Model-Based Performability and Dependability Evaluation of a System with VM Migration as Rejuvenation in the Presence of Bursty Workloads. Journal of Network and Systems Management. 1573-7705. 10.1007/s10922-021-09619-3. 09/14/2021

433. Transaction Processing Performance Council. http://www.tpc.org/. Retrieved at 9/20/2020.

434. http://www.tpc.org/tpcc/detail5.asp. Retrieved at 8/7/2020.

435. T. Triebel, M. Lehn, R. Rehner, B. Guthier, S. Kopf and W. Effelsberg, "Generation of synthetic workloads for multiplayer online gaming benchmarks," 2012 11th Annual Workshop on Network and Systems Support for Games (NetGames), Venice, 2012, pp. 1-6, doi: 10.1109/NetGames.2012.6404028.

436. Triola, E. F., Elementary statistics (second edition), Pearson Education, 2013.

437. Kishor S. Trivedi. Probability and Statistics with Reliability, Queuing, and Computer Science Applications, 2nd Edition. John Wiley & Sons. 2001.

438. Robin A. Sahner, Kishor S. Trivedi, Antonio Puliafito. Performance and Reliability Analysis of Computer Systems - An Example-Based Approach Using the SHARPE Software Package. s.l. : Kluwer Academic Publishers. p. 404. 1996

439. Trivedi, K. S., Grottke, M. (2007). Fighting Bugs: Remove, Retry, Replicate, and Rejuvenate. IEEE Transactions on Computers, 4(20), 107–109.

440. T. K. Tsai, Mei-Chen Hsueh, Hong Zhao, Z. Kalbarczyk and R. K. Iyer, "Stress-based and path-based fault injection," in IEEE Transactions on Computers, vol. 48, no. 11, pp. 1183-1201, Nov. 1999, doi: 10.1109/12.811108.

441. Dimitri P. Bertsekas, John N. Tsitsiklis. Introduction to Probability,2nd Edition. Hardcover. 544 Pages. Published by Athena Scientific ISBN-13: 978-1-886529-23-6. ISBN: 1-886529-23-X. 2008

442. Tukey, John W., Exploratory data analysis,1977, Reading, Mass.

443. https://www.ubuntupit.com/most-comprehensive-list-of-linux-monitoring-tools-for-sysadmin/ Retrieved at 4/29/2020.

444. James Rumbaugh, Ivar Jacobson, and Grady Booch. 2004. Unified Modeling Language Reference Manual, The (2nd Edition). Pearson Higher Education.

445. Ushakov, Igor. IS RELIABILITY THEORY STILL ALIVE?, e-journal Reliability: Theory & Applications. March 2007, Vol. 2, No 1.

446. Ushakov, Igor. IS RELIABILITY THEORY STILL ALIVE? e-journal Reliability: Theory & Applications. March 2007, Vol. Vol. 2, No 1.

447. Valmari, Antti, The state explosion problem, Lectures on Petri Nets I: Basic Models: Advances in Petri Nets, pages:429–528,isbn:978-3-540-49442-3, Springer Berlin Heidelberg, 1998.

448. Vassiliou P., Mettas A., El-Azzouzi T. Quantitative Accelerated Life-testing and Data Analysis. In: Misra K.B. (eds) Handbook of Performability Engineering. Springer. London. 2008. https://doi.org/10.1007/978-1-84800-131-2˙35

449. W. E. Vesely, F. F. Goldberg, N. H. Roberts, D. F. Haasl. Fault Tree Handbook. Systems and Reliability Research Office of Nuclear Regulatory Research U.S. Nuclear Regulatory Commission Washington, D.C. 20555. Date Published: January 1981

450. Vishay Semiconductors. Reliability. VISHAY INTERTECHNOLOGY. Document Number: 80116. Rev. 1.3, Feb-2002.

451. Vishay Semiconductors. Quality and Reliability. VISHAY INTERTECHNOLOGY. INC. ENVIRONMENTAL, HEALTH AND SAFETY POLICY. Document Number: 82501. Rev. 1.3, 26-Aug-2005.

452. HP Insight Dynamics - VSE and HP VSE Management Software 4.1 Getting Started Guide, January 2009.

453. Implementing a Virtual Server Environment: Getting Started, January 2009.

454. Introduction to the HP Virtual Server Environment, January 2009

455. Christian Walck. Hand-Book on Statistical Distributions for Experimentalists. Internal Report SUF–PFY/96–01 Stockholm, 11 December 1996, first revision, 31 October 1998, last modification 10 September 2007

456. Josephine L. Walkowicz. Benchmarking and Workload Definition. A Selected Bibliography with Abstracts Systems and Software Division. Institute for Computer Sciences and Technology. National Bureau of Standards. U.S. DEPARTMENT OF COMMERCE. Washington, D.C. 20234. 1974.

457. David Watts. Lenovo x86 Servers Top ITIC 2020 Global Reliability Survey. Information Technology Intelligence Consulting Corp. March 2, 2020.

458. Wei-Lun Kao and R. K. Iyer, "DEFINE: a distributed fault injection and monitoring environment," Proceedings of IEEE Workshop on Fault-Tolerant Parallel and Distributed Systems, College Station, TX, USA, 1994, pp. 252-259, doi: 10.1109/FTPDS.1994.494497.

459. Weicker, Reinhold P. "Dhrystone: a synthetic systems programming benchmark." Communications of the ACM 27, no. 10 (1984): 1013-1030.

460. Weicker, Reinhold P. 1990. An Overview of Common Benchmarks. Computer 23, no.12. 65-75 (December 1990), 65–75. DOI:https://doi.org/10.1109/2.62094

461. Wendai Wang and D. B. Kececioglu, "Confidence limits on the inherent availability of equipment," Annual Reliability and Maintainability Symposium. 2000 Proceedings. International Symposium on Product Quality and Integrity (Cat. No.00CH37055), Los Angeles, CA, USA, 2000, pp. 162-168. doi: 10.1109/RAMS.2000.816301

462. Peter H. Westfall. Kurtosis as Peakedness, 1905–2014. R.I.P. The American Statistician. Vol:68. Number:3. Pages:191-195. Taylor & Francis. 2014

463. https://www.netlib.org/benchmark/whetstone.c. Retrieved at 10/7/2020.

464. Mark Wilding and Dan Behman. Self-Service Linux. Prentice-Hall. ISBN 0-13-147751-X. 2005

465. Wilmink F.W., Uytterschaut H.T. Cluster Analysis, History, Theory and Applications. In: Van Vark G.N., Howells W.W. (eds) Multivariate Statistical Methods in Physical Anthropology. Springer, Dordrecht. https://doi.org/10.1007/978-94-009-6357-3'11. 1984.

466. https://www.winpcap.org/windump/. Retrieved at 5/19/2020.

467. https://www.wireshark.org/. Retrieved at 5/19/2020.

468. Cluster Analysis, Wolfram Language Documentation Center. 2020. https://reference.wolfram.com/language/guide/ClusterAnalysis.html. Retrieved at 12/22/2020.

469. Wayne B. Nelson. Accelerated Testing: Statistical Models, Test Plans, and Data Analysis. Wiley Series in Probability and Statistics. Book. ISBN: 9780470317471. 2009. Wiley.

470. https://docs.microsoft.com/en-us/windows/win32/perfctrs/performance-counters-portal. Retrieved at 4/29/2020.

471. K. Lai, D. Wren. Fast and Effective Endpoint Security for Business – Comparative Analysis. Edition 1, PassMark Software. 15 June 2010.

472. J. Han, D. Wren. Consumer Security Products Performance Benchmarks. Edition 2. PassMark Software. 13 January 2020.

473. Device Reliability Report Second Half 2020 UG116 (v10.14). https://www.xilinx.com/support/documentation/user'guides/ug116.pdf. April 23, 2021. Retrieved at 5/10/2021.

474. Yeo, In-Kwon, and Richard A. Johnson. "A New Family of Power Transformations to Improve Normality or Symmetry." Biometrika, vol. 87, no. 4, 2000, pp. 954–959. JSTOR, www.jstor.org/stable/2673623.

475. Yim, O, & Ramdeen, K. T. Hierarchical Cluster Analysis: Comparison of Three Linkage Measures and Application to Psychological Data, The Quantitative Methods for Psychology, 11(1), 8-21. doi: 10.20982/tqmp.11.1.p008. 2015.

476. J. Yin, X. Lu, X. Zhao, H. Chen and X. Liu, "BURSE: A Bursty and Self-Similar Workload Generator for Cloud Computing," in IEEE Transactions on Parallel and Distributed Systems, vol. 26, no. 3, pp. 668-680, 1 March 2015, doi: 10.1109/TPDS.2014.2315204.

477. Young, Derek Scott. Handbook of regression methods. CRC Press, 2018.

478. Zenie, Alexandre. Colored Stochastic Petri Nets. International Workshop on Timed Petri Nets. IEEE Computer Society. pages: 262–271, 1985. isbn: 0-8186-0674-6

479. Zimmermann, Armin. Stochastic Discrete Event Systems: Modeling, Evaluation, Applications. isbn.: 3540741720. Springer-Verlag. 2007.

480. Zuberek, W. M. Timed Petri Nets and Preliminary Performance Evaluation. Proceedings of the 7th Annual Symposium on Computer Architecture. Pages: 88–96. ACM. 1980. La Baule, USA.